People Management and Development

Human Resource Management at Work

SECOND EDITION

Mick Marchington is professor of human resource management at the Manchester School of Management, UMIST. He is author of fourteen books and monographs as well as numerous papers in refereed journals on a range of aspects of human resource management and industrial relations. He has been the principal investigator on grants awarded by ESRC and EPSRC, various government departments and the CIPD. He has been a CIPD chief examiner for many years and took over as chief moderator, standards in 2001. He is a companion of the CIPD.

Adrian Wilkinson is professor of human resource management and director of research at Loughborough University Business School. He is author of ten books and monographs and numerous papers in refereed journals in the field of human resource management and industrial relations. He has been principal investigator on grants awarded by the ESRC, EPSRC, CIPD, the Department of Health and the European Regional Development Fund. He is a fellow of the CIPD.

● Other titles in the series

The Chartered Institute of Personnel and Development is the leading publisher of books and reports for personnel and training professionals, students, and all those concerned with the effective management and development of people at work.
For details of all our titles, please contact the Publishing Department:

tel 020 8263 3387
fax 020 8263 3850
e-mail publish@cipd.co.uk
The catalogue of all CIPD titles can be viewed on the CIPD website:
www.cipd.co.uk/publications

People Management and Development

Human Resource Management at Work

SECOND EDITION

Mick Marchington
and
Adrian Wilkinson

Chartered Institute of Personnel and Development

© Mick Marchington and Adrian Wilkinson 1996, 2000, 2002

First published in 1996
Reprinted 1997 (twice), 1998
Updated edition 2000
Reprinted 2000

This edition first published in 2002

Design by Pumpkin House

Typeset by Fakenham Photosetting Ltd, Fakenham, Norfolk

Printed in Great Britain by
the Cromwell Press, Trowbridge, Wiltshire

British Library Cataloguing in Publication Data
A catalogue record of this book is available from
the British Library

ISBN 0 85292 926 9

Chartered Institute of Personnel and Development, CIPD House,
Camp Road, London SW19 4UX
Tel: 020 8971 9000   Fax: 020 8263 3333
E-mail: cipd@cipd.co.uk Website: www.cipd.co.uk
Incorporated by Royal Charter. Registered Charity No. 1079797.

Contents

13 Managing the Learning and Development Process   381

14 Structures and Processes for Effective Employee Relations   416

15 Using Employee Relations Procedures to Resolve Differences and Engender Commitment   448

16 Motivating Staff and Rewarding Contributions   476

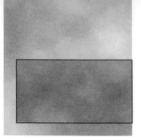

• Editor's foreword

HRM is now more important than ever. Organisations increasingly compete with each other on the basis of effective people management and development by tapping into the ideas of workers and organising their work in more efficient ways. Much of this relies on line managers in their day-to-day interactions with the people who work for them. However, line managers are busy individuals who need the support of HR specialists – internal or external to the organisation – to help them make sense of what is happening in the field. Contemporary initiatives in learning and development, recruitment and selection, employee relations, reward management, appraisal and performance review need to be interpreted for different organisational contexts. HR specialists not only need to display a sound understanding of the main HR issues, but also show awareness of business issues and have an acute sensitivity to how change can be managed effectively. In addition, HR specialists need to demonstrate a commitment to professional and ethical standards, and be able to provide sound advice based on an extensive knowledge of high-quality research and contemporary organisational practice.

With this in mind, the CIPD is publishing a series of books designed to address key issues in people management and development. This book is one of the series focusing on the CIPD Standards in People Management and Development, Learning and Development, Employee Relations, People Resourcing, and Employee Reward. The series provides essential guidance and points of reference for all those interested in learning more about the management of people in organisations. It covers the main sets of CIPD Standards in a systematic and comprehensive manner, and as such is essential reading for all those preparing for CIPD examinations. In addition, however, the books are also excellent core texts for those studying for courses in human resource management at postgraduate and advanced undergraduate levels. Moreover, practitioners should also find the books invaluable for information and reference to sources of specialist advice. Underpinning the series is the CIPD notion of 'the thinking performer' that is central to the Professional Development Scheme.

People Management and Development: HRM at Work, written by Mick Marchington and Adrian Wilkinson, analyses the essential knowledge and understanding required of all personnel and development professionals. The book comprises a number of sections, commencing with an examination of the factors shaping HRM at work – including the legal and institutional forces as well as the changing nature of work and employment. A recurring theme throughout the book is the integration of HRM with business objectives and the degree to which it is able to add value. Later chapters in the book consider each of the main components of HRM at work, seeking to show how these interrelate with each other in a wide range of differing organisational contexts. The authors are both well-known researchers and professors of HRM at two of the UK's premier management schools – UMIST and the University of Loughborough. Professor Marchington is also Chief Moderator, Standards for the CIPD.

Learning and Development is written by the CIPD's Chief Examiner for the subject, Rosemary Harrison. Building on her extremely popular previous book on training and development, this also provides an extended analysis of learning and development that is based on the CIPD Standards. The book focuses on the main areas of the field – national policy frameworks, professional and ethical considerations, the delivery of learning and development, and career and management development. Given the comprehensive treatment of learning and development in this book, it is also eminently suitable for students on all courses – including CIPD – as well as for practitioners.

Employee Reward has also been fully revised and restructured to address the CIPD Professional Development Scheme Standards in the area. The author, Michael Armstrong, is a well-known and experienced writer and consultant in employee reward, and he was one of the CIPD's chief examiners until 2001. The book is divided into nine sections, each of which analyses a key component of reward management. This includes chapters on reward processes, job evaluation and competency frameworks, pay structures and systems, performance management and employee benefits. The book provides a highly practical and systematic coverage of employee reward that is likely to offer students an invaluable resource as well as give practitioners vital sources of information and ideas.

Employee Relations, like all the other books in the series, has been thoroughly updated in order to cover the CIPD Standards in the subject. The authors, John Gennard and Graham Judge, have an immense amount of academic and practical experience in employee relations, and they have combined forces again to offer students on CIPD courses an unparalleled text. The book deals systematically with all of the key components of employee relations. It provides an overview of the economic, corporate and legal environment and it focuses on the increasing influence of the European Union on employee relations. Subsequent parts of the book examine the processes and policies used by organisations, and the practice and skills required of HR professionals. John Gennard is Professor of HRM at the University of Strathclyde and Graham Judge is an independent consultant.

People Resourcing is written by Stephen Taylor, who is a senior lecturer at Manchester Metropolitan University, one of the CIPD's centres of excellence. This is an updated version of his earlier book on employee resourcing, and it provides a highly practical and accessible text for students taking CIPD examinations. All the main elements of people resourcing are examined in detail in the book. There is a particular focus on human resource planning, recruitment and selection, performance management, dismissal and redundancy. A wide range of examples drawn from different sectors and occupational groups illustrates the core concepts. The author is one of the CIPD's national examiners for Core Management and has a wide range of experience marking scripts in the people management and development area.

Essentials of Employment Law, now in its seventh edition, is firmly established as the most authoritative textbook on employment law for all students of human resource management. The authors are both from Middlesex University – David Lewis is professor of employment law and Malcolm Sargeant is reader in employment law. The text covers the CIPD employment law specialist elective and is an invaluable source of reference to students studying any area of HRM. It covers the key areas of employment law from the formation of contracts of employment to human rights and discrimination issues.

In drawing upon a team of such distinguished and experienced writers, this series provides a range of up-to-date, practical and research-led texts essential for those studying for the CIPD qualifications. Each of the books provides a systematic and comprehensive analysis of their subject area and as such can be used as core texts for all students on postgraduate and advanced undergraduate courses.

Mick Marchington
CIPD Chief Moderator, Standards

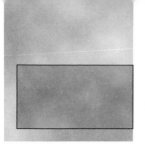

Acknowledgements

It is always difficult when writing a book of this size to acknowledge all the support that has been given to make the process work, but listed below are those people that to us seem to have offered the most important contributions. We have both been fortunate to receive grants from a wide range of funding bodies over the years who have also provided much of the data that has been used in this book. We would therefore like to mention grants, since the last book was written, from the Economic and Social Research Council, the Department of Trade and Industry (as it then was), the European Regional Development Fund and the Chartered Institute of Personnel and Development. We are both immensely lucky to work with such good colleagues at the Manchester School of Management, UMIST and Loughborough University Business School who provide the space and the support that is needed when putting together a textbook. It would be invidious to single anyone out for special mention because they have all contributed in some way by giving ideas or helping us to retain our sanity. Great support is also received from people at CIPD, especially Rob Foss who has been responsible for taking this book and the series to publication in such a short time-period, as well as colleagues in the PKI Group such as Mike Emmott.

The bulk of the word processing has been undertaken by Lindsay Endell and Rebecca White, and Lindsay has also put together all the references. Without them, we would have been in a mess! Our families have also given special support, so thanks again to Lorrie, Jack and Lucy, and to Jackie, Erin and Aidan. Jackie Wilkinson also made a major contribution to Chapters 3 and 5. However, the largest acknowledgement for this edition is to Lorrie Marchington. She has tracked down publications, references and websites, contacted organisations for data and helped substantially with the grammar and with proofreading. Her contribution to the chapters on learning and development has been especially important because there have been massive changes in this area since the last edition of the book. It is impossible to acknowledge just how much support she has provided.

Mick Marchington
Adrian Wilkinson
Manchester and Loughborough, February 2002

Acronyms and Weblinks

ACAS: The Advisory, Conciliation and Arbitration Service: www.acas.org.uk

ALI: Adult Learning Inspectorate: www.ali.gov.uk

BACP: British Association for Counselling and Psychotherapy: www.counselling.co.uk

BPS: British Psychological Society: www.bps.org.uk

CAC: Central Arbitration Committee: www.cas.gov.uk

CBI: Confederation of British Industry: www.cbi.org.uk

CIPD: Chartered Institute of Personnel and Development: www.cipd.co.uk

CPD: continuing professional development

CRE: Commission for Racial Equality: www.cre.gov.uk

DDA: Disability Discrimination Act (1995)

DfES: Department for Education and Skills: www.dfes.gov.uk

DOCAS: deduction of contribution at source

DPA: Data Protection Act

DRC: Disability Rights Commission: www.drc-gb.org/drc

DTI: Department for Trade and Industry: www.dti.gov.uk

EAP and EAPA: Employee Assistance Programmes and Employee Assistance Programmes Association: www.eapa.org.uk

EAT: Employment Appeals Tribunal: www.employmentappeals.gov.uk

ECJ: European Court of Justice: http://europa.eu.int/cj/en/

EDAP: Employee Development and Assessment Programmes

EDB: Employee Development Bulletin (IRS)

EEF: Engineering Employers Federation: www.eef.org.uk

EHB: Employee Health Bulletin (IRS)

EI: employee involvement

Eiro: The European Industrial Relations Observatory: www.eiro.eurofound.ie/

EOC: Equal Opportunities Commission: www.eoc.gov.uk

ESF: European Social Fund: www.esfnews.org.uk/

ETUC: European Trade Union Confederation: www.etuc.org/

EU: European Union: www.europa.eu.int

EWC: European Works Council: www.europeanworkscouncils.org/

GoodCorporation: www.goodcorporation.com

GNVQ: General National Vocational Qualification

HASAWA: Health and Safety at Work Act 1974

HCM: high-commitment management

HRD: human resource development

HRM: human resource management

HSC: Health and Safety Commission: www.hse.gov.uk/hsehome.htm

HSE: Health and Safety Executive: www.hse.gov.uk/

IDS: Incomes Data Services: www.incomesdata.com/

IES: Institute for Employment Studies: www.employment-studies.co.uk/

IIP: Investors in People: www.investorsinpeople.co.uk

ILO: International Labour Organisation: www.ilo.org

IPA: Involvement and Participation Association: www.ipa-involve.com/

IPD: Institute of Personnel and Development (now CIPD)

IRS: Industrial Relations Services

IT: information technology

ITBs: Industry Training Boards

ITOs: Industry Training Organisations

JCC: Joint Consultative Committee

KM: knowledge management

LEA: local education authority

learndirect: www.learndirect.co.uk

LO: learning organisation

LSCs: Learning and Skills Councils: www.lsc.gov.uk

MBA: Masters in Business Administration

MSC: Manpower Services Commission

NCTO: National Council for Training Organisations (superseded by Sector Skills Development Agency in 2002): www.nto-nc.org

NIACE: National Institute for Adult and Continuing Education: www.niace.org.uk/

NGOs: non-governmental organisations

NHS: National Health Service

NLSC: National Learning and Skills Council: www.lsc.gov.uk/

NSTF: National Skills Task Force

NTOs: National Training Organisations (superseded by the SSCs in 2002): www.nto.org.uk

NVQs and SVQs National/Scottish Vocational Qualifications

OCN: Open College Network: www.nocn.ac.uk/

OFSTED: Office for Standards in Education: www.ofsted.gov.uk/

PBR: payment by results

PDS: Professional Development Scheme

PMS: performance management systems

PQS: Professional Qualification Scheme (forerunner of the PDS)

PRP: performance-related pay

PVA: production value added

QCA: Qualifications and Curriculum Authority: www.qca.org.uk

RBV: resource-based view

R&D: research and development

RDAs: Regional Development Agencies: (Department for Regional Development): www.drdni.gov.uk

SAYE: Save As You Earn

SME: small and medium-sized enterprises

SSCs: Sector Skills Councils: www.ssdauk.co.uk

SSDA: Sector Skills Development Agency: www.ssdauk.co.uk

TECs/LECs: Training and Enterprise Councils

TQM: Total Quality Management

TUC: Trades Union Congress: www.tuc.org.uk

TURERA: the Trade Union Reform and Employment Rights Act 1993

UMIST: University of Manchester Institute of Science and Technology: www.umist.ac.uk

UNICE: Union of Industrial and Employers' Confederations of Europe: www.unice.org/

VET: vocational education and training

WERS: Workplace Employee Relations Survey, 1998

Human Resource Management at Work

The effective management and development of people is now seen as critical to gaining improvements in organisational performance. This is potentially good news for those involved in human resource management (HRM) because it means that there is greater interest in our subject than ever before. Other managers – who might in the past have been scathing about the HR profession and its contribution – are being forced to take notice of research that suggests that 'people really do make the difference'. The fact that it is a particular approach to HRM based on the 'high-commitment' model gives it even greater credence, as it centres on the notion that investing in human resources makes good business sense. Perhaps this finally paves the way for HR professionals to argue convincingly that 'people really are the organisation's most important resource'. Having arrived at this point, it could be argued that the main task is now to work out how to turn the principles into practice.

There are plenty of success stories in which links are made between HRM and business strategy. Examples might include situations where a new customer-focused strategy has apparently led to superior levels of performance, or where the existing culture has been transformed by the creation of a learning organisation. The principles underpinning initiatives such as Investors in People or Knowledge Management assume that organisations are likely to be successful if they commit themselves to more professional approaches to recruitment, training, communications and reward management. There has been a much wider recognition – by all parties – that investing in training does help organisations to be more successful, and may help to shift Britain from its traditional position as a low-skill, low-cost, low-performance economy. Communications, involvement and teamworking appear to be very important components of HR systems that generate enhanced levels of employee commitment and satisfaction, which lead ultimately to better performance. Even structures of collective employment relations, partnership schemes in particular, are promoted as beneficial for employers after years of being derogated for contributing to the ills of the British economy.

Appealing as this evidence is, however, serious doubts remain about whether or not managements really do invest in employees in practice, and equally whether or not this leads to competitive advantage. A number of studies show that it is the lack of professionalism in recruitment, a paucity of effective training, a failure to communicate with the workforce, and an unsystematic approach to employee relations that still predominate. Even when 'best practice' or 'high-commitment' HRM has apparently been adopted, it is often implemented without clear and careful planning, and taken up as the latest fad or fashion without considering how it might actually contribute to competitive advantage. As with many other aspects of organisational life in Britain, short-termism and the requirement to achieve immediate financial returns often assume priority over the sustained development of policies that will be beneficial in the longer run.

The purpose of this book is to address these issues by delving beneath the surface and adopting an analytical and evaluative stance to assess how HRM works in practice. The book provides readers with knowledge and understanding in the core areas of HRM, as well as facilitating the acquisition of skills that are central to the field. It differs from many of the existing prescriptive and descriptive texts by encouraging readers to raise questions, engage in a critical assessment of theory and practice, and evaluate the extent to which broad policies and procedures can be converted into reality. It repeatedly asks the question 'Why?', and demands of readers that they consider the relevance of specific human resource practices for different organisations.

In this sense, the book is an essential reference for those aiming to meet the CIPD Standards in the area of People Management and Development. It has relevance not only for those individuals who are studying full-time or part-time on college- or university-based programmes, but also for those who are undertaking flexible learning or are aiming to meet the CIPD Standards through experience and competence-based methods. The book is ideal also for students taking modules in human resource management and employment relations on business and management studies or other degree courses. It is also appropriate for courses at postgraduate level, but in this case – as with advanced undergraduate courses – it is essential to supplement the book by referring to specialist material in books and academic journals, in publications such as *People Management* and *IRS Employment Review*, and through electronic media. Tutors should find the web pages helpful when planning their sessions for examples of slides that may be useful and for points to raise when tackling the mini-questions and case studies.

The meanings of human resource management: an overview

From an academic perspective, 'HRM' is still a relatively new term that is struggling to gain credibility and sit alongside more established disciplines. It is often contrasted with 'industrial relations' and 'personnel management', the former laying claim to represent the theoretical basis of the subject while the latter is viewed as the practical and prescriptive homeland for issues concerning the management of employment. In addition, there are so many variants of HRM it is easy to find slippage in the use of the term, especially when critics are comparing the apparent *rhetoric* of 'high-commitment' HRM with the so-called *reality* of life in organisations that manage by fear and cost-cutting. Rather than explore this issue in depth here, we focus on some key distinctions and terms used in the subject.

There is little doubt that the HRM terminology originated in the USA, and that it emerged subsequent to the human relations movement. Two schools of thought predominate: Fombrun *et al*'s matching model and the Harvard framework. The former (Fombrun *et al*, 1984) emphasises the links between organisational strategy and the management of people, dividing people management into selection, development, appraisal and reward. The focus is on ensuring that there is a 'match' or 'fit' between the overall direction of the organisation and the way in which its people should be managed. It is essentially a unitarist analysis of employment relations – one in which the management of people is 'read off' from the broader objectives of the organisation. By contrast, the Harvard framework (Beer *et al*, 1985) suggests that a mix of situational factors and stakeholder interests combine to guide an HRM policy which then feeds through into HR outcomes – such as commitment, competence, congruence and cost-effectiveness. While acknowledging a role for alternative stakeholder interests, including the government and the community, this framework is essentially positivist in that it assumes a series of one-way links from policy to outcomes. As we see in Chapter 7, the frameworks used by David Guest in a series of studies adopt a line similar to this (Guest *et al*, 2000a). Neither approach pays a great deal of attention to the realities of work inside organisations, and especially not to the contested, contradictory and fragmented nature of the employment relationship.

The British debate has focused rather more on the distinction between 'hard' and 'soft' models of HRM (Storey, 1989; Legge, 1995). The 'hard' model – as with Fombrun *et al*'s approach – stresses the links between business and HR strategies and the crucial importance of a tight fit between the two. From this perspective, the human resource is seen as much the same as any other resource – land and capital, for example – and it is used as management sees fit. In this scenario there is no pretence that labour has anything other than commodity status, even though it may be treated well if the conditions are conducive – that is, when it is in short supply or it is central to the achievement of organisational objectives. By way of contrast, the 'soft' model focuses on the management of 'resourceful humans' and it assumes that employees are valued assets and a source of competitive advantage through their skills and abilities. Within this conception of HRM, there is one best way of managing staff, and it requires managers to gain the commitment and loyalty of staff in order to ensure that they deliver their best performance. Whereas the 'hard' model allows for a range of different styles to emerge for the management of people, the 'soft' variant argues that one style is superior to all others. In short, in this version it is appropriate to conceive of HRM as a particular *style* of managing that is capable of being measured and defined, as well as compared with an ideal.

This is the version that has attracted most interest in recent times, especially in those seeking links between HRM and performance. This version of HRM has also been compared with personnel management and industrial relations by a number of people, and has since stimulated a series of somewhat sterile debates about whether the management of employment in any organisation equates with HRM or industrial relations or personnel management. Legge (1995) outlined the similarities and distinctions between HRM and personnel management some time ago in terms of how each of these terms related to strategy, to the role of line managers and to the contribution of the specialist function. Storey (1992) compared HRM with personnel management and industrial relations, identifying 27 points of difference between the two in terms of beliefs and assumptions, strategic aspects, line management and key levers. Broadly, HRM – again seen as one distinct style – was perceived as less bureaucratic, more strategic, more integrated with business objectives, and substantially devolved to line managers. Guest (2001) differentiated between workplaces on the basis of high or low HRM activity and high or low industrial relations activity, thus leading to four alternative ideal types of workplace – partnership, traditional pluralism, individualism, and black hole.

Although each of these frameworks is useful in categorising employment relations, they all assume a particular model of HRM – the universalist, high-commitment, 'best practice' model that we explore in detail in Chapter 7. Conversely, if we assume that HRM is a field of study rather than a distinct style, it is then possible to examine how the management of employment may vary between workplaces and over time depending on a range of influences. It also allows us to examine the extent to which factors external to the workplace – such as legislative changes – can impact differentially depending upon management choice, management-employee relations and worker attitudes and behaviours. With this conception of the subject area, HRM can exist just as easily in a small owner-managed sweatshop as it can in a large and sophisticated high-tech organisation. HRM can therefore be defined as *the management of employment*, so incorporating individual and collective relations, the whole range of HR practices and HR processes, line management activities and those of HR specialists, managerial and non-managerial actions. It is not just another version of the 'hard' model because it allows for different styles to emerge in different workplaces, and for influence from a range of different stakeholder interests. HRM may or may not therefore include a key role for unions, it may or may not place an emphasis on training and development, it may or may not commit to employment security, and it may or may not have line managers at the helm of organisational change. But it may still centre on the notion that employers should be seeking to enhance the contribution of HR practices to performance irrespective of the approach adopted.

HRM and people management and development: the key assumptions

The CIPD's Professional Development Scheme was launched in 2001. As with its predecessor – the Professional Qualification Scheme – it was designed by small teams of experienced specialists following extensive consultation with the membership. The broad design of the Standards retains much from the previous PQS, especially in terms of there being a compulsory module – this time, People Management and Development – and a set of specialist modules from which students have to choose four. There have been a number of name changes, such as in the Learning and Development modules, as well as substantial updating and reconfigurations of the material. There are two further changes. First, the requirement to present a management report has been strengthened and reinforced by the addition of extra material on project management and research skills contained in this book as Chapter 5. Samples of management reports are now to be seen by the Chief Moderator – Standards. There is also a requirement to develop

Table 1   The CIPD notion of the thinking performer

Personal drive and effectiveness	Sets out own professional objectives with a prioritised plan for managing time and service delivery
People management and leadership	Demonstrates a level of knowledge and understanding about managing people and leadership that meets the CIPD Professional Development Scheme Standards
Business understanding	Demonstrates an understanding of the business needs and issues of various types of organisation
Professional and ethical competence	Meets a defined range of the CIPD's professional standards
Added value	Identifies opportunities for adding value and makes appropriate recommendations
Continuing learning	Adopts a considered approach to continuing learning and professional personal development
Analytical and intuitive/ creative thinking	Demonstrates use of a range of analytical, intuitive and creative abilities, tools and processes
Customer focus	Shows empathy for and responsiveness to customers of the PM&D function(s) and of employing organisations generally
Strategic capabilities	Understands the concept of strategy and the required contributions to it at all levels
Communication, persuasion and interpersonal skills	Uses 'active listening' with feedback, communicates clearly and positively; generates empathy with others

Source: CIPD Professional Standards for the Professional Development Scheme

and maintain a learning log as part of the CIPD's expectation that all members need to engage in continuing professional development (CPD) as good, professional practice. This subject is addressed as part of Chapter 6 in this book. The second change is the more explicit articulation of the notion of the 'thinking performer', a set of competencies that should guide CIPD members through their studies and their careers. These are outlined in Table 1. In reality they describe 'good practice', something that professional managers should be expected to follow.

The rationale underpinning the PM&D Standards specifies clearly the importance of acquiring a sound professional base for activities in the area, irrespective of the precise position that is occupied or the type of organisation for which a person works. The skills, knowledge and understanding that are developed are also appropriate for individuals who are not involved in specialist HR activities for an employer but are employed as consultants, academics or line managers. It is now increasingly common for practitioners to move between functions and organisations throughout their working lives, as well as between different forms of employment status. As a consequence it is important that all HR practitioners are aware not only of their own area of specialist expertise but also of the wider contribution which HRM can make to organisational success. They need to be able to justify how they contribute to improved performance and to understand how HRM integrates with other organisational activities. In addition, specialists in discrete areas – recruitment and selection, training and development, reward management or employee relations – must understand how their own activities fit in with other elements of HRM, and the extent to which they may support or conflict with overall strategies. A major theme underlying the PM&D Standards, and indeed the whole Professional Development Scheme, is the need for HR specialists to gain the commitment of line managers to their advice. Being able to persuade colleagues of the merits of particular ideas, and their contribution to organisational and departmental goals, is a skill of the utmost importance.

There are four key assumptions behind the PM&D standards, and these are reinforced continually throughout this book. First, as we saw above, the subject area of HRM is taken as those aspects of people management and development that are required to be understood by all CIPD graduates irrespective of their precise role or position in organisations. Using Torrington's medical analogy (see Chapter 6), these are the standards the 'general practitioner' needs to understand, and which remain important for the specialist consultant even though he or she is not explicitly aware that they are being used. These principles and practices are categorised in the Professional Development Scheme, as well as in this book, into the four generalist areas of resourcing, development, relations, and reward.

Second, the notion of integration is central to the standards. This takes two forms:

- vertical integration, which refers to the links between HRM and wider business strategies and organisational contexts

- horizontal integration, which refers to the 'fit' between different HR policies and practices, and the degree to which they support or contradict one another.

Readers will find similar topics being addressed at a number of places in the standards. This should be recognised as a positive sign of complementarity, integration and reinforcement rather than unnecessary repetition. A key assumption behind the standards is that both vertical and horizontal integration must be strengthened in order to maximise the HR contribution as well as to minimise the likelihood of conflicting messages.

Third, a thread running through the entire Professional Development Scheme, not just the PM&D module, is that HR specialists must be able to gain line management commitment for their proposals and recommendations. It matters little that a course of action impresses other HR specialists if it fails to convince line managers – the people who have to put most policies into effect. This is not to say that HR specialists should become the servants of line managers, merely recommending what the line managers want to hear in order to gain 'customer' approval. It does mean, however, that HR specialists have to be acutely aware of their audience, of the purpose of human resource policies, and of their contribution to organisational success. On some occasions the existing views of line managers will have to be challenged and the basis for their perspectives questioned, while on others their needs can be fulfilled with clear professional judgement and sound practical advice.

The final thread running through the standards is that of ethics and professionalism. As we see in Chapter 6, HR specialists might be able to make a distinctive contribution by adopting a clear ethical and professional stance on issues other managers might wish to ignore. This means that HRM can never be a simple technical exercise in which answers are read off according to some scientific formula and implemented without problem. HR professionals have to become accustomed to the fact – especially as they reach the higher echelons of the occupation – that their work is going to be fraught with tensions and contradictions, and with situations that are characterised by uncertainty, indeterminacy, and competing perspectives.

Outline of the Book

Following on from this introductory chapter, which forms Part 1, there are a further 17 chapters organised into five more parts.

Part 2 comprises three chapters on how the HR agenda is shaped by a number of issues and institutions. In Chapter 2, the changing nature of work and employment is addressed, with a particular focus on the changing nature of the labour market. Here a series of tables are presented detailing trends in the number of people in work and their hours of employment, the changing gender balance, and the reduction in overt conflict between employers and employees. We also examine the flexible firm, the meanings that people associate with work, and the changing psychological contract. This brings to the fore questions about employment insecurity. Chapter 3 outlines how the legal framework shapes and influences HR practice at the workplace, noting that this is increasingly driven by EU Directives and traditions. The law is much more significant than it was 30 years ago, both in terms of the way in which it has helped to formalise good practice in areas such as discipline and dismissal, and in its influence over contemporary patterns of employment relations. This chapter can do no more than provide an overview of employment law, and readers are advised to consult specialist legal texts – such as Lewis and Sargeant (2002) for more detail. The final chapter in the second Part of the book examines economic and institutional frameworks. The focus in Chapter 4 is on trade unions and on employers' associations, both of which continue to play a role in the development of HR practice at the workplace, although they are much less influential than they were 30 years ago. ACAS is another institution to have influenced management-employee relations, so this is also examined briefly. The training infrastructure has changed beyond recognition in the last few years, and the development of a new agenda and set of institutions – such as the Learning and Skills Council – promises to shape HRM yet further. Whether or not these structural changes have much impact in the workplace is something we leave to a later section of the book.

Part 3 considers the contribution of practitioners to research and project management and to the ethical and professional development of HRM. Chapter 5 is specifically designed to provide readers with guidance on how to devise, manage and complete projects – such as the management reports that are required as part of the CIPD Professional Development Scheme and on many other courses. It explains how to undertake a project, and it focuses on the key personal and interpersonal skills required to complete work on time and considers how others can be persuaded of the ideas contained in projects. Chapter 6 describes the history and development of HRM as well as assessing the degree to which the CIPD can be regarded as a professional body. It also examines how HR specialists can adopt an ethical stance at work, in terms both of their own activities and of those of their employing organisations. The chapter acknowledges that it is not always easy for practitioners to persuade others of the importance of ethics but that it is one of the obligations on any professional.

Part 4 examines the way in which the HR contribution can be integrated into the business and the extent to which HRM has an impact on organisational performance. This is the core of the book in that it not only introduces more detailed analysis of different HR practices, it also assesses the links between HRM and organisational strategies and performance. Chapter 7 considers in some detail the 'high-commitment' or 'best practice' model, explaining how this model is put together and reviewing it in the light of both US and UK literature and practice. Although acknowledging that the model appears very attractive, the argument is that it is not necessarily achievable in all workplaces, nor would employers necessarily want to invest so heavily in their workers. The research examining the high-commitment HRM–performance link is also reviewed, and we compare the 'positive' result that this model of HRM contributes to improved performance with the rather more sceptical conclusion that high performance might just as easily have occurred due to intensified working practices and regimes. Chapter 8 examines the proposition that HR practices are likely to vary depending upon organisational objectives and context. This, the 'best fit' notion of HRM, is reviewed using a number of frameworks, and the major limitations of these sorts of model are outlined. Another way in which to view the strategy–HRM link is through the resource-based view of the firm, and this is analysed briefly in Chapter 8 as well. We conclude this chapter with an assessment of the blocks and barriers that make it problematic to convert strategy into practice in any workplace. Finally in Part 4, we address the question of who has responsibility for HRM, comparing and contrasting the roles of HR specialists, consultants and line managers in the delivery of HR policies and practices. It is noted that consultants and line managers now assume greater responsibility for HRM – often for very good reason – but there is no guarantee they will perform better than their HR colleagues within the organisation. Initiatives to devolve HRM to line managers and consultants require to be considered carefully to make sure that benefits will arise from them. Chapter 9 concludes with an assessment of the HR contribution in terms of the influence that HR specialists are able to enjoy within organisations and also in relation to how performance may be benchmarked against that of other similar employers. Despite its attractions, we caution against simplistic comparisons.

Part 5 is the longest section in the book, and it is here that we examine different HR practices in rather more detail. The section is designed in line with the CIPD Standards, so there are two chapters each on people resourcing, learning and development, employee relations, and employee reward. Chapters 10 and 11 look, respectively, at cost-effective recruitment and selection, and managing performance for added value. In Chapter 10 we deal with human resource planning, a topic frequently stressed as a key element in a professional and strategic approach to HRM. The practice of human resource planning is generally much more mundane, however, and organisations are often typified by 'ad hocery' and reactive management than they are by systematic planning. The remainder of Chapter 10 examines recruitment and selection, emphasising that decisions at this stage have a major consequence for subsequent employment relations. We assess interviews and selection testing in a little more detail, and alert readers to the fact that they should be ready to seek advice from experts if they are not qualified. Chapter 11 analyses the management of performance, starting with the critical role that induction plays in socialising new recruits in to the culture of the organisation. Appraisal and performance review form the core of this chapter, but we also look in some detail at how the problems of poor performance may be addressed by examining both capability and attendance issues. Although the end-result of this review process might be discipline or dismissal, it could just as easily point to a need to provide counselling and support for staff, and here we identify strategies and external agencies that may be able to help in this field.

Chapters 12 and 13 address learning and development. The first of these chapters looks at how employee skills and contributions may be maximised, examining in particular the way the national framework for vocational education and training (VET) has impinged upon the workplace. As well as describing some of the recent changes to the system, we focus on specific interventions such as Modern Apprenticeships and Investors in People. The latter in particular has been regarded as a significant policy initiative, and many organisations have been accredited for this award. Despite its success, there remain some concerns about IiP. Similarly, there have been plenty of positive reports about learning organisations and knowledge-intensive firms, and in theory these offer tremendous opportunities to improve both individual learning and organisational performance. Again, we review evidence of how these initiatives have worked in practice. Chapter 13 focuses more specifically on the training cycle within organisations. The importance of identifying training needs correctly, of designing and delivering training programmes effectively, and of evaluating whether they have attained objectives, are all critical to the success of training interventions. One major issue is the extent to which learning and training actually make a difference to individual and organisational performance, and how they tie in with other aspects of HRM.

Chapters 14 and 15 are concerned with employee relations. In the first of these chapters, we analyse the structures and processes for effective employment relations. This includes a review of management objectives in employee relations, as well as a comparison of union and non-union organisations. We argue that the differences between union and non-union firms are probably exaggerated, given the sizeable differences within each of these broad categories – say, between a large, 'household name' non-union firm and a sweatshop from which unions are excluded. Collective bargaining and employee involvement (EI) is also dealt with. It is accepted that the former has become less influential in recent years – though it is still relevant for pay determination and grievance resolution in a large number of workplaces. EI has grown in significance, both in its collective form through partnership agreements and works councils and specifically through individual schemes designed to communicate with and tap into ideas from workers. Chapter 15 discusses the role of procedures in employee relations, with particular reference to discipline and grievance-handling, as well as to the role that HR specialists play in the bargaining process. We conclude that procedures still have an important part to play in the management of employee relations, and urge caution on those employers who might see them as little more than a legacy of previous bureaucratic rules which should be discarded in the pursuit of flexibility.

The final two chapters of Part Five examine reward management. Chapter 16 reviews the motivational base for reward strategy and practice by describing briefly the work of some of the classical management theorists – Taylor, Maslow and Herzberg – and the implications for reward management and choices of payment system. We consider a range of different payment schemes, explaining their nature and reviewing their comprehensiveness, as well as considering how they work in practice. We focus particularly on performance-related pay and profit sharing/employee share ownership given their popularity as a potential device for gaining performance improvements. As with other areas of the book, however, we caution against implementing such schemes on the basis of their supposed appeal, and advise readers to conduct a thorough review of their appropriateness to different workplaces and situations. Chapter 17 assesses how equity and fairness – key concepts in reward management and HRM – can be delivered in organisations. This chapter reviews job evaluation and considers equal value issues for the design of reward schemes. We also examine employee benefits – such as pension schemes, harmonisation and non-financial recognition and reward. This last area is increasingly perceived as one which can and should be developed, not only because of cost constraints on employers but also because the provision of more interesting work and prizes can have important motivational and recognition effects.

Chapter 18 – Part 6 of the book – offers readers an opportunity to review their understanding of the whole book by providing a range of examination questions. These are designed to be of particular assistance to students taking the CIPD Professional Development Scheme and in particular the People Management and Development module. However, they should also be useful to other readers and students on other programmes. In addition, some general advice is provided for students on how to address examination questions and in particular how to increase their chance of success.

2 • The Changing Nature of Work and Employment

CHAPTER OBJECTIVES

By the end of this chapter, readers should be able to:

● access, use and interpret data from a range of internal and published sources on work and employment

● benchmark indicators of employee satisfaction, commitment and loyalty against national averages

● contribute to decisions about the use of flexible forms of working in their own organisation.

In addition, readers should understand and be able to explain:

● the impact of broader economic and employment trends on the character of HRM at work

● the nature, meaning and extensiveness of the flexible firm

● the costs and benefits of moves to more flexible forms of employment.

Introduction

The employment relationship is central to the study of people management and development, whether in terms of the direct employment of staff by an organisation, or in the subcontracting of work to external bodies. This relationship is characterised by conflict and co-operation, by confusion and contradiction, and by varying imbalances in the distribution of power between the parties. As we see in Chapter 3, on the legal context, contracts are incomplete and change in nature during the period of a person's employment due to broader political, legal, economic, social and technological trends. In addition, changes come about through interactions between representatives of employers and employees at national and international level, senior managers and employee representatives at establishment level, and the actions of first line managers and individual employees on the shop floor or in the office. None of these influences is paramount in defining the way in which employment relationships are forged at the workplace, although some may have a stronger influence at some times than others. All may point in the same or in different directions.

It is tempting to assume that the broader influences leave little room for choice at the workplace. Over the last 20 years, changes at the macro level – especially in patterns of employment and in legislation – have clearly affected the nature of the employment relationship as well as HR practice. Nevertheless, it is important to stress that although these wider developments do have a significant impact on employment relations at workplace level, their precise influence is heavily dependent upon the specific circumstances in which organisations operate. For example, despite the fact that many of these changes strengthened the hand of employers and provided an opportunity for managers to exert firmer control, organisations remain in which line managers still have difficulty in persuading their staff to work harder and smarter, or in dealing with 'problem' employees. In the contrasting situation – at times when broader influences have placed more severe constraints on managements' freedom of action – at some workplaces employees were harshly treated and received little protection from arbitrary actions by managers. HR practitioners need to understand how these influences combine together, as well as appreciate the impact of specific actions on HRM.

In this chapter we focus on general trends in the area of work and employment. First, we present data on the changing nature of employment, referring in particular to sectoral and structural trends in employment, in addition to looking at working hours, unemployment rates and strikes (stoppages of work). In combination, these illustrate graphically the degree to which British employment relations changed over the last two decades, even more so when seen alongside the decline in union membership that we outline in Chapter 4. Second, we review the material on flexibility and the so-called flexible firm by examining functional and numerical flexibility in particular. This discussion leads us into debates about new organisational forms and the way in which these – for example, outsourcing and public-private partnerships – are reshaping work and employment relations. Finally, we move on to consider the changing nature of work. While accepting that the employment relationship is incomplete and constantly changing, we address questions about job satisfaction, motivation and commitment, the psychological contract and work intensification. Each of these themes recurs throughout the remainder of the book.

Labour markets and changing patterns of employment

The last 25 years have seen major changes in the labour market and to employment patterns in Britain. In particular, there have been major sectoral shifts in employment, a growing proportion of workers employed on what are termed 'atypical' contracts, and considerably enhanced female participation in the labour market. Unemployment dipped towards the end of the century, having remained stubbornly high for a long time, and patterns of strike action and union membership changed significantly over this period. All of these have significant implications for the nature of HRM. Many of these issues are bound up with, and exemplified by, the growth of flexibility, and increasing distinctions between a core and peripheral workforce. Before analysing the nature and impact of flexibility in Britain we must first briefly describe some of these major economic and labour market factors.

There has been a fundamental sectoral shift in employment away from manufacturing and the public sector – sectors renowned for more formalised HR systems, high levels of trade union membership, and larger employment units – towards the more informal, relatively union-free, and smaller employment units of the service sector. For example, in 1970 nearly 8 million people worked in manufacturing, a figure which fell to about 7 million by 1980 and has now dropped to around 4 million. In other words, the number of people working in manufacturing in Britain halved in about 30 years. Public-sector employment also declined significantly in the latter part of the twentieth century, falling from around 30 per cent of all those employed in 1979 to about 25 per cent by 2001. Much of this decline has been due to long-running problems in the productive public sector (eg coal) and to privatisations of what were previously public service sector employers (eg gas, water, electricity and telecommunications). In addition, there have been declining numbers of public sector workers in healthcare, local and central government organisations due to the contracting-out of a wide range of ancillary and other services to the private sector. Taken together, however, in 2001 there were still more than 2 million people employed in public and private sector education, and more than 2.5 million in health and social work (*Labour Market Trends*, November 2001).

The principal growth area over the last 30 years has been the service sector. As a whole, including both public and private services, this grew from around 10 million employees in 1970 to well over 20 million at the turn of the century. Indeed, numbers employed across the economy increased altogether by nearly 2 million in the six years to 2001 to over 29 million. During this period, service employment increased by more than 2 million workers, with the largest growth area – about 20 per cent – in finance and business services. Other industries that grew over this period included distribution, hotels and restaurants (8 per cent), transport and communications (15 per cent), and public administration, education and health (4 per cent). The industries that declined the most over this period were agriculture and fishing (15 per cent) and energy and water (20 per cent). The changing nature of employment has implications for all areas of HR practice, and the growth of 'new' firms is particularly significant in the employment relations area   as we see in later chapters. It is evident that new firms tend to adopt quite different HR practices from those of their 'older' counterparts.

Much of the growth in numbers employed can be accounted for by the increased participation rate of women in the economy. Table 2 shows that over 2 million more women were employed in 2000 than had been in 1985, compared with a growth rate for men of about 1 million.

Nevertheless, the employment rate (the number in employment divided by number in the 16–59 age-group) for women remained below that for men at just under 70 per cent as opposed to a little below 80 per cent for men in the 16–64 age-group (*Labour Market Trends*, February 2001). Over the longer term, the growth rate for women in employment has been much higher. In 1960, for example, women comprised about 33 per cent of the labour force, a figure that rose to nearly 45 per cent by the year 2000. Extrapolating from these trends suggests that the proportion of women and men in the labour force could well equalise within the next 20 years. The labour market is heavily segmented, however, with many more women than men working part-time, and with women concentrated in the service sector and in jobs with lower pay and lower status. The equal opportunities implications of labour market segmentation are considered further in Chapter 4.

Associated with the growth in female participation in the labour market has been a major shift in the distribution of employment between full-time and part-time work, as well as some changes to the number of people working on temporary contracts or self-employed. There are many different ways of defining part-time employment and it clearly makes a difference to the figures whether we are talking about jobs that are less than 35 hours or 30 hours or 21 hours, for example. Equally, we might expect to find differences depending on whether the classification is based on self-reporting or on actual hours worked. The number

Table 2   Men and women in employment (millions) between 1985 and 2000

	1985	1990	1995	2000
Women aged 16 to 59				
All women	16.32	16.70	16.94	17.29
In employment	9.73	11.12	11.12	11.92
Full-time	5.58	6.52	6.34	6.77
Part-time	4.15	4.60	4.78	5.15
Employment rate (%)	59.7	66.6	65.6	68.9
ILO* rate of unemployment (%)	11.0	6.6	7.0	4.9
Men aged 16 to 64				
All men	17.94	18.31	18.54	19.02
In employment	13.96	15.03	14.11	15.05
Full-time	13.46	14.30	13.13	13.83
Part-time	0.50	0.73	0.98	1.22
Employment rate (%)	77.9	82.1	76.1	79.1
ILO rate of unemployment (%)	11.7	7.1	10.2	6.1

*International Labour Organisation
Source: adapted from *Labour Market Trends*, February 2001; derived from labour force surveys from spring 1985 to 2000

of people who stated that they were employed on full-time contracts grew by about 7 per cent (a little under 1.5 million) between 1985 and 2000 whereas part-time employment increased by more than one third (about 1.7 million) over the same period (*Labour Market Trends*, February 2001). On this count, the proportion of jobs that are part-time increased from less than 20 per cent in 1985 to approximately 25 per cent by the turn of the century. More recent data, using different measures, estimated that workers in part-time employment comprise about 33 per cent of those employed (*Labour Market Trends*, November 2001). Either way, part-time work has become a much more prominent feature of the UK employment scene over the last few decades, a little way above the EU average. This is a higher proportion than all other EU countries but for France and the Netherlands, and it is significantly higher than Spain or Finland (European Foundation for the Improvement of Living and Working Conditions, 2000). It is interesting to note that the growth in part-time work may be due more to sectoral change, and the emergence of new firms in the service sector that are more likely to employ part-timers, than to the extension of part-time working at 'continuing' workplaces (Millward *et al*, 2000: 44).

Positive benefits from part-time working

- 'Part-time staff provide the flexibility that the organisation needs operationally.'

- 'Our experience of part-timers is that they are very hard-working and loyal to the company, and are often more productive than a comparable full-timer.'

- 'Part-time workers are essential both to the organisation and to the community.'

- 'We generally find that our part-timers are extremely productive, eager to learn and committed to the business.'

- 'It is a good way of retaining skills and experience within the company.'

- 'Gives greater flexibility of cover, because if one leaves or is off sick you can still have some cover and can request extra hours.'

This is a set of comments made by employers about the value of employing people part-time. How do your own experiences compare with this, and can your own organisation make greater use of part-timers?

Source: IRS Employment Trends 735, September 2001

About 40 per cent of all temporary jobs across the EU are part-time, compared with slightly over a quarter of all so-called 'permanent' jobs – ie those with open-ended as opposed to fixed-term contracts. The UK figures are very similar for temporary employment but rather higher for people in permanent positions. Temporary employment has grown in the last 20 years from less than 5 per cent of the working population (excluding the self-employed) to about 7 per cent, a growth that has been more marked amongst those in full-time jobs than in part-time employment (*Labour Market Trends*, November 2001). Nevertheless, this still comprises a fairly small proportion of full-time jobs (about one in 20) whereas it is a much larger percentage of those in part-time employment at 15 per cent (Robinson, 2000: 32). The fastest spurt in the growth of temporary jobs occurred after 1990, particularly in public administration, education and health, and it was also most marked for those in professional positions (Robinson, 2000: 33–4). Britain has rather more temporary workers than the USA, but many less than its main European competitors: for example, in Germany and France, temporary workers comprise 11.5 per cent and 12.2 per cent of the total workforce respectively, and in Spain approximately one quarter of the workforce is on temporary contracts (Hudson, 2002: 41).

Finally, there has been a substantial growth in the number of people who are classified as self-employed since the late 1970s. In 1979, for example, just over 1.8 million people were self-employed, a figure which increased dramatically to over 3.2 million by 1989, only to flatten out in the 1990s (Robinson, 2000: 33). In the spring of 2001, for instance, 3.17 million people were self-employed (*Labour Market Trends*, November 2001). Many of the self-employed are people made redundant during the 1980s, who decided to set up their own businesses due to the relative scarcity of 'standard' employment opportunities. Unfortunately, many of these businesses have since gone into liquidation or their owners have made only limited financial returns for their investments. The proportion who are self-employed full-time has now fallen below 10 per cent of all those in employment, although there has been a growth in the part-time self-employed (Robinson, 2000: 33). This latter figure could include a whole range of people who otherwise work full-time but have self-employed status for tax reasons. It is not a good indicator of self-employment because of this. The number of agency workers from private recruitment bureaux has more than trebled during the last decade (Druker and Stanworth, 2001) to almost 300,000 by the turn of the century, getting on for 20 per cent of all temporary workers being supplied through this route.

> Workers on temporary contracts may offer advantages to employers in terms of cost savings and flexibility, but do they add other costs for the employer (in terms of quality, productivity or commitment, for example)? What do temporary workers gain from this form of employment, if anything?

Whereas the employed segment of the labour force has changed significantly in the last 30 years, unemployment levels remained high for most of this period, falling back around the turn of the century. Back in the 1960s, unemployment typically stood at about 3 per cent – that is, at around 600,000 people. The effects of a variety of world-wide shocks on the system during the 1970s pushed the figure steadily up beyond 1 million and to over 5 per cent by 1979. Since then numerous changes in the way in which unemployment is defined have made it difficult to make precise comparisons, but by the International Labour Office (ILO) definition it has oscillated between about 1.5 and 3.5 million over this period. In percentage terms, the figure has varied from about 5 to 12 per cent, and even at the lower levels this is higher than would have been considered reasonable in the 1960s. By the end of 2001, the (ILO-defined) unemployment rate stood at a little over 1.5 million, approximately 5 per cent of the potential workforce (*Labour Market Trends*, December 2001). Certain pockets of unemployment persist, chiefly among young people in inner-city areas, and in those in their fifties who have been made redundant and are unable to find comparable work. The number of redundancies announced varied little each year between 1995 and 2000, with about 180,000 per spring quarter each year, although women had a slightly lower redundancy rate than men, and younger workers (less than 25 years old) were more likely to be made redundant than older workers. Not surprisingly, the rate was also much higher in manufacturing than in services. Re-employment rates are now higher for women than for men, as well as for workers aged less than 50 than for older workers (*Labour Market Trends*, June 2001).

The next 30 years are likely to see further pressures on the labour market due to an ageing population, and perhaps calls to lift the retirement age beyond 65. In Britain, for example, the ratio of pensioners to the working population is currently about 1:3, a ratio that could rise – on current projections – to over 2:5 by 2030. This is not just a British problem either, in the light of estimates for Germany of over 3:5 by 2030, and for Italy of 7:10. We are already seeing the impact of these demographic changes upon pension provisions and on the ability of society to cope with the recent spate of early retirements.

The extent of strike action in Britain also illustrates the degree to which labour markets have changed over the last 20 years. Table 3 (derived from *Labour Market Trends*, June 2001) shows how the nature and extent of stoppages varied over the period between 1980 and 2000. The principal points to note about this table are that the number of working days lost to industrial action fell sharply from an average of about 10 million in the early part of the 1980s to less than half a million in the years up to 2000. The number of workers involved in stoppages also fell dramatically over this period. The typical figure now averages out at about 200,000 per annum, compared with levels more than six times as high in the early 1980s. The number of recorded stoppages dropped by similar proportions, from well over 1,000 per annum in the early 1980s to approximately 200 at the turn of the century. Yet more notable are the length of stoppages, the last 10 years recording just six strikes that lasted longer than 100,000 working days, a figure that was typically achieved in a single year during the 1980s (*Labour Market Trends*, June 2001). In short, industrial action has become a relatively rare phenomenon in the UK. When it does occur, it is often short-term in nature, designed to achieve maximum effect without having to suffer long-term losses in earnings. Yet occasionally it results in a long-drawn-out strike. For example, a cursory inspection of the statistics appears to show that the number of working days lost through strikes varies significantly by region. However, the fact that Scotland had a figure substantially higher than any other region in 2000 can be explained by the fact that virtually all of this was accounted for by one stoppage of work.

Table 3   Stoppages in progress, United Kingdom 1980–2000

Year	Working days lost (000s)	Working days lost per thousand employees	Workers involved (000s)	Stoppages	Stoppages involving the loss of 100,000 working days or more
1980	11,964	492	834	1,348	5
1981	4,266	184	1,513	1,344	7
1982	5,313	234	2,103	1,538	7
1983	3,754	168	574	1,364	6
1984	27,135	1,207	1,464	1,221	11
1985	6,402	282	791	903	4
1986	1,920	85	720	1,074	2
1987	3,546	155	887	1,016	3
1988	3,702	157	790	781	8
1989	4,128	172	727	701	6
1990	1,903	78	298	630	3
1991	761	32	176	369	1
1992	528	23	148	253	–
1993	649	28	385	211	2
1994	278	12	107	205	–
1995	415	18	174	235	–
1996	1,303	55	364	244	2
1997	235	10	130	216	–
1998	282	11	93	166	–
1999	242	10	141	205	–
2000	499	20	183	212	1

Source: Davies J. 'Labour disputes in 2000', *Labour Market Trends*, Vol. 109, No. 6, 2001. p302

It can be seen that the employment patterns have gone through some fundamental adjustments during the last 20 years, and the 'old' images of workers as principally male, full-time and permanent have now been shattered. Similarly, the extent of sectoral shifts in employment, away from manufacturing and to the service sector, has had major implications for the way in which work is organised and for the role of HR professionals. Having outlined briefly each of the component parts of the changes in employment, we can now move on to examine how these might hang together around the notion of flexibility and the flexible firm.

Flexibility, the flexible firm and inter-organisational relations

Popular and managerial interest in workforce and organisational flexibility grew following the publication of Atkinson's work on the flexible firm in the mid-1980s (Atkinson, 1984; Atkinson and Meager, 1986; Atkinson, 1987). Since then other writers have taken up the idea,

Figure 1   The flexible firm

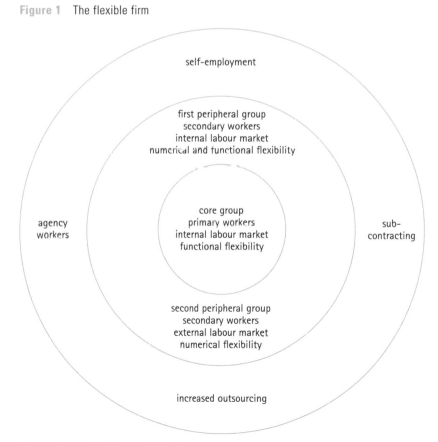

Adapted from J. Atkinson, 1984: 29

notably Handy (1991) with the terminology of a 'shamrock organisation'. Both make distinctions between a core and a peripheral workforce, albeit in slightly different ways and with different foci, but because Atkinson's was the first to be publicised it is still widely referred to in other research. There have been some refinements to the model in the last 20 years, notably by Ackroyd and Procter (1998), but the essential framework remains the same and it provides a straightforward graphical representation of flexibility. In simple terms, organisations can be divided into a core and a periphery in employment terms, as illustrated in Figure 1.

The core comprises workers who are drawn from the primary labour market, who have the security of 'permanent' (ie not fixed-term) contracts, and who have skills that are extremely important to the employer. In return, these core employees are expected to be functionally flexible by applying their skills across a wide range of tasks. Flexibility can be both vertical and horizontal. Vertical flexibility refers to employees who take on tasks that are at a higher or lower skill level than that for which they have been recruited. A good example would be craft workers who undertake labouring duties – such as sweeping up – or semi-skilled employees who assume responsibility for certain skilled tasks, such as making minor repairs to keep production lines running. Horizontal flexibility refers to employees who undertake a wider range of tasks at the same broad skill level, as for example in the case of craft workers who operate across previous skill boundaries by doing both mechanical and electrical work. Employees who work in teams may be both vertically and horizontally flexible if they are responsible for a complete task. For example, process workers in some chemical plants operate in the control room, undertake routine maintenance tasks on the plant and take it in turns to act as team leader (Marchington, 1999; Frobel and Marchington, 2001). Each of these forms of functional flexibility is driven by employer needs for increased productivity and quality so as to survive in highly competitive (often international) product markets.

The periphery can be subdivided into several segments. The first peripheral group comprises workers from the secondary labour market but who are still internal to the organisation in the sense that they are employed on contracts that have some degree of permanence. They are typically full-time (though some part-timers could also be included in this category), but due to their lower level of skills these workers cannot expect similar degrees of security as their colleagues from the 'core'. They may display some functional flexibility, but typically their work is characterised by little responsibility, low levels of discretion and lower material rewards. These employees are numerically flexible and employers feel that they can be laid off relatively easily since applicants with similar skills can be hired quickly if necessary.

The second peripheral group comprises individuals who find greater difficulty breaking into internal labour markets and whose employment experiences tend to be precarious. This group includes individuals with little prospect of employment security. Many part-timers, temporaries, and public subsidy trainees would fit into this category, and for some a move into the internal labour market is a possibility, provided work continues and they are seen to do a good job and 'fit' with the organisational culture. As we saw in the previous section, the number of part-timers and temporaries increased over the past 25 years, but for many of those on fixed-term contracts there is little prospect that their employment will extend beyond the end of their current contract.

Beyond the second peripheral group are those individuals who are clearly external to the host organisation – that is, employed by another employer or in self-employment. As we noted above, the size of this group has expanded significantly since the 1970s, especially where work has been sub-contracted to other organisations. Agency workers would clearly fit into this category, the types of people included ranging from secretaries to accountants, nurses, teachers and lecturers (Druker and Stanworth, 2001; Ward et al, 2001). Ward et al (2001: 9) put forward a number of reasons why host organisations are becoming more likely to recruit temporary workers through specialist agencies, most of which relate to numerical flexibility and the shifting of risk to agencies and the temporaries themselves. It is clear that some organisations are now vetting temporary agency workers during their contracts to see whether or not they may be suitable for appointment to permanent positions should these fall vacant (Forde, 2001). In other words, the initial responsibility for certain aspects of recruitment and selection transfers to an agency, leading in some cases to the development of quasi-internal labour markets that may be advantageous both to the host employer and to the agency.

Whereas the Atkinson model views this group as very much within the secondary labour market, and at a major disadvantage to those in the primary internal labour market, some of these workers may be in a relatively powerful position. The more highly-skilled workers could well be in great demand, and may choose to remain outside mainstream organisational life in order to maintain greater control over their own lives, as well as earn larger amounts of money for their efforts. Obviously, some HR consultants could fall into this category, as would other individuals whose skills are in demand (eg information technology specialists).

> How well do these models compare with patterns of flexibility in your own organisation, and how easy is it to distinguish between these categories in practice?

There is some evidence to illustrate that organisations now have more flexible employment policies and practices, in particular through the increased use of part-timers and in the growth of sub-contracting and self-employment. The public sector – in particular health trusts and local authorities – has been at the forefront of these developments, with government requirements to extend outsourcing through a range of means in recent times. The move to compulsory competitive tendering (CCT), best value and public-private partnerships has increased the extensiveness of fixed-term contracts (Colling, 1999) and the use of TUPE transfers of employment have become commonplace (Cooke *et al*, 2002). Despite some well-publicised success stories, however, there remain doubts about the extensiveness of the 'flexible firm' in reality, and some scepticism about whether or not such new organisational forms are the product of strategic thinking or muddling through. At least four sets of issues need addressing in relation to the flexible firm concept.

First, there are doubts about the conceptual standing of the terminology. Publications on the subject seem to veer between descriptions of flexibility at work, to predictions that the flexible firm is the design of the future, through to prescriptions that this represents what organisations ought to look like in order to be successful. At times it is difficult to tell which is being used, and it has led to allegations that flexibility has been 'talked up' in order to support successive governments' ideological stance on market deregulation and 'lean' organisations (Legge, 1995: 172). It is also argued that despite its obvious intuitive appeal, the model itself lacks clarity in terms of the core-periphery distinction. For example, rather than viewing part-timers as peripheral, it is clear that some part-time workers may be critical to organisational success given the closeness of their contact with customers or their contribution to business goals (Rubery *et al*, 2002). A question arises therefore as to whether these workers should be classified as core because of their roles, or peripheral because they are part-timers. The fact that service sector organisations frequently employ part-timers in customer-facing jobs shows that they are prepared to treat them as if they occupied a core rather than a peripheral role – as the IRS (2001) survey quotes above indicated clearly. Similarly, the extensive use of agency staff in call centres (Carroll *et al*, 2001a) or students in hotels and supermarkets (Curtis and Lewis, 2001) also demonstrates the limitations to the model.

Second, there are questions about the extensiveness of flexibility in practice and the reasons for its growth. Robinson (1999: 90) suggests that the more dramatic assertions about the impact of the core-periphery model are not really backed up by the data. We have already presented data on numerical flexibility in the previous section, and from that it can be seen that there has been growth in so-called 'non-standard' employment. The 1998 WERS survey (Cully *et al*, 1999: 35) data on this is summarised in Table 4 From this, it would appear that sub-contracting is well established in both sectors, as is the use of fixed-term contracts for staff in the public sector. Temporary agency workers are used in about a quarter of all workplaces and freelancers by one in

Table 4   Sub-contracting and the use of non-standard labour (% of all workplaces)

	Private sector	Public sector	All workplaces
Sub-contract one or more services	91	88	90
Temporary agency workers	29	26	28
Fixed-term contract employees	34	72	44
Freelance workers	16	7	13
Homeworkers	8	3	6
Zero-hour contract workers	6	2	5
None of these used	5	6	5

Source: Cully *et al* (1999), *Britain at Work, as depicted by the 1998 Workplace Employee Relations Survey*. Routledge, London, p35

eight, though rarely in the public sector. Homeworkers and zero-hours contract workers, despite the popular media interest in these forms of employment, remain relatively under-used if one ignores those who work at home in addition to or instead of their normal workplace (Felstead *et al*, 2001. Moreover, although large numbers of people claim to work at home occasionally, it is almost impossible to establish how often this occurs and for what length of time.

The other important finding from Table 4 (Cully *et al*, 1999) is that very few workplaces make no use whatsoever of non-standard labour. Of course, there are questions about the extent to which the growth in 'non-standard' or 'atypical' work is indicative of strategic management practice to change working hours so as to increase flexibility. Many of the reasons put forward by employers for employing part-timers and temporary workers relate to cost savings, as does the move to greater outsourcing of core or ancillary services. Increasing customer demand for longer opening hours – for example, in supermarkets or in call centres – also makes it more difficult to staff these activities with 'conventional' full-time work systems, and has led many employers to increase the use of people on part-time or temporary contracts. In short, much of the growth in non-standard working patterns can be explained by sectoral shifts within the economy.

Thirdly, there are questions about the costs and benefits of flexibility. It is widely assumed that the flexible firm is naturally and automatically more efficient than its 'inflexible' counterpart, and that part-time workers, temporaries and sub-contractors offer employers advantages over secure and permanent staff. This question is reconsidered at many points in this book, but particularly later in this chapter when we analyse the arguments for and against the intensification of work, as well as in Chapter 7 when we review the notion of high-commitment HRM. It is difficult to estimate whether part-time workers are more productive than their full-time colleagues or whether they are more costly due to differing levels of absenteeism, commitment and quality (Hunter *et al*, 1993: 348). There have been continuing concerns about levels of quality, for example, in work that has been sub-contracted from the NHS and local authorities to the private sector (Colling, 1999; Marchington *et al*, 2002). There are also questions about whether core workers maintain previous levels of commitment when many of their colleagues lose jobs through rationalisation due to fears for their own future security (Redman and Wilkinson, 2001). At the same time, it should not be assumed that workers automatically lose out through working non-standard hours. It is clear that some prefer to be able to work part-time and would not want to move into full-time employment despite the lower level of earnings (Thompson and McHugh, 2002: 161). The increased number of students in part-time and temporary jobs clearly influences these figures, but even among people with a long-term presence on the labour market there are often good reasons for wanting part-time work.

Who do you think gains most from flexible working, and why? Put together lists for employees and employers in relation to functional and numerical flexibility before making a judgement.

Finally, it could be argued that the model of the flexible firm is restricted because it is based too much on the notion of a single firm and its HR practices, rather than being dynamic enough to account for major developments in inter-organisational relations (Rubery *et al*, 2002). Most analysis continues to be based on the relationship between a single employing organisation and its employees, even though this is probably no longer an entirely accurate characterisation of HRM. A series of changes – such as increasingly globalised capital markets, unstable and flexible labour markets, and breakdowns and fragmentation in the world of work – have brought about major adjustments to this picture. Many of the most significant changes to the nature of employment and work relations have been stimulated by adaptations in ownership patterns and state policies that have amended the shape of both private and public sector organisations. Spin-off companies, joint ventures and strategic alliances have redrawn the boundaries between organisations in the private sector, especially in the newer high-technology sector. The public-private divide has become increasingly blurred through a range of initiatives such as compulsory competitive tendering, Private Finance Initiative (PFI), 'best value' and Public-Private Partnerships (PPPs), and the associated transfer of staff. Multi-employer sites have become much more common in the service sector in particular, with the expansion of firms to cover activities such as postal services and banking, often through franchising, or in call centres or other workplaces increasingly staffed by agency workers. Other developments in inter-firm collaboration that are less visible but equally significant are also increasing through supply-chain linkages, through exchanges of staff, and through joint problem-solving and new relational links.

Ongoing research at UMIST (see for example Grimshaw *et al*, 2001; Carroll *et al*, 2001; Marchington *et al*, 2002; Rubery *et al*, 2002) is exploring these issues in several public and private sector organisations. It is apparent from these cases that work is becoming increasingly fragmented, that conventional boundaries between organisations are becoming blurred, and that existing hierarchies are being disordered. In order to meet performance targets, organisations are fragmented and traditional divisions within and between organisations break down. In many cases work becomes more pressurised and controlled rather than liberated and empowered. So-called 'old' notions of skill, career and learning – which worked on the assumption of extended time horizons – are being replaced by new visions that rely increasingly on short-term and superficial levels of training and development where discontinuities are the norm. Simultaneously, the nature of worker representation is changing as trade unions find that their role, already under threat, is further marginalised as systems for worker representation are weakened following transfers of workers to other organisations. Boundaries are becoming increasingly blurred as organisations break up and re-form, change their names and areas of activity, and place additional responsibilities on more junior staff. The boundaries within organisations are also becoming more blurred, both in terms of managerial relations and the traditional gender segregation of jobs. Low-paid employment is not just dominated by women but also by younger males and older people with few transferable skills. Shifting boundaries may open up opportunities, but they also create more insecurity and confusion for people, and often fail to deliver the improved performance expectations that are promised to customers or clients. The growth of inter-organisational relations also leads to a disordering of hierarchies as responsibility for the management and control of staff is diffused, and customers are increasingly seen to influence the management of employment. There are cases in which powerful client organisations specifically ask for certain staff to be utilised on 'their' contracts, or in which workers are rebuked following a customer-feedback survey. The increased use of agency staff, sometimes as a permanent feature at call centres, means that the responsibility for managing staff who have direct contact with customers is split between different organisations. In many cases, new jobs are created for 'boundary-spanning agents', people whose prime responsibility is to manage relations across organisational boundaries.

In other words, models based around the concept of a flexible firm may no longer be adequate to analyse changes within and between different organisations that are tied together with a variety of commercial contracts. For example, a professional who works at the site of a client for long periods of time may be a peripheral worker so far as the client is concerned, but may well be a core worker for the management consultancy by whom she is employed. Equally, how can the self-employed person who routinely sells his services to an agency be classified: as self-employed, as a core agency worker, or as a peripheral contract worker? Even greater confusions can occur in circumstances where several employers operate from the same site. The case studies below give a flavour of these new organisational forms.

CASE STUDY: Working across organisational boundaries

Teacher supply agencies have become more prominent from the 1990s following changes in legislation and with the introduction of LMS (local management of schools). Teachertemp provides a large number of supply teachers to the market on a temporary basis even though it refers to them as employees. These supply teachers do not receive sick pay or holiday entitlement, nor do they receive payments into pension funds from Teachertemp. Some teachers do however receive a base payment (about 60% of daily rate) if placements are not found for them on the days that they are available for work. The agency also provides training courses for the teachers on their books so as to update their skills.

Call centres are now a prominent feature of the UK employment scene, and many of these employ temporary workers in order to service contracts. One of the companies in the sector – TCS (Total Customer Solutions) – provides business processing outsourcing facilities to a range of clients. Some 1,200 people work at its North Western site on contracts with five different clients, each of which is for a different type of service and makes different demands on customer service representatives who work at the site. The recruitment of staff for these contracts has been outsourced to an agency (Beststaff) which maintains an office on the site. Teams on these contracts contain a mixture of permanent and temporary staff, and it is usual for staff to move onto permanent contracts

some time after they have started working at the site. The different demands by the clients and the different skill levels and training needs mean that there is little transfer between contracts on a short-term basis even though this would help to smooth out fluctuations in workload.

Airport S is a major international airport that used to be under local authority control. Now, following a series of organisational changes, some of the work is retained by the parent company, but large amounts of this is now undertaken by specialist contracting firms that have offices at the site. There is a complex web of relations between these different firms, and work tends to be transferred between them so as to ensure that it is completed to tight time schedules. Given the need for speed and efficiency at turnaround times, staff may end up working for organisations other than their employer – even wearing their uniforms. Cleaning, baggage-handling, refuelling, and airline staff may all be vying for space on the aircraft at the same time, and their work is co-ordinated by dispatchers who are employed by companies different from those of most of the staff whose activities they are overseeing.

Each of these cases raises interesting HR issues relating to control and discipline, identity and commitment, recruitment and training, performance management and reward, as well as voice and representation.

The contested nature of work

Most publications on employee relations and organisational behaviour include some material on the nature of work (see, for example, Blyton and Turnbull, 1998; Thompson and McHugh, 2002; Noon and Blyton,

2002). Typically, this portrays the employment relationship as a mixture of conflict and co-operation, both of which are present to differing degrees in different workplaces at any one time. In addition, it is acknowledged that the balance between these two forces can vary over time and between different countries as well (Lansbury *et al*, 2002). By way of contrast, it is rare for texts on other aspects of HRM (eg recruitment and selection, learning and development, reward management) to conceive explicitly of the employment relationship in such terms. Instead, there is likely to be some discussion of motivation or commitment which deals with conflict solely in terms of management's failure to engender employee attachment to the organisation. In other words, the notion of conflict between the buyers and sellers of labour typically tends to be compartmentalised as an employee relations issue.

Issues of conflict and co-operation are explicitly embedded in employee relations, most obviously in analyses of industrial action and in collective bargaining between employers and trade unions. But conflict and co-operation pervade other aspects of people management and development as well. In the resourcing field, for example, the recruitment of new staff prepared to demonstrate loyalty and commitment, as well as work effectively with a minimum of supervision, raises major issues about the base upon which such co-operation is founded. As we see in Chapter 10, alternative paradigms of the selection process question the so-called 'objectivity' and scientific justification for psychometric approaches. The contested terrain is also apparent in questions about how managers aim to deal with absenteeism. In learning and development, conflict and co-operation is also ever-present, particularly in terms of individuals' attitudes to training, and their willingness to take on extra skills and responsibilities and to work towards the achievement of organisational goals as opposed to against them. This is apparent in more recent analyses of learning and training that differentiate between short-term organisation-specific benefits of training and those that focus on the longer-term development of people – see Chapter 12 for a fuller examination of these issues. Employee reward also manifestly includes subjects that go right to the heart of the employment relationship, concerning equity and fairness, harmonisation, and internal and external differentials. Too often, however, these issues are treated in straightforward technical terms – for example, in how to develop a training programme. It is important to recognise therefore that every aspect of HRM incorporates issues concerned with the way in which the employment relationship is constructed and developed, and that conflict should not be considered solely within the employee relations subject area.

There are many different perspectives on the employment relationship. Some of the early labour process writers (for example, Braverman, 1974; R Edwards, 1979) saw it as typified solely by conflict and a struggle for control between managers and those whom they seek to manage. According to this viewpoint, the interests of workers automatically collide with those of employers, since what is good for employers (capital) is inevitably bad for workers (labour) because surplus value – which is required in order to finance and reward capital – can only be achieved through the exploitation of workers. Again according to this viewpoint, workers who co-operate with employers, and who take part in participation and involvement schemes by offering their advice and ideas to management, are effectively doing themselves out of jobs by helping organisations to become more efficient. In addition, by sharing their expertise with management, it is argued that workers make it more likely that their jobs will become deskilled (or disappear altogether) as employers replace labour with new technology.

Other writers are more interested in the balance between conflict and co-operation in the employment relationship. Paul Edwards (1995: 13) argues that in relation to the introduction of new technology, employees have shared interests with employers – for example, in the development of new skills and the greater employment security that may derive from a more successful business in the longer term. At the same time, however, there are also potential conflicts between the parties in this process – for example, in new demands on employees and disputes between management and labour about appropriate rewards for taking on new responsibilities. Edwards (1995: 15) regards the employer-employee relationship as characterised by 'structured antagonism' which is created by the indeterminacy of the employment relationship. This relationship can never be constructed precisely enough to specify every aspect of an individual's work, and it relies upon both employer and employee to show some degree of trust and discretion for it to be discharged effectively. Because of this, Edwards sees the employment relationship as both contradictory and antagonistic. It is contradictory because managers have not only to exercise control but also to learn how to tap into and release creativity, and it is antagonistic because workers offer the only opportunity by which employers can realise surplus value. Although employees may have much to gain from co-operating with employers, this should not disguise the fact that employers need to maximise employee efforts to gain competitive advantage. It also needs stressing, particularly given the low levels of strike action in recent times, that an absence of overt conflict does not guarantee co-operation, and neither does a bout of industrial action necessarily indicate a fundamental breakdown in the employment relationship.

Debate with your colleagues the proposition that 'Conflict is now a thing of the past in the modern UK employment scene'.

Given the incompleteness of the employment contract (Cooke *et al*, 2002), it should be clear that, irrespective of the skill levels of their jobs, all employees possess 'tacit skills'. This refers to the knowledge and understanding that workers accumulate throughout their lives, and in many cases it is extremely difficult for this to be codified, written down and copied. Tacit skills can be seen in many areas of paid and unpaid employment – in the ability to realise from the sound of a machine or a car engine, for example, that a problem is lurking, or in the 'simple' act of washing up dishes, or in gardening. Thompson and McHugh (2002: 187) itemise more than 20 detailed activities undertaken by a waiter when taking an order, but even these fail to include the more hidden interactive skills that are crucial to ensure that this task is completed effectively. Increasingly, tacit skills are required to ensure that the inter-personal relations between customers and agents in a call centre oper-ate to the benefit of good customer service. Certain skills can be copied by watching other people or reading manuals, but others have to be 'learned' through practice or by doing similar jobs, sometimes outside of work. The key thing, however, is that most people are unaware of these skills and attributes, typically dismissing them as 'common sense' or as something that 'you are born with' – see Chapters 12 and 13.

Tacit skills can be used in a variety of ways by employees, and it is important for managers to be aware of how they can be tapped into or turned against the employer (Marchington, 1992: 155). First, they can be used as a potential weapon against employers, either as part of a col-lective dispute or as an individual response to managerial domination. Tacit skills can be used overtly by refusals to 'work beyond contract' or covertly in order to undermine a management instruction. In the case of the latter, actions may have to be done in secret if they are unlawful or involve sabotage, or they may have to be concealed if workers fear dis-missal if their actions are discovered. What unites these cases is that workers use tacit skills in order to 'get back at' an employer and chan-nel their creative energies into opposing, rather than co-operating with, employer objectives (Blyton and Turnbull, 1998: 312–13).

Tacit skills can also be used to make time at work more tolerable, but with no intention of offering employers any more than the basic mini-mum required to fulfil the terms of their employment contract. Often this approach results in game-playing – what Burawoy (1979: 81–2) refers to as 'making out' and Marchington (1992: 156) terms 'getting by'. Under this scenario, employees dream up games to keep their minds occupied while at work. Anybody who has been employed on rou-tine, mundane jobs for any length of time should recognise how games can be used to pass the time. For example, thinking up names for cus-tomers, producing a certain number of components in a 30-minute period, or dreaming about how to spend £1 million on a TV quiz pro-gramme. In some cases, this may actually improve performance, as workers set themselves targets for achievement or prevent their get-ting bored by talking with other members of staff. As workers appear to be consenting to management rules on the surface, their low level of attachment only comes to light when they are asked to agree with the introduction of new technology, take part in the latest employee involve-ment initiative or sign up for a learning and development programme. Since their major life interests are fulfilled outside work, they resent what is seen as an intrusion into their private lives (Thompson and McHugh, 2002).

The final way in which tacit skills can be used is in working towards what employers would like to achieve – this is where employees actively contribute to the attainment of employer goals by 'getting on' at work. This takes several forms, such as working hard to gain promotion, taking on extra responsibilities to ensure that the organisation manages to satisfy customer orders, or in working hard because that is perceived as the 'right thing to do'. The idea of 'doing a good job' – turning out high-quality work, resolving difficult problems at work, or providing superior customer service – is central to much of our socialisation, and also to much of the activity we undertake outside paid employment (Ackers and Preston, 1997). To a large extent, our identity and feelings of self-worth are reinforced by 'getting on' at work, by helping a customer, finishing a project late at night, or just clearing the in-tray. As we see at various points within this book, management gurus have repeatedly exhorted line managers and HR specialists to tap into this knowledge, expertise and commitment, and to get rid of the syndrome by which workers 'leave their brains on the coat-hangers' on the way into work.

Think about three different types of job that you have either done or about which you have some knowledge. What was the mix of 'getting back', 'getting by' and 'getting on' in these jobs, and what might have been done to increase the likelihood of workers' wanting to 'get on'?

Expectations from work and the psychological contract

A number of the classic studies have analysed what employees want from their working lives. Writers like Maslow (1943) and Herzberg (1966) point to factors intrinsic to work, motivators such as interesting and varied work, the opportunity to develop, to be recognised for doing a good job, and so on. Others (eg Goldthorpe, Lockwood, Bechofer and Platt, 1968) suggest that factors such as job security and decent wages, which were seen as hygiene factors by Herzberg, are important, especially for people who do not regard work as of central life interest. There is not the space to consider these ideas in detail here, but readers may like to consult sources such as Mullins, 2001; Noon and Blyton, 2002; Thompson and McHugh, 2002 for a fuller discussion. However, since these classic studies were carried out some time ago, to what extent do their findings still have resonance today?

The Employment in Britain survey (Guest, 1995) provided some information about what people want from work. There are four broad sets of factors that seem to matter to people, in the sense that over 70 per cent of those questioned felt these were essential or very important in their work:

- the type of work they are doing, the opportunity to use their initiative and abilities while at work, in effect to be stretched in terms of problem-solving and creativity

- job security

- working with friendly and supportive people, having a good relationship with their supervisor

- good pay and satisfactory physical working conditions.

The fact that work is expected to fulfil an important social and creative role probably explains why such a large proportion of people indicate that they would continue working even if they no longer had any economic need to do so. The so-called 'lottery question' has been asked on many occasions, both in Britain and elsewhere. Although there are variations, a substantial majority of people state that they would continue to work even if they won sufficient money to keep them comfortably off for the rest of their working lives. British workers had the lowest level of commitment to remaining in work, but even here it was over 66 per cent of all those questioned; in Japan, the corresponding figure was over 90 per cent, whereas in the USA, Israel, the Netherlands and Belgium it was well over 80 per cent.

Recently there has been a renewed interest in the 'psychological contract' between employer and employee, first described by Schein (1965). Herriot (1998: 106) defines this as 'the beliefs of each of the parties to the employment relationship, the individual and the organisation, as to what their mutual obligations are'. According to Herriot (1998: 107) there are two fundamental implications of the psychological contract – it differs between individuals and it is a two-way exchange process rather than one that is unilaterally imposed. The 'contract', which is actually implicit rather than written down, is based upon a series of assumptions about relations between employer and employee. These are outlined by Mayo (1995: 48):

- that employees will be treated fairly and honestly, and that information will be provided about changes at work, so as to meet the need for equity and justice

- that employees can expect to have some degree of security and certainty about the jobs in return for their loyalty to the employer, thus fulfilling the need for security and relative certainty

- that employees can expect employers to recognise and value their past and future contribution, so as to satisfy the need for fulfilment, satisfaction and progression.

This set of reciprocal arrangements may have been present in organisations during the 1970s, according to Herriot (1995: 146), but it has now disappeared from many workplaces. The last decade has been characterised by instrumentality and uncertainty, an imbalance in what is offered by the individual compared with that offered by the employer. Consequently, in contemporary Britain, he argues, the individual offers flexibility, accountability and long hours, and gets in return a job with a high salary – although for many peripheral workers even that cannot be taken for granted. The insecurities that now characterise the new psychological contract are felt particularly strongly by middle managers, according to Herriot (1995b). In the early part of the 1990s, it was widely reported that managers felt under-valued and over-worked, essentially being taken for granted by employers. Might this have changed by now, not just for managers but for all workers?

Guest and Conway have carried out a series of surveys for the CIPD on the psychological contract since the mid-1990s, and the most recent report – at the time of going to press – was conducted and published in 2001. Below we present some of the findings from that survey in Tables 5, 6 and 7, and provide a commentary on these results and their implications. Readers are encouraged to get the results from subsequent surveys themselves in order to trace changes over a longer period of time. The 2001 survey included 2,000 respondents (workers) drawn in equal proportions from the private sector, central government, local authorities and the health sector. There is not space here to do justice to the findings, especially those that compare attitudes between workers in the different sectors and industries, so for the most part the

Table 5 Promises made by the employer, and how well they are kept

Promise or commitment by the organisation to:	Promise made (% of all employees)	Promise fully kept (% of all who made promises)	Promise not kept (% of all who made promises)
Provide a reasonably secure job	74	65	1
Provide fair pay for the work done	72	48	5
Provide with a career	58	51	3
Provide interesting work	48	45	1
Ensure fair treatment by managers	89	44	2
Ensure equality of treatment	92	51	3
Keep employees fully informed about changes affecting them	88	44	2
Involve and consult employees about changes affecting them	81	39	4

Adapted from Guest, D. and Conway, N. (2001), *Public and Private Sector Perspectives on the Psychological Contract.* CIPD, London, p24

findings are presented in aggregate form with occasional reference to differences between the workers' responses. One interesting finding is that central government workers have the largest number of progressive HR practices of any of the groups but they report lower levels of morale and less satisfaction with changes taking place at work (Guest and Conway, 2001: *xi*). Chapter 7 provides a much more extensive examination of what is meant by progressive HR practices and high-commitment HRM. Table 5 presents data on the degree to which promises are made and kept by employers according to this group of respondents.

From this it can be seen that the vast majority of employers made promises about equality and fairness of treatment, about information and consultation with staff, and to a slightly lesser extent about security and pay. Hardly any workers felt that management did not keep their promises at all, but a large proportion felt that they did not keep them fully. This is apparent in relation to most of the promises made by employers, particularly regarding information and consultation, but there were also concerns about broken promises regarding equality and fairness, the provision of interesting and fair paid work and a career. About two-thirds felt that promises had been kept in relation to employment security. In general, private sector workers are more likely to say that promises have been kept than those working for central government (Guest and Conway, 2001: 25). If 'delivery of the deal' is an indicator of the state of the psychological contract, these results are mixed, especially in parts

Table 6   Trust, loyalty and pride at work (% of all employees)

	A lot/ very much	Somewhat/ quite a lot	Only a little	Not at all
To what extent is your employer open and up-front with you?	40	40	17	3
To what extent do you trust your immediate manager to look after your best interests?	58	25	11	6
To what extent do you trust senior management to look after your best interests?	24	40	25	12
How much loyalty would you say you have to the organisation you work for?	54	33	9	4
Are you proud to tell people who you work for?	26	43	22	10

Adapted from Guest, D. and Conway, N. (2001), *Public and Private Sector Perspectives on the Psychological Contract*. CIPD, London, pp26 and 36

of the public sector, but then it may be unrealistic to expect employers to achieve all their promises in full.

Respondents were also asked whether or not they felt that they were rewarded fairly for the work that they did. Just under a quarter answered these questions very positively and just over a third thought that this was probably the case. The remaining 40 per cent felt that they were not well rewarded. Not surprisingly, given the constraints on public sector pay for a number of years, those in public employment were rather less positive that they were fairly treated. A series of questions were posed about trust, loyalty and pride at work, and the results for these are presented in Table 6.

The vast majority of respondents felt that their employers were relatively open with them, which is interesting, given the somewhat more sceptical response to the previous set of questions about the promises made and kept in relation to information and consultation. Whereas immediate line managers are trusted, their senior colleagues are not to anything like the same degree, more than a third of the sample saying that they trusted them only a little or not at all. Conversely, over half the respondents stated that they owed a lot of loyalty to their organisation, and a quarter were very proud to tell people who they worked for. Once again, it is central government workers who display the lowest levels of trust, especially in senior management, leading Guest and Conway (2001: 27) to conclude that workers here feel the psychological contract is in a poor state. Organisational commitment – as measured by loyalty and pride – is highly dependent on the way in which workers feel they are treated by their employer, on the amount of support they receive, and on a positive psychological contract (Guest and Conway, 2001: 37). Those in the health sector are particularly committed to their organisation – or perhaps it is to their profession and occupation instead.

Table 7 shows the changes that have taken place in attitudes since the survey was first conducted in 1996. At one level, the findings show limited consistency or trends, and variations occur from year to year. However, there is some evidence that there has been 'a general deterioration in the experience and evaluation of work in the public sector and an improvement in the private sector' (Guest and Conway, 2001: 74). In the former, this is perhaps best exemplified by the fact that the amount of pride public sector workers feel in their employer is declining, yet at the same time levels of loyalty have increased since 1996. Satisfaction has declined in the public sector whereas it has improved in the private sector, but even within the public sector, those working in health are considerably more positive than those in local and central government. Teachers and nurses report high levels of satisfaction with work, but that they are working harder and/or struggling with finances. Overall, scores that average three out of four or seven out of ten suggest that by far the most workers are satisfied on balance with most aspects of their working lives. Yet the authors conclude that 'there is not a great

Table 7   Changes in employee attitudes in the public and private sectors over the period 1996–2001

Attitude	1996		1998		2000		2001	
	Public	Private	Public	Private	Public	Private	Public	Private
Trust	2.86	2.93	3.02	3.01	2.97	3.00	2.95	3.16
Loyalty	3.12	3.18	3.44	3.31	3.36	3.32	3.37	3.38
Pride	2.92	2.93	3.08	2.99	2.89	2.84	2.73	3.05
Motivation	*	*	3.18	3.16	3.23	3.11	3.22	3.28
Work satisfaction	*	*	7.12	6.87	7.13	6.99	6.89	7.20

Trust, Loyalty, Pride and Motivation are scored on a 4-point scale: the higher the score, the more positive the attitude. Work satisfaction is recorded on a 10-point scale, on which 10 indicates very high satisfaction.

Adapted from Guest, D. and Conway, N. (2001), *Public and Private Sector Perspectives on the Psychological Contract.* CIPD, London, p75

deal of encouragement to be taken from these results' (Guest and Conway, 2001: 80).

The conclusions drawn from a large survey of the UK working population by the Gallup Organisation (Buckingham, 2001) also suggest that employers are failing to get the best from their workers. Apparently, less than 20 per cent are actively engaged with their work, and of the remainder – worryingly for employers – 20 per cent are actively disengaged. There is a strong correlation between 'engaged' employees and factors such as high levels of attendance at work, a low intention to quit and willingness to recommend their workplace to friends. More surprisingly, the longer that workers stay with an organisation, the less engaged they become, and the more they feel that the employer is not providing them with the resources or the support to do their jobs effectively.

Rose (2000) has undertaken several analyses of job satisfaction on the British Household Panel Survey and from WERS 1998 data for the Future of Work programme. In these, workers tend to report higher levels of satisfaction with the same sorts of factors – intrinsic items such as use of initiative or the work itself – and the lowest levels of satisfaction with extrinsic items such as pay levels or chances of promotion. Rather than taking this as a sign that workers are happy with their lot, Rose suggests that aspirations in relation to intrinsic factors tend to be lower. One of the other key findings is that managerial and professional workers are consistently more satisfied with their jobs than are less-skilled manual workers. It is therefore very important to take great care when benchmarking levels of job satisfaction since these vary so much between occupations and grades.

> Do you feel engaged at work or with your studies, do you feel satisfied with your life, and do you feel loyalty to or pride in the organisation for which you work or at which you are studying? Why is this?

Insecurity, work intensification and the long hours culture

The last few years have seen plenty of debate about the extent to which work is becoming more insecure and intensive and about how people are routinely working longer hours as well. The so-called 'insecurity thesis' (Heery and Salmon, 1999: 1) includes at least three separate elements. These are that:

- risk is being transferred to employees through the growth of temporary and precarious employment so as to increase insecurity

- insecurity is damaging to economic performance

- reduced economic performance leads to severe consequences for individuals and the wider society.

Although many analysts (eg Hutton, 1998) agree that work is now much more insecure than in the immediate past, exemplified in particular by the growth of non-standard jobs and the decline of the 'job for life', Doogan (2001) disagrees. He argues that rather than work becoming more insecure, there is now an even greater likelihood that people will remain in their existing employment than 20 years ago. Table 8 presents a selection of his evidence drawn from various labour force survey sets.

Since 1992, the proportion of workers with 10 or more years' service in the same employment has grown from less than 7.5 million to over 9 million, from 28.6 per cent of the working population to 33 per cent (Doogan, 2001: 423). The same picture emerges in relation both to women and men, and indeed the growth in long-term employment is considerably greater for women (21 per cent to 29 per cent) than for men (35 per cent to 37 per cent). This trend also holds across shrinking sectors of the economy such as manufacturing and public administration as it does for expanding sectors. For example, the rate of long-term employment in manufacturing stood at 38 per cent in 1999 compared with 32 per cent in 1992, whereas the increase in construction was most marked of all – rising from 30 per cent to 40 per cent of total employment. In declining sectors, there had been an absolute decline in the number of long-term employees, hardly surprisingly, alongside a rather slower decline in the rate of long-term employment. Perhaps contrary to expectations, part-timers were also more likely to have a higher rate of long-term employment than they had at the beginning of the 1990s, and indeed the rate of increase was actually higher than for full-timers. This increase for part-timers, however, was almost totally confined to those over the age of 30, thus suggesting that younger workers bore the brunt of short-term and unstable work patterns. Finally, all categories of worker saw an increase in the long-term rate of employment, varying from the higher skill levels to a miniscule improvement (0.1 per cent) for those in the most basic jobs. In short, there is compelling evidence to support the proposition that a larger percentage of workers now have long employment tenure, and that for some workers at least job insecurity may be less of a problem than is sometimes imagined.

Of course, this analysis does not examine statistics relating to the length of job tenure for those people who experience frequent job changes and move in and out of employment. As we saw in earlier sections of this chapter, the increase in numbers engaged in temporary work alone indicates that this is potentially a major source of job insecurity. Moreover, focusing solely on job tenure only tells half the story, in that workers may *feel* much more insecure without actually losing their jobs, and, perhaps more crucially, anticipated opportunities for promotion and advancement may be lessened. As Burchell *et al* (1999: 39) note, 'Many of the employees we spoke to were not unduly worried about losing their job *per se* but were, nevertheless, extremely concerned about the loss of valued job features such as their status within the organisation or their opportunity for promotion.' This shows how job insecurity is multi-dimensional and driven by a number of different forces. Hudson (2002: 81), drawing on the same survey data, notes

Table 8 The rate of long-term employment – those in same employment for ten years or more

Sector	1992			1999		
	Total employment (000s)	Long-term employment (000s)	Rate of long-term employment	Total employment (000s)	Long-term employment (000s)	Rate of long-term employment
Manufacturing	5,390	1,731	32%	4,882	1,824	38%
Public administration	1,749	738	42%	1,632	851	52%
Mining	178	87	49%	101	44	43%
Utilities	314	175	56%	187	97	52%
Construction	1,790	538	30%	1,929	768	40%
Hotels and catering	1,165	143	12%	1,154	168	15%
Education	1,741	595	34%	2,180	803	37%
Health and social services	1,518	432	28%	2,989	960	32%
Full-time	19,577	6,271	32%	20,556	7,465	36%
Part-time	5,863	1,105	19%	6,774	1,569	23%
Managers	3,564	1,322	37%	4,068	1,703	42%
Technicians	2,052	585	29%	2,390	768	32%
Clerical	4,349	991	23%	4,504	1,355	30%
Craft	3,537	1,163	33%	3,238	1,321	41%
Elementary	2,270	509	22%	2,077	468	22%

Adapted from tables in Doogan, K. (2001), 'Insecurity and long-term employment', *Work, Employment and Society*, Vol 15(3), pp 419–441

how the vast majority of workers felt that they had increased their skill level, responsibility and task variety during the past few years but nevertheless did not have improved career and promotion prospects. She refers to this as 'broken ladders' and 'disappearing pathways', and it demonstrates well that even though people may be secure in their jobs – in the sense that they are not made redundant – they may find that longer-term expectations have deteriorated considerably. The respondents to the Burchell *et al* study put down reasons for feeling insecure to factors such as organisational restructuring – eg mergers or rationalisations – or to anxieties about future product market or financial circumstances. Broadly, workers were more insecure if there was a lack of clear communications from management, if they did not trust managers, or if they lacked confidence in getting another job should they need one (Burchell *et al*, 1999: 22). This echoes our previous examination of the psychological contract.

Another way to assess whether or not work patterns have changed is to examine working hours. Plenty of space is typically devoted to features on the length of the working week, driven in part by the Working Time Regulations, as well as by the potentially deleterious effects of this on productivity, health and family relations. Cooper (2000a) reports that 10 per cent of the 5,000 managers he surveyed in a joint UMIST-Institute of Management project reported that they worked more than 61 hours per week, and a third that they worked more than 51 hours each week on average. Fewer than 20 per cent worked a 40-hour week. A CIPD survey (2001a) found that the vast majority of those working 48 hours per week or more felt that they had no option because of increased workloads, whereas only a very small number (4 per cent) worked additional hours in order to earn extra money. Those who had reduced their working hours in the last few years had done so primarily because of changes in work requirements, and just 14 per cent quoted family reasons as the stimulus to change their working patterns. Interestingly, about half the sample did not mind doing so many hours, and only 10 per cent felt reluctant to work additional time.

> Why do you think that people work such long hours? Do you think anything could, or should, be done to reduce this?

Data from *Labour Market Trends* (November 2001) shows that full-timers put in an average of 38.1 hours and part-timers an average of 15.7 hours per week, giving a combined average of 33 hours per week. Men employed full-time work slightly longer hours than women at 39.9 hours compared with 34.4 hours per week. This has hardly changed over the last five years, but if we compare figures for the last decade with those from some time ago, the length of the working week has actually declined. As Green (2001: 56) notes, in the mid-nineteenth century, work took up about 60 hours per week on average; in the

1950s it was much higher than now; and even in 1968 the average working week was 40 hours. However, the average figures mask some quite large dispersions in working time. For example, the proportion of people who work at least 48 hours per week has increased over the last 20 years, but equally the proportion of those people who work less than 20 hours per week has increased as well. Even more significantly, in 1977 just 12 per cent of households who included people of working age had no one working, a figure that had nearly doubled by 1998 (Green, 2001: 59). In short, there has been an increasing bifurcation in patterns of working time – some work very long hours while others work rather fewer hours, either because of choice or due to exclusion from the labour market. Relatedly, the composition of those who work long hours has also changed, and it is now more likely that this group is made up of professionals and managers rather than manual workers on overtime.

The picture in relation to work intensification is rather more straight-forward. People appear to be working harder, both in terms of the speed at which they work and in the amount of effort that they feel they are putting into work. For example, just under 66 per cent of the employees interviewed by Burchell *et al* (1999: 30) felt they were working faster and more intensively, about 33 per cent felt that things had not changed over the last few years, and a handful felt that work was less intense. The wider range of tasks undertaken, the extra effort that had been devoted and the responsibility they had shouldered had not been rewarded in their view. According to Burchell *et al* they felt 'under press-ure from managers, colleagues and, above all, from the "sheer quantity of work" '. In his analysis, Green (2001) differentiated between 'discre-tionary effort' – work beyond that which is normally required – and 'con-strained effort' – the work required merely to complete the job. He concludes, from analysis of various data sets covering the last 20 years, that work has been intensified, both in terms of discretionary and con-strained effort. Other studies also support this conclusion. For example, the 1998 WERS survey (Cully *et al*, 1999; Green, 2001) showed that 60 per cent of worker representatives felt that effort had increased a lot at their establishment during the past five years, an additional 20 per cent saying that it had increased a little. Managers were less convinced about the extent of the increased effort, but nevertheless 39 per cent of them felt it had gone up a lot and 37 per cent a little. Very few of either group felt effort levels had decreased.

The implications of this degree of work intensification are considerable. Wichert (2002: 99) provides a long list of health problems that workers felt had been instigated or worsened by working so hard and to tighter deadlines. These include headaches, muscular problems, stomach-aches, stress, sleep problems and irritability. Nolan (2002: 122) refers to the time squeeze caused by working longer hours as well as more intensively with fewer breaks, and evidence shows that tensions at home are greater if workers feel more insecure, are under greater work pressure, and work too many hours. There are also doubts that any productivity increases secured via more intensive working are sustainable in the longer-term.

CONCLUSION

There is little doubt that working patterns and expectations have changed considerably over the last two decades. The proportion of women in work has increased significantly, there has been an ongoing shift in employment from manufacturing to the service sector, and the 'old' notion of working 40 hours per week, from 9 to 5 on Monday to Friday, has been undermined. Although unemployment fell back at the turn of the century towards levels last seen in the 1960s, there are major concerns about insecurity at work, about deteriorating conditions for some groups of workers, and about opportunities for promotion and career advancement. To be sure, some workers enjoy high levels of employment security, and in aggregate terms the length of the typical working week has fallen and levels of job tenure have increased. The way in which work is experienced varies greatly between different occupations and sectors, with a continuing increase in levels of satisfaction in the private sector combined with increased feelings of insecurity and lack of worth for many in the public sector. Much of this is driven by continuing moves to sub-contract work from the public to the private sector and the growth of inter-organisational contracting between the two sectors. Although progressive employers might be encouraged to adopt high-commitment management systems, the reality is that far too many workers are employed under regimes that emphasise cost reduction rather than quality enhancement (see Chapter 7). Having reviewed the changing nature of work and employment, we can now move on to consider the legal context within which HRM operates.

Useful reading

BUCKINGHAM M. 'What a waste', *People Management*, 11 October 2001. pp36–40.

BURCHELL B., LADIPO D. *and* WILKINSON F. (eds) *Job Insecurity and Work Intensification*. London, Routledge. 2002.

CULLY M., WOODLAND S., O'REILLY A. *and* DIX G. *Britain at Work: As depicted by the 1998 Workplace Employee Relations Survey*, London, Routledge. 1999.

FELSTEAD A., JEWSON N., PHIZACKALEA A. *and* WALTERS S. 'Working at home: statistical evidence for seven key hypotheses', *Work, Employment and Society*, Vol. 15, No. 2, 2001. pp215–231.

GUEST D. *and* CONWAY N. *Public and Private Sector Perspectives on the Psychological Contract*. London, CIPD. 2001.

Labour Market Trends – each edition carries useful statistical information on work and employment.

NOON M. *and* BLYTON P. *The Realities of Work*. London, Macmillan Business. 2002.

RUBERY J., EARNSHAW J., MARCHINGTON M., COOKE F. *and* VINCENT S. 'Changing organisational forms and the employment relationship', *Journal of Management Studies*. 2002.

THOMPSON P. *and* McHUGH D. *Work Organisations: A critical introduction*. 3rd edition. London, Palgrave. 2002.

WARD K., GRIMSHAW D., RUBERY J. *and* BEYNON H. 'Dilemmas in the management of temporary work agency staff', *Human Resource Management Journal*, Vol. 11, No. 4, 2001. pp3–21.

The Legal Framework for HRM

CHAPTER OBJECTIVES

By the end of this chapter readers should be able to:

- supply accurate and timely advice on the rights and obligations of employers and employees arising from the contract of employment and associated legislation, bearing in mind conflicts of interest and issues of confidentiality

- identify and access key sources of information on employment law issues

- provide advice on the effect that major pieces of legislation have on the employment contract.

In addition, readers should be able to understand and be able to explain:

- the context within which HRM takes place in terms of government actions, legal requirements and wider societal needs

- the role played by legal and national institutions in setting the standards for HRM

- the way that employment law shapes HR practice in the workplace.

Introduction

In the previous chapter we analysed the way in which the work and employment context provided a backcloth for the practice of HRM at workplace level. One of the key points to recall from that chapter is that the precise nature of the employment relationship depends upon the interplay between local, national and international forces. In this chapter we move on to examine the legal framework. As we saw in Chapter 2, there has been a major growth in legislation over the past 30 years, and lawyers have played an increasingly important role in setting the parameters within which HRM is enacted. For the vast majority of employers, the most immediate and obvious influence on their activities, especially in the area of employment rights, comes from the employment tribunal system. But the employment tribunals are themselves overseen and explicitly influenced by the Employment Appeals Tribunal and higher-level courts. Increasingly, this includes European legal institutions – such as the European Court of Justice – whose influence over the adjudication of employment rights has grown enormously over the last 20 years, and has led to major changes in employment law. Readers who are keen to find out more about the legal institutions and the framework might like to consult law books, such as those by Lewis and Sargeant (2002), Pitt (2000), or specialist employee relations texts such as Gennard and Judge (1999) or Farnham (2000). *People Management online* also publishes a legislative timetable listing upcoming legal changes that affect HR professionals. Other statutory bodies have also played a sizeable part in the HR area. In relation to equal opportunities, this has been through the Equal Opportunities Commission and the Commission for Racial Equality, whereas the resolution of grievances, disputes and dismissal cases has comprised a key part of the Advisory, Conciliation and Arbitration Service's duties (see Chapter 4).

The material in this section aims to set the scene for the more detailed analysis of HRM that comprises the rest of the book. Firstly, it looks at the role of the law in shaping HRM. Secondly, it examines individual rights and the nature of the employment contract as this underpins most other aspects of work, before moving on to look at collective employment rights. Finally, it reviews institutions such as employment tribunals (ETs) and the various Commissions that have a central role to play in the area. It is important also to state at the outset what this section does *not* do. It does not aim to provide a comprehensive and detailed coverage of all aspects of employment law, nor is it intended as a replacement for more specialised employment law publications. HR practitioners must be especially aware of the limits of their expertise in this area, and seek specialist advice if in doubt. Legal and political influences receive additional coverage elsewhere in the book – for example, in relation to equal opportunities in Chapter 4, recruitment in Chapter 10, discipline in Chapter 15, and equal value in Chapter 16.

Shaping HRM at work

In Britain the law has traditionally played a minor role compared with legal institutions in many other countries. The character of the British system has been moulded by employers and trade unions rather than by legal enactment. 'Voluntarism' has been the generally prevailing philosophy, with 'collective *laissez-faire*' (Kahn-Freund, 1959: 224) regarded as the appropriate process to resolve employee relations issues – the law was seen only as a mechanism of last resort, to be used when other voluntary means had failed. However, legal intervention has to be assessed not only against its desirability but also against its likelihood of attaining the modifications expected from its operation.

According to Kahn-Freund (1965: 302), the law performs a number of different roles in the rule-making process. Firstly, there is the *auxiliary* role through which the state provides a statutory framework of what is called 'organised persuasion'. This provides benefits – financial or otherwise – for those who observe agreements, and a number of pressures that may be applied against those who do not. A good illustration of this type of role can be seen through the actions of ACAS in providing services such as conciliation, mediation and arbitration.

Secondly, the law has a *restrictive* role in that it provides a set of rules that stipulate what is allowed and what is forbidden in the conduct of industrial relations. Thus, rules defining legitimate strike action and picketing have existed for a long period, but have been the subject of major reforms during the last 25 years.

Thirdly, the law has a *regulatory* role in that it sets a 'floor of employment rights' for employees. Again, this is a long-standing role which dates back to the nineteenth and early twentieth centuries when it was introduced to provide protection in industries such as mining, and over issues such as pay in sweatshops. In the 1970s the employment protection legislation took on a wider remit, incorporating all employees rather than just those in particular industries or working under especially harsh conditions. It has been extended considerably since the Labour government took office in 1997. Apart from actively setting certain rules and regulations, the law also has a wider impact. For example, the legislation on unfair dismissal has led to changes in the way people are recruited and selected, the formalisation of disciplinary procedures and the keeping of records (see Chapter 15). The law is not simply influential in directing what is required to be done but in shaping ideas about acceptable good practice beyond legislative requirements as well as potentially stimulating new ways of doing things. Nevertheless, the law is clearly an influential trigger of change. In *IRS Employment Review 740* (2001), 98 per cent of respondents report this as influential in their decision to introduce or amend HR policies.

Following the 1960s, voluntarism came under attack due to the poor performance of the British economy, leading the state to intervene more in employee relations both through economic policies and in the legislative arena. For example, the Industrial Relations Act 1971 attempted to replace voluntarism with a more American-style system of legal regulation. Despite its failure, it did signify increasing concern over what were seen as the costs of voluntarism. The Conservative government that was elected in 1979 saw industrial relations at the centre of the 'British disease' and intervened with a step-by-step dismantling of union protections, ostensibly designed to free up the labour market. During the period from 1979 to 1997, labour law in Britain took a different direction. The market was used to regulate labour standards. This included the programme of privatisation of the nationalised industries and the associated programmes contracting out to the private sector large parts of the public sector which remained – compulsory competitive tendering in local government and market testing in central government. Where employees enjoyed the safety of an expanding raft of regulatory legislation, this was gradually dismantled. Initiatives were taken to diminish the influence of collective bargaining and reduce the power of trade unions on the one hand, and to diminish the role and influence of regulatory legislation on the other (Ewing, 2002).

There were eight major pieces of legislation during this period – in 1980, 1982, 1984, 1986, 1988, 1989, 1990, and 1993. The strategy was notable for several main features. First, the reduction of trade union power – including withdrawal of existing legal support for trade unions and the ending of union membership agreements (closed shops) which required workers at a particular place of work to be members of a trade union. Second, indirect support for collective bargaining was removed, involving such measures as the termination of the ability to extend collectively-agreed terms and conditions of employment to other workplaces, the Fair Wages Resolution, and the creation of Wages Councils. In effect, trade unions were cut adrift from the support of the state. Third, the trade unions' ability to bargain with employers was constrained by legal restrictions on the right to strike (see below). In addition, there was no regulation of working time, and following a number of changes to the law on unfair dismissal, there was no protection against arbitrary management conduct for the first two years of the employment relationship. While steps were taken to reduce or remove the regulatory burden from employers, new regulatory restraints were imposed on trade unions. As Ewing (2002) notes, 'It would be difficult to exaggerate the extent to which regulation had been compromised during the period from 1979 to 1997.'

However, there were constraints – in particular, a number of barriers erected by EU law which protected important regulatory initiatives such as equal pay for work of equal value, the protection of employees' rights in the event of a transfer of an undertaking, and the introduction of information and consultation machinery for redundancy, business transfer, and health and safety issues in enterprises where there was no recognised trade union. More recently a number of EU decisions have strengthened the position of workers – for example, in relation to redundancy, maternity, equal value and hours of work. In 1997 the election of a Labour government led to a change in the perspective of the state (Gennard, 1998; Farnham, 2000). The new approach is concerned with general economic well-being, and not only with the rights of workers in employment. There is both a renewed commitment to trade union recognition and an expansion in individual rights legislation. The contract of employment remains the cornerstone of the employment relationship, but this is now a contract which, for most workers, is regulated by legislation rather than by collective bargaining. Fewer workers are now dependent on collective bargaining to regulate working conditions, and more are dependent on legislation to set minimum terms and conditions (Ewing, 2002).

The impact of the national minimum wage (NMW)

Around 10 per cent of the working population benefited from the introduction of the NMW in 1999. Of these, 1.5 million were women, more than half of whom worked part-time. Other groups most affected were homeworkers, lone parents, ethnic minority workers and 18–20-year-olds. Excluded groups included workers under the age of 18, apprentices, au pairs or nannies (who are treated as family members) and family members working in the family business. Initial research findings showed that the NMW did not reduce employment levels or lead to a significant increase in inflation. This was partly because the rate was set at a 'prudent' level and partly because it was introduced at a time of economic growth and prosperity. The impact on pay differentials was found to be minimal.

(Arthurs, 2002)

The Labour government appears to be shifting to an employee relations policy based on five pillars. These are:

- encouraging employment flexibility

- protecting minimum employment standards in the workplace

- promoting family-friendly policies at work

- supporting partnership at work

- supporting union recognition.

The main strategy is via legal enactment and signing up to the Social Chapter of the EU. The Labour government's 'New Deal' on employee relations incorporates support for a flexible labour market, underpinned by an extended but limited range of legal protections at work, largely for individuals but also, to a lesser degree, for trade unions (Farnham, 2000: 347). It is noteworthy that the legislation on the closed shop, picketing, secondary action, ballots and notices prior to industrial action, unofficial action, elections for certain trade union offices, rights to join a trade union of one's choice, and the right of members in specified circumstances not to be disciplined by unions according to rule have remained in place. In addition, financial reporting rules and sanctions continue to be imposed on unions (Smith and Morton, 2001: 121).

The new system of labour law is thus a synthesis of competing values. It accepts a great deal of the Thatcher inheritance but is also shaped to accommodate new values. For example, there are rights to trade union recognition where there is a prescribed level of support, but tight restrictions on trade union government and on industrial action. The emphasis has changed in terms of a more comprehensive role for legislation rather than treating collective bargaining as the basis for setting minimum standards (Ewing, 2002). The DTI Fairness at Work paper summarised this clearly: 'In offering new rights we will demand that employees in return accept their responsibilities to co-operate with employers. There will be no return to the days of industrial conflict' (DTI, 1998: 14). The provision of minimum standards for all employees was seen as important so as to promote improved competitiveness, enhance workplace democracy and provide greater 'fairness' in the employment relationship. However, the government was keen to avoid excessive labour market regulation and to promote labour market flexi-bility by active labour market policies and employability linked to new skills (Gennard, 1998: 13). The Employment Relations Act 1999 intro-duced new rights for members of unions and individual employees including a route for statutory recognition, a national minimum wage and extended rights for individual employees.

To what extent do you think the state should intervene in HRM? Discuss this question with colleagues on your course, and consider who has gained most from state intervention over the years.

Legal and political issues set the scene for all aspects of HRM, and at each stage of the employment relationship. For example, there are clear legal standards that influence decisions on recruitment and selection, and at the induction stage of employment. Legislation affects issues relating to equal opportunities in all aspects of HRM, such as in access to recruitment (people resourcing) and training (learning and develop-ment), as well as in areas covered by employee relations (discipline) and employee reward (equal value considerations).

The Europeanisation of employment relations

The influence of European law is more complex than that resulting from domestic legislation. It is also complicated – in the minds of many HR practitioners, at least – in that four separate sets of proposals can be put forward by the European Commission. These are:

- *recommendations* that do not bind member states but that it is hoped will be followed

- *regulations*, which take immediate effect once adopted by the Commission

- *directions*, which affect only the parties involved in a specific case

- *Directives*, which are binding on member states but require appropriate legislation from each member state within a set period of time to comply with the objectives of each Directive. They are formulated in broad terms, allowing member states flexibility to interpret specific provisions (Reid, 2000b).

In addition, the Commission has also issued codes of practice. Cases are heard at the European Court of Justice, which is responsible for interpreting European legislation and for providing preliminary rulings on disputed or unclear points of law. These then have to be incorporated into domestic law.

European Union (EU) social policy has evolved over time. The Treaty of Rome in 1957, which founded the European Economic Community (EEC), stated a commitment to common action on economic and social progress, (but mainly on equal opportunities and equal pay). Two developments have accelerated the development of EU social legislation. First, in the 1970s the case law of the European Court of Justice (ECJ) began to grow significantly, especially in the field of equal opportunities. Second, with growing trade among member states and the increased mobility of workers and organisations across borders, there was pressure to add a social dimension to the 'economic' community and to incorporate adequate protection of workers so that the interests of owners and other stakeholders were balanced. This led to legislative developments in relation to employment protection in the 1970s, and in workplace health and safety in the 1980s and early 1990s (Reid, 2000b). As Gennard and Judge (1999) observe, collective redundancies, transfers of undertakings, acquired rights, written proof of the employment relationship, pregnancy and maternity leave and payment, paternity leave, working time and equal opportunities are now all areas in which EU legislation impacts on the everyday work of the UK HR profession.

Major developments in European integration since 1951

Treaty of Paris 1951
- created the European Coal and Steel Community
- promoted living and working conditions of coal and steel workers

Treaty of Rome 1957
- created the European Economic Community (EEC) by removing barriers to the free movement of labour, capital, goods and services (the 'Common Market')
- created the European Atomic Energy Community
- included the Free Movement of Workers Chapter enshrining the right of citizens of member states to live and work where they wished
- included the Social Chapter promoting improved working conditions and better standards of living for workers and the right to equal pay for equal work for men and women

Single European Act 1987
- set a deadline for establishing the single European market
- replaced unanimity in the voting procedures of members states by qualified majority voting (QMV), through allocating votes

---

according to the populations of member states, thus removing the power of veto by single member states
- formalised the European Community's commitment to involving the 'social partners' in European decision-making procedures
- enabled health and safety provisions to be harmonised by QMV

Treaty on the European Union 1993
- created the European Union (EU)
- provided for the creation of a common currency, starting in January 1999
- restated the principle of 'subsidiarity', giving competency to the EU when common objectives could be better achieved by harmonised action rather than by member states acting alone
- formalised the EU's commitment to involving the 'social partners' in EU decision-making machinery
- amended the Social Chapter, so that through the Social Policy Agreement member states (except the UK) could extend the employment and social issues to be harmonised by QMV

Treaty of Amsterdam 1997
- empowered the Council of Ministers to combat discrimination on the grounds of sex, ethnic origin, religion or belief, age and sexual orientation
- pledged to remove remaining restrictions on the free movement of labour
- introduced an Employment Chapter making the achievement of high and sustainable employment opportunities in the EU a strategic goal
  required EU institutions to encourage 'social dialogue' on employment, working conditions, the right to work, training and social security
- incorporated the Social Policy Agreement into the Treaty as the Social Chapter, making it applicable to all member states of the EU (including the UK)

Source: Farnham D. *Employee Relations in Context.* London, CIPD. 2000. p362.

The Single European Act 1987 extended the areas in which the EEC could legislate to social policy (including employment) and also increased the use of qualified majority voting for measures designed to increase harmonisation of the internal market and progress to a 'people's Europe'. Although unanimity was required in relation to employment issues, majority voting could be used for health and safety – this was particularly important given the Conservative government's opposition to working life legislation in the 1980s (Pitt, 2000). The scope of EU social policy has widened since the adoption of the Social Chapter in the

1992 Maastricht Treaty – and its incorporation, along with the 1989 Social Charter, into the 1997 Treaty of Amsterdam. Hence, national labour markets are increasingly regulated by legislation adopted at EU level (Reid, 2000c). As Gennard and Judge (1999: 77) note, the increase in European business is undoubtedly a result of the development and enlargement of the European single market, and this has led UK employers to expand operations into other member states. In turn this is likely to increase the range of experiences and influences on personnel managers in the UK. The new social model advocated by the Commission (Bach and Sisson, 2000: 34) seeks to:

balance the employer's demand for flexibility with the employee's hopes for security. Equally important, education and training are increasingly seen as a way not only of helping individuals to become more adaptable in their present employment, but also of providing opportunities to acquire knowledge and skills so that they can find alternative employment should the number of jobs be reduced in their present workplace.

Some 50 Directives had been adopted in the field of social policy by 2001, covering equal opportunities, employment protection, working conditions, health and safety at work, and employee relations – see the box below for examples.

Examples of Directives

1975	Equal Pay Directive
1976	Equal Treatment Directive
1996	Parental Leave Directive
1997	Parental Leave (UK Extension) Directive
1997	Burden of Proof in Sex Discrimination Cases Directive
1998	Burden of Proof in Sex Discrimination Cases (UK Extension) Directive
1997	Part-time Work Directive
1998	Part-time Work (UK Extension) Directive.
1975	Collective Redundancies Directive
1977	Transfers of Undertakings/Acquired Rights Directive
1992	Directive amending the Collective Redundancies Directive
1994	European Works Council Directive
1997	European Works Council (UK Extension) Directive
1998	Directive amending the Transfers of Undertakings/Acquired Rights Directive.
2000	Race Discrimination Directive

European legislation is a complex process, but is determined in the following ways, depending upon the issues concerned (Farnham, 2000: 363):

- unanimous vote of the Council of Ministers

- qualified majority voting (QMV) in the Council of Ministers

- a co-decision procedure involving the Council of the EU and the European Parliament

- a 'framework agreement' involving the 'social partners', who can either suggest that the European Commission draft a Directive for approval by the Council of Ministers (by unanimous decision or QMV) or jointly negotiate an EU-level framework agreement.

Areas of employment in which European-Union-wide legislation affects the work of the UK personnel/HR professional

Equality issues
Equal pay (1975)
Parental leave (1996)
Equal treatment (1976)
Part-time work (1997)
Fixed-term contracts (1999)
Burden of proof in sex discrimination cases (1997)

Employment protection
Redundancy (1975 and 1992)
Transfer of undertakings (1977 and 1998)
Contracts of employment (1991)
Posting of workers (1996)
Insolvency (1980)

Employment relations
Consultation and information (1994 and 1997)

Health and safety
Organisation of working time (1993)
Safety and health at work for pregnant employees and new mothers
Safety and health at work for workers with a fixed-duration employment relationship or a temporary employment relationship

Source: Gennard and Judge, 1999, p97

Where provisions of a Directive are clear and unambiguous, and confer rights on individuals, Directives can be said to have a so-called direct effect. This has been important in relation to equal pay (Reid, 2000b). If a member state fails to transpose a Directive into domestic legislation by the stipulated date (or transposes the Directive incorrectly), the Commission may bring action against the member state before the European Court of Justice (ECJ). Because EU legislation prevails over national legislation, a ruling by the ECJ can have significant consequences in national legislation (Reid, 2000b).

The signing by the UK government of the Social Chapter of the 1997 Amsterdam Treaty brought an end to the British opt-out from European

Union (EU) social policy negotiated at the Maastricht European Council in 1991. Consequently, EU social policy-making now takes place within a single decision-making institutional framework (Reid, 2000c). Article 136 of the Treaty (the so-called Social Chapter) outlined the objectives of EU social policy as the promotion of:

- employment
- improved living and working conditions
- proper social protection
- dialogue between management and labour
- the development of human resources
- the fight against exclusion.

This became operational in the UK on 1 May 1999, but is not a set of detailed regulations. As Farnham (2000: 362) notes, 'It merely allows states to make legislation at EU levels on a range of social issues by a variety of institutional means, which member states have to implement.'

The Social Chapter – the basis on which issues can be decided

Qualified majority voting
Health and safety
Working conditions
Information and consultation of workers
Equal treatment and equal opportunities for men and women
The integration of persons excluded from the labour market

Unanimous vote
Social security and protection of workers
The protection of workers whose employment contracts are terminated
The representation and collective defence of the interests of workers and employers, including co-determination
Conditions of employment for third-country nationals legally resident in the EU
Financial contributions for the promotion of employment and job creation

Excluded issues
Pay
The right of association
The right to strike
The right to lock out

Source: Gennard and Judge, 1999, p95

The Treaty introduces a number of amendments to the original Treaty of Rome, which established the European Community. The equal pay provisions have been amended to include a direct reference to the principle of equal treatment. Such a reference – the first reference to the principle of equal treatment – should make it 'directly effective' – that is, it provides private sector employees the same rights as those currently enjoyed by employees of the state to rely on principles of European law in national courts and tribunals. The Treaty of Amsterdam also contained Article 13, which enables the EU to take action against any form of discrimination, whether based on sex, racial or ethnic origin, religion or belief, disability, age or sexual orientation.

In deciding the basis of social policy, the EU can utilise the ideas behind the Social Charter (which was incorporated into the Treaty of Amsterdam). The Charter – not to be confused with the Chapter – provides a floor of rights in respect of:

- freedom of movement
- employment and remuneration
- the improvement of living and working conditions
- social protection
- freedom of association and collective bargaining
- vocational training
- equal treatment for men and women
- information, consultation and participation for workers
- health protection and safety at the workplace
- the protection of children and adolescents
- elderly persons
- disabled persons.

Although the Social Charter has no legal force but is a series of recommendations and minimum standards, it has nevertheless formed the basis for EU action in the area of social policy through the Social Action Programme (Farnham, 2000). This reflects the view that social policy had fallen behind developments in the single market.

The new framework of EU social policy-making includes provision for the European social partners – the European Trade Union Confederation (ETUC), the Union of Industrial and Employers' Confederations of Europe (UNICE) and the European Centre of Enterprises with Public Participation (CEEP) – to be consulted about both direction and the content of EU legislation in the social field. They can also negotiate framework agreements as a substitute for legislation. The social partners may similarly engage in negotiations (social dialogue) at their own initiative, as has happened in relation to accident prevention and improving working conditions. Framework agreements have been negotiated on parental leave (1996), part-time work (1997) and fixed-term work contracts (1999). When the social partners decide not to negotiate, the Commission may submit its legislative proposal through the normal decision-making procedures.

The legal basis for proposals can be challenged. For example, the 1993 Working Time Directive came into force in the UK under the Working Time Regulations 1998, covering not just management working hours but holidays and rest periods (Bone, 2002). It was considered by the UK government an issue of working conditions, not a health and safety issue as put forward by the Commission. This was because health and safety was then subject to QMV, while working conditions were subject to unanimity, and therefore susceptible to a UK veto. The UK government took its case to the ECJ but lost (Gennard and Judge, 1997; Reid, 2000b). However, the UK voluntarist tradition with minimal legislation is reflected in how this Directive was implemented in the UK allowing individuals to opt out of the limits (Fenton O'Creevy, 2001a).

Other European developments to affect the UK include the Race Directive 2000 – covering discrimination on grounds of race or ethnic origin – which has to be implemented by 2003. In addition an Equal Treatment Directive 2000 – covering discrimination on grounds of religion or belief, disability, age and sexual orientation – also has to be implemented by 2003, although provisions relating to age or disability may be deferred until 2006.

The Human Rights Act 1998 came into force on 2 October 2000 and incorporated into UK law certain rights and freedoms set out in the European Convention on Human Rights. According to Lewis and Sargeant (2002: 339–44), the key sections of the Human Rights Act relating to employment issues likely to affect the UK are:

- Article 8 – on the right to privacy
- Article 9 – on freedom of thought, conscience and religion
- Article 10 – on freedom of expression
- Article 11 – on freedom of assembly and association, including the right to join a trade union.

Article 8 may be of importance when employers interfere with communications by staff, such as intercepting telephone calls, monitoring e-mail or interfering with Internet use. The disclosure of personal information about an employee to third parties without that employee's consent may breach Article 8, particularly if it is confidential medical information. Article 9 might for example affect dress code, religious observance and the expressing of political views (Williams, 2000: 19). Article 10 has been tested in relation to issues of disclosure of confidential information. Article 11 has been utilised in relation to staff who work in positions where national security is at risk and their rights to trade union membership have been questioned. Disability as well as sexual orientation and mental status is thought to fall under this area as well. It remains to be seen how tribunals will apply these rights in practice. European influence will continue to grow in importance. As Gennard (2000: 120) notes:

Unless the UK withdraws from the EU or is able to re-negotiate the Social Chapter of the Treaty of Rome then the EU will continue to establish common standards for the UK employee relations system. Increasingly, these common standards may be established by collective bargaining between the Social Partners, thereby increasing the influence of trade union behaviour on non-union organisations.

The EU is about a lot more than beef bans. For employees the EU has given minimum standards in the fields of working time, hours of work, holiday entitlement, information and consultation in pan-European companies, in redundancies and transfers of businesses and parental leave. These are protections UK governments have been less than enthusiastic to give. The EU is an integral part of the UK employee relations system and not something entirely external to it.

Individual rights at work

Employer–worker relations are organised principally around the concept of the employment contract. The main terms of this contract are outlined in various texts (Lewis and Sargeant, 2002: 18–58; Pitt, 2000: 79–134), sources which should be consulted for further advice. At the outset, however, it is important to clarify the difference between the employment contract and the statement of terms and conditions. The contract may or may not be written, and in practice the parties enter into a contract after the stages of advertisement, interview, offer and acceptance. In most cases employers provide a statement of the main terms and conditions of employment or a written contract, but a contract is still formed even if no written material changes hands. It is also important to realise that a breach of contract, which can lead to an action for wrongful dismissal, is different from a claim for unfair dismissal. Not only is each case typically dealt with through different channels (wrongful dismissal through the court system, and unfair dismissal through the employment tribunals), they each cover different issues (Pitt, 2000). Since 1994 jurisdiction has been extended to include breach of contract cases (Lewis and Sargeant, 2002: 225). There are several sources of contractual terms.

Express agreement between employer and employee

These are the terms of the contract that are spelled out, either in writing or orally. They may include the terms of an advertisement, oral terms outlined at interview, or a written contract provided after the interview, either at the time the individual starts work or some time thereafter. The express terms may differ from what is contained in a job advertisement, but are clearly laid down as part of the individual contract or are expressly incorporated from a collective agreement (Lewis and Sargeant, 2002: 20; Earnshaw, 2002: 44–5).

Terms implied by common law

These are the terms inferred by the courts as inherent in all contracts of employment. They can arise in either of two ways. First, an implied term may result from what is understood to have been the intention of the parties. This is either through the 'officious bystander' test, which means that a term is so obvious that it need not be stated, or the 'business efficacy' test, in which it can be presumed that such at least was the intention on the part of both parties within a business context. The second influence of common law is that certain terms are implied in every contract (Pitt, 2000: 116–34). In this connection every employer has a duty:

- to pay wages if an employee is available for work and there is no express term that limits this in the event of the employee's being laid off

- to provide work in certain specified circumstances, such as when an employee's earnings are dependent upon work being provided (eg if employees are paid by commission), or when the lack of work could lead to a loss of publicity or affect the reputation of the employee, or when the employee needs practice in order to maintain his or her skills

- to co-operate with the employee, in that the employee is to be treated by the employer in a manner that will not destroy any mutual trust and confidence upon which co-operation is built (eg making false accusations on the basis of flimsy evidence, seeking to enforce contractual obligations that are impossible to comply with, or persistently varying an employee's conditions of service)

- to take reasonable care for the health and safety of the employee by providing a standard of care which any prudent employer would take in the circumstances (eg providing safe premises and working environment, and avoiding risks which are reasonably foreseeable).

In return, the employee also has obligations under common law. These are:

- to co-operate with the employer, by obeying lawful and reasonable instructions so as not to impede the employer's business. The situation in which employees are asked to take on duties falling outside the scope of their contract is complicated. Depending upon the nature of the request, this may be construed as a fundamental breach of contract, but the employer may be able to justify the decision on the grounds of a necessary business reorganisation and so avoid an accusation of unfair dismissal (Pitt, 2000: 124–5).

● to be faithful to the employer, and not engage in actions that cause a conflict of interest with the employer (eg in competing directly with the employer, in disclosing confidential information that may be of benefit to a competitor or some other third party, or in relation to patents and copyright)

● to take reasonable care in the performance of his or her duties such that he or she does not put himself or herself or other employees at risk.

Collective agreements

Terms may be derived from collective agreements as well as being individually negotiated, either by express provision or by implication. Pay and conditions of service are routinely incorporated into an individual's contract of employment if the contract contains an express provision that it is subject to the terms of a particular collective agreement. In addition, the terms of a collective agreement may be legally enforceable if trade union officers act as agents of their members for the purpose of making a contract on their behalf; this is really likely only where the number of workers is small.

Works rules

These can be incorporated into the contract in two ways: first, if employees are required to sign an acknowledgement at the time of entering employment that works rules will form part of the contract; second, if 'reasonable notice' is given by the employer that works rules are to form part of the contract. Questions then ought to be asked about whether the terms of the contract in any way vary with the rules, how adequately and how prominently the rules are displayed, and whether or not the employee would regard this notice as likely to include contractual conditions. Works rules are dealt with again in Chapters 14 and 15.

Custom and practice

In the absence of express terms, 'custom and practice' may help to define what constitutes the employment contract. To be implied into a contract, custom and practice has to be 'reasonable, certain and notorious'. It is 'reasonable' if it fits with norms in the industry in question, and would be interpreted in this way by a court. Custom and practice is 'certain' if it is capable of precise definition and not interpreted in substantially different ways by different people. Finally, it is 'notorious' if the custom is well-known by all those to whom it relates. The requirement to provide employees with written statements limits the scope for there to be customary terms in the contract (Pitt, 2000: 115).

Statute

These are terms Parliament has decreed are to be put into all contracts of employment, such as the provision for pay equality through the Equal Pay Act 1970, as amended by the Equal Value Amendment Regulations 1983. The amount of employment legislation regarding employer–worker relations has expanded considerably in the UK since the early 1970s, under a whole series of legal enactments. These include the Industrial Relations Act 1971; the Trade Union and Labour Relations Act 1974; the Employment Protection Consolidation Act 1978; the Sex Discrimination Act 1975; the Race Relations Act 1976; the Equal Pay Act 1970 as amended by the Equal Pay Amendment Regulations 1983; the Transfer of Undertakings (Protection of Employment) Regulations 1981; the Wages Act 1986; the Trade Union and Labour Relations (Consolidation) Act 1992; the Trade Union Reform and Employment Rights Act 1993; the Disability Discrimination Act 1995; the Employment Rights Act 1996; the Data Protection Act 1998; the Employment Relations Act 1999; employment tribunals 1996; the Collective Redundancies and Transfers of Undertakings (Protection of Employment) Amendment Regulations 1999; the National Minimum Wage Act 1998; the Human Rights Act 1998; the Maternity and Parental Leave Regulations 1999; and the Working Time Regulations 1998. The legislation in relation to equal opportunities and discrimination on the basis of sex, race and disability is taken up again in Chapter 6 when we examine the ethical and professional context of HRM.

Employment rights of individuals

The main employment protection rights of individuals include the right:

- to join or not to join a union
- not to be refused employment on the grounds of union membership
- not to be dismissed, or have action short of dismissal taken, because of trade union membership
- to receive written particulars of the main terms of the contract of employment
- to receive an itemised pay statement
- not to have unlawful deductions made from wages
- to receive guaranteed payments when not provided with work by an employer on a normal working day
- to receive medical suspension payments

- to receive statutory sick pay
- to be afforded equal treatment in terms and conditions of employment, irrespective of sex
- not to be treated less favourably as a part-time worker than a full-time worker
- to take time off work for antenatal care, to receive maternity pay and maternity leave for female employees and, after giving birth, to return to work
- to take parental leave
- to be able to take time off work to care for dependants
- to be able to take time off work for public duties
- not to be discriminated against on the grounds of sex, marital status, disability or race
- not to be dismissed in connection with medical suspension
- to receive a minimum period of notice
- to receive at least the statutory minimum wage
- to be accompanied by a fellow worker or trade union representative at certain disciplinary or grievance hearings
- to receive a redundancy payment when a job disappears
- to be able to take time off work to look for work in a redundancy situation or to arrange training
- to obtain payment from the Secretary of State in the event of the employer's insolvency
- to be afforded protection from detriment or dismissal for refusing to sign personal contracts excluding employees from collectively negotiated terms
- to disregard 'waiver clauses' for unfair dismissal in fixed-term contracts
- not to be unfairly dismissed
- not to be unfairly dismissed during the first eight weeks of lawful industrial action
- to receive a written statement of the reasons for dismissal

Source: Farnham, 2000, pp93–4

A written statement of particulars should be provided by the employer not later than two months after the start of employment of a person whose employment continues for a month or more (Employment Rights Act 1996). This is not meant to be a constraint on employment but to represent the employer's own formal statement of what has been agreed (Lewis and Sargeant, 2002: 33). It should include:

- the names of the employer and employee
- the date on which the period of continuous employment is to commence or commenced
- the scale or rate of remuneration, and the interval at which it is to be paid

- terms and conditions relating to hours of work, holidays and holiday pay, and sick pay

- terms relating to pensions arrangements

- the length of notice employees are required to receive and obliged to provide

- the title of the job

- the name of persons to whom the individual employee can apply in the event of a grievance or dissatisfaction with a disciplinary decision

- the place(s) of work at which the employee is required or allowed to work

- details regarding collective agreements which directly affect the employee's terms and conditions of employment

- where the employment is temporary, the period for which it is expected to continue, or, if it is for a fixed term, the date when it is to end

- any arrangement by which the employee is required to work outside the UK for more than a month.

Employers collect and hold information on workers, but there is an issue over misuse of information. The Data Protection Act 1984 provided some protection for employees. Its main purpose was to 'regulate the use of automatically processed information relating to individuals and the provision of services in respect of such information' (Lewis and Sargeant, 2002: 344–7).

The Directive on the Protection of Personal Data 1995 (PPD Directive) led to the passing of the Data Protection Act 1998 (DPA 1998), which replaced the 1984 Act (Pitt, 2000: 120). One of the main extensions of the law in DPA 1998 is that it now applies to manual records as well as computerised information. Under the DPA employers have a duty to ensure that personal data is obtained only for specified, lawful purposes and is likewise used only for those purposes. The information kept must be accurate, up-to-date, relevant and not excessive – suggesting that personnel records should regularly be culled of old and irrelevant information. The Act contains strict limitations on the processing of such information, which includes its disclosure. Although there are exceptions to these principles, the general thrust of the Act requires employers to respect the privacy of employees through limitations on the use of information about them (Pitt, 2000: 120–21). There are also transitional provisions which exempt many existing manual records – manual data held before 24 October 1998 is exempted until October 2007. Key words in the Act include the phrase 'relevant filing system'. According to Hansard 'we do not wish the definition to apply to miscellaneous collections of paper about individuals, even if the collections are assembled in a file with the individual's name or other unique identifier on the front, if specific data about the individual cannot readily be extracted from the collection . . .' (16.3.98, cited in Bone, 1999). There are many potential legal wrangles over the meaning of such words as 'processing', the majority of organisations in a recent poll agreeing that they are at risk of breaching their obligations. In a recent case, the health insurer Western Provident Association (WPA) settled out of court for £45,000 from Norwich Union after libellous e-mail messages about WPA were circulated on the Norwich Union company e-mail system (Bone, 1999: 6). The Data Protection Act covers several aspects of HRM, such as recruitment, the provision of references, internal assessments, career planning, and wage administration and payments.

Collective rights at work

The period between 1979 and 1997 was characterised by a piecemeal and gradual reform of employer–union relations. At the same time it was driven by a continuing and persistent objective: to weaken the power of trade unions, both by limiting their ability to engage in industrial action, and by making it harder for trade union leaders to gain mandates from the membership. Not many employers have actually taken out injunctions to delay industrial action, and even fewer have gone beyond the injunction stage to seek damages against trade unions because of the potential detrimental effect on employee relations (Farnham, 2000: 394–400). On the other hand, the threat of the law has probably acted as a severe constraint on union leaders and members, and may well have prevented many deep-seated conflicts from being translated into strike action. Most commentators agree that the law has played a significant part in changing the balance of power since 1979, but it would be unwise to overestimate its influence, given other factors, most notably relatively high levels of unemployment throughout the 1990s and increasingly competitive product market pressures.

Throughout the twentieth century up until 1979, public policy in Britain had encouraged the support and development of collective bargaining. Most of this period was characterised by voluntarism, leaving employers and trade unions to sort out their own arrangements without any explicit state intervention. As we saw earlier in this chapter, the law played an auxiliary role, persuading the parties that employee relations could be improved by the development and extension of collective bargaining. For example, the terms of reference of ACAS are a prime example of this, in that up until 1993 it had a general duty to 'encourage the extension of collective bargaining', although there were no formal powers to impose changes on employers or employees. The period from 1979 to 1997 saw a gradual erosion of collectivist legal principles in employee relations, being presented as 'enhancing individual freedom, freeing employers from the abuses of union power, and improving efficiency and competitiveness' (Dickens and Hall, 1995: 275).

Legislation directed at employer–union relations includes: the Trade Union Act 1984; the Employment Act 1988; the Employment Act 1989; the Employment Act 1990; the Trade Union and Labour Relations (Consolidation) Act 1992; the Trade Union Reform, Employment Rights Act 1993, and the Employment Relations Act 1999. These affect union organisation (and in particular the closed shop) and industrial action (strikes and picketing).

What is your view on the position of the law in relation to trade unions? Does the 'balance' between employers and unions seem about right or should it be adjusted? Do the current restrictions make it harder or easier for HR practitioners? Why do you say this?

The dismantling of the closed legislation which allowed union membership to be a condition of employment – albeit with exceptions and escape clauses for employees with fundamental objections to the principle – was achieved through legislation between 1980 and 1990. The Trade Union Reform and Employment Rights Act 1993 (TURERA 1993) made it harder for unions to organise at the workplace by restrictions on check-off or deduction-of-contribution-at-source (DOCAS) arrangements. Under TURERA individuals had to provide written consent every three years that they were prepared to have union subscriptions deducted from payroll and also had to authorise subscription changes. There were employer objections to this provision on the grounds that it could destabilise employee relations and lead to greater confusion and complexity at the workplace, and the 1998 Deregulation Order (deduction from pay of union subscriptions) restored the previous position. In the intervening period unions encouraged staff to pay subscriptions by direct debit (Pitt, 2000: 355). However, DOCAS remains the predominant method of collection: 66 per cent of unionised workplaces operated in this way in 1998 (Cully *et al*, 1999: 89).

The legislation on strikes and picketing has followed a similar gradualist route, to the point where it is now extremely difficult for trade unions to organise industrial action. Prior to the Employment Act 1980, picketing was allowed at any place other than an individual's home. In 1980 picketing was effectively restricted solely to a person's place of work, although there were exceptions for individuals with no fixed workplace. A code of practice issued by the Employment Department also recommended a limit of six on the number of pickets, although this has not been rigorously applied by the police who have preferred to control picket lines via the use of public order offences. There have been a number of attempts to restrict strike activity, falling broadly into three categories:

- Definitions of a lawful trade dispute have been narrowed progressively since the Employment Act 1982. Inter-union disputes have been excluded from immunity, as are those deemed to be of a 'political character' – that is, seen to be wider than those concerned wholly or mainly with conditions of employment. Secondary industrial action (ie that which relates to disputes beyond the initial employer–employee dispute) was also restricted in 1982, and is now effectively outlawed.

- The dismissal of strikers was made easier following the Employment Act 1982. This prevented individuals who were dismissed during a lawful dispute from claiming unfair dismissal if all strikers at a workplace had been dismissed and none had been re-engaged within three months. The Employment Act 1990 allowed for the selective dismissal of strikers engaged in unofficial action.

- The requirement to hold ballots of members before taking industrial action has been extended, first on a voluntary 'auxiliary' basis by providing public funds to pay for postal ballots in the 1980 Act, and through the removal of immunity if ballots are not held. At first unions were allowed to hold workplace ballots (Trade Union Act 1984) but this has now restricted to postal ballots alone. The wording on the ballot paper has been specified more precisely; there are now time limits regulating the use of industrial action after a ballot, and notice has to be given to an employer that a ballot is to be held. There is little doubt that these requirements now make it much harder for trade unions to organise, and much easier for employers to plan their defence against, industrial action, given that prior notice has to be given. Interestingly, the ballots provisions have tended to increase the support for industrial action rather than decrease it in a majority of cases (Martin *et al*, 1991).

The 1999 Employment Relations Act included statutory recognition procedures but applied to only employers with at least 21 workers – hence excluding some 8 million workers (Smith and Morton, 2001). It also provided some protection for workers taking industrial action in that it became automatically unfair to dismiss those taking part in lawfully-organised action for eight weeks. If all reasonable steps are taken to resolve the dispute after this time, dismissal is likely to be fair (Bone, 1999). In addition, ballots before action contain new wording explaining the new protection. Smith and Morton (2001: 130) point out that employers' freedom to dismiss workers has been regulated, not abolished. Recognition can be achieved through several routes.

- recognition by agreement – In companies that employ 21 or more workers, an independent trade union can make a request to the employer for recognition. If there is no agreement after 28 days, ACAS can be called in to intervene.

- recognition from an application to ACAS – If voluntary negotiations fail, the Central Arbitration Committee (CAC) assesses the extent to which a 'bargaining unit' exists for the purpose of recognition. The CAC is required to help both sides reach agreement about the bargaining unit and consider whether the trade union has majority support of workers within the defined unit. The CAC can then issue a declaration that the union is recognised for those workers. There is no agreed definition of a 'bargaining unit', although it should be consistent with existing structures of management, and ideally avoid small fragmented groups of workers within an undertaking.

- recognition ballots – The CAC has the discretion to conduct a ballot to assess the extent of support for trade union recognition if three conditions are met: (a) if it thinks this is in the interests of good industrial relations, (b) if a 'significant number' of employees within a bargaining unit inform the CAC they do not want trade union recognition, or (c) if there is evidence that leads the CAC to conclude that a 'significant number' of union members do not want the trade union to bargain on their behalf. The employer is obliged to co-operate with the ballot, and if at least 40 per cent of those eligible to vote support union recognition, the CAC will declare that the union is recognised (Dundon 2002a; Farnham, 2000: 316–21).

However, Dundon (2002a: 253–4) notes that the procedure has been criticised:

On one hand employers prefer the voluntary approach and view the law as impeding further regulation within the labour market. On the other hand, trade unions regard the 40 per cent voting threshold as unworkable. They suggest it will be extremely difficult to achieve recognition for workers in those organisations for which the law was intended, particularly in smaller undertakings where membership is low (or non-existent) and employers are extremely hostile.

Have there been any strikes at your place of work in recent years, and if so what were they about? If there have not been any strikes, but there has been some discontent, how have employees shown their displeasure? Has this situation been easy to resolve?

The tribunals

Before we describe the tribunal system, it is important that readers are aware of the differences between criminal and civil law. Although the vast majority of HR issues are dealt with through the civil law, there are times when the criminal law comes into play, and individuals may be able to seek redress through either branch of the law. Criminal law is concerned with preventing breaches of society's rules, and with punishing offenders; cases are normally dealt with through the magistrates' courts or Crown courts. In contrast, civil law is concerned with settling disputes between private parties, such as between two individuals or between a worker and an employer. Employment issues are typically dealt with through the tribunal system, whereas other matters go through the County Court or High Court system. Two examples of employment issues that could go through either or both routes are those concerned with safety and accidents, and with dismissal due to a breach of contract.

The vast majority of HR practitioners who become embroiled in legal issues are likely to be involved in employment tribunals. Originally called industrial tribunals, these were set up under the Industrial Training Act 1964 to hear employers' appeals against levies, and their work was extended in 1965 to include redundancy payments issues. It was only really after the Industrial Relations Act 1971 that tribunals started to play a major role in the HR field, largely in dealing with claims for unfair dismissal. More recently, however, a growing proportion of their caseload has involved equal opportunities and redundancy payments issues. Over the years, the tribunal system has had a significant influence on the way in which managements handle employment issues, and it has led to an increasing formalisation of procedures in employing organisations. This topic is dealt with more fully in Chapter 14 when we examine grievance and disciplinary procedures.

Employment tribunals mostly sit and hear cases to do with:

- unfair dismissal
- health and safety at work
- race discrimination
- equal pay, sex discrimination and maternity
- redundancy, reorganisation and transfers of undertakings
- pay and other terms of employment
- trade union membership and non-membership
- time off for public duties
- dismissal due to a breach of contract.

Individuals who have a complaint against an employer start the process by completing an originating application (IT1), typically, though not necessarily, after consulting with their trade union, the Citizens Advice Bureau, a friend, or a solicitor. The application is received by the Employment Tribunal Office and a copy of the application is sent to the employer, who has 21 days to respond. Copies of the employer's response are then sent to the employee or his or her representatives. At this point, ACAS contacts both

Table 9   Employment tribunal applications

Year	Applications registered
1990–91	43,243
1991–92	67,448
1992–93	71,821
1993–94	71.661
1994–95	80,061
1995–96	108,827
1996–97	88,910
1997–98	80,435
1998–99	91,913
1999–2000	103,935
2000–01	130,408

Source: Employment Tribunal Office

parties to see if a conciliated settlement can be achieved. ACAS concili-ation officers have the task of making speedy and informal contact with the parties, and a duty under the law to seek a conciliated settlement if either party requests it or if ACAS believes there is a reasonable prospect that its intervention may be successful. Following conciliation, a substan-tial proportion of cases are settled, and in many cases this results in an out-of-court settlement to the applicant. It is rare for a dismissed individ-ual to be reinstated or re-engaged, however.

The number of originating applications more than doubled between 1990 and 2000 to well over 100,000 per annum. The range of cases has broadened as well, and matters have been complicated yet further by the influence of European judgements on British employment relations. This led to what some see as a growing 'compensation cul-ture' (Fairclough and Birkenshaw, 2001: 4).

Go to the library and find a recent copy of one of the specialist employment law publications – such as the *Industrial Relations Law Report* or *IRS Employment Trends*. Choose a recent case, examine the details, and write a short report for your manager outlining any lessons to be learned by your organisation.

The Employment Rights (Disputes Resolutions) Act 1998 empowered ACAS to draw up an arbitration scheme for individual disputes so as to reduce the load on tribunals, to minimise delays, and to contain demands on public expenditure.

Within the tribunal system itself there has been a continuing tension between its initial aim of providing a cheap, speedy and informal route to resolve employment rights problems, and the increasing tendency to legalism and reference to legal precedents. The latter is inevitable as the body of case law has built up and both parties (respondent and applicant) seek specialist representation at the tribunal. In addition to the increasing likelihood that both parties are represented by solicitors, employers' organisations and trade unions also provide specialist expertise, and some employers have their own legal experts to deal with these cases. Because the costs of losing a case can be quite high for an employer, not just in terms of direct employment costs but also in compensation, payment for representation and negative public relations, the incentive to win has become even greater. Attempts to retain some measure of informality are made by many tribunal chairmen, who have been encouraged to adopt a more investigative approach, and to assist unrepresented applicants or respondents with their line of questioning. The lay members of the tribunal provide knowledge and expertise from industry.

Appeals against tribunal decisions are made to the Employment Appeals Tribunal (EAT), a body with the same status as a High Court, which was established under the Employment Protection Act 1975. It hears appeals on any question of law stemming from a tribunal decision. Such appeals may be based on claims that the tribunal has misunderstood or misdirected itself as to the law applicable in the circumstances, that there is no evidence to support a particular finding, or that the tribunal has come to a perverse conclusion. Appeals can be remitted to the same or to a fresh tribunal for a rehearing if they are neither upheld nor dismissed. Appeals on a point of law are tightly circumscribed, and there have been repeated warnings that points of fact are not to be dressed up in the garb of points of law in order to bring an appeal. Appeals against EAT decisions can be made in certain circumstances to the Court of Appeal, then to the House of Lords and to the European Court of Justice. In addition, individual employment tribunals can refer matters directly to the ECJ for interpretations of Community law. The ECJ is becoming increasingly influential in several areas of employment law – for example, in relation to equal pay, maternity rights, sex discrimination, and health and safety.

The Commissions: equal opportunities, racial equality, health and safety, and trade union issues

The Equal Opportunities Commission (EOC) was established under the Sex Discrimination Act 1975 with the general duties of working towards the elimination of discrimination, promoting equality of opportunity between men and women generally, and reviewing the operation of the relevant legislation – such as on sex discrimination and on equal pay. The EOC is empowered to bring proceedings under the various pieces of legislation, carry out formal investigations on its own initiative, and publish reports and recommendations. Enforcement relating to employment matters falls within the domain of the employment tribunals, and the last decade has seen a great increase in the number of cases that centre on equal opportunities issues. Although most cases brought before tribunals relate to women's attempts to receive equal treatment with men, the EOC also investigates cases in which men feel they are being discriminated against in favour of women – for example, in the case of a male secretary. The EOC issued a Code of Practice on how to eliminate discrimination in employment (as the CIPD has also done), and it can issue 'non-discrimination' notices. The European Commission has produced a Code of Practice on measures to combat sexual harassment, and tribunals can take the provisions of the code into account when deciding if harassment has taken place. Shaw (2002: 77–8) notes that inequality is still evident in the UK, and the EOC is committed to using its statutory powers to advise the government on legislative reform and to seeking an extension of its investigative powers. One suggestion has been that following the incorporation of the European Convention on Human Rights, the EOC should merge with the Commission for Racial Equality and the newly-established Disability Rights Commission to form a single Human Rights Commission.

In many respects, the Commission for Racial Equality (CRE) performs a role similar to that of the EOC. It was established under the Race Relations Act 1976, with similar general duties to the EOC, but with an added requirement to promote good relations between people of different racial groups. The CRE has three principal functions: to conduct formal investigations into any discriminatory matter, and (like the EOC) issue non-discrimination notices; to institute legal proceedings in the case of persistent discrimination and in relation to advertisements; and to assist individual complainants in taking their case to an employment tribunal. Like the EOC, it has produced a Code of Practice on how to eliminate discrimination in employment which can be used in evidence at a tribunal. Racial inequality in employment still exists in Britain, and in this context a number of shortcomings have been identified in the Commission's structure and powers. The Race Relations Amendment Act which came into force in 2001 outlaws discrimination in all public services and makes it a statutory duty as a public body to promote race equality. Both these equal opportunities issues are taken up again in Chapter 6, when we review the ethical and professional context of HRM.

The Disability Discrimination Act 1995 imposes requirements on employers in respect of disabled workers. These are people with a mental or physical impairment that has lasted or is likely to last at least 12 months, and which has a substantial adverse effect on their ability to 'carry out normal day-to-day activities'. This applies to employers with 15 or more employees. It prohibits employers from treating such workers less favourably and by requiring employers to make 'reasonable adjustments' to their premises and the way in which they operate (James, 2002: 4). The Disability Rights Commission Act 1999 established a Disability Rights Commission (DRC) for Great Britain. The Act also sets out the functions of the DRC, which are similar to those of the Equal Opportunities Commission and the Commission for Racial Equality.

Penalties for breaches of the Act's requirements can be enforced through individual complaints to an employment tribunal, and the Disability Rights Commission can conduct formal investigations and issue non-discrimination notices (Bone, 1999: 4).

The Health and Safety Commission (HSC) has some similarities with ACAS in that it operates with an independent chair and a council composed of part-time members drawn from a variety of backgrounds but broadly representative of both sides of industry and commerce. The Health and Safety at Work Act (HASAWA) 1974 brought together the myriad different bodies which had previously held responsibility for safety and health issues, thus providing the HSC with a unified and integrated set of powers. The general duties of the HSC are:

- to assist and encourage people to secure the health, safety and welfare of persons at work, and protect those not at work

- to undertake and encourage research, to publish findings, and to train and educate people in relation to the purposes of the legislation

- to provide an advisory and information service

- to make proposals for regulations.

The HSC therefore has a wide remit, including more obvious safety issues – such as the wearing of protective clothing and the investigation of accidents – through to less obvious, but equally important, areas concerned with health at work. Recently this has involved issues connected with stress-related illnesses and the provision of management support for employees who are under intolerable pressures at work. The HSC has an operational arm, the Health and Safety Executive, which is responsible for the work of the various inspectorates. There are several instruments of enforcement open to inspectors. These are:

- 'improvement notices', which require a fault to be remedied within a set period of time

- 'prohibition notices', which can lead to closures of workplaces and buildings as unsafe if insufficient attention has been paid to an improvement notice, or the risk of serious injury is considered to be high

- prosecutions.

The Certification Officer has the following areas of responsibility:

- trade union political activities, such as approving the rules for a political fund, and dealing with complaints from union members about breaches of the rules in this respect

- trade union mergers and transfers of engagements, ensuring that these take place in accordance with union rules, and that individual members who complain have their cases dealt with

- maintaining a list of trade unions, and determining whether or not they can be classified as independent. This is a major role which requires the Certification Officer to establish whether or not a trade union is 'independent' of an employer, and able to continue in existence without support from the employer. A certificate of independence entitles trade unions to secure tax relief on parts of their income and expenditure, as well as to have access to information from employers about various proposals. To retain a certificate of independence, the trade union has to submit membership returns and agree to scrutiny of its rules.

- ensuring that trade unions keep up-to-date membership returns for election purposes, and investigating complaints from members about the administration of elections.

The ERA 1999 abolished the offices of the Commissioner for the Rights of Trade Union Members (CROTUM) and the Commission for Protection against Unlawful Industrial Action. The Act gave the Certification Officer powers to hear complaints involving most aspects of the law in which CROTUM had previously been empowered to assist (Farnham, 2000: 1). Union members must now choose between two routes of complaint: a court or the Certification Officer (CO). Whereas the CROTUM could only advise and support complaints by union members, the CO now has a quasi-judicial function. Various declarations and enforcement orders made by the CO in relation to a wide range of issues relating to union government and administration (breach of rule or statutory duty by a union) have the status of court orders, and may be enforced as such. Wedderburn (2000: 7) noted that the CO 'has become a court'. Non-compliance may lead to contempt proceedings (Smith and Morton, 2001).

Which of these Commissions or Commissioners do you consider has made the greatest impact on the workplace? Do you think that the impact has been broadly positive or negative? Why?

CONCLUSION

In this chapter we have reviewed the legal framework for HRM, focusing on the legal institutions and bodies central to the management of employment. There is little doubt that legal institutions such as the employment tribunal system and the various Commissions (Equal Opportunities, Racial Equality, Health and Safety) have had a major impact on HR policies and practices. It is not just their direct impact on individual employers and employees that matters, but the indirect influence of their activities on all employers. For example, although the employment tribunals hear a large number of cases each year, their decisions also send messages to other employers about how to deal with dismissal and other employment issues. As we see in Chapter 15, procedures have been extensively formalised since the 1970s, to a large extent because of this influence. In addition, managements are now more likely to take care when advertising, recruiting and selecting, when dealing with equal opportunities cases, and in promoting health and safety awareness at work, than they were 30 years ago.

'Faced with the need to manage more and more laws, HR managers have less and less time to introduce the business-driven HR practices that can help their organisations to achieve their goals. In short, the weight of legislation is forcing HR professionals into "reactive mode" ' (Reid, 2000).

Discuss.

Although legal changes have significantly reduced the ability of trade unions and their members to engage in collective action, EU legislation and judgements from the ECJ have forced the British government to introduce some new protections for certain categories of staff (eg part-timers).

The effect of changes introduced since 1997 has been to extend the scope of employment protection legislation to cover the most vulnerable groups of workers and to widen the range of issues over which employment regulation applies. The legislation has also started to address questions such as the role of work as part of a relationship in which individuals are involved – relationships which both affect work and which are affected by it (Ewing, 2002). A second major change has been in relation to the range of issues now covered by regulatory legislation. It can now be said that British labour law has reached the stage at which we now have a comprehensive labour code, although it has also been criticised as minimalist – for example, workers can opt out of the 'maximum' 48-hour working week.

There is little doubt that individual employees are more informed and prepared to challenge employer actions because of the cumulative impact of legally enforceable rights at work – most of which are drawn from a European agenda (Taylor, 2002). As Taylor notes:

> *From the regulation of working time to equal rights for part-time, sub-contracted and temporary workers as much as full-time, permanent employees, from the rights of migrant workers to those of women and the disabled, the world of work in the new century is witnessing an uncertain but inexorable growth in the juridification of the employment relationship. The enormous growth of litigation, the tendency of workers to resort to employment tribunals in search of justice or financial compensation for employer wrongdoings, has begun to reshape workplace attitudes.*

Useful reading

EQUAL OPPORTUNITIES COMMISSION, *Equality in the 21st Century: a New Approach*, Manchester, EOC. 1998.

EWING K. 'Industrial Relations and Labour Law', in P. Ackers and A. Wilkinson (eds) *Reworking Industrial Relations*, OUP. 2002.

FARNHAM D. *Employee Relations in Context.* 4th edition. London, CIPD. 2000.

GENNARD J. 'Labour government: change in employment law', *Employee Relations*, Vol. 22, No. 1, 1998. pp12–25.

GENNARD J. *and* JUDGE G. *Employee Relations*, London, CIPD. 2002.

LEWIS D. *and* SARGEANT M. *Essentials of Employment Law*, 7th edition. London, CIPD. 2002.

PITT G. *Employment Law.* 4th edition. London, Sweet and Maxwell. 2000.

SMITH P. *and* MORTON G. 'New Labour's reform of Britain's employment law: The Devil is not only in the detail but in the values and policy too', *British Journal of Industrial Relations*, Vol. 39, No. 1, 2001. pp119–138.

Institutional Forces Shaping HRM at Work

CHAPTER OBJECTIVES

By the end of this chapter, readers should be able to:

- demonstrate the benefits to be gained from membership of an employers' organisation

- advise their management team on the services available from ACAS

- explain the principles behind, and structure of, the NVQ/SVQ system to a group of learners.

In addition, readers should understand and be able to explain:

- the role played by institutions in shaping the practice of HRM at work

- the ways in which trade unions and employers' organisations impact on HR practice

- the changing nature of vocational education and training, and current initiatives in the field of learning and development.

Introduction

In previous chapters, we analysed the way in which the changing nature of work and employment and the legal context influence the way in which HRM is put into effect at workplace level. One of the key points to recall from those chapters is that work is characterised by both conflict and co-operation, and that the nature of employment depends upon the interplay between local, national and international forces. The legal framework also provides a context within which managers and employees interact with each other, and which has to be interpreted and applied in day-to-day relations. In this chapter we move on to analyse some of the principal institutional and national forces that shape people management and development at the workplace. The framework used for this chapter is derived from work by Rubery and Grimshaw (2002), and shows clearly the relatively limited role played by such forces in Britain compared with their influence in shaping work relations in countries – such as Germany – with a 'strong' institutional structure. On the other hand, some of the institutions in the UK play a greater role than is often recognised – ACAS being a prime example – and in some industries employers' associations and trade unions shape and constrain major aspects of HR practice at the workplace.

First, we analyse briefly the role played by organisations representing employees and employers: trade unions and employers' associations. In one sense, both these sets of institutions are external to any single employer because their officials may not be employees of that employer, and they have interests extending way beyond the specific workplace in which HRM takes effect. For example, employers' organisations have many different employers in their membership and speak on trade issues as well as employment relations, while most trade unions have members in many different workplaces and speak on political issues that are not always immediately relevant to all workplaces. However, they are also internal in the sense that collective agreements negotiated between employers' organisations and trade unions can form part of the employment contract, and in the case of trade unions their members are also employees. Shop stewards are paid by employers, yet are the voice for unions and their members in the workplace. In this section, we not only review briefly some of the vast amount of material on trade unions and employers' organisations, but also consider the respective roles of the 'peak' bodies – the Trades Union Congress (TUC) and the Confederation of British Industry (CBI).

Second, we review the role of ACAS (the Advisory, Conciliation and Arbitration Service), one of the most important external bodies that influences employment relations in the workplace. We examine its changing nature as well as its impact upon a range of HR practices – most importantly, discipline and dismissal and trade union–management relations. The ACAS Codes of Practice, especially the successive codes on disciplinary and grievance procedures, are regarded as exemplars of 'best practice' and a key contributor to the improvement of employment relations in many organisations. Recently, the Central Arbitration Committee (CAC) has had a new lease of life following the changes to union recognition procedures in the Employment Relations Act 1999, and we review this role very briefly here because it is likely to help shape union–management relations during the next few years. Of course there are other institutions that shape and influence HR practices at the workplace – such as the Equal Opportunities Commission and the Commission for Racial Equality – that we considered in Chapter 3.

The final part of this chapter examines the changing nature of the training system, from its earlier roots in industrial training boards through to Sector Skills Councils (SSCs) and the Learning and Skills Councils (LSCs). There is also some discussion of NVQs and SVQs (National/Scottish vocational qualifications) which prepares the ground for some of the later chapters – especially on recruitment and selection, and on learning and development. Given space limitations, readers should not expect to find a highly sophisticated and comprehensive analysis of these institutions here but are advised to search for more detailed treatments elsewhere. Also, because this area is currently part-way through a major upheaval, readers must ensure that their knowledge is up-to-date by accessing other sources of information – such as *People Management* – rather than relying on this chapter alone.

Trade Unions and the Trades Union Congress (TUC)

The British trade union movement has a long and proud history, stretching back at least to the early part of the nineteenth century. As Britain became the cradle of modern industrialisation, unions were formed to provide workers with protection against unscrupulous Victorian employers. The union movement can be categorised in either of two ways: as craft, general or industrial; or as open or closed (Turner, 1962). Readers who wish to find out more about the union movement are advised to consult one of the specialist texts on employment relations or trade unions (such as Blyton and Turnbull, 1998; Salamon, 2000; Farnham, 2000; Waddington and Hoffman, 2000).

What is the level of union membership in your organisation (or in one with which you are familiar)? To what extent has this changed over the last few years, and what are the reasons for this?

Taking the former categorisation, the earliest unions were for craftsmen (for it *was* men) who experienced a high level of autonomy in their work, and sought to maintain and extend job control by preventing a dilution of their skills. These craft unions were based on single trades – such as printing, carpentry and milling – and they were organised typically at a local and regional level, with no real attempt to form national federations before the 1850s. Each trade union jealously guarded its own specialist field, both against other craft unions and against encroachment by unskilled workers, and union strength came from the ability to regulate entry to a particular set of jobs by maintaining strict controls over numbers. The fact that early developments were restricted to craft workers meant that unskilled and semi-skilled workers had to look elsewhere in order to build organisations for themselves. The traditions of this group – the general unions – are very different from their craft-based colleagues' in a number of ways. They were established in the 1880s and 1890s at national level and adopted a more overtly political stance. They were willing to accept almost anybody into membership, and subscriptions were kept at a low level so as not to deter new members. The third category is industrial unions, formed to represent a wide range of workers in a particular industry or sector. These unions vary somewhat in structure and orientation, but prominent among the industrial unions were those for workers in coal-mining and the railways, as well as for office workers and managers in the public sector. In recent years, however, often due to privatisation and rationalisation, these unions have gone through major upheavals and have often merged with other unions purely to survive. Merger activity since the early 1980s has rendered the old craft/general/industrial classification increasingly obsolete, and the emergence of more 'super-unions' will make it even less appropriate as an instrument of categorisation.

The alternative classification – open and closed – has the benefit of focusing on the recruitment methods of the union, and the extent to which it seeks to expand or restrict membership. Good examples of closed unions were those originally formed for craft workers or in some industrial sectors – such as coal-mining; few of these now remain in

Table 10   The largest British unions

| Union | Membership (000s) | | | Summary description |
	1980	2000	% change	
UNISON	1697	1272	−25	Public services; white-collar and manual
Transport and General Workers' Union	1887	872	−54	General/open; has white-collar section
Amalgamated Engineering and Electrical Union*	1690	727	−57	Ex-craft; now fairly open
General, Municipal and Boilermakers' Union (GMB)	1180	694	−41	General/open; has white-collar section
Manufacturing Science and Finance Union (MSF)*	683	405	−41	White-collar, technicians and supervisors
Royal College of Nursing	181	327	+81	Professional union; largest union not in TUC
Union of Shop, Distributive and Allied Workers	450	310	−31	Based in retailing, but wider
National Union of Teachers	273	295	+8	School teachers
Communication Workers' Union	334	281	−16	The 'industry' union for communications
Public and Commercial Services union	–	259		Civil servants/executive agency staff
National Association of Schoolmasters & Union of Women Teachers	156	252	+62	School teachers
Graphical, Paper and Media Union	286	201	−30	Ex-craft; printing/paper industries
Association of Teachers and Lecturers	90	183	+103	School and some college teachers

*The AEEU and the MSF merged on 1 January 2002 to form AMICUS
Source: Marchington M., Goodman J. and Berridge, J. 'Employment relations in Britain'. In G. Bamber and R. Lansbury (eds), *International and Comparative Employment Relations: A study of industrialized market economies*, 3rd edition, Allen & Unwin, Sydney. 2002

existence. In the printing industry, for example, technological change has accelerated mergers of what were once closed unions. The open unions, by contrast, seek to expand membership in order to increase their strength and influence. Trade unions can thus be categorised in terms of the degree to which they are open or closed in nature.

The overall number of unions has declined consistently since the early part of the twentieth century, from nearly 1,400 in 1920 to a little over 200 now. Membership has become more concentrated as well, the 21 unions whose membership is in excess of 50,000 accounting for 86 per cent of all trade union members (*Labour Market Trends*, September 2001). It has been the aim of the Trades Union Congress for a number of years to create a small number of super-unions that can work together rather than, as in the past on some occasions, do battle with one another. Multiple unionism has diminished markedly. According to WERS in 1998, 55 per cent of workplaces employing 25 or more employees did not recognise trade unions. Of those that did, the largest proportion (43 per cent) recognised only a single trade union, and just 23 per cent recognised more than three (Cully *et al*, 1999: 91). Union mergers have contributed to the reduction in multi-unionism yet also to the greater heterogeneity of membership of some of the larger unions. The thirteen largest unions are shown in Table 10.

The changing sectoral nature of employment, outlined in the previous chapter, has had significant implications for the trade unions. It is estimated now that about 30 per cent of those in employment are union members, a dramatic decline since the zenith of 1979 when the proportion stood at approximately 55 per cent of all employees. Interestingly, there has been a slight growth in union membership since the late 1990s, stimulated by a number of factors – including the new regulations on union recognition. There are major variations in union density. Non-manual workers now constitute a much greater proportion of total union membership, and are now as likely to be unionised as manual staff. According to the 2000 Labour Force Survey (*Labour Market Trends*, September 2001) union density is no longer higher among men than women, with both at about 30 per cent, but there remain differences between full-time workers (32 per cent) and part-timers (21 per cent), as well as between different age-groups. Broadly, workers over the age of 30 are more likely to join unions than those who are younger. There are significant differences in density between industries. Private sector services have lower union density – for example, only 11 per cent in retailing and 5 per cent in hotels and restaurants, compared with 27 per cent in manufacturing. There is also a wide differential in union density between the public sector (60 per cent) and the private sector (20 per cent).

If the current figures are seen against a longer backdrop, however, the decline over the last two decades looks slightly less stark. Between 1945 and 1970, for example, membership density was relatively stable at 40 to 45 per cent, and it was only the major surge during the 1970s that took it well above half the workforce by the end of the decade. Although some of the decline since the late 1970s can be attributed to more aggressive government and employer policies towards the unions, there are many other structural and employment factors that are equally important (Salamon, 2000: 109). These include:

- higher union density in the 'old' declining industrial regions of Britain, and lower density in 'new' areas of employment growth

- decline in large units of employment and an increase in the number of smaller establishments

- higher union density in the contracting sectors of employment and lower density in the expanding sectors

- contraction in manual occupations and an increase in non-manual occupations.

Further analysis of the 1998 WERS data by Machin (2000) shows that the 'age' of the workplace is a critical factor underlying these figures. Newer workplaces are much less likely to be unionised than their 'older' counterparts – something that has become more pronounced over the last 20 years as Table 11 shows clearly. Machin (2000: 642) points to the failure by trade unions 'to organise workers, and to gain recognition

Table 11   Changes in union density between 1980 and 1998

| | Percentage of employees who were union members | | | |
	1980	1984	1990	1998
Workplace size				
25–49 employees	36	26	19	8
50–99 employees	39	30	25	14
100–199 employees	47	39	32	21
200–499 employees	59	47	49	32
500 employees or more	77	68	53	45
Organisation size				
Fewer than 100 employees	27	20	14	6
100–999 employees	46	31	24	17
1,000–9,999 employees	60	50	39	28
10,000 employees or more	70	56	48	40
Workplace age				
Less than 5 years	42	30	23	19
5–9 years	43	37	19	14
10–24 years	49	37	32	16
25 years or more	62	48	44	38

Source: Cully *et al*, 1999, p237

for collective bargaining purposes, in establishments and firms [in the private sector] that have been set up since 1980'. Waddington (2000: 589) suggests that employers at 'new' sites appeared to have used the legislation available during the 1980s and 1990s to restrict unionisation. It has long been acknowledged that senior managers' attitudes towards trade unions have a major influence on whether or not they gain recognition. It is interesting to note that a number of organisations, such as Vertex, which were initially avowedly non-union have now decided to recognise unions following changes in the law and the political climate (Walsh, 2001).

Unlike most other Western European countries, Britain has only one main union confederation: the Trades Union Congress (TUC), established in 1868. In 2000, 75 unions representing around 85 per cent of British union members were affiliated to the TUC. The TUC has no direct role in collective bargaining and cannot implement industrial action, largely because British unions have generally been too jealous of their own autonomy to allow it such powers. Instead, the TUC's primary role has been to lobby governments, with the EU now an additional focus, and its political influence and participation in tripartite bodies and quasi-governmental agencies peaked in the 1970s (Marchington *et al*, 2002). The return of Labour in 1997 presaged a more fruitful role for the TUC as a social partner with the government, although this has proved to be much less close than under previous Labour governments, despite the moderate, 'modernised' stance it has adopted. Since the unions were instrumental in the establishment of the Labour Party in 1906, this has led to some friction between them in the last few years.

The TUC has also long played an important role in regulating inter-union relations in a number of ways (Salamon, 2000: 175–6). It has occasionally become involved in trying to settle industrial disputes by putting pressure on the strike leaders or in attempting to widen the dispute by encouraging other unions to become involved, typically through moral and financial support. The role of the TUC in inter-union disputes has a long history through the Bridlington Principles that encouraged unions to take care before trying to recruit members from another union or in an organisation where another union had representation or bargaining rights. Although it is impossible for the TUC to regulate union membership following legislation in the early 1990s, it can try to bring moral pressure to bear on competing unions. The TUC can also expel affiliates that do not comply – but this is something not undertaken very often.

Membership decline among affiliates over the last 20 years has reduced its income, necessitating cost-cutting, while its virtual exclusion from the 'corridors of power' during nearly 20 years of Conservative governments reduced its lobbying effectiveness. In the late 1990s, a shift in emphasis appeared with the commitment to engage in partnerships with 'good' employers – see Chapter 14 – in a move that seeks to displace the traditionally more adversarial orientation. This has been an approach that has not been universally welcomed, and some (eg Kelly, 1996) have argued that trade unions have rather more to lose from engaging in partnership deals than they are likely to gain. It is suggested that unions and employers have different objectives for partnership, such that employers are more interested in using it as a device to improve performance and unions are more committed to issues to do with quality of training and 'good' employment practices. Moreover, because the focus of partnership (in Britain, at least) is at the level of the organisation, it is unlikely to be applied to broader social issues – such as unemployment or working time – and it also runs the risk of undermining union activity across different workplaces and organis-ations (Waddington, 2000: 613). In addition, the adoption of a more con-tinental European-style approach – ie pressing for broader statutory rights for all employees (including non-unionised) – has brought into question the old voluntarist philosophy (Marchington *et al*, 2002). There has also been a greater willingness to accept new unions as affiliates, most notably when the Association of Teachers and Lecturers joined the TUC in 1997, and the only large union still outside the TUC is the Royal College of Nursing.

These changes and other adaptations to the new realities were associ-ated with the re-launch of the TUC in 1994 as a more `encompassing', more widely networking organisation, with a campaigning approach to 'world of work' issues relevant to all workers. The TUC also underlined the imperative of stemming membership decline via more effective recruitment strategies and set up an Organising Academy to train a new generation of union organisers (Heery, 1998). The need to priori-tise recruitment of new members led some unions to focus on broader services to individual members, and to adopt models closer to 'cus-tomer servicing' than to the traditional fraternalist ideals and collective consciousness (Salamon, 2000). The servicing model focused on links with union officials external to the workplace and on providing members with financial products such as credit-card facilities, cheap loans and independent legal advice. According to Waddington (2000: 617), this had little impact on the rate of unionisation either in the expanding areas of the economy or in those of traditional membership strength. The 'organising' model takes a different approach and focuses on pro-viding support for workplace representatives who receive training, guid-ance and advice from their unions in how to recruit and retain members. Heery *et al*'s (2000: 413) analysis of the first two years of the Organising Academy's work led them to conclude that there had been a number of problems, not least in the lack of support from some large private sector unions. On the other hand, they felt that sufficient suc-cessful outcomes resulted from the experiment – in terms of new union members being recruited – which guaranteed that it could be con-verted into a permanent programme. The feeling is that unions ought to invest in new approaches in order to prevent levels of membership, power and influence falling yet further (Machin, 2000: 643). One such approach would be the use of electronic means of communication, which the TUC is now instituting. A report in IRS (October 2001; *Employment Trends*, 737) suggests that the new TUC website is likely to receive most enquiries from union members for advice about rights at work, information about current and prospective employers, and pensions. In reality, of course, the distinction between the 'servicing' and the 'organising' models is less clear-cut, and trade unions must identify ways of responding to members' needs that are appropriate to their own particular circumstances – either through full-time officials or through lay representatives at the workplace.

There is little doubt that British trade unions are less powerful agencies than they were two or three decades ago. Their membership has almost halved and they now represent less than a third of employees. Almost all have lost their militancy – in both rhetoric and action – and strikes have been at very low levels for the last decade. Despite changes in both methods and emphasis, most unions are still perceived as being collectively-oriented in an age of enhanced individualism and as associations that aim to protect producers in an age of overt consumerism. Although the value of an independent and influential employee voice may be conceded, in practice British trade unions continue to face difficulties in adopting anything other than a co-operative stance towards employers (Marchington *et al*, 2001).

Taking into account what you have read here and elsewhere, including the article by Gregor Gall in *People Management*, 13 September 2001, do you believe that trade unions still have a future?

Employers' associations

Organisations of employers have a history as long as the trade union movement, but in recent times their prominence and influence over employment issues has also declined. Employers' associations can be defined as 'any organisation of employers, individual proprietors, or constituent organisations of employers whose principal purpose includes the regulation of relations between employers and workers or between employers and trade unions' (Farnham, 2000: 42). Their numbers have declined in much the same way as have trade unions', from well over 1,000 in the mid-1960s to well under 200 by the turn of the century (Certification Officer, 2001). In the early 1980s, about one quarter of all workplaces were in organisations that were members of a relevant employers' association, but that figure fell to 13 per cent by the mid-1990s, rising slightly by 1998 (Cully *et al*, 1999: 228). However, the latest figures were derived from a wider definition of an employers' organisation, leaving Millward *et al* (2000) in no doubt that membership levels did not increase during the 1990s. Membership seems most likely for smaller and for larger organisations, whereas medium-sized firms are the least likely to join.

Employers' associations differ widely in their structure and organisation, and can be categorised into three broad groupings (Salamon, 2000: 271). First, there are national associations or federations with local branches or affiliates, such as the Engineering Employers' Federation (EEF) which has about a dozen regional affiliate organisations – like those of the West Midlands or the North-West. Other well-known organisations are the Chemical Industries' Association or the Electrical Contractors' Association, both of which retain a key role in their respective industries. Second, there are specialist bodies that represent a distinct segment of an industry, such as in printing where there are a number of different bodies for newspaper printing, book publishing and general printing (Salamon, 2000). Others would include the England and Wales Cricket Board, the National Hairdressers' Federation or the Vehicle Builders and Repairers Association. Finally, there are small local associations such as the Hinckley and District Knitting Industry Association or the Lancaster, Morecambe and South Lakeland Master Plumbers' Association (see the annual report of the Certification Officer for the entire list). The largest employers' association in the late 1990s, in terms of numbers of members (127,000) and income from members (£100m) was the National Farmers' Union (Salamon, 2000), although the onset of foot-and-mouth disease certainly reduced the number of farmers in the UK.

Historically, industrial associations of employers played an important part in shaping the old British voluntarist system of employment relations. Initially at local level and then (more importantly) at national level they brought together and acted as representatives for employers in each industry, reaching agreements with unions over recognition, disputes procedures and the substantive terms and conditions to apply in member companies. They tended to shift the determination of basic wages, hours and other employment conditions beyond the level of individual companies. They offered forms of mutual defence against union campaigns and to some extent took wages 'out of competition' among British employers competing in the same product market. With the extensive establishment of multi-employer, industry-level collective bargaining, employers' associations became crucial actors, along with trade unions, by the 1950s. Signs emerged during the next two decades that national agreements were losing their regulative effectiveness due to the growth of establishment-based incentive payment and job evaluation systems, the escalation of overtime working, and the broadened scope of joint regulation (Marchington et al, 2002). Since that time, their membership and influence has declined considerably, although they still play an important role in shaping employment relations activities at the workplace, especially in single-industry firms and in specialist sectors.

Employers' associations have traditionally offered four major sets of services to members:

- collective bargaining with trade unions
- assisting in the resolution of disputes
- providing members with general advice
- representing members' views.

Collective bargaining with trade unions

This role was central to the activities of employers' associations for many years, and is still particularly important when some form of collective bargaining takes place at industry level. In a small number of industries, agreements are comprehensive in scope and coverage, specifying wage rates and other terms and conditions of employment which apply broadly at each establishment. Comprehensive agreements were much more prevalent in the past than they are now, but they remain highly influential in many parts of the public sector despite moves towards single employer bargaining. As Cully *et al* (1999: 228) noted in the late 1990s, multi-employer bargaining covered 47 per cent of all employees in the public sector, 25 per cent in manufacturing, and just 12 per cent in the private services sector – figures way down from 1980. Despite the decline in direct influence through this source, nationally negotiated rates of pay – and perhaps more importantly, patterns of working time – still create a climate of expectation and help to shape the practice of employment relations in other industries. For some employers, such as conglomerates whose interests span many different industries or those organisations that prefer to negotiate locally or across the firm as a whole, the collective bargaining role does not offer any advantages. Conversely, for employers with a single-industry focus and intense labour market competition in a specific region or area, the employers' association can fulfil a very useful role.

Assisting in the resolution of disputes

To some extent, this is linked with the previous role, in that the employers' association and the recognised trade unions abide by joint grievance, disputes, and disciplinary procedures if there is a 'failure to agree' at establishment or firm level. The major purpose of these procedures is to allow for an independent view of problems in a particular workplace to be put forward by individuals who have a good knowledge of the industry, and so assist the parties to reach an agreement. It also has the advantage of encouraging the parties to channel their discontent into agreed procedures rather than taking unilateral action – such as going on strike or dismissing a worker without appeal. The use of employers' associations for this role declined slightly during the 1990s, but these provisions were still widely used (IRS, *Employment Trends* 653, 1998). At the same time, other employers have resigned their membership and chosen to appoint their own appeals body, or to seek external advice from other sources, rather than to remain tied into these formal arrangements (see Chapter 15).

Providing members with general advice

This can take a variety of forms, ranging from seminars for member companies on the impact of new legislation or important developments in HRM through to informal assistance in the event of a query about how to resolve a specific employment problem. According to an IRS survey (1998, *Employment Trends* 653), this was seen as the most widely-used activity provided by the employers' association, in particular for advice on health and safety, industrial relations and employment law. Overall, however, Millward *et al* (2000) report a reduced reliance on the use of employers' associations as a major source of external advice. For employers seeking advice from an external body in 1980, the most likely source was an employers' association or a full-time trade union officer, with ACAS and outside lawyers the next most popular, and management consultants rarely used. By 1998, the date of the last WERS survey, lawyers were by far the most popular source of advice, followed by ACAS and other government agencies, and management consultants. The use of employers' associations was much lower, less even than the use of external accountants. Interestingly, there is a much greater reliance on external sources than there was 20 years ago, well over half of all work-places resorting to this route for advice compared with under one third back in the 1980s.

Representing members' views

This role takes two forms; first, employers' associations, and in particular the Confederation of British Industry (CBI), act as a pressure group for employers generally, both in relation to national government and

Table 12   External sources of advice for employee relations managers

Sources of advice	Cell percentages		
	1980	1990	1998
ACAS and other government agencies	10	12	23
Management consultants	4	6	6
External lawyers	1	16	32
External accountants	2	2	14
Employers' associations	12	6	10
Other professional bodies	–	1	19
Other answers	12	13	6
None of the above	69	68	44

Source: Millward *et al*, 2000, p73

with the European Commission. In some industries they play a major role in widening the awareness of the general public – say, in relation to the employment consequences of tax increases on tobacco or alcohol, or on the value of attracting inward investment to a particular region. Second, employers' associations also provide specialist representation for member firms that have to appear at employment tribunals – 90 per cent of the respondents to the IRS survey did this on occasion (*Employment Trends* 653, 1998: 14). As we saw above, however, some employers now prefer to use lawyers or consultants instead for this purpose; we examine the role of consultants in rather more detail in Chapter 9.

> Choose an industry-based employers' association and find out how it serves its members nowadays in terms of the four roles discussed above. In particular, assess the extent to which it shapes HR practice at the workplace.

The peak body for employers is the CBI. It was formed in 1965 by a merger of three existing organisations so as to concentrate resources on the more effective co-ordination and representation of industrial opinion to the government and other bodies. Its membership includes individual employers as well as employers' and trade associations. Indirectly, it can claim to articulate the views of 250,000 organisations with a combined employment of approximately 10 million people (Salamon, 2000). Its objectives, according to Farnham (2000: 45), are to:

- provide a voice for British industry and influence general industrial and economic policy, and to act as a national point of reference for those seeking industry's views

- develop the contribution of British industry to the national economy

- encourage the efficiency and competitive power of British industry

- provide members with information and advice.

In addition to the CBI, a number of other organisations claim to speak for employers' interests. The Institute of Directors achieved a higher profile during the 1980s and 1990s, largely because of its commitment to free market principles and its support for the Conservative government's policies. It can also claim to be more representative of the views of small employers. The CBI has probably regained some influence since the election of the Labour government in 1997 due to its better – though not always close – relationship with the TUC. The Institute of Management has a membership of 600 companies and 80,000 managers, thus providing it with a voice on behalf of line and general managers. We consider the role of the CIPD, and its voice for specialist human resource managers, in several other chapters of this book. With a membership of well over 100,000 and an increasing prominence at national level both with government departments and with the TUC, as well as a significant education and professional profile, it is also well placed to help shape HR at workplace level. At European level, employers are represented by the Union of Industrial and Employers' Confederations of Europe (UNICE).

The Advisory, Conciliation and Arbitration Service (ACAS) and the Central Arbitration Committee (CAC)

Third-party involvement has long been a prominent feature of the British employment relations scene. For most of the twentieth century, these services were provided by the state – following the Conciliation Act of 1896 and the Industrial Courts Act of 1919. Respectively, these allowed the government to investigate and conciliate in disputes, and to set up an arbitration body to settle a dispute that had exhausted its internal machinery. The Employment Protection Act 1975 set up ACAS, and it brought together a number of duties previously handled by government departments under a single structure. ACAS is now chaired on a part-time basis and its council comprises a number of part-time members drawn from employers' organisations (not just the CBI), employees' organisations (not just the TUC) and independent members such as lawyers and academics. ACAS is independent of government, and this is regarded as vital in maintaining its reputation as a genuine third party in the employee relations area, and in its ability to help resolve problems at work, both of a collective and an individual nature. Its general duty, under the 1975 Act, was 'to improve industrial relations and to encourage the extension of collective bargaining'. It was assumed that 'good' industrial relations were synonymous with the reform of collective bargaining and its development, where appropriate. The clause relating to collective bargaining was deleted in the Trade Union Reform and Employment Rights Act 1993, but following the Employment Relations Act 1999, ACAS is now charged with the general duty of promoting the improvement of industrial relations (Lewis and Sergeant, 2000: 11). Much of the information outlined below is drawn from the ACAS Annual Report for 2000/2001; readers should update their knowledge by looking at the most recent report – these are available free from ACAS offices or can be sent by post for a small fee (www.acas.org.uk).

CASE STUDY: Shaping better employment relations: the role of ACAS

An employee relations forum was established in Yorkshire and Humberside during 1999 following a joint initiative by Ken Hall (Director of ACAS Northern Region) and Professor Peter Nolan (University of Leeds). Membership of the forum consists of senior employer and trade union representatives, leading law specialists and researchers from local universities. The forum seeks to make a real contribution to the prosperity of the region by promoting the principle of business success through employers, employees and their representatives working together. The forum is useful because it acts as a key resource for business, trade unions and researchers to engage in constructive dialogue about the changing world of employment relations.

Adapted from the ACAS Annual Report 2000-2001. London, ACAS, 2001, p42

ACAS services cover six main areas:

- *resolving collective disputes* – This is where ACAS provides assistance through its officers at the request of either party to a dispute, or on its own initiative – although that has to be done with great care and sensitivity. ACAS officers encourage the parties to use their own internally-agreed procedures to resolve disputes, but on some occasions the intervention of ACAS makes headline news. For the most part, however, the collective conciliation work is done quietly and unobtrusively, proactively but necessarily 'unsung' (Goodman, 2000). ACAS was involved in approximately 1,500 disputes in 2000–2001, of which about one quarter were concerned with trade union recognition cases. This aspect of its work has grown slightly in recent years following a period of gradual decline since the early 1980s. As Goodman (2000: 38) notes, the conciliator's role is 'to facilitate a voluntary agreement', acting as an intermediary, maintaining communications between the parties, clarifying issues, eroding unrealistic expectations, establishing common ground and pointing out the costs and disadvantages of not settling the dispute.

- *arbitrating and mediating in disputes* – This aspect of its work is not actually conducted by ACAS officials themselves but by appointed independent experts – such as academics – who investigate the issue and make an award which the parties agree to accept in advance. Some disputes procedures provide for ACAS arbitration following the exhaustion of internal procedures and a breakdown in negotiations. Arbitration can take several forms in reality, varying from the conventional practice of reaching a compromise through to pendulum arbitration, in which a decision is made entirely in favour of one party or the other. In 2000–2001, about 60 cases fell under this heading, a much smaller number than in the early 1980s (Hawes, 2000).

● *building better employment relations* – Advisory work is undertaken by ACAS in order to help the parties prevent problems arising in the first place, and it is an area of activity which ACAS officers regard as very important. It is perhaps best viewed as 'fire prevention' rather than the 'fire-fighting' that takes place following a breakdown in negotiations or after a contested dismissal. This aspect of ACAS work focuses on the processes of employment relations, getting the parties to work together more effectively – such as through joint working parties (Purcell, 2000). The issues investigated include those relating to payment systems, the design of grievance and disciplinary procedures, and job evaluation. In 2000–2001, ACAS carried out visits to nearly 3,000 workplaces to advise on improvements in employment relations, involving major projects in over 500 of these to resolve workplace problems, facilitate the management of change and build workplace partnerships. Although this area of activity has been declining gradually in numbers since its peak in the early 1980s, it remains a critical part of moves to shape and help improve employment relations. The 2000–2001 Annual Report (p29) shows clearly the role that ACAS plays here in helping to

> build better employment relations by promoting an atmosphere of trust and co-operation within workplaces and through developing a joint approach to problem-solving. ACAS can provide practical help and assistance with the tools and techniques to facilitate the development of modern, effective employment relations.

● *settling complaints about employee rights* – Unlike the situation with collective conciliation, the area of individual conciliation is a statutory part of ACAS activity, as a prelude to consideration by an employment tribunal. In sheer volume terms, this represents one of the major aspects of ACAS work, involving over 167,000 complaints in 2000–2001, and it is probably the area in which HR practitioners have greatest contact with the service. The total number of applications to employment tribunals more than doubled between 1980 and 2000, to some extent due to a widening in the range of cases that can be dealt with. In 2000–2001, ACAS officials managed to achieve a conciliated settlement in 43 per cent of cases and a further 28 per cent were withdrawn, leaving less than 30 per cent to find their way to an employment tribunal. As with other areas of its work, this generally receives very positive feedback from users even though spending limits and workforce reductions at ACAS itself have meant that most individual conciliation has to be conducted over the telephone rather than face-to-face (Dickens, 2000). The Employment Rights (Dispute Resolution) Act 1998 allowed ACAS to set up an arbitration scheme to enable parties to unfair dismissal disputes to submit their dispute to arbitration instead of going to an employment tribunal. This can be done only with the agreement of all parties to the dispute, and they must also agree to be bound by the arbitrator's decision. Its advantages are that the process is likely to be quicker and more private, although there is no right of appeal (Lewis and Sargeant, 2000: 13). Delays in enacting this provision have meant that it only came into effect during 2001, and it is too early to gauge its success. However, critics of the scheme argue that it is bound to fail because employees are unlikely to choose a system that deprives them of the right to appeal (*People Management*, 17 May 2001).

- *providing impartial information and advice* – Inquiries are the fifth broad aspect of the ACAS workload, and in 2000–2001 there were approximately three-quarters of a million of these to the Public Enquiry Points (PEPs). The range of topics is very broad, and many questions are about the law – for example, inquiries from employers about what to do if no work was available once fuel supplies dried up, or from employees about their rights if they could not get to work. ACAS's own surveys show very high levels of satisfaction with the quality of these services. This area of work – which is free, of course – is now much more extensive than it was 20 years ago.

- *promoting good practice* – There are two aspects to this area of work: events to promote good practice, such as conferences and seminars, and the issuing of Codes of Practice that contain practical guidance on how to improve employment relations. The former of these activities in 2000–2001 involved over 500 separate events around the country, of which a little over half were charged for on a self-funding basis. In recent years, these events have focused more on small businesses, although it is still only a minority of the seminars offered. ACAS has issued four Codes of Practice, the first three of which – on disciplinary practice and procedures in employment, on disclosure of information, and on time off work for trade union duties and activities – have been around for some time and are regularly updated. In September 2000, the first of these Codes was extended to cover grievance procedures as well as those relating to discipline and dismissal. As we shall see in Chapter 15, there is little doubt that the first of these Codes of Practice has been widely used throughout industry and commerce, and has led to major changes in the last 30 years in the design and extensiveness of disciplinary procedures.

Get hold of a copy of the most recent ACAS Annual Report, and assess whether or not your organisation (or one with which you are familiar) is getting maximum benefit from its services.

The Central Arbitration Committee (CAC), like ACAS, is not subject to ministerial direction. It is a permanent independent body whose main function, under the Employment Relations Act 1999, is to adjudicate on applications relating to the statutory recognition and derecognition of trade unions for collective bargaining purposes. The CAC receives the application for recognition and supervises the process – including ballots – before deciding whether or not recognition should be granted. The panel that is set up by the CAC comprises one of its deputy chairmen – typically academics – and two other members drawn from employer and employee representatives. In addition, the CAC has a statutory role in determining disputes about disclosure of information for collective bargaining purposes, and has recently acquired further responsibilities regarding the establishment and operation of European Works Councils. In its first year of operation, between June 2000 and March 2001, the CAC received 59 references regarding union recognition, nine relating to disclosure of information and one about the transnational information and consultation regulations (CAC Annual Report, 2000/2001). The number of references to the CAC has increased markedly since then, doubling to 138 by the end of October 2001.

The importance of the CAC's role cannot be estimated solely from the relatively small number of cases with which it deals, but from its influence on employers and employees in reaching settlements regarding union recognition that might not have been achieved without its presence. It is also clear that some lessons have been learned from the government's previous attempt to create a statutory framework for union recognition in the late 1970s, in particular in relation to the balloting provisions (Wood, 2000: 142). Although some would argue (Gall, 2000) that the spectre of CAC intervention has prompted a surge in voluntary recognition agreements, it is not clear whether the first wave of deals is representative of future activity. Perhaps these were among the easier ones with which to deal, for example. At the same time, there are also concerns that the quality of union–management relations following a reference to the CAC is never likely to be as good as with a voluntary arrangement (Wood, 2000: 148). Trust is unlikely to be particularly strong if the parties find themselves unable to agree without external intervention – see Chapters 14 and 15 for further consideration of union recognition and grievance resolution.

Vocational education and training

The UK 'training problem' has been with us for a very long time. It has been recognised by all political parties, and over the years there have been a wide variety of initiatives aimed at developing a coherent national policy. However, most of these have not proved particularly successful, and have involved regular reviews and revisions. The voluntarist approach to vocational education and training (VET) has persisted throughout, with the exception of the period from 1964 to 1981 when the Industry Training Boards (ITBs) operated a statutory system of levies. Even then, there was no evidence of a coherent national training policy. Attempts were made to produce long-term policies from 1981 onwards, but the government continued to rely on a decentralised, voluntary, market-led system. The 1980s and early 1990s were characterised by long-term unemployment, and the VET system focused on ways in which to deal with it. During the period in which the Manpower Services Commission (MSC) was in existence there was centralised control, but throughout the decade of TECs/LECs, it became fragmented yet again.

The Conservative government started reform of the VET system in the early 1990s. This was taken over by the incoming Labour government in 1997, after which there was an accelerated rate of VET initiatives, although it still relies on a voluntarist approach. The main aim has been to produce a coherent strategy to which all key players could contribute – including the trade unions that had been marginalised under the Conservative administration. Through the formation of the Learning and Skills Council (LSC) and Sector Skills Development Agency (SSDA) systems in 2001 and 2002 respectively, a rationalised system based on partnership was established. Readers wanting a fuller picture of the history of the national framework up to this time should consult Harrison (2000: 23–59) or Reid and Barrington (2001: 33–57).

Vocational education and training in Britain since the 1960s

1964   System of Industry Training Boards (ITBs) established with statutory levy and subsidies given to companies carrying out approved training.

1973   Employment and Training Act. Manpower Service Commission set up.

1981   ITBs abolished with the Employment and Training Act which stressed the importance of employers *voluntarily* investing in training.

1986   National Council for Vocational Qualifications launches National Vocational Qualifications (NVQs). Manpower Services Commission (MSC) takes responsibility for a national VET strategy.

1988   MSC disbanded and the Training Agency formed.

1989   TECs (LECs in Scotland and Northern Ireland) established.

1990   MSC disbanded and role divided between the Employment Department and Training, Enterprise and Education Division.

1991   National Vocation Education and Training (NVET) vision embedded in lifelong learning. White Paper *Education and Training for the 21st Century*. National Learning Targets established. Investors in People established.

1992	Tax concessions introduced for those taking VET courses.
1993	NACETT (National Advisory Council of Education and Training Targets) established to promote NVQs. GNVQs piloted. Modern Apprenticeships introduced.
1994	Merger of Departments of Education and Science and Employment to make the DfEE.
1995	National Education and Training targets set for 2000.
1997	Labour government begins major review of VET policy. Training credits introduced for all 16–17-year-olds leaving full-time education giving them up to £1,000 to spend on further VET and statutory right to paid time off for study. Qualifications and Curriculum Authority (QCA) formed.
1998	UK National Skills Task Force highlights major skills deficiency. Green Paper *The Learning Age:* 'Investment in human capital will be the foundation of success in the knowledge-based global economy of the 21st century. That is why the government has put learning at the heart of its ambition.' Green Paper *Lifelong Learning,* which stresses learning for the economy, social cohesion, and the development of individuals with the aim of creating a learning society. New Deal – welfare to work. Industry Training Organisations merge with occupational standards councils to form state-owned employer-driven national training organisations (NTOs) under the auspices of the National Council (NCTO). Regional Development Agencies established to improve the economic performance of the regions. University for Industry Ufl (now called *learndirect*). Labour reduces some of the 1995 education and training targets and extends the deadline to 2002. Targets relating to skills for those aged over 19 are dropped.
1999	Introduction of Individual Learning Accounts (ILAs). White Paper *Learning to Succeed* (DfEE).
2000	Financial grants made available to the poorest students aged 16 and 17 enhancing their access to a wide range of vocational and educational courses that should increase their employment prospects. Last report of NSTF published.
2001	47 Learning and Skills Councils (LSC) and National Learning and Skills Council established to replace the T/LECs with a budget of £6b. Announcement that the NTOs and the National Council are to be replaced by a Sector Skills Development Agency and a Sector Skills Council network. ILAs suspended following allegations of fraud by providers

NVQs and SVQs (National Vocational Qualifications and Scottish Vocational Qualifications)

NVQs were developed in the late 1980s with the aim of establishing a wide range of employer-led vocational qualifications with national accreditation. At this time, less than one third of UK workers held vocational qualifications compared with two thirds in Germany (Harrison, 2000: 33). It was acknowledged that there was a need a) to extend qualifications into areas in which none existed, b) for qualifications to reflect real workplace requirements, c) for industries to own and develop their own qualifications, and d) for there to be a recognised Europe-wide framework against which attainment could be measured. The National Council for Vocational Qualifications (NCVQ) was established in 1986 to rationalise and reform vocational qualifications in England and Wales, and SCOTVEC was formed in Scotland. The NCVQ was subsumed within the QCA from 1997.

NVQs are based on National Occupational Standards which describe what competent people in a particular job are expected to be able to do. They cover all the main aspects of an occupation, including best practice and the ability to adapt to future requirements, as well as the knowledge and understanding which underpins competent performance. Although NVQs may require employees to be trained to reach a set of standards, they do not themselves constitute a training programme, nor is there a prescribed learning method. The NVQ concept is based on four main principles. Firstly, it is an industry-led scheme, in theory making the qualifications acceptable to employers rather than educationalists or trainers. Secondly, it is based on performance on the job rather than on knowledge. Thirdly, it is aimed at making access to qualifications easier by removing barriers or restrictions on individuals. Finally, the qualifications are flexible and transferable because they comprise units (some of which are compulsory) of competencies which enable individuals to accumulate units over time. Furthermore, Accreditation of Prior Learning (APL) provides a means of proving past achievements. Given that NVQs specify outcomes and not learning methods, there is flexibility in teaching and learning.

NVQ/SVQ Levels of competence

There are five levels of the award reflecting increasingly demanding competence requirements and more complex knowledge.

Level 1   Competence which involves the application of knowledge in the performance of a range of varied work activities, most of which may be routine and predictable.

Level 2   Competence which involves the application of knowledge in a significant range of varied work activities, performed in a variety of contexts. Some of these activities are complex or non-routine and

---

there is some individual responsibility or autonomy. Collaboration with others, perhaps through membership of a work group or team, may often be a requirement.

Level 3 Competence which involves the application of knowledge in a broad range of varied work activities performed in a wide variety of contexts, most of which are complex and non-routine. There is considerable responsibility and autonomy, and control or guidance of others is often required.

Level 4 Competence which involves the application of knowledge in a broad range of complex technical or professional work activities performed in a variety of contexts and with a substantial degree of personal responsibility and autonomy. Responsibility for the work of others and the allocation of resources is often present.

Level 5 Competence which involves the application of a range of fundamental principles across a wide and often unpredictable variety of contexts. Very substantial personal autonomy and often significant responsibility for the work of others and for the allocation of substantial resources features strongly, as do personal accountabilities for analysis, diagnosis, design, planning, execution and evaluation.

Assessment might include: observation in the workplace, examination of the work or products that the candidate has produced, statements from people whom the candidate works with, and discussion with the candidate. When the candidate has sufficient proof of competence, the assessor signs off the appropriate units.

Full information is available from the DfES website: www.dfes.gov.uk/nvq.

On the whole, the new framework has been welcomed, although it has not escaped criticism. In particular, the 1996 Beaumont Report made roughly 80 recommendations to improve the qualification. These were mainly concerned with making the system more accessible to employers and giving employer-run lead bodies and occupational standards councils greater responsibility for assessment and quality. In addition, there were calls to adjust the expensive and bureaucratic delivery system as well as to rationalise systems for funding and standards (Beaumont, 1996). However, one of the main criticisms is still being hotly debated – that there is disagreement over whether a competence gained in one context is transferable to another, and whether the ability to carry out a series of discrete tasks implies that the person can do a complete job.

Despite criticisms, the total number of NVQ certificates awarded up to 30 June 2001 was over 4 million, with the fastest growth at NVQ level 4 (www.qca.org.uk). Additionally, the majority of occupations offer

NVQs within the national framework, in theory allowing standards to be compared between different jobs at the same level. Moreover, an increasing number of SMEs are embracing NVQs (Harrison, 2000: 35) and they have been popular with employers, particularly in those sectors which previously had few recognised qualifications – eg the retail industry.

Yet problems remain in that many employers fail to see their relevance and continue to run traditional and NVQ systems in parallel, and costs for colleges remain high. Central to the criticism is the principle of competence as a transferable notion. Grugulis (2000: 95–6) is concerned that defining any occupation rigidly runs the risk that the fundamental aspects (say, enthusing students or conveying ideas, in the case of teaching) will be overlooked in favour of those that are more readily observed. Consequently, the meaningful element of the work is lost. More seriously, she argues that the claim of competence-based qualifications to be relevant is based on a bureaucratisation, routinisation, and documentation of what are often the less important elements of work.

Find out about NVQs/SVQs in an occupation of your choice, and assess how effective they are in providing an appropriate and relevant qualification structure for that occupation.

Sector Skills Councils *www.ssda.org.uk*

In the 1960s Industry Training Boards (ITBs) were set up in order to raise funds for training and development and to disseminate good practice. It was felt that there was a need for a national body to link each ITB, and in the early 1970s, when the Manpower Services Commission was established, this was one of its many roles. Over the decade the MSC grew and took over the Job Centres and the training schemes that were delivered through Area Manpower Boards. The MSC and the Area Boards were tripartite organisations comprising government, employers and trade unions. When the Conservatives came to power in 1979, they immediately deregulated the levy system and abolished all but three of the ITBs. The unions were still part of the MSC, but in the late 1980s this too was abolished in order to make way for TECs which were employer-led organisations with no union involvement and independent of the government. At this stage the VET system was totally deregulated and lacked a coherent framework. The quality of TECs varied widely. By the time Labour was elected in 1997, the great skills debate had been in flow for some years, and it was inevitable that there would be radical changes to the infrastructure.

The few remaining ITBs became known as Industry Training Organisations (ITOs). The development of NVQs in the late 1980s required 'lead bodies' to produce occupational standards, and some of the lead bodies were ITOs. The picture became more confusing as the number of NVQs and SVQs increased. In the mid-1990s the situation was once more rationalised, all existing ITOs, lead bodies, and Occupational Standards Councils being asked to apply for recognition as an NTO under the auspices of a National Council. The NTO network was launched in 1998, with SCONTO in Scotland, Cyngor NTO Cymru in Wales, and the Training and Employment Agency in Northern Ireland. By 2001 the network comprised 72 NTOs acting as the voice of employers on the skills and people development needs of each sector.

The NTO and the National Council became key players nationally, particularly in providing labour market information. The Labour Market Intelligence Network was launched in 2000 and comprised DfES, LSC, RDAs and the NTO National Council. In October 2001, the government announced the development of Sector Skills Councils (SSCs) to replace the NTOs. The aim is to streamline and strengthen the role of the sectors enabling them to bring greater influence on VET provision. The stated goals of the Sector Skills Councils are to:

- reduce skills gaps and shortages and anticipate future needs, through leverage on the supply side, and help employers and individuals to make informed career and personal development choices

- improve productivity, business and public services performance through specific strategic actions based on analysis of sectoral priorities

- increase opportunities to develop and improve the productivity of everyone in the sector's workforce, including action to address equal opportunities

- improve learning supply, including the development of apprenticeships, higher education and of national occupational standards.

The Councils are expected to lead the drive to boost skills and workforce development, produce intelligence and analysis of future skills needs, influence the planning and funding of education and training across the UK, link with employers and providers of education and training, and share best practice. They are owned and run by employers, but work in partnership with trade unions, professional bodies and other stakeholders in each sector. In the same way that the NTOs were co-ordinated by the National Council (NCTO), the Sector Skills Councils are supported and funded by a new UK-wide Sector Skills Development Agency (SSDA). This fills any gaps not covered by the SSCs, ensures quality and consistency across sectors, and facilitates communications between sectors and with major stakeholders. Speaking in 2001 shortly after the announcement of the creation of the SSDA, Andy Powell the chief executive of NTO National Council said:

Up until now a strong sector voice has been missing in the demand drive for the way we deliver our education and skills in this country. The UK-wide employer-led Sector Skills Councils will provide this voice – building on the advances already made by National Training Organisations to rise to the skills and productivity challenge.

The Regional Development Agencies (RDAs)

Eight RDAs were created in 1999 with the aim of furthering the economic development and regeneration in each area. Because they have small budgets, their chief input is to influence other key players. Their stated aims in relation to VET reflect those of the government:

- to raise employers' demands for skilled people, to increase their skills investment and improve their workforce development capacity

- to raise individual demand for skills

- to invest in equal opportunities

- to invest in improvements to the regional labour and learning market, and to encourage employers to recognise the importance of investing in training through boom and bust.

The RDAs establish Regional Intelligence Units in order to predict future skills needs in the area.

Learning and Skills Councils

The Learning and Skills Councils were established in 2001: 47 local councils were set up in England, and a new council in Wales, replacing the 72 TECs and the Further Education Funding Council. The National Learning and Skills Council (NLSC) is now responsible for planning and delivery of all post-16 education and training up to higher education; adult and community education; work-based training for young people; information, advice and guidance for adults; and education business links. A new Adult Learning Inspectorate (www.ali.gov.uk) was established at the same time to ensure high-quality learning and training for those aged 19 and over, with the Office for Standards in Education (OFSTED) continuing its inspection role for those aged up to 19 years. Each of the 47 local councils works to NLSC's national learning targets, but is given some freedom, and a proportion of its budget, to meet local needs and to pump-prime innovation. Unlike the TECs, employers do not form the majority of LSC board members. Responsibility for work-based learning for adults has been transferred to the Employment Service, to integrate provision with New Deal. Key stakeholders are the RDAs, the Small Business Service, the Employment Service, Sector Skills Councils and the SSDA, Connexions, further-education and sixth-form colleges, and representatives of community groups. Their key tasks [*The LSC Strategic Framework to 2004: Corporate Plan*: www.lsc.gov.uk) are to:

- raise participation and achievement by young people

- increase demand for learning by adults and equalise opportunities through better access to learning

- raise skill levels for national competitiveness

- improve the quality of education and training delivery

- improve effectiveness and efficiency.

---

learndirect www.learndirect.co.uk

learndirect was launched in late 1999 as the University for Industry (UfI), but because it was neither a university in the usual sense, nor only for industry, its name was changed. *learndirect* is not a provider of courses but an infrastructure enabling people to access courses at all levels. By the end of 2001, over 700 *learndirect* centres had been established in a wide range of locations. The aim is to get a geo-graphical spread, and to open centres in places not commonly associated with learning, such as leisure centres, cafes or pubs. As well as generic centres, there are sector hubs that concentrate delivery on those in a particular occupational area, and corporate hubs set up by large companies or public sectors – eg Virgin Trains, the NHS, the Army, Sainsburys, etc. Each hub provides access to IT and learning materials so that people can learn in the centres using computers and materials, at home, or at work. The majority of the *learndirect* courses are online and there is a free helpline which gives information about courses and a certain amount of guidance. Initial priorities for *learndirect* included basic skills, IT, and management development for small businesses. At the time of writing, it is not known whether *learndirect* is succeeding in attracting those who do not ordinarily opt for education, or whether its reliance on technology-based learning is discouraging adult returners who are not accustomed to computers.

Liz Davies, director of one the largest LSCs (Greater Manchester), speaking at the CIPD conference on Learning and Skills Councils – A New Approach to Training (2001), stressed the importance of local delivery within the overall framework. The aims of the NLSC are to increase participation and achievement rates and to maximise economic performance by generating a framework in which enterprise and creativity can flourish. One of the initial tasks of each LSC is to establish benchmarks against which progress can be measured, and to analyse local business needs. This will then allow the LSC to identify gaps, over-laps, and deficiencies, and to establish networks of partners to ensure coherence and synergy. Liz Davies acknowledged that achieving their aims – particularly in relation to national targets – was not going to be easy. She used the example of the proportion of young people in the UK who were not in education or training post-16: the average was 9 per cent in 2001, but with huge regional variations. In Cheshire this figure was 2–3 per cent, whereas in Salford (Greater Manchester) it was 18–20 per cent. Although each LSC will strive to help the government to meet national targets, it was accepted that some of these will not be met locally. For example, the national target – for 85 per cent of young people aged 19 to be qualified to NVQ level 2 by 2002 – will not be achievable in the Greater Manchester area. A major problem is that many firms do not see the need for training and development and/or lack management skills, but it is also a considerable task to meet the basic literacy and numeracy needs of 7 million people.

Learning and Skills Council Targets

In July 2001 the LSC published its corporate plan outlining its main aims. By 2004 it aims to:

- raise the proportion of 16- to 18-year-olds in education and training from 75 per cent to 80 per cent

- raise the proportion of 19-year-olds attaining a level 2 qualification from 75 per cent to 85 per cent

- raise the proportion of 19-year-olds attaining a level 3 qualification from 51 per cent to 55 per cent

- improve the literacy and numeracy skills of 750,000 adults who currently have difficulties

- increase the proportion of adults attaining a level 3 qualification from 47 per cent to 52 per cent.

www.lsc.gov.uk/news

The LSC has been welcomed because of its coherence, and because it is likely to have more wide-reaching impact than the TECs. However, there have already been criticisms of the new LSC, particularly from employers who are angered that they are no longer a majority, and because they fear that each LSC will have limited powers within the centralised structure. A further cause for concern is that the division between training for the unemployed (now the responsibility of the Employment Service) and that for the employed may lead to a two-tier system of training. This is particularly worrying at a time when it is expected that people will increasingly move in and out of work. Finally, educationalists are worried about probable changes in further education, sixth-form colleges, and school sixth forms. Further information is available from the LSC website: www.lsc.gov.uk.

Do you think that the Learning and Skills Councils will succeed where many other bodies have failed in the past? Why/why not?

CONCLUSION

This chapter has reviewed the institutional and national framework, building on earlier chapters to complete our analysis of the major forces that shape HRM at work. There is little doubt that the legal system has become much more significant over the last 20 years and that, combined with sizeable sectoral and demographic changes in the nature of employment, this has transformed many of the 'old' established views of work. The influence of trade unions and employers' associations, by contrast, has declined, but there are many workplaces where trade unions continue to have a significant presence, and where employers' associations are still used for specific advice and/or collective bargaining and dispute resolution. Although Labour governments have placed greater priority on social partnership than the Conservatives, trade unions and employers' associations are unlikely to regain the positions of prominence and influence they enjoyed in the 1960s and 1970s. Bodies such as ACAS and the CAC have continued to play a significant part in shaping the framework of HRM, more through their role in disseminating good practice than in terms of specific interventions at workplace level. The recent legal changes have given a boost to the CAC, and ACAS was able to maintain its presence as a tripartite body at times when that was out of fashion. Training policy has been fragmented and *ad hoc* for the most part in Britain, but the latest attempt – building on the work of the NTOs – through the SSDA may result in further weakening of the position of employers' associations. The introduction of a centralised and coherent approach linked to tough targets is likely to bring about some changes, but only time will reveal whether this strategy is sufficient to encourage employers to invest in VET in order to enhance the UK's competitive position. It could well be that the future might bring a return to training levies or tax incentives, but at the time of writing the precise way forward is uncertain.

Useful reading

BLYTON P. *and* TURNBULL P. *The Dynamics of Employee Relations.* London, Macmillan. 1998.

FARNHAM D. *Employee Relations in Context.* London, CIPD. 2000.

GALL G. 'Back to terms', *People Management*, 13 September 2001. pp40–42.

GRUGULIS I. 'The Management NVQ: a critique of the myth of relevance'. *Journal of Vocational Education and Training*, Vol. 52, No. 1. 2000.

HARRISON R. *Learning and Development.* London, CIPD. 2002.

HEERY E., SIMMS M., DELBRIDGE R., SALMON J. *and* SIMPSON D. 'The TUC's organising academy: an assessment', *Industrial Relations Journal*, Vol. 31, No. 5, 2000. pp400–415

Labour Market Trends

LEWIS D. *and* SARGEANT M. *Essentials of Employment Law*, 7th edition. London, CIPD. 2002.

TOWERS B. *and* BROWN W. *Employment Relations in Britain: 25 years of the Advisory, Conciliation and Arbitration Service.* Oxford, Blackwell. 2000.

5 ● Research and Change Management Skills

Introduction: the research project

HR specialists are often involved in project work with other managers and achieving outcomes through the actions of other people. The skills required to do this include interviewing, communication and presentation, assertiveness, time management, negotiating, influencing and persuading. In addition to these general transferable skills, for any project work to be successful, researchers have to deploy a wide range of analytical skills. These include identifying key issues, planning and organising work individually or in teams, information search and retrieval, and data analysis and presentation. Project work forms a critical part of the HR manager's job, and it has been suggested that it is particularly important as an effective tool to influence line managers (Pickard, 2001: 14).

This chapter elaborates on how to carry out a research project and introduce change into organisations. We examine research design and method, structure and layout, and we consider the role of the HR manager and the skills required to implement projects. The chapter is somewhat different from the rest of the book in that it provides

Figure 2   Seven-stage sequence for a research project

IDENTIFY BROAD AREA

SELECT TOPIC

DECIDE APPROACH

FORMULATE PLAN

COLLECT INFORMATION

ANALYSE DATA

PRESENT FINDINGS

With acknowledgement to Howard K. and Sharp J. A. 'The Management of a Student Research Project', in J. Gill and P. Johnson, *Research Methods for Managers*, 2nd Edition, London, Paul Chapman Press, 1997, p.3

guidance on how to produce a research project. Naturally, this will be particularly helpful to those who have limited experience, but it should also be a useful reminder for more experienced practitioners. The word 'researcher' is used throughout but is intended also to apply to 'project manager', 'CIPD student' and 'change management specialist'.

When planning projects, a seven-step sequence proposed by Howard and Sharp (1983) which builds on the earlier work by Rummel and Ballaine (1963) is commonly used. This is illustrated in Figure 2, and is used as a framework for the remainder of the chapter.

Each step in the sequence should be given sufficient attention if time is to be saved in the longer term. A common error is to give insufficient attention to defining clearly the topic to be investigated (Gill and Johnson, 1997: 3). This is similar to answering the wrong question in an examination – still the most common reason for failure. As a result the project may be too broad, it may take up too much time, and the recommendations may be difficult to justify, or may not flow from the content of the report.

Identifying the broad topic area

A number of issues are important when identifying the broad area. These include terms of reference, access and collaboration. The *terms of reference* indicate what the researcher is being asked to do and what access and budget are provided. If the report is for a CIPD Management Report, the terms of reference are normally a part of the brief. Clarifying the terms of reference shows what the report is about – and also indicates what the report is not about. In short, it delineates the boundaries of the report (Johns, 1996).

The prospect of gaining *access* and the type of access are very important issues (Saunders *et al*, 2000: 114–24). Topics concerned with, for example, redundancy, competitive product markets, or managerial stress – while potentially interesting and useful research areas – may be difficult to study (Gill and Johnson, 1997: 13). Similarly, topics that are politically sensitive – such as executive pay for senior managers – may make access to information difficult as determined by the power-base of the people commissioning the research. For those already employed in the HR function, access to the organisation itself may not be a problem but access to data and people may be trickier. For researchers who are starting 'cold', one common approach is to send a project proposal (no more than two pages) to targeted organisations, and then follow this up with further letters or telephone calls. It is often difficult to gain access, and luck tends to play a large part in this.

The next issue is *collaboration and research partners*. Because projects often depend heavily on working closely with prospective respondents and practitioners, it might be useful to involve these people in the definition and management of research. This very often brings an immediate relevance to the work (practitioners are likely to have many 'hot' topics they feel need researching) and the findings can be disseminated quickly across user networks. However, work must be theoretically grounded in a way that makes its contribution to knowledge obvious, and this cannot be traded off in the interests of 'practical utility'. When working within an employing organisation, it is similarly important to ensure that the needs of the researcher match organisational needs in relation to a project – otherwise, it is possible to end up doing two quite different projects. Additionally, there are confidentiality and ethics issues. As Brewerton and Millward (2001: 4) note:

The researcher must be conscious of and respect any ethical issues raised. Research projects involving participants of any kind are likely to raise expectations, or have other implications for the organization or the participants involved. Confidential information gained from whatever source must remain confidential, and the researcher must retain a high degree of integrity in conducting research within a 'live' setting.

Selecting a topic for the project

The choice and definition of topic is determined by a number of issues, including the amount of time available as well as the personal capabilities and interests of the researcher. Among the questions that must be addressed are:

- What is the purpose of the project, and how realistic is it to investigate?

- Will it usefully add to the existing store of knowledge?

- Will the subject chosen for investigation be manageable and not be too open-ended?

Further considerations are presented in the boxed checklist below.

Checklist of the attributes of a good research topic

Does the topic fit the specifications and meet the standards set by the examining institution?

Is the topic something with which you are really fascinated?

Does the topic involve issues that have a clear link to theory?

Do you have, or can you develop within the project time-frame, the necessary research skills to undertake the specific research for the topic?

Is the research into the topic achievable within the available time?

Is the research into the topic achievable within the scope of the financial resources that are likely to be obtainable?

Are you reasonably certain of being able to gain access to the data you will require for this topic?

Are you able to state your research question(s) and objectives clearly?

Will your proposed research be able to provide fresh insights on this topic?

Does the topic relate clearly to the overall idea you have been given (perhaps by an organisation)?

Are the findings of your research likely to be symmetrical – that is, of similar value to the topic – whatever the outcome?

Does the topic complement your career goals?

To what extent does your research fulfil the characteristics of a good project?

Adapted from Saunders M., Lewis P. and Thornhill A. *Research Methods for Business Students*, 2nd edition. London, FT-Prentice-Hall. 2000, p.15

The overall purpose of the project must be clear. It is important to have several ideas and be flexible over the choice and treatment of the research topic. Where possible, it is important to choose something interesting with enough depth, but that is not too broad. A topic for research such as 'What impact does organisational change have on the everyday life of employees?' is far too vague, whereas 'What is organisational change?' needs a clearer definition in terms of strategy, structure, and culture (Thietart *et al*, 2001: 44–5). In short, the topic should be manageable, precise and achievable in the time available. It is better to say a lot about a relatively specific problem than a little about a very broad issue. Another trap is what Silverman (1993) terms 'tourism' – that is, examining only the novel, and ignoring the routine aspects in your research.

Time management is a crucial consideration. With limited time available there may be a temptation to select a topic before doing the preliminary groundwork. This is short-sighted, for no time will be saved in the long run. It is generally the case that the time taken to accomplish a piece of research is underestimated. The duration can be lengthened by delays, illness or job pressures (Gill and Johnson, 1997: 14). In addition, external factors may have a bearing on the time needed, especially when relying on the goodwill of others who may prove difficult to pin down in practice. There may also be unforeseen organisational changes that make it difficult to carry out the original project. Research may depend on the organisation not experiencing major upheavals throughout the period of the project because that may cause problems with continued access and support.

A *research plan* showing the phases of the research and dates for completion can assist in the management of any unforeseen delays. It is useful to keep a research diary including targets, progress and ideas, and to review these regularly. In the business and management world, planning ahead with any precision is often very difficult, but that does not mean such planning should be eschewed. Few research projects are as elegant and unproblematical as their eventual published form suggests. Companies may drop out, people go on holiday, and circumstances change – this is part of the normal process of research. There is a danger of assuming that all research projects are undertaken with fully articulated objectives at the commencement of the study – an error compounded by the rational and logical way in which results are written up after the event! As Pettigrew (1985: 222) honestly admits, 'It is more easily characterised in the language of muddling through, incrementalism, and political process' than in terms of a rationally-contrived act. Similarly, access is often assumed to be unproblematical, and that researchers have total freedom to inquire into the exact details in the precise location where their theoretical preconceptions lead them. Unfortunately, reality rests more on good fortune and opportunism – for example, making contact at a time when the 'gatekeeper' in the organisation wants outside intervention, or in not 'losing' sites through closure or takeover. As Buchanan *et al* (1988: 53) observe:

Fieldwork is permeated with the conflict between what is theoretically desirable on the one hand and what is practically possible on the other. It is desirable to ensure representativeness in the sample, uniformity of interview procedures, adequate data collection across the range of topics to be explored, and so on. But the members of the organisations block access to information, constrain the time allowed for interviews, lose your questionnaires, go on holiday, and join other organisations in the middle of your unfinished study. In the conflict between the desirable and the possible, the possible always wins.

Gill and Johnson (1997: 15) point out that a researcher with strong capabilities in the behavioural sciences but low numeracy skills should hesitate before choosing a topic that involves complex statistical analysis. Similarly, a researcher with poor analytical and writing skills might be unwise to embark on an ethnographic study. If possible, projects should make use of existing skills, and of course, it helps greatly if the topic is of particular interest to the researcher. Finally, the value of the project is important. Gill and Johnson suggest that 'motivation and interest is higher if the work is clearly making a contribution to the solution of a significant problem'.

There are a number of techniques used to generate and refine research ideas. Some of these are shown in the box below.

Frequently-used techniques for generating and refining research ideas

Rational thinking

- Examining your own strengths and interests
- Looking at past projects
- Discussion
- Searching the literature

Creative thinking

- Keeping a notebook of ideas
- Exploring personal preferences
- Using past projects
- Relevance trees
- Brainstorming

Source: Saunders M., Lewis P. and Thornhill A. *Research Methods for Business Students*, 2nd edition. London, FT-Prentice-Hall. 2000, p16

Deciding on the approach and formulating the plan

Writing a *project proposal* is an important first step, whether it is going before a managerial meeting, a research committee, or a student's tutor. It is a process that repays very careful attention (Saunders *et al*, 2000: 29). For example, writing can be a good way of clarifying thoughts and ideas, and it can also help organise ideas into a coherent statement of research intent. The proposal must convince the audience that the objectives are achievable in the time-frame allowed. If asked to carry out a project for a client or for their own organisation, researchers need a clear proposal to submit for approval. Acceptance of the proposal by the client forms part of the contract, and implies that the proposal is satisfactory (Saunders *et al*, 2000: 29–30).

A struggle to finish on time often comes about because ideas were not focused at the earliest stage or the viability was not thoroughly investigated. A proposal should have:

- *a title* – one that should reflect the content of the proposal, even if this title is provisional

- *a rationale* – something that says why the research is important and worth the effort

- *objectives* – a precise statement of what it is hoped to achieve

- *themes/issues* – a statement of what will be investigated and why, and how it will be used to guide the project research. If the research is expected to prove or disprove hypotheses, they should be stated up front.

- *a note of the existing literature* – a short annotated list of existing work on the topic, demonstrating how the proposed research will fit in

- *a note on the proposed methodology* – a brief account of how the work might be carried out, an indication of the proposed sources of information, the research approach and methods (justified in the light of project objectives) and an indication of analytical or statistical tools to be used. The research design and data collection phases are both important. The latter is more concerned with detailing how the data is collected (for example, how many interviews are to be carried out, and how long each will last).

- *a proposed timetable* – a provisional outline of how the research will be completed over a period of time, suggesting how many days/weeks will be spent on each of the various stages involved. Always assume it will take longer than you first think (Saunders *et al*, 2000: 32).

- *a list of potential problems* – something to indicate the sort of problems the researcher is likely to encounter. Resources may be an issue here: to what extent do you have the resources, time, money, assistance in collecting data, software packages, etc, to carry out the project? Another key issue is to do with access. If you are suggesting an interview with every personnel director in all the major competitors in the region, you might want to think through whether it is actually viable.

Think about a potential (or actual) project that you are doing. Write down four key questions that the project seeks to address. Which of these is the central question?

The research process: a framework for crafting research

What?

- What puzzles/intrigues me?
- What do I want to know more about/understand better?
- What are my key questions?

Why?

- Why will this be of enough interest to others to be presented as a thesis/book/paper/guide to practitioners or policy-makers?
- Can the research be justified as 'a contribution to knowledge'?

How – conceptually?

- What models, concepts and theories can I draw on/develop to answer my research questions?
- How can these be brought together into a basic conceptual framework to guide my investigation?

How – practically?

- What investigative style and techniques shall I use to apply my conceptual framework (to both gather material and analyse it)?
- How shall I gain and maintain access to information sources?

Source: Watson T. J. 'Managing, crafting and researching: words, skill and imagination in shaping management research', *British Journal of Management*, Vol. 5, Special issue June 1994. p80

The project must be mapped out into clear stages – eg planning and preparation, project design, project implementation, data analysis/interpretation, report, and various sub-stages. This might include meeting with contacts, seeking feedback on methods, acquiring ethical approval, and agreeing logistics. In addition, measurable milestones

Figure 3 Using a Gantt chart to document the schedule

Activity/ task	January 2002	Feb'ry 2002	March 2002	April 2002	May 2002	June 2002	July 2002
Literature review	▬▬						
Complete first round of interviews		▬▬					
Finalise questionnaire			▬▬				
Second round visits				▬▬			
Analyse responses					▬▬		
Preliminary report						▬▬	

have to be established, although it is sensible to build in contingency times (Brewerton and Millward, 2001: 23–4). There are different ways of documenting the time-planning, but one of the best is by using a Gantt chart as shown in Figure 3.

Methodology is about choosing the most appropriate methods of research to fit the aims and projected outcomes. It provides a rationale for the particular methods utilised. Methods are the business end of the researcher's methodological and theoretical assumptions (Ackroyd and Hughes, 1992). A distinction is often made between quantitative and qualitative research: *quantitative research* is held to be concerned with figures, and *qualitative research* with words (Miles and Huberman, 1984).

Quantitative research refers to studies concerned with measurement and quantification of data to answer research questions. To be useful, data has to be analysed and interpreted, and quantitative analysis techniques assist this process. The archetypal approach is the application of a formula, a statement or hypothesis to be tested; an account of sampling and methods; and, finally, a description of results and a discussion of the implications. With quantitative work, the process of data collection becomes distinct from analysis (Easterby-Smith *et al*, 1996: 116).

Qualitative research is more fashionable than in the past when there was greater stress on 'objectivity' and 'reliability' and an attempt to impose scientific use of theory. Qualitative research puts emphasis on individuals' interpretation of behaviour and their environment. The emphasis tends to be on understanding what is going on in organisations in participants' own terms rather than in those of the researcher (Bryman, 1989: 30). As Fineman and Mangham (1983: 296) observe: 'If behaviour is viewed as situationally specific, idiosyncratic, multi-variate or holistic, then a "richer", more descriptive analysis may well be taken to be worthwhile.' The scientific model has been criticised on the grounds that research in the real world does not fit the textbook model. In contrast, qualitative research tends to generate data in a non-standard fashion and has therefore been described as 'an attractive nuisance' (Miles, 1979: 590).

In practice the differences between quantitative and qualitative approaches can be exaggerated, and both can be equally useful. Qualitative material can be generated from quantitative data – for example, interviews and surveys can incorporate open-ended questions which allow for qualitative analysis to be used (Easterby-Smith *et al*, 1996: 116). Both approaches are frequently used together. For instance, recent research into best practice in teacher-capability procedures involved quantitative research (analysis of questionnaires sent to head teachers) as well as qualitative data (analysis of interviews with head teachers). The conclusions and recommendations resulting from the research were informed by both sets of data (Earnshaw *et al*, 2002).

Glaser and Strauss (1967) emphasised the evolutionary nature of research, especially in the fieldwork phase. They stress the limitations of sticking to a prescribed research plan when events unfold that highlight different issues much more important than those originally identified. Mintzberg (1979: 587) is particularly critical of quantitative researchers who never 'go near the water' and who collect data from a distance 'without anecdote to support them'. He argues that this may lead to 'difficulty explaining interesting relationships'. His approach to inductive research is in two parts. First there is detective work which involves tracking down patterns and seeing how pieces fit together. Second, there is the 'creative leap', which effectively requires researchers to generalise beyond their data in order to describe something new. However, he warns that this kind of research can tend to be haphazard and harder to plan than testing simple hypotheses in the relative security of the laboratory.

An understanding of theory and related research is an essential part of a good project and it is important to present the *theoretical background* to a project. This is the sum of what is already known about a subject-area, and its related problems, in general terms. It should outline and provide a critique of the generally accepted models on which the common understanding is based. This may provide a rationale for the proposed project, where it supplements existing theory, or fills a gap in theoretical knowledge. A critical review of other researchers' published work can be included as a part of an examination of the general theoretical background. In most projects it is necessary to make comparisons with similar studies or similar problems in some detail. It is certainly necessary to identify and discuss the key studies in the field, so that their implications may be considered in the choice of research approach and method, and their results and conclusions may be compared.

There are generally accepted methods for choosing research sites, making data observations, collecting data, and analysing it. Usually they depend upon on some common consensus held by a research community on what they think are the known facts, and what constitutes a subject-area, as well as what are appropriate research styles and approaches. It is important to take care over the sources of data and literature to identify the studies closest to the project. The research should relate to these studies, and if different findings emerge, explanations must be found. Sometimes, however, it happens that there are competing schools of thought, or different research and theoretical traditions, so it is important to establish the state of knowledge and the different views that prevail. The perspective to be adopted in the project and an explanation of how the research fits into the general picture should be provided. Research methods should then be selected to match this. It is important to state the reasons for the choice of approach, and later, perhaps in the project discussion, to state something about the validity of methods (Witcher and Wilkinson, 2002).

> Critically assess the research approach, sample and methods used in a project that has been done recently in your organisation or in a recent paper in one of the main academic journals in the field.

Research hypotheses are often necessary to guide and direct the research process. Often, however, they do much more than this – they dictate quite precisely the nature of the research process itself. Many accounts of how to carry out research suggest the following process:

1 Read other people's work.

2 Construct a general model.

3 Propose hypotheses.

4 Design a survey and/or a questionnaire to operationalise the hypothesis.

5 Process the results to see if the hypothesis is confirmed.

6 Assess the results in terms of implications for the usefulness of the model.

The role and purpose of different research styles, and the methodologies they suggest, constitute a major subject-area in itself, and would take too long to outline here. However, it is important to note that while, in principle, this general approach is correct, in practice it can often prove too simplistic. Research is often messy and plans continually evolve, perhaps due to unexpected changes in the organisation being studied. Perfection and planning are difficult to achieve in practice, and the researcher should be aware that although taking a systematic approach is important, analytical quality in a project is also crucial. It can be difficult in management and organisational studies to prove or disprove hypotheses. The level of required theoretical abstraction is often too high, and the results are too specific to be meaningful for statements of theory that have a general application. Research in organisations is typically exploratory as well as investigative in its nature. Often, it is based around 'solving' a practical and clearly-defined problem within a particular context. Solving a problem or issue in one particular case means that the emphasis is on achieving insights rather than about formulating general theoretical statements. Where hypothesis-directed research is going to be used in its narrow and strict sense, such as to prove or disprove ideas, it must be clear how the research hypotheses is to be operationalised in terms of data collection and quantitative analysis (Witcher and Wilkinson, 2002).

What is, and what is not, theory

There is more agreement on what theory is *not* than on what theory *is*.

- *References are not theory.* Listing reference to existing theories and mentioning the names of such theories is not the same as explicating the causal logic they contain.

- *Data are not theory.* Data describe *which* empirical patterns were observed and theory explains *why* empirical patterns were observed or are expected to be observed.

- *Lists of variables or constructs are not theory.* A theory must also explain why variables or constructs come about or how they are connected.

- *Diagrams are not theory.* The logic underlying the portrayed relationships needs to be spelled out. Good theory is often representational and verbal.

- *Hypotheses (or predictions) are not theory.* Hypotheses do not (and should not) contain logical arguments about why empirical relationships are expected to occur. Hypotheses are concise statements about *what* is expected to occur, not *why* it is expected to occur.

Source: Sutton R. and Shaw B. 'What theory is not', *Administrative Science Quarterly*, Vol. 40, No. 3, 1995. pp371–384

Collecting information and analysing data

Literature search and review

Data that has already been collected is normally referred to as secondary data. There is always a huge amount of secondary data available from newspapers and government departments that publish a huge volume of information, statistics, and official reports. Trade organisations and professional bodies (including the CIPD) also provide plenty of material. Most of these have websites that are continually updated. The

Figure 4   Types of secondary data

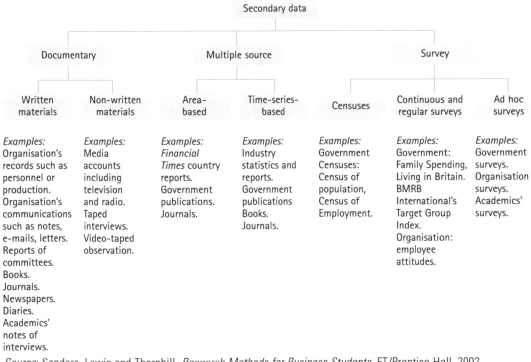

Source: Sanders, Lewis and Thornhill, *Research Methods for Business Students*, FT/Prentice Hall, 2002

CIPD website has material on a wide range of issues, usually written from an HR or personnel perspective.

Some data held by companies may not always be accessible. Basic factual data is easily available through annual reports and websites, but data such as company minutes and reports may be much more difficult to obtain.

A classification of secondary data is given in Figure 4.

Books and articles represent a good starting-point, and there may also be material on the web. See Redman and Wilkinson (2002: 272–6) for a list of useful sites on HR issues, and Saunders *et al* (2000: 42–83) for advice on identifying literature and information. When carrying out the literature search, it is useful to look for work that has used theory and methods similar to those identified for the project.

The *literature review* has been referred to as 'a means of thought organisation' (Brewerton and Millward, 2001: 36): the most common approach is to start broadly and then narrow down when a more specific focus is achieved. It is important to be reflective and think critically. For example, if investigating Total Quality Management – the researcher could look exclusively at books on this subject. However, the management of quality, is by no means new and could be traced back to the building of the pyramids! Rather than assume that a so-called 'hot topic' is new, it may make sense to contextualise it by looking at other relevant literature rather than to restrict focus at the start. Reinventing wheels can be a needless task. Today, literature searches can be undertaken much more quickly and efficiently using computerised databases – such as AB Inform – that provide considerable detail on management topics. It is important to keep a good list of references and also to try to write up notes before the box-files of material become too large. Writing notes helps to make sense of the material gathered and how it fits together, and is infinitely better than simply collecting it in an unfocused way. The danger otherwise is the accumulation of 'mountains of facts piled up on plains of human ignorance'! The literature should generate issues and questions to help choose the main objective. Once the main objective has been decided, it may then be possible to derive more specific questions.

Approaches to research

There is no one single model for project research, but a number of different approaches. Here we briefly examine three: the experiment, the survey and the case study. Each has its own advantages and disadvantages, and it is important to identify what is most appropriate for the project. All three can be used for exploratory, descriptive or explanatory purposes (Yin, 1984: 14). The type of research question (ie Who?, What?, Where?, How?, Why?) influences the choice of strategy. A survey may be the best approach for 'What?'-type questions, whereas 'How?' and 'Why?' questions are more appropriately addressed through exploratory and case study research. Table 13 outlines these different research strategies and the types of questions they are designed to address.

The experiment
This is the common 'classical' approach in the physical sciences (Saunders *et al*, 2000: 93). The researcher sets up a project in a

Table 13   Relevant situations for different research strategies

Strategy	Form of research question	Requires control over behavioural events?
Experiment	How? Why?	yes
Survey	Who? What?* Where? How many? How much?	no
Case study	How? Why?	no

*'What?' questions, when asked as part of an exploratory study, pertain to all strategies
Adapted from Yin R. *Case Study Research: Design and methods*. London, Sage. 1984, p.17

laboratory with a number of variables (usually controllable) and conducts the experiment by altering one variable at a time, so that he or she can study the relationship between the different variables. In the terminology, the researcher controls the independent (or input) variables while measuring the effect on the dependent (or output) variables and simultaneously keeping intervening factors constant (Bennett, 1983). The social experiment takes place in a field setting where the researcher follows the above pattern by treating different groups of people in different ways. For example, evaluating the effect of a training course on a group of managers involves the measurement of knowledge or attitudes before and after the course and a comparison of their responses with those of a group of similar managers who did not attend the course. This assumes that nothing 'happens' to the 'control' group (those not on the course). Easterby-Smith *et al* (1996: 37–8) remark that this is naïve, and provide the example of a course they evaluated. While the course was ongoing, those not on the course (the control group) took the opportunity to improve relationships with their bosses and strengthen their political standing – in effect shutting out some of those who were absent because they were on the course. This meant that the original topic – assessing the impact of a course – was rendered meaningless by changes elsewhere in the organisation.

> To what extent is it possible to draw meaningful conclusions from studies that have used laboratory experiments – for example, on sleep patterns of students in order to predict the effects of shiftwork on long-term health?

The case study

Here research is carried out in an organisation to examine a particular topic or event. Case studies have formed an essential plank of research in a variety of disciplines, from medicine and psychology through to political science. According to Yin (1981: 59), the case study is an attempt to 'examine a contemporary phenomenon within its real-life context; when the boundaries between phenomenon and context are not clearly evident, and in which multiple sources of evidence are used'. Mitchell (1983: 191) describes the case study as 'a detailed examination of an event (or series of related events) which the analyst believes exhibits (or exhibit) the operation of some identified general theoretical principle'. In short, the case study method tries to capture the whole, is intensive in nature, and is open-ended and flexible at all stages of the research process. A comparative case approach could involve the researcher in examining a particular topic via visits to several different organisations to interview staff and collect data. Such an approach could for example be used to examine the impact of a particular pay system on employees in different organisational contexts. It has been argued that the technique utilised by case study researchers can lead to bias in the results, either via the inherent limitations of any single method (Denzin, 1970: 13) or due to the effect of the researcher on the situation itself (see the examination of interviews below).

The survey

This is also one of the most widely adopted approaches in social science, business and management research. Surveys are cheap, quick to administer, and provide a much wider coverage than, say, an experiment or case study (Bennett, 1983). The main method of data collection is via the questionnaire (see below), although other survey methods include structured observation. The primary aim of the survey is to collect information from, or about, a defined group or 'population' (Easterby-Smith *et al*, 1996: 122). The data is standardised so as to allow for comparison. Saunders *et al* (2000: 94) note that the data is less wide-ranging than that collected by qualitative methods because there is a limit to the number of questions that can be asked. An example of this would be WERS surveys that collected data from a representative sample of 2,000 workplaces on various aspects of employee relations.

Methods of collecting research data

Whatever the broad approach adopted, researchers may use a number of different techniques to collect data. This is particularly apparent in case study research.

Observation

According to Ackroyd and Hughes (1992: 127), 'The most well-known of the observational methods is participant observation, which requires researchers to involve themselves in the lives of those being studied – looking, listening, enquiring, recording, and so on.' Observations are directed towards an understanding of how interaction patterns are linked – such that symbols and intentions are used to interpret behaviour, rather than the frequency and distribution of events. Participant observation, according to Denzin's wider meaning of the term, is a method of qualitative analysis that requires observer submersion in the data, and uses analytical induction and theoretical sampling as the main strategies of analysis and discovery. A major advantage is that it allows the 'simultaneous generation and verification of theory' since the researcher tries to share his or her life with those being studied (Denzin, 1978: 187). There are four variants of participant observation:

- *The complete participant* – In this role the researcher aims to become an ordinary member of the group and his or her full intent is not revealed. The researcher may perhaps need to collect information without revealing his or her identity for fear that this might either undermine access or affect the results. An example of this might be a study of the extent to which companies observe the minimum wage or health and safety legislation.

- *The participant as observer* – The role of observer is made clear to the research subjects. Although the researcher undertakes the same tasks as the people being observed – as in the work on assembly lines undertaken by Delbridge (1998) – his or her reason for being there is made explicit.

- *The observer as participant* – In this role the contact is brief and tends to take the form of interviews. There is no attempt to create a longer-term relationship. This is probably the most typical of research situations in the HR area.

- *The complete observer* – The researcher is removed completely from interaction with his or her subjects, and merely administers questionnaires or observes their behaviour – perhaps through a one-way mirror, as in some psychological research.

A balance between involvement and distance is needed. The researcher must get close enough to the actors in order to empathise with them, but maintain enough distance to retain a theoretically informed and detached viewpoint (Pettigrew, 1985: 228) and avoid 'going native'.

Interviews

Interviews have been defined by Ackroyd and Hughes (1992: 100) as 'encounters between a researcher and a respondent in which the latter is asked a series of questions relevant to the subject of the research. The respondent's answers constitute the raw data analysed at a later point in time.' It is based on the assumption that the answers offered by respondents are valid indicators of the subject under investigation, and that these answers provide access to observable and reportable behaviour. Put another way, the information collected is 'presentational data' – based upon symbolic projections and appearances – rather than 'operational data' which is behaviour actually observed by the researcher. This analytical distinction is critically important for interpretation, since there is a danger that 'the presentational data will literally swamp the operational data, thus masking the difference between fact and fiction in the findings' (Van Maanen, 1979: 542–3). Questions asking line managers how they have handled grievance and disciplinary cases is presentational data, whereas with operational data, their handling of actual cases would be observed. By using multiple triangulation (see below) and longitudinal research, as well as a degree of common sense, researchers can remain aware of any potential shortcomings in their analysis and interpretation of results, and can minimise them by using a range of techniques.

The interview may be classified in three major forms/types, according to the degree of standardisation or structuring (Denzin, 1970: 123–8; Brewerton and Millward, 2000: 70–1; Saunders *et al*, 2000: 242–77).

The most rigid and formalised is *the schedule or standardised interview*, in which there is strict adherence to a prearranged schedule both in terms of the wording of the questions and the order in which questions are put to respondents. In addition, other features of the situation are also standardised across different interviews, such as location, in order to minimise the possibility of variance between responses (Ackroyd and Hughes, 1992: 103).

Rigidity is relaxed in the second type, the *non-schedule standardised or semi-structured interview*. In this type, the researcher aims to elicit certain information from all respondents, but the phrasing of questions and their order is varied in order to allow for the special characteristics of each respondent, and to maintain rapport throughout the interaction. However, the same sorts of questions are posed to each interviewee.

Finally, there is the *non-standardised (unstructured) interview*, which is sometimes compared with a conversation (Denzin, 1970: 126; Ackroyd and Hughes, 1992: 103). In this situation the interviewer can work from a list of topics, indicating broad areas in which issues are to be pursued – or the interaction can be totally free of prearranged sets of questions. The principal advantage of this latter type of interview is that it does not attempt to fit respondents into predetermined categories, and so enables the interviewer to explore issues as they arise. The interviewer is free to adopt whatever mode of behaviour seems appropriate in the circumstances in order to elicit information from the respondent. This type of interview is particularly useful at the commencement of the research, and with more senior managers who could amplify their views with examples, especially when the researcher 'plays dumb' (Denzin, 1970: 131). It may be less effective in situations where the respondents feel less at ease in the interviews, or where the range of their experiences (in relation to the research) is more limited.

One of the principal criticisms of the interview – and especially of the non-standardised variety, given its less rigid and more open structure – is that bias can invalidate the results from the research process. Bias can enter into the process at any of a number of stages:

- in the construction of interview questions, their precise order and wording and the context in which they are posed (Ackroyd and Hughes, 1992: 110–20; Brewerton and Millward, 2001: 71), and in the extent to which the interviewer poses leading or bland questions

- due to physical characteristics of the interviewer, such as age, gender, class, and colour, none of which can be rendered invisible in the typical research programme. Other factors – such as mode of dress or gestures – are more easily controlled, although it should be remembered that whatever the interviewer's characteristics, they always create some impression with the respondents (Denzin, 1970: 140–1).

- through respondents not conforming with the rules which govern the interview – for example, by telling lies or by providing answers that they imagine the researcher wants to hear

- due to the situation in which the interview takes place, its location and timing, and the way in which this may limit or facilitate rapport in the interaction. It is often assumed that good rapport is an essential precondition of a successful interview, to the extent that the researcher must communicate trust, avoid technical language, and adapt to the type of interviewee (Brewerton and Millward, 2001: 71). However, although good rapport may be a necessary requirement for successful interviews in most cases, it is not sufficient to guarantee such an outcome. Indeed, it may actually be counterproductive in some instances, leading to over-identification between researcher and respondent.

- in the recording and interpretation of results. Data from the interview can be recorded either by hand, relying upon rough notes taken verbatim by the interviewer(s), or by taping the proceedings and later transcribing the tape. Tape-recording has been used in a variety of research studies and has the principal advantage of ensuring that everything the respondent says is noted, so that the transcript can be reanalysed to tease out the meanings and subtleties in the interviewee's responses. Of course, it also has the associated disadvantages that transcription takes a considerable amount of time and the presence of a tape-recorder may inhibit the respondent from providing open answers. Taking notes during the interview is a more manageable process, and can ensure relatively full accounts of the interview, particularly if the notes are written up very soon after the interaction, and the notes are kept in case they have to be re-examined. It is possible to recall with some precision the words used by respondents so that verbatim quotes can be used to supplement the argument of the research report. Nonetheless, there is still the danger that the interviewer consciously – or more likely, unconsciously – may fail to report accurately the respondents' words or nuances in the write-up, thus introducing another source of bias into the process.

Assess what can be done to minimise the effect of bias on the results gathered from a set of interviews.

Focus groups are a specific form of interview that simultaneously uses multiple respondents to generate data. It is used to get close to participants' understanding and perspectives of issues, and is more appropriate as a technique for generating ideas than for testing hypotheses (Brewerton and Millward, 2001: 80–1). It can be used either as a self-contained means of data collection or as a supplementary approach. However, the results must be interpreted in the context of group dynamics.

Documentary data

In addition to the techniques described above, data can be collected via the inspection of documentary information produced by individuals within the organisation involved. Personnel departments can provide a range of statistics and information to go alongside the material that emerges from the use of other techniques. Minutes of meetings can also be inspected. However, it is foolhardy to rely too heavily upon such data for a number of reasons. They do not provide a detailed account of meetings; they are not sensitive enough to capture the nuances which generally lie behind specific items; and they tend to represent one version of reality – that of management, since management is usually responsible for their completion. Yet even when these limitations are taken into account, minutes are of some value in that they can help the researcher appreciate the kind of issues that have arisen over time, and the arena in which they were raised, as well as the manner in which they were subsequently formally resolved. If the data is combined with observation of current-day meetings, the adequacy or comprehensiveness of previously-recorded minutes can also be assessed, and their worth evaluated with a little more precision.

Checklist for the use of books and other documents

When using books or other documents you should feel confident about answering 'Yes' to the following questions:

Am I satisfied that *the documents are genuine* in terms of what they purport to be (not drafts, forgeries, misleading second versions, etc)?

Have I considered *the credibility of the documents* in terms of:
-   the *type* of document (published book, journal article, official statistics)?
-   the *author(s)* of the document (status, role)?
-   the *sponsorship* of the document (organisation, funding, pressure-group)?
-   the *accessibility* of the information they use (public domain, restricted, secret)?

Am I satisfied that I have taken account of possible bias in the documents arising from:
-   the *purpose* of the document (description, theory, persuasion)?
-   how *representative* the document is (typical, extreme)?
-   the editing and *selection of extracts* used by the author(s)?
-   the *interpretation* of facts, theories or statistics given by the author(s)?
-   the *sensitivity* of the information contained?

Source: Denscombe M. *The Good Research Guide*. Milton Keynes, Open University Press. 1998

Questionnaires

Questionnaires are perhaps the most widely-used research tool in social sciences and management studies. They are attractive because they require minimal resources and are of low cost but can provide a large sample. However, Saunders *et al* (2000: 278–9) warn that questionnaires are not easy to design, administer and interpret. It is necessary to ensure that precise data is collected to answer the specific research questions, for it is not usually easy to go back to respondents if too late it seems that the questionnaire has been badly designed or is inappropriate. Broadly, three types of data can be collected using a questionnaire: firstly, demographic or background data; secondly, behavioural data; and thirdly, attitudinal data (Millward and Brewerton, 2001: 108).

The main decisions in questionnaire design relate to the type of questions to be used and the overall format of the questionnaire (Easterby-Smith *et al*, 1996: 119). It is important to distinguish between questions of 'fact' and questions of 'opinion'. Biographical data such as age, length of service or job title are factual and capable of a 'correct' answer, although there are sometimes problems with the last of these in that people may define a job in more than one way. Other questions may ask for opinions, such as 'Do you think you have enough say in decisions made at your work?' The response to such a question can vary significantly across a sample.

There is also a distinction between 'closed' (or forced choice) and 'open' questions. The former – as in the question above – can be answered with a yes or no response. But if the question is phrased as 'In what areas do you feel you have enough say in decisions made at your workplace?', then the answer could be several lines long. Once all the data has been collected, it has to be coded by assigning numbers to each answer category so that common answers can be aggregated (Bryman, 1989: 49).

With closed questions, yes or no responses may be rather crude, and a Likert scale is commonly used instead to provide some idea of the strength of opinion. A statement – such as 'Do you think you have enough say in decisions made at your work?' – is provided, and respondents are asked to indicate their views by choosing from the options set out. Typically, a five-point Likert scale would be used (although of course there are six- or seven-point variants):

– Strongly agree – Agree – Neither agree nor disagree –
– Disagree – Strongly disagree –

Certain general principles should be followed when drafting a questionnaire (Easterby-Smith, 1996: 120; Bryman, 1989: 50–4; Brewerton and Millward, 2001: 104–8). It is essential to ensure that:

- questions are clear and unambiguous

- questions are short

- questions avoid jargon or specialist language

- 'double-barrelled' questions – in which the respondent is asked about two things in one question – are avoided

- leading questions and 'presuming' questions (which suggest indirectly what the right answer might be) are avoided

- personal questions are avoided unless essential to the research.

It is normal for questionnaires to begin with relatively simple, non-threatening and closed questions, before moving on to questions which are more involved, complex or 'open' towards the end of the document (Thietart *et al*, 2001: 174). This is done to ensure that respondents are not discouraged from continuing with the questionnaire.

There are also a number of issues relating to layout which are important in terms of achieving comprehensibility. Among the key issues identified by Brewerton and Millward (2001: 108) are:

- The instructions and covering letter must be clear, outlining the background and aims of research, explaining why the respondent's involvement is important, and stressing confidentiality and anonymity.

- It should normally be possible to complete the questionnaire in no more than 45 minutes, so the document should be a maximum of 10 pages in length.

- The type font and size must make it easily legible. Using a miniature type size to keep the number of pages down is not a good approach!

- Correct spelling and grammar are critical to reassure the respondent that the researcher is competent and professional.

Finally, it is a good idea to 'pilot' the draft questionnaire to check that all the questions make sense and that respondents are able to understand them. It is also vitally important to ensure that respondents are able to answer questions in the way that was intended and that their replies are meaningful. If a large number of questionnaires are to be distributed, it is necessary to use statistical packages such as SPSS to help with the analysis. In this case, issues of scaling are also critically important. These must be sorted out during the drafting of the questionnaire so as to avoid problems at a later stage in the analysis. It is impossible in this book to provide details of all the issues relating to questionnaire design and analysis, so researchers are referred to the standard texts indicated in the Useful reading section at the end of the chapter.

Think of the last time you filled in a questionnaire, and try to recall how you felt about it. Is there something you could learn from this experience that might help in the design of questionnaires in the future?

Triangulation

Denzin's (1970: 13) commitment to multiple triangulation is clear: 'If each method leads to different features of empirical reality, then no single method can ever completely capture all the relevant features of that reality.' So there is a need to 'learn to employ multiple methods in the analysis of the same empirical events'. Denzin articulates four basic types of triangulation: data, investigator, theory, and methodology.

By *data triangulation* he means that information should be collected from different people, at different times, and in different places, in order to create a fuller picture of a single event. Simultaneously, data should be drawn from a range of levels as well. *Investigator triangulation* is fairly straightforward, meaning that more than one researcher should be employed, wherever possible, on the data collection parts of a project so as to remove the potential bias that comes from a single person, and to ensure greater reliability in observations. *Theoretical triangulation* requires researchers to approach the study with multiple perspectives and hypotheses in mind. In addition, it permits the widest possible use of theoretical findings. Finally, there is *methodological triangulation*, which can be within an individual method – for example by using separate scales In a questionnaire for measuring the same construct (say, personality) – or between methods. Denzin (1970: 308) regards the latter as essential because 'the flaws of one method are often the strengths of another, and by combining methods observers can achieve the best of each while overcoming their unique deficiencies'.

In sum, multiple triangulation combines all the features (data, investigator, theory, methods) simultaneously in analysing the same set of events.

Presenting findings: the structure of the report

The precise form of the report obviously depends upon the subject matter, the individual writer and the terms of reference. The introduction would typically include something on the terms of reference or on the basic hypotheses, and maybe a discussion of research methods, and a rough balance should be achieved between subsequent sections. It must be remembered that the report – especially if commissioned – could be seen as an exercise in persuasion, so the researcher should do everything possible to ensure that its presentation maximises impact.

A typical format would be:

1   *The executive summary* – A short report to management or the sponsoring organisation summarising the key points and recommendations is very useful. This is particularly pertinent where the report may be presented to several audiences, some of whom may not read the report in its entirety. For example, it is to be hoped that the senior management of the organisation in which the research takes place and the academics asked to assess the work will read the whole thing through very carefully. On the other hand, managers at other organisations may wish only to consult the executive summary. The executive summary is thus likely to reach the widest possible audience – so it is very important that it is well presented, clear and unambiguous.

2   *Introduction* – A clear statement of the terms of reference for the project, and its principal objectives. This should indicate the way the research on the topic has been directed, the issues connected with the project, and how these have been interpreted and clarified. A summary of the structure of the report is helpful to the reader. It may be necessary at an early stage in the project to acquaint the reader with some background information that is useful for a full understanding of the project argument. This may include some complex issues. If such information is detrimental to a fluent reading of the text, it could be presented as an appendix.

3   *A literature review* – There should be a concise and critical review of the relevant literature, an appreciation of the range of theoretical bases upon which the study has drawn, and an evident awareness of current practice in the matter being investigated. The review is not a separate part of the report. It should inform the research approach and must be re-examined in the conclusions so as to locate the findings within the wider body of knowledge about the subject.

4   *The methodology* – An account of, and justification for, the research methods (for example, qualitative and/or quantitative) selected. The writer should be able to demonstrate an understanding of the different methods and an appreciation of which methods are appropriate in the specific set of circumstances. The influence of different methods on the results emerging from the investigations should be explained. For example, different results may be obtained by asking personnel managers and employees about the success of performance-related pay. The former may have designed and implemented the scheme whereas the employees have it applied to them.

5   *Data description and background* – An account of the investigation stating what has actually been done. It is crucial that data is presented in a concise and logical manner and makes appropriate

use of tables, statistics, quotations and observations so as to guide the reader through the mass of information in the report. It is important not to mix together evidence and analysis in the same place but deal with these things separately. Other people's work may provide evidence, but it must be clear which is the project work and which is the work and findings of others. It is better to present project findings first, and then bring in other evidence in a separate analysis of these findings, and an examination of them.

§ *Analysis and discussion* is the most important part of the report. It is about the significance of the findings in terms of the overall project argument. It also involves evaluating the project findings as well as the theoretical literature and other published work. Discussion should be open and speculative, as the wider meaning of the findings are analysed and interpreted to achieve different ways of understanding. It is important to be original and show initiative and imagination in the work, and not to hide 'ifs' and 'buts'. Also, when examining findings from the fieldwork, it should be clear what the researcher is concluding and what others have claimed. In other words, if a company says it has implemented Total Quality Management, equal opportunities or empowerment, make it clear that this is *what the people there claim*, not necessarily what the researcher believes. Beware of using confidential, sensitive or personal material obtained from respondents, especially via the interview process.

§ *The conclusion* – This draws together the evidence from the investigation, and explains it with reference to the introduction and the literature survey, and relates the findings to the hypotheses or terms of reference for the project. There should be an explicit statement indicating the value of the investigation, and the way in which it supplements, refines, or disputes existing wisdom. Researchers should also show their awareness of the limitations of the study, and indicate what they have personally learned from their investigation. This process of reflection is vital for researchers, and it can help with continuing professional development (CPD) – see Chapter 6 – because it may prevent mistakes from being made more than once.

§ *Recommendations* – Recommendations are usually presented as simple statements of follow-up actions. It is important to be specific, especially if asked to provide these. Vague statements about 'a need to review x and y' or to the effect that 'more thought needs to be given to z' or 'we should involve people more' are not really very helpful. If recommending greater involvement of staff, suggestions on how to effect this are important. Also bear in mind that recommendations exist in a context – issues of practicality and affordability must always be considered. If there are recommendations, they should not be confused with conclusions.

§ *Appendices* – These can be used for information that is necessary to provide a fuller understanding of the research, but would be a distraction to the key arguments if put in the main body of the text. Typically, such material comprises organisational documents, forms or internal publications central to the research, but which are not the researcher's own work. The status of such material should be clearly stated. However, information put into an appendix should not be there just for padding.

10 *References* must be appropriate, accurate, and easy to follow. They should provide details of the sources used, and they can help to give the reader a good understanding of the approach that has been taken as well as indicate other sources that have been useful to the project.

The style of the report is also very important. The use of very *brief introductions* and *summaries* in each chapter, to link each stage of the argument in terms of its purpose and structure, will greatly help the reader. It may be useful to think of the report as a story: each section should follow from the previous one and be signposted. Good presentation cannot redeem an unsatisfactory report, but it helps to make its processes and findings more accessible. Avoid the use of too many bullet points. These can be helpful – providing brief snapshots of some of the key issues – but they may carry different weights. Think of the case of Hannibal Lecter and whether to invite him to dinner. He is educated, erudite, cultured and charming, and has exceptional knowledge of fine wine and food (all pluses). There may be just one downside – he might decide to eat you – but that is a pretty significant one!

> Having read this section, look again at the last report you wrote, and critically review the process in terms of what you did, how you organised the report, and how it was presented. How can this reflective learning be used to improve your skills?

Implementing recommendations for change

Unintended consequences

For an HR practitioner it is important to continually be aware that actions taken as a result of recommendations can have unintended consequences. Any action invariably impacts on other areas, and finding solutions to one problem in turn may well create further unforeseen problems. For example, systems set up to ensure that things run smoothly may gradually become more bureaucratic and become ends in themselves – and in some cases may turn into a sledgehammer used to crack a nut. The application of a specific technique to improve a process can become viewed as a universal panacea for all problems, with the result that the user(s) become blinkered to the use of other more appropriate tools and techniques. A good example might be a situation in which senior management aims to get middle managers to take quality seriously. They may do this by setting up an elaborate appraisal system which middle managers do not have the time to implement. Similarly, payment systems introduced to motivate staff – such as payment by results (PBR) – may lead to increased output, but at the expense of quality.

Overcoming resistance to change

There is overwhelming evidence that the best way to reduce resistance to change is to involve those whom it is going to affect in the decision-making process. Individuals who have been involved in the diagnosis, planning, devising and implementation of change are far more likely to feel positive about it. In general, they do feel more committed, which should lead to speedier and improved implementation.

In the ideal situation, all the necessary information is freely available and decisions are taken by consensus. There will, however, be occasions when it is not possible to be totally open (for example, if some of the information is commercially sensitive). As Makin *et al* (1989) emphasise, the general rule should be that good communication and feedback channels should be established between the change agents and those who are to be affected. Even where there are short-term costs, such as need for retraining, it is necessary to show that there will be long-term benefits, such as improved pay, improved job security, better working conditions, or the award of more customer contracts. Obviously, it will be easier to effect change if there is a general climate of trust in the organisation, such that people feel their fears will be listened to, and their problems recognised and dealt with in a sympathetic manner.

HR managers as effective change agents

According to Buchanan and Boddy (1992: 88–116), there are five competence clusters required for people to be effective change agents. The definition of competence adopted by the authors concerns actions and behaviours identified by change agents as contributing to their perceived effectiveness as implementers of change. The framework below draws heavily on Buchanan and Boddy (1992: 92–3).

Goals

- *Sensitivity to changes* in key personnel, top management perceptions and market conditions – and to the way in which such changes impact on the goals of the project in hand – are vital. The project does not take place in a vacuum and events will shape the direction of the project, which itself may have unintended consequences.

- *Clarity in specifying goals*, in defining the achievable, is important for internal communication and motivation (and external relationships). Goals must be realistic and be perceived as realistic.

- *Flexibility* in responding to changes outside the control of the project manager is also important. This may require major shifts in project goals and management style, and engender risk-taking in response to unforeseen events.

Roles

- *Team-building abilities*, including bringing together key stakeholders and establishing effective working groups, to define and delegate respective responsibilities, are essential. The project should not be based on the efforts of a single person.

- *Networking skills* in establishing and maintaining appropriate contacts within and outside the organisation are usually crucial.

- *Tolerance of ambiguity*, to be able to function comfortably, patiently and effectively in an uncertain environment, is vital so that the project manager can live with delay and disappointment.

Communication

- *Effective communication* enables the project manager to transmit effectively to colleagues and subordinates the need for changes in project goals and in individual tasks and responsibilities.

- *Interpersonal skills* – including selection, listening, collecting appropriate information, identifying the concerns of others, and managing meetings – are also vital.

- *Personal energy and enthusiasm*, in expressing plans and ideas, is essential.

- *Stimulating the motivation and commitment of others* involved in the process is crucial.

Negotiation

- *Vision* – part of the project manager's role is to sell plans and ideas to others via a desirable and challenging vision of the future.

- *Negotiating* with key players for resources, or for changes in procedures, and to resolve conflict in a context of limited resources and varied agendas, is a vital competency.

Managing-up

- *Political awareness* is something else project managers have to demonstrate in identifying potential coalitions, and in balancing conflicting goals and perceptions.

- *Influencing skills*, to gain commitment to project plans and ideas

Table 14   Key features and methods of the change management strategy

The three phases of the strategy	The steps of the strategy	What kinds of actions are appropriate to each step?	What tools and techniques are available to help?
Diagnosis	0 Begin	Start by recognising that change is a complex process.	Make use of the concepts of 'mess' and 'difficulty'.
	1 Make a description	Structure and understand the change in systems terms. Get other points of view on the change problem or opportunity.	Use diagrams. Set up special meetings. Create a model of things as they are.
	2 Identify objectives and constraints	Set up some objectives for the systems you are examining. Think of the objectives of the change itself.	Set up an 'objective tree'. Prioritise your objectives for change.
	3 Formulate measures for your objectives	Decide on ways of measuring if an objective is achieved.	Use £ or quantities where possible. Scaling or ranking methods elsewhere.
Design	4 Generate a range of options	Develop any ideas for change as full options. Look at a wide range of possibilities. Your objectives may suggest new options.	Brainstorming. Idea-writing. Interviews and surveys. Comparisons with best practice in other organisations.
	5 Model options selectively	Describe the most promising options in some detail. Ask of each option: What is involved? Who is involved? How will it work?	Diagrams are simple models. Cost-benefit analysis. Cash-flow models. Computer simulations.
Implementation	6 Evaluate options against measures	Test the performance of your options against an agreed set of criteria.	Set up a simple matrix to compare the performance of your options. Score each option against the measures.
	7 Design implementation strategies	Select your preferred options and plan a way of putting the changes into place.	Look for reliable options. Check back to the 'problem owners'. Plan time and allocate tasks.
	8 Carry through the planned changes.	Bring together people and resources. Manage the process. Monitor progress.	Sort out who is involved. Allocate responsibility. Review and modify plans if necessary.

Source: Mayan-White B. 'Problem-solving in small groups: team members as agents of change', in C. Mabey and B. Mayan-White (eds) *Managing Change*, 2nd edition. London/PCP. 1993, p136

from potential sceptics and resisters, are important, in the light of the fact that the project manager may not be in a position to force through change.

- A 'helicopter perspective', with which to stand back from the project and take a broader view of priorities, is required.

From their research, Buchanan and Boddy (1992: 108) argue that change management now places a much greater emphasis on these five competence clusters rather than on traditional project management and content agenda skills.

CONCLUSION

This chapter has examined the topics of research and change management. Personnel and human resource managers today no longer simply act as administrative agents or 'clerks' of the work but are being asked to play a more direct role in the running of the organisation rather than simply watch from the sidelines. Research has a vital role to play in this, and it is usually linked to a wider change management role.

In carrying out projects, the parameters are often clearly defined by those outside the function. However, allowing 'customers' to define the role of the HR function contains some dangers (Wilkinson and Marchington, 1994). Although most people would agree with Giles and Williams (1991: 29) that it is important to remind personnel departments 'to accept that their role is to serve their customers and not their egos', this begs the question of how customer needs are defined. If a narrow conformist role is adopted, by which needs are defined by line managers, advice from the HR function may often be rejected. In such circumstances, the function can do no more than reflect the competencies and values of line managers who expect it to adopt a passive role. A paradigm in which 'hard data' or meeting contractual obligations is required to justify personnel activity means that HR can lose its distinctive role. We would argue that much thus depends on the function's playing a 'creative' role in organisations. Responding simply to the stated requirements of line managers while perhaps providing some short-term credibility may backfire in the longer run when it becomes apparent that this response is inappropriate or makes little contribution to organisational goals. The HR function is regarded by some managers as free from the typical conflicts that take place between production, marketing and design, and thus more likely to be 'objective' in its approach to managing change. This offers real opportunities to help define the agenda. Using the Torrington (1989) analogy, HR specialists need to maintain their 'general practitioner' role and should not be seen as a street chemist dispensing services on demand. It may well be up to the HR function to highlight the contradictory nature of the organisational cures that have been suggested.

Useful reading

BELL J. *Doing your Research Project*, Milton Keynes: Open University Press, 1987.

BREWERTON P. *and* MILLWARD L. *Organizational Research Methods: A guide for students and researchers*. London, Sage. 2001.

BUCHANAN D. *and* BODDY D. *The Expertise of a Change Agent*, Hemel Hempstead, Prentice-Hall. 1992.

BURNES B. *Managing Change*, London, Pitman. 2000.

DARWIN J., JOHNSON P. *and* MCAULAY J. *Developing Strategies for Change*, FT/Prentice-Hall. 2002.

EASTERBY-SMITH M., THORPE R. *and* LOWE A. *Management Research: An introduction*, London, Sage. 1996.

GILL J. *AND* JOHNSON P. *Research Methods for Managers*. London, PCP. 1997.

HOWARD K. *and* SHARP J. *The Management of a Student Research Project*. Aldershot, Gower. 1983.

SAUNDERS M., LEWIS P. *and* THORNHILL A. *Research Methods for Business Students*, 2nd edition. London, FT-Prentice-Hall. 2000.

The Professional and Ethical Contribution of HRM

Introduction

In earlier parts of this book we examined the major economic, legal and institutional forces that help to shape the character of HRM at the workplace. It was argued that although these contextual factors can have a major influence over the nature of the environment within which people management and development is practised, none of them determines its precise operation. There are frequent complaints that legal regulations allow managers little freedom of action at the workplace, but irrespective of the legislation employers are usually able to adopt HR practices that suit their own goals. HR specialists are more than mere organisational ciphers, largely because there is a body of professional knowledge that is able to guide and inform their activities. This is most apparent through the work of the CIPD, its code of conduct, its membership and education function, and its professional knowledge and information resources. Members are expected to comply with a whole host of obligations, ranging from a requirement to engage in continuing professional development (CPD) through to an expectation that certain ethical stances – especially in relation to equal opportunities and diversity – will be adopted.

Commitment to certain agreed standards is central to this discussion. Personnel management had its origins in activities designed, in part at least, to ameliorate the worst effects of industrial capitalism, and its pioneers were individuals with a strong social conscience – such as Seebohm Rowntree and Jesse Boot. On occasions, the HR function has been regarded as the conscience of employers, there to ensure that in the pursuit of more productive and efficient work the human dimension is not overlooked. The ethical and professional perspective is demonstrated by what some would see as obsession with rules, compliance with legal standards or the maintenance of employee voice. But professionalism should also relate to how organisations can achieve greater productivity and efficiency through the adoption of up-to-date and proven HR practices. Accordingly, efforts to persuade line managers to implement 'best practice' HRM is also a clear sign of professionalism, in much the same way that engineers would be expected to disseminate new ideas on the latest technology.

Equal opportunities is one area in which the professional and ethical influences coalesce, and in the final part of the chapter we focus on employers' attempts to introduce family-friendly policies into the workplace. As with many aspects of HRM, two essentially distinct sets of arguments tend to be used to extend equal opportunities – the moral and the economic. The moral case rests upon injustice and inequality, on the limited access that certain categories of people (women, the disabled, and minority ethnic groups) have to employment in certain occupations, and especially into more senior management. The economic case rests upon the claim that it makes good business sense to increase access – in terms of productivity and quality, customer care, and managerial skills – in order to ensure the most effective use of all talents in the workforce.

The emergence of personnel and development

A number of books provide potted histories of personnel and development, some describing the major changes from its early roots in Victorian Britain (see, for example, Crichton, 1968; Farnham, 1990), others presenting a sociological critique of the occupation (Watson, 1977; Legge, 1995). Rather than dwell on these analyses here, instead we focus on two key features of HRM – the range of activities it covers, and the tensions and contradictions in its meaning. This is illustrated by a historical analysis of how the key elements of people management and development have altered over the years. Readers who require a fuller treatment are advised to consult one or more of the sources mentioned above.

First, it is clear that a wide range of activities is included within the boundaries of HRM. The early roots were in welfare, championed by social reformers who displayed a genuine paternalistic concern for their workers. Often driven by strong religious motivations, such as Quakerism and Non-conformism, they were keen to improve working conditions and provide their employees with assistance should they fall on hard times. However, it is clear that reforms were implemented within a clear business framework, in which tight controls were maintained in relation to discipline, time-keeping, and output (Crichton, 1968: 15). Many of the earliest welfare workers were women, especially in munitions factories during World War I, and these specialists were brought in to make work more tolerable for the female workers who worked on production lines at these factories. Some of the first companies to invest in personnel and welfare are still well known names: Boots, Cadbury's, Lever Brothers, and Rowntree (now owned by Nestlé).

Although most observers agree that the roots of people management and development resided in the welfare tradition, there are alternative interpretations about how the specialist function and the subject as a whole has developed since then. Its history can be viewed sequentially, different aspects of the subject coming to the fore in different time-periods so as to confront changing pressures. Alternatively, it can be seen in a summative fashion, each new set of activities representing an addition to the HR portfolio (Torrington, 1988). In a sense, both perspectives have validity, given the range of different types of employing organisations and the different pressures with which each is confronted. The other activities are:

- *administration* – This comprises much of what is now seen as the transactional aspects of HR work, and indeed administration is likely to form a large part of a new personnel assistant's or training officer's job. Included within the administrative duties could well be to advertise posts, to write to applicants, to organise induction programmes, to set up training sessions, to keep employee records (on matters such as absence levels and discipline), and to look after the payroll. In other words, it is not possible to pigeonhole this set of activities into any one of the 'generalist' categories (resourcing, development, relations, reward) because the set covers all aspects of the employment contract. Administrative activities have formed a central part of the role since the 1940s, and have become increasingly important as a support and trigger mechanism within a fully integrated computerised personnel information system.

- *negotiation* – This aspect of HRM became prominent in the 1960s and 1970s as employers responded to growing trade union influence, especially through collective bargaining, over the way in which people were managed and developed. The context for the negotiation role is one in which trade unions have substantial membership and are prepared to use (or threaten to use) bargaining power to put pressure on employers to change their decisions. It is most apparent in the set-piece negotiations that take place between employers and trade unions at the time of wage settlements, although it is also seen when managers engage in discussions about changes to working practices, redundancies or subcontracting of services. The skills needed for this set of activities are somewhat different from those required in welfare or administration. Good negotiators not only have to demonstrate competence in interpersonal skills such as persuasion, but should also work well in teams, be able to operate under stress, and keep calm under pressure. We take up some of these issues in Chapters 14 and 15, but leave the full treatment of negotiating skills to books such as Gennard and Judge (1999).

- *legal expertise* – We have already seen that employment relations in Britain remained relatively free from overt legal intervention until the 1960s. Since then there has been a mass of EU and UK legislation, and HR professionals are required to understand it all – if not in fine detail, then sufficiently well to ensure that mistakes are not made. In Chapter 3 we examined the law in terms of employment protection and individual rights, as well as in the area of collective regulation. There has been a substantial amount of procedural reform in the employment protection area over the last 30 years, and now most HR professionals are likely to have a decent working knowledge of the law. In the 1970s this was principally in the area of unfair dismissal, but more recently employment tribunals have dealt with a growing number of increasingly complex cases about sex and race discrimination, equal pay, working time, and transfers of undertakings. Several chapters in this book include a legal component but this is integrated into the discussion of the specific HR practice being considered.

- *organisation development* – Although there was some interest among a number of large multinational companies in models of organisation development during the late 1960s and early 1970s, this has taken up a more central position during the last decade. It is especially apparent in the body of work recently undertaken on the psychological contract – see Chapter 2. Often connected with ideas on change management, learning and organisation culture, it is realised in such terms as 'de-layering', 'empowerment' and 'knowledge management'. Its recent rise to prominence coincided with a period of intense competitive pressures, and it has been influenced by writers such as Tom Peters and Rosabeth Moss Kanter, and the examples of large US organisations which 'turned themselves around' during the 1980s and 1990s. We deal with this part of HRM in Chapters 12 and 13, and it is mentioned elsewhere when we consider performance management, non-union firms, and harmonisation.

- *being a business partner* – Many of these aspects of people management and development are now pulled together under the banner of strategic human resource management. Of course, much depends upon the version of HRM employed, and whether the emphasis is on 'human *resource* management' or the 'management of *resourceful humans*'. This has led some analysts to differentiate between personnel management and HRM, viewing the latter as a new, strategic and more business-focused activity than the former. We do not address the differences between the various forms of HRM here (but see Chapter 1), nor do we consider whether or not HRM is different from personnel management or industrial relations. The debate about the distinct meanings of personnel management and HRM has now become rather sterile, and in practice many organisations do not differentiate between these labels in a clear way. The business partner role has achieved prominence through the work of Ulrich (1998), amongst others, and we analyse this more systematically in Chapter 9. Broadly, within this conception, the HR function makes a more significant contribution by helping senior managers to implement people management practices that can help to achieve and sustain high levels of performance.

How many of these aspects of people management are evident at your place of work? Are some more prominent than others?

The second key feature is that HRM is ambiguous, beset with conceptual and practical tensions and contradictions. Legge (1995: 10) summarises this as a 'tension between two potentially incompatible orientations': the 'caring' and the 'control' elements of the role. Both of these were apparent in the initial category of personnel practitioner as welfare agent, whereby employees were given assistance at work largely – though not exclusively – to ensure that their contribution could be enhanced. It is also illustrated by the dual usage of the term 'counselling'. On the one hand, this denotes an activity that is undertaken in a non-directive way to help staff come to terms with anxieties, whereas on the other it is used as a shorthand for the preliminary stages of a disciplinary process. The fact that the expertise of HR practitioners is bound up in their dealings – either directly or indirectly – with the 'human' resource, as opposed to other inanimate resources, means that they are inextricably linked with questions of caring and control. For other managers, human resource considerations tend to be hidden and implicit in their thinking rather than overt and explicit.

HR practitioners are often seen as intermediaries between managers and employees, ready to listen to both but on the side of neither. It is not unknown for applicants for personnel posts to say at interview that they want the job because they 'like working with people' or because they see themselves as conciliating between warring factions. In reality, of course, HR specialists contribute directly to the achievement of employer objectives whether or not they are aware of this. The new CIPD Standards, like the profession as a whole, are now much more explicitly oriented towards adding value and making a contribution to the business, as we see in Chapters 7 to 9. For example, the Standards recognise that it is important to improve recruitment and selection decisions so as to maximise performance, develop better learning systems to enhance customer service, or introduce employee involvement to improve product quality. In this respect, the HR function is just as much a part of management as production, finance or marketing, and it is on these criteria that its contribution is increasingly being assessed (see Chapter 9 for a review of this). If it fails to make a positive contribution that can be measured and evaluated, there is a danger that the function could be outsourced or its activities devolved in their entirety to line managers. At the same time, measurement and quantification are also risky, for the HR function then is forced to take on board an accountancy perspective on the world (Armstrong, 1989).

Connected with this is the continuing debate about the responsibility for HRM, and in particular whether it is a specialist occupation or an activity that forms part of every manager's job. To some extent, of course, both perspectives are accurate. Obviously, anyone who manages other people at work has responsibilities for HRM since he or she deals with issues of motivation, discipline, reward, learning and training on a regular basis, irrespective of whether or not a specialist function is in existence. In organisations that do have specialists, the balance of responsibilities between HR professionals and line managers is important. Various studies have shown that line managers are increasingly taking over the day-to-day practice of HRM while functional specialists retain responsibility for drawing up policy and reviewing procedures. We explore this question of responsibility for human resource issues more fully in Chapter 9.

Tensions can also occur between different elements of the HR function, especially if it is highly specialised and differentiated, or if certain issues fall within the province both of personnel and other management functions. The latter problem is best illustrated in the area of corporate communications. This may be the responsibility of specialist functions such as sales and marketing, public relations, or planning, as well as HR. Moreover, it is likely that line managers expect to be in charge of disseminating information without interference from specialist support functions. It is also possible, given different traditions and backgrounds, for different parts of HR to come up with alternative 'solutions' for employment problems. The employee relations manager, for example, may regard many of the 'new' HRM initiatives as little more than 'soft and naïve' management, whereas the learning and development manager might see his or her employee relations colleague as a throwback to the collectivist world of the 1970s. Although the latter might be keen to pursue policies designed to strengthen individualism, the former might believe that it is critically important to maintain co-operative relations with local trade union officers. These themes are examined more fully in subsequent chapters of the book.

> Specify *four* ways in which the HR function contributes towards the achievement of organisational goals, either directly or indirectly. Use examples to illustrate them.

The role of the CIPD in maintaining standards

The first seeds for a professional body for personnel practitioners were sown in 1913 when Seebohm Rowntree invited firms to send representatives to a conference of welfare workers in York. The 48 people present decided to form an Association of Employers 'interested in industrial betterment and of welfare workers engaged by them' (Niven, 1967: 36). The Welfare Workers' Association, as it became known, joined with the North Western Area Industrial Association six years later to form the Welfare Workers' Institute, with a membership of 700 (Farnham, 1990: 22). After World War I membership fell as the welfare tradition lost ground, and the association was renamed the Institute of Labour Management in 1931, a name it kept until after World War II. During this time the type of duties undertaken by practitioners in the field broadened to include wages, employment, joint consultation, health and safety, employee services and welfare, as well as education and training (Farnham, 1990: 22–3). In 1946 the Institute of Personnel Management was formed, thus reflecting this broader orientation, and it remained in existence until 1994 when the IPM joined with the Institute of Training and Development (ITD) to form the Institute of Personnel and Development (IPD). Chartered status was granted in 2000 when the name was changed to the Chartered Institute of Personnel and Development (CIPD).

Table 15 Membership of the main professional body for personnel and development – selected years

Year	Number of members
1913	48
1919	700
1939	760
1956	3,980
1971	14,260
1981	22,620
1990	41,000
1994	75,500
2001	110,015

Table 16   Distribution of members by grade in 2001

Grade of membership	Numbers	Percentage of members
Companion	232	0.21
Fellow	7,653	6.95
Corporate Member	28,646	26.03
Graduate	21,914	19.91
Associate/Licentiate	27,296	24.81
Affiliate, etc	24,274	22.05

Source: CIPD Consolidated membership statistics at year end, August 2001 (CIPD, 2001b)

Since 1913 membership has grown dramatically, although there were periods in the early part of the twentieth century when numbers fell. Table 15 illustrates the growth of the professional body, showing how membership increased substantially during certain periods, often in the earlier days following mergers and re-badging. The number of members has more than doubled in the last decade and gone up fivefold in the last 20 years. The merger between the IPM and the ITD added about 20,000 to the membership of the IPM, so the vast increase at that point was due to new members. The dramatic growth in numbers showed no sign of abating during the period after the merger.

Table 16 presents information on the breakdown of membership across different grades. A very small proportion of the membership is at the Companion level, a grade that is awarded solely by invitation. About a third of the membership are Fellows and Corporate Members, and there is little doubt that this would be much higher if members upgraded when they were eligible. There are many CIPD Graduates who have just never taken the time and trouble to upgrade. These four grades account for well over half the membership of the Institute. The remainder are part-way through their studies or have affiliate membership. The proportion of Associates, Licentiates and Affiliates is now slightly higher than it was five years ago.

The CIPD is Europe's largest professional body for individuals specialising in the management and development of people. Its mission is:

- to lead in the development and promotion of good practice in the field of the management and development of people, for application both by professional members and by their organisational colleagues

- to serve the professional interests of members

- to uphold the highest ideals in the management and development of people.

The CIPD's stated objective is to 'promote the art and science of the management and development of people for the public benefit'. In other words, in addition to ensuring a contribution from each member to the success of his or her employing organisation, the CIPD believes that the public should benefit from this activity as well. This illustrates yet again some of the potential tensions in the objectives and activities of the profession. CIPD members are expected to fulfil these objectives in a number of ways, as specified in the CIPD Code of Professional Conduct. These include:

- endeavouring to enhance the standing and good name of the profession

- continually seeking to improve their performance and update their skills and knowledge

- seeking to achieve the fullest possible development of people both for the needs of the organisation and for their own self-development

- adopting people management processes and structures that enable their employing organisation to best achieve its present and future objectives

- maintaining fair and reasonable standards in the treatment of people

- promoting policies that remove unfair discrimination for any reason

- respecting the legitimate needs and requirements for confidentiality

- exercising due diligence and providing both employers and employees with timely, appropriate and accurate advice

- exercising integrity, honesty, diligence and appropriate behaviour in all their activities, both within and outside work.

In this fairly impressive list of professional standards, do you see any potential tension between the different standards, especially between those commitments to the public benefit and those to improvements in organisational performance?

To what extent does the CIPD fulfil criteria typically associated with a professional body? And do its members deserve the description 'professional'? Freidson (1973: 22) defines 'professionalisation' as:

a process by which an organised occupation, usually but not always by virtue of making a claim to special esoteric competence and to concern for the quality of its work and its benefits to society, obtains the exclusive right to perform a particular kind of work, [to] control training for and access to it, and [to] control the right of determining and evaluating the way the work is performed.

The CIPD, despite the substantial growth in membership over the last 20 years, is still not able to claim exclusivity in the performance of HR work because managers in the field are not required to gain professional qualifications before being able to practise. It is well known that there are many people who carry out work in the HR area who are not in membership, and of course every manager has responsibility for HRM at work. Although line managers may actually implement HR practice, it is typical for HR specialists to have designed the policies and procedures governing and structuring this work. Moreover, even if an employer does not employ a dedicated specialist, 'good practice' in the field may well have been developed initially by experts in the function – either through research or the experiences of other employing organisations that do possess specialist expertise. Glover and Hughes (1996: 308) believe that HRM represents a 'sensible and useful coming together of professionalism and managerialism'.

The CIPD meets some of the other elements in Freidson's definition quite well. The Professional Development Scheme (PDS) lays down a set of standards (in the form of performance outcomes) to be met by all aspiring members, and these have to be updated by continuing professional development (CPD) on a regular basis. CPD is particularly important when it comes to upgrading decisions, and all members not only have to demonstrate what they have done but also indicate the impact this has had on their employing organisations and the broader specialist community – CPD is considered in more detail later in this chapter. Standards for the majority of new entrants are maintained by a formal coursework and examination assessment scheme overseen by the CIPD vice president and director for membership and education, as well as by chief examiners appointed for their expertise in the area. Graduate membership can be gained through other routes as well – for example, through exempted courses or by the professional assessment, Accreditation of Prior Certificated Learning or NVQ/SVQ routes. CIPD Standards are monitored by external examiners and professional advisers and are subject to regular re-accreditation – typically on a five-year basis. The Chief Moderator – Standards, introduced along with the new PDS in 2001, plays a central role in maintaining comparable standards across the whole range of entry routes (Whittaker, 2001).

Despite this impressive array of qualification structures and systems, the CIPD does not have exclusive control over entry to the profession – unlike the regulation of lawyers, doctors or dentists, for example (Morris and Pinnington, 1999). Apart from accountancy, however, the CIPD is in a much stronger position than most management bodies, and its research activity has become much more influential with government and industry. The professional knowledge and information (PKI) group at the CIPD produces a wide range of publications in the form of fact-sheets, surveys, guides and issues papers. The topics cover areas such as recruitment and selection, labour turnover, absence, performance management, learning and development, the working time regulations, the national minimum wage, and stress at work (Griffiths, 2000).

The Code of Professional Conduct has processes in place to deal with claims that a particular member is not complying with its provisions and is acting in a way that could discredit the CIPD. This could lead, ulti-mately, to expulsion from the Institute, as of course could a failure to pay subscriptions. Since it is unlikely that CIPD membership could ever become a condition for employment as an HR specialist, there will always be questions about the extent of professionalisation. However, in terms of qualifications, research and influence, the CIPD comes close to fulfilling many of Freidson's criteria.

The CIPD operates a series of committees at national and local level, as well as having a sizeable number of staff at its London headquarters – including a library service. There are a number of national committees, such as membership and education or employment relations, compris-ing members from the branches, as well as HQ staff and *ex-officio* mem-bers. It is at local level that most CIPD members have the initial opportunity to be more involved in the work of the institute, and this is a critical part of the whole structure. There are approximately 50 dif-ferent branches across the country, the largest in London and the south-east of England, but there are also large branches in Manchester and the west of Scotland. The smallest branches – in terms of numbers – are in rural parts of the country such as Cumbria and south-west Wales. In addition, the Irish Republic has its own CIPD branch that had well over 4,000 members in 2001. Volunteers are drawn from industry and commerce, or from further- and higher-education staff branches, and all branches lay on a wide range of activities including visiting speak-ers, surgeries and legal updates. Establishing and maintaining links with student members is a key aspect of branch policy, and each taught course has its own professional adviser for students. Branches are organised by small teams of dedicated members. Despite their best efforts, attendance at meetings – as with most other voluntary bodies – is not generally that high as a proportion of membership in the branch. It is all the more important, therefore, that student members do attend whenever they can, not only to learn from visiting speakers and to update their CPD, but also for the opportunity to meet more senior and established members of the profession.

> If you are a CIPD member, make sure the next time that you go to a branch meeting you talk with someone from another organisation and compare notes on an aspect of HR practice.

Continuing Professional Development (CPD)

Ideas about learning styles and learning cycles have influenced the growth of interest in continuous development, both in a broad sense and in relation to the CIPD. It has now become rather more widely accepted that people learn in different ways, and that traditional models of sequential and tutor-led training are not appropriate for everyone. Moreover, it is acknowledged that learning can take place in a wide range of different settings, not just at work, and that it can incorporate personal life activities as well as those undertaken during hours of employment. In addition, as we see in Chapters 12 and 13, so-called 'tacit' skills can even be acquired without being recognised overtly by the individual learner. CPD enables the integration of learning with work in a way that should be meaningful and relevant to the individual, largely because it is self-directed and therefore relevant to an individual's own development needs. It is also important to stress that CPD is a process, not a technique, which has relevance for all employees and not just for managers. Learning undertaken in this way can become a habit, 'thinking positively about problems and viewing them as opportunities for learning' (Wood 1988: 12).

The whole concept of CPD is underpinned by terms such as 'learning to learn' and 'reflective practitioners', and material on the 'learning organisation' (see Chapter 12) paints a very positive picture of current practice. It is seen as inevitable that employees will be motivated to learn and search for continuous improvement at work, but this cannot be taken for granted. Many employees see little point in investing time and energy in working beyond the minimum required, and the growing insecurity of employment for many workers only serves to reinforce feelings such as these. Equally, not all individuals look forward to being given the opportunity of being 'stimulated' to learn at work, preferring to focus their creative energies on leisure activities. Not all employers are enamoured by concepts of CPD either, and some continue to take the view that 'workers are not paid to think', and that any investment in training and development is wasted due to lost production time or labour turnover among trained staff. However, a growing number of professional bodies are re-emphasising the importance of CPD, and looking for new ways in which to encourage its extension. For example, Glover (2001) reports that the inter-professional forum – covering over 50 bodies and chaired by the CIPD – is leading developments in making CPD a more user-friendly and effective process. Other organisations that are interested in improving CPD include the Law Society, the Royal Institute of British

Architects and the General Social Care Council. A survey of CIPD members found that most members were convinced of the long-term value of CPD in terms of learning responsibilities, but less sure of the immediate benefits that it might bring to their career development through promotion (Sadler-Smith and Badger, 1998: 74).

Broadly, there are two rather different ways of trying to ensure that members actually complete their CPD. The first focuses on the sanctions to be applied to those individuals that do not complete their CPD as required. Professional bodies can refuse to upgrade those who do not comply, and at the extreme, people could be expelled from the profession altogether. The alternative is to encourage individual members to engage in CPD by reminding them of the benefits that ought to accrue from its completion (Stansfield, 2001: 43). This may involve the establishment of support systems at work or at the educational institution where people are studying (Megginson, 2001).

It is CIPD policy that all members are expected to structure their learning and maintain a record of their CPD, and evidence is required for upgrading. The Institute surveys a sample of members annually. The essential principles of CPD are that:

- it should be continuous because professionals should always be seeking to improve performance

- it should be owned and managed by the individual learner

- it should be driven by the individual learner's current state of development

- it should have clear learning objectives that aim to satisfy individual and organisational needs

- it should be seen as an essential part of professional life, not an optional extra.

CPD is now a compulsory aspect of the Professional Development Scheme for all aspiring CIPD Graduates, and it is evaluated as part of the Applied Practitioner Standards along with the Management Report – see Chapter 5 for a full examination of the latter. The sort of activity that can be put forward as part of CPD breaks down into three broad areas. First, there is evidence related to the CIPD or related qualification, such as research for course work, group activities and role-playing, and presentations. Second, there are work-related activities such as new projects or assignments, report-writing, attending training courses, and secondments. Finally, there are personal development activities such as learning a new language, acting as a school governor, e-learning and organising sports or social events. A much longer and indicative list is available from the CIPD, but the key point to stress is that CPD can be achieved via a range of different routes provided that learning takes place. The advantages of undertaking CPD are numerous, as can be seen from the box below.

The benefits of continuing professional development

Becoming a better learner
- Developing reflection skills for now and in the future at work

Profiting from learning opportunities
- Transferring ideas from courses to the workplace by understanding the principles of learning

Becoming a reflective practitioner
- Developing the skills of being a 'thinking performer' by re-evaluating activities in relation to leading research findings

Managing self-development
- Providing a template and a way of thinking to manage your own learning needs

Helping with career advancement
- Compiling a list of achievements can help to focus your mind when deciding whether or not to apply for promotion

Upgrading CIPD membership
- Keeping a record of achievement and a learning log makes it easier to apply for upgrading as soon as it is possible

There is no perfect way to compile a learning log, but the CIPD provides a number of templates that could be used. One option is to divide learning into development plans and development records, the former indicating what is intended over the next year and the latter comprising a record of what has been achieved. Table 17 presents two corresponding templates for this. Of course, this approach can also be used in relation to assignments in order to ensure that continuing learning actually takes place. Further information is available from the CIPD.

Table 17   Templates for planning and recording CPD

Development plan	Development record
What do I want/need to learn?	Key dates
What shall I do to achieve it?	What did you do?
What resources or support will I need?	Why did you do it?
What will my success criteria be?	What did you learn from it?
Target dates for completion	How will/have you use/used it?

Source: CIPD Requirements of the Applied Personnel and Development Standards (CIPD, 2001c)

Business ethics and social responsibility

There has been a considerable degree of scepticism about the concept and practice of business ethics – indeed, suggestions are made that 'business ethics' is a contradiction in terms. It is not hard to see why people may be sceptical, given the range of examples that can be used to illustrate a lack of ethics: allegations of sleaze in public life, environmental catastrophes, and arms sales to military dictatorships. In addition to these general examples, others can be quoted which are firmly within the realm of HR activity – for example, very high levels of boardroom remuneration at a time of pay restraint and redundancies of staff, misappropriation of pension funds, and racism, sexism and ageism in organisational practice. On some occasions HR specialists may even be accused of duplicity, such as in relation to low wage levels, selective redundancies, and the use of selection tests that have not been properly validated. Unethical behaviour is not confined just to managerial staff acting explicitly or implicitly to further employer policies, but is also evident in the actions of non-managerial staff – for example, where staff receive gifts in return for influence or read other people's mail.

Such examples have stimulated a growth of interest in business ethics and social responsibility in an effort to extend managerial concern beyond short-term profit maximisation and the satisfaction of shareholders. As we shall see below, this leads us into an analysis of stakeholder interests, but some commentators believe that the only social responsibility that a business has is to maximise profits. The leading proponent of this view is Milton Friedman (1970). He argued that there is 'one and only one social responsibility of business – to use its resources and engage in activities designed to increase its profits so long as it stays within the rules of the game ... [that is, it] engages in open and free competition without deception or fraud'. It is claimed that businessmen (*sic*) who talk of social responsibility in terms of environmental protection, the prevention of discrimination or the provision of employment, are guilty of 'pure and unadulterated socialism' (Chryssides and Kaler, 1993: 249). Friedman sees social responsibility solely in terms of costs to the employing organisation, whereas promoting 'good' values should be the responsibility of the government, and should only be undertaken if the government has electoral support for such a programme.

The Friedman view is challenged by the stakeholder model based on the premise that business and HRM should concern itself with the well-being of individuals and society. According to Mullins (2001: 148–9) there are several reasons why firms go down the stakeholder route. It is fashionable, it keeps the campaigners and lobbyists quiet, and it may bring increased profitability and long-term survival. The most persuasive argument is that the stakeholder model makes economic sense, and that an ethical business is likely to be more successful longer-term because of its reputation with customers and improved motivation among employees. In any case, economic arguments are not appropriate for the public sector, non-governmental organisations (NGOs), not-for-profit organisations, and the voluntary sector (Winstanley and Woodall, 2000: 5). Corporate ethics include employee secondments to community work, charitable donations, responsible/fair trading, human rights, and ethical investment. Internal workplace issues relate to the fair treatment of staff, and environmental policies such as recycling, the use of chemicals and the control of emissions, packaging, and sourcing.

There are a large number of categorisations of business ethics (Ethical egoism, Kantian rights-based, justice-based, teleological, stakeholding, discourse, inclusiveness and communitarianism, ethics of care, virtue, etc) and readers who require additional information are referred to Winstanley and Woodall (2000), Ackers (2001: 379–82) or Storey (2001: 44–53).

The idea that ethical principles make good business sense runs into a number of problems. Some commentators feel that employer commitment is superficial, at the level of rhetoric rather than of reality. Ethics 'in use' may be somewhat different from the broad and benign visions that are published in mission statements. For example, there may be an expectation that staff work long hours despite a public commitment to healthy working practices, or some staff may be paid low wages despite a commitment to the concept of best-practice HRM. There is a danger that ethical and socially responsible practices may become even more elusive as organisations devolve HR activities to line managers who are required to meet corporate targets that stress production and service goals as their first priority (see Chapter 9). Legge (2000: 23–40) raises the more fundamental question about whether it is indeed possible to impose ethical considerations on organisations that operate in the global marketplace and that have the ability to transfer business to countries unfettered by such constraints.

> Where do you stand on this argument? Do you believe it is right for employers to try to promote business ethics and social responsibility, or should these be left to the government and to society at large?

There are major problems in defining ethical issues, largely because both ethics and morality are essentially subjective and value-laden concepts. Ackers (2001: 377) takes the Collins dictionary definition of ethics – 'the philosophical study of the moral value of human conduct and the rules and principles that ought to govern it' – and suggests that there are two dimensions: the personal and the corporate. The personal dimension involves the way in which individuals behave in relation to work. For some this may involve decisions not to take up employment with companies whose business contravenes personal codes of morality – for example, those operating in the tobacco, nuclear or genetic fields. The subjective nature of ethics means that each individual may put a different spin on what is right and wrong, and issues can involve considerations of which course of action might result in least harm. Legge (2000: 24) cites the case of child labour in the stitching of footballs. The children in Pakistan were employed to provide Nike, Reebok and Adidas with footballs despite a pact by most manufacturers to end this practice. To get around the agreement, work was subcontracted out to villages making monitoring almost impossible. However, a report by the Save the Children Fund found that many of the children worked with their parents to help pay their school fees and fears were expressed that if the children stopped this work, they might be forced to take more risky work, or to go into prostitution. Some people would feel that despite this concern, the ban on child labour should remain, whereas others would feel that until alternatives were made available the ban should be put on hold. Of course, a third (ethical) way is the payment of a fair wage, and there now exists a powerful customer-led demand for increased availability of Fair Trade products together with boycotts and lobbying of international firms to discourage them from unethical practices.

The key influences on ethical and environmental stances are the government, shareholders, and customers, as well as directors and employees. The UK mixed economy steers a middle course between *laissez-faire* and state control, legislation now ensuring a national minimum wage, reasonable working hours and holiday entitlement, protection against discrimination, and statutory trade union recognition. The introduction of these basic minimum rights has come about through EU regulations, and these are expected to go further, involving worker participation and representation in the first decade of the twenty-first century. A recent statutory provision also offers protection for whistle-blowers (Ackers, 2001: 383–4).

Shareholders can exert considerable influence, as the revolt at Shell's 1997 AGM (in protest against human rights abuses in Nigeria) clearly demonstrated. There have also been changes in corporate governance which have promoted increased stakeholder influence on corporate ethics. The Cadbury Report (1992) was mainly a reaction to the Robert Maxwell scandal and provided guidelines to enable shareholders to oversee best practice so that they could protect their interests. Other reports followed Cadbury (Greenbury and Hampel), and The Centre for Tomorrow's Company – a think-tank which promotes an ethical approach to business – and the Labour Party are encouraging shareholders to exercise greater influence over company policy (Mullins, 2001: 155–6).

Collectively, customers have massive potential to bring about changes in corporate ethics. There is evidence that some consumers are becoming more outspoken, and this has led some organisations to publicise their ethical stance more widely to demonstrate that it is worth doing business with them. Two examples of organisations with systemic ethical philosophies are the Co-operative Bank and the BodyShop. For example, the Cooperative Bank periodically consults its customers on issues in order to refine its Ethical Policy. The BodyShop involves itself in many environmental campaigns – its electricity is generated by its own wind-farms and surplus is fed into the national grid – as well as championing fair trade with the Third World. For many other organisations, ethics are usually a bolt-on extra and may have been prompted by a scandal. Examples here might be the food giant which used 'nurses' to promote its baby milk in the Third World, or the more recent Triumph Bra campaign which is subject to a boycott because of its funding of the Burmese military dictatorship (*Ethical Consumer*, 74: 27). The impact of bad publicity and the power of publications like the *Ethical Consumer* in sustaining boycotts often results in a flurry of ethical/green public relations in order to make the company's activities appear more responsive.

Does your organisation have an ethical policy, and are there gaps between the rhetoric and the reality? If there are, what have you done – or what could or should you do – about it?

Employers and managers are instrumental in the delivery of an ethical workplace. It has been proposed that the HR function is best placed to take on the role of 'ethical stewardship' because it has traditionally overseen disciplinary and grievance procedures (Winstanley and Woodall, 2000: 6–7). However, Ackers argues that the new HRM model does not always fit this mould. He suggests that the rhetoric reveals HR to be central to the strategic aims of improving business performance, the champion of labour as a precious resource and the proponent of employee participation. In practice Ackers suggests that it is only in a few mainstream unionised companies where rhetoric and reality align, but that in the large non-union sector, the reality belies the rhetoric and labour is all too often viewed as a cost rather than as a resource. In the latter cases ethical concerns relate only to staying within the law and to practising effective public relations (Ackers, 2001: 391). Hart (1993) also argues that HR has lost any pretence to professionalism because it has sided with employers, casting itself firmly as a part of the management process, and seeking to develop arguments which are principally economic and business-oriented in character. For example, in pursuing the extension of equal opportunities, fairness and justice within organisations, HR specialists are concerned solely with whether and how they 'add value', not with their inherent moral and ethical qualities. A professional, by way of contrast, would expect to signal the potential divergence between professional and managerial values, and if there was conflict between them automatically pursue the former. Ackers (2001) even suggests that HRM's total commitment to the profit goal means that it sells its soul in a Faustian pact in return for a strategic place at the heart of the organisation. As we saw in Chapter 2, the changing nature of the psychological contract has left many employees relatively powerless in relation to their employers, and unsure about how their legitimate concerns might be articulated and dealt with – unless by the 'conscience' of the organisation. Miller too (1996: 16) worries that ethical considerations are often overlooked so that, in the short term, 'employees may be as expendable as the ozone layer'.

The IRS survey of ethics at work (IRS *Employment Trends* 675, 1999) produced a low response rate (39 out of 1,000), and this may be indicative of a lack of interest in the subject by the majority of firms surveyed. Moreover, for many of those that did respond their ethical/environmental stances were marginal activities. The results of the survey showed that 92 per cent were involved in community or other charitable projects, and that 82 per cent had a written environmental policy (commonly covering energy use), although there was considerable support for the introduction of compulsory environmental reporting. About one third had already achieved ISO 14001 (see below), approximately half had written codes on business ethics covering how employees should deal with gifts or bribes, and 11 (out of 39) required their suppliers to commit to the principles of ethical trading; 24 of the 39 organisations had written codes covering the fair and ethical treatment of their employees. The companies' main motivating factors were: corporate image, moral obligation, employee satisfaction, and the development of staff potential. Only six of the 39 mentioned a wish to improve profitability. Cynics might conclude that many of these policies are merely tinkering at the margins, and some result in large savings for the company. For example, Ladbrokes' energy policy resulted in an annual saving of more than £200,000 a year at the same time as reducing carbon dioxide emissions by 1,700 tonnes (IRS *Employment Review* 739, 2001: 10).

For most firms, concern about loss of customers, investors, and even employees is providing the push to adopt ethical/environmental stances, although there are doubtless some whose moral codes also exercise powerful influence. The growing awareness of ethical and environmental concerns has led to a proliferation of firms established to produce ethical/environmental products and for whom such concerns are their *raison d'être*. In addition to the BodyShop and the Co-operative Bank, other examples include financial institutions such as Triodos Bank, the Ecology Building Society and Friends' Provident. Other companies espousing Fair Trade and/or selling organic products based on environmental sustainability include organisations such as Traidcraft and Green & Black's chocolate. There are also firms that produce environmentally-friendly products – for example ECOS paint and Green Fibres.

This has led some major producers to develop their own rival products and more vigorously promote their ethical and environmental credentials. To this end there are a number of awards that validate ethical and/or environmental stances. Examples include the ISO 14001 standard for environmental management. The SA 8000 initiative provides an internationally-recognised ethical trading standard (IRS *Employment Trends* 675, 1999: 11–13). The GoodCorporation (www.goodcorporation.com) has established a Charter Mark which recognises the way an organisation treats its employees, customers, suppliers, and finance providers, protects the environment and makes a commitment to the community (Trapp, 2001a: 34). Additionally, the London Stock Exchange has produced an 'ethical index' – FTSE4Good (www.ftse4good.com) (IRS *Employment Review* 739, 2001: 6), the European Commission has published a Green Paper on corporate social responsibility, and the government has introduced a website giving examples of good practices (www.societyandbusiness.gov.uk). Perhaps the ultimate ethical question is how far an organisation working in an unethical sector (such as armaments or gambling), but with a host of ethical and environmental policies, together with large charitable donations, can be held up as a model of good practice.

The GoodCorporation Charter

While we are accountable to our shareholders (or equivalent for not-for-profit organisations), we take into account the interests of all our stakeholders including our employees, customers and suppliers as well as the community and environment in which we operate.

The organisation respects the dignity and rights of all **employees**. *We:*

- Provide clear and fair terms of employment
- Provide clean, healthy and safe working conditions
- Have a fair remuneration policy everywhere we operate
- Strive for equal opportunities for all present and potential employees
- Encourage employees to develop skills and progress in their careers
- Do not tolerate any sexual, physical or mental harassment of our employees
- Do not discriminate on grounds of colour, ethnic origin, gender, age, religion, political or other opinion, disability or sexual orientation; and
- Do not employ underage staff.

The organisation treats its **customers** *with respect. We:*

- Seek to be honest and fair in our relationships with our customers

- Provide the standards of products and services that have been agreed
- Take all reasonable steps to ensure the safety and quality of the goods and services we provide.

*The organisation treats its **suppliers and subcontractors** with respect. We:*

- Seek to be honest and fair in our relationships with our suppliers and subcontractors
- Have a policy not to offer, pay, or accept bribes or substantial favours
- Pay suppliers and subcontractors in accordance with agreed terms
- Encourage suppliers and subcontractors to abide by the principles of this charter.

Community and environment

The organisation seeks to be a good corporate citizen respecting the laws of the countries in which we operate. We:

- Aim to make the communities in which we work better places to live and do business
- Aim to be sensitive to the local community's cultural, social and economic needs
- Endeavour to protect and preserve the environment where we operate.

Shareholders (or equivalent) and other suppliers of finance

The organisation is responsible to those who provide its funding. We:

- Are accountable to our shareholders for financial reports that are accurate and timely
- Communicate to shareholders all matters that are material to an understanding of the future prospects of the organisation
- Aim to protect shareholders' funds, manage risks and ensure that funds are used as agreed.

We [managers] will do all in our power to conform to the letter and spirit of this charter.

Source: GoodCorporation

Discrimination and disadvantage at work

The government's position (www.dti.gov.uk/er/equality/) is stated as follows:

> *Discrimination is bad for individuals. But it has a negative impact on productivity and profits too. It denies employers access to valuable knowledge, experience and skills. It causes stress-related illnesses, poor-quality work and long-term absences. And formal complaints tie up the time of staff, their managers and trade union representatives. No one benefits from this cycle of events – particularly if it ends in employees leaving to find a new job or career.*
>
> *Practical action on equality and diversity can help to avoid these costs. It also brings wider benefits for business. Good recruitment practices often lead to a more diverse workforce. Diversity, in turn, can help access new markets. It can also help improve a company's image as an employer.*

There has been a whole host of initiatives to combat discrimination at work, as we saw in Chapter 3. According to a report by the Employers' Forum, age discrimination is costing the UK economy up to £26 billion a year. In common with other forms of discrimination, the CIPD suggests that age discrimination is wasteful of talent. This is because age is not a genuine employment criterion, it is a poor predictor of performance, and to equate physical and mental ability with age is misleading (CIPD, 1999b). The government's Age Positive campaign is voluntary, although legislation will be in place by 2006 to reflect new EU requirements (Worman, 2001).

The situation for women has improved slightly over the years. By the winter of 2000–2001 their employment rate was 69 per cent, compared with 79 per cent for men, and 12 million women were in employment. However, as we saw in Chapter 2, the majority of the increase is in part-time employment and there is considerable evidence of gender segregation between sectors. Working part-time obviously has a massive impact on women's earning potential as well as income (Grimshaw and Rubery, 2001). Only 8 per cent of male employees of working age work part-time compared with 43 per cent of female employees (*Labour Market Trends*, May 2001: 236). Women are disproportionately represented in clerical and secretarial occupations, and men are disproportionately represented in plant- and machine-operative work and in craft-related occupations, as can be seen from Table 18. With regard to pay, female employees working full-time earn on average 82 per cent of the average hourly earnings of male full-time employees, and women working part-time earn on average 39 per cent less per hour than men working full-time (EOC, 2001: 1). The pay gap varies between sectors, women earning 90p for every £1 that a man earns in education, and only 55p for every £1 earned by a man in banking, insurance, and pensions – see also Chapter 16. The UK is bottom of EU nations in relation to the pay gap when full-time and part-time earnings are compared (EOC *Newsreleases*, 5 December 2001; www.eoc.gov.uk).

With regard to women in management, despite initiatives and hype there is some evidence that the 'glass ceiling' is 'as tough as it was 10 years ago'. A survey by Pye of 10 large UK companies found that in 1989 2 per cent of executive and non-executive directors were women, and by 1999 this had risen to only 7 per cent, but with very low numbers of women appointed to non-executive director positions (Mahoney, 2000).

Ethnic minorities accounted for 7.2 per cent of the working population in 2000. The position in relation to ethnic minority groups is complicated, and is heavily influenced by the specific group (Black, South Asian, or Chinese), as well as between women and men, and by age. Research by Owen *et al* (2000: 505) revealed some key points:

- White economic activity rates are well above those for people from ethnic minority groups as a whole. Among men of working age, only Black Caribbean and Indian men have economic activity rates (80 per cent and 82 per cent respectively) that are close to Whites (85 per cent).

- An important influence on women's activity rate is whether or not they are single. Black Caribbean women have the highest economic activity rate (83 per cent), while Pakistani and Bangladeshi women are more likely to be economically active if they are single.

Table 18   UK employment by occupation (employees and self-employed aged 16 and over)

Major occupational groups	Women %	Men %
Managers and administrators	33	67
Professional	40	60
Associate professional and technical	51	49
Clerical and secretarial	74	26
Craft and related	7	93
Personal and protective	67	33
Sales	64	36
Plant and machine operatives	18	82
Other occupations	47	53
All occupations	45	55

Source: EOC analysis of Labour Force Survey Spring 2000, Office for National Statistics: taken from EOC *Facts about Women and Men in Great Britain*, 2001

Table 19 Economic activity rates by age group, sex, and ethnic group, Great Britain, averaged between Spring 1999 and Winter 1999–2000

| | Percentage | | | | | | | |
| | MEN | | | | WOMEN | | | |
	16–64	16–24	25–44	45–64	16–59	16–24	25–44	45–59
White	85	78	94	78	74	70	78	71
All ethnic minority groups	77	59	88	70	56	47	60	55
Black	78	69	86	69	68	54	72	72
Black Caribbean	80	77	89	65	75	63	78	72
Black African	76	50	84	77	61	40	65	71
Other Black*	81	78	83	S	67	59	72	S
South Asian	77	59	91	67	47	45	51	41
Indian	82	62	95	74	63	56	69	56
Pakistani	74	56	89	62	30	35	31	21
Bangladeshi	65	55	81	40	22	36	S	S
All other groups	74	47	85	78	57	46	58	64
Chinese	63	S	83	73	57	S	63	64
Other Asian	77	46	85	82	58	52	58	64
Other	76	58	86	77	55	49	55	66
All ethnic groups**	85	76	93	77	73	68	76	70

S = Sample size too small for reliable estimate
*Includes Black mixed
**Includes those who did not state ethnic origin
Source: Owen *et al*, 2000, p506

- Men from ethnic minority groups are less likely than White men to be employed as managers and administrators. Within this, Black Caribbean, Black African, and Bangladeshi men are poorly represented (10 per cent, 13 per cent, and 16 per cent respectively).

- The proportion leaving the New Deal Gateway for an unknown destination was higher for all ethnic minority groups in aggregate (24 per cent) than for the White group (15 per cent).

Table 19 clearly demonstrates the differences for younger workers: the economic activity rate for young White males at 78 per cent compares with a figure of 69 per cent for young Black males, and 59 per cent for young South Asian males. Comparable figures for young women are 70 per cent for the White group, 54 per cent for Blacks and 45 per cent for South Asians. In the spring of 2001, 4 per cent of White people of working age were unemployed, compared with 11 per cent among ethnic minority groups. Within these unemployment figures the rates were 11 per cent for Asian-British, 7 per cent for Indian, 20 per cent for

Bangladeshi and 13 per cent for Black British (*Labour Market Trends*, September 2001: 429). Overall, it is apparent that people from ethnic minorities are disadvantaged, compared with Whites, not just in terms of the type of work they do but also in terms of lower average pay levels (at least 10 per cent less) and crucially in their access to employment (www.cre.gov.uk).

The government has acted – possibly as a result of the 1999 Stephen Lawrence Inquiry Report – with the Race Relations (Amendment) Act 2000 to give greater powers to the Commission for Racial Equality (CRE). This places a positive and enforceable duty on public authorities to promote race equality in carrying out their duties in order to avoid race discrimination *before* it takes place, and the CRE now has a stronger enforcement capability. The TUC has also responded to the Lawrence Inquiry and has established a 'Stephen Lawrence Task Group' chaired by its General Secretary, John Monks. The TUC Report *Black Workers Deserve Better* (TUC, 2001) states that 'Despite improved educational qualifications, black workers still face barriers in accessing the labour market. This is a message of despair for the black community that flies in the face of the old adage that if you work hard in school, you will succeed.' The Report does, however, cite examples of good practice that is attempting to eradicate institutional racism.

> These figures demonstrate clearly that certain groups of people are disadvantaged in relation to the population as a whole. How can you explain this? To what extent do you think it is due to discrimination (overt or covert) by employers as a whole or by individual managers?

Nearly one in five (6.8 million) of the UK working-age population was disabled in the summer of 2000, of whom only one eighth (around 85,000) were in employment. A disability is defined as a physical or mental impairment that has a substantial and long-term adverse effect on the ability to carry out day-to-day activities (Hammond Suddards, 2000: *ix*). People with disabilities are six times more likely to be unemployed than the able-bodied (Twomey, 2001: 241).

The legislation on disability has a long pedigree but has only recently been strengthened through the Disability Discrimination Act (DDA) 1995 and the Disability Rights Commission Act 1999. The DDA states that firms must make 'reasonable' adjustments in their workplace while taking into account the resources available individually to them. The 1999 Act established the Disability Rights Commission (DRC) and recommended new legislation that is due to come into force in 2004. This will extend the provisions of the DDA to organisations that employ two or more employees (down from 15) and will include people with HIV and cancer. It means that small businesses (which account for 80 per cent of all employers in the UK) will have to ensure that their premises and

CASE STUDY: Centrica pilots the New Deal for Disabled People

Centrica employs approximately 55,000 people. As part of the New Deal for Disabled People it offered permanent employment to 40 long-term disabled people in the Manchester area. Previously, very few people with disabilities had applied for jobs. Centrica worked closely with the Employment Service to identify potential recruits and to provide technical advice and financial support for appro-priate aids and adaptations such as work-station modifications for people with restricted mobility, and voice-activated, synthetic-speech and large character software for people with visual impairment.

Adapted from IRS *Employment Trends* 708, 2000

employment practices do not discriminate against disabled people. Recent government initiatives include a New Deal for Disabled People, a disabled person's tax credit, and provision of disability employment advisers and Access to Work schemes. In addition, job retention pilot schemes place an emphasis on helping employers retain employees who are developing an illness or disability rather than making them redundant (IRS *Employment Trends* 708, 2000: 5–6).

Despite the recent focus on rights for disabled people, a 2001 IRS survey on managing disability found that UK organisations were not adopting a multi-departmental approach. The research shows that the process of accommodating a disabled employee in a particular workplace is greatly enhanced when the organisation utilises a cross-department strategy, but that HR departments were taking the lead role in more than 80 per cent of organisations surveyed (IRS *Employment Review* 738, 2001: 6). A recent CIPD survey report *Adapting to Disability* showed that one third of surveyed personnel managers found that changing people's attitudes to disability was the hardest part of complying with the DDA. Just over one third of managers felt that there were problems in changing the attitudes of fellow workers and supervisors, whereas 80 per cent of personnel managers reported that they had found it easy to adapt workplace procedures to comply with the act (Higginbottom, 2001: 16–17).

One major problem with the DDA is the definition of ' reasonable'. The work of Earnshaw *et al* (2002) showed how many LEA personnel departments were unsure about what constituted 'reasonable' adjustments in relation to the continued employment or re-employment of teachers, particularly those suffering from mental ill-health problems. Concern has also been expressed on behalf of small firms that will have to comply with the legislation after 2004, in part because some of them may inadvertently fall foul of the law through lack of information. As a response to the criticism, the Disability Rights Commission plans to allocate 20 per cent of its annual £11 million budget to helping employers (Higginbottom, 2001: 16–17).

The issue of 'work–life balance' has also become increasingly topical over the last few years. A survey carried out by Ceridian/Institute of Management in 1999 revealed that 73 per cent of managers regarded work–life balance as important – and that only professional challenge, recognition of contribution, and security of employment rated more highly. At the same time almost half of these managers said that they felt guilty about leaving work on time, and only one third said that they had time to enjoy the money they earned (IRS *Employment Trends* 688, 1999: 2). However, there is increasing evidence of the business benefits of 'family-friendly' policies. CIPD research into 12 companies that had adopted family-friendly policies showed that business benefits included increased employee satisfaction and the ability to recruit and retain good employees (Coussey, 1999). Most organisations have brought in family-friendly policies in a piecemeal manner, typically introducing part-time or term-time work, career breaks and workplace nurseries.

The government's concern resulted in the launch of the Work–Life Balance Campaign in the spring of 2000 while at the same time it undertook a Baseline Study (for full details contact DfES publications or visit the website: www.dfes.gov.uk/research). The key findings of recent government research (Hogarth *et al*, 2001: 371–3) are reproduced below:

- Employers felt that they had a responsibility to help employees get the balance right.

- Most workplaces reported that staff worked more than their con-tracted hours, by an average of 9 hours per week.

- In about two-thirds of workplaces some staff were allowed to vary their usual hours.

- Part-time working was commonly available, but a small proportion of employers offered flexible arrangements such as flexitime, term-time contracts, and reduced hours.

- Approximately one fifth of workers worked from home occasion-ally. About one-third of those not working from home would like to.

- The majority of women returning from maternity leave prefer to switch to part-time work and to have greater flexibility in their working arrangements. Roughly one fifth of workplaces provided some help with childcare needs, but this usually meant providing information – only a very small proportion provided a crèche.

- Most employers felt that work–life balance practices improved work relations, staff motivation and commitment and helped retain employees.

The recent CIPD survey (CIPD, 2001a: 3) revealed that one in three partners of people who work more than 48 hours in a typical week says that this has a negative effect on their personal relationship. The effects varied from being too tired to hold a conversation (29 per cent), to having a deleterious effect on their sex lives (54 per cent), and resentment over having to bear most of the domestic burden (43 per cent). Additionally, those working long hours said that they might have made mistakes as a result of fatigue. A recent European Foundation study (Fagan and Warren, 2001: 7) showed that many full-timers would like to work fewer hours, even though this would mean reducing income, and that many part-time workers would like to work longer hours. The optimum arrangements fall within the bands of substantial part-time hours (20–34 hours a week) or moderate full-time hours (35–39 hours a week).

Family-friendly provisions in the Employment Relations Act of 1999 gave working parents with children born on or after 15 December 1999 rights to unpaid parental leave. All workers were given rights to take a reasonable amount of unpaid leave to deal with emergencies involving others who rely on them. There was also an increase in paid maternity leave from 14 to 18 weeks. However, the legislation may still not solve the problem. Some employees are reluctant to ask for unpaid parental leave for fear that do so may damage their careers, and others may not be able to afford to take time off (IRS *Employment Trends* 704, 2000: 12–16). IRS *Employment Review* 742b, 2001, provides answers to the most common concerns about parental leave entitlement.

In the meantime, the government proposes to intervene on the subject of the parental right to request shorter working hours. It is anticipated that legislation will be introduced in 2003 that requires employers to seriously consider requests for shorter hours from working parents (IRS *Employment Review* 742b, 2001).

Equality management and managing diversity

The management of equality has now become the main avenue for addressing equal opportunities issues in employing organisations. This usually includes gender, age, ethnicity, disability, sexual orientation, and nationality (Hicks-Clarke and Iles, 2000). The CIPD position paper states that 'managing diversity is based on the concept that people should be valued as individuals for reasons related to business interests, as well as for moral and social reasons. It recognises that people from different backgrounds can bring fresh ideas and perceptions which make the way work is done more efficient and products and services better' (CIPD, 1999). This typically involves stating the business case for equal opportunities and making direct links with business strategy. The CIPD's case study research (1999c: 1) found that there were powerful business benefits:

- improved customer satisfaction and market penetration by employing and supporting a diverse workforce whose composition is similar to that of the local population

- recognition that a diverse workforce brings a range of skills and is the best use of human resources

- improved supply of labour

- avoidance of costly discrimination cases.

Much of the current research also points to the potential competitive advantage gained by those organisations that embrace diversity (CIPD, 1999c; Hick-Clarke *et al*, 2000: 236–7; Cassell, 2001: 407). The main advantages not already mentioned by the CIPD research include increased employee commitment and satisfaction and the ability to attract ethical investors. Equal opportunities policies and practices may help to increase the motivation and commitment of employees – particularly those from disadvantaged groups – and they may also lessen the likelihood of industrial unrest. This is well illustrated by the experience at Ford in the spring of 1996, when it was found that a number of black faces had been painted white for an advertising poster to be used in Poland. After a short stoppage of work and complaints from the trade unions, Ford management soon issued an apology in order to prevent a further deterioration in employee relations. Respondents to the CIPD Survey (Coussey, 2000) reported that the additional administrative costs were more than balanced by the advantages to the firm. Moreover, employees reported that they were determined to put in extra effort and flexibility to be more highly productive because the firm had responded to their needs.

Employers not only want to avoid a bad press – both locally and nationally – they also want to convey a more positive image as a 'good employer' so as to attract high-quality applicants as well as ethical

CASE STUDY: The Halifax Fair's Fair diversity programme

The Halifax invited members of Manchester's Chinese community to apply for work within the bank. In the past, the company had few customers and staff from this large community. Bilingual posters were placed in the main Chinatown advice centre asking 'Are you interested in working for the Halifax?' No fewer than 40 people were attracted to attend a presentation, leading finally to the employment of six Chinese people in the Manchester area. A consequence of the policy has been increased business from the Chinese community, possibly because some staff can now speak Mandarin or Cantonese. Since 1998, the Halifax has increased the proportion of employees from ethnic minorities from 4% to 6.4% nationally, and increases are locally even higher – for example, from 9 to 27% in Keighley.

The Fair's Fair diversity programme is also about women, older workers, and people with disabilities, and the company utilises a diversity team including a disability manager and an equal opportunities adviser. Results include 'glass ceiling' events for women managers and an increase in flexible working conditions, including managers working part-time or job-sharing.

Source: Merrick, N., *People Management*, 8 November 2001, pp52–3

investors. In addition to having a direct impact upon applicants (potential employees), organisational image also has an impact upon customers and citizens in the local community. This has led many public and private service sector organisations to publicise their equal opportunities policies and reflect the wide mix of employees in their advertising and HR policies. One example centres on the experience of the Halifax Building Society described in the box on the previous page.

Despite these positive findings, doubts remain about the durability and likely conversion of these potential benefits into practice within organisations. The 'business case' can be quite fragile since it depends upon the specific circumstances confronting each organisation, as well as changes in the wider legal, political, economic and social context. These may lead management to downgrade equal opportunities arguments if they are not seen to be of pressing concern. For example, Cassell (2001: 418) cites the Midland Bank's programme in the early 1990s for 200 crèches. The programme stopped after only 115 crèches had been set up because the labour market changed and made it easier for the bank to recruit as the level of unemployment rose. Similarly, some employers may be unconvinced by the cost-effectiveness arguments because they may gain substantially (in the short term, at least) from pockets of low-paid labour that enable them to keep down the organisation's cost-base. Diversity may likewise be valued among professionals whose skill is scarce, whereas this may not be the case with casual or unskilled employees (Cassell, 2001: 419). Moreover, despite the existence of national policies that support the extension of equal opportunities, union officials may find themselves under pressure from existing male, white, and able-bodied members to protect their interests rather than those of disadvantaged groups.

At the heart of effective equality provision is, of course, a new set of attitudes, beliefs and values. Yet it is very difficult to change beliefs that may be deep-rooted, implicit, and resistant to alternative arguments. Kandola and Fullerton (1998) argue that for diversity management to work, it must be systemic so that all staff are committed to maximising the potential of the workforce, regardless of their age, gender or sexual orientation. Dickens (1999) also criticises the predominant use of the business-benefit arguments for promoting equality because this excludes those not within organisations and may actually increase disparities within groups – for example, between white women and ethnic-minority women. Moreover, even within an organisation, equality practices may be selective and partial and operate only when equal opportunities and business needs align. Liff (1999) argues that in organisations which subscribe to equal opportunities, the policies are not always put into practice, as evidenced by the number of tribunal cases. Secondly, she suggests that white males usually establish the norms, and that this immediately disadvantages members of other groups. Thirdly, a top-down approach might have little impact on attitudes and beliefs.

> Make out a case for equal opportunities at your workplace, either to
> extend current provision or to ensure that it is not reduced due to
> other pressures. To what extent would you draw upon the 'business
> case' to convince line managers of the value of equality provisions?

A good example of the differences between equal opportunities and
managing diversity can be seen in their approaches to the concept of
family-friendly policies. Equal opportunities would focus primarily on the
way in which employers could introduce policies and practices which
make it easier for women to balance the competing demands of childcare (or eldercare) and continued employment. The emphasis would
therefore be on flexible working patterns – such as part-time employment, term-time-only contracts, flexitime, and extended career breaks –
as well as consideration of nursery and crèche provision. The key point,
however, is that equal opportunities would focus on the obstacles to
women's continued employment, and how these might be overcome to
allow women to reduce the tension between work commitments and
domestic responsibilities. As Dickens (1994: 288) notes, the main concern is that the equal opportunities prescription rests upon an inadequate conceptualisation of the 'problem', and it pays insufficient
attention to the resistance that may be created by such interventions.
Moreover, the prescription generally focuses on 'helping individuals from
disadvantaged groups get in and get on within existing organisations,
with no real challenge being mounted to the nature, structure and
values of the organisations themselves'. Since members of 'advantaged'
groups typically establish prevailing norms, it is not surprising that even
the best achievements fall well short of equality in employment. Hicks-
Clarke and Iles (2000: 236–7) also maintain that power in most organisations still lies with white males whereas it is women and ethnic
minorities who are more likely to support an organisation attempting to
embrace diversity.

By contrast, managing diversity starts from the assumption that the
focus should be on the workforce as a whole and what it can contribute,
rather than on the removal of obstacles for specific sections of the
workforce. It is appreciated that differences can actually be strengths
for the organisation as a whole, and that different people can introduce
alternative perspectives and ideas that can bring competitive advantage. It is only when 'women's issues' are recast as 'people's issues' that
any real moves towards equality are likely, and diversity is recognised
and commended – both in its own right and for its contribution to
improved organisational performance.

Goss (1994: 157) provides a two-dimensional categorisation for the
form that equal opportunities policies and practices can take in organisations. First is the *depth* of management's commitment to equality,

and this can range from shallow and instrumental through to deep and principled. The second dimension, the *breadth* of its focus, ranges from a narrow list of practices driven largely by economic and legal expediency through to a broad set that includes a whole range of issues. This allows for four alternative agendas in practice. The short agenda is shallow and narrow, little more than a lip-service commitment to legal imperatives. The broad agenda combines a broad focus with a shallow commitment to equality. The focused agenda is built upon a narrow base, but at least has the advantage of a deep management commitment to achieve real change. Finally, the long agenda is broad and deep, essentially concerned with changing how the whole organisation is managed, and aiming to develop the talents of all employees. This final agenda is rare, according to Goss, except in some local authorities and large private sector employers where an essential component of the equality policies is likely to be positive action. Under this agenda, employers aim to ensure that members of under-represented groups have the skills and credentials necessary to reach the selection pool, prepare for the selection interview and gain training in areas where their skills may be lacking.

Are equal opportunity policies at your workplace monitored? If so, what does this show, and where does it place your organisation on the categories outlined by Goss? If equal opportunities policies are not monitored, why is this the case, and what do you intend to do about it?

CONCLUSION

In this chapter, we have examined the professional and ethical aspects of HRM. The history and development of the profession has been intertwined with these sorts of issue, in particular in relation to the 'side' that HR professionals take in relation to ethical and equality issues that confront their own organisations. Both the welfare heritage and the CIPD Code of Conduct demonstrate the tensions that can arise when HR specialists are expected to join in and strive for organisational goals when these are perceived to conflict with professional standards. However, a strong professional and ethical stance also provides HR practitioners with a potentially distinctive contribution to improved performance, one that recognises the need for consistency, fairness and equity in the handling of people management and other issues. Other managers will not always appreciate the value of this contribution, and HR practitioners who do their jobs effectively may well make life uncomfortable for their colleagues at times. There are likely to be disagreements about the validity and suitability of recommendations, especially in the short term, but it is up to HR specialists to demonstrate that they can be beneficial for the organisation, as well as for the wider public good.

Useful reading

ACKERS P. 'Employment ethics', in T. REDMAN and A. WILKINSON (eds), *Contemporary Human Resource Management*. London, FT/Prentice-Hall. 2001.

COUSSEY M. *Getting the Right Work–Life Balance*. London, CIPD. 2000.

DICKENS L. 'Beyond the business case: a three-pronged approach to equality action', *Human Resource Management Journal*, Vol. 9, No. 1. 1999. pp9–19.

INDUSTRIAL RELATIONS SERVICES (2001) *Businesses Behaving Responsibly*. IRS *Employment Review* 739. November. pp6–11.

INSTITUTE OF PERSONNEL AND DEVELOPMENT *Key Facts: Age and Employment*. London, IPD. 1999.

KANDOLA R. and FULLERTON J. *Diversity in Action: Managing the mosaic*. London, IPD. 1998.

SADLER-SMITH E. and BADGER B. 'The HR practitioner's perspective on continuing professional development', *Human Resource Management Journal*, Vol. 8, No. 4, 1998. pp66–75.

ULRICH D. 'A new mandate for human resources', *Harvard Business Review*, Jan-Feb 1998, pp125–134.

WHITTAKER J. 'Remaking the grade', *People Management*, 27 September 2001. pp44–46.

WINSTANLEY D. and WOODALL J. *Ethical Issues in Contemporary Human Resource Management*. London, Macmillan Business. 2000.

INTEGRATING THE
PM&D CONTRIBUTION

Best-Practice HRM: Improving organisational performance through the high-commitment bundle

CHAPTER OBJECTIVES

By the end of this chapter, readers should be able to:

- implement appropriate HR policies that maximise the contribution of people to organisational objectives and to wider societal needs

- convince other managers that there are business benefits to be gained from adopting 'best-practice' HRM

- benchmark their own organisation's HR practices against those of other comparable organisations.

In addition, readers should understand and be able to explain:

- the meaning of 'best-practice'/'high-commitment' HRM, and the ways in which bundles of HR practice can be combined together

- the contribution of people management and development policies and practices to improvements in organisational performance

- the limitations of claims that best-practice HRM can be applied universally in all organisations.

Introduction

There has been a continuing search for a set of human resource practices that consistently deliver higher levels of organisational performance. Most of the interest over the last decade or so has been in models of high-commitment or best-practice HRM, stimulated initially by the work of a number of US academics but developed more recently by people in Britain as well. Basically, the idea is that a particular bundle of HR practices has the potential to contribute improved employee attitudes and behaviours, lower levels of absenteeism and labour turnover, and higher levels of productivity, quality and customer service. This has the ultimate effect of generating higher levels of profitability. Since the HR practices that supposedly contribute to an improved bottom-line performance are generally perceived as 'good' for workers – for example, employment security, training and development, information and consultation, and higher levels of pay – this looks like an attractive scenario for employers and employees alike. However, not all the studies report such glowing and positive links between best-practice HRM and performance, and there are some doubts about the precise mix of practices that comprise the high-commitment bundle, about their attractiveness to employees and about their universal applicability. The purpose of this chapter is to review this debate and present evidence from a range of sources to allow readers to make informed judgements about the role of best-practice HRM. We use the terms 'best-practice' and 'high-commitment' HRM interchangeably.

Defining and measuring 'best-practice' HRM

In recent years, there has been a considerable degree of interest in the notion of 'best-practice' human resource management (HRM). Sometimes this is referred to as 'high-performance work systems' (Berg, 1999; Applebaum *et al*, 2000), 'high-commitment' HRM (Walton, 1985; Guest, 2001) or 'high-involvement' HRM (Wood, 1999a). Whatever the terminology, the idea is that a particular set (or number) of HR practices can have the potential to bring about improved organisational performance for all organisations. Over the last decade, there have been a large number of US publications exploring the links between HRM and performance (eg Arthur, 1994; Pfeffer, 1994; Huselid, 1995; MacDuffie, 1995; Delaney and Huselid, 1996; Delery and Doty, 1996; Huselid and Becker, 1996; Ichniowski *et al*, 1997; Youndt *et al*, 1996; Pfeffer, 1998; Applebaum *et al*, 2000). This has been supplemented by an increasing number of studies in Britain (eg, Wood, 1995; Wood and Albanese, 1995; Patterson *et al*, 1997; Guest and Conway, 1998; Wood and de Menezes, 1998; Wood, 1999b; Guest *et al*, 2000a, 2000b), several of which have been published by the CIPD. Despite this output, it is still difficult to draw generalised conclusions from these studies for a number of reasons. There are differences in the HR practices that have been examined, in the proxies deployed for each of these practices, in the methods used to collect data, and in the respondents from whom information was sought. Guest (1997: 263) argued some time ago that there is 'little additive value in these, and whilst statistically sophisticated, they lack theoretical rigour'. Despite a plea for more theoretical models to underpin empirical research, this has not prevented even more of these sorts of studies from taking place, and there remains concern about the strength of the conclusions that can be drawn from them.

Rather than review all of the studies mentioned above – which would be lengthy and repetitive – we have decided instead to focus on the list of high-commitment HR practices outlined by Pfeffer (1998), and adapt these to make them more meaningful for a UK audience. For example, our analysis makes use of a wider definition of employee involvement and information sharing that incorporates the notion of employee voice (Marchington and Grugulis, 2000; Marchington *et al*, 2001).

> **Components of 'best-practice'/'high-commitment' HRM**
>
> - Employment security and internal promotion
>
> - Selective hiring and sophisticated selection
>
> - Extensive training, learning and development
>
> - Employee involvement and voice
>
> - Self-managed teams/teamworking
>
> - High compensation contingent on organisational performance
>
> - Reduction of status differentials/harmonisation.
>
> Adapted from Pfeffer, 1998

Employment security and internal transfers

Pfeffer (1998: 180–1) regards employment security as fundamentally underpinning the other six HR practices, principally because it is regarded as unrealistic to ask employees to offer their ideas, hard work and commitment without some expectation of security on their part. In emphasising the importance of employment security, Pfeffer draws a parallel between organisation and home life, and the expectation that loyalty can be achieved via temporary appointments:

Try going home to your spouse and children with the following redefinition of the 'new family contract': 'Because of increasing instability in the economy, I can no longer make credible long-term commitments for your support and education. I face career instability, and, therefore, how can I promise that I will provide ongoing financial support? In this era of rapid change, we need more family unit flexibility to deploy our personnel resources as the situation dictates. In fact, what I will help you to do is to become family-circumstance resilient, so that you are better able to cope with changing family circumstances.'

There are limits to employment security however. It does not mean that employees are necessarily able to stay in the same job for life, nor does it prevent the dismissal of staff who fail to perform to the required level. Similarly, a major collapse in the product market that necessitates reductions in the labour force should not be seen as undermining this principle. The most significant point about this practice is that it asserts that job reductions will be avoided wherever possible, and that employees should expect to maintain their employment with the organisation – if appropriate, through internal transfers. Employment security can be enhanced by well-devised and forward-looking systems of human resource planning (see Chapter 10) and an understanding of how organisations may be structured to achieve flexibility (Chapter 2). It is perhaps best summed up by the view that workers should be treated not as a variable cost but as a critical asset in the long-term viability and success of the organisation. Indeed, there is also a business case for employment security. As Pfeffer (1998: 66) notes, laying people off too readily 'constitutes a cost for firms that have done a good job selecting, training and developing their workforce ... Layoffs put important strategic assets on the street for the competition to employ.'

In the various studies, employment security has been operationalised in many different ways, and the measures used for each of these elements of HR vary considerably between studies depending on whether information is sought about policy or practice. For example, Wood and Albanese (1995) include three measures in reaching their assessment of employment security: a policy of no compulsory redundancy, the use of temporary workers primarily to protect the core workforce, and an expectation on the part of senior managers that new employees will stay with the firm until retirement. Guest *et al* (2000a), drawing on the 1998 WERS survey, use the presence or absence of a 'job security guarantee for non-managerial employees', finding that this is reported by only a very small number of workplaces – 5 per cent in the private sector, 15 per cent in the public. Delaney and Huselid, (1996) use 'filling vacancies from within and creating opportunities for internal promotion' as a proxy for employment security. Guest *et al* (2000b) actually ask about practice rather than policy, and inquire about whether or not compulsory or voluntary redundancies have occurred in the last three years. Over half of these organisations acknowledged that compulsory redundancies had taken place during this period. It will be recalled from Chapter 2 that many employees felt concerned about the quality of their psychological contract with their employer. However, the WERS survey (Cully *et al*, 1999: 167) reported that a majority of employees felt their jobs were relatively secure.

Pfeffer (1998: 183) reckons that compulsory lay-offs and downsizing undermine employment security, and sees the following as alternatives: proportionately reducing working hours to 'spread the pain' of reduced employment costs across the entire workforce; reducing wages to reduce the labour costs; freezing recruitment to prevent overstaffing; or putting production workers into sales to build up demand. This is some way short of full-blown employment security, and in reality it may be little different from the policies adopted by many progressive organisations. Equally, it is not assumed that employment security is to be achieved by compromising corporate profits. The employer's financial flexibility is maintained by increasing employee workloads and by ensuring that salaries are related to organisational performance in the event of a downturn in demand.

CASE STUDY: Employment security provisions at various organisations

Inland Revenue

'The Inland Revenue is committed to avoiding compulsory redundancies except as a very last resort, and one which it will do its utmost to avoid.'

The Co-operative Bank

'... to jointly recognise that effective use of the revised organisational change process (agreed with UNIFI) will require continued commitment to maintain an approach which keeps the number of redundancies to a minimum and achieves redundancies on a voluntary basis, as far as possible.'

AGCO (manual workers)

'... there will be no compulsory redundancies arising from: improvements in productivity, make-versus-buy decisions, changes in workflow or processes [or] reduction of non-value-added time.

Indefinitely and in all circumstances we will make use of redeployment, early retirement and voluntary redundancy.'

Welsh Water

'Partnership gives employment security – in these days of rapid change it is impossible to give a guarantee of job security – that is, doing the same job at the same location doing the same things. But it does mean that permanent staff who want to continue working for the company can continue to do so provided they understand their obligations – to share responsibility for continual improvements in meeting business objectives and providing the highest levels of customer service.'

Adapted from *Sharing the Challenge Ahead: Informing and consulting with your workforce.* Involvement and Participation Association, Guide to Good Practice, London, 2001

Selective hiring and sophisticated selection

This is seen as an effective way to achieve 'human capital advantage' by recruiting outstanding people and 'capturing a stock of exceptional human talent' (Boxall, 1996: 66–7) as a source of sustained competitive advantage. Even though employers have always wanted to recruit the best people available, this is nowadays more likely to be systematised through the use of sophisticated selection techniques and taking greater care when hiring. Increasingly, employers are looking for applicants who possess a range of social, interpersonal and teamworking skills in addition to technical ability. For example, Wood and de Menezes (1998) asked about the importance of social and teamworking skills as selection criteria, and Wood and Albanese (1995) found that two of the major facets sought by employers were trainability and commitment. Hoque's (1999) study of large hotels also identified trainability as a major selection criterion. Indeed, in a growing number of situations, it would appear that employers feel that they can provide technical training for people so long as they have the 'right' social skills, attitudes and commitment (Sturdy *et al*, 2001; Marchington *et al*, 2001; Callaghan and Thompson, 2002).

The proxies used to measure 'selective hiring' vary widely. They include:

- the number of applicants per position (Delaney and Huselid, 1996)

- the proportion administered an employment test prior to hiring (Huselid, 1995)

- the sophistication of (selection) processes, such as the use of psychometric tests (Patterson *et al*, 1997) and realistic job previews (Hoque, 1999; Guest *et al*, 2000b).

These measures capture quite different practices, and it could be argued that the number of applicants for a position is actually indicative of poor HR procedures due to failures to define the job and the field adequately prior to advertising. As we see in Chapter 10, it is also possible that selective hiring – especially when it focuses on how well new recruits might fit with the prevailing organisational culture – can lead to under-represented groups being excluded from employment. Moreover, an excessive 'cloning' of employees can be problematic if the organisation is keen to promote initiative and diversity, as well as if there are changes in business objectives (Becker and Gerhart, 1996: 789).

Recruiting high-quality committed staff is seen as central to 'best-practice' HRM, and the use of psychometric tests, structured interviews and work sampling is likely to increase the validity of selection decisions. Competencies to be sought at the selection stage include trainability, flexibility, commitment, drive and persistence, and initiative. The key point about 'best-practice' selection is that it should be integrated and systematic, making use of the techniques that are appropriate for the position and the organisation, and administered by individuals who have themselves been trained. It must also be recalled that recruitment methods have to be capable of attracting a pool of high-quality candidates, and that a comprehensive induction programme represents the final stage of successful recruitment and selection – see Chapters 10 and 11. The two recent surveys undertaken by Guest *et al* (2000a, 2000b) show performance tests to be more widely used in the public than in the private sector, but there are still a large number of organisations (53 per cent in the CIPD survey) that do not use testing for any appointments.

Extensive training, learning and development

Having recruited 'outstanding human talent', employers must ensure that these people remain at the forefront of their field, not only in terms of professional expertise and product knowledge but also through working in teams or in interpersonal relations. Boxall (1996: 67) views this as one element in 'human process advantage', the idea that organisations aim to synergise the contribution of talented and exceptional employees. There is little doubt that there has been a growing recognition during the last decade of the importance of individual and organisational learning as a source of sustained competitive advantage as employers introduce more skills-specific forms of training and experience continuing skills shortages in some areas. Pfeffer (1998: 89) defines this in terms of the amount of training provided and of the budget devoted to training, especially in lean times.

This is arguably one of the most important elements of 'best-practice' HRM, both in seeking to ensure continuing training and development for all employees, but also in terms of improving organisational performance. The use of the word 'learning' is crucial because it demonstrates employer willingness to encourage and facilitate employee development rather than just to provide specific training to cover short-term crises. Different types of measure can be employed to indicate best practice, such as fully-fledged 'learning companies' (Hoque, 1999), employee development and assessment programmes (EDAPs) or task-based and interpersonal skills training (see Chapter 13). The time and effort devoted to learning opportunities is also important. A range of proxies are used for this, such as the number of days training received by all workers, the proportion of workers who have been trained, the budget set aside for training, or the establishment of agreed training targets over a two-year period. The WERS survey used a simple absence/presence distinction in relation to induction training and formal job training, finding that well over half of all workplaces engaged in this. Training was provided at fewer workplaces in the private sector than the public sector. The CIPD survey (Guest *et al*, 2000a: 15) reports, quite surprisingly, that almost one quarter of respondents claimed to offer at least one month's training per annum to their staff, although 13 per cent admitted that they provided none at all. Chapters 12 and 13 focus on learning and training.

Of course, there are problems in trying to measure and evaluate the training contribution. While it is clearly important to establish how much time and resources employers invest in formal training covering the entire workforce, it is also crucial to identify the type of training that is provided and who has the responsibility for managing it. Some of the researchers focus solely on extensiveness (eg Huselid, 1995), whereas others go further and attempt to establish whether formal training programmes are directed at issues not specifically related to the individual's immediate work area (Arthur, 1994). More broadly, questions must be asked about whether or not longer-term budget safeguards are established so as to protect training provision (Wood and Albanese, 1995) or if training is tied in to 'increased promotability within the organisation' (Delery and Doty, 1996). The quality of training, in terms of both its focus and its delivery, is clearly more important than a simple count of the amount provided. In their study of eight large UK organisations, Truss *et al* (1997: 61) found that even where training opportunities were provided, 'these were not necessarily equated with a soft, developmental HRM perspective ... [There] was no explicit aim within the training of increasing the individuals' skill-base or broadening their experience.'

> How much time has been devoted to training in your organisation –
> or in one with which you are familiar – over the last 12 months? What
> sort of training has been available? To what extent has this training
> supported other aspects of HRM at your place of work?

Employee involvement, information-sharing and employee voice

There are two reasons why information-sharing is essential, according
to Pfeffer. Firstly, open communications about financial performance,
strategy and operational measures conveys a symbolic and substantive
message that employees are trusted as well as reducing the role of the
grapevine in spreading rumours. Secondly, if teamworking is to be successful and employees are to be encouraged to offer ideas, it is essential that they have information upon which to base their suggestions and
know something about the financial context in which their organisation
operates. Information-sharing or employee involvement (EI) appears in
just about every description of, or prescription for, 'best-practice' or
high-commitment HRM. Employee involvement can include downward
communications, upward problem-solving groups and project teams, all
of which are designed to increase the involvement of individual
employees in their workplace. The precise mix of EI techniques depends
upon the circumstances, but a commitment to its philosophy appears to
be the key factor – see Chapter 14.

The range of measures used and the 'flexible' definition of involvement
are potentially confusing. Many of the studies restrict this to downward
communications from management to employees which measure the
frequency of information disclosure (Patterson *et al*, 1997) or the regularity of team-briefing or quality circles (Wood and Albanese, 1995). The
regularity of attitude surveys also features strongly in many of the
studies (eg Huselid, 1995; Hoque, 1999; Guest *et al*, 2000a). Some go
further and enquire about the percentage of employees who receive
training in group problem-solving (Arthur, 1994) or the level at which a
range of decisions is made (Delaney and Huselid, 1996). Wood and de
Menezes (1998) specifically asked whether or not team briefings or
problem-solving groups took place at least once a month. The WERS
survey analysis only included briefing in its estimates if at least 25 per
cent of the time at the meeting was devoted to employee questions and
discussion (Guest *et al*, 2000a: 16). This apparently happens at about
half the workplaces, and a similar proportion had administered an attitude survey during the previous three years.

Again, the range of proxies used is so wide that it is difficult to compare
results across these studies and arrive at any firm conclusions about
the importance of information-sharing and EI to high-commitment HRM.
The fact that EI is often little more than a cascade of information from

management to employees means that any meaningful employee contribution is unlikely. Indeed, one of the objectives of schemes such as team briefing is to reinforce the supervisor's role as an information-disseminator who adapts messages to suit specific operational requirements. This one-way version of information-sharing – rather than being perceived as educative, empowering and liberating as the terminology might imply – could more easily be interpreted instead as indoctrinating, emasculating and controlling (Marchington and Wilkinson, 2000).

Only two authors (Huselid, 1995; Roche, 1999) specifically include voice as an aspect of best-practice HRM, but it seems essential that employees should have the opportunity to express their grievances openly and independently, in addition to being able to contribute to management decision-making on task-related issues. Employee voice may be achieved through trade union representation and collective bargaining as well as through formally-established grievance and disputes procedures, but in addition it could be through speak-up schemes which offer employees protection if their complaints are taken badly by managers (Marchington et al, 2001). Such a stance can be reinforced by 'symbolic egalitarianism' (Pfeffer, 1994: 48, and see the section on 'harmonisation' below), but these are insufficient in themselves without a firm commitment to employees having an independent voice. Employees can also articulate their voice through partnerships between employers and trade unions – see Chapter 14.

Self-managed teams/teamworking

This practice has become more prevalent over the last decade for a variety of reasons, not least as a way of pooling ideas and improving work processes in response to Japanese competition. It is now identified by most employers as fundamental to organisational success (Marchington, 1999). It is one of the key attributes that employers look for in new recruits, something asked for in references, and it even plays a part in courses organised for school students. Teamwork is typically seen as leading to better decision-making and the achievement of more creative solutions (Pfeffer, 1998: 76). Evidence suggests that employees who work in teams generally report higher levels of satisfaction and are more motivated than their counterparts working under more 'traditional' regimes (Wilkinson et al, 1997; Edwards and Wright, 1998; Geary and Dobbins, 2001).

The range of measures used by researchers to assess teamworking has been rather narrower than those used to assess many of the other 'best practices'. Generally, it refers to the proportion of (production) workers in teams (MacDuffie, 1995), the use of formal teams (Patterson et al, 1997; Guest et al, 2000a), or the deliberate design of jobs to make use of workers' abilities (Hoque, 1999). However, this measure is not really capable of determining the degree to which these teams actually manage themselves or act as autonomous groups, and much depends upon decisions concerning, *inter alia*, the choice of team leader, responsibility for organising work schedules, and control over quality (Frobel and Marchington, 2001). We see in Chapter 14 that although 65 per cent of workplaces claim to have teamworking, just 5 per cent of these 'teams' could actually be categorised as autonomous groups in which team members have responsibility for managing their own time and appointing their own leaders (Cully *et al*, 1999: 43).

There is also a less optimistic perspective on self-managed teams which suggests that they are intrusive and difficult to implement in practice, and that they serve to strengthen – rather than weaken – management control. It may also be impossible to introduce any realistic version of teamworking when workers are unable to enlarge their jobs to embrace higher-level skills or where there are legal, technical or safety reasons that prevent workers from making certain types of decision. Moreover, the prospect of teamworking is limited where the rotation of a range of low-level jobs means that one boring job is merely swapped for another boring job on a regular basis. In situations such as these, teamworking may only serve to make work more stressful and intrusive, and add nothing to the skills or initiative which workers are able to deploy. Although these criticisms of self-managed teams can be seen as indicating failures of implementation, some analysts see this form of organisation as potentially flawed because it gives the *impression* of control without devolving any real power or influence. Barker (1993: 408), for example, suggests that self-managing teams produce 'a form of control more powerful, less apparent, and more difficult to resist than that of the former bureaucracy' because the locus of control shifts from management to workers – what he terms 'concertive control'. The consequence of this is that peer pressure and rational rules combine to 'create a new iron cage whose bars are almost invisible to the workers it incarcerates'.

> What is your experience of working in teams? Do you think that peer pressure is more likely to generate better performance than supervisory control? Is teamworking automatically 'positive' in your view?

High compensation contingent on organisational performance

Pfeffer (1998) reckons that there are two elements to this practice – higher-than-average compensation and performance-related reward – although both send a signal to employees that they deserve to be rewarded for superior contributions. To be effective, this needs to be at a level which is in excess of that for comparable workers in other organisations so as to attract and retain high-quality labour. In addition, rewards should reflect different levels of contribution and either be paid along with basic rates of pay or provided through profit-sharing schemes. Despite the extensive criticisms of performance-related pay (see Chapter 16), it is included in all the lists of 'best practice' outlined above. It may be appropriate to include the entire reward package in this HR practice so that it is not restricted to pay alone, and it can then relate to employee contributions to organisational performance – whether on an individual, team, departmental, or establishment-wide basis.

Huselid (1995) includes two measures for this factor: the proportion of the workforce who have access to company incentive schemes, and the proportion whose performance appraisals are used to determine their compensation. MacDuffie (1995) refers to contingent compensation. The UK studies also focus on merit or performance pay. Wood and de Menezes (1998) enquired about merit pay and profit sharing, Guest *et al* (2000a) included performance-related pay for non-managerial staff, and Hoque (1999) asked about merit pay and appraisal schemes for all staff. Not surprisingly, the proportion of workplaces covered by these sorts of arrangement were rather less widespread in the public sector than in the private (Guest *et al*, 2000a: 16). Surprisingly, given the degree of practitioner interest in incentive pay schemes, about two-thirds of the respondents to the CIPD survey (Guest *et al*, 2000b: 16) said that their organisations did not make use of individual performance-related pay for their non-managerial employees.

Reduction of status differences/harmonisation

Symbolic manifestations of egalitarianism have been rather more common in Japanese companies than is typical in other organisations. They are meant to convey messages to manual workers and lower-grade office staff that they are valuable assets who deserve to be treated in a way similar to their senior colleagues. It is also seen as a method of encouraging employees to offer ideas within an 'open' management culture. This can be seen through egalitarian symbols, such as staff uniforms, shared canteen and car-parking facilities, but it is also underpinned by the harmonisation of many terms and conditions of employment – such as holidays, sick-pay schemes, pensions, and hours of work. The principal point behind moves to single status and harmonisation, as we see in Chapter 17, is that it seeks to break down artificial barriers between different groups of staff, so encouraging and supporting teamworking and flexibility. Extending employee share ownership to the workforce as a whole is a further way in which status differences can be reduced, typically through schemes under which staff are allocated shares according to some predetermined formula. Pfeffer (1998: 38) argues that 'Employee ownership, effectively implemented, can align the interests of employees with those of shareholders by making employees shareholders too.' He also comments that firms with high shareholder returns also often have some form of employee ownership – this aspect of reward policy is considered in more detail in Chapter 16.

The proxies used for harmonisation and the reduction of status differentials are also wide and variable. For example, Wood and de Menezes (1998) ask about whether or not any employees have to 'clock in' to work, and about the existence of employee share schemes and welfare facilities/fringe benefits. Hoque's (1999) questions relate very broadly to harmonisation and single status. Guest *et al* (2000a and 2000b) vary between the highly specific (harmonised holiday entitlements for all staff) through to whether or not the organisation has a formal commitment to achieving single status. Over 80 per cent of the organisations in the CIPD survey (Guest *et al*, 2000b) claimed to have harmonised holidays, and just under a half reckoned to have a formal commitment to single status. A majority of the hotels sampled by Hoque also reckoned that they were well on the way to harmonised terms and conditions.

Table 20   The extent of high-commitment HR practices in the public and private sectors (data drawn from WERS 1998)

Human resource practice	Percentage of workplaces with this practice in place	
	Public sector	Private sector
Use of performance test for selection	58	44
Preference for internal candidates in selection	16	30
Standard induction programme for new recruits	80	76
40% or more received formal job training in last year	68	37
Employees have a lot of variety in their work	52	41
40% or more work in formally designated teams	54	40
At least 25% of the time at meetings is devoted to employee questions	63	49
40% or more take part in problem-solving group	28	16
Attitude survey in last three years	54	40
Formal appraisals for 40% or more of non-managerial staff	77	87
Formal grievance procedure in place	100	90
All employees have standard contracts	91	79
Formal policy on equal opportunities	97	66
Family-friendly policy	55	17
Job security guarantee	15	5
Performance-related pay for non-managerial staff	20	38
All-employee share-ownership scheme	n/a	25

Source: Guest *et al*, 2001a, p16

Table 20 shows clearly that some of these practices are relatively widespread in UK organisations. For example, a very sizeable proportion of the workplaces surveyed for WERS (Guest *et al*, 2000a) have grievance procedures in place, have a formal policy on equal opportunities, make extensive use of appraisals for a large percentage of their non-managerial staff, and have a standard induction programme for all recruits. These features are especially marked in the public sector. Around half of all workplaces use performance tests, provide some degree of formal training, engage in teamworking and administer attitude surveys. On the other hand, hardly any offer job security guarantees, only a small number have problem-solving groups for a sizeable proportion of the workforce, and not many of the private sector firms have a family-friendly policy or an all-employee share-ownership scheme. The CIPD survey by Guest *et al* (2000b: 37) reports different figures, but the conclusion is much the same – that is, 'human resource practices are not well embedded in a majority of workplaces'. Moreover, few of these workplaces 'have put in place a coherent range of practices of the sort commonly associated with "high-commitment" or "high-performance" HRM'.

This is disturbing because, when considered from a positive stance, high-commitment HR practices are very appealing in that they offer the prospect of a more pleasant and stimulating working environment than might be experienced in traditional 'Taylorist' regimes. For example, the provision of employment security is attractive, the opportunity to earn above-average wages and to be rewarded for performance is enticing, and the chance to gain extensive levels of training is highly desirable. Most attitude surveys have shown for years that employees would like to have more information about their organisation and a chance to contribute to and influence decisions that affect their working lives, as well as to remove status differences between separate categories of workers. Selective hiring is less obvious as a source of direct benefit to employees, although it might reduce the likelihood of having to work alongside what might be seen as incapable or ineffective co-workers. In addition, delayed recruitment or the use of temporaries instead of permanent staff might enhance the employment security of those permanent staff in the event of a downturn. Put together – especially in comparison with the 'bleak house' policies described by a number of authors – best-practice HRM seems very attractive. However, as we have also seen, digging beneath the surface implies that some of these 'best practices' may not be quite as appealing in reality.

Look at Table 20 and compare your own organisation – or one with which you are familiar – against the 17 HR practices outlined there. Develop a business case arguing for an increase in the range of practices used at your workplace.

Bundles of human resource practices

It should be clear from the previous section that there are potential links between these high-commitment HR practices. For example, employees are more likely to welcome involvement and information-sharing if their future employment is seen as relatively secure and their workplace is seen as relatively status-free. Equally, they are more likely to show an interest in teamworking if their efforts are rewarded with performance-related incentives, share ownership, and access to training opportunities. Similarly, if sufficient care has been taken at the recruitment and selection stage, new recruits are more likely to adopt flexible working practices and welcome teamworking, as well as be striving for internal promotion in the future. In isolation, or without the support of a strong organisational culture, each of these practices can easily be dismissed as nothing more than a short-term fad or fashion. Success is rather more likely in the context of a long-term, integrated and comprehensive philosophy of high-commitment HRM.

A key point about best practice HRM is that individual practices can not be implemented effectively in isolation, and that combining practices into a coherent bundle is what matters (MacDuffie, 1995). There is certainly theoretical support for the notion that bundles of HR practices should operate more effectively when combined together. For example, it could be argued that extensive training is essential for self-managed teams to run effectively, or that higher-than-average rewards are likely to have a positive impact on numbers of applications for jobs. An employer may feel more inclined to promise employment security if selective hiring has taken place, self-managed teams are extensive throughout the organisation, and rewards are contingent upon performance. Wood and de Menezes (1998: 485) find an 'identifiable pattern to the use of high-commitment HR practices' and confirm that they are being used in conjunction with each other. Similarly, despite finding a low take-up of the high-commitment model across his sample of Irish workplaces, Roche (1999: 669) notes that 'organisations with a relatively high degree of integration of human resource strategy into business strategy are very much more likely to adopt commitment-oriented bundles of HRM practices'.

Guest (1997: 271) categorises previous attempts to examine internal fit across HR practices into three distinct groups. First, there are criterion-specific studies, such as that by Pfeffer, which outline a number of 'best practices' and suggest that the closer organisations get to this list the better their performance is likely to be. The danger with such universalist approaches is that they ignore potentially significant differences between organisations, sectors and countries, and posit a particular model – in this case, the US model – as the one to be followed. With this approach, the principal job is to detect the bundle that seems to work and then get all organisations to apply this without deviation. Second, there are two sets of criterion-free categories, 'fit as Gestalt' and 'fit as bundles'. In the case of the former, it is assumed that the synergies are achievable only with the adoption of *all* these practices, and that if one is missing the whole effect will be lost. These approaches are termed 'multiplicative', and it is assumed that the whole is greater than the sum of its parts. In this scenario, an organisation that adopted a majority of the practices would be no better off than one that adopted none of them because the chain tying together the different elements of HRM would be broken. By contrast, bundles are 'additive'. Generally, the more practices that are in place the better, so long as some distinctive core exists. In other words, it may be possible to adopt a large number of high-commitment HR practices and ignore others, but still gain from the interactive effects of those that are in place. Questions then arise as to how many practices are needed to make a difference, and from what areas of HRM these are to be drawn. As we see in the section on HRM and performance later in this chapter, much of Guest *et al*'s recent work has differentiated between organisations on the basis of how many HR practices they use. Their analysis of the WERS data led them to conclude that 'despite trying a variety of approaches and combinations, we could not find any coherent pattern of bundles of practices in the private or the public sectors. The only combination that made any sense was a straightforward count of all the practices' (Guest *et al*, 2000a: 15). Provided a certain minimum number of practices are in place, it is likely that high-commitment HRM will be found in a range of different areas of practice – such as selection, training, EI and harmonisation.

It is assumed that contradictions between 'best practice' in one area and 'worst practice' in another will undermine the package as a whole. Employees, it is argued, soon notice differences between employment practices, and are quick to spot inconsistencies between policy statements and workplace practice. There have certainly been many occasions when a high-profile cultural change programme, for example, which majors on learning and development as a key principle, has been undermined by the announcement of massive redundancies. Similarly, it has not been unknown for an organisation to introduce a new set of EI policies without first consulting employees about its shape. More generally, Wood and de Menezes (1998: 487) note that most studies indicate a lack of consistency, reporting fragmentation, a 'pick-and-mix' approach to managing human resources, *ad hoc*ism, pragmatism and short-termism, rather than the deployment of consistent, integrated and long-term packages of HRM. Truss *et al* (1997: 66–7) sum this up by stating that their research 'found little evidence of any deliberate or realised coherence between HR activities. For instance, one HR officer commented that the firm could be recruiting someone in one department and laying-off someone with a similar profile in another.' Moreover, they saw no evidence of any coherence among HR activities in different parts of the organisation, and although the language of the soft HRM model was in evidence, so too was that of the hard model – emphasising financial control. Perhaps the lack of any sizeable take-up of these HR practices should not surprise us. Pfeffer suggests that even smart organisations often do 'dumb things', failing to learn from other examples or being driven by criteria which are ultimately wide of the mark.

> Compile a list of the HR practices used by your own organisation and assess whether or not these combine with or contradict each other. Then, check with fellow students whether the same issues have arisen in their assessment of a different organisation, and work out why there are similarities or differences in your conclusions.

Although the principle of bundling together HR practices may appear sound, what happens if the achievement of one of these practices contradicts with or undermines (some of) the others? For example, employers may make employment security conditional on an agreement that pay rates can be reduced in order to maintain the guarantee through lean times. Selective hiring on the basis of future potential rather than immediate contribution may require existing staff to work harder and longer in order to induct new staff. This may be acceptable at the margins, but if the profit-sharing or performance-related component of rewards is a significant proportion of overall income, then it could be problematic (see Pfeffer, 1998: 84). Equally, if staff routinely have to commit to long working hours, their own quality of life can be adversely affected. Presumably, there is a point at which the value of employment security is outweighed by the need for a certain minimum salary or work–life balance. Individual employees are offered security, but at a price in terms of flexibility in working hours, locations and tasks.

One of the many advantages of self-managed teams, according to Pfeffer (1998: 77), is that they can remove a supervisory level from the hierarchy:

> *Eliminating layers of management by instituting self-managing teams saves money. Self-managed teams can also take on tasks previously done by specialised staff, thus eliminating excess personnel.*

It is not self-evident that the personnel who are 'eliminated' are actually found other jobs, so the implementation of self-managed teams – even if it does empower certain groups of workers – may result in others' losing their employment security. There are further potential contradictions between the different practices. For example, teamworking may be undermined by the use of individual performance-related pay. It is also hard to square the notion of an organisation without major status differentials with one in which senior managers are able to collect

substantial bonuses because their pay is linked with company performance. In other words, although there is strong support for bundling – in
one form or another – it is also clear that contradictions and tensions
may arise between the different HR practices in the bundle.

Human resource management and performance

Analysing the links between HRM – and in particular, high-commitment
HRM – and performance has now become a major research area.
Originally, this stemmed from the USA, but latterly there have been several studies in the UK, most notably by David Guest and his colleagues.
Before reviewing their work in more detail, it is worth mentioning some
of the earlier studies that first claimed to have established a link
between HRM and performance. Huselid (1995) drew his conclusions
from a survey of nearly 1,000 US organisations. He divided high-commitment work practices into two broad groupings – employee skills and
organisational structures, and employee motivation. The former
included items concerned with the proportion of workers taking part in
attitude surveys, the number of hours training received in the previous
year, and the proportion of workers required to take an employment
test as part of the selection process. The latter included items such as
the proportion of the workforce with performance appraisals linked to
compensation and the number of applicants for those posts where
recruitment took place most frequently. Output measures included
labour turnover, productivity and corporate financial performance.
Huselid (1995: 667) concluded that 'the magnitude of the returns for
investments in [what he calls] high-performance work practices is substantial. A 1 per cent standard deviation increase in such practices is
associated with a 7.05 per cent decrease in labour turnover and, on a
per-employee basis, 27,044 US dollars more in sales and 18,641 US dollars and 3,814 US dollars more in market value and profits respectively.'

The results from the survey by Patterson *et al* (1997) published by the
Institute of Personnel and Development, were quoted widely by the
media and put forward as evidence for the importance of HRM as a
driver of, and contributor to, improved performance. The research was
based on longitudinal studies of 67 UK manufacturers that were predominantly single-site and single-product operations. It has been claimed
– on the basis of this research – that HRM had a greater impact on productivity and profits than a range of other factors including strategy,
research and development, and quality. For example, it was argued that
17 per cent of the variation in company profitability could be explained
by HRM practices and job design, as opposed to just 8 per cent from
research and development, 2 per cent from strategy, and 1 per cent
from both quality and technology. Similar results were indicated for productivity. The authors are currently extending this research to provide a
longer time-frame over which to assess the HRM-performance link.
Other researchers have also examined the links between best-practice

Table 21   A selection of major studies examining the links between HRM and performance

Author (year)	Location, nature of sample and industry, nature of study
Arthur (1994)	USA: 30 mini-mills in the steel industry Cross-sectional study
Huselid (1995)	USA: 968 US-owned firms with more than 100 employees Cross-sectional study
MacDuffie (1995)	USA: 62 automotive plants Cross-sectional study
Delery and Doty (1996)	USA: 114 banks Cross-sectional study
Youndt *et al* (1996)	USA: 97 manufacturing plants Longitudinal study
Applebaum *et al* (2000)	USA: 40 manufacturing plants in steel, apparel and medical electronics and imaging Cross-sectional study
Patterson *et al* (1997)	UK: 67 manufacturing firms employing fewer than 1,000 Longitudinal study
Wood and de Menezes (1998)	UK: use of data from WIRS (1990) and Employers' Manpower and Skills Practice Survey – approximately 2,000 workplaces with more than 25 employees, all sectors Cross-sectional study
Guest *et al* (2000a)	UK: use of data from WERS (1998) – approximately 2,000 workplaces with more than 25 employees, all sectors Cross-sectional study
Guest *et al* (2000b)	UK: 835 private sector companies with more than 50 employees, interviews with HR professionals and CEOs Cross-sectional study

Sources: Richardson and Thomson, 2000; Wood, 1999a

HRM and various outcome measures, and there have been comprehensive reviews of these studies by Richardson and Thomson (1999), Wood (1999a) and Boxall and Purcell (2002). Guest (2001) has also written a short paper that addresses the principal issues involved in these quantitative studies. Some of the best-known studies are outlined in Table 21.

On the basis of these studies, and in particular those by David Guest, there have been some forceful claims about the impact of high-commitment HRM on performance. Two recent reports by the CIPD (2001d, 2001e) argue that the economic and business case for good people management has now been proved. One notes (2001d: 4) that:

> *more than 30 studies carried out in the UK and the USA since the early 1990s leave no room to doubt that there is a correlation between people management and business performance, that the relationship is positive, and that it is cumulative. The more and more effective the practices, the better the result.*

This leads the CIPD (2001e: 2) to argue that:

> *senior personnel practitioners now agree that the case for people management and development making an impact on organisational performance is not in dispute. What they are more interested in is establishing the best means to make that impact.*

A number of articles in *People Management* published during 2000 and 2001 – under the heading of 'HR and the bottom line' reinforced this view (see Caulkin, 2001, for example). From a US perspective, Pfeffer (1998: 306) agrees that best-practice HRM has the potential to have a positive impact on all organisations, irrespective of sector, size or country, but he doubts if senior managers will actually take this advice. However, 'for organisations that have leaders possessing both insight and courage, the evidence demonstrates that the economic returns can be enormous'.

Although Guest and his colleagues published the results analysing two separate data sets on the links between HRM/employment relations and performance during 2000, we focus here on the CIPD survey – rather than WERS – because it takes into account some estimate of whether or not HR practices are effective. This seems to make a difference, as we see later. Although it varies slightly between the publications and with the detailed analyses, the broad theoretical framework guiding the analysis is outlined in Figure 7.5 below (Guest *et al*, 2000b: 5). Broadly, this proposes a path model linking together the business and HR strategies at the left-hand side of the framework (the input in positivist terms) with performance outcomes on the right-hand side. These include indicators such as financial performance, quality and productivity, as well as employee outcomes in terms of competence, commitment and flexibility. The overall framework is glued together by a number of HR practices covering all the usual areas of people management and development, as well as by HR effectiveness. The HR practices are training and development, recruitment and selection, appraisal, financial rewards, job design, communication, job security and harmonisation. The

Figure 5   Model of the link between HRM and performance

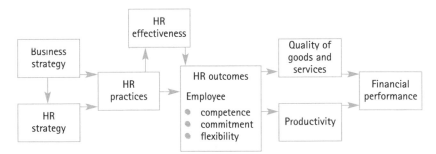

Source: Guest *et al*, 2000b, p5

inclusion of a factor assessing effectiveness is particularly important because this allows for some evaluation of how well the practices are working, in addition to whether or not they are actually in place in organisations.

The Guest *et al* study is based on the findings from telephone interviews with 610 managers responsible for HRM and 462 chief executive officers from a cross-section of companies in the UK. The interviews were conducted in July 1999. Matched pairs of HR professionals and chief executives were interviewed in 237 organisations, and in total responses were available from over 800 different organisations. In order to assess the sorts of strategy used by these companies, the questions allowed for differentiation between a cost-reduction approach (termed 'customer focus') and a quality-enhancement/innovation strategy – see Chapter 8 for amplification of these terms. The sample tended towards a quality-enhancement rather than a cost-reduction strategy. Whereas just 10 per cent of the organisations felt that being the lowest-cost producer in the industry was what really mattered, nearly half felt that offering a range of specialised products was the crucial factor, while 62 per cent regarded high quality after sales service as critical (Guest *et al*, 2000b: 12). There were some differences of emphasis about the extent of integration between business strategy and HR strategy, with the managing directors more convinced than their HR counterparts that the strategies were integrated. It was revealing that although 70 per cent of the chief executives felt that their business strategy relied a lot on people as a source of competitive advantage, considerably less than half felt that 'people issues' were more important than financial or marketing issues (Guest *et al*, 2000b: 14).

We have already considered the range of HR practices deemed central to best-practice HRM, but it is worth bringing the results on extensiveness together in order to assess which practices are most widely used. Some of the findings merely reinforce what we already know from other surveys, but some are surprising. There seems to be a systematic attempt to provide staff with information on business and performance issues, the vast majority claim to have harmonised holiday entitlements in place, and over half of all the companies said that all non-managerial employees received formal appraisals. Rather more surprisingly, about half the respondents reported that new staff were given at least one month's training in their first year of employment, and almost a quarter were trained in subsequent years. In addition, 70 per cent of these organisations apparently provide all recruits with realistic job previews. Employment security – regarded by some observers as essential to underpin high-commitment HRM – seems to be rare among these companies, more than half of them reporting that they had made compulsory redundancies in the last three years while about a third had made these on a voluntary basis. Individual performance-related pay was rather less widespread across this sample than is generally

Table 22   The nature and distribution of HR practices in the CIPD sample

The nature of the HR practice	The distribution of the HR practice
Training days given in the first year of employment to a new recruit	47% of organisations claimed to offer at least one month's training during the first year, 2% said that none was provided.
Training days per year for experienced employees	23% of organisations claimed to offer at least one month's training each year, 13% said that none was provided.
Deliberate attempt to provide a realistic job preview, including the negative aspects	70% of organisations said that they did this as part of recruitment and selection.
Percentage of employees given a performance, ability or personality test during selection	17% of organisations said that this was given to all recruits, 53% to none of them.
Percentage of non-managerial employees having regular performance appraisal	54% of organisations said that all employees received this, 23% none of them.
Percentage of non-managerial employees receiving feedback on performance from multiple sources (eg customers)	41% of organisations said that all their employees received this, 29% said none of them did.
Percentage of non-managerial employees covered by system of individual performance-related pay	13% of organisations said that this covered all staff, 66% none of them.
Percentage of employees eligible for deferred profit-related payments or bonuses	9% of organisations said that all their employees were eligible, 85% said none of them was.
Percentage of employees with flexible job descriptions	32% of organisations said that all of their employees had these, 28% said none of them did.
Percentage of employees qualified to perform more than one job	15% of organisations said all of them were; 48% said that more than half their employees were; 4% said that none was.
Percentage of employees regularly participating in work improvement teams	14% of organisations said more than half did this, 46% said that none of them did.
Percentage of employees regularly participating in problem-solving groups	19% of organisations said that more than half did this, 32% said that none of them did.
Information on firm's performance targets is provided for all employees	60% of organisations said information was made available, 40% that it was not.
Information on business plans is regularly provided for all employees	43% of organisations said information was made available, 57% said that it was not.
Compulsory redundancies have occurred in the last three years	55% of organisations said that they had occurred, 45% that they had not.
Voluntary redundancies have occurred in the past three years	34% of organisations said that they had occurred, 66% that they had not.
Formal commitment to achieve single status	47% of organisations said that there was a formal commitment to this, 53% that there was not.
Harmonised holiday entitlement for all employees	83% of organisations said that there was such an entitlement, 17% that there was not.

reported, two-thirds of these organisations indicating that none of their staff was a recipient of a merit-type payment. Similarly, less than 10 per cent of these companies made profit-related bonus arrangements available to all staff and teamworking was not particularly well established. A summary of the responses is presented in Table 22.

Taking the full sample of 610 organisations, not one of them has more than 15 of the 18 practices in place, and under 2 per cent use more than three-quarters of the list. At the other extreme, 20 per cent have less than one-quarter of the practices in place. The median figure is six practices, and nearly half the sample operates with between five and seven practices. In short, these results indicate a relatively low take-up of high-commitment HR practices across the UK (Guest *et al*, 2000b: 17).

Even if organisations do operate a wide range of HR practices, that does not mean they are applied effectively or that they have any impact on workers or managers. For example, although it is important to know whether or not an employer makes use of regular appraisals or provides information about performance targets, this gives us no clue as to whether the appraisals make any difference or the information is supplied in a meaningful and timely fashion. That is why measures of effectiveness are so useful. Managing directors and HR professionals were asked to assess the effectiveness of each practice area, and in most cases they were judged to be either slightly or highly effective. The results are outlined in Table 23. It can be seen that there are relatively small differences between the respondents, the HR professionals being

Table 23   The effectiveness of HR practices, according to managing directors and to HR professionals

HR practice	Managing directors' assessment		HR professionals' assessment	
	Quite effective	*Highly effective*	*Quite effective*	*Highly effective*
Recruitment and selection	41	13	41	12
Training and development	40	17	39	17
Appraisal/performance management	34	14	27	11
Job design	31	7	27	4
Communication, consultation, EI	43	23	39	12
Financial flexibility	24	9	22	6
Harmonisation	32	20	34	17
Employment security/labour market practices	39	23	45	26

Source: Guest *et al*, 2000b, p19

slightly more circumspect about the effectiveness of the practices. The most positive responses were in relation to employment security, which is strange, bearing in mind the fact that over half of the sample had made compulsory redundancies during the previous three years. The HR practices deemed to be least effective were those related to financial flexibility, job design and appraisal, and it is notable that the HR professionals felt they were less effective (Guest *et al*, 2000b: 18–19).

The HR performance outcomes in this framework are concerned with commitment, quality and employee contribution, measured by responses to questions about employee motivation and identification with the organisation's core values, and by replies from managers asked to determine whether or not employees came up with novel and innovative ideas. Flexibility was assessed in terms of the responsiveness of employees to changes in their work environment, and their willingness and ability to move between jobs in different departments. The overall view is highly positive, although we must remember that these responses are made by senior managers *on behalf of* employees rather than by the employees themselves (Guest *et al*, 2000b: 22–3). Other information was collected on levels of labour turnover and absence, as well as on the number of grievances raised and the incidence of industrial action. Indicators of wider performance outcomes were also collected, and in this study respondents were asked about comparisons with other organisations in the same industry. Not surprisingly, both managing directors and HR professionals felt that their own organisations fared rather better than did their competitors'. For example, in terms of financial performance, 55 per cent of managing directors and HR professionals felt that their own company was better than average, whereas just 9 per cent and 6 per cent, respectively, felt it was below average (Guest *et al*, 2000b: 25). It is interesting to note that both sets of managers were slightly less positive about their comparative performance in relation to HR practices and labour productivity – although even on these counts, they still believed they were well above the industry average.

Guest *et al* (2000b: 27) conclude their study by stating that the link between high-commitment HRM and performance is endorsed very strongly. It is clear that the link is not direct but is mediated through the apparent relationship between the range of HR practices and employee outcomes such as employee commitment, quality and flexibility. In short, the greater the number of HR practices employed, the higher the levels of commitment, quality and flexibility. These, in turn, are related to higher levels of reported productivity and quality. Finally, productivity and quality of goods and services are associated with higher estimates of comparative financial performance. HR effectiveness – both of the practices themselves and of the personnel department – increase the strength of the relationship between HRM and performance, again because of its impact on employee commitment, contribution and flexibility. In short, the more HR practices that are used, and the more effectively they appear to be used, the better is the organisational performance.

Find a copy of the latest survey results analysing the links between HRM and performance, and prepare a presentation to give to your senior management team (or its equivalent) on the benefits that can be gained from investing in high-commitment HRM. In order to get hold of an up-to-date study you may need to search for sources other than Guest *et al*, but that will provide a good grounding and framework.

Alternative interpretations of the HRM-performance link

Persuasive as they are, findings from the studies supporting a link between high-commitment HRM and performance have not escaped criticism, including some by the authors themselves. For example, Guest *et al* (2000b: 27–8) remind readers that they should be very cautious when interpreting the results of cross-sectional analysis, especially when scores are dependent on self-reporting. It is impossible to be certain whether or not 'good' HRM has led to improvements in performance or whether financial success has paved the way for the implementation of capital-enhancing HR practices. There are other concerns that require us to exercise caution in asserting that the link between HRM and performance is proven:

- questions about which HR practices are included in the bundle of high commitment management

- variation in the proxies used for HR practices and for the measures of performance

- the dangers of relying on self-reported scores, especially where they are made by managers who lack specialist expertise or who make judgements about employee responses.

As previously mentioned, one of the problems with the various lists of 'best-practice' HRM is that there are inconsistencies between the studies, some of them ignoring one factor but including others. For example, despite the importance attached to employment security by Pfeffer, this is not included in quite a number of the other lists (eg Delaney and Huselid, 1996; Youndt *et al*, 1996; Patterson *et al*, 1997; Wood and de Menezes, 1998). Equally, whereas other authors include some measure of employee voice other than that achieved through self-managed teams and employee involvement, Pfeffer does not. Perhaps this does not matter if we are clear as to *why* certain HR practices should be included or excluded – but that does not seem to be the case. The lists seem to have been developed on the basis of individual preference, by looking at what other researchers have used, or by constructing groupings of practices on the basis of factor analysis and then attempting to impose some theoretical justification for this *post facto*. Huselid (1995: 645–7) uses two groups of practices, entitled 'employee skills and organisational structures' – which includes job design, enhanced selectivity, formal training, various forms of participation, and profit sharing – and 'employee motivation' – which comprises performance appraisal linked to compensation and a focus on merit in promotion decisions. It seems strange that participation and profit sharing should be in the first grouping rather than the second, given the supposed importance of these as techniques that enhance employee motivation. Patterson *et al* (1997) also emerge with two groups of practices, subtitled 'acquisition and development of employee skills' and 'job design', and on this occasion, participation and teamworking find their way into the second grouping rather than the first.

One way out of this problem is to use models derived from the resource-based view of the firm (Barney, 1991). In applying this to HRM, Boxall (1996: 66–7) makes the useful distinction between *human capital advantage* and *human process advantage*. The former is concerned with 'recruiting and retaining outstanding people through capturing a stock of exceptional human talent, latent with productive possibilities', whereas the latter may be understood as 'a function of causally ambiguous, socially complex, historically evolved processes such as learning, co-operation and innovation'. In other words, while the former is designed to ensure that the best people (in our view, those who are most appropriate for the circumstances rather than the most able in general) are recruited and retained, the latter is necessary in order to ensure that they work together effectively. Following Barney's development of the concept of inimitability, it is the latter that is hardest to imitate, largely because it is complex, often unarticulated, and is the product of many different sets of people in organisations over a lengthy period of time – that is, it is path-dependent. This opens up the potential for a model of HRM that identifies a series of objectives – such as attracting and retaining the best candidates, managing performance, or providing the environment for synergistic endeavour. These can then be linked to a series of HR practices that are essentially interdependent (eg effective selection techniques, opportunities for training and development, employee involvement and voice, reward systems), but can be tailored to different organisational priorities. The resource-based view of the firm is discussed in the next chapter (Boxall and Purcell, 2002).

A further criticism of the quantitative studies is that they make use of a range of different proxies for the same HR practice – see above for specific details. There are problems with the nature of these proxies. For example, some are straight yes/no or absence/presence -type measures, whereas others ask for the percentage of the workforce covered by a particular aspect of HRM – such as performance-related pay. In some cases, the proportions vary between studies with, say

25 per cent in one and 90 per cent in another. Worse still, they can vary within a particular study between different items. Differences in the way in which practices are counted as present or absent have a major effect on the construction of the overall bundle, and it is rare for there to be explicit information on why certain levels have been set. Notably, Guest *et al* (2000b) do openly explain why they went for a figure of 90 per cent in some of their questions. More seriously, as we have already mentioned, the mere absence or presence of a practice is irrelevant because what matters is how it is used. Take the example of grievance procedures, one of the HR practices used in the analysis based on the WERS study (Guest *et al*, 2000a). These are almost universally employed in organisations, so a proxy based around absence or presence tells us nothing about how people take up grievances, how many they take up, and whether they regard the processes as open and reasonable. Arguably, this is a more useful way in which to differentiate between organisations. A similar point arises in relation to days spent on training. Knowing that the typical employee is trained for about five days per annum is hardly evidence of high-commitment HRM if those employees are trained merely in how to conform to strict rules and procedures – as sometimes happens in call centres (Sturdy *et al*, 2001).

Potential problems also arise when compiling scores of high-commitment HRM in deciding whether or not each practice should be weighted equally. This is clearly a problem where there are more measures of one particular item than of others – for example, as often occurs with employee involvement. It is possible in this situation that the overall measure gives too much weight to the one factor compared with others. Moreover, what happens when, as in the WERS analysis, one practice is widely used – such as a formal statement on equal opportunities – and another, such as job security, is rarely provided? Do these deserve to be equally weighted, or is the relatively rare practice something that could provide organisations that offer it with an opportunity to stand out and achieve competitive advantage?

One of the major problems with the survey technique is that it is difficult to know which practices are likely to have a greater impact on any one organisation. In any case, the impact is likely to vary depending on the context. For example, workers in a research laboratory may regard employment security as a critically important component in their decision on whether or not to co-operate in teams, whereas those in a sales environment may feel that the opportunity for performance-related pay is what makes a difference for them. A straight count of HR practices, as undertaken by Guest *et al* in their studies may get us around the immediate problem, but it does not overcome the wider issue that the list of HR practices is pre-defined and can not be adjusted during a survey. Other problems arise with the measures used for performance, shown graphically by the fact that so many respondents feel that their organisations are doing better than the industry average. Some of the other intermediate employee outcome measures are simple to quantify but less easy to interpret. For example, it may be important for an organisation to have low labour turnover or absence levels compared with the average for the industry as a whole, but there are questions about whether or not a zero figure is actually indicative of good employment relations. In the case of labour turnover, work may be so pleasant that very few people ever want to leave, but if productivity levels are poor, then this is hardly evidence of high-commitment HRM. Similarly, absence levels may be low because people are scared to take a day off for fear of harsh reprisals from management or because they have so much work to do that they feel it is impossible to stay at home even when they are unwell. It is clear that what appears initially to be a technical measurement problem actually obscures rather more serious conceptual weaknesses.

Finally, differences can also arise depending on who completes the questionnaire for a company and the basis of their expertise and commitment in so doing. For obvious reasons, questions used in telephone surveys tend to be those that are capable of an immediate answer that can be coded easily rather than those that require some consideration. As Purcell (1999) notes, this may not get us very far in establishing what factors really make a difference to employee commitment or organisational performance. Further problems arise because personnel specialists, who are often the respondents in these surveys, often lack detailed knowledge about the competitive strategies utilised by their organisations and the proportion of sales derived from these strategies. Anxieties such as these mean that considerable caution is needed when interpreting conclusions from these quantitative studies. At least the Guest *et al* study did overcome a number of these shortcomings by including managing directors and HR professionals in their sample, but they were unable to get opinions from employees themselves.

Having read the above section in this chapter, now read the paper by David Guest in the *International Journal of Human Resource Management*, Vol. 12 (7), 2001, entitled 'Human resource management: when research confronts theory'. Compare and contrast the arguments used, and have a discussion with your colleagues about the value of survey-based research.

In addition, there is also a more radical critique that questions whether or not the findings actually support a link between high-commitment practices and performance, as the interpretation of this material takes for granted. Ramsay *et al* (2000) propose an alternative, labour process explanation that suggests that higher levels of organisational performance are achieved not through 'progressive' employment practices but instead through work intensification. Basically, both the high-commitment and the labour process versions agree that a distinctive set of HR practices is likely to contribute to improved levels of organisational performance, and that employees represent the mediating factor between HR practices and performance. However, as Ramsay *et al* (2000: 505) argue, 'It is at this point that the two approaches part company. The labour process critique holds that while high-performance work systems practices may provide enhancements in discretion, these come to employees at the expense of stress, work intensification and job strain, the latter being a key explanatory factor in improved organisational performance.' The interpretation of the practices and the links is quite different, therefore, mirroring the discussion above when we considered competing versions of specific HR practices such as teamworking.

In order to test this proposition, Ramsay *et al* used the 1998 WERS survey material, focusing in particular on employee outcomes. They also included other factors in their analysis related to job strain and work intensification – measured by questions about the lack of time to complete work, worrying about work outside working hours, and changes in productivity. Their conclusions are at odds with those of the high-commitment school in the sense that they find little support for the notion that positive performance outcomes flow from positive employee outcomes. They suggest that the high-commitment approach has been adopted without sufficient analysis of whether or not employees really do have positive attitudes to such regimes. At the same time, however, they find little support for the labour process interpretation either. Although they acknowledge that lack of support for either model may be due to problems with the methodology, they conclude instead that neither bears much resemblance to reality. This is due to the inability of senior managers to implement strategic thinking – either to treat workers as resourceful humans or as costs to be minimised. Once it is accepted that workers play an active part in the creation and maintenance of HR practices at work, it is likely that any simplistic one-dimensional model will be unable to explain the links between strategy and practice.

> What do workers want from their employment, and does this equate with the high-commitment bundle of practices considered above?

The universal application of best-practice HRM

One of the key features of the Pfeffer (1998: 33–4) argument is that best-practice HRM may be used in any organisation, irrespective of product market situation, industry, or workforce, and evidence is produced from a range of industries and studies which he claims demonstrates the case for 'putting people first'. He notes that the industries in which a 'best-practice' approach has been shown to work:

range from relatively low-technology settings such as apparel manufacture to very high-technology manufacturing processes. The results seem to hold for manufacturing and for service firms. Nothing in the available evidence suggests that the results are country-specific. The effects of high-performance management practices are real, economically significant, and general – and thus should be adopted by your organisation.

Support for this line of argument is provided by the results from several other studies. For example, Huselid (1995: 644) states that 'all else being equal, the use of High-Performance Work Practices and good internal fit should lead to positive outcomes for all types of firms'. He has some confidence in his conclusion because the results are 'consistent across diverse measures of firm performance' and take into account selectivity and simultaneity bias. Delery and Doty (1996: 825), after comparing the universalistic, contingency and configurational perspectives, find 'relatively strong support' for the first of these and some support for the other two. They expand on this by suggesting that 'some human resource practices *always* [our emphasis] have a positive effect on performance'; these were profit sharing, results-oriented appraisals and employment security. There is support from a non-US study as well, Wood and Albanese (1995: 242) agreeing that certain HR practices have a universal effect.

There are criticisms of this view, ranging from minor adjustments through to downright rejection of the case that 'progressive' HR practices can always provide sustained competitive advantage. Youndt *et al* (1996: 837) suggest that 'the universal approach helps researchers to document the benefits of HR across all contexts, *ceteris paribus*, [whereas] the contingency perspective helps us to look more deeply into organisational phenomena to derive more situationally-specific theories and prescriptions for management practice'. Purcell (1999: 36) is particularly sceptical of the claims for universalism, which lead us, he argues, 'down a utopian cul-de-sac'. He stresses that we need to identify 'the circumstances of where and when [high-commitment management] is applied, why some organisations do and some do not adopt HCM, and how some firms seem to have more appropriate human resource systems than others'.

At a conceptual level, however, there are a number of reasons to doubt that best practice is universally applicable (Marchington and Grugulis, 2000). First, it is apparent that the 'best-practice' approach is underpinned by an assumption that employers have the luxury of taking a long-term perspective or that, with a bit of foresight, they could do so. For example, they are encouraged to hire during the lean times when labour markets are less tight rather than seek to recruit when they have a pressing demand for staff and it is harder to attract the type of applicant desired (and desirable). Similarly, employers are advised to invest in employees with non-specific skills who will offer most over the longer term rather than seek to fill posts with staff who can solve immediate needs and no more. It is suggested that employees should be retained during downturns because it will only cost more to rehire them when the market improves – a practice that also ties in with employment security guarantees. Similarly, instead of cutting back on training when times get tough or cash is in short supply, employers are urged to spend more money on training during the lean times because it is easier to release employees from other duties when production schedules are less tight. There are good economic and labour market reasons for employers to do all of these things, but they all depend, to a greater or lesser extent, upon the luxury of a long-term perspective and the prospect of future market growth.

Second, it is rather easier to engage in this list of high-commitment HR practices when labour costs form a low proportion of controllable costs. In capital-intensive operations it probably does not make sense to cut back on essential staff who have highly specific and much-needed skills – say, in a pharmaceutical or chemical plant or with research scientists. When labour costs are more significant, as in many service sector organisations, for example, it is much more difficult for managers to persuade financiers that there are long-term benefits from investments in human capital. It is unlikely, given their previous behaviour, that bankers and lenders in Britain will perceive the benefits of taking a strategic perspective on human resources and sacrifice short-term gains for longer-term accumulation. In contrast, it is immensely difficult to persuade employers to adopt a 'best-practice' approach if they operate in situations where labour costs are sizeable, and where it is difficult to increase pay rates or offer training when resources are constrained. Moreover, it is unlikely that customers or users will accept inferior levels of service even if it is helping to develop talent over the longer term (eg in the health service, pubs and restaurants).

> Think about whether or not customers really do gain from 'best-practice' HRM, or whether it is just an expensive nicety for people who are prepared and able to pay higher prices.

Third, so much depends upon the categories of staff which employers are trying to recruit. MacDuffie (1995: 199) is often quoted as someone whose research is supportive of the universality argument, but it is apparent from his studies that 'best-practice' HRM may actually be situationally specific. He suggests:

Innovative human resource practices are likely to contribute to improved economic performance only when [our emphasis] *three conditions are met: when employees possess knowledge and skills that managers lack; when employees are motivated to apply this skill and knowledge through discretionary effort; and when the firm's business or production strategy can only be achieved when employees contribute such discretionary effort.*

This seems to indicate clearly that the circumstances under which best-practice HRM will make a difference are quite specific. For example, when employee skills and attributes are essential to achieve organis-ational goals – such as in high-technology industries where work systems and processes cannot be easily codified or overseen by managers and qualified workers are in short supply – it may make considerable economic sense to hoard labour. In many other situations, the time taken to train new staff is relatively short, work performance can be assessed simply and speedily, and there is a supply of substitutable labour readily available. Here, the rationale for arguing that employers should adopt a best-practice approach is hard to sustain. In addition, some jobs are so boring or so unpleasant that it is inconceivable that many people would see employment security, basic training or infor-mation sharing – for example – as any kind of benefit. On the contrary, such employees would undoubtedly resent being expected to take an interest in their organisation beyond routine work performance, and find it stressful and intrusive. In short, the best-practice model may be relatively unattractive or inappropriate in some industries or with cer-tain groups of workers.

Finally, the dramatic growth in 'non-standard' contracts over the past few years has led many commentators to question if 'flexible' employ-ment is compatible with best-practice HRM, and whether or not the latter can be applied to *all* employees in an organisation. As we saw in Chapter 2, the changing nature of the psychological contract has led to worries that employment insecurity is now widespread (Boxall, 1996: 68). Support for this perspective comes from the survey by Gallie *et al* (1998: 124) which indicates that between the mid-1970s and the early 1990s the proportion of people who had experienced a spell of unem-ployment almost trebled across the 20 years from 7 per cent to approximately 20 per cent of the population. Other data presented here and in Chapter 2 also reinforces case study and anecdotal evidence that employees now feel rather more insecure than they did 20 years ago. However, it is also clear that some groups of employees are gain-ing more from best-practice HRM than others. Burgess and Rees (1998: 630) show that the average elapsed job tenure barely changed between the mid-1970s and the early 1990s, 40 per cent of men and 20 per cent of women having worked for the same employer for more than 20 years. Over the last decade, the number of employees with 10 or more years' service has grown, and this has been particularly marked for women. Part-time workers over the age of 30 have also experienced an increase in the rate of long-term employment as well (Doogan, 2001: 423). This suggests that distinctions are arising between long-serving core workers on the one hand – who might have to be nurtured because of their contribution to sustained competitive advantage – and non-core peripheral or subcontracted workers (Purcell, 1999).

CONCLUSION

The focus in this chapter has been on best-practice or high-commitment HRM, and we have examined the way in which HR policies and practices support one another so as to provide coherent and comprehensive human resource bundles. This has led to suggestions that there is one best way in which people management and development should be delivered, and moreover that this has a positive impact on organisational performance. There is currently a good deal of interest in the high-commitment-HRM–performance link, and ideas that a specific bundle of human resource policies and practices is inherently superior and capable of making a major contribution to organisational success in all workplaces. We have reviewed this argument in the chapter, providing alternative and competing interpretations of the research findings, as well as calling for some reflection on whether or not best-practice HRM really can make a difference to bottom-line performance in all workplaces. The appeal of the high-commitment model is obvious in that it supports the case for implementing 'good' people management practices on business grounds – that is, best-practice HRM leads to improved performance. However, there are also strong theoretical and empirical grounds for arguing that high-commitment models cannot be – and are not being – applied in all workplaces and to all groups of staff. Having considered the 'best-practice' school at some length in this chapter, we are now in a position to analyse an alternative – the 'best fit' scenario – in Chapter 8.

Useful reading

BOXALL P. *and* PURCELL J. *Strategy and Human Resource Management.* London, Palgrave. 2002.

CAULKIN S. 'The time is now', *People Management*, 30 August 2001. pp32–34.

GUEST D. 'Human resource management: when research confronts theory', *International Journal of Human Resource Management*, Vol. 12, No. 7. 2001. pp1092–1106.

MARCHINGTON M. *and* GRUGULIS I. ' "Best practice" human resource management: perfect opportunity or dangerous illusion?', *International Journal of Human Resource Management*, Vol. 11, No. 4, 2000. pp905–925.

PFEFFER J. *The Human Equation: Building profits by putting people first.* Boston, Harvard Business School Press. 1998.

PURCELL J. 'The search for best practice and best fit in human resource management: chimera or cul-de-sac?' *Human Resource Management Journal*, Vol. 9, No. 3, 1999. pp26–41.

RAMSAY H., SCHOLARIOS D. *and* HARLEY B. 'Employees and high-performance work systems: testing inside the black box', *British Journal of Industrial Relations*, Vol. 38, No. 4, 2000. pp501–531.

RICHARDSON R. *and* THOMSON M. 'The impact of people management practices on business performance: a literature review', *Issues in People Management*, London, Institute of Personnel and Development. 1999.

WOOD S, 'Human resource management and performance', *International Journal of Management Reviews*. Vol. 1, No. 4, 1999. pp367–413.

Exploring the Links between Business Strategy and HRM

CHAPTER OBJECTIVES

By the end of this chapter, readers should be able to:

- contribute to the choice of appropriate human resource policies that can lead to enhanced organisational and individual performance.

- apply business planning models to benchmark their own employer's approach to HRM against those of other organisations.

- recognise and overcome barriers to the effective implementation of human resource strategies.

In addition, readers should understand and be able to explain:

- competing meanings of the term 'strategy', and their implications for the management and development of people

- links between business strategy and HRM at work

- the nature of the barriers that prevent the achievement of business strategy in employing organisations.

Introduction

We saw in Chapter 7 that it has become commonplace for management gurus to extol the virtues of investing in people and treating employees as the vital component in the achievement of competitive advantage (see, for example, Prahalad, 1995; Ulrich, 1997; Pfeffer, 1998). At one level it is clear that the development of management systems which encourage employees to 'work beyond contract' makes good business sense. Other things being equal, it is likely that committed and motivated employees will provide higher levels of customer service that lead to increased productivity and improved quality. However, there is not a lot that committed and excellent staff can do if the organisation has low-quality products, poor designs and an insufficient investment in technology, or if there are unstable exchange rates, collapsed economies, or political upheavals. Equally, even if senior management believes in 'best-practice' human resource management, this does not guarantee that first-line supervisors have either the skills or the motivation to put it into effect. It was apparent from Chapter 7 that 'best-practice' HRM may not be appropriate for all situations and that, despite the claims, other approaches to people management may have greater success in generating high levels of performance (Hoque, 2000). This brings us neatly onto an analysis of 'best fit' (or contingency and configurational analyses) as an alternative way of looking at HRM and assessing the extent to which there is vertical integration between business strategy and HRM.

Before engaging in that discussion, we provide a very brief resume of 'strategy', drawing on established perspectives and using Whittington's (1993) framework as a way to structure the material. We then move on to consider three different contingency/configurational frameworks – life-cycle models, Schuler's adaptation of Porter, and Delery and Doty's extension of Miles and Snow – so as to examine the links between business strategy and HRM. This is followed by a consideration of resource-based views of HRM and strategy. We also present material showing that employing organisations are beset by political rivalries, departmental splits and functional conflicts that make it difficult to translate broad corporate goals into specific workplace practices. To complicate matters yet further, strategies do not emerge in a simple, unilinear top-down direction, but – as we see below – are complex, multi-faceted phenomena. In other words, we must consider the inter-relationship between business strategy and HRM rather than viewing the combination solely from a top-down perspective.

Business and corporate strategies

Most definitions of strategy in the business and management field stem from the work of Chandler (1962), who argued that the structure of an organisation flowed from its growth strategy. To be worthy of the title 'strategy' in the classical sense of the word, actions should:

- be derived from the broad intentions of senior decision-makers in the organisation

- encompass the enterprise (or business unit in devolved organisations) as a whole

- co-ordinate resources in a meaningful way that is designed to achieve sustained competitive advantage

- identify future actions based on an analysis of internal strengths, markets and competitors

- determine the scope of the organisation's activities over the medium to long term.

One of the leading British texts on strategy (Johnson and Scholes, 2002: 10) defines strategy as:

the direction and scope of an organisation over the long term, which achieves competitive advantage for the organisation through its configuration of resources within a changing environment and to fulfil stakeholder expectations.

Within this perspective, strategy is seen to operate at three levels. Corporate strategy relates to the overall scope of the organisation, its structures and financing, and the distribution of resources between its different constituent parts. Business or competitive strategy refers to how the organisation is to compete in a given market, its approaches to product development and to customers. Operational strategies are concerned with how the various sub-units – marketing, finance, manufacturing, and so on – contribute to the higher-level strategies. The management of people would be seen as an element at this third level, although Johnson and Scholes, in common with most writers on strategy, do not devote much space to considering the human aspects of organisations.

How would you define the word 'strategy'? Ask your colleagues or fellow students what they understand by the word and compare their answer(s) with the perspectives outlined below.

This top-down perspective, in which it is assumed that strategies are formulated by boards of directors and then cascaded down the organisation, represents the dominant view of strategy in most published literature on the subject, and is derived from military roots. The 'classical' model is not the only way in which to look at strategy however (Hussey, 1998), and an alternative approach is put forward by writers such as Quinn and Mintzberg that treats strategies as emergent rather than deliberate. Quinn (1980: 58) regards the most effective strategies as those that tend to 'emerge step by step from an iterative process in which the organisation probes the future, experiments, and learns from a series of partial [incremental] commitments rather than through a global formulation of total strategies'. This is very useful in that it quite rightly casts doubt on the perspective that organisations make decisions on the basis of cold, clinical assessments in an 'objective' manner. Decisions are taken by people whose own subjective preferences and judgements clearly influence the outcome. Mistakes are made for a variety of reasons, and conditions change so as to render decisions that seemed sensible at the time totally inappropriate at a later date. Interpersonal political tensions and battles also play a major part in the outcome of decision-making processes within organisations. More recently, Mintzberg and his colleagues (1998: 11) have suggested that strategies are neither purely deliberate nor purely emergent, for 'one means no learning, the other means no control. All real-world strategies need to mix these in some ways; to exercise some control while fostering learning.' Deliberate and emergent strategies form the poles of a continuum along which actual practice is expected to fall (Stiles, 2001).

Figure 6   Whittington's typology of strategy

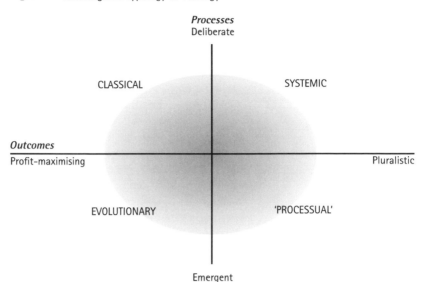

Adapted from Whittington, R. *What is Strategy and Does it Matter?* London,
Routledge, 1993

Whittington (1993) proposes a fourfold typology of strategy as depicted
in Figure 6. This is based upon distinctions between the degree to which
outcomes are perceived purely in profit-maximising or pluralistic terms,
and the extent to which strategy formulation is seen as deliberate or
emergent.

The four types are:

- *classical* (profit-maximising, deliberate) – Under this conception,
  strategy is portrayed as a rational process of deliberate calculation and analysis, undertaken by senior managers who survey
  the external environment searching for ways in which to maximise
  profits and gain competitive advantage. It is characterised as non-
  political, the product of honest endeavour by managers who have
  nothing but the organisation's interests at heart, and who are able
  to remain above the day-to-day skirmishes which typify life at lower
  levels in the hierarchy. This notion of independent professionalism
  is something that is often used to legitimise management action.
  Using the military analogy by separating formulation from
  implementation, Whittington (1993: 15–17) notes that 'plans are
  conceived in the general's tent, overlooking the battlefield but sufficiently detached for safety ... the actual carrying-out of orders is
  relatively unproblematic, assured by military discipline and obedi-
  ence.'

- *evolutionary* (profit-maximising, emergent) – From this angle,
  strategy is seen as a product of market forces, in which the most

efficient and productive organisations win through. Drawing upon notions of population ecology, 'the most appropriate strategies within a given market emerge as competitive processes that allow the relatively better performers to survive while the weaker performers are squeezed out and go to the wall' (Legge, 1995: 99). Taken to its extreme, it could be argued that there is little point in planning a deliberate strategy since the winners and losers will be 'picked' by forces beyond the influence of senior managers. They might, however, see some advantage in keeping their options open and learning how to adapt to changing customer demands, a process that Lovas and Ghoshal (2000) refer to as 'guided evolution'. Boxall and Purcell (2002) make a useful differentiation between the problem of viability (remaining in business) and the problem of sustained advantage (playing in the 'higher level tournament' through superior performance). Because so much of the debate about strategy focuses on the latter, this is a valuable corrective; we return to the subject later in this chapter.

- *'processual'* (pluralistic, emergent) – This view stems from an assumption that people are 'too limited in their understanding, wandering in their attention, and careless in their actions to unite around and then carry through a perfectly calculated plan' (Whittington, 1993: 4). There are at least two essential features of this perspective. First, as Mintzberg (1978) argues, strategies tend to evolve through a process of discussion and disagreement that involves managers at different levels in an organisation, and in some cases it is impossible to specify what the strategy is until after the event. Indeed, actions may only come to be defined as strategies with the benefit of hindsight, by a process of *post hoc* rationalisation through which stories are recounted that appear to be sequential and carefully planned in retrospect. Quinn's (1980) notion of 'logical incrementalism' – the idea that strategy emerges in a fragmented and largely intuitive manner, evolving from a combination of internal decisions and external events – fits well with this perspective. The second essential feature of the 'processual' view is that it takes a micro-political perspective, and acknowledges the fact that organisations are beset with tensions and contradictions, with rivalries and conflicting goals, and with behaviours that seek to achieve personal or departmental objectives (Pettigrew, 1973; Marchington *et al*, 1993a).

- *systemic* (pluralistic, deliberate) – The final perspective suggests that strategy is shaped by the social system in which it is imbedded – factors such as class, gender, legal enactment, educational systems and national culture. Within this viewpoint, strategic choices are shaped not so much by the cognitive limitations of the actors involved but by the cultural and institutional interests of a broader society. State intervention in countries such as France and Germany have helped to shape HRM in a way that can be contrasted easily with those that are more typical of Anglo-Saxon countries such as Britain and the USA (Lane, 1989; Ferner and Quintanilla, 1998; Rubery and Grimshaw, 2002). A further advantage of viewing strategy from this perspective is that it enables us to appreciate how – under the classical approach – management actions are legitimised by reference to external forces, so cloaking 'managerial power in the culturally acceptable clothing of science and objectivity' (Whittington, 1993: 37).

What types of forces beyond the level of the organisation shape HRM? Consult *People Management* and/or ask someone that you know who has worked abroad or for a foreign-owned firm about how choices relating to employment are shaped by national cultures and frameworks, legislation and educational systems. Note that this is becoming more significant for HR professionals in Britain in the light of more EU legislation and the growing recruitment of workers from other countries.

This discussion of strategy has interesting implications for how we view the notion of vertical integration. Under the classical perspective it can be seen as unproblematical – merely a matter of making the right decision and then cascading it through the managerial hierarchy to shop floor or office workers, who then snap into action to meet organisational goals. The evolutionary view complicates the situation slightly, in that it puts a primacy upon market forces and the perceived need for organisations (which are perceived in unitarist terms) to respond quickly and effectively to customer demands. This introduces notions of coercion, power and flexibility into the equation, as opposed to the objectivity that supposedly underpins classical perspectives. The two pluralist perspectives highlight the contested nature of organisational life and demonstrate the barriers to fully-fledged vertical integration in practice, whether due to tensions within management or to challenges that may be mounted from workers. The systemic perspective also causes us to look beyond the level of the employing organisation and so to be aware of the limits to employer choice. It is worth bearing these problems in mind before we examine the principal attempts to link business strategy and human resource management, because many of these have assumed the predominance of classical perspectives on strategy – with obvious limitations.

'Best-fit' HRM: contingency and configurational ideas

There have been a number of attempts to develop categorisations linking HRM with business strategy, competitive circumstances or national business systems. The models used include the Boston Consulting

Group (BCG) matrix, product or organisational life-cycles, and derivations from Porter's ideas on competitive advantage, strategic behaviour, and organisational flexibility. Authorities and commentators include Delery and Doty (1996), Kochan and Barocci (1985), Lengnick Hall and Lengnick Hall (1988), Marchington and Parker (1990), Marchington and Wilkinson (1996), Peck (1994), Purcell (1989), Purcell and Ahlstrand (1994), Schuler (1989), Sisson and Storey (2000), Storey and Sisson (1993), Streeck (1987), and Thomason (1984). For the purposes of this book, we focus on just three of these: life-cycle models (Kochan and Barocci), competitive advantage (Schuler), and strategic configurations (Delery and Doty). The different models are outlined first, followed by a general critique of contingency approaches.

Life-cycle models

A number of US researchers (for example, Kochan and Barocci, 1985; Lengnick Hall and Lengnick Hall, 1988) have attempted to apply business and product life-cycle models of strategy to the management of human resources in an effort to explain why employers adopt different policies in different situations. Sisson and Storey (2000) have related this to a British employment context, using just four categories: start-up, growth, maturity, and decline.

Start-up
During the early stages of business growth, it is felt that flexibility of operation and response is necessary to enable the organisation to grow and develop, with a strong commitment to entrepreneurialism. The human resource implications of this phase suggest that there ought to be an emphasis on flexible working patterns, and the ability to recruit and retain staff with the motivation to work long hours and develop themselves. Employers aim to gain employee commitment to the business, and although there may be some return in the form of highly competitive salaries in some circumstances, it is more likely that employees will be encouraged to look forward to the potential benefits that may accrue to them in the future. There is likely to be little or nothing in the way of formalised practices – for example, in relation to learning and development or structured performance management systems. In the most unlikely event that trade unions are present, their role will probably be minor. It is also unlikely that a specialist HR manager would be employed, so this role would either be combined with other managerial tasks or it may be more cost-effective to employ consultants to undertake those activities.

Growth
As the organisation grows beyond a certain size, formal policies and procedures probably begin to emerge in order to ensure that it builds upon earlier successes. There is a need to retain expertise and ensure that earlier levels of commitment are maintained, so more systematic HR procedures and systems are introduced. For example, in order to

recruit staff, it is likely that managers will make use of more sophisticated methods for recruitment and selection, management development, training, appraisal, pay and reward and organisation development. In employee relations, priorities become the maintenance of peace, and the retention of employee motivation and morale (Kochan and Barocci, 1985: 104). As the need for specialist expertise becomes apparent throughout the business as a whole, so too does the pressure for professional HR services internal to the organisation. If human resource policies remain informal and *ad hoc*, there is a danger that problems will emerge due to a failure to apply grievance and discipline procedures, pay systems and performance management consistently. However, the entrepreneurs who set up the organisation in the first place may resist any shift to greater formalisation.

Maturity

As markets begin to mature, and surpluses level out, the business has to take stock of its activities and shift priorities so as to cope with much lower levels of growth – and even a complete flattening out of performance. By this stage there is likely to be a range of formalised procedures, covering everything from HRM to purchasing. The human resource implications of this phase centre on the control of labour costs – something that is often hard to achieve since employees have become accustomed to enjoying the continuing fruits of prosperity. Staff who leave may no longer be replaced automatically, training and development programmes may become harder to justify, promotions become less common, and the overall wage bill is kept firmly under control. Union representatives, if they are present, are likely to find that previously good relationships may start to become strained, and management is likely to find itself under increasing pressure to control all types of costs. This is the time at which employees and managers start to question the viability of continued employment into the future, and doubts emerge about management's ability to sustain a positive psychological contract. Staff may be encouraged to leave the organisation or become more mobile around the business as efforts are made to improve productivity against a backcloth of worsening competitive prospects.

Decline

The process of decline brings to a head many of the problems that were beginning to become apparent in the previous phase, as the business struggles to survive. In this stage the emphasis shifts to rationalisation and redundancy, with obvious implications for HR philosophy. Most of the policies that have developed through previous years are reconsidered, and indeed may be ditched as the employer seeks desperately to reduce costs. The specialist HR function could well be disbanded, there may be pay cuts, training opportunities become focused on re-skilling and outplacement counselling, and there is an increasing tendency to contract-out services. The culture can become tense and difficult, and trade unions may find that they are marginalised or de-recognised.

> Can you see any problems in applying the life-cycle model to a large organisation, from either the public or the private sector, which offers a range of different products or services? What are the implications of this for the ways in which people are managed?

Competitive advantage models

Such models seek to apply Porter's ideas on competitive strategy to HRM. Porter (1985) argues that employers have three basic strategic options in order to gain competitive advantage: cost reduction, quality enhancement and innovation. Schuler and Jackson (1987) draw out the

Table 24   Competitive strategies and HRM

HR practices	Competitive strategy		
	Cost-reduction	*Quality-enhancement*	*Innovation*
Resources	*Ad hoc* methods predominate, use of agencies/subcontractors	Sophisticated methods of recruitment and selection	Focus on core competencies and transferable skills
	Tight performance management	Comprehensive induction and socialisation	Agreed performance outcomes
Learning and development	Poor or non-existent training in specific immediate skills	Extensive and long-term focus	Provided if necessary
		Focused on learning and career development	Personal responsibility for learning
	Little EI or communications	Well-developed systems for employee voice	Preference for informal communication systems
	Non-union workplace, or unions tolerated	Partnership arrangements	Professional associations
Reward management	Low pay levels	Competitive pay and benefits package	Cafeteria reward system
	No additional benefits	Harmonisation	Share ownership/profit-sharing
HR function	Slimmed down	Works closely with line managers	Advice and support for employees
	Lacking in influence	Potentially large influence	Potentially some influence

Adapted from Sisson K. and Storey J. *The Realities of Human Resource Management*. Open University Press. 2000

human resource implications of these strategies, and in a later work Schuler (1989) attempts to combine this with life-cycle models. The original paper has also been developed by Sisson and Storey (2000): see Table 24.

The 'cost-reduction' employer seeks to produce goods and services cheaper than the competition's, with no frills and an emphasis on minimising costs at all stages in the process – including people management. The human resource implications of this are similar to the 'bleak house' or 'black hole' employer (Guest, 2001b), with no systems for independent employee representation and no evidence of high-commitment HRM. Recruitment and selection is likely to be *ad hoc*, especially for low-grade tasks, and the employer may well use agencies or sub-contractors to perform some of the more mundane jobs. Training is likely to be poor or non-existent, with no recognition that employees deserve to be provided with opportunities for learning and development. Pay levels are unlikely to be much above the minimum wage, and may well be less if the employer can get away with it. There are likely to be minimum health and safety standards, tight performance monitoring, little emphasis on employee involvement and communications, and little empathy with staff who are experiencing problems. Non-unionism is likely, although if unions do make an approach they are ignored, or tolerated provided they are not seen as problematic. If a specialist HR function exists, it is likely to be slim and have little influence. The cost-reducer category is undoubtedly the most common form in Britain, largely because so many people work for small firms that have neither the resources nor the commitment to develop resourceful humans.

The 'quality-enhancement' employer operates with a set of HR practices that are the exact opposite of the cost-reducer because the goal is to

---

CASE STUDY: HRM in a 'cost-reducer' hotel

This hotel is located in the centre of a large city and is part of a small chain. It employs 115 staff, many of whom are casual workers passing through the UK and seeking to finance their stay here. Most stay for no longer than six months or a year at the very most. The hotel management emphasises cost control and the efficient control of staffing levels, and this is reflected in the benefits package available to staff – low levels of base pay, no sick or holiday pay, and no written contract of employment. Wage costs are controlled very tightly, and managers are expected to remain within budget. There is no obvious sign of har-monisation between different groups of staff, some of them – such as the chefs – receiving much better terms and conditions of service. Although there is basic training for all staff, it is limited to health and safety courses, customer service and hygiene. There has been some attempt to improve communications across the hotel via team briefings, and the 'open door' system provides staff with access to managers relatively easily.

Adapted from Hoque K. *Human Resource Management in the Hotel Industry*. London, Routledge. 2000

produce goods and services of the highest quality possible in order to differentiate itself from the competition. People management and development in this situation is likely to resonate with the best-practice HRM approach described in the previous chapter. This includes: carefully controlled recruitment and selection, comprehensive induction programmes, empowerment and high-discretion jobs, high levels of employee involvement, extensive and continuous training and development, harmonisation, highly competitive pay and benefits packages, and a key role for performance appraisal. There is no mention of unions in the Schuler model, but if they are recognised it is probable that both parties are keen to maintain co-operative relations and a *de facto* (or *de jure*) partnership arrangement would be in place. The HR function is likely to be well-staffed and highly proactive in helping to shape organisational cultures and change programmes. Close co-operation between HR and line managers would be desired so that competitive advantage could be sustained. A growing number of large organisations are likely to aspire to this model, and offer the more favourable employment package that this implies, if only to attract and retain key staff at times of labour market shortage. The extent to which they are able to sustain this style, other than for their core staff, during periods of downturn and recession is open to question.

The 'innovation' category of the Schuler framework is likely to be the least extensive of the three. Here, groups of highly-trained specialists work closely together to design and produce complex and rapidly-changing/adaptable products and services in an effort to stay ahead of the competition. The consequences for HR policy are similar in many respects to the quality-enhancement model outlined above, but there is much greater emphasis on informality, problem-solving groups, a commitment to broadly-defined goals, and flexibility. Employee development is likely to be seen as a personal responsibility rather than the employer's obligation, and basic pay rates are likely to be supplemented by access to share-ownership schemes that enable employees to link their fortunes to that of the employer. Schuler does not mention unions, but in view of the emphasis on individualism they are unlikely to figure prominently in the organisation. Because it is unlikely that entire organisations will be located in the 'innovation' category, it is possible that this set of HR practices may be preserved for small groups of highly-qualified staff or those engaged in 'leading-edge' activities. This opens up the possibility – as we saw in Part 2 of this book – that different groups of staff may be employed on quite different terms and conditions from one another.

How can 'cost-reducers' continue to recruit and retain staff if their conditions are so much worse?

Strategic configurations

One of the principal criticisms of traditional, bivariate contingency theory is that it simplifies reality far too much by seeking to relate one dominant variable external to the organisation (say, product market position) to another internal variable (say, human resource management) in a deterministic manner. For example, it is assumed that HRM style can be 'read off' from product market circumstances or position in the product life-cycle. The choice of an alternative external factor (say, labour market circumstances) might indicate that the employer should adopt a different style altogether, and it is at this point that contingency

Table 25   Strategic configurations and HRM

HR Practices	Strategic configuration	
	Defenders – internal employment system	*Prospectors – market employment system*
Resources	Great care over recruitment and selection	Buying-in of labour to undertake specific tasks
	Well-developed internal labour markets	Tight performance standards and expectations
Learning and development	Extensive and long-term focus	Likely to be extensive
	Well-defined career ladders	Personal responsibility for learning and development
Employee relations	Emphasis on co-operation and involvement	Emphasis on responsibility and performance
	Voice through grievance procedures and trade unions	Little attention paid to voice
Reward management	Clear grading structures and transparent pay systems	Pay determined by external market comparisons
	Employee share ownership	Bonus and incentive payments
HR function	Well-established	Limited role
	Potentially large influence	Managing external contracts

Adapted from Delery J. and Doty H. 'Modes of theorising in strategic human resource management: tests of universalistic, contingency and configurational performance predictions', *Academy of Management Journal*, Vol. 39, No. 4, 1996. pp802–835

models are found wanting. Delery and Doty (1996: 809) propose the notion of configurational perspectives in an attempt to overcome this problem, by identifying ideal-type categories of both the HR system and the organisation's strategy. The principal point about this perspective is that it seeks to derive an internally consistent set of HR practices that maximise horizontal integration (see Chapter 7) and then link these to alternative strategic configurations in order to maximise vertical integration. Delery and Doty do this by linking an 'internal' employment system with Miles and Snow's (1978) 'defender' strategy and a 'market-type' employment system with their 'prospector' category. This is presented in Table 25.

Defenders concentrate on efficiency in current products and markets, on narrow product ranges, and have a centralised organisation structure. They tend to 'build' their portfolios and extend their activities slowly and carefully. The internal employment system of a defender offers the most appropriate fit with the strategic goals and capabilities of such an organisation, and it allows for the derivation of a bundle of HR practices that support each other. Recruitment, wherever possible, is through specific ports of entry, and then employees deemed acceptable are promoted internally to fill other positions. Career ladders are well-defined, training and development activities are extensive, and socialisation into the dominant organisational culture is high on the managerial agenda, both through formal induction programmes and through day-to-day reinforcement. Appraisals are principally for developmental purposes, and the reward structure is geared up to long-term employment with the organisation – for example, through clear grading structures and increments, as well as via employee share ownership. Employment security is likely to be high for those who make it through probationary periods, and there are plenty of opportunities for employees to exercise their voice through grievance procedures, problem-solving groups and (where recognised) trade unions. The HR function is well-established and may be encouraged to play a major part in management decision-making.

Prospectors, by contrast, are inclined to change and adaptability, exploring new product markets and business opportunities, and therefore less reliant on existing skills and abilities. Consequently, their HR strategies are less internally-oriented, and they search the external labour market so as to buy in staff rather than 'build' them as do the defenders. Recruitment tends to be from the external labour market, and there is little use of internal career ladders, other than for a specialist core group of staff who have a range of transferable skills that might be appropriate in different environments. Given the emphasis on external recruitment to meet new demands, training is not organised in the same way as in the defender firms – it is likely to be much less extensive and typically related to short-term needs rather than long-term learning and development. Appraisals are likely to be results-oriented, and incentive pay systems – such as performance-related pay – tend to be prominent, as do other short-term financial incentives. Participation and voice are unlikely to be extensive, and are likely to be tolerated rather than encouraged. The role of the HR function in such organisations can be expected to be limited to administration and support rather than acting as a strategic business partner, unless this is as an expert in managing external contracts, interpreting the legal situation and leading on rationalisation and change.

> Apply one of the models discussed above to (a) two different organisations of your choice in different markets, and (b) two in the same market. You will obviously need plenty of information in order to do this, so find published material or talk with other course members about their organisations.

Limitations of the 'best-fit' models

There are clear similarities between these models, and parallels can be drawn between HR practices in some of the different categorisations – for example, between the cost-reducer and the start-up, or between the quality-enhancer and the internal employment system. There are also some general shortcomings.

Firstly, each of them has a tendency to determinism: each assumes that it is possible to 'read off' a preferred human resource strategy from a knowledge of business strategy or competitive prospects. There are several problems with this assumption. Many organisations do not have clear business strategies, and it is impossible to claim that there are links with HRM if there is no strategy in place (Boxall and Purcell, 2000: 187). In addition, the contingency approaches adopt the classical perspective on strategy, in which logical, rational decision-making takes place in an ordered and sequential manner between non-political actors. We have already seen that such an assumption is unrealistic. Drawing on research with companies in the oil and chemicals industries, Ritson (1999: 170) argues that the relationship between HRM and strategy is much more interactive than the classical models suggest. Part of the reason for this is the supposition that HRM is owned by and undertaken in specialist departments rather than being integrated into the line management of the organisation, and thus inseparable from all other managerial functions and activities. Moreover, these models are normative – they rely on 'what ought to be' rather than 'what is' – resting upon yet another assumption, that there is a best way to run businesses and manage people in particular situations. Problems also arise if different factors external to the organisation suggest the adoption of different types of HR strategy, or if different parts of a business operate in quite different market circumstances. On the other hand, Ogbonna and Whipp (1999: 82) found that two of the UK's leading supermarket chains tended to adopt a rational model for strategy formulation derived from sophisticated computer packages that simulated environmental scenarios.

Secondly, the models follow traditional scientific management principles in assuming that managers are omniscient and omnipotent in their dealings. We already know that it is impossible for anyone to retain sufficient information in his or her head to make judgements that take into account all possible effects and scenarios; this concept of 'bounded rationality' is widely understood and accepted. Moreover, the models also assume that even if a preferred strategy can be identified, there is no problem putting it into effect. Although it has to be acknowledged that employers typically have greater bargaining power than employees, it is still unrealistic to pretend that no thought must be given to how to meet the 'baseline needs of employees whose skills are crucial to the firm's survival' (Boxall and Purcell, 2000: 187). Even in workplaces that utilise computer technology to monitor performance – such as call centres – it is clear that there are strict limits to the extent to which managers are able to fully control the activities of their staff (Taylor and Bain, 1999; Kinnie *et al*, 2000). Employer goals and visions are not determined in a vacuum but emerge through negotiated processes within the managerial hierarchy and with employees/trade unions, as well as being shaped by governmental and institutional forces.

The third problem is that the approaches are all rather static and fail to focus on the processes involved. Evidence suggests that, for example, organisations do not travel in the direction indicated by the life-cycle model, but instead move through a series of recurrent crises as they grow and develop (Hussey, 1998; Legge, 1995). Assumptions also tend to be made about the size, shape and structure of organisations in each of the phases and categories, so that a start-up business is typically assumed to be small and a mature business large. It is difficult to gauge when an organisation moves from one stage of the life-cycle to the next, and at what point there might be a change in HR practice to reflect – or drive – this change. In addition, even if it was possible to identify the precise moment when an organisation moved from one stage to the next, it would be a major task to adjust the terms and conditions of staff in order to realign the business and HR strategies. It may also be totally inappropriate for a whole series of reasons to do it in case it might damage management-employee relations.

Finally, the categorisation of 'real' organisations can also be difficult, as Crawshaw *et al* (1994) have shown with their analysis of Sainsbury's. 'Good food costs less' implied that the company was stuck in the middle – neither a quality-enhancer nor a cost-reducer. The differences in HR practices between organisations as diverse as a research-led pharmaceutical company and a service-oriented fast-food chain are probably apparent to most observers, but it is more problematical to assess differences between two organisations in separate – or even the same – segments of the same broad product market. Why, for example, has

General Motors developed its HR policies in a certain way whereas Ford has taken a quite different stance (Mueller, 1994)? Or why did Tesco choose to work closely with trade unions while Sainsbury's preferred to minimise union involvement? Bird and Beechler (1995: 40) did find that organisational performance (in a sample of Japanese companies in the USA) was higher when there was a match between their business and

CASE STUDY: Business strategy and HRM in Spain

This study was undertaken by a group of academics from Spain who gathered questionnaire returns from a sample of 200 firms in the south-east of the country. Over half employed less than 50 staff, and a large number had been in operation for at least 20 years and were under family control. The researchers used factor analysis to develop a series of clusters that approximated to the model outlined above which differentiated between quality-enhancement, cost-reduction and innovation. A range of HR practices were investigated, including recruitment and selection, type of employment contract offered (temporary or permanent), training and development, reward and compensation, and appraisal. A number of statistical differences were found between the categories for business strategy, and these were broadly supportive of the Schuler predictions. That is, the cost-reduction firms were the least likely to invest in human resources, whereas the other two categories were much more likely to. Differences were found between the firms with quality-enhancement and innovation strategies on a number of factors. The most important of these were:

- Lower levels of training, teamwork, internal labour markets, employee participation and pay were found — as might be expected — at the firms with cost-reduction strategies.

- Higher levels of teamwork, temporary contracts and promotion plans were found at the innovative companies.

- Higher levels of hierarchy in payment systems operated at the companies with a quality-enhancement strategy. A number of other HR practices — such as training, promotion

plans, pay, and employee participation — were found at the firms with innovation strategies.

- Despite the statistical differences between these categories, only a minority offered temporary contracts. There were similar levels of training offered compared to sales turnover, pay levels were reportedly above the sector average, and all firms said that they engaged in employee participation.

The authors note that these results should be treated with caution, for a number of reasons. On average, the firms were much smaller than in most other studies and the HR function was more developed at the quality-enhancement and innovation firms than at the cost-reduction firms. In addition, the research was dependent on management interpretations of issues, and it is well-known that — on wage level or productivity comparisons for example — respondents typically over-estimate their own organisation's performance. Moreover, some HR issues — such as voice, trade union representation or employment security — were not examined in this study. Furthermore, there are also questions about the ability to generalise from results derived from analysis in different countries. Nevertheless, this does provide an empirical test of, and some support for, the Schuler categorisation.

Adapted from Sanz-Valle R., Sabater-Sanchez R. and Aragon-Sanchez A. 'Human resource management and business strategy links: an empirical study', *International Journal of Human Resource Management*, Vol. 10, No. 4, 1999. pp655–671

HR strategies than where there was a mismatch. However, they suggested that a more holistic approach was needed by which strategies in other functional areas – such as production, sales and R&D – was considered as well. Kelliher and Perrett (2001: 433) are less convinced on the basis of their examination of the strategy–HRM links in 'designer restaurants'. Unlike much of the industry, these sorts of establishment focus very strongly on the importance of a quality experience and adopt an 'innovation' strategy. Applying the contingency approaches would imply that a similar HR strategy would emerge, but there was little evidence that any alignment had taken place. The dominant HR practices were hard-nosed and short-term, relying on the use of a transient workforce, particularly at the front-of-house, that received only average levels of pay and few other benefits. Yet it was apparent that certain 'key' groups of staff – notably in the kitchens – did receive an employment package that was in line with the strategy.

Examples such as these indicate clearly that it is not appropriate to focus on one particular factor – say, competitive strategy – and ignore the effect of others in shaping HR practice. It also shows that internal political issues are critical in working out why particular organisations choose to develop a specific set of HR policies that are then changed when a new chief executive is appointed. This is not to say that contingency approaches are useless, but that different factors evidently have different levels of importance at different times, and it is the mix of factors that is important. Moreover, within a large, diversified company, some HR practices may appear inappropriate for certain businesses while being in line with those for others. This raises important questions about how decisions on HRM are made in large organisations, as well as about the choices over the balance between centralisation and decentralisation (Purcell and Ahlstrand, 1994).

On the other hand, these models are useful for at least two sets of reasons, especially if they are used as a tool for guidance rather than a technique for reading off the approach to be adopted. First, each model attempts to predict appropriate human resource strategies from an analysis of business strategies. At the polar extremes this may fit quite well. For example, it may explain why so many British manufacturing companies that failed to move out of mature markets suffered so badly in the 1980s, with such disastrous consequences for the people employed by them at the time. Equally, it is easy to see how the HR activities of many new firms can be aligned with start-up or innovation business strategies. In short, it causes us to question the prescription that all employers should adopt 'best-practice' HRM policies irrespective of their market fortunes or business strategies. Second, these kinds of analysis lead personnel practitioners to think more carefully about how they might usefully contribute to the business, and in particular frame proposals in ways that can be 'sold' to senior managers. The case for a new human resource initiative might have a better chance of success if it is seen to 'fit' with business strategy (Legge, 1978).

Write down two separate lists, one suggesting reasons why the 'best-fit' approach might be more useful, the other doing the same for the 'best-practice' approach.

HRM and the resource-based view of the firm

The resource-based view (RBV) of the firm has been a recent entrant into the literature on strategy and HRM, and it is now widely accepted as a (if not the) dominant perspective in strategic management. Drawing on Penrose (1959), Hoskisson *et al* (1999: 417) argue that a focus on the internal resources at the disposal of the organisation (and its agents) has produced a useful corrective from earlier paradigms, such as those discussed in the previous section, which analysed performance in terms of external competitive forces. It is the range of resources, including human resources, that gives each organisation its unique character and may lead to differences in competitive performance across an industry. In its most recent manifestation, the notion of RBV was rediscovered by Wernerfelt (1984) and developed into a more meaningful concept by Barney (1991: 99). Barney argued that organisations 'obtain sustained competitive advantage by implementing strategies that exploit their internal strengths, through responding to environmental opportunities, while neutralising external threats and avoiding internal weaknesses'.

The potential for sustained competitive advantage requires four specific attributes (Barney, 1991: 105–6) – value, rarity, imperfect imitability, and a lack of substitutes. Value means that the resource must be capable of making a difference to the organisation in the sense that it adds value in some way. Rarity means that there must be a shortage of these particular resources in the market to the extent that there are insufficient to go around all organisations. Imperfect imitability refers to the idea that it is very difficult, if not impossible, for other employers to copy (imitate) these specific rare and valuable resources, even if there are sufficient available in the market as a whole. Finally, these resources must not be easily substitutable by other factors so that they are rendered obsolete or unnecessary. It is the combination of these resources (human and non-human) that provides an organisation with the opportunity to gain sustained competitive advantage.

There are three sets of reasons for imperfect imitability, according to Barney (1991: 107–11). Unique historical conditions make it difficult for a competitor to copy another organisation's resources, even if it knows what they are, because of its particular path through history. Second, due to causal ambiguity, it is difficult for competitors to understand how these resources are put together to produce a coherent bundle, or indeed the precise nature and mix of the resources that lead to competitive advantage. Third, an organisation's resources are 'very complex social phenomena, beyond the ability of firms to systematically manage and influence'. For example, the web of interpersonal relations that develop in an organisation or the firm's reputation in the local labour market are both sources of competitive advantage, but both are highly complex and difficult to replicate even if the individual elements could be copied.

Although RBV is very useful in helping us understand why differences exist between firms, and consequently how certain organisations may be able to gain competitive advantage, it neglects the forces that lead to similarity in the same industry. Oliver (1997: 701) deals with this issue well by advocating the combination of RBV with the new institutionalism of organisation theory (DiMaggio and Powell, 1983). Oliver sees firms as being influenced by powerful forces for difference and for similarity. The former would include factors such as an orientation towards efficiency and deliberate decision-making, whereas the latter would, by contrast, imply that decisions are deeply embedded in specific norms and traditions. The pressures for similarity within industries include a mixture of external coercion (for example, laws), mimicking other successful organisations, and normative traditions (for example, professional networks). These forces can be formal and informal, as well as explicit and implicit, codified and uncodified. Deephouse (1999: 154) proposes a theory of 'strategic balance' by which organisations aim to achieve a balance between differentiation and conformity. Whereas RBV focuses on how firms may seek competitive advantage through differentiation, he suggests that firms which are too different from the rest of the industry face legitimacy challenges since they do not represent what customers expect or want. He argues that an attractive niche 'is one that is different from other firms' niches yet similar enough to be rational and understandable. In sum, the need for legitimacy limits the organisation's ability to differentiate into specialised niches.' This is likely to be particularly important where conformity is associated with legitimacy – for example, in professional services or those where confidentiality is critical.

Wright *et al* (1994) were the first to apply RBV ideas to HRM. They argued that human resources are deemed to be *valuable* to the extent that there is heterogeneity both in the supply of and in the demand for labour that can make a difference in organisations. The quality of labour available varies to the extent that there are large differences between the skills and competencies of individuals in the labour market as a whole, but also between those with similar formal qualifications. Human resources are *rare* to the extent that irrespective of overall levels of unemployment, it is not unusual for organisations to experience persistent skill shortages in specific areas – such as with teachers in recent years, or with certain types of skilled manual labour for some time. On *inimitability*, the issue is rather less clear. Human resources are potentially highly mobile, but then there are often substantial transaction costs involved in moving from one workplace to another, and the more that skills become organisation-specific the harder this is likely to become. Wright *et al* (1994: 311) argue that it is through the 'combination of social complexity, causal ambiguity and unique historical circumstances with imperfect mobility that the value created by human resources is accrued by the firm'. Human resources are seen as *non-substitutable*, even by technology ultimately, because they have the potential (a) not to become obsolete, and (b) to be transferable across a variety of situations. Accordingly, the contribution of human resources to competitive advantage is felt to be just as significant as, if not more so than, other firm resources. A number of issues emerge from the Wright *et al* (1994: 313) paper and from a series of papers by Boxall.

How would the RBV approach apply to your organisation – or one with which you are familiar? How could human resources be considered valuable, rare, imperfectly imitable and non-substitutable – and how might this impact upon the types of HR policy and practice that the organisation currently uses?

First, there is the issue of whether RBV relates to the entire human capital pool or just to senior managers who are not only likely to be rarer in quantity but also have the potential to exert greater influence over organisational performance. Wright *et al* are clear that it is the former because employees as a whole are directly involved in making products or delivering a service, they are typically less mobile (although that is open to question) and they are less able to claim excessive wages for their efforts. Mueller (1996: 757) is even more convinced that the social architecture that resides in an organisation is likely to have developed over a considerable length of time, slowly and often in an uncodified manner. He suggests that 'social architecture is truly valuable [due to] ongoing skill formation activities, forms of spontaneous co-operation, the tacit knowledge that accumulates as the unplanned side-effects of intentional corporate behaviour'. This shows how difficult it is for other organisations to imitate practices that evolve in this way, and it demonstrates the potential contribution of people to performance.

A second issue is whether RBV relates to human capital itself – that is, the people who are employed – or to the HR practices that are used to manage staff. As we saw in Chapter 7, Boxall (1996: 66) makes the useful distinction between *human capital advantage* and *human process advantage*. Combined together, they form 'human resource advantage', the idea that competitive advantage can be achieved by employing better people *and* by using better HR processes. Each element is therefore important, whether it is an individual's inherent ability to learn or his or her manual dexterity, or the policies and practices that are implemented in order to 'secure, nurture, retain and deploy human resources' (Kamoche, 1996: 216). It is therefore clear that the employment of highly-qualified and talented people can be useless without effective processes to ensure that they work well in combination and wish to contribute to organisational goals (Wright *et al*, 1994: 320). The interdependence of people and processes, the complete bundle of HR practices that combine together, and the integration with other managerial systems is illustrated graphically by Leonard (1998: 15–16):

> *Competitively advantageous equipment can be designed and constantly improved only if the workforce is highly skilled. Continuous education is attractive only if employees are carefully selected for their willingness to learn. Sending workers throughout the world to garner ideas is cost-effective only if they are empowered to apply what they have learned to production problems.*

Third, RBV provides a particularly useful framework for analysing HRM because it recognises the importance of historical conditions and the different paths that are taken in organisations over time, as well as industry movements (Boxall, 1996: 65). A number of major studies in the area have demonstrated the importance of processes, as well as procedures and outcomes, for understanding the nature of the employment relationship. This is particularly apposite in relation to the degree of trust (or lack of it) that develops over time between different organisational actors (see, for example, Purcell, 1980). The informal relations that emerge at workplace level are especially difficult to imitate. On the other hand, RBV has limitations in that it is focused at organisational level, and therefore downplays the significance of institutional arrangements at national and industry level beyond the workplace. As Boxall and Purcell (2002) note, some firms have an immediate advantage in international competition because they are located in societies that have much better educational and technical infrastructure than do others. This reminds us that choices about HRM are shaped not just by managers but by external forces as well.

Finally, it is worth noting that the important issue of differentiation and conformity has also been addressed in the HRM literature on RBV. Boxall and Purcell (2000: 15) suggest that:

> *caution is needed before we get too carried away with the idea of differentiation. It is easy under the RBV to exaggerate the differences between firms in the same sector. All viable firms in a sector need some similar resources in order to establish their identity and secure some legitimacy.*

It is suggested that a set of minimum human resource policies is necessary merely in order to 'play the competitive game' in any industry, what has been termed 'table stakes' (Boxall and Purcell, 2000) or 'enabling capabilities' (Leonard, 1992). Rather than viewing these resources as necessary for a firm to gain competitive advantage, as classic RBV would, their argument is that certain resources are critical for organisations even to remain viable. In other words, firm resources that are valuable, rare, imperfectly imitable and non-substitutable may well be needed merely in order to survive and achieve satisfactory performance. In industries where significant numbers of firms go out of business, as is the case with small firms in particular, this may be a more appropriate way to apply the ideas of RBV than it is to focus on the 'differentiation' route alone.

CASE STUDY: The application of RBV to HRM in the road haulage industry

This study was undertaken in the highly competitive 'hire and reward' sector of the British road haulage industry. As with most of the firms in this sector, those studied for this project were relatively small – employing on average about 50 drivers – and the majority had been in business for several generations. Aside from major problems with the cost of fuel, a major constraint on continued growth of these firms was the shortage of good drivers.

In RBV terms, the drivers were *valuable* in that they did make a difference to these organisations, not only in allowing the firm to put more trucks on the road but also in the way that they interacted with customers. Drivers were seen as a critical factor for survival, let alone success. Drivers were *rare* even though many more people were trained to LGV level than the industry needed, but had left for other jobs with more money and better working hours. There was great reluctance to use agencies to supply drivers for fear that they would damage customer relations, crash the trucks (which were expensive) or just not turn up for work. There were no obvious *substitutes* for drivers either, unless the company chose to move out of the 'hire and reward' market and set up an alternative transport organisation, using other forms of travel such as the railways. However, these did not take away the need for some form of road transport for at least some stage of the journey. Finally, in an effort to keep staff, the firms tried to engage in HR practices that were felt to differentiate them from

the rest of the market. They used 'word of mouth' recruitment to attract suitably qualified staff, they tried to offer them working conditions that might retain the better drivers, and they made efforts to make the environment preferable to that at other haulage firms. Some sought to offer additional incentives for drivers with longer service, others tried to organise social events and offer opportunities for greater involvement in the business, and some set up internal promotion ladders for drivers. But this was not easy in the face of competition from other companies, reductions in pricing for contracts, and tighter performance specifications from the firms for which these hauliers worked. Ultimately, staying in business was as much as many of them could manage.

This study is useful given its application to SMEs as well as to a business sector that is typically in a highly dependent product market position. Moreover, the industry is not renowned – unlike some of the 'best-practice' organisations in pharmaceuticals – for its progressive HR practices. The research also illustrated well the distinction made by Boxall between the 'table stakes' that are necessary for mere survival and the HR processes that can catapult a firm into a dominant market position and sustained competitive advantage.

Adapted from Carroll M. and Marchington M. *The Recruitment and Retention of Drivers: Evidence from small UK road haulage firms.* Manchester School of Management Working Paper 9912, UMIST. 1999

One of the few studies to apply RBV to HRM has been Boxall and Steeneveld's (1999: 456-9) study of the engineering consultancy sector in New Zealand. Five of the leading firms were examined over several years, although one of these actually went out of business during the period of the study. Of those that remained in the industry, there were many common elements in their approach to managing employment. In particular, certain key staff, known as 'rainmakers' who generated significant business opportunities, were seen as critical to continued viability and success. This distinction between HRM for viability and HRM for industry leadership is a very useful corrective to the obsession with competitive advantage. It was apparent that all the firms were obliged to recruit and retain 'rainmakers' merely to remain in business because they were judged by clients on the quality of their senior employees and the ability to retain this 'critical core' of contract-winning staff. The study demonstrated that firms which fail to maintain viable operations are 'doomed, sooner or later, to receivership or to take-over by better-managed companies' (Boxall and Steeneveld, 1999: 459). Only once this is secure can organisations tackle the more difficult task of introducing the HR strategies necessary for industry leadership.

Carroll and Marchington (1999) also demonstrated the critical importance of survival, as opposed to industry leadership, in their study of small firms in the road haulage sector. Recruiting and retaining drivers had become a major problem for these firms, and a number felt that the amount of business they could undertake was limited by their ability to find sufficient suitable staff. In other words, drivers were rare due to skills shortages, valuable because they were needed to drive trucks, and not substitutable unless the firm moved into a different area of transportation. The key to attracting and holding on to staff lay in the distinctiveness of the HR practices the firms used and the degree to which their managerial systems and approaches were incapable of being imitated. The case study on the previous page provides more detail on this.

Converting strategy into practice: blocks and barriers

Much of the management literature is based on classical versions of strategy that presuppose an unproblematic conversion of strategy into practice. Because it is felt that managers merely need to find the most appropriate methods to put their ideas into effect, the focus tends to be on the tools and techniques rather than on values and behaviour. Once the plans have been laid, therefore, individual managers from different functions and departments are expected to follow the senior management line without question. However, if we reject such superficial assumptions about organisational life, it is then possible to appreciate how senior management strategies may not be operationalised. In this section, we consider the blocks and barriers inherent within management circles alone, rather than employee and trade union resistance to management initiatives – these are covered in Chapters 14 and 15.

The distinction which Brewster *et al* (1983: 63–4) make between 'espoused' and 'operational' policies offers a useful starting-point for this discussion. *Espoused* policy is a 'summation of the proposals, objectives and standards that top-level management hold and/or state they hold for establishing the organisation's approach to its employees.' These may or may not be committed to paper, and in many cases they are little more than broad philosophical statements about how senior management feel towards staff – such as those within a mission state-ment, for example, about employees being 'a key and valued resource'. Obviously, the phraseology used in these documents is very general, and is capable of interpretation in different ways depending on the cir-cumstances. In contrast, *operational* policy describes 'the way senior management are seen to order industrial relations [and human resource] priorities vis-à-vis those of other policies'. This may well be done subconsciously, as well as with intent, since it is reflected in managerial value systems and is clearly moulded by the issues con-fronting them on a daily basis. If two policies are seen to be in conflict – say, a commitment to healthy and safe ways of working, and a desire to be customer-responsive – then, it is argued, the human resource policies tend to take a lower priority. There are many examples from different industries illustrating the way in which espoused policies are ignored, amended or downgraded in the face of conflicting pressures on organisations.

In order to put strategies into effect, 'champions' are required within organisations. Champions are managers who have the energy and the ability to lead new initiatives and to ensure that others are persuaded of their merits, and who are prepared to commit themselves to seeing that strategies are embedded in the workplace. By their nature, how-ever, champions tend to be mobile and career-oriented, often moving to new positions soon after introducing fresh initiatives. As Ahlstrand (1990: 23) notes, in relation to a succession of productivity deals at Esso's Fawley refinery, each initiative received a high-profile launch and commanded powerful symbolic significance within the company. The champions made great use of what Barlow (1989) calls 'impression management', making their activities visible to more senior managers, with the result that they were often promoted soon after implementing a new deal. In short, soon after making an impression, champions tend to move on to other posts, either within or beyond the organisation. Those left with responsibility for maintaining these new initiatives feel little ownership of them, are less committed to making them work, and in any event want to introduce their own ideas in order to gain pro-motion themselves. A cycle is set in motion, with the inevitable conse-quence of fads and fashions, cynicism, and short-termism (Marchington *et al*, 1993a; Marchington, 2001).

Which of the following statements do you think is more accurate?

a)   'champions are necessary to achieve organisational change'
b)   'champions are ultimately the major cause of failures to achieve change in organisations'

Review the arguments in favour of and against both of these statements.

Conflicts and contradictions can occur within the ranks of management both on a hierarchical and a functional basis. In this chapter we deal with the former, in view of the fact that this relates to questions of vertical integration and the conversion of strategy into practice. The question of interdepartmental conflicts is considered in Chapter 9 as part of the discussion about horizontal integration and links between line managers and their HR colleagues.

Broadly, there are five separate sets of blocks and barriers to the vertical integration and the implementation of strategy, caused by:

- managers and supervisors regarding themselves as distinct from senior management

- work overload

- lack of training

- desire on the part of supervisors for flexibility

- inadvertent rule-breaking by managers.

Division between managers and senior management
First, many middle managers and supervisors do not identify closely with the goals of the employer, but instead view themselves as distinct from senior management (Thompson and McHugh, 2002: 94–6). There are several parts to this argument. Scase and Goffee's (1989: 186) conceptualisation of 'reluctant managers' sees persisting class divisions within British employing organisations as the reason why supervisors fail to share senior management views. First line managers might feel that they have escaped from the working class but are not accepted into the managerial class, to some extent stuck in the middle and unable or unwilling to align themselves either with workers or with managers. They may also have doubts about the validity of senior management's ideas, especially those philosophies which espouse employee involvement and use the language of 'resourceful humans', regarding attempts to empower workers as akin to soft management (Marchington *et al*, 1993a; Denham *et al*, 1997; Heller *et al*, 1998). The language of teamworking and empowerment, for example, while potentially attractive to more senior managers, can appear highly threatening and problematic to first line managers whose authority has been built on technical

expertise and the restriction of information to the shop floor (Marchington, 2001: 241). They are often cynical about the value and potential life-span of new management initiatives, arguing that they 'have seen all this before' (Yong and Wilkinson, 1999).

Feelings of role ambiguity and insecurity have been reinforced by events of the past two decades during which large numbers of supervisors and middle managers have lost their jobs or found that their existing skills are increasingly irrelevant to modern organisational needs. Although written some time ago, Scase and Goffee's (1989: 191) conclusion may still be very apposite: 'Corporations may succeed in cultivating "cultures of excellence" and introducing more flexible organisational forms, but predominant practice in Britain will tend, we suspect, to lead mainly to the compliance of reluctant managers.' Supervisors often doubt the sincerity of support from senior management, an anxiety that is fuelled as their own job security is lessened and they find little attempt to 'involve' *them* in management decisions. An important first step in any change programme may well be to involve line managers in the process and give them increased responsibility and authority as 'a central part of the agenda' (Fenton O'Creevy, 2001b: 37).

Work overload
A second constraint to the achievement of vertical integration is that line managers and supervisors are already suffering from work overload, conflicting requirements from senior management, and a lack of explicit rewards for undertaking the human resource aspects of their jobs. Like most staff, supervisors are being asked to take on extra duties, and are finding it difficult to squeeze yet more into their working hours. Fenton O'Creevy (2001b: 36) found that de-layering and job loss put even greater pressures on line managers by reducing the time and energy available for implementing new initiatives. However, rather than seeing negative attitudes as the problem, and therefore regarding supervisors as scapegoats, Fenton O'Creevy (2001: 37) reckons that it is management systems that are to blame. He questions whether or not reward and appraisal mechanisms are appropriate to encourage positive behaviours or if there is sufficient time left in the working day to devote to staff development. It is hardly surprising if line managers concentrate on the achievement of targets they know will be used to assess their performance at appraisal (Bach, 2000). If meeting production deadlines, having zero defects, or reducing queue lengths gains a higher priority when they are appraised than does the regularity of team briefings, opportunities for their staff to engage in self-development, or levels of absenteeism, then they are bound to focus on the former set of goals. First line managers pick up signals from their more senior colleagues about the ordering of priorities irrespective of what is contained within the formal mission statement and, understandably, aim to meet these demands rather than more ephemeral 'soft' human resource goals. In other words, the heavier the workload, the more difficult it is for line managers to satisfy HR objectives. Even in the 'leading edge'

organisations studied by Gratton *et al* (1999), it was clear that a series of pressures led the line managers to place a low premium on HR activities at work. In a separate paper (McGovern *et al*, 1997: 26), they conclude that:

- there are limited institutional pressures to reinforce the importance of carrying out HR activities

- the short-term nature of managerial activity leads them to put a greater emphasis on the achievement of numbers *per se* rather than the achievement of numbers through people

- downsizing and de-layering places tremendous pressures on the time that line managers can allow for people matters generally.

Lack of training

The third obstacle to converting strategy into practice is the lack of training typically provided for line managers and supervisors. Given the prominence accorded in mission statements to 'investing in employees', it might be expected that considerable time and effort would be expended on developing first line managers. The reality, however, is rather different, and in practice training in people management tends not to be a key priority. Yet more worrying is the feeling that line managers and supervisors may not be sufficiently competent in interpersonal skills to cope with the responsibilities required to lead change programmes at workplace level (Cunningham and Hyman, 1995; Marchington *et al*, 2001). Too often, it would appear, insufficient time is allocated to the training of first line managers because senior managers are keen to implement new initiatives with a minimum of delay. This has been particularly apparent from our own studies of employee involvement over the years. Training in how to run a quality circle, for example, could consist of little more than a half-hour session on 'how not to communicate' followed by an amusing video illustrating how things went wrong elsewhere. Occasionally, a speaker may be invited from another organisation to explain their approach and answer questions, but there is little attempt to give supervisors the chance to practise their skills (Marchington and Wilkinson, 2000). At one of the banks studied by Marchington *et al* (2001: 56), there was an explicit recognition that 'We haven't done enough training to support our line managers in how to hold team meetings ... certainly the style of managing in an organisation as big as ours is always going to be a problem.'

Flexibility for supervisors

A fourth problem is that supervisors do not like to be constrained by instructions from senior managers, but wish to retain some flexibility to adapt rules in the workplace. This aspect of behaviour – termed 'management commission' by Brown (1973) – allows supervisors to vary the application of rules, to provide themselves with leeway so as to reward, ignore or discipline workers on a selective basis. This can work not only to reinforce managerial control over recalcitrant employees, but also as a way of showing leniency or providing a negotiating counter in cases where it is deemed appropriate. This notion of 'deal-making' (Klein, 1984) gives supervisors discretion in dealing with employees, by allowing staff some flexibility (say, in taking time off) in return for an expectation that they will work harder or stay later in order to complete a rush job. In a sense, this allows supervisors to be seen as independent from the more oppressive face of management. In each of these cases, it is apparent that management can gain from a degree of rule-bending. However, this can also work to the detriment of their plans or policies, such as when unacceptable precedents are set in relation to disciplinary issues, or custom and practice is established which lowers worker performance or customer service.

Managers unaware of the rules

The final reason why it is difficult to achieve vertical integration is that managers may be unaware that they are breaking or not following organisational rules, and in the process creating precedents which may run counter to employer goals: Brown terms this 'management by omission'. In these situations, first line managers may not realise that rules are being broken, as in the case of workers who appear to comply with health and safety instructions but deliberately flout them when the supervisor is elsewhere. Equally, senior managers may agree to requests from staff undermining agreements made previously by the departmental manager, so creating awkward precedents. This is particularly problematical in the employee relations area when an agreement in one department may be used as a bargaining counter by workers elsewhere in efforts to improve their pay and conditions. What makes acts of omission so hard to manage is that they are often not noticed until a later date – for example, when being used to support a case against disciplinary action (Earnshaw *et al*, 1998).

Some might see this discussion as being unduly pessimistic, in its assumption that supervisors are unlikely to support management actions. Can you come to a more optimistic conclusion?

CONCLUSION

This chapter has reviewed material relating to 'best-fit' HRM, the idea that HR practice should and does vary between organisations depending on business strategy, product market circumstances or national business systems. There is much value in this proposition, particularly because it counters the more simplistic versions of 'best-practice' HRM, but also because it appears to reflect organisational reality – at least at a broad level. The notion that HRM in a leading pharmaceuticals firm may differ from that in a small textiles factory, or that a local authority may manage its staff differently from a restaurant, can be explained to some extent by the best-fit analyses. Greater problems emerge when we attempt to explain differences between two firms in the same market position, for example. Part of the difficulty is that the models used tend to be top-down and deterministic, driven by classical strategic theory, and it is clear that a range of factors can influence HRM in practice. Among the most important of these are the style and philosophy of senior management and the differing ways in which organisations seek to achieve competitive advantage. The resource-based view of the firm is especially helpful here in that it focuses on the specific, sometimes unique, factors that enable organisations to retain their position in the market as well as contribute to superior competitive performance. However, any analysis of organisations has to take into account internal politics, and examine the ways in which broad management strategies may be adapted, ignored or resisted by managers at lower levels in the hierarchy or in different departments. To conceive of management as a cohesive, omnipotent and omniscient entity is clearly wide of the mark, and it is important to recall that different managerial functions often battle for control and influence within the organisation. This theme runs through much of the material in the next chapter as well.

Useful reading

BOXALL P. *and* PURCELL J. 'Strategic human resource management: where have we come from and where should we be going?', *International Journal of Management Reviews*, Vol 2, No. 2, 2000. pp183–203.

BOXALL P. *and* PURCELL J. *Strategy and Human Resource Management*. London, Palgrave. 2002.

COFF R. 'Human assets and management dilemmas: coping with hazards on the road to resource-based theory', *Academy of Management Review*, Vol 22, No. 2, 1997. pp374–402.

DELERY J. *and* DOTY H. 'Modes of theorising in strategic human resource management: tests of universalistic, contingency and configurational performance predictions', *Academy of Management Journal*, Vol. 39, No. 4, 1996. pp802–835.

FENTON O'CREEVY M. 'Employee involvement and the middle manager: saboteur or scapegoat?' *Human Resource Management Journal*, Vol. 11, No. 1. 2001. pp24–40.

HOSKISSON R., HITT M., WAN W. *and* YIU D. 'Theory and research in strategic management', *Journal of Management*, Vol 25, No. 3, 1999. pp417–456.

JOHNSON G. *and* SCHOLES K. *Exploring Corporate Strategy*. Prentice-Hall, London. 2002.

OLIVER C. 'Sustainable competitive advantage: combining institutional and resource-based views', *Strategic Management Journal*, Vol 18, No. 9, 1997. pp697–713.

SISSON K. *and* STOREY J. *The Realities of Human Resource Management*. Open University Press. 2000.

WHITTINGTON R. *What is Strategy and Does it Matter?* London, Routledge. 1993.

Changing Responsibilities for the Management of HRM

CHAPTER OBJECTIVES

By the end of this chapter, readers should be able to:

- identify the most appropriate roles for the HR function in different types of organisation

- work in partnership with other stakeholders to overcome blocks and barriers to change

- make recommendations about the advantages and disadvantage of outsourcing some or all elements of HRM.

In addition, they should understand and be able to explain:

- the different models available for analysing the role of the HR function

- the implementation of HRM by line managers, HR specialists and consultants, and how these interact with each other

- the contribution that HRM can make to organisational success and the measures used to illustrate this.

Introduction

The last decade has seen an increasing challenge to the assumption that organisations should have personnel or HR departments comprising, for the most part, their own specialist staff. Although this arrangement still exists in many organisations, HR departments have been forced to justify their existence and demonstrate how they 'add value'. They have been slimmed down, and in a number of cases their role has been outsourced completely to consultants. Many HR tasks are undertaken now by line managers and supervisors. These changes have often coincided with restructuring and rationalisation, a determination by large organisations to focus on their core competencies, and an expectation that all activities will be seen to contribute to improvements in shareholder value.

The purpose of this chapter is to consider the question of who has responsibility for the management of human resources. A primary focus of this discussion is the extent to which it is either possible or appropriate for the HR function to adopt a business partner model, following Ulrich's major contribution to the issue (1998). We also evaluate the idea that it is more realistic to acknowledge that the HR function can (and should) fulfil a number of roles dependent on the issues involved and its current position within the organisation. A number of organisations have increased their use of HR consultants, in terms of responsibility either for the complete function or for parts of it. An increasingly popular way in which to deliver HR is through shared services between employers, and in some cases call centres have been set up to provide advice for managers and staff working for several organisations. The link between line managers and HR specialists is also examined to discover how these relationships are managed, and to whose benefit. Although there may be advantages in expecting line managers to take principal responsibility for managing their own staff, it is also important to be aware of the limits to this. The chapter concludes with an assessment of whether HR departments are making a positive contribution to organisational performance – not just in terms of economic value added or short-term financial measures, but also in relation to their influence and involvement in decision-making and in assessments by their internal customers.

> Before reading on, write down the main activities involved in your job and identify how much time each of them takes up in a typical working week. Return to this question at the end of the chapter and critically assess what you have written. *[If you are working in HR currently or have experience of this sort of role, this should be easy. If you do not have HR experience, ask someone else to work with through this question with you.]*

Human resource managers and their roles

As we saw in Chapter 6, membership of the CIPD grew enormously in the latter part of the twentieth century, reaching over 110,000 in 2001. However, because not all managers with specialist responsibility for HRM are in the CIPD, there are obviously more people working in HRM than this. WERS 1998 found that about 30 per cent of all workplaces with 25 or more employees had an HR specialist although about three-quarters had access to a specialist beyond the workplace. Not surprisingly, the presence of a specialist became more likely the larger the workplace, and nearly 90 per cent of those employing more than 500 had an HR professional on site (Cully *et al*, 1999: 51). Other factors that increased the likelihood of an HR presence were foreign ownership, being in the public rather than the private sector, and being part of a wider organisation rather than a stand-alone workplace. Industry also mattered, with high numbers of personnel specialists at workplace level or above in the former utilities, public administration and financial services, whereas there were lower numbers in construction and manufacturing in general. In other words, there is considerable diversity in whether the HR function is located at workplace level or above (Cully *et al*, 1999: 52).

It is commonly perceived that there are major differences in the HR function between the public and private sectors: by stereotype the public sector HR function is a bureaucratic backwater staffed by less well-qualified and effective people (Lupton and Shaw, 2001: 34). It is apparent that few HR staff transfer between the two sectors, and it is probable that the public sector employs a greater number of administrative staff. Indeed, many private sector employers, especially in smaller firms, are unlikely even to have a personnel function. The WERS study (Cully *et al*, 1999: 52) found that personnel specialists were more likely to be found in the public sector – albeit above the level of the workplace – than in the private sector. Similarly, high-commitment HRM was also more prominent in the public than the private sector (Guest and Conway, 2000: 10). On the other hand, due to differences in decision-making structures, and especially in the role of councillors in local government, HR practitioners are likely to be given less authority than their private sector counterparts in more sophisticated organisations might be. Public sector HR practitioners regularly make reference to 'breaking out' and escaping to the 'promised land' of the private sector – although Lupton and Shaw (2001: 35) note that that may be caused by mythical expectations.

Although some feel that the debate about the title – 'personnel' or 'HRM' – is sterile and of little worth (Gennard and Kelly, 1994; Hall and Torrington, 1998), others feel that the terms have quite different meanings (Grant and Oswick, 1998). Using the WERS survey data, Hoque and Noon (2001: 18) suggest that 'titles do matter' and that managers using the HR label differed significantly from those who reckoned to be 'personnel'. Apparently, the former are more likely to have a formal related qualification and claim that they have strategic influence. In addition, they are more likely to work for organisations that have adopted a larger number of 'high-commitment' HR practices and have devolved personnel activities to line managers. Interestingly, however, those who thought they belonged to 'personnel' were three times more common than those with the HR badge.

> Do you think that job titles are important? Do you believe that your influence would change if you had a different title?

Over the years, there have been many attempts to categorise the work of the HR function in order to analyse the variety, diversity and complexity of the role. Some writers argue that it is possible to identify discrete roles that are logically distinct from one another, even if tied together by a single continuum. Others regard the different categories as cumulative, with each role building upon the previous one, resulting in

Table 26   Models of the human resource function

Author (date)	Categories for the HR role	Reasons for differentiation
Legge (1978)	Conformist innovator Deviant innovator Problem-solver	Ways to gain power and influence
Tyson and Fell (1986)	Clerk of the works Contracts manager Architect	Time-span for decision-making Degree of discretion Involvement of HR
Storey (1992)	Handmaiden Regulator Adviser Change-maker	Level – strategic or tactical Degree of interventionism
Wilkinson and Marchington (1994)	Facilitator Internal contractor Hidden persuader Change agent	Level in the hierarchy – senior or junior Profile – high or low
Ulrich (1998)	Administrative expert Employee champion Change agent Business partner	Level, focus and time-frame Managing processes or people

categories of increasing complexity. Yet others argue that individuals or departments display multiple roles, and that it is possible for more than one category to be in evidence at any organisation at the same time. Each of the categorisations explicitly or implicitly assesses how the HR function can best contribute to improved performance. Table 26 presents a summary of some of the major categorisations.

One of the oldest, and arguably still one of the best, models was that proposed by Karen Legge (1978) more than 20 years ago. She argued that in order to gain power and influence within their organisations, personnel managers had to adopt one of a series of strategies. The first of these is *conformist innovation* by which HR managers attempt to relate their work and efforts clearly to the dominant values and norms in the organisation, aiming simply to satisfy the requirements of senior managers. An alternative approach is *deviant innovation*. Here, the personnel specialist subscribes to a quite different set of norms, gaining credibility and support for ideas driven by social values rather than by strict economic criteria. This might include concerns about stress, equal opportunities, long working hours or empowerment. Finally, there is a contingent role, that of *problem-solver*, in which the HR contribution is assessed through its ability to identify and resolve problems for the employer.

An alternative classification is Tyson and Fell's (1986) analogy to a 'building site' in which three roles are identified for the personnel function. These are differentiated along a single continuum defined by factors such as the planning time adopted for HR activities, the degree of discretion exercised by personnel specialists, and the extent to which they are involved in creating the organisation's culture. The role with least discretion is termed *clerk of the works*, where the HR system operates in an *ad hoc* manner merely to serve line managers. The activity of the personnel function is predominantly administrative and clerical, concerned with record-keeping and welfare – what is now sometimes termed 'transactional' work. In the middle of the continuum is the *contracts manager*, a role most likely in industries with a significant trade union presence, where systems and procedures are heavily formalised, and the underlying emphasis is on trouble-shooting. The final role – that of the *architect* – is the most sophisticated. As the name implies, this is concerned with grand design at a senior level, with the integration of human resource issues into broader business plans, and with a creative and innovative approach. In this scenario, HR practitioners are able to influence change and are expected to take the lead in creating the 'right' culture and philosophy for the organisation as a whole. The architect is regarded as a business manager first and a personnel professional second (Caldwell, 2001).

Although it is tempting to view the Tyson and Fell (1986: 24) continuum as one where the role of HR assumes greater maturity as it develops, the authors reject this assumption. They argue that the choice of role is contingent upon organisational circumstances, and that each of the variants may be found at each level in the hierarchy. Tyson and Fell's model has been refined by Monks (1993). Based on research on a sample of Irish organisations, she suggests that it is possible to identify four categories rather than three, with an extra role in between the contracts manager and the architect. These four categories are to be regarded as a continuum running from simple to complex, but Monks (1993: 36) also suggests that the roles are cumulative rather than discrete. That is, in organisations where the architect-type role is present, each of the other three are also in evidence.

> How much of your work is 'transactional'? Although this might be low-level and routine, does it add value to the organisation? What would happen if that work was not done?

A further set of categorisations is based on ideal-types created by differentiating between roles along two separate independent axes. The best-known of these is the work of Storey (1992a). He proposes a four-fold 'map' based on two cross-cutting dimensions: the degree to which HR is strategic or tactical, and the degree to which it is interventionary or not. The former dimension makes the simple distinction between policy and practice, long- and short-term time horizons, and the level in the hierarchy at which decision-making takes place. The latter dimension reflects continuing tensions about the contribution which HR specialists put in to organisational decision-making, and the extent to which it is possible to measure their contribution in quantitative or financial terms. There are four main 'types of personnel practitioner'. *Advisers* operate at the strategic level and are non-interventionary, providing support for line managers as required, and often working behind the scenes to help shape policies and practices. *Handmaiden* is a particularly apt term to describe the role which is tactical and non-interventionist, predominantly led and defined by the needs of their 'customers', the line managers. Very much like the clerk of the works, the handmaiden is involved mainly in clerical and administrative tasks, and in responding to other people. Storey sees this group as submissive, subservient and attendant, responding to short-term requests from customers, and not seeking to change or influence the direction of the organisation. The third type is the *regulator*, a role which is highly interventionist at the tactical level, very much operating as 'old-style' industrial relations fire-fighters who work closely with shop stewards to smooth over problems and manage discontent. As Storey notes (1992a: 176), just because their interventions are at a tactical level, in some organisations such a role is critical in helping to facilitate stoppage-free production. The final type is the *change-maker*, a role that aims to establish new HR cultures, seeking ways in which to elicit employee commitment and encouraging staff to 'go the extra mile'. He also suggests (1992a: 181–2) that change-makers can be proponents of either soft or hard HRM.

Figure 7   The role of HR practitioners in Total Quality Management

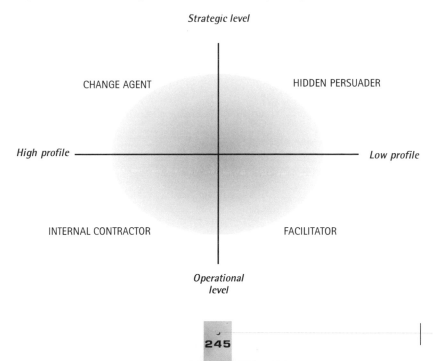

There are some suggestions in Storey's work that HRM within a single organisation may be represented by more than one role (eg in relation to the handmaiden and contracts manager), but this is not amplified. In Marchington *et al*'s (1993b) research for the IPM – as it then was – on quality management and the human resource dimension, the notion of multiple roles is explicit. In a categorisation similar to that of Storey, the four types are differentiated along two cross-cutting dimensions of level (strategic versus operational) and profile (high versus low). These four types are shown in Figure 7 on the previous page (Wilkinson and Marchington, 1994). Although this categorisation was devised initially to analyse the role of HR practitioners in quality management, it is also relevant to other aspects of HRM.

The *change agent* is similar to Storey's change-maker, and is characterised by a board-level appointment (or equivalent) that is highly visible to other senior managers. In this study, the view which best summed up the change agent role was the 'engine of change', providing a culture and structure in which TQM could thrive. This view emerged from discussions with managing directors, line managers, quality managers and union representatives. The *hidden persuader* also operates at a strategic level, but does so in a low-profile manner, working behind the scenes providing 'cabinet office' support for the senior management team. The third category – *internal contractor* – is rather different from Storey's regulator in that the latter is so closely identified with industrial relations. The internal contractor's main contribution is at the operational level in learning and development, for example, just as much as in employee relations. There is little doubt that this role has become more extensive as HR practitioners have been required to demonstrate their contribution to business goals. Finally, at operational level and in low profile there is the *facilitator*, a traditional role providing support of a routine, administrative nature for line managers.

Perhaps the most important point about this framework is that it stresses that the HR function at one site or one organisation typically plays more than one role. There was evidence of a facilitator role at each of the 15 organisations studied by Marchington *et al* (1993b: 36), but at only four sites was this the only role observed. Although there were no cases where all four categories were present, at one third of the sites three roles were evident. A study of the NHS by Procter and Currie (1999) provides support for this framework, and especially for the suggestion that the HR function can best be understood in terms of its multiple roles and contributions. This is likely to vary depending upon the issues that confront HR and the organisational context in which it is located.

Of course, there are dangers with each of these roles as well. The change agent, while potentially the most influential because of its high profile and strategic contribution, also runs the risk of significant costs if problems occur with any interventions. By taking such a visible role, the HR function may create enemies within the organisation, and interventions therefore have to be successful in order to prevent the build-up of overt dissent from elsewhere. The problem for the hidden persuader is almost entirely the opposite, since the managing director may have chosen to use personnel as a confidant(e) or adviser precisely because of its assumed neutrality. However, continued effectiveness is dependent upon sustained support from its champion, and the basic problem is that other managers may be unaware of this contribution. The facilitator suffers from a similar problem, in that the support which personnel provides for line managers is often hard to evaluate and is difficult to isolate from what is expected of the function on a daily basis. This is not a problem for the internal contractor, due to the very clear and public commitments made by the HR function to its internal customers. However, there is a risk that the function may be contracted-out if it fails to meet targets. The setting of targets must be undertaken carefully because of this.

> Consider whether there are circumstances (internal and external to the organisation) under which each of these roles is more likely to occur. Is it possible for HR practitioners and departments to simply 'choose' the role – say, change agent – that they like the best?

The final model is that developed by Ulrich (1997, 1998). He acknowledges that there is 'good reason for HR's beleaguered reputation. It is often ineffective, incompetent and costly; in a phrase, it is value-sapping' (Ulrich, 1998: 124). In order to overcome this reputation, he argues that HR must adopt four roles – see Figure 8 below. These are:

- *business partner* – HR acts as a partner with senior managers in strategy execution, not in the making of strategy but in ensuring that it is developed and put into effect. HR defines the 'organisational architecture', carrying out audits and renovating those aspects of the organisation in need of repair. In short, it is expected that the HR function will play a major part in creating the systems and processes that make organisations work effectively.

- *administrative expert* – HR acts as an expert in the way that work is organised and executed, and delivers administrative efficiency both in terms of its own function and for the organisation as a whole. Information technology is used widely in order to reduce the burden of routine tasks. This has been put into effect in call centres and shared service operations that deal with the transactional aspects of work – such as salary administration and personnel records. Ulrich (1998: 129) argues that success in this role can help HR to gain higher status: 'Improving efficiency will build HR's credibility which, in turn, will open the door for it to become a partner in executing strategy.'

Figure 8   Ulrich's four roles for the HR function

Focus
Strategic and forward-looking

STRATEGIC PARTNER   CHANGE AGENT

Activities   *Management of*
                                                         people
Management of
processes

ADMINISTRATIVE EXPERT   EMPLOYEE CHAMPION

Operational and day-to-day

Developed from Ulrich, 1998

- *employee champion* – HR acts as a voice for employees both in representing their concerns to senior managers and in working to improve their contribution, their commitment and engagement. Ulrich suggests that the HR function should be held accountable for ensuring that employees are motivated and willing to do more than the basic duties that are required of them. Of course, this cannot be done in isolation, and a major role for the HR function lies in orienting and training line managers to achieve employee engagement.

- *change agent* – HR acts as 'an agent of continuous transformation, shaping processes and a culture that together improve the organisation's capacity for change'. Ulrich (1998: 125) argues that the HR function must help the organisation embrace and capitalise on change, as well as transform vision statements into practical realities in the workplace.

There is little doubt that Ulrich's contributions have had a major impact on the HR profession. In particular, there is plenty of interest in how personnel practitioners can create the tools necessary for achieving a business partner role, as well as in ideas concerned with shared services and e-HR. In a sense, the excitement about the Ulrich models is strange, in that they do not differ dramatically from those reviewed above. After all, at least one of the dimensions (level/focus) used by Ulrich is similar to those that were employed by Storey. Tyson's architect has much in common with the business partner role, and his employee champion makes a similar contribution to Legge's deviant innovator. Moreover, his view that the HR function should adopt multiple roles tells us nothing more than Wilkinson and Marchington did. A more careful analysis of the roles suggests that they may not be quite so influential as may be assumed. For example, the business partner has a severely constrained role as 'an architect within an already constructed building' – perhaps little more than choosing the right colours of wallpaper! The administrative expert is responsible solely for the ways work is organised and executed within the HR area alone and not for work redesign throughout the organisation. The employee champion is tasked with doing jobs that trade unions ordinarily do in most large organisations in Britain, and the idea that HR should act as the 'voice' of employees smacks of paternalism rather than organisational justice. Change agents are not actually managers who execute change themselves or play a major role in the decision-making process but instead facilitate the work of other senior managers. In other words, rather than offering the vision of a new and more strategic role for HR managers, the Ulrich model may merely confirm their position as useful support staff who lack a unique set of specialist professional skills.

Read Dave Ulrich's paper in the *Harvard Business Review* (January– February 1998), and draw conclusions about the potential role for the HR function in your organisation.

Consultants and the delivery of HR practice

Until the 1980s there were very few consultants who offered HR services to organisations because most activities – aside from training – were provided in-house. Since then there has been a rapid growth in their number, although it is virtually impossible to arrive at a precise figure because there is no obligation on consultants to register their activities. Studies suggest that there has been a spectacular growth in the use of consultants over the last decade. For example, an IRS survey (IRS *Employment Trends* 698, 2000) reported that the combined fee income of the 20 largest consultancy firms had grown by over 20 per cent per annum since the beginning of the 1990s. Moreover, around 90 per cent of the UK's largest companies now use external consultants. Within this, there is little doubt that the extent of HR consulting has grown significantly. An article in *People Management* (1999) also referred to 'outsourcing fever' in the area of human resource management. Certainly, many organisations, both from the private and the public sectors, have now outsourced some or all of their HR activities. The case study below gives an example.

Not all HR consultants are the same, of course (Adams, 1991). Some organisations, for example, have set up internal consultancies that not

CASE STUDY: Oil or grit in the wheels of the personnel function?

The decision by BP to outsource its entire personnel administrative function to Exult, a US-owned organisation, late in 1999 created a lot of interest in the press. At the time it was one of the biggest deals yet made, at approximately £400m over five years, covering over 100,000 staff, and it involved an organisation that already had a well-established HR function. About 500 staff worked at two centres, one in Glasgow. A small proportion of the staff came from BP itself, the rest being recruited from other organisations. Exult provided basic transactional services for BP, such as updating personnel records when a member of staff got married or was promoted. The objective was that all employees, not just managers, would be able to access records electronically through a system known as MyHR.

There were a number of reasons for the decision to outsource, but most of them stemmed from the merger of BP with Amoco, and the fact that the new company had a mass of different types of HR system that were desperately in need of standardisation. In addition, the opportunity to outsource administrative aspects of HR to an organisation that had extensive experience in the use of new technology was very attractive, especially because BP did not have to invest time and resources in a project that was not central to its core competencies. Moreover, it was felt that once HR managers were released from dealing with day-to-day transactional activities, they could devote more time to adding value for the organisation by working with line managers on the ground. Exult had a clear rationale for wanting to take this service over: 'to help its clients achieve service level improvements, cost savings and tangible business benefits by assuming complete management, ownership

and accountability for the entire HR management process.' It also agreed to absorb any excess costs if the deal ended up costing more.

It was acknowledged at the outset that HR managers were still needed at the workplace so as to deal with issues that arose there, and that BP could now use its staff at the centre to focus on strategic activities. BP made it clear that there should be a strict division of labour between the work of the two companies, and that strategic issues would never be outsourced.

Approximately one year after the initial deal, in October 2001, BP announced that it had decided to put the project on hold because of teething problems. In particular, it proved difficult to convince employees to accept the changes brought about by outsourcing, and many preferred to continue with face-to-face contacts with HR professionals on the ground rather than log on to deal with issues remotely. One of the BP vice-presidents reported that one reason for the problems was that the project had been led by the HR and IT communities and not by the businesses.

It will be interesting to see how this situation develops, and readers are advised to consult *People Management* and other sources for further information.

Sources: *People Management*, 3 February 2000, 'The truth is out there'; *People Management*, 23 November 2000, 'A sell-out strategy'; *People Management*, 5 April 2001, 'Keep HR strategy in-house, warn outsourcing leaders'; *People Management*, 8 November, 2001, 'BP learns outsourcing lessons'

only provide services for their own staff on a profit centre basis, but also market themselves to other organisations as well. In other cases, the consultant is totally external to the organisation for which services are provided, although the contract between the host firm and the consultant may be short-term and tightly specified or long-term and partnering in its philosophy. Additionally, different arrangements are likely to be in place for different aspects of HRM. This 'balkanisation' of HR practice means that some areas may be heavily outsourced, such as training and development, executive search and selection, recruiting temporary staff, and outplacement and redundancy counselling. Other activities may well be retained principally by in-house units – for example, graduate recruitment and general counselling. Even in the case of training and development, however, it is clear that no one category of consultancy is used exclusively, and almost as many organisations use in-house agencies as use external consultants.

It makes sense to differentiate HR consultants into several distinct categories (Armstrong, 1994; IRS *Employment Trends* 698, 2000). These are:

- large strategy consultants, such as McKinsey and Company, that deliver extensive and far-reaching change management programmes, of which HR support is one key element

- the 'Big Five' accountancy firms, such as Pricewaterhouse-Coopers, which provide a whole range of services – including HR – and have now developed large and thriving businesses in the area of HR consulting. Their expertise originally was on the 'harder' end of taxation, reward and remuneration, but has now extended to other areas of HR practice.

- specialist human resource firms such as Towers Perrin that provide a full range of services or smaller and specialised 'boutiques'

- small firms or independent consultants that specialise in one particular HR field or region, or those that operate across the whole HR spectrum

- academics, some of whom provide consultancy expertise in specific areas as a supplement to their research, and who may be a source of up-to-date findings

- organisations such as the Industrial Society and ACAS, which provide consultancy services in addition to their other functions.

Training and management development are the most widespread areas of HR work undertaken by consultants, according to Hall and Torrington (1998: 126), followed by recruitment and selection and outplacement. Over half of the organisations they surveyed had employed consultants to undertake at least some part of their training and development during the previous year. It was rather less likely for these organisations to outsource employee relations, communications and work design. Even where an employer did outsource sizeable elements of a particular area of HR work, it was unlikely for this to be given over entirely to external consultants. For example, induction training would be retained in-house while specialist technical support would be provided by an independent outside body. Executive search and selection is now routinely handled by specialist agencies whereas the recruitment of manual workers or customer service representatives, for example, is more likely to be delivered by internal HR practitioners. A survey by IRS (IRS *Employment Trends* 698, 2000: 8) found that most employers who used outsourcing looked for external support in the areas of international assignments, reward and remuneration, employee relations and change management, and rather fewer in legal services. It is clear that management consultants as a whole now offer services in a wide range of generalist and specialist areas for a large number of clients. In a small, but increasing, number of cases vast tracts of the HR function are currently delivered by external consultants – especially in transactional services such as personnel records that can be dealt with via an electronic interface.

Take an organisation with which you are familiar and undertake an audit of the HR activities currently outsourced. Find out whether or not outsourcing has increased in recent years, and why this is the case.

There are four sets of reasons why employers turn to external consultants in preference to an in-house service (Armstrong, 1994; IPD, 1998; Hall and Torrington, 1998; IRS *Employment Trends* 698, 2000). First, if consultants are able to provide expertise or time that is not available internally, then there may be a strong case for using an external organisation. The expertise may be in a particular subject (eg European Works Councils, executive reward or psychometric testing) or it may relate to process skills. In the former situation, assistance comes from a specialist consulting firm or leading academic known to be at the forefront of its/his/her subject. Smaller firms may use a local person who has wide experience of HR across the board but is no longer in full-time employment or rather someone from an interim management agency. In the case of process consultancy, help is offered to senior managers in how to introduce a transformational programme of cultural change, for example. In short, consultants provide expertise that is not available within an organisation (IPD, 1998: 2). Consultancy firms have the resources to set up extensive databases of information, to offer benchmarking and – in the case of the large, multinational firms – to provide support in several different countries (IRS *Employment Trends* 698, 2000: 9).

Second, consultants tend to be regarded as independent and able to provide an expertise that is (theoretically) free from internal influence. This may be particularly useful in complex and multi-faceted situations in employee relations in a variety of ways. Independent consultants can also conduct attitude surveys under the auspices of a representative steering-group or make recommendations on organisational restructuring. It is sometimes felt that an outsider's view of issues can help to resolve problems which had previously seemed insurmountable, and that consultants are able to use the language of independence, objectivity and so-called 'rational' solutions (Baxter, 1996). A fresh perspective on a problem may be beneficial, and a summary of views collected by an independent consultant can help to shift attitudes or behaviour.

Third, it is argued that the HR function can make itself into a more strategic player by contracting-out routine, clerical, and/or transactional duties to an external agency that is skilled in providing systems and support for these activities. Once it is agreed that these sorts of HR activity are hardly central to the core competencies of the organisation, there is a clear rationale for outsourcing. In cases where HR activity has been outsourced, it has been common to retain a small core of staff to work with senior managers on issues such as culture change or organisation development. Moreover, this group defines performance criteria and monitors arrangements for dealing with contractors. The attraction of

---

CASE STUDY: A capital piece of outsourcing?

Westminster City Council was the first local authority to outsource its personnel support services in late 1998, to Capita Business Services, an organisation that was firmly established in the public sector market. A deal was agreed under the provisions of compulsory competitive tendering (CCT). Because Capita already ran a number of other local authority services, such as housing benefits, it was accustomed to this environment. The local authority was required to meet a number of criteria in the agreement: there was a need to deliver value for money; for no duplication of roles between the two organisations; and for the interests of the council not to be jeopardised by the deal. Twenty of the council's HR staff transferred to Capita, five left its employment and 10 were retained in-house to provide core services.

The agreement ensured that personnel strategy was retained by the council in areas such as employment law, national conditions of service, remuneration and corporate objectives, as well as the giving of advice to members about employee relations. Capita took over the provision of professional advice and guidance to managers on personnel policy on subjects such as attendance levels and sickness, maternity leave, working time and questions of pay and benefits. Responsibility for the provision of training courses also passed to Capita. Not only are there face-to-face surgeries for managers but there is also a telephone helpline to deal with queries.

The council feels that it gained by not having to deal with the usual daily headaches and questions, and also feels secure that its services are being provided for a fixed fee. Capita has provided wider career opportunities for some of the HR staff who transferred from the council, and its experience in Westminster has been valuable in gaining business elsewhere. UNISON found that it did not have the same level of information that it was used to in the local authority days, and there are times that it has felt sidelined.

Look in the pages of *People Management* or elsewhere to find out how this deal has developed over time.

Sources: IRS *Employment Trends*, 684, July 1999, 'Privatising personnel'; *People Management*, 19 August 1999, 'Premier division'

the 'business partner' model (Ulrich, 1998) has seduced many HR practitioners into thinking that they should dispose of the more mundane aspects of their work to focus on strategy.

The final, and arguably the most important, reason is cost savings. This is especially important if large parts of HRM or a major project are contracted-out. When consultants are used on a temporary basis, the costs of employing them are likely to be much less than maintaining an in-house expertise that may not be fully utilised at other times of the year. If senior managers are unhappy with the service provided by the consultants, it is easier to dispense with their services than with in-house personnel. Undoubtedly there are short-term attractions to employers seeking to reduce quasi-fixed costs in order to retain a competitive edge. Should employers decide to use consultants on cost grounds, however, they ought to be fully aware of the complete financial implications. The budget must include both the direct and the opportunity costs of internal management time in putting together the tender in the first place, as well as the costs of implementing recommendations and monitoring performance with a continuing contract. There also has to be some assessment of employee reactions to outsourcing.

There are several problems with employing consultants rather than using an in-house function. First, there is a loss of internal synergy if the entire HR function is outsourced. For the HR function to remain in-house provides an opportunity for benefits to be derived from internal teams learning across and within the organisation. Tacit skills that are difficult to codify and formalise are lost if the HR function is outsourced. The importance of shared cultures or histories is important in most organisations (as the resource-based view of the firm would argue), and the loss of them once HR expertise is provided by an external organisation is difficult to counteract. One of the best ways to develop future directors is to plan their career development so that they are familiar with all aspects of HR and with the business as a whole. That opportunity is missed if routine activities are subcontracted to an external consultancy (Hall and Torrington, 1998: 191–2). Moreover, some of the best HR managers have moved around between different functions and jobs during their working lives. Sometimes this may involve a stint as a research chemist or plant engineer, whereas for others it may be in marketing or purchasing. Either way, immersing HR professionals in other aspects of the business is beneficial for enhancing the contribution of the HR function.

Second, there are limits to 'best practice'. It is likely that external consultants can provide better technical solutions given their greater knowledge of HRM across a whole range of different organisations and situations. However, the best technical solution is not necessarily the most appropriate. Much depends on what is acceptable to the parties involved, and this is heavily influenced by the culture of the organisation – see the box headed *Oil or grit in the wheels of the personnel function?*

on page 250 for an example of this. There are clearly limits to the extent to which benchmarking against other organisations is appropriate, and in many circumstances it would appear that external consultants come along with 'solutions looking for problems' (Baxter, 1996; Fincham and Evans, 1999). In other words, practices that have worked effectively in other organisations tend to be recommended for quite different sectors and situations. The obsession with benchmarking relies upon the spurious assumption that imitating successful organisations is the route to performance improvement. As Fincham and Evans (1999: 38) suggest, 'Benchmarking is thus held out as a short-cut to success. Clients are given the chance to "learn from the best practices developed by world-class companies", and so are being offered cut-price membership of an exclusive club.'

The third problem relates to the definition and monitoring of performance standards. Clearly, there have to be agreed performance indicators to govern and control the relationship between the host organisation and the supplier. In many cases, these are very tightly specified – in terms of answering the telephone within five rings, responding to a letter within a certain number of days, or reducing the levels of labour turnover. In themselves, none of these performance indicators is necessarily problematical. However, when treated in isolation, there is a danger that HR activities become distorted in order to meet these particular standards. A situation can arise when 'the law of unanticipated consequences' comes to the fore, and the achievement of one objective leads to an obsession with it at all costs. By singling out particular goals as the most important to be achieved, there are dangers that other issues are ignored or indeed that the holistic HR contribution is overlooked. In addition, the factors that are generally measured are those that are relatively easy to define, and many HR processes critical to the business are actually very difficult to define precisely.

> Set up a debate with your colleagues about the question of whether or not it makes sense to outsource the HR function. Make use of the arguments outlined here, as well as others, and find contemporary examples to support your case.

Consultants do not always enjoy a good press. They have been referred to as modern witch-doctors 'recommending half-baked, theoretical, expensive and unsuccessful remedies to problems they have mis-diagnosed in the first place' (quoted in Baxter, 1996: 67). It is acknowledged that there are 'cowboys around whose only mission is to sell their simplistic prescriptions to any or all of the problems which beset management' (Armstrong, 1994). On the other hand, good consultants can provide expertise that may be lacking internally and they can help to facilitate changes that might otherwise not have come to fruition. Clearly, it is important to avoid problems when choosing consultants, and it is important that basic project management skills are used in drawing up specifications for consultants before they are offered a contract. Drawing upon a variety of sources (Armstrong, 1994; IPD, 1998; IRS *Employment Trends* 698, 2000; Rippin and Dawson, 2001), these can be summarised as:

- Take care to ensure that there is a valid and justifiable reason for employing consultants in the first place, and that their work cannot be done just as well in-house.

- Do your homework in choosing which consultant to use, by examining previous work, asking questions about the services and support that will be provided, and making sure that they can deliver what the organisation wants in each case.

- Ensure that the objectives and deliverables for the assignment are specified in a way that clearly indicates the desired results. Plan the project so that terms of reference, deadlines, methods of monitoring and review, and reporting arrangements are laid down clearly. Ensure that both parties fully understand their respective roles in the relationship.

- Take care that the project is managed according to deliverables, and that you continue to receive value-for-money services by a thorough review of performance at regular intervals. Wherever possible it is desirable to foster a partnership approach.

- Because consultancy projects involve change, special care is needed over implementation, involvement and communication processes during and after the assignment.

Line managers and HR specialists – working together?

Many of the criticisms concerning the lack of contribution by HR specialists to organisational performance have come from line managers. Such criticisms broadly take one or more of four forms. First, personnel practitioners are regarded as out of touch with commercial realities, and unable to comprehend much about the nature of the business, its customers, or its corporate goals. The allegation is that HR professionals base their decisions upon a set of principles and ideas, such as welfare or employee rights, which have little relevance for competitive prospects. Second, HR is often thought to constrain the autonomy of managers to make decisions that they feel are in the best interests of the business. Line managers are particularly frustrated by legal constraints, especially in the area of equal opportunities or individual rights, or about having to negotiate and consult with union representatives. The third criticism is that HR managers are unresponsive and slow to act, always wanting to check options thoroughly rather than pursuing a series of actions and not worrying about the consequences until later (Cunningham and Hyman, 1999: 17). The cautious nature of the role is probably most apparent in relation to legislation and employee relations. Finally, HR practitioners are criticised for promulgating policies that may be fine in theory but hard to put into effect, or inappropriate for their particular workplace. For example, although line managers may support the principle of appraisal, they are often annoyed by the practical requirement to keep records of meetings. The HR function is caught in a cleft stick, criticised both for being too interventionist and too remote. In his classic book, Watson (1986: 204) sums this up well:

If personnel specialists are not passive administrative nobodies who pursue their social work, go-between and fire-fighting vocations with little care for business decisions and leadership, then they are clever, ambitious power-seekers who want to run organisations as a kind of self-indulgent personnel playground.

Legge (1995: 27–8) terms this problem the 'vicious circle in personnel management'. Because senior managers do not involve the HR function in mainstream decisions and planning, 'people' issues are not accorded sufficient attention at an early stage in the decision-making process. Problems inevitably arise with new initiatives or with routine business issues because HR has not been involved – such as difficulties with poor recruits, inadequately-trained staff or stoppages of work. At this stage, the HR practitioners are asked to help resolve the crisis. The short-term solutions to immediate difficulties merely store up trouble for the future because insufficient time is allowed to introduce the solutions properly. Accordingly, the personnel function gets the blame for not being able to resolve the problem, and so continues to be excluded from major decisions, thus completing the vicious circle.

This provides a rationale for line managers to take even greater responsibility for people management activities, although of course at one level this has always been one of their jobs (Lowe, 1992). Because line managers operate at the workplace alongside the people they manage, their reactions can be more immediate and appropriate. Rather than waiting for an 'answer' from the personnel department, issues can be resolved instantly. Moreover, solutions are more likely to be in tune with business realities, and therefore contribute more overtly to organisational goals and performance. Having ultimate responsibility is also likely to enhance line management ownership of these issues, and so increase their commitment to integrating HR with other objectives. Some practitioners have even suggested that the HR function could be disbanded if line managers are given and accept this responsibility (Cooper, 2001b).

For most observers, however, the solution is not to get rid of the function but to encourage HR practitioners to be accepted as 'business partners' by their senior management colleagues. As Ulrich (1998: 129) notes, 'To be truly tied to business outcomes, HR needs to join forces with operating managers to systematically assess the impact and importance of initiatives.' It is likely to include a significant role for training and developing line managers. This recognises the fact that, ultimately, it is line managers who have overall responsibility for putting HR into effect, and that trying to create partnerships with HR specialists represents a viable way forward.

Several surveys indicate that line managers now have far greater responsibility for HR issues, typically in conjunction with HR practitioners where they are employed. Storey (1992) detected some shifts in the early 1990s. Line managers were at the forefront of various change initiatives, and communicated with their staff through team-briefings, appraised them for pay purposes, and dealt directly with employees rather than channelling issues through trade union representatives. By the mid-1990s, Hutchinson and Wood (1995: 9) noted – on the basis of interviews with senior line and personnel managers in 27 organisations – that 22 of them reported greater line management involvement in personnel issues since 1990. The devolution was often accompanied by decentralisation within the organisation, with greater local financial autonomy and responsibility, sometimes due to privatisation or deregulation. This trend has continued. For example, Hall and Torrington (1998: 50) report that there are very few areas in which the HR function now makes a decision on its own, but that typically first line managers make decisions in conjunction with HR specialists. The 1998 WERS survey (Cully *et al*, 1999: 56) also found that supervisors were much more likely to play a part in HR-type decisions than they had previously, as did an IRS survey of 60 organisations conducted in 2000. Unfortunately, the latter survey did not differentiate between sole and shared responsibilities and was therefore only able to conclude that first line managers had a heavy involvement in decisions about HR issues relating to their own staff. The limits to supervisory control of decisions are abundantly clear both in the WERS and the IRS surveys. In both, it is rare for first line managers to have final authority over decision-making. For example, in the WERS survey (Cully *et al*, 1999: 57), just 30 per cent of supervisors in the private sector and 17 per cent in the public sector had the final say over the selection of staff for their teams. For other issues (eg pay rises and dismissal) it was much lower.

> What is the division of responsibility and activity between HR and line managers at your place of work, or one with which you are familiar?

Which aspects of HRM are line managers most likely to undertake, and are there differences between responsibilities for policy and practice? Hutchinson and Wood (1995: 17) found that the HR function took the lead in the determination of *policy* across all areas, either having sole responsibility or deciding on policy in conjunction with line management. It was rare that line managers took the lead on policy issues – either on their own or in consultation with personnel colleagues. There were no great variations across the whole HR spectrum, although the personnel influence is slightly more marked with resourcing policies such as human resource planning or recruitment and selection.

If the HR function took the lead in developing policy, the picture in relation to *practice* is somewhat different. Here, line managers played a much greater part, according to the respondents, especially in resourcing and employee relations, while in employee development and employee reward the HR professional still had a significant role in most issues. Hall and Torrington (1998: 57) found that HR managers had the biggest role in issues to do with pay and benefits, and the least in appraisals, quality initiatives, health and safety, and communications. In general, it would appear that HR involvement tends to remain highest where issues of consistency and specialist expertise are most important and lowest when line managers are responsible for dealing with everyday management issues. Nevertheless, the conclusion from most studies is that HR specialists and line managers tend to work in conjunction with each other across a wide range of issues.

Of course, much depends on the respective power bases of the line managers and HR practitioners. A study by Lupton (2000: 62) provides a useful corrective for any personnel specialists who believe that decisions about devolution rest solely with them. This examined the role played by personnel in the selection of doctors, and concluded that it was little more than 'pouring the coffee', acting as an administrative support while the consultants made decisions. In this situation the personnel professionals were on low grades and had little opportunity to influence the highly-paid and very influential consultants who made it clear that they resented any interference from an external source. On occasions, the consultants short-circuited the formal procedures, as well as making it clear to candidates that they felt questions asked by the personnel officer were of little importance.

The 2000 IRS survey found that about 60 per cent of its respondent organisations had experienced problems with the devolution of HR to line managers. Drawing on this and several other studies it would appear that there are four major concerns. First, it is suggested that line managers do not possess the skills and competencies necessary to perform the HR aspects of their jobs effectively without the support and involvement of personnel practitioners. IRS (IRS *Employment Trends* 698, 2000: 12) quoted a number of examples where skills gaps had been identified in relation to the breadth of management responsibilities and confidence in the role. Drawing on a study of 28 organisations, Gennard and Kelly (1997: 34–5) suggest that line managers are unlikely to acquire sufficient skills in the HR area without continuing support from HR specialists. McGovern *et al* (1997: 14) reckon that the low educational and technical base of line managers in Britain is a significant constraint on the effective devolution of HRM in Britain. Changes tend to occur so rapidly that training is carried out neither properly nor systematically, and line managers pick things up as they go along. Cunningham and Hyman (1999: 18) provide examples of insufficient training for line managers expected to take on extra responsibilities. The faddish nature of many management interventions, and the demand for instant success, also relies upon new initiatives being implemented without full and effective preparation (Marchington and Wilkinson, 2000). It also helps to explain why line managers fail to take new ideas seriously because they expect them to be jettisoned when the next fashion appears.

> Why should it matter that line managers typically have a low educational and technical base in Britain, and how is this a problem when it comes to the management of people? Are there any industries in which this might be less of a problem?

The second concern is even more problematic. We have already argued that line managers probably need further training and development in HRM if they are to be more effective at work. However, there is also a feeling among line managers that they do not actually need any training in HRM, a point that comes out strongly from Cunningham and Hyman's (1995: 18) interviews. They note that many supervisors and line managers feel that competence in the area is gained from a mixture of common sense and experience, and that training is unnecessary. Two quotes from their study sum this up well:

'Most of this is common sense anyway. We have had some training but when an issue comes up it's always in an area where you have had no preparation ... you can deal with it if you consider matters carefully.'

'If I went for a personnel manager's job, I would know what to do ... I have had no formal training in these matters – it has just been on-the-job experience using manuals.'

This disdain for learning and development is very worrying. It contrasts sharply with what they (the line managers) believe is needed to fulfil their own traditional work roles, especially if this is a technical area where knowledge and skills in science or engineering would be considered essential. Most line managers have received little more than rudimentary training in the area, and for those who were recruited from university more than 20 years ago it would have formed only a minor and insignificant part of their degree programmes. Moreover, it is often assumed that the skills held by personnel specialists are either irrelevant, because this is all common sense, or inappropriate because it is based on models of human behaviour that are seen as naïve and idealistic. This is very apparent in small organisations that do not have a specialist HR presence and where personnel work is undertaken by people without any training and whose main responsibility is to ensure that wages are paid correctly and on time. The case of doctor recruitment mentioned above (Lupton, 2000: 56) is a clear, if extreme, example of how the personnel presence can be marginalised in the workplace even if it is required as part of the organisation's policy. The doctors refused to work with person specifications, feeling that they could 'spot a good doctor' when they saw one without any interference from personnel. Moreover, the consultants who led the interview panels were sometimes quite explicit in their undermining of personnel officers who tried to prevent improper questions being asked of applicants.

Third, as we saw in Chapter 8, line managers have many other more pressing priorities than managing and developing the people who work for them. At the 'leading-edge' organisations studied by Gratton *et al* (1998), line managers did not feel any institutional pressure – through their own performance criteria – to consider HRM issues seriously because they were low on their list of priorities. Even at these supposedly forward-looking organisations, issues to do with people management did not appear in formal or unwritten performance expectations. Line managers report frustration that they are not able to devote sufficient time to HR issues – such as appraisal – because 'harder' priorities tend to dominate (Cunningham and Hyman, 1999: 25). Without explicit proactive support from senior managers, and recognition and rewards for their work in the HR area, it is easy to understand why line managers do not take this part of their job too seriously.

> How would you convince a line manager that it was important to take the HR aspects of her/his job seriously in the absence of any explicit performance criteria?

The problem leads on to the final concern – without specialist HR support and clear procedures to follow, it is highly likely that inconsistencies will appear in the management of human resources. This is most apparent in relation to compliance with employment legislation – although we believe this does little more than formalise 'good practice'. Earnshaw *et al*'s research (2000) on discipline and dismissal in small firms demonstrates clearly the potential problems that can occur if line managers fail to follow correct procedures. Dismissals arose after 'heated rows' at the workplace or due to personality clashes, without following any procedure whatsoever. Evidence, due process and the opportunity to appeal all tended to be lacking. Moreover, action taken on one occasion in relation to a particular member of staff is ignored on a subsequent occasion in relation to another. It appears that managers tend to adopt a lenient stance in relation to a worker who is liked or valued while treating another much more harshly if he or she 'fails to fit in'. On some occasions, dismissals are deferred until after the completion of an urgent order or a replacement is available. In short, line managers assess their work situation before acting or vary their decision according to the individual worker.

The shifting of HR issues into the hands of line managers has several implications for the work of HR professionals – not least in terms of numbers employed by organisations. New skills are likely to become more important in the future. For example, HR professionals might play a larger part in the formulation of HR policies and procedural frameworks – such as in recruitment or grievance-handling – to ensure adherence to corporate policy and legal requirements. They might also provide expert advice and guidance on all personnel matters perhaps through guidance manuals. Finally, there is likely to be an even greater demand to train line managers so that they have sufficient skills to enable them to devise a job description, conduct an interview, or harness employee commitment. This new role is likely to be strengthened by the effective use of information technology in areas such as absence monitoring, standard letter production, spreadsheets and personal records. (See the box below.)

How HR can support middle managers

- HR strategies should be composed of broad themes that can then be contextualised by middle managers at an operational level.

- Middle managers should be encouraged to contribute towards an elaboration of these broad themes.

- Opportunities should be provided for middle managers to span boundaries within the organisation through membership of project groups.

- The HR function should be organised to allow HR professionals to work closely with middle managers at the point of delivery.

- The development of middle managers is directed towards their contribution to strategic change.

Adapted from Currie G. and Procter S. 'Exploring the relationship between HR and middle managers', *Human Resource Management Journal*, Vol. 11, No. 3, 2001. pp53–69

In order to convince line managers to take advice about human resource issues seriously, two sets of arguments seem relevant. Both of these demand that HR managers acquire better financial awareness and the ability to provide costings for their recommendations. The first set of arguments concerns the cost of getting things wrong, and it is worthwhile estimating the financial implications of mistakes. Examples include the cost of a tribunal case for an unfair dismissal, a lapse in safety awareness resulting in an accident, or the cost of lost orders due

CASE STUDY: How can HR and line managers work together more effectively?

This case concerns the education department of a local authority, and it demonstrates clearly that major problems can arise without clear lines of accountability and a systematic framework for relations between different managers.

The organisation in question has a personnel presence both at corporate and at departmental level, with some element of dotted-line relationships between the two. Broadly, however, the personnel function in each department is left to get on with its own work within a framework that applies to the council as a whole. The head of HR for the Education Department had no previous personnel experience but worked as a line manager in the service for many years and was well-known to staff there. The chief officer for the Education Department felt that one of his strengths was HR and he was therefore keen to run this himself – indeed, he made a point of stressing that he wanted 'someone who knew the service, rather than an expert in human resources'. The other HR staff in the Department were on low grades and part-way through their CIPD courses at the local college. Accordingly, they had little experience of HRM beyond their current jobs but they were aware of the main professional issues.

The department was run in a very hierarchical way, and all decisions had to be approved by senior managers. Line managers were allowed relatively little freedom to make decisions, and this often resulted in long delays. Many of the front-line staff in the department had been transferred in from other jobs in the council, as part of its employment security policy, and some were renowned around the authority for being difficult to manage. This led to a number of issues at workplace level, set within a context of an increasingly problematical employment relations agenda at national level.

During the past year there have been problems with time-keeping, with poor performance, and with fraudulent use of the council's property. In some cases, the evidence is clearly available whereas in others it is more difficult due to differing interpretations of the situation. The line managers have tried to address these issues, but on each occasion the matter has had to be referred up the chain for a decision. It has not been unusual for there to be delays of several months as more senior managers work out what to do. Because the head of HR in the Education Department knows so many of the staff, and worked there himself for so long, he finds difficulty in taking a hard line with disciplinary issues. This inertia is also reinforced by the fact that some of the senior managers are in a similar position.

The authority of the line managers is often undermined because long-serving front-line staff go directly to the senior manager if they have problems and effectively short-circuit the management chain. They also ensure that their views about line managers are made known. The head of the Education Department always expects to be involved in HR decisions and this causes yet more problems. The junior HR staff – the only ones that have any professional training in the subject – are on low grades and find it difficult to impose their own views on the situation. Indeed, this lack of influence has led several of these staff to leave the organisation in frustration.

Clearly, the situation is a mess. *What would you do to address these issues, and what advice would you provide about (a) the organisation of the HR function, (b) the authority to be vested in line managers, and (c) how relations between line managers and HR could be made more effective?*

to a strike because an employee relations issue was badly handled. Organisations with a poor public relations profile can suffer costs at the recruitment stage through a lack of high-quality applicants or because staff leave disappointed that the organisation has not met their expectations. If the reputation is particularly poor, customers may decide not to buy goods or services from the organisation (see Chapter 6). Costs can also be viewed in 'softer' motivational terms reflected in low levels of productivity, unsatisfactory customer service and inadequate quality standards, or through poor levels of attendance and time-keeping, and high levels of labour turnover, stress, and general dissatisfaction. A realistic view has to be taken about costs. The costs of high labour turnover, for example, must not just be assessed in terms of the 'lost' employee, but must also include the costs of re-advertising, re-interviewing and re-inducting – as well as the time it takes for a new member of staff to reach the top of the learning curve.

The second set of arguments relate to the benefits of getting it right. Many of these are the converse of those outlined above. Financial benefits can accrue through the higher value that is added from each well-motivated and productive employee, and public relations benefits can emerge so that the image of 'a good employer' leads to the attraction of high-quality applicants. Moreover, 'softer' motivational benefits can flow from low levels of absenteeism, from the positive impact which committed employees make on customers, and from the higher levels of productivity and quality which appear to result from high-commitment HRM. All these ideas can be applied to the case study on the previous page.

Enhancing the contribution of the HR function

On several occasions, we have noted the distinction between HRM as a discrete function staffed by specialist managers and HRM as an integral part of every line manager's job. Sometimes this distinction is forgotten in evaluations of the impact of human resource issues on organisational performance, or the ambiguity causes problems in our attempts to assess whether or not HRM adds value. It also helps to explain why human resource specialists appear to be so critical of their own contribution to organisational goals in a way that does not appear to concern other specialist functions (Torrington, 1998). Guest and Hoque (1994b) suggest three reasons why this might be the case. First, the history and emergence of the profession has always put it in an ambiguous position, with the debates about welfare or efficiency, or intermediary or managerial control function, for example. Following considerable rationalisation in most organisations over the last two decades, questions have been raised about the need for a separate specialist personnel function, either at headquarters or at the workplace. Second, an ambivalence for people management issues is created and reinforced by a UK national culture which puts a primacy on financial control and short-termism to the neglect of longer-term human resource development considerations. Third, the contribution of human resource specialists has always been hard to quantify because they work closely with line managers and are dependent on the latter to put systems and policies into effect. Consequently, although 'we may be able to identify the impact of personnel decisions, we cannot always be sure whether the personnel specialists contributed towards them' (Guest and Hoque, 1994b: 41). In other words, although the philosophy and framework for HRM is set by the HR function, it is ultimately dependent on line managers to put them into effect.

Several observers have concluded that the HR function has a minor impact on organisations, summed up well by Skinner's quote that the personnel function is just 'big hat and no cattle' (Guest, 1991). Fernie *et al* (1994: 12), drawing on the 1990 WIRS database, concluded that 'workplaces with a personnel specialist and/or director responsible for personnel matters have very much worse relations than those without such workplace or board specialists'. However, detailed analysis of their work reveals severe methodological and conceptual problems, both in terms of the respondent base for their research and in the interpretation of the results. Because 93 per cent of the sample rated the employee relations climate at their workplace as good or better, and only 2 per cent considered it to be poor or very poor, their conclusion is perverse.

One way to increase the likelihood that organisations take HR issues seriously is to have a specialist personnel presence on the board. Millward *et al* (2000: 76) review data from the successive WIRS/WERS surveys to show that by the late 1990s 64 per cent of workplaces in the private sector were in organisations where there was a specialist presence on the board. In fact, the proportion had declined since the mid-1990s when it stood at 76 per cent, and it was particularly marked in manufacturing companies where well under half had a specialist presence on the board. However, it appears that the decline is due to a change in the composition of workplaces over this time rather than organisations deciding to clear out their HR directors (Millward *et al*, 2000: 77). Indeed, the proportion of workplaces in large multinationals that had an HR director remained constant, and in workplaces where trade unions were recognised it actually rose slightly. WERS (Cully *et al*, 1999: 81) also found that workplaces with a personnel specialist and an integrated employee development plan were substantially more likely to use a wide range of HR practices than those without them. The vast majority of workplaces do not utilise 'bundles' of HR practice, and this is more pronounced where there is no specialist HR presence (Sisson, 2001: 89).

Although most observers feel that an HR presence on the board is likely to mean that issues of people management are taken seriously, Torrington is less convinced. He suggests (1998: 33) that 'formal positioning on the board, or the lack of it, did not seem to make much difference to the extent of personnel's influence.' Hope-Hailey *et al* (1997) also suggest that it may be possible for HRM to be treated as a strategic issue without a specialist presence on the board. However, this is only possible if the chief executive is convinced of the value of HRM and these values are embedded throughout the entire organisation via line managers.

The extent of influence may depend rather more on the attitudes of chief executives towards personnel issues and the career paths of the HR directors themselves. Drawing on interviews with HR and managing directors in 60 organisations, Kelly and Gennard (2000) identify three different routes for personnel to the board. A very small number of HR directors were 'parachuted' into the role, usually because the chief executive needed a more general expertise. About one third had taken what was termed a 'vertical' route through personnel, undertaking a range of generalist rather than specialist HR duties over their careers. The largest proportion, however, had taken a 'zigzag' route spending periods of time in general or line management as well as in personnel. They felt that this had equipped them well for the wide range of skills needed to perform effectively at board level. Three factors seemed to be important in selecting a specialist HR board member: professional and technical competence, business focus, and being a team player. Appointment decisions are made in order to plug specific gaps in current expertise, although interpersonal and teamworking skills seem to be paramount (Stiles, 2001: 643). In short, while HR representation on the board may help to ensure that people management issues are given due consideration, it would also appear that HR directors are usually appointed because they can make a general contribution to the business. In Caldwell's study (2001: 45), one of the HR directors said that he 'was a director first and an HR director second', someone able to bring both boardroom credibility and operational expertise to resolve issues. CIPD research (Guest and King, 2001) suggests ways in which HR directors can improve their contribution – see *Voices from the boardroom* box below.

Voices from the boardroom

Research for the CIPD by David Guest and Zella King has been investigating the views of directors about, among other things, the importance of people management to organisational performance and the standing of the HR function. Most directors considered it self-evident that good people management impacted on performance, but that there was plenty of room for improvement. The most important elements of HRM were identified as performance management, training, selection, career development and harmonisation. Many comments referred to the relationship between HR and the line, quite a number stressing that the role of the HR function was to support line managers rather than acting as 'corporate police'. Whereas more

---

than two-thirds of the directors claimed to be aware of current research on people management and performance, only a quarter gave a convincing answer showing they knew what it was. Because HR directors are a major source of information for chief executives, there is an opportunity here for HR to strengthen its contribution by helping their senior colleagues to understand the 'hows' of people management. They also need to ensure that their departments are staffed with professionals who are aware of business issues, who use language other managers understand and whose initiatives can make a tangible contribution to their organisation.

Source: adapted from Guest D. and King Z. 'Personnel's paradox', *People Management*, 27 September 2001

An alternative way to assess the effectiveness of HRM and human resource specialists is to ask key stakeholders in the organisation for their views (Guest and Peccei, 1994; Wilkinson and Marchington, 1994). The views of line managers, chief executives or employees – each of whom is a 'customer' or 'end-user' of HR services – can be sought. Mayo (1999: 33) believes that HR managers gain influence by using their expertise in helping other managers achieve their goals. Moreover, they should escape from the balance-sheet mentality and regard all staff as knowledge workers whose intellectual capital must be developed. Tesco adopted a balanced scorecard approach in the late 1990s by developing a 'steering wheel' with four quadrants – people, finance, customers and operations (IRS *Employment Trends* 703, 2000). Moreover, the senior management team at store level – including the personnel manager – take it in turns to manage the store for about 20 per cent of their working time. This provides valuable opportunities for the HR function to learn about other aspects of the business and at the same time identify the services that other managers rely on to run the store. The balanced scorecard at Sears (Yeung and Berman, 1997: 324) focused on the creation of a vision that the company was a 'compelling place to invest', a 'compelling place to shop' and a 'compelling place to work'.

The services and support valued by other managers varies depending upon their level in the hierarchy. Buyens and de Vos (2001: 82) asked senior managers, line managers and HR managers to indicate (a) the value of various HR practices to the organisation, and (b) the value that the HR function added to the organisation in general. Using Ulrich's model outlined earlier in this chapter, the senior managers in their study valued HR's role principally in the areas of change and transformation – such as balancing organisational and individual needs, and overcoming barriers to change. The line managers were not really bothered about HR as a strategic partner but felt that added value came from administrative expertise, managing costs and delivering core HR services such as recruitment and training. The HR managers interestingly felt that the role of employee champion added the greatest value – either in terms of regarding employees as 'the heartbeat of the organisation' or providing a bridge between different interest groups. Additionally, it is important to note that HR managers were not just valued for their proactive, strategic contribution but also for their ability to resolve problems and fight fires that arose.

The assessments made of the HR contribution by directors and chief executives are clearly very important. Guest and King (2002) interviewed 48 directors for the CIPD, drawn equally from chief executives, operational directors and HR directors. Rather more were positive than negative about the contribution of the HR function, and indeed the most critical were the HR directors themselves. Views were split on whether there should be an HR presence on the board. One of the quotes from a chief executive suggested that without an HR presence on the board, the message given out would be that people management is not as important as other activities. In contrast, one of the operations directors felt there was no need for specific HR representation on the board because HR was the responsibility of all members. If present, HR directors were expected to operate as 'thinking partners'. Considerably more directors felt that HR made a positive contribution to the business than did not, especially in setting the tone as well as challenge other directors if HR issues did not receive proper treatment.

Debate with your colleagues whether it is possible for the HR contribution to be effective without a specialist personnel presence on the board.

There are few published surveys seeking the views of employees about the performance of the HR function, so it is often hard to work out what these end-users think about its work. Gibb's (2001) survey of over 2,600 employees in 73 organisations is particularly useful because it specifically asked employees for their opinion of how HR was performing on a number of counts. In general terms, HR tended to do best in areas concerning interpersonal relations (such as being approachable, helpful and prompt) and professionalism and knowledge (such as confidentiality and advice). Estimates of the function were rather less positive in the delivery of practice – such as recruitment, absence, and appraisal. There were positive ratings across all issues, and this consistency seems to 'indicate that employees have a favourable view of the work of specialist HR staff' (Gibb, 2001: 330). The results show that HR staff are seen in a more positive frame of light than HR practices. Perhaps this suggests that the HR function is perceived more favourably when it is totally responsible for delivery and less well when delivery has to be mediated through line managers.

It is difficult for HR professionals to measure the effectiveness of their own function, given that their contribution to organisational goals is mediated through line managers. Two broad options are available. First, use can be made of external benchmarking exercises through industry clubs, consultants and employers' organisations. One such process is APAC (the audit of personnel activities and costs), described by Burn and Thompson (1993), that adopts a three-tier approach to assessing the performance of the human resource function. Other services are provided by consultants such as PricewaterhouseCoopers (IRS *Employment Trends* 721, 2000). A number of key statistics are produced for benchmarking, but these are clearly subject to considerable variation between organisations, regions and occupational group, as well as over time depending on the state of the external labour market. Drawn from a range of sources (Mayo, 1995; Ulrich, 1997; IRS *Employment Trends* 698, 2000), some of the most widely used measures are:

- the ratio of HR staff to full-time equivalent employees
- the costs of the HR function as a percentage of total costs or as a cost per employee
- recruitment costs per new recruit
- the time taken to fill each vacancy
- the average number of days lost per annum through absenteeism
- the level of labour turnover
- the training costs per employee per annum
- the percentage of employees involved in training
- the percentage of employees who receive formal appraisals
- the ratio of salaries and wages to those of competitors
- the percentage of employees involved in problem-solving groups
- the speed and effectiveness of response to employee grievances
- the degree of employee satisfaction evinced in attitude surveys.

An IRS *Guide to Benchmarking the HR Function* (IRS *Employment Review* 742, 2001) presents data from 80 organisations covering a broad spectrum of employers in Britain. It found that the most widely-used measures were 'levels of staff turnover' (80 per cent of organisations), 'absence rates' (74 per cent) and 'employee attitude surveys' (68 per cent). However, great care must be exercised with benchmarking to make sure that the measures used are appropriate and accurate. For example, recruitment costs vary considerably between occupations, as do training costs. Levels of absenteeism and labour turnover differ significantly across the economy and much depends on the nature of the external labour market. Equally, figures for absence levels can vary depending on whether or not all forms of absence are included. Levels of worker satisfaction show differences between industries and countries, as well as between men and women (Rose, 1999). Even if we can be sure that the comparisons are valid, the problem remains that all the measures are related to costs rather than to value added. It may well be that higher costs are offset by, or contribute to, much higher levels of performance in the short or the long term. A single, blanket figure for the costs of replacing a member of staff assumes that all employees are worth retaining because they perform at or above expectations. Indeed, it may actually be cost-effective for people whose performance is not up to standard to leave the organisation. Complexities such as this make comparisons of raw figures on labour turnover rather less useful.

Pfeffer (1997: 360) actually questions whether or not benchmarking exercises ever have value because 'what is easily measurable and what is important are often only loosely related'. One set of figures produced in the IRS *Guide* enables readers to generate a ratio of the number of permanent HR staff to the number of employees. This shows sizeable variations between industries as well as between organisations within the same industry. For example, in chemicals the ratio varies from 1:22 to 1:167, in finance from 1:45 to 1:200, and in public services from 1:16 to 1:610. It is difficult to draw firm conclusions from this information. If one's own organisation is above the average, does this justify a reduction in the number of HR staff without a consideration of how these people operate and some estimate of the value that is added by their contribution? If a reduction in staffing levels is demanded, a cunning HR director might find a way round the figures by subcontracting certain aspects of the function in order to reduce the number of direct staff, perhaps with little benefit. Although it is conceivable that an organisation may decide there is under-investment in HRM, it is rather more likely that investigations will focus on how to reduce costs to bring it back to the industry norm. This may be a dramatic example, but similar questions can arise about the meanings behind raw figures of labour turnover, absence or training, for example.

> Write a short report for your manager outlining the limitations of benchmarking and explaining what other measures might be used instead.

The alternative option is to focus on internal evaluations – by drawing up service-level agreements, for example. This has become much more common in recent years, either as part of a contracting-out exercise or when an HR function is required to justify its expenditure. Service-level agreements can cover a whole range of aspects of HRM, such as payroll management, recruitment advertising, induction, and personnel information systems. According to Mayo (1995: 249), service-level agreements offer several advantages to employers, not least in enabling a more specific statement of service provision that can facilitate the making of auditing, benchmarking, and outsourcing decisions. There are also dangers with this approach. The HR function may find that in trying to satisfy the needs of internal customers it becomes the servant of other functions – it is forced into making agreements that create greater problems in the medium term. As we saw earlier in this chapter, allowing HRM to be defined by line managers downplays the judgement of professionals. This has major drawbacks because the need to satisfy short-term cost-effectiveness is given prominence without any consideration of the problems that can be created in the longer run (Sisson, 2001: 94).

The HR function can apply TQM processes to audit its activities as part of a service-level agreement. The precise list of practices obviously depends on the organisation and function involved, but some of the more typical might be:

- preparing offer and contract letters within one day

- providing advice on disciplinary matters within two days

- advising staff on terms and conditions of employment within five days

- preparing, disseminating and analysing absence and labour turnover data to line managers on a monthly basis

- evaluating training provision on an annual basis.

It is not assumed that the more of these that are undertaken the better. Indeed, going down this route might result in poorer performance because resources are spread too thinly, or the HR function may come to be seen as the purveyor of the latest fads and fashions that are irrelevant to organisational needs. The main issue is to find ways in which the function can continually improve its service to stakeholders and its contribution to organisational success.

Prepare a paper for a general manager which demonstrates the way in which the personnel function is still able to 'add value' in an organisation that has devolved many of its HR practices to line managers. Choose any type of organisation for this exercise.

It is important to realise that by attempting to quantify the HR contribution, the function basically succumbs to the accountants' vision of how organisations are meant to operate. As Peter Armstrong (1989: 160) cautioned many years ago, this cedes too much to 'the dominant accounting culture and may also, in the end, achieve little security for the personnel function'. Pfeffer (1997: 363) makes a similar point when he argues that HR is unlikely ever to win the numbers game because other departments have much more experience of this – and they also set the rules! He warns that 'if all HR becomes is finance with a different set of measures and topic domains, then its future is indeed likely to be dim'. The use of figures and ratios to measure the costs of the HR contribution might make it easier for the function to be subcontracted without a proper analysis of its contribution in the longer term. As we have suggested on several occasions, the focus on costs is too narrow, and it is better to direct attention to how the HR function can add value to the organisation as a whole. One option is to set up shared service centres (Arkin, 2001a) to provide answers to routine enquiries – see the case study below.

CASE STUDY: Shared services for the HR function

One of the more recent innovations in HR has been the development of shared service centres, usually provided by the host organisation rather than by a specialist outsourcing company. The pressures to introduce these kinds of facility are similar to those that lead to outsourcing, but the organisations concerned feel that more can be gained from retaining an in-house service than going for a consultancy firm. An Institute for Employment Studies (IES) report found that cost reduction (to avoid duplication), quality improvement (through consistent messages) and organisational restructuring were the principal forces behind the setting-up of shared service centres. Among the organisations that have established such centres are BOC, J P Morgan, IBM and Scottish & Newcastle, and shared service provision is also appearing in the NHS.

Shared service centres tend to be involved in the provision of HR advice about a range of issues, including personnel policies and procedures, recruitment, employment legislation, payment queries, and promotion and development opportunities. Some are open solely to managers whereas others provide a service for all employees. The importance of providing a consistent and accessible service is particularly critical in organisations that are geographically dispersed and have small workplaces – such as in many parts of retailing. The organisations that have

gone down this route would appear to have been satisfied by the initiative. It is also emphasised that although shared services are run on a call centre principle, they are very different from the 'assembly line in the head' image, and rely on knowledgeable staff who do not perform according to a standard script.

There are a number of issues that must be considered in respect of shared service centres, however. The time that HR staff spend at these centres should be carefully monitored so that individual career paths are not destroyed – some organisations have set a limit of less than a year before people move back to other HR jobs. There are also concerns about the sophistication of the technology employed, as well as about the lack of face-to-face interaction. As with any initiative, the reasons for entering into shared services must be evaluated systematically, and they should not be solely to reduce costs. Obviously, there may well also be teething problems. But overall it would appear that shared services may offer an opportunity for large organisations to provide consistent and timely HR advice at lower costs.

Sources: Peter Reilly and Jane Pickard, 'HR service centres: called in to question', *People Management*, 6 July 2000; IRS *Employment Trends* 721, 'Dial-up HR at Scottish and Newcastle', February, 2001

CONCLUSION

In this chapter, we have reviewed the changing nature of the work undertaken by HR departments in Britain. There has been a great deal of interest in the notion that the function needs a presence on the board in order to make a contribution, and that this may be best achieved via a strategic partner role. There is little evidence that this has actually occurred in the vast majority of organisations, although it is clear that high-commitment HRM is more likely in workplaces that have a personnel presence. On the contrary, the tendency to subcontract HR work to consultants, either in its entirety or in a piecemeal fashion, has become more extensive. Moreover, line managers have continued to take over activities that were once the preserve of the HR function. This has led some (for example, Cunningham and Hyman, 1999) to question whether there will be a role for HR departments in the future. The situation is made worse by an increased tendency to seek quantitative assessments of HR work, sometimes using indicators that are inappropriate or too simplistic to allow a fundamental review of departmental performance. Although the dominant tradition in management more generally is driven by accountancy versions of performance, it is important for students to be aware of the severe limitations of such models. The fact that they focus on easily-measurable, cost-driven indicators does not sit easily with models that rest upon the assumption that HRM – especially high-commitment HRM – provides benefits over the longer term.

Useful reading

ARKIN A. 'Central intelligence', *People Management*, 22 November 2001. pp38–41.

CUNNINGHAM I. *and* HYMAN J. 'Developing human resource responsibilities to the line: Beginning of the end or a new beginning for personnel?', *Personnel Review*, Vol. 28, No. 1/2, 1999. pp9–27.

GIBB S. 'The state of human resource management: evidence from employees' views of HRM systems and staff', *Employee Relations* Vol. 23, No. 4, 2001. pp318–36.

GUEST D. *and* KING Z. 'Personnel's paradox', *People Management*, 27 September 2001.

INDUSTRIAL RELATIONS SERVICES. 'Flexible working – new rights for parents, more work for tribunals'. IRS *Employment Review* 742, 17 December 2001b. pp46–49.

KELLY J. *and* GENNARD J. 'Getting to the top: career paths of personnel directors', *Human Resource Management Journal*, Vol. 10, No. 3, 2000. pp22–37.

PFEFFER J. 'PITFALLS on the road to measurement: The dangerous liaison of human resources with the idea of accounting and finance', *Human Resource Management*, Vol. 36, No. 3, 1997. pp357–365.

PROCTER S. *and* CURRIE G. 'The role of the personnel function: roles, perceptions and processes in an NHS trust', *International Journal of Human Resource Management*, Vol. 10, No. 6, 1999. pp1077–1091.

SISSON K. 'Human resource management and the personnel function', in J. Storey (ed.), *Human Resource Management: A critical text*, 2nd edition. London, Thomson. 2001.

ULRICH D. 'A new mandate for human resources', *Harvard Business Review*, Jan-Feb 1998. pp125–134.

Cost-effective HR Planning, Recruitment and Selection

By the end of this chapter, readers should be able to:

- undertake the main aspects of the recruitment and selection process

- implement and operate cost-effective processes for recruiting and retaining the right calibre of staff in their own organisation, and for evaluating these processes at contractors

- contribute to the design, implementation and evaluation of selection decisions.

In addition, readers should understand and be able to explain:

- the links between human resource planning, recruitment and selection and other aspects of people management and development

- the nature of the recruitment process and its principal components

- the major advantages and disadvantages of the most important selection methods, and their contribution to organisational effectiveness.

Introduction

Recruitment and selection is a crucial element of HRM in all organisations, irrespective of their size, structure or sector. Over the last two decades this area of HR practice has become more sophisticated, involving the assistance of organisational psychologists or consultants to improve the reliability and validity of selection decisions. This is important because new recruits provide managers with an opportunity to acquire new skills as well as to amend organisational cultures. Too often, however, decisions are made in an informal, *ad hoc* and reactive manner without a proper analysis of whether or not specific jobs are needed, other than to fill a vacancy. Moreover, there is often little recognition that the characteristics required by post-holders should perhaps be specified or that techniques other than an unplanned interview might be used when recruiting and selecting staff.

It is the purpose of this chapter to review the entire recruitment and selection cycle, from human resource planning through to the decision on appointment. The process incorporates a number of stages, each of which must be completed effectively if a satisfactory appointment is to be made. The situation has to be analysed in order to establish whether or not a particular post is to be filled internally on a permanent, open-ended contract, on a temporary basis, or externally through an agency. A job description and person specification/accountability profile should guide the process, and care should be taken at each stage to ensure that the organisation continues to convey the message it wants to the outside world. Once a suitable pool of candidates has been found, choices have to be made over selection methods, although it is generally advisable to employ multiple methods to increase the validity of selection decisions.

The implications of poor selection decisions for the business as a whole are potentially catastrophic. There may be expense in terms of the management time required to deal with disciplinary cases, in retraining poor performers, and in having to recruit replacements for those individuals who have been wrongly selected and/or who choose to quit soon after starting. The likely effects on customer service and product quality are also significant, whether workers are employed on a supermarket checkout or in an engineering factory or a hotel. The problem is not just one of recruiting someone who is under-qualified, lacks the relevant skills or is uncooperative, even though that is what inevitably comes to mind. Equally serious problems may arise with employees who are over-qualified and/or soon become bored with their work. Selecting the right person for the task and for the organisation is what matters.

Human resource planning, turnover and retention

At a time when world markets were characterised by greater stability and predictability, human resource planning was prominent in HRM, personnel management and labour economics. There were many books on the subject, and considerable emphasis in large organisations on planning their future employment needs – especially in the managerial hierarchy. This has been referred to as the 'golden age of manpower planning', since which time it 'caught a cold in the chill economic winds of the 1980s' (Cowling and Walters, 1990:3). The techniques in favour at the time drew heavily upon statistical techniques – making use of Markov models, for example (Bowey, 1975; Bramham, 1975, 1994; Walker, 1992; Sisson and Timperley, 1994). Most of the major texts on HRM now devote very little attention to the principles and practice of human resource planning, often tending to fall back on more general discussions of strategy or management control systems (Liff, 2000; O'Doherty, 2001; Iles, 2001). In what are now characterised as 'new, flexible' organisations, the mention of human resource planning conveys images of bureaucracy, rigidity, and a lack of real-life awareness of these uncertain times. It is sometimes implied that planning is irrelevant or misguided in a turbulent and increasingly insecure competitive environment.

Such a view, however, misunderstands the nature and uses of the planning process, and can be used to justify '*ad-hoc*ery' and reactive management. Planning is just as important, if not more so, during turbulent times to ensure that employers have staff of the right quality and quantity available at the right time. Compared with some of our international competitors, Britain has typically suffered from recurrent skill shortages at both a national and an organisational level. More effective long-term HR planning may have lessened the problems associated with this. Indeed, it could be argued that current pressures to control labour costs and protect tighter profit margins demands an increasing – rather than decreasing – emphasis on human resource planning.

Moreover, employers faced with declining markets must start planning well in advance for reductions in numbers employed so as to maintain long-term employment security for as many staff as possible and minimise the need for compulsory redundancies. Planning ahead provides managers with the opportunity to consider alternative forms of contract in advance or to subcontract work that is unpredictable in nature. Accordingly, long-term human resource planning has potentially positive implications for many features of the psychological, as well as the legal, contract in organisations that engage in it, although it may lead to worsened conditions in those to which the work is subcontracted. Hall and Torrington (1998: 160–1) indicated that HR planning was more important and took up more of HR managers' time in the mid-1990s than in the mid-1980s, but it is difficult to find firm evidence about its overall distribution now. It is even harder to determine the processes being used. As Liff (2000: 125) notes, 'Perhaps the most one can say with any certainty is that many UK companies continue to express a commitment to the idea of human resource strategy and planning. How this translates into practice, however, is less clear.'

Do you believe that human resource planning is worthwhile in your organisation (or one with which you are familiar)? What do you see as the organisational benefits of spending time making plans about future employment projections?

Human resource planning can be regarded as important for at least four sets of reasons:

- *It encourages employers to develop clear and explicit links between their business and human resource plans, and so integrate the two more effectively*. There are two ways in which this linkage can be viewed. First – following on from Chapter 8 – it can be seen solely in terms of the degree of 'fit' between HR planning and broader strategic plans, and the ability of human resource plans to deliver precisely what is required by the business as a whole. Second, it can be viewed in terms of an interactive relationship between corporate and human resource plans, with the latter contributing to the development of the former, and at least demonstrating that longer-term business goals may not be achievable if there are problems with labour supply. Either way, HR planning is perceived as a major facilitator of competitive advantage.

● *It allows for much better control over staffing costs and numbers employed.* It is important for employers to make projections about anticipated staffing needs, irrespective of whether a growth or decline in numbers is predicted. By so doing, employers are better able to match supply and demand, and make decisions about recruiting from the external labour market, relocating staff, or preparing for reductions in numbers employed. In each case, better control over staffing costs is the likely result. For example, if short-term product market demand is expected to be highly variable, a decision can be made on whether or not to subcontract work or to use workers on temporary contracts.

● *It enables employers to make more informed judgements about the skills and attitude mix in the organisation, and prepare integrated HR strategies.* Although it is important to ensure a match in numbers employed, it is just as necessary to achieve the right skills mix among the workforce. Choices about the skill mix can be linked to decisions about the future shape and nature of the business, and shifts can be planned in advance. For example, senior management in an organisation that is becoming more customer-oriented in its approach might well consider how existing staff can be retrained to cope with future demands. If new staff are needed, choices have to be made about the HR implications of that decision.

● *It provides a profile of current staff (in terms of age, gender, race and disability, for example) which is necessary for moves towards an equal opportunities organisation.* Without accurate and up-to-date figures on existing staff numbers and their breakdown by grade and position, it is impossible for employers to make decisions about how equality management can be achieved (Schuler and Huber, 1993: 129). In each of the areas discussed above, but especially here, the use of information technology makes this a much more manageable task.

> If human resource planning is meant to derive so many benefits, why is so little written about it, and why do so few organisations appear to devote much time to it?

Several techniques have been used to derive 'hard' human resource plans. Broadly these have been applied to three sets of issues: forecasts of the demand for labour, forecasts of internal supply, and forecasts of external supply. Each of these is considered in turn below, although the greatest emphasis is on internal supply forecasts because this has traditionally been where HR contributions have been required

Forecasting future demand

There are basically two sorts of method for assessing future demands for labour – the objective and the subjective. The objective method relies upon the projection of past trends and, to be of any value, must take into account shifts brought about by changes in technology and organisational goals. Simple projections from the past to indicate the amount or type of labour required in the future can be related to results from work study exercises or ratios of customers to staff. For example, in the case of education, there are certain norms for the number of full-time equivalent (FTE) students per member of staff, or class sizes deemed appropriate for effective learning to take place. Arguments for increases, decreases or replacements are typically made with these figures in mind, and comparisons made with similar schools/departments in similar situations. However, technological changes may lead to major shifts in demand for certain types of labour, and simple extrapolations are of little value in these circumstances.

Fears that objective systems may be unresponsive to local needs have fuelled arguments that subjective methods are more appropriate. At its most basic this may be little more than managerial judgement about future needs, perhaps an excuse for speculation based on limited amounts of data. Subjective approaches can be either 'top-down' or 'bottom-up', or indeed a mixture of both. A top-down approach relies heavily on estimates from senior managers, a group of people who ought to have a clear idea about the direction in which the organisation is moving. The bottom-up method, conversely, focuses on departmental and workplace managers making estimates about future staffing requirements based upon their experience and judgement (Walker, 1992: 162), and is susceptible to 'inflated' demands to ensure that they do not lose out. In reality, both methods are combined to arrive at meaningful estimates of future demand.

Forecasting the demand for staff depends on assumptions about projected product demand, and the implications this has for the numbers and type of employees required. This is not a central task for HR specialists but is more likely to involve business planners, finance and marketing managers. It is much easier to forecast future demand in certain sectors than in others. For example, based upon past projections, reasonable assumptions can be made about overall levels of demand for health care, primary school education or food products in the next five years, thus allowing for sensible estimates of future labour demand. However, it is much more difficult to estimate the numbers of patients, schoolchildren or shoppers likely to attend a *specific* hospital, school or supermarket in the light of mobility patterns and, in principle, a wider degree of choice for consumers. Because classes at school are run in broad unit sizes (of, say, 30), problems arise if an extra 10 children are enrolled across two age-groups. Also, the decision to take on extra children leads to further questions about the need for more facilities, buildings and infrastructure. HR planning is even harder in companies that operate in highly competitive or volatile international markets.

The demand for jobs in 2010

Although many employers feel comfortable forecasting the internal supply of labour, trends for the overall market, broken down into sectors and occupations, remain more of a mystery. Research by the Institute for Employment Research and Cambridge Econometrics has produced forecasts for recruiters' needs up to the year 2010. This is worked out by adding or subtracting changes in the overall job levels from the underlying number of replacements required for staff that leave the particular labour market so as to calculate net demand. Overall, recruiters will have to fill over 13.5 million vacancies in the first decade of the 21st century in the main occupations in the UK. Five times as many will comprise vacancies in existing jobs as will be newly-created posts in expanding occupations and sectors.

The major areas in which greater numbers of recruits will be required are:

Administrative and clerical occupations	1.34 million
Caring work below para-professional level	1.14 million
Sales assistants and cashiers	1.11 million
Teaching and research professionals	0.82 million
Business and public service associate professionals	0.79 million

The major areas of decline will be in the following:

Elementary occupations such as cleansing, security, sales and personal services	1.17 million
Managers in hospitality and leisure services, farming, horticulture, forestry and fishing	0.50 million
Elementary occupations in agriculture, construction, goods handling and storage	0.46 million
Plant and machine operatives, assemblers, and construction workers	0.46 million
Skilled metal and electrical trades	0.45 million

Examine this set of figures, as well as other data, and prepare a brief paper outlining the implications of this for the following:

- a recruitment agency specialising in secretarial and administrative work

- government departments overseeing the training of health staff and teachers

Forecasting internal supply

Once the likely demand for labour has been forecasted, attention can turn to establishing the balance between external recruitment, developing staff internally, or, if necessary, seeking workforce reductions. This section examines factors internal to the organisation, while the next considers external supply.

The principal techniques cover two sorts of estimate: wastage/labour turnover, and internal job and grade movements. Data about these issues can be used for a variety of purposes, and can point to problems that are likely to emerge for the organisation. High levels of labour turnover, for example, can indicate problems with a whole range of HR policies and practices, possibly including not only inappropriate methods of recruitment and selection but also poorly-designed and uncompetitive pay systems, ineffective grievance and disciplinary procedures and practices, inadequate levels of training and development, and major blockages in communication systems. External factors that could account for these problems as well include the presence of new competitors for labour in the area or reduced levels of public transport to the workplace.

Two schools of thought dominate research and practice on turnover: the labour market/economic and the psychological (Morrell *et al*, 2001). The former tends to focus on factors external to the organisation – such as the level of unemployment, wage differentials and the availability of alternative jobs in the local or national (even global) economy depending on occupation. The latter tends to focus on individuals and their decisions to quit the organisation voluntarily, relating labour turnover to factors such as job satisfaction and employee commitment. Readers who wish to explore these approaches in greater detail should consult publications by Chang (1999), Kirschenbaum and Mano-Negrin (1999) and Tang *et al* (2000). Morrell *et al* (2001: 240) are clear that neither school is capable on its own of providing sufficiently good explanations or predictions of labour turnover.

Two measures are typically used to calculate rates of labour turnover. First, there is the *wastage rate*, which divides the number of staff who leave over a specified period by the number of staff employed overall; the formula is presented in Table 27 below. Typically, about 15 per cent of staff leave their employer each year for a mixture of voluntary and other reasons (IRS *Employment Review* 742c, 2001: 37). Both the numerator and the divisor can include different elements and be applied to different departments in the organisation. For example, 'leavers' may refer solely to those people who quit the organisation voluntarily, or it can include those made redundant, those at the end of fixed-term contracts, or those dismissed, each of which inflates the numerator. The divisor can be calculated on the basis of the number employed at the beginning of the year, at the end, or the average of the two figures. Comparisons of raw data are inevitably clouded by such considerations, and care should be taken in interpreting material without a clear understanding of the basis on which the statistics are derived. Exit interviews may shed some light on the problem, but people are often unwilling to provide an honest answer to explain their resignation. The most fundamental problem with these indices, however, is that they do not differentiate between leavers in terms of their length of service, grade or gender. As Morrell *et al* (2001: 222) note, 'This is because any single-figure measure of turnover will be inadequate in so far as it treats all those who leave as a homogeneous group.'

Problems such as this have led to the development of the second type of measure – *stability* indices. With these, the number of staff who have enjoyed a certain minimum period of service (say, one year) at a certain date is divided by overall numbers employed at that date – Table 27 shows this calculation. Stability indices provide a good indicator of the proportion of staff who have been with the organisation for a longer period, and conversely the extent to which labour turnover is a problem specific to new recruits.

This latter phenomenon is referred to as the 'induction crisis' because it occurs several months after new staff are recruited and realise that the job is rather different from what they expected, or that their previous post may not have been as bad as they felt at the time. Data from successive Labour Force Surveys (IRS *Employment Review* 742c, 2001: 33) show that over 20 per cent of workers leave within the first 12 months, a further 12 per cent leave during the second year of their employment, and thereafter it falls to under 5 per cent per annum. In short, about one third of people leave within the first two years of employment, at some cost to both parties. Levels of labour turnover vary from year to year. During the 1990s they ranged from a low of

Table 27   Indices of labour turnover

Wastage rate

$$\frac{\text{Leavers in year}}{\text{Average number of leavers in year}} \times 100$$

Stability rate

$$\frac{\text{Number of staff with at least one year's service at date}}{\text{Number of staff employed exactly one year before}} \times 100$$

about 12 per cent to a high of around 20 per cent (IRS *Employment Trends* 698, 2000: 8). Although reporting slightly higher overall figures due to different samples, the most recent CIPD survey (2001f) showed a large jump in levels of labour turnover between 1999 and 2000. In the latter year it had reached over 25 per cent – that is, more than one in four people left his or her organisation in any one year. Despite claims from the competing schools, lower levels of unemployment do have an influence on rates of turnover.

How have labour turnover rates changed recently, and what factors do you think help to explain that? *You may need to find more up-to-date information from the CIPD or IRS to do this properly.*

Tables 28 to 32 provide data on variations in labour turnover on the basis of occupational group, sector, region and organisation size, as well as some estimates about the costs of turnover in different occupations. Although an estimate of costs might be useful in emphasising the importance of improving recruitment and selection, as well as other HR practices, it is necessarily limited because of the assumptions made in reaching such figures. Perhaps the most serious of such defects is that all cases of labour turnover are treated in the same way, with no allowance for the performance levels and potential of the employees who leave. Clearly, managers may be relatively happy if a poor performer were to leave yet devastated if a high-flier with great potential were to join a competitor or a long-serving and experienced member of staff were to quit. Moreover, if an organisation is aiming to reduce the numbers employed or has to reduce costs, a high rate of labour turnover may actually be advantageous (Sadhev *et al*, 1999).

Tables 28–32   Labour turnover fact-file
Labour turnover for main occupational groups (2000)

Occupational group	Percentage
Managers	14
Professional	22
Associated professions, technical and scientific	21
Secretarial and administrative	24
Sales	23
Personal services	70*
Craft and skilled manual	17
Operative and assembly manual	22
Unskilled manual	25

* very small sample
Source: Chartered Institute of Personnel Development. *Labour Turnover*. London, CIPD. 2001f

Labour turnover for selected industries and sectors (2000)

Industrial sector	Percentage
Manufacturing	21
Retail, hotel and leisure, and consumer products	55
Professional services	31
Public sector	17
Transport, construction and other industries	19

Source: Chartered Institute of Personnel Development. *Labour Turnover*. London, CIPD. 2001f

Estimated total costs of labour turnover per leaver (2000)

Occupational group	£
Managers	6,086
Professional	5,813
Associated professions, technical and scientific	4,591
Secretarial and administrative	2,215
Sales	4,179
Personal services	1,589
Craft and skilled manual	1,736
Operative and assembly manual	1,225
Unskilled manual	895
Average	3,933

Source: Chartered Institute of Personnel Development. *Labour Turnover*. London, CIPD. 2001f

Labour turnover by region (1998–99)

Region	Labour turnover
South-west	26%
London	22%
North-east	22%
South-east	21%
North-west	20%
East	18%
East Midlands	17%
West Midlands	17%
Yorkshire and the Humber	15%
England	20%

Source: Industrial Relations Services. 'Benchmarking labour turnover 2001/02, Part 1', IRS *Employment Review* 741, 3 December 2001. pp31–38

Labour turnover per annum according to workplace size (1998–99)

Workplace employee numbers	Labour turnover
25–49	29%
50–99	26%
100–199	17%
200–499	14%
500+	12%
All	20%

Source: Industrial Relations Services. 'Benchmarking labour turnover 2001/02, Part 1', IRS *Employment Review* 741, 3 December 2001. pp31–38

Forecasting external supply

Most texts on human resource planning devote rather less attention to forecasts of external supply than to analyses of internal supply. This probably explains why so many employers are shocked to discover there are skill shortages or a lack of suitably qualified staff when they are recruiting. The so-called 'demographic time-bomb' in the 1990s is a good illustration of this. Due to a decline in the birth rate in the late 1970s, it was apparent that the number of school- and college-leavers entering the labour market in the early to mid-1990s would be significantly less than in previous years. This stimulated a spate of recruitment and advertising schemes designed to attract school-leavers, but also the introduction of new policies to retain existing female and elderly staff, and the employment of individuals past the normal age of retirement.

There are a number of factors that determine the supply of staff from the external labour market, at both a local and a national level. Obviously, local labour market and social information is more important for certain grades and types of staff – such as manual workers – whereas national and global trends and educational developments matter more for professionals. Broadly, the major factors influencing external labour supply *locally* include:

- the level of unemployment in the travel-to-work area

- the opening or closure of other workplaces in the area which compete for the same types of labour

- the number/qualifications of school- and college-leavers from the local educational system

- the cost of housing and the availability of transport to and from work

- the reputation of the employer compared with that of others in the area, measured by such things as wages and working conditions, employment record, and general public relations image.

The major factors that influence labour supply at a *national* level, and by implication locally, include:

- the level of unemployment in general, and in particular occupations

- the number of graduates in general, and in specific fields

- the UK and EU legal frameworks governing working time, equal opportunities, employment protection, and employee relations

- government and industry-wide training schemes.

Take *two* occupational groups in an organisation with which you are familiar, and draw up a list of the factors that influence labour supply for each group. What can the organisation do to ensure that there is an adequate supply of labour in each case?

Job and role analysis

Job and role analysis is the next stage in the recruitment and selection process, and it has a crucial part to play in identifying the tasks that new recruits are expected to undertake. In firms with relatively buoyant product markets and high levels of labour turnover, in which recruitment takes place on a frequent and continuing basis, it is probably not necessary to re-analyse jobs every time a vacancy has to be filled. However, it is useful to examine whether or not existing job descriptions and person specifications (or competency profiles) are appropriate for future requirements. Indeed, it may even demonstrate that there is no need for further recruitment or that the type of job and person required is somewhat different from that which had been anticipated. It may be rare for some organisations to recruit new staff, and in these cases rather more attention should be focused on redeploying employees to other roles. Job and role analysis is clearly equally relevant in this context, as it is in many areas of HRM. For example, it can help with the classification and ranking of different jobs, in identifying necessary changes in work design, and in relation to formulating training requirements and learning plans (Taylor, 1998; Armstrong, 1999).

Job analysis refers to 'the process of collecting, analysing and setting out information about the content of jobs in order to provide the basis for a job description and data for recruitment, training, job evaluation and performance management' (Armstrong, 1999: 190). This emphasis on gathering information is what differentiates job analysis from job descriptions, the latter being seen quite clearly as an output of the former. 'Role analysis' is probably a more accurate and useful term to use because it focuses on the importance of the activity to the

organisation (Pearn and Kandola, 1993; Armstrong, 1999), and emphasises the purpose of the role, as opposed to its individual components.

Various methods are used to analyse jobs and roles. Broadly, they vary
in terms of their sophistication, cost, convenience and acceptability, and
these factors must be borne in mind when deciding which method to
employ. The issue of cost is particularly pertinent, for the benefits from
any technique always have to be weighed up against the time, effort and
money involved in its application. Similarly, the methods used must be
acceptable to the staff involved and be capable of gaining their agreement and commitment. No one method is inherently more suitable than
any other, and choices should be made on the basis of the jobs to be
analysed and the context in which job and role analysis takes place. For
example, the use of sophisticated techniques is unlikely to be cost-effective if a small number of low-skill jobs are to be analysed. Moreover, it
may well be better to use relatively simple methods rather than employ
untrained or unqualified staff to undertake a sophisticated role analysis.
There are four broad types of method that can be used (Cooper and
Robertson, 1995): observation, diaries, interviews, and questionnaires.
The first three are relatively simple to employ and are the most widely
used. Each of the techniques is reviewed briefly below, but readers who
want more detailed information and analysis should consult Cook
(1998), Taylor (1998) or Armstrong (1999).

Observation is potentially the most straightforward and readily available
method, and it forms part of job analysis even if other techniques are
employed. It is also one of the least costly methods, and if there are any
problems, clarification can be sought from the job-holder in person. On
the other hand, it may be difficult to interpret precisely what tasks are
being undertaken, especially if there is a high intellectual or cognitive
content to the job, and the fact that someone is being observed can also
have an impact upon job behaviour.

Work diaries are also commonly employed. These operate on the principle that job-holders record their activities over a period of time – say,
each hour over the course of a week, or every time they change the task
on which they are engaged. To be effective this requires a high degree
of commitment and co-operation from the job-holder, and a willingness
to spend time explaining items in the diary. It is heavily reliant on job-
holders keeping a comprehensive record of their activities, and not
excluding items because they are deemed unimportant or common
sense, or omitting items that are done frequently.

Interviews are the third broad type of method employed, ranging from
the relatively unstructured – in which job-holders are asked to describe
their job while the interviewer probes to get more detail – through to
the more standardised format by which similar questions are asked of
each job-holder. The major advantages of interviews are cost, convenience and the opportunity for interaction between interviewer and interviewee. The major disadvantages relate to bias and reliability, and

interviewer skills. A further and rather more sophisticated technique that involves interviews and focus groups is repertory grid analysis, although this requires skilled specialist interviewers (Roberts, 1997: 82; Taylor, 1998: 81).

Questionnaires are the most sophisticated of the methods employed for job and role analysis, and some make use of computer packages. There is a range of techniques on offer, and a number of these have been redesigned in recent years (Visser *et al*, 1997). The best-known and most widely-used in the UK and the USA are the Position Analysis Questionnaire (PAQ), the Work Profiling System (WPS), and the Work Performance Survey System (WPSS). According to Taylor (1998: 82), the Medequate Job Analysis Questionnaire developed by KPMG has been used in the NHS. Because they require specialist training and expertise, more detailed analysis of these methods is beyond the scope of this book. Roberts (1997: 91) reiterates that several techniques should be used to ensure that the end-result is 'comprehensive and balanced' and that it 'develops a clear specification of the person being sought'.

Has your organisation ever used the more sophisticated methods of job analysis? If so, evaluate their use and consider whether or not they could be extended to other types of job. If these methods have not been used, explain why.

Job descriptions, person specifications and competency frameworks

The results from a job analysis provide the basis for some description or definition of the job(s) to be filled. This can be very specific or relatively broad in character, and the tendency in recent years has been to focus on the skills that employers need not just in the short term but over a longer time-frame. Most organisations continue to use job descriptions, according to successive IRS and CIPD surveys – the 1999 IRS survey, for example, found that 95 per cent of their sample of over 100 organisations still made use of them, a figure that was even higher in the public sector (IRS *Employment Development Bulletin* 117, 1999: 19). Various pieces of information are typically included in a job description (Fowler, 2000); see Chapter 3 for an examination of the contract of employment and statements of terms and conditions. The list below indicates what should be included:

- job title – a clear statement is all that is required, such as employee relations manager or wages clerk

- location – department, establishment, name of organisation

- who the employee is responsible to – job title of the supervisor to whom the member of staff reports

- who the employee is responsible for – job titles of members of staff who report directly to the job-holder (if any)

- the main purpose of the job – a short and unambiguous statement indicating precisely the overall objective and purpose of the job, such as 'assist and advise customers in a specific area', 'to drill metals in accordance with manufacturing policy'

- responsibilities and/or duties – a list of the main and subsidiary elements in the job, specifying in more or less detail what is required, such as maintaining records held on computer system or answering queries

- working conditions – a list of the major contractual agreements relating to the job, such as pay scales and fringe benefits, hours of work and holiday entitlement, and union membership if appropriate

- other matters – information such as requirements relating to geographical mobility and performance standards

- any other duties that may be assigned by the organisation.

Notwithstanding the extent of their usage, job descriptions have been subject to criticism as being outmoded and increasingly irrelevant to modern conditions, symptomatic of an earlier collectivist, inflexible and more rules-oriented culture. It is argued that employers should not be concerned with the precise definition of 'standard' behaviour but rather with how 'value' can be added through personal initiative. Instead of 'working to contract' and abiding by explicit and published rules, staff should be encouraged to work 'beyond contract' under a regime of 'high-performance work systems', 'blame-free cultures' or 'high-trust philosophies'. This has led to the replacement of highly specific job descriptions by more generic and concise job profiles or accountability statements that are short – say, less than one page – and focused on the outcomes of the job rather than on its process components (Storey and Wright, 2001: 237). Another alternative is to use role definitions and 'key result area' statements (KRAs) that relate to the critical performance measures for the job (Armstrong, 1999: 200). Examples of KRAs are 'prepare marketing plans that support the achievement of corporate targets for profit and sales revenue', or 'provide an accurate, speedy and helpful word-processing service for internal customers'.

In view of the criticisms, it is surprising that job descriptions continue to be so widely used. Job descriptions or role profiles provide recruits with information about the organisation and their potential role, and without them people would apply for jobs without any form of realistic job preview. Having to outline critical results areas or accountability profiles can help managers decide whether or not it is necessary to fill a post, and if so, in what form and at what level. Moreover, vague and 'flexible' accounts of what is needed in a job may only serve to store up trouble if there are subsequent concerns about levels of performance. There is a danger that commentators are seduced by the language of liberation and empowerment that articulates these ideas, without being mindful that some employers exploit their new-found freedom to redesign people's jobs without consultation or negotiation. It is worth noting that the CIPD Recruitment Report (2001g: 9) found that most employers still determine their recruitment requirements on the basis of immediate vacancies and how these may change in the short run rather than the more ambitious exercise of assessing what might be needed in the future. Just 20 per cent of the sample undertook their recruiting with an eye to longer-term organisational needs or career development.

Have job descriptions been abandoned in your organisation? Has their removal led to greater autonomy or greater stress? If detailed job descriptions still exist, how well do they work?

Whereas job descriptions relate to the tasks to be undertaken, person specifications outline the human characteristics and attributes regarded as necessary to do the job. The best-known and most widely-used methods are the seven-point plan (Rodger, 1952) and its later adaptation by Fraser (1966) in the form of the five-point plan. These describe and categorise the principal features required for any job, with a differentiation between those aspects that are essential to perform the job and those that, in an ideal world, are desirable. The two methods are outlined in Table 33.

Although both sets of person specifications are now rather dated, they still appear to be used very widely, albeit in an adapted form, in many organisations (IRS *Employment Development Bulletin* 117, 1999: 19). Most texts on the subject (Newell and Shackleton, 2000; Maund, 2001; Storey and Wright, 2001) focus on these methods, sometimes referring to other competency-based approaches as well. A major problem with the traditional methods is that they were devised at a time when it was considered acceptable to ask questions about an individual's domestic circumstances or private life. Although the broad framework may still be valid, it is now unethical, inappropriate and potentially discriminatory to probe too deeply into some of these areas of the person specification. Moreover, it does not make business sense to restrict applications to people with specific educational qualifications or length of experience in a particular job.

Both the Rodger and the Munro Fraser frameworks suffer from a heavy reliance on personal judgement to specify the human qualities associated with successful performance (Newell and Shackleton, 2000: 115).

Table 33   A traditional view of person specifications

Rodger's seven-point plan	Munro Fraser's five-point plan
● Physical make-up – physical attributes such as the ability to lift heavy loads or differentiate between colours ● Attainments – educational or professional qualifications considered necessary for undertaking the work ● General intelligence – the ability to define and solve problems, and to use initiative in dealing with issues that have arisen ● Special aptitudes – skills, attributes or competencies that are specifically relevant to the particular job ● Interests – pursuits both work-related and leisure that may be relevant to performance in the job ● Disposition – attitudes to work and to other members of staff and customers, as well as friendliness and assertiveness ● Circumstances – domestic commitments, mobility, and family support.	● Impact on others – this covers much the same sort of issues as 'Physical make-up', but is more focused on impact on other employees and customers ● Acquired knowledge and qualifications – see Rodger's 'Attainments' category (left) ● Innate abilities – see Rodger's 'General intelligence' category (left) ● Motivation – a desire to succeed in particular aspects of work and a commitment to achieve these goals ● Adjustment – characteristics related specifically to the job, such as the ability to cope with difficult customers or to work well in a team

Before moving on to the next part of this chapter – on competency frameworks – analyse these two plans in a little more detail. Focus in particular on the specifications used, explain what they are looking to find, and assess how easily and effectively they can be measured.

What are the major shortcomings of these approaches?

Accordingly, the traditional person specification is giving way to competency frameworks, the most significant advantage of these being that the focus is – or should be – on the *behaviours* of job applicants. There is therefore no need to make inferences about the personal qualities that might underpin behaviour (Newell and Shackleton, 2001: 26). Although job descriptions and person specifications are still widely used, nowadays this tends to be alongside competency approaches in order to provide depth and breadth to the recruitment process (CIPD Recruitment Report, 2000a).

There are several advantages of using competency-based approaches, not the least because they set a framework within which subsequent HR practices – such as performance management, training and development, and pay and grading – can be placed (Whiddett and Hollyforde, 1999). In addition, the competencies can be related to specific performance outcomes rather than being concerned with potentially vague processes, such as disposition or interests outside work. Moreover, these approaches do not use criteria that are easy to measure – such as educational qualifications or length of service – but not necessarily closely related to job effectiveness. The focus on outcomes also means it is possible to exclude behavioural measures that appear at first sight to be relevant but are not central to effective performance at a particular workplace.

Roberts (1997: 71–2) differentiates between four types of competency. These are:

- *natural* competencies – made up of the 'big five' dimensions of personality: extraversion/intraversion, emotional stability, agreeableness, conscientiousness, and openness to experience

- *acquired* competencies – knowledge and skills acquired through work or other avenues

- *adapting* competencies – the ability to adapt natural talents and acquired skills to a new situation

- *performing* competencies – observable behaviours and outputs.

Whiddett and Hollyforde (1999: 14) give an example of a three-level competency framework for a job that involves working with people, which demonstrates clearly how the levels are derived.

- Level 1: builds relationships internally

- Level 2: builds relationships externally

- Level 3: maintains external networks.

The behavioural indicators that are appropriate for each level can then be defined. For Level 3, for example, these are:

- Takes account of different cultural styles and values when dealing with external organisations.

- Actively manages external contacts as a business network.

- Identifies and makes use of events for developing external network.

These indicators tend to focus on 'softer' customer service skills relationships rather than 'harder' technical skills, and it is clear from various sources that attitudinal and behavioural skills are sought by an increasing number of employers. There has been a shift from recruiting on the basis of qualifications and experience to one that focuses on what employers see as positive employee attitudes – such as a preparedness to work flexibly, a willingness to change, and a responsiveness to customers (Morris *et al*, 2000: 1053). Royle (1999) suggests that McDonalds is keen to recruit an acquiescent workforce unlikely to resist management control, and the target is therefore people who are in a weak labour market position with minimal work experience. In short, the strategy is to recruit on the basis of attitude and train staff in the requisite technical skills (Callaghan and Thompson, 2002). However, there must come a point by which customers find the soothing tones of the customer service operator do not compensate for the poor-quality service provided by the bank, the train company or the food retailer that is attempting to run operations with reduced staffing levels. See the *Looks good* box below.

Looks good, sounds right – lousy product!

It has become part of modern business language that employers are now recruiting staff who have the right attitude or 'smile' down the telephone rather than those who have well-developed technical skills. A recent report by Warhurst and Nickson (2001) took this to an even higher level when they reported that workers are being selected on the basis of their looks or their voices. This is referred to as 'the commercial utility of aesthetic labour' where image and design pervade the new economy. It means that certain groups of workers – who are the wrong weight or speak in the wrong way – may be excluded from an increasing range of employment opportunities.

Drawing on your own personal experience, talk this through with your colleagues and friends. Do you think that it makes commercial sense to focus so much on attitudes rather than on technical skills? If you are annoyed about a product (eg a cancelled train, a shop-soiled expensive item from a store, or a mistake by your bank), do you feel that your irritation can be overcome just because someone listens attentively to your complaint? Is it ethically or morally right that people should be excluded from jobs in a clothes shop on the basis of their looks or from a call centre on the basis of their accent? Consider these issues in relation to person specifications and competency frameworks

Source: Warhurst C. and Nickson D. *Looking Good, Sounding Right: Style counselling in the new economy.* London, The Industrial Society. 2001

Recruitment methods

Recruitment is often regarded as the poor relation of selection, with rather less space devoted to it in most publications. Whereas selection has caught the attention of organisational psychologists keen to increase the reliability and validity of selection methods, recruitment has received scant attention. However, as Watson (1994: 203) argued cogently some time ago, 'Recruitment provides the candidates for the selector to judge. Selection techniques cannot overcome failures in recruitment; they merely make them evident.' Important decisions have to be made about whether or not to recruit, from which sources, using

Table 34 External recruitment methods used by employers

Recruitment methods used by employers	Percentage of respondents in 2001	Percentage of respondents in 1999
Closed searches		
Word of mouth	58	53
Links with schools and colleges	41	40
Headhunters	30	33
Responsive methods		
Speculative applications	57	69
Open searches		
Local newspaper adverts	89	82
Adverts in specialist press	79	91
National newspaper adverts	77	80
Job centres	73	69
Employment agencies	70	60
The Internet	64	42
Local radio adverts	11	13

Source: Chartered Institute of Personnel Development. *Recruitment*. Survey Report. London, CIPD. 2001g

which media, and at what cost. Moreover, the documentation used in the recruitment exercise has an impact beyond HRM in that it conveys images of the organisation, its products and its overall philosophy. A number of legal issues have to be borne in mind when recruiting new staff, not only in the design and wording of any adverts but also in ensuring protection if people choose to apply for posts on-line (Leighton and Proctor, 2001). Furthermore, if the recruitment process generates too few applications, or too many unsuitable ones, it will prove expensive to make appointment decisions. The choice of cost-effective recruitment methods depends on a host of factors specific to each organisation and to each vacancy.

Rather than produce a long list of recruitment methods, with associated advantages and disadvantages, it makes more sense to classify them into four broad categories, and add a few comments about each. The first of these is *internal recruitment*. This often takes the form of using the internal labour market for filling vacancies, something used more frequently during rationalisation than in periods of boom and expansion. Posts can be filled following a search of employee records, and then redeploying staff from one task or area to another. At its best this can be seen as a form of career development in which staff are moved around the organisation to make effective use of their skills and abilities as part of a wider HR plan. At its worst, however, in situations where external recruitment is frozen, it may simply entail shifting staff from one department to another, resulting in untrained and/or demotivated employees. Alternatively, staff can be transferred from temporary posts to open-ended contracts or from agency work onto the payroll. This provides employers with a form of quasi-internal labour market where they can observe people at work before committing to an offer of more secure employment (Rubery *et al*, 2002). This form of recruitment is prevalent in small firms as managers 'take a "good hard look" at potential staff before deciding to offer direct employment' (Earnshaw *et al*, 1998: 547).

Moving on to methods that make use of the external labour market, the second approach can be termed *closed searches*. There are several strands to this. It can use 'word of mouth' recruitment by existing staff to identify potential recruits through their personal contacts or on the part of managers to recruit people who have worked for another local firm. An IRS survey (IRS *Employment Development Bulletin* 135, 2001) suggested that this form of recruitment has been used more widely than agencies and newspaper advertising put together, although this may alter if online recruitment becomes more prominent. Some organisations actually pay 'bounties' or referral payments to staff who recommend a friend who then remains in employment for more than three months. The amounts paid vary according to the nature of the post filled. For example, Pret-à-Manger paid £50 for a basic-level job and up to £2,000 for a manager, and it was estimated that over 10 per cent of their recruits came from this source (IRS *Employment Development Bulletin* 135, 2001: 6). The biggest advantage of this source of recruitment has been the quality of the candidates provided, for most employees are unlikely to recommend friends they deem to be unsuitable or someone who would not 'fit in' with the culture of the organisation. Indeed, all 40 of the firms investigated by Carroll *et al* (1999: 244) used this method, often in tandem with more formal approaches, and two-thirds had rehired former employees. As with internal recruitment, this is a cheap option in that recruits are readily available, are known to existing members of the workforce, and their selection requires little in the way of sophisticated techniques. On the other hand, such 'ring-fencing' may reinforce existing imbalances (gender, race and disability), thwarting attempts to encourage greater workforce diversity.

Debate with your colleagues the justification for continuing to employ 'word of mouth' recruitment methods. Consider both the performance and the professional implications of this approach.

Closed searches also take the form of relying upon external contacts (say, in schools, colleges or universities) to identify suitable candidates from among their class, if this has worked well in the past. Obviously, this is especially appropriate for the recruitment of younger workers

(IRS *Employment Development Bulletin* 138, 2001). Some organisations make use of headhunters for higher-level appointments, and particularly for those that require to be handled sensitively or confidentially, or for those where the executive search agency has extensive contacts. This method is expensive, and it is used rather less in the public sector than in the private (IRS *Employment Development Bulletin* 117, 1999: 11). Practice is overseen by the Association of Executive Search Consultants, a worldwide body, that operates according to an explicit list of ethical principles and guidelines for good practice (IRS *Employment Review* 740, 2001) – although of course, membership is not obligatory.

A slight variant on this set of methods is the *responsive* approach, whereby employers interview casual callers or former applicants whose names and addresses are on file. Many employers tend to place notices outside their factories or offices when there are vacancies, and in some locations this may be a very good source of applicants. This had become rather less extensive between the 1999 and 2001 CIPD studies, and is now one of the least widely-used of the techniques. In the study by Carroll *et al* (1999), over half the sample of 40 small and medium-sized enterprises (SMEs) made a point of contacting former applicants if there was a vacancy, and a similar proportion had offered work to casual callers. This method is more 'open' than the previous two categories, although it does rely on people actually making the effort to search for work rather than applying for a vacancy that is advertised in the press. Indeed, many of the managers interviewed in this study felt that it showed initiative and potential commitment by applicants, making these people stand out from the rest of the field.

The final method is the *open search*, and this covers the largest number of techniques. Advertisements in national and local papers are the most widely-used methods, and for specialist posts it is usual to advertise in the trade press. The CIPD 2001 survey showed that local advertising had grown recently whereas radio adverts were rarely used. On some occasions, employers make use of specialist agencies so as to reap the benefits of cheaper advertising costs. The Internet has become a much more significant tool in recruitment over the last few years – see Table 34 and the box on *Online recruitment* below – its use increasing by over 50 per cent between 1999 and 2001.

The advertising media used depends on the vacancies to be filled and the resources the employer is prepared to commit to the exercise. The state of the external labour market is also important, and the most appropriate methods vary depending upon local and/or national levels of unemployment, on specific skill shortages, and on competition from other employers for the same types of labour. For example, a company seeking to recruit a semi-skilled manual worker for a job that requires little training may target the local job centre and put advertisements in local newspapers very cheaply. Conversely, when trying to recruit for technical jobs, specialist trade magazines, schools and further-education colleges might be a more fruitful source of applicants. The recruitment of graduates probably includes visits to universities on 'the milk round', and adverts in the national press and the Internet. In this situation, the cost of recruitment is likely to be high but justified in terms of expected contributions from graduates in general, and potential high-fliers in particular (IRS *Employment Review* 742c, 2001: 31–40).

Online recruitment

The Internet has now come of age with online recruitment. As the CIPD Recruitment Report, 2001, found, this has been the fastest growing technique in the field over the last few years. But what exactly does recruiting online entail, what do employers think about this as a source of applicants, and what worries do they have about its increasing use? Most employers responding to the IRS Survey in 2001 appear positive and enthusiastic about the potential of the Internet for recruitment. However, they are sceptical about whether or not it will become more prominent than traditional techniques as well as concerned about the practical problems they may have to face with e-recruitment. It is recognised that although a good site can help to cement a positive image of the employer, a poorly-designed site can discourage applications.

Employers' use of the Internet

- 39 per cent use it to post vacancies on an external provider's site

- 32 per cent use it to post vacancies on their own Internet site

- 30 per cent use it to post vacancies on their own intranet network

- 27 per cent use it for background information about the organisation for candidates

- 1 per cent include a self-selection exercise on the site

- 0 per cent administer selection tests via the Internet.

Reasons given by this group of employers for advertising jobs on the Internet include:

- It is more cost-effective than regular advertising.

- It is easy to update and to refer people to other information on the site.

- It gives access to a much wider pool of candidates.

The Internet is regarded by most employers as a much more important source of applications in the future as well as a very effective marketing tool in attracting applicants. Employers are more divided over whether it will replace existing methods, and they are not yet convinced that it has really improved their recruitment processes. There is a tendency to fall back on tried and trusted methods that appear to have worked well in the past, although there is an awareness that the world has now changed and that they have to move with the times.

Have you ever used the Internet to apply for a job or to collect more information about an organisation that you are interested in? Did the exercise leave you more or less positive about the employer? Why/why not?

Sources: IRS *Employee Development Bulletin 134*, February 2001; Industrial Relations Services, 'The Internet comes of age with online recruitment', *IRS Employment Development Bulletin*, 141, 2001

Employment agencies and job centres are also widely used, with the former particularly active in the field of professional, secretarial and administrative posts, and especially in the area of temporary employment (Druker and Stanworth, 2001; Ward *et al*, 2001). This is also evident in the provision of supply teachers (Grimshaw *et al*, 2001). There are often concerns about the quality of provision and the extent to which agency workers are committed to organisational goals. In particular, Ward *et al* (2001: 17) feel that the use of temporary agency workers is not sustainable for a variety of reasons – high levels of labour turnover, limited career opportunities, differential rates of pay, and other employment conditions. Agency workers may offer employers a short-term solution but there are worries about the consistency with which temporary labour is managed. Concerns about quality of provision were repeatedly made by the owner-managers in Carroll *et al*'s (1999) study of road haulage firms, a majority expressing significant anxieties about allowing temporary workers to drive 'expensive and potentially lethal trucks' without proper training. Job centres now handle over one third of all published vacancies in Britain (IRS *Employment Development Bulletin* 139, 2001), including a very large proportion of posts at manual, clerical and secretarial grades. The concerns that employers have about job centres as a source of recruitment relate partly to the quality and commitment of candidates, and partly to problems with the patchy levels of delivery across the country (IRS *Employment Development Bulletin* 139, 2001: 15–16). However, the move to online recruitment and the opening-up of websites to other employers and agencies may help to improve levels of service in this area through the operation of 'Employer Direct' (IRS *Employment Review* 738, 2001b).

The choice of selection methods

We now move on to review briefly the choice of selection methods, examining interviews and tests in more detail. It is beyond the scope of this book to analyse the whole range of methods – such as references, application forms, work-sampling, assessment centres and graphology – in greater depth. However, readers who want more information should consult Cooper and Robertson (1995), Cook (1998) and Taylor (2002) for a more comprehensive discussion of selection in general, and Woodruffe (2000) and Lievens and Klimoski (2001) for material on assessment centres. No single technique, irrespective of how well it is designed and administered, is capable of producing perfect selection decisions that predict with certainty which individuals will perform well in a particular role. In the vast majority of cases, employers use more than one method. Interviews are used on a very large proportion of occasions and in most organisations, along with application forms and references. Practice varies as to whether references are sought prior to or after interviews, whether they are consulted before or after interviews, or merely sought as a final vetting device prior to making an appointment. Although references may be taken up, the weight accorded to them also varies, and most HR practitioners know of cases when excellent references have been provided in respect of staff that the existing employer would be happy to lose.

The 2001 CIPD Recruitment Report, based on a matched sample of employers responding to the surveys over a number of years, shows the

Table 35 Trends in selection techniques

Selection technique used by employers	Percentage of respondents in 2001	Percentage of respondents in 1999	Percentage use in some jobs in 1999	Percentage use in all jobs in 1999
Application form	86	86	90	58
Curriculum vitae	68	73	67	18
Covering letter	61	56		
Interview	100	100	100	75
Telephone screening	18	16	15	3
Personality questionnaire/ Personality test	41	40	64	0
Ability test			70	8
Assessment centre	34	29	41	0
Biodata	14	7	2	0
Graphology	4	not asked		

Sources: Columns 2 and 3 Chartered Institute of Personnel and Development. *Recruitment*. Survey Report. London, CIPD. 2001. Columns 4 and 5 adapted from Industrial Relations Services. 'The business of selection: an IRS survey', IRS *Employment Development Bulletin* 117, 1999. pp5–16

extent to which different techniques are used, as well as trends in usage. It can be seen from Table 35 that interviews were used by every organisation, followed closely by application forms, curricula vitarum and covering letters. Personality questionnaires and assessment centres were used by less than half of the sample, and other techniques – such as telephone screening and graphology – employed by relatively few. It is apparent that different techniques are used for the selection of different groups of staff. For example, much fewer organisations use CVs as part of the selection process for manual workers than do for professionals. Unfortunately, questions were not asked in this survey about the overall distribution of work-sampling, something that is more likely to be used for manual and clerical staff. Presentations – a form of work-sampling – are used widely when selecting professional and managerial staff.

It is also apparent that selection techniques vary in popularity between countries. Newell and Tansley (2001: 199) found that interviews are most widely used in Britain and North America, graphology in France (and French companies in other countries), and assessment centres in Britain, Germany and the Netherlands. Tests in general are more popular in France and Belgium, although integrity tests are rarely used but are becoming much more popular in the USA. There are clear societal and organisational effects on choices over which techniques to use, and applicants are likely to have quite mixed views about their legitimacy (Iles and Robertson, 1997; Schmitt and Chan, 1999).

Smith (2002) presents data (see Figure 9) indicating that most techniques have very low levels of accuracy in terms of producing effective

Figure 9   The accuracy of selection methods

1.0	perfect selection
0.65	intelligence tests *and* integrity tests
0.63	intelligence tests *and* structured interviews
0.60	intelligence tests *and* work sampling
0.54	work sample tests
0.51	intelligence tests
0.51	structured interviews
0.41	integrity tests
0.40	personality tests
0.37	assessment centres
0.35	biodata
0.26	references
0.18	years of job experience
0.10	years of education
0.02	graphology
0.0	selection with a pin

Adapted from Smith M. 'Personnel selection research', *International Journal of Organisational and Occupational Psychology*, 2002

selection decisions. Of techniques used on their own, work-sampling offers the highest likelihood of success, closely followed by intelligence tests and structured interviewing. References score fairly low on accuracy levels, and graphology – so widely used in France – is regarded by some as hardly better than random selection. Schmidt and Hunter (1998: 270) argue that it is not so much the characteristics of writing that leads to different estimates of people's abilities and personalities but its content – clearly quite a different factor. It is also apparent from this research that combinations of techniques greatly increase the accuracy of selection decisions. The combination of intelligence tests with structured interviews, integrity tests or work-sampling leads to a substantial improvement in validity (Schmidt and Hunter, 1998: 272).

What really matters, though, is choosing the most appropriate selection techniques for each situation, because it is clear that no one method is a panacea. An IRS study (IRS *Employment Development Bulletin* 124, 2000) found that telephone screening was very appropriate as the initial stage for the selection of call centre operatives, whereas tests were felt to be more appropriate for secretarial staff, as were presentations for professional engineers. Cooper and Robertson (1995: 47–65) and Newell and Shackleton (2000: 119–23) examine in detail the criteria needed to assess the value of each method:

- practicability
- sensitivity
- reliability
- validity.

Practicability, according to Smith and Robertson (1993: 94), is the most important criterion of all. The method chosen has to be acceptable to all parties – senior managers and candidates, as well as statutory bodies such as the EOC and CRE, and professional organisations such as the CIPD and the British Psychological Society. It also has to be economical in terms of costs and benefits, the time that is required to administer the exercise, and be within the capabilities of those people who are to run the selection process. The issue of cost is particularly critical. There is little point in running a sophisticated and complex personality test if just one candidate applies or if it is for a temporary post.

Sensitivity is a key feature in the choice of selection methods because it represents the ability of any particular technique to discriminate between candidates. Such discrimination is desirable provided it relates to the applicants' ability to do the job, and is not used as a smokescreen for making employment decisions which disadvantage particular groups of applicants on grounds of race, gender, age or disability.

Reliability has several different aspects, but refers essentially to 'the consistency of a method used to select individuals' (Newell and Shackleton, 2000: 119). It should not be influenced too much by chance factors. Cooper and Robertson (1995: 50-3) and Newell and Shackleton (2000: 119-20) both describe various forms of reliability – between different raters, when the same technique is used on different occasions, and/or between different methods. If inter-rater reliability is low, for example, great care must be exercised when using a number of interviewers because one is likely to reject candidates that others would have selected. Tests may prove to be unreliable if applicants are able to improve their performance from one occasion to the next.

The final criterion is *validity* – the correctness of the inferences that can be drawn from the selection method. Newell and Shackleton (2000: 121) define this as 'the relationship between the predictors (the results from the selection method used) and the criterion (performance on the job)'. Much of the competency debate revolves around this issue, as selectors attempt to define the key attributes and skills demonstrated by high (or satisfactory) performers and then use these as a benchmark against which to assess applicants. This is a difficult task to undertake, not least because it is hard to find proxies for these characteristics – for example, in deciding upon the best questions to discern how effective someone is at running teams or managing change. It is also hard to draw inferences about future job performance from statements made at interview or characteristics displayed during an assessment centre. A whole host of other variables influence subsequent job performance, many of which occur outside the workplace, and their effects may be unknown at the time of appointment

Interviews

We have already noted that interviews are extremely widely used in selection. Indeed, IRS (*Employment Development Bulletin* 117, 1999: 13) noted that 76 per cent of its respondents felt that this was the most influential of all the techniques used in selection, considerably more so than any other technique on offer. Interviews are also the most widely condemned of all selection techniques, criticised in particular for their unacceptable unreliability, poor predictive validity and low sensitivity, although they do have the advantage of being relatively cheap – at least in terms of direct costs. There are many legal issues surrounding the interview, in terms of bias and equal opportunities, data protection and confidentiality, as well as human rights (Leighton and Proctor, 2001). Frequently, however, the interview – as a *technique* – is blamed when the real problem resides in the fact that it is planned and conducted by untrained and inadequately prepared interviewers. One way to reduce this problem is to use interviews in conjunction with other methods. Nevertheless, there is a deeper question here about the purpose of the interview. To what extent is it seen as a two-way decision-making process involving choices both for the organisation and the applicant? Or is it principally a technical exercise in which the employer seeks a perfect selection decision with high predictive validity?

> Consider two interviews – one you think was well handled and one
> that was poorly handled – in which you have taken part, either as an
> interviewer or as an applicant. Identify the reasons for the differ-
> ences between them. What can you learn from this to improve the
> validity of interviews as a selection device?

Interviews for selection purposes can take a number of forms – see
Roberts (1997), Cook (1998) and Taylor (2002) for much lengthier
treatments of this issue. First of all, they can be between individuals on
a one-to-one basis. These have the advantage of greater informality, the
encouragement of rapport, and the generation of more open and frank
discussions. They also suffer from problems of interviewer bias (both
the 'halo' and the 'Satan' effects), from low levels of reliability, and from
lack of coverage of the subject matter. This type of interview is particularly prone to the accusation that the interviewer makes up his or her
mind about an applicant in the first few minutes, before spending the
remainder of the interview finding reasons to justify this viewpoint. The
sequential interview is a slight adaptation of this format, in that candidates are seen by a series of managers in one-to-one situations, each
probing for evidence about different aspects of the job.

The second broad variant is the small group or tandem interview, where
two or three people interview a candidate together, making their judgement on the same event. They may explore different aspects of the job
or even take on specific roles during the interview. In the case of a
supervisory appointment, for example, it may be appropriate for a line
manager and an HR specialist to interview together to explore both the
technical elements of the job and the individual's management style.
This has the advantage of enabling more than one manager to observe
the candidate at first hand and reach a joint decision.

The final type of interview is the panel, typically comprising between
three and five interviewers drawn from different parts of the organisation, and fulfilling – if their roles have been allocated beforehand – different duties. Panel interviews for senior academics and public servants
often involve 12 or more people – in which case the interview really
does become something of a ritual or trial, depending upon which side
of the table one is sitting. The arguments in favour of using a panel are
much the same as for the tandem interview. It allows several people to
see a candidate at the same time, it minimises the potential for overt
bias, and it ensures – in theory, at least – that decisions are made by
those individuals with an interest in who is to be appointed. The disadvantages are also well known. It is more difficult for interviewers to build
up rapport with candidates, some interviewees may be extremely nerv-
ous about the prospect of facing a large number of people in a formal
setting, and panel members often lack training in how to interview. Bias

is a particular concern in this situation because some panel members exert much greater influence over the decision than do others, yet this is often hidden and covert.

Most commentators agree that selection interviews are riddled with problems, some of which are due to the nature of the interview process, others to the skills of interviewers. The major problem was clearly articulated by Plumbley (1991: 103) many years ago when he wrote that interviewing is:

> an everyday occurrence and is the most widely-used assessment technique. It is part of the popular vocabulary. It looks easy, and everyone is inclined to believe they are good at it. Therein lies the danger and the confusion.

Much of this can be explained by attribution theory – the view that applicants are defined as 'good' if they obey the rules of the interview as seen by the interviewer, and 'bad' if they do not comply (Smith and Robertson, 1993: 201). Similarly, interviewers have a tendency to select candidates who display attributes that they regard as important, who behave – or even look – like others for whom they have positive feelings, or who say something early in the interview with which the interviewer agrees (Taylor, 2002). The converse also applies, but such 'halo' or 'Satan' effects are not visible to other members of the panel (nor often to interviewers themselves) and are therefore extremely hard to take into account. It is also widely understood that interviewers have highly selective memories for what has been said, typically picking up on one point to support their predetermined opinion while not being aware of contra-indications (IRS *Employment Development Bulletin* 122, 2000). The ritual of the interview is more important than is often admitted, for both parties perceive it to be a key aspect of the selection process. It is unusual for hiring decisions in Britain to be made without face-to-face contact, although it does happen with the overseas recruitment of teachers and nurses as part of the drive to overcome skill shortages here (Johnson, 2001).

Structured interviews are seen as a way of improving the validity and reliability of the exercise. According to Cooper and Robertson (1995: 81–5), three features are particularly important: questions should be developed from the job analysis, each candidate should be asked standard – though not necessarily identical – questions, and a systematic scoring procedure should be used, preferably based upon a behaviourally-anchored rating-scale. Dipboye (1997: 461–5) provides a good set of arguments in favour of the structured interview. These include the fact that it is tied into job analysis and competency profiles, that there is an increased focus on job-related questions, and that multiple interviewers tend to be used. In some local authorities, as part of the drive to ensure that selection decisions are free from gender and race bias, applicants are asked precisely the same set of questions – which are agreed in advance – in the same order, and the answers are rated in a systematic manner. It is also recognised that there are major cultural and structural barriers to the acceptability of structured interviews, not least because senior decision-makers prefer to avoid rigid, fixed and standardised processes. It is also acknowledged that the interview is not a one-way exercise (Cook, 1998: 66). Structured interviews do improve reliability but problems remain with validity. For example, some individuals may be extremely good at articulating their achievements and plans but poor at putting them into effect, whereas others may do the job well but not act in a very convincing manner at the interview. A slight variant of this is the behavioural interview in which candidates are asked to describe how they have operated in previous situations rather than hypothesise about how they would act if a particular situation were to arise – as in situational interviews. Barclay (2001: 88) cites evidence from a sample of organisations that used behavioural interviews to show they felt this format yielded better selection decisions due to improved quality of information. It more than offset the additional training costs incurred for interviewers.

Which selection techniques would you advise using for the appointment of (a) a worker in a call centre, (b) a manager in a restaurant, and (c) a research scientist? Justify your answers.

Selection testing

Selection tests have become more popular over the last decade as dissatisfaction with interviews has grown and employers have sought to achieve higher levels of validity from their selection decisions. We have already seen that tests are used in some form or another by a large number of organisations. They are most likely to be used for selection to junior and middle management, supervisory and professional positions, and especially when assessing graduates (Newell and Shackleton, 2000: 125). In the latter case tests are used regularly as part of a battery of selection techniques. Although tests are used for other HR decisions, their use in selection far outstrips that in training and development or career planning.

It must be stressed that this section of the chapter is not designed to enable readers to design, administer, and interpret tests, but rather to make them aware of the major types of tests that are available, their principal merits and shortcomings, and their part in selection decisions. It is crucial that HR practitioners understand the limits to their own role in this area, knowing when to seek advice on test usage, and from which suppliers. Acting beyond their own professional competence can have severe consequences, not only in the area of recruitment and selection but also for the public relations image of the organisation as well as on applicants. Readers who want more detailed analysis of these techniques are advised to consult Toplis *et al* (1994), Cooper and Robertson (1995), and Cook (1998), as well as the CIPD and British Psychological Society (BPS).

Smith and Robertson (1993: 161) have defined psychological tests as:

> *carefully chosen, systematic and standardised procedures for evoking a sample of responses from a candidate, which can be used to assess one or more of [his or her] psychological characteristics by comparing the results with those of a representative sample of an appropriate population.*

This definition highlights several important features – the fact that tests should be chosen carefully and be appropriate for the situation, that they should be applied systematically in a standard manner, and that the results should be capable of comparison with norms for the particular group in question. The CIPD Quick Facts guidance on Psychological Testing (2001) stresses that tests must be supported by a body of evidence and statistical data that demonstrates their validity in an occupational setting. Toplis *et al* (1994: 15) distinguish between two broad categories – psychometric tests and psychometric questionnaires/personality tests. As we see below, the latter has been subject to the most forceful criticisms.

Psychometric tests are designed to measure mental ability, and they take several different forms in practice. First, there are tests of achievement that purport to measure the degree of knowledge and/or skill a person has acquired at the time the test is administered. This would include school examinations, for example. Second, there are tests of general intelligence which are designed to assess 'the capacity for abstract thinking and reasoning within a range of different contexts and media' (Toplis *et al*, 1994: 17). Among the better known of these are Wechsler's Adult Intelligence Scale (WAIS), AH4, and Raven's Progressive Matrices (RPM). This category of tests also aims to assess what a person could learn (Cook, 1998: 98). The third set of psychometric tests is for special aptitudes or abilities, such as the assessment of verbal, numerical or spatial ability, and manual dexterity. A number of these are outlined in Toplis *et al* (1994: 19–26), including tests for clerical speed and accuracy, computer aptitudes, or sales skills. Sometimes they are compiled into batteries of tests for use in organisations. Cook (1998: 135) states confidently that 'validity generalisation analysis has proved that tests of natural ability predict work performance very well. For a vast range of jobs, the more able worker is the better worker.' Stairs *et al* (2000: 28) are not totally convinced, however, and suggest that such techniques are most appropriate for testing managerial abilities.

The second broad grouping is *psychometric questionnaires or personality tests*. These are based around 'trait' or 'type' theories, which involve 'the identification of a number of fairly independent and enduring characteristics of behaviour which all people display but to differing degrees' (Toplis *et al*, 1994: 28). The 'Big Five' personality factors mentioned in an earlier section are agreed by the scientific community as generally applicable across all contexts. However, this does not mean that all five factors are applicable in all situations and for all occupations, nor does it mean that the correlations between these factors and performance is strong across the board (Robertson, 2001). Results of meta-analysis (Barrick *et al*, 2001) show that conscientiousness and emotional stability seem to be relevant for selection decisions in all occupations, whereas the other factors – agreeableness, extraversion and openness to experience – are more specific to particular jobs and situations. For example, extraversion appears to be useful in predicting performance amongst managers (Barrick *et al*, 2001: 22). Other factors seem to be growing in importance as employers demand more flexible work patterns, and there is an increasing amount of evidence that personality may be strongly associated with organisational citizenship behaviour (Robertson, 2001: 43).

Can selection decisions ever be truly *objective* tests of a person's suitability for employment?

Choosing which test is most appropriate has to be judged on the basis of existing evidence in similar situations and perceived organisational needs. There are now many of these types of test on the market, some of which were designed and tested on the US market and therefore have to be treated with caution if they have not been validated in Britain. Among the most common types of personality questionnaire are Cattell's 16PF, the SHL Occupational Personality Questionnaire (OPQ), the Myers-Briggs Type Indicator and the Californian Psychological Inventory (CPI). There are sometimes several versions of each type. In addition to personality questionnaires, there are also interest questionnaires (such as the Rothwell-Miller Interest Blank and a range of SHL questionnaires for different levels), values questionnaires, and work-behaviour questionnaires. So many of these are now available that just to list them would cover several pages; further information can be obtained from the sources already quoted.

Not surprisingly, this increase in use has highlighted a number of problems, particularly in the choice of tests and in their deployment. Major criticisms have been raised by professional bodies such as the CIPD and the BPS about the emergence of disreputable providers and untrained assessors who do not know how to interpret the results of tests (Fletcher, 1998; Stairs *et al*, 2000). In addition, there have been concerns that some tests may discriminate against particular groups of people, most notably ethnic minorities and women (Schmitt and Chan, 1999: 56; Newell and Shackleton, 2000: 126). Other problems arise if individuals are able to fake their responses in order to present an image that might increase their chances of being selected (Arthur *et al*, 2001: 665–6). Even more serious is the case where people provide a 'true' answer to a question – say, about never having stolen anything – only to find that they are penalised because this has been inserted to check on lying or response distortion (Arthur *et al*, 2001: 668). In other words, it is taken for granted that everyone will have stolen something during their lives.

Nevertheless, it is widely accepted that tests have a useful role to play in selection decisions provided they are used properly, preferably in tandem with other tests or selection methods. Indeed, Stairs *et al* (2000: 30) argue that tests should never be used in isolation but always as part of a broader selection process. On their own, tests are not particularly good predictors of future job behaviour, according to Newell and Shackleton (2000: 127) because of strong situational pressures in work that lead to alternative solutions in practice. Moreover, they argue that many jobs, especially those with discretionary potential, can be done perfectly well in a variety of different ways.

There are occasions when financial or other pressures on organisations may encourage them to take short-cuts in the use of tests, or there may be inconsistencies in their usage. In addition, although HR managers may raise professional objections to the inappropriate use of tests, organisational politics sometimes means that they are ignored (Baker and Cooper, 2000: 78). There are other concerns with testing as well, many of which relate to their administration and their legal and ethical standing (Palmer, 2002). Issues such as these have led the CIPD to provide advice on Psychological Testing – see the box below. Drawing on a number of studies (Smith and Robertson, 1993; Fletcher, 1998; Schmitt and Chan, 1999; Baker and Cooper, 2000), the following issues must be taken into account before using tests:

- Tests should be sold only to qualified users, carried out under standard conditions, and released only after adequate research.

- Tests should not be used which are known to discriminate against particular groups of individuals, such as ethnic minorities, women or the disabled.

- Candidates must understand the place of tests in the selection process, see their relevance to the job in hand, and be convinced of their accuracy.

- Test administrators must be qualified to use tests and able to interpret the inferences that can be drawn from them, and candidates must be reassured about this.

- Candidates should not be coached for tests.

- The results should be confidential and held with the full knowledge of those tested, and provision must be made to feed back results to candidates.

CIPD guidance on selecting psychological tests

Before finally selecting a test to use, which appears to be appropriate for their needs, users should ensure that they receive satisfactory answers from the test suppliers to the following questions:

- How reliable is the test and how consistent is it as a measure?

- How valid is the test and does it really identify the attributes or skills which the supplier claims?

- What evidence can suppliers provide that their tests do not unfairly disadvantage certain groups?

- Will the test seem appropriate in the eyes of those taking it, and what have previous reactions been to this test?

- Has the test been used effectively in similar circumstances?

- Are the norms provided by the supplier for comparative purposes up to date and appropriate for the user's requirements? Do the norm results apply to a sufficiently representative mix of occupations, gender or ethnic groups to allow fair comparison with the user's group?

- Is the method of test evaluation and scoring appropriate to the purpose for which the test will be used?

If the answers to these questions are not available or are unsatisfactory, *the test should not be used*.

Differing paradigms of selection

It will be apparent from the textual information throughout this chapter that there are competing definitions and paradigms operating within the field of selection – for the most part implicit rather than explicit. In this final section of the chapter, while acknowledging that the distinctions between them are not always clear-cut, we review four of these perspectives: social exchange, scientific rationality, socialisation, and socially constructed reality, knowledge and power.

Social exchange
For many personnel managers, the selection process has typically revolved around the interview, an example of social exchange. As such, it is not unrealistic to view it as 'a controlled conversation with a purpose', the purpose being to 'collect information in order to predict how successfully the individual would perform in the job for which they have applied, measuring them against predetermined criteria' (Torrington and Hall, 1995: 272). The idea of a conversation – albeit controlled –

conjures up images of a pleasant chat to share experiences, and plays down the fact that the selector is in a rather more enviable and powerful position, especially at times of high unemployment. But there is some substance to this view. After all, applicants make decisions about whether or not they want to work for an organisation, and at times of labour market shortage or in jobs where it is difficult to attract people because of competition, the process is a rather more equal exchange. Potential applicants may decide, after reading the literature from an organisation, that they will not bother to apply for a post. Similarly, candidates may decide not to attend an interview or may turn down a job after it has been offered (Newell and Shackleton, 2001: 25). Moreover, applicants 'may create and maintain impressions of themselves which they believe the assessor is looking for' (Newell and Shackleton, 2001: 37), thus undermining the validity of the selection process. The same process can also occur on the part of the selectors who are keen to persuade someone to work for the organisation and give unrealistic job previews. Problems such as these make it clear why it is so important to minimise the possibility of 'contamination' in selection by using methods with higher validity and reliability.

Scientific rationality

The second paradigm is that of scientific rationality, an approach that tends to be led by organisational and occupational psychologists searching for the 'perfect' selection device. The emphasis here is to focus on ways of making selection more scientific by using structured interviews, tests and work-sampling. This psychometric perspective has dominated the field for some time (Newell and Shackleton, 2001: 24), and it operates with a number of clear and unambiguous premises:

- Excellent job performance can be identified and codified.

- There is one best way to work.

- Competencies can be derived and used to define the key characteristics of a post.

- Selection techniques can be devised to assess these competencies.

- The validity and reliability of the process can be improved by sticking to pre-planned and determined methods.

This is termed the 'actuarial method' of selection by Newell and Shackleton (2001: 32) because 'it is based purely on a numerical calculation of the collected data'. However, this semblance of rationality is a myth, and these approaches actually increase the opportunity for 'injustice, because they are based on the assumption that there is one best way to do a job'. Newell and Shackleton (2001: 42) go further and claim that the psychological perspective simply hides behind a façade of objectivity so it remains easy to perpetuate discrimination while presenting the whole process as fair. Confidence in the apparent objectivity of testing can be undermined by inappropriate and poorly-applied tests. Moreover, the idea that any selection technique can be 'objective' is problematical, because decisions have to be made along the way which render the exercise open to management choice – for example, in terms of the choice of test, the items contained within it, the perceived validity for the job in question, and the cultural norms surrounding their use. The use of standard tests may also contribute to organisational cloning and limit the achievement of a 'diverse' workforce.

Socialisation

The third paradigm sees selection as the first stage in a process of socialisation (Anderson and Ostroff, 1997). Anderson and Ostroff argue that the selection decision is too often perceived as a closed process of which the purpose is to achieve a fit between the person and the job, and not regarded as part of a wider exercise in achieving person-job-organisation fit. It is suggested that 'Selection and socialisation are more accurately conceived as stages in a single, longitudinal process of newcomer integration ... Socialisation begins during selection as the applicant experiences the organisation's formal procedures for the first time' (Anderson and Ostroff, 1997: 413). The socialisation aspects of selection take a number of forms depending on the methods that are used. These are:

- information provision – the extent and accuracy of communications

- preference impact – procedural and distributive justice and personal liking for methods

- expectational impact – assumptions about organisational climate and the psychological contract

- attitudinal impact – the degree of investment in the selection process

- behavioural impact – the extent to which the selection methods create/affect subsequent behaviour.

Socially constructed reality, knowledge and power

The final paradigm revolves around the idea that the selection process is not just something that is enacted within organisations – and therefore principally affected by selectors – but is an event that takes place within a wider societal framework (Ramsay and Scholarios, 1999). The notion of *socially constructed reality* considers issues concerning knowledge and power, and with social structures and expected norms within societies. Consequently, 'an integrated model of selection should accommodate the subjective, discursive, power-laden, contested, negotiated and transient nature of each aspect of the process' (Ramsay and Scholarios, 1999: 77). This approach contrasts starkly with the notion of scientific rationality and objective decisions, and it provides a better understanding of why selection decisions vary so much between countries (and between organisations, for that matter). Ramsay and Scholarios (1999: 81) describe the case of senior executive selection to illustrate their argument, suggesting that techniques regarded as highly appropriate for other positions – say, graduates – would be seen as totally unacceptable for appointments at this level. The whole process is managed sensitively and confidentially, making use of informal sources of information, and constitutes an exercise in which both parties can influence the final decision. Normative pressures clearly shape levels of expectation in this situation.

Which of these paradigms makes sense to you? Why is that the case?

CONCLUSION

This chapter has reviewed briefly the major elements in an organisation's recruitment and selection policies and practices, and it has argued that recruitment should not be treated as the poor relation of selection. Because of increasing sophistication in selection decisions, it is often forgotten that without effective recruitment practices the field of applicants from which to choose is likely to be small and unsuitable. Unsatisfactory performance at later stages in employment can sometimes be traced back to poor recruitment and selection decisions and processes. Conversely, effective policies and practices increase the likelihood that staff will be appointed who are capable of meeting targets. This is one area of HRM in which assistance might usefully be sought from consultants and specialists, especially in relation to recruitment advertising and psychometric testing. Being aware of the limits to one's expertise is just as important as knowing which techniques to use. In view of the fact that selection decisions are increasingly devolved to line managers, it is even more important that these processes are well organised, delivered and evaluated, and that advice is sought where appropriate.

Useful reading

BARRICK M., MOUNT M. *and* JUDGE A. 'Personality and performance at the beginning of the new millennium: what do we know and where do we go next?' *International Journal of Selection and Assessment*, Vol. 9, No. 1/2, 2001. pp9–30.

CHARTERED INSTITUTE OF PERSONNEL AND DEVELOPMENT. Recruitment Report. London, CIPD. 2001.

COOPER D. *and* ROBERTSON I. *The Psychology of Personnel Selection*. London, Routledge. 1995.

FOWLER A. *Writing Job Descriptions*. London, CIPD. 2000.

INDUSTRIAL RELATIONS SERVICES. 'Graduate recruitment 2001/02: diversity and competition, IRS *Employment Review* 742c, 17 December 2001c. pp31–40.

MORRELL K., LOAN-CLARKE J. *and* WILKINSON A. 'Unweaving leaving: the use of models in the management of employee turnover', *International Journal of Management Reviews*, Vol. 3, No. 3. 2001. pp219–244.

NEWELL S. *and* SHACKLETON V. 'Selection and assessment as an interactive decision-action process' in T. Redman and A. Wilkinson (eds) *Contemporary HRM*, London, FT/Prentice-Hall. 2001.

RAMSAY H. *and* SCHOLARIOS D. 'Selective decisions: challenging orthodox analyses of the hiring process', *International Journal of Management Reviews*, Vol. 1, No. 4. 1999. pp63–89.

ROBERTSON I. 'Undue diligence', *People Management*, 22 November 2001. pp42–43.

TAYLOR S. *People Resourcing*. London, CIPD. 2002.

Managing Performance for Added Value

Introduction

It should now be clear that horizontal and vertical integration are key themes in HRM, and nowhere is the concept of integration more important than in the management of performance. As we see below, performance management aims directly to link together individual goals, departmental purposes and organisational objectives. It incorporates issues that are central to many other elements of HRM, such as appraisal and employee development, performance-related pay and reward management, and individualism and employee relations. Indeed, it has been argued that performance management is synonymous with the totality of day-to-day management activity because it is concerned with how work can be organised in order to achieve the best possible results.

In this chapter we stretch beyond conventional definitions of performance management to include other aspects of the employment relationship. Here we deal with the induction of new staff – following on from the previous chapter where we considered recruitment and selection – since this is a key component of HRM. While it is obviously crucial to select the right people, it is also imperative to ensure that, from the outset of their employment, employees understand not only the nature of their tasks but also how they and their tasks fit into broader organisational cultures. These principles are reinforced during employment both through the informal daily interactions between managers and their staff, and through formal reviews of performance on a regular basis. Carried out effectively within a systematic performance management system, such reviews can do much to reinforce and strengthen the links between organisational goals and individual performance expectations. Too often, however, appraisals and reviews are treated as a bureaucratic necessity undertaken as a chore by indifferent managers and disinterested employees.

Even if great care has been taken with recruitment and selection, as well as during induction, the performance standards of some employees fall below expectations at subsequent stages of their careers. Decisions have to be taken about how to address this, and whether or not to instigate disciplinary processes or to provide assistance through counselling and support. Problems may arise due to events outside of work (relating to family issues, for example) or within work (relating to career blockages or a change in management style, for example). These can manifest themselves in poor attendance, in a lack of interest in work, or in psychological problems – with which management may be able to assist through counselling or welfare policies. Overall, our purpose in this chapter is to focus on the management of effective and ineffective performance. It is impossible to deal with every aspect of performance management in a single chapter, however, so elsewhere we examine learning and development (Chapter 12), disciplinary procedures (Chapter 15) and performance-related pay (Chapter 16).

Performance management systems

Since becoming part of the HR vocabulary there has been a massive growth in performance management systems (PMSs) as well as a shift of emphasis towards developmental approaches at the expense of reward-driven systems (Bach and Sisson, 2000: 244). There are many reasons for this growth in popularity and overall distribution. Drawn from Williams (1998: 2–8) and Sisson and Storey (2000: 87–9), they include:

- increased competitive pressures which put an emphasis on performance improvement

- attempts to achieve a clearer correlation between organisational goals and individual targets

- restructuring and devolution which have put a primacy on delegating tasks and responsibilities down organisational hierarchies

- the shift from collectivism to individualism, which has allowed for a more rigorous specification of individual performance standards and measures

- government policies introducing performance management frameworks into the public sector.

Like many supposedly well-known terms, however, 'performance management' has a variety of meanings (Bach and Sisson, 2000: 243–4), and has been used to describe just about any HR initiative. For most writers it is seen as 'the policies, procedures and practices that focus on employee performance as a means of fulfilling organisational goals and objectives' (Lowry, 2002: 129). Mabey et al (1998: 129) see the essence of performance management as establishing 'a framework in which performance by individuals can be directed, monitored, motivated and refined'. Armstrong and Baron (1998) promote performance management as a process of aligning or integrating organisational and individual objectives to achieve organisational effectiveness, with development as the prime purpose. The 'framework' approach emphasises a top-down system, whereas the 'process' approach recognises upward communication and is better suited to the theory of modern organisational structures. The key aims of performance management are to measure effectiveness, identify training needs and promote motivation through feedback (Lowry, 2002: 132).

Performance management systems have a number of central characteristics – according to various writers (Armstrong and Baron, 1998: 80–1; Williams, 1998: 3; Lowry, 2002: 130–1) they:

- clarify and help translate corporate goals into individual, team, departmental and divisional goals

- provide regular communications about business plans and progress in achieving objectives

- create a shared understanding of what is required to improve performance and how it is to be achieved

- encourage self-management of individual performance

- require a management style that is open and honest, and encourage two-way communication between superiors and subordinates

- systematically measure and assess all performance against jointly agreed goals

- are a continuously evolving process in which performance improves over time.

In addition, PMSs should apply to all staff, they should rely on consensus and co-operation rather than control or coercion, and they require continuous feedback. The main frameworks of performance management are broadly similar, in that they each link together planning (including integration with business/departmental goals), employee socialisation, monitoring/reviewing progress, reinforcing performance standards, and supporting individuals to achieve performance expectations. The principal components of the process are illustrated in Figure 10.

Figure 10   The performance management process

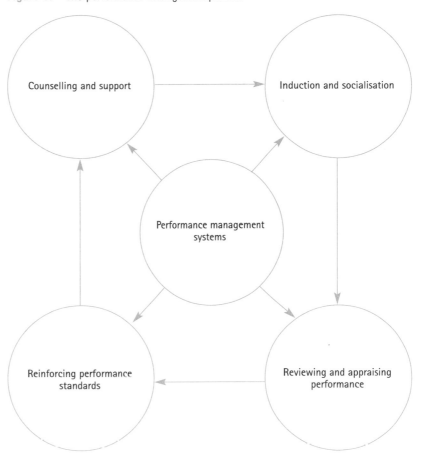

The first stage of a PMS is when new recruits are briefed about performance standards during *induction*, and where attempts are made to
socialise them into the organisation. Typically, this is expressed through
mission statements that articulate organisational goals, mediated
through departmental purpose analyses. Much of the literature on performance management assumes that this phase of the cycle/process
is concerned with corporate communications, job descriptions and key
accountabilities, each of which are considered elsewhere in this book.
Induction training and initial socialisation into employment are rarely
mentioned, but this is a critical time for establishing understanding of,
and commitment to, wider corporate or departmental goals. Most texts
now stress the importance of induction as a process that starts with
recruitment and leads into continuous development. Individual performance expectations and targets are set at this stage, and learning needs
established.

Review and appraisal is the second stage of performance management.
This refers both to the day-to-day informal interaction between

managers and their staff and the formal processes of appraisal and review. The former includes continuous monitoring and the provision of resources and systems that facilitate achievement of individual targets. Although it is clearly necessary to establish formal mechanisms, performance management requires ongoing and unsolicited support in order to be effective. These include the telephone call or the 'chance' conversation just to check that all is going well – something that busy managers tend to overlook in their efforts to satisfy formal organisational demands. Formal review and appraisal is often seen as synonymous with performance management. As with any formalised system, however, there are dangers that the appraisal interview comes to be viewed as the sole event at which performance is reviewed, when staff are praised or criticised for meeting or not meeting targets, and when training and development needs are identified. In many cases, and in particular when appraisals are assessment-based, one purpose of this phase is to determine pay levels or bonuses due to employees – see Chapter 16. With developmental appraisals the emphasis is on how improved performance can be facilitated and sustained, on training and development, and on assisting staff to achieve targets that have been set for the future.

However, it is important to note that appraisals might just as easily focus on failures to achieve standards, on poor performance, and on any problems that may be affecting work. This is the third stage of the PMS, the phase of *reinforcing performance standards*. There are several possible issues that could be dealt with here, ranging from minor lapses in performance or one-off problems through to a more serious and potentially long-term deterioration in standards. This could well be expressed through problems with capability, either due to a lack of expertise or knowledge, a failure to cope with changes in the nature of work, or absenteeism. Incapability issues are often ignored by managers rather than addressed. There are many reasons for this, but managers are frequently unwilling to address the nature of problems, and in any event they harbour a vague hope that the problem will disappear or that the employee concerned will leave. Sometimes the problem becomes so severe that it explodes and the organisation is faced with a difficult situation, perhaps culminating in an application to an employment tribunal.

Finally, PMSs involve *support* for individuals to meet performance requirements through welfare and counselling services. This may involve little more than informal support from an individual manager, perhaps through a quiet conversation in the office – and in some cases that may be all that is required to improve things both for the individual and the organisation. On other occasions, external professional support is needed, and there are several bodies that provide services and information that is of use when counselling employees. The increasing tendency is to use external services for counselling – even via the web – to ensure that employees have confidence that an independent person is able to listen to their concerns and help them devise strategies to over-come problems. In view of the increasing pressures that face employees – manifested in intensified working conditions and resultant stress – counselling and support is an essential component in any PMS, even if it is used only by a minority of staff.

Is there a performance management system (PMS) in your organis-ation? Could it be improved, and if so how? If your organisation does not have a PMS, what value might it add?

Induction and employee socialisation

Induction forms a critical element of the employee socialisation phase of PMS. Induction can be defined as 'a planned and systematic process, structured and implemented by the organisation, to help new employees settle into their new jobs quickly, happily and effectively' (Fowler, 1999: 4), or more informally, 'the way we do things around here' (also Fowler, 1999: 1). Many definitions mention the importance of welcoming new staff into the organisation, and arranging for them to get to know other workers. Writers stress that a formal induction programme need not be expensive, and that the benefits to be gained from a systematic process far outweigh the costs of recruiting new staff if large numbers of people leave at the time of the so-called 'induction crisis' (Reid and Barrington, 2001: 281).

Irrespective of whether or not a formal or structured programme is in place, all employees go through an induction phase on joining a new organisation or department. In many organisations, especially those that do not have a specialist HR function or manager, this may be little more than a rudimentary greeting before being shown to their place of work. New recruits may be told to ask questions if they need assistance and they are left to get on with the job, because it is assumed they have the required technical or administrative skills to cope. In many work-places the introductory phase may consist of practical jokes and tricks (for example, 'Go and find a left-handed screwdriver') as the new recruit is socialised into the norms of the workplace and the workgroup. There may be little attempt to explain anything about the company mission, its policies on customer service or quality assurance, or its underlying phil-osophy. Even information about health and safety, disciplinary rules and company procedures may be dealt with in an informal way, despite their importance in setting the tone of the workplace and establishing what are regarded as acceptable behaviours.

The problems associated with such a lack of systems are obvious. Employees often feel isolated and confused, unaware of company rules and procedures. They may struggle to learn how to do the job because they have received only limited assistance at the outset. They may end up breaking safety or disciplinary rules, receive a warning and become embittered about the employer. They may decide that the initial enthusiasm associated with the new job was misplaced, and leave to take up a position elsewhere. Each of these problems represents a cost to the employer, either in direct financial terms (poor-quality work, time spent on disciplinary issues, re-advertising jobs) or in public relations terms, as potential recruits and customers choose to go elsewhere. In circumstances such as these it is hardly surprising that employees question the depth of employers' commitments to people as their most important resource. As we saw in the previous chapter, about one quarter of new recruits leave their employment within the first year.

For organisations that do invest time and effort in induction, there are three broad perspectives on the nature and purpose of the process: induction as an administrative exercise, induction as a means of promoting social integration, and induction from an HRM viewpoint.

As *an administrative exercise*, induction's sole purpose may seem to be to impart information about the job, the procedures and the organisation. From this perspective the principal points at issue appear to be what topics to include and when to deal with them so as to prevent information overload. Drawn from the lists produced by Fowler (1999: 17–26) and Reid and Barrington (2001: 282–3), necessary elements in the induction package would appear to be:

- the terms of employment, involving such information as the hours of work, shift arrangements, time-keeping and clocking-on and -off systems

- housekeeping and security issues, such as catering facilities, energy conservation and speed limits on site

- health and safety regulations, such as safety procedures, protective clothing and the hazards of office equipment

- wages and benefits, such as starting salary, holiday and sick pay, profit sharing, expenses claims, welfare

- company rules and policies, such as disciplinary and grievance procedures, trade union membership, works rules, time off for statutory or trade union duties, equal opportunities

- employee development opportunities, sports and social amenities

- information about the company and the industry, such as a mission statement, history, product markets, organisational structure, communications

- job performance issues, such as job description, standards, appraisal, and role within the department.

The role of the HR specialist is regarded as particularly relevant in maintaining quality assurance standards during the induction process, as well as in delivering some parts of the programme – such as information about welfare, wage and salary administration, and grievance and disciplinary procedures. Fowler (1999: 63–6) suggests that specialists can help line managers enhance their contribution to induction programmes by designing policies and training in conjunction with them, and by monitoring the effectiveness of existing systems. Data on labour turnover crisis points, on the results of exit interviews, on the degree to which all aspects of the induction checklist are being covered, and on evaluating the experiences of recent recruits should all feed back into the induction planning process.

The second and third perspectives differ not so much in the type of information that is to be imparted during induction but on the underlying philosophy of the process and its interpretation. The *social integration perspective* is best illustrated by Fowler (1999: 31–2), who argues that the speed of inclusion into informal groupings is a powerful influence on how quickly a newcomer settles in. Some organisations allocate a 'friend' to help employees join in with the formal and informal social gatherings – for example, joining in sports activities, or having someone to eat lunch with. There may be groups of workers for whom some cosseting is particularly appropriate, such as school-leavers who are entering employment for the first time, or young catering staff who have just left home to work in a hotel. Other workers may face special problems at work, and also need a fair amount of initial assistance. For example, employees with disabilities will need to know immediately where and how special arrangements can be made for them, and members of ethnic minorities may wish to be put in touch with support groups.

The final perspective views induction as an altogether more hard-nosed business issue, in which employers make use of various techniques to 'educate' employees about the company ethos, aiming to integrate them with existing organisational cultures. This, the *HRM perspective*, is rarely to be found in mainstream HR publications, which view induction as a relatively value-free device for helping employees settle down in a new job. Accordingly, the advice mainly prescribes how to design induction programmes or balance different activities to ensure that effective learning takes place. It is hardly acknowledged that induction can be a powerful device for integrating new employees, gaining their commitment, and inculcating them with a sense of belonging and identity that forms a basis for effective performance 'beyond contract'.

Harrison (2000: 248) suggests that dialogic learning is a major element of induction in that 'it should help [new recruits] to understand and adapt to the vision of the organisation and its implicit values and norms'. By interpreting the policies and practices used, new recruits are able to appreciate the meaning and purpose of them in operation, and to grasp the fact that such policies – equal opportunities, for example –and practices constitute an important aspect of organisational life.

CASE STUDY: The Body Shop induction

The Body Shop employs approximately 800 people in its two head offices. Its commitment to values and its reputation for progressive personnel policies are well known. In 2000, a new induction programme was launched in part because the company was restructuring and also in recognition that people would leave if the induction process was not sufficiently motivating. The induction process spans six months, starting with a full first day of formal basics mixed with social interaction (at breakfast or lunch) with team members. A 'buddy' is allocated so that the new worker has someone to turn to at any time. Throughout the first month a series of meetings are arranged with a wide variety of people outside the immediate work team, but with whom the new worker may have to make contact. In the second month a full day is spent learning more about the company values, campaigns, and products. During the third month head office staff work in a shop for 2–5 days. During the fourth month time is spent on a community project (all staff are given half a day a month to take part in a community project). The fifth month covers health and safety and human resources. And during the final month a personal development workshop is held to emphasise the long-term development of staff. All staff should have prepared a personal development plan by the time of the first annual appraisal. Evaluation takes place after each session as well as at the end of the six-month period.

Adapted from Sanders D. 'Improving retention and performance through induction'. IRS *Employee Development Bulletin* 130, 2000

There is some evidence that dialogic learning and the human resource management perspective comprises a major component in the employment strategies and practices of many Japanese and US companies, exemplified by artefacts such as similar uniforms, badges, baseball caps and company credit cards. Harrison (1992: 284) mentions the fact that new recruits at Fujitsu are invited to join the 'family of employees' and some US computer companies are noted for their commitment to philosophies that emphasise open communications. Similarly, Delbridge (1998: 46) reports on a process known as 'intensive induction' during which new recruits are developed into loyal and trusting members of staff. More recently, using data from a UK company, Dundon *et al* (2001: 445–6) describe the innovative approach taken at 'Consultancy Co.' where a full-time culture manager was appointed. When recruiting new staff, personality was valued above job competence in order to ensure that all staff fitted the culture in which 'having fun at work' was top of the company's 'culture statement'. There are numerous other examples of the HRM approach to induction, involving team activities and physical exercises, as well as learning about the philosophy and motives of the company. It could be argued that in this situation induction is more appropriately termed 'indoctrination'.

Do you think there is any substance in the view that induction can be interpreted as indoctrination?

Performance review and appraisal

A PMS typically incorporates a formal appraisal or review on an annual or more frequent basis, with informal meetings taking place more frequently. Like other elements of HR, appraisal/review systems have become more widespread over the last decade, involving an increase in use with non-managerial staff – by 1999, 75 per cent of organisations used appraisal in respect of all their full-time employees (Redman, 2001: 59) – and widespread adoption by the public sector. This was stimulated in some cases by governmental pressures to introduce compulsory competitive tendering, and by moves to increase employee involvement, to seek better ways of identifying training needs, and monitoring employee performance more effectively – all aimed at improving service delivery. A large number of local authorities regarded performance management as a very significant development in their activities, tied in with appraisals and attendance management.

Randell (1994: 221) defined performance appraisal in broad terms as 'the process whereby current performance in a job is observed and discussed for the purpose of adding value to that level of performance'. In itself this seemingly simple definition contains a number of contentious issues, not least who has responsibility for, and what is included in, appraisals. Randell divides appraisal into three categories: reward review, potential review, and performance review. Problems arise where the primary purpose of the review is reward or potential, in which case the employee is unlikely to openly discuss performance problems, and it may be that different people and different systems are needed depending on the main purpose of the interview. We concentrate below on the appraisal/review system for performance analysis. Fowler (1999: 5–6) suggests the following main aims of appraisal: making reward decisions, improving performance, motivating staff, succession planning and identifying potential, promoting manger-subordinate dialogue, and making a formal assessment of unsatisfactory performance.

The development of performance management in ICI Pharmaceuticals (now Zeneca) has been quoted extensively over the years (Armstrong and Baron, 1998: 159–68). The pressures that led the company into performance management were similar to those facing most organisations – most notably, international competition. The company had a task-oriented culture in which staff felt disassociated from the business as a whole, and it was decided to shift towards a learning organisation – one in which there was a holistic understanding of issues. The focus at ICI was development-based rather than assessment-based, and the system was introduced and integrated by 'performance management' coaches – who were line managers. Two key features of the system particularly worthy of note are the close involvement of individuals in setting their own targets, and the fact that the administration of the performance-related pay system is devolved to departmental and functional level.

The most prevalent model in the past has been the individual performance review (IPR) – usually conducted by line managers. Where the
focus is on development, the interview should be an honest and open
conversation with the aim of improving performance and motivation.
Armstrong and Baron (1998: 64–5) believe that the word 'appraisal'
suggests a top-down approach, whereas 'review' more accurately
describes a process in which the manager and individuals, or team
leaders and teams, can reflect and examine structured feedback on a
more equal footing. In theory, the review should summarise and draw
conclusions from what has happened since the last review based on fact
rather than opinion. Moreover, there should be no surprises because
issues should have been dealt with as they arose, and successes and
problems should be recognised and learned from, and developmental
opportunities identified. The interview may give employees an opportunity to comment on leadership, support and guidance from their managers. In this context the manager uses counselling skills to actively
listen and to offer constructive feedback, as well as to agree on future
aims. Drawn from the work of Armstrong and Baron (1998: 64–6),
Lowry (2002: 133) and Redman (2001: 60), the areas for discussion
might include:

- the link between business and individual objectives

- clarification of the performance 'agreement'

- a measurement of individual contribution, including discussion on
  the achievement of objectives and an analysis of why they have or
  have not been achieved

- the identification of training and development needs

- career and succession planning

- a general discussion on feelings about work and aspirations.

What are the main aims of a performance review and an appraisal?
Do you think they are incompatible?

Redman (2001: 60) suggests that control may also be one of the purposes of appraisal and cites evidence that the 'harder' approach is
increasing while 'softer' developmental approaches are declining. He
suggests that there has been a shift away from using appraisal for
career planning and determining future potential to one of using it for
improving performance and allocating rewards. Bach and Sisson (2000:
255–6) also discuss appraisal in the context of Foucault's concept of
power, in which appraisal is perceived as 'a form of disciplinary gaze'.
What is clear is that the *purpose* of the appraisal/review must be absol-
utely clear before determining the type of system to adopt. Similarly,
the formal annual process should not replace continuous informal

discussions which should go on as and when required. Nor should regular informal meetings be seen as a replacement for the formalised annual or bi-annual meeting which ensures that adequate time is devoted to overview all performance issues in a structured and focused manner.

As we saw earlier, it is usually line managers who carry out the appraisal/review, but others may be involved. Choices of the people to act as appraisers often depend upon prevailing organisational culture and the group to be appraised. There are many other options, including self-assessment, peer assessment (by colleagues at the same grade/level), upward assessment (by the appraisee's subordinates), external assessors (by such means as consultants or assessment centres) and feedback from internal or external customers about the individual's services.

Reviews conducted by the immediate supervisor are particularly appropriate where reward is linked to performance, and where control is seen to be one of the aims of the process – but such reviews are still prevalent where the aim is developmental. This method may be instrumental in strengthening relationships, but only where the relationship is already sound, and where the manager has the skills to conduct the review (Lowry, 2002: 135–6). If the aim is developmental, both the organisational culture and the manager's approach are critical, for a 'control' focus is likely to stifle open discussion and thereby hamper progress. As Harrison (2000: 252) points out, it is the relationship between the parties that has the single most powerful influence on the success of the review, and is one of the major problems related to it. Many disagreements may arise during the review – for example, in relation to identifying and prioritising learning needs – and in extreme cases may end in allegations of victimisation or discrimination (Harrison, 2000. 252–4). Indeed, where either party does not subscribe to the goals or philosophy of the system, genuine communication can quickly break down. Certainly the review/appraisal process can be a balancing act between control/judgement and support/development, with the manager cast in the conflicting roles of judge and helper. In recent years there has been a shift away from relying solely or predominantly on managers' appraisals in order to incorporate a greater number of independent reviews of performance and so build up a more rounded picture of the individual. As Grint (1993: 74) argues, we should escape from the labyrinthine implication that schemes can be objective, and instead accept our subjective fate by collating a number of different perspectives on performance, including those of subordinates. We return to the issue of 360-degree appraisals later in this section.

Customer appraisal is becoming more widespread, sometimes feeding into the setting of performance targets, especially if there are service guarantees that involve compensation to customers. Customer surveys might include a wide variety of techniques, including electronic surveillance, and it is now common for call centres to record a random sample of conversations. A more controversial means is the use of individuals posing as customers or 'spies' to check quality of service.

Upward appraisal is relatively common in the USA and has been adopted by UK companies such as WH Smith and the Body Shop. Employees comment on their manager's performance, usually by using an anonymous questionnaire. However, for managers, these can be very threatening and/or undermining. Moreover, they rely on employees not feeling intimidated, nor using the opportunity to register unjustified complaints against their supervisors – factors that may explain the lack of widespread use of upward appraisal in the UK (Redman, 2001: 64–5).

Self-assessment is often combined with other forms of assessment, and works well for those with high levels of autonomy or for employees with

---

CASE STUDY: Janet as appraiser and appraisee

Janet line-managed 20 staff, and on appraising them found that she adopted a different approach to each appraisee. She strongly believed in the appraisal process, but felt that her own appraisal often ended up being of little use to her.

Rose and Janet

Rose came into work merely to collect her salary, and had no interest in the aims of the organisation, nor of improving her performance through training or any other means. She tended to be a law unto herself, and people approached her with trepidation. From Rose's point of view the idea that she should be managed and should have to attend review meetings was new, and she resented the intrusion of both on her way of working. Janet felt that Rose's work and attitude were often very poor, although she could work hard and well when she felt inclined. Janet tried very hard to harness Rose's motivation using positive tactics and by giving her a relatively high degree of autonomy, but Rose's workstyle remained unchanged, or possibly worsened. Rose quickly showed that she resented Janet's role. At the review meetings Rose was usually sullen. Janet maintained an open style during review, but felt that she would eventually have to use the reviews as a tool for setting targets based on 'control' rather than 'equality'. In the end, she felt that recourse might have to be made to the capability procedures.

Selina and Janet

Janet also line-managed Selina, and they met regularly to discuss work issues, to allocate responsibility and to look to future needs. Notes were taken at the meetings, and as their relationship developed, the meetings widened to discuss developmental concerns. They both felt that there was still need for an annual review in order to allocate quality time to discuss issues that had been mentioned in their more regular meetings.

Janet and John

Janet was line-managed by John, who had been in the service for many years. Janet felt that he had been promoted beyond his capability and when she took problems to the review meetings they remained unresolved. On one occasion she suggested to John that she desperately needed proactive support to deal with particularly entrenched problems, and he responded that he always gave such support when asked for it. John never initiated meetings, and usually neglected to produce or pass on to Janet the record of the meetings. The review meetings continued increasingly irregularly, but became a paper exercise of little added value. Janet put less and less effort into the self-assessment that she was required to produce in advance of meetings with John.

scarce skills. The main problem with this form of assessment is that it often does not correlate with supervisory assessment, and that women tend to rate themselves lower than men (Lowry, 2002: 135–6; Fletcher, 1999: 39–40).

Other approaches include *team-based and competency-based reviews*. Although it is assumed that one approach to appraisal will be used within any organisation, in practice managers may adopt a wide variety of approaches depending on circumstances – see the case study below. As Fletcher (1999: 3) notes, appraisal is certainly here to stay, but it will not remain a universally-applied standard procedure because what suits one set of circumstances is impracticable in another – even within the same organisation.

The 360-degree performance review

Because of problems with other forms of appraisal, 360-degree performance reviews have been growing in popularity. Such reviews include some of the appraisal systems already mentioned because they incorporate feedback from peers, subordinates, supervisors, and sometimes customers. These are usually voluntary, confidential, self-determining, and learning-oriented, rather than linked to assessment. However, there are a range of types and purposes for 360-degree feedback, and although it is sometimes linked to managerial reward, many feel that this does not help working relationships and affects the quality of feedback (Chivers and Darling, 1999: x). Its use is based on two assumptions

CASE STUDY: 360-degree appraisal in Humberside TEC

Storr (2000) reports on the way in which Humberside TEC introduced an informal system of 360-degree appraisal. The system was started with team leaders and was subsequently extended to cover almost all staff. The scheme was unusual, for it was paper-free – appraisees and appraisers met eye-to-eye together as a group. The appraisee 'owned' the process, and decided on who should appraise, and what questions should be asked. Some appraisees initially chose safe groups and /or safe questions, moving to use different sets of appraisers and more challenging questions when they gained confidence. There were no rules on frequency of appraisal, although it was expected that most people would go through the process annually. The scheme emphasis was on celebrating achievement as well as performance and

development. All participants were given support and training before participating in the scheme. One person used external clients and reported that this brought out subtle issues about the way they communicated with each other. Another reported that her feedback was similar to that given by her line manager, but that it had far more impact because it came from six different people. Most of the feedback was very positive, participants reporting that the system was very useful for focusing on pertinent targets, promoting self-development and autonomy, improving communications, and enhancing a more open organisational style.

Adapted from Storr F. 'This is not a circular'.
People Management, 11 May 2000

– firstly, that self-awareness increases when feedback is based on a number of assessments, and secondly, that self-awareness is a prerequisite for improved performance as well as an initial building-block for leadership and management development programmes (Leopold, 2002: 141).

There are a number of reasons why upward and 360-degree appraisals have recently become popular (Mabey, 2001: 42; Grint, 1993: 73; IRS *Employment Trends* 705, 2000; Chivers and Darling, 1999: *viii*; Leopold, 2002: 142):

- They involve multi-rater rather than single-rater assessments. Traditional top-down approaches provide only a single viewpoint, and that may be influenced by factors subject to personal bias or prejudice, either positive or negative. Having upward or 360-degree appraisals provides an instrument with potentially much greater validity, and one that stands a greater chance of acceptance – and therefore action – by the appraisee.

- Information from the process is valuable for strategic planning purposes, in particular to inform resourcing, training, and development strategies. It can be used to identify organisation-wide strengths and weaknesses.

- As people become used to giving and receiving feedback, they are more likely to use feedback daily, creating more open communications.

- They provide a framework for the effective assessment and development of poor performers.

In addition, 360-degree performance review may be more appropriate for new organisational forms:

- If an organisation genuinely believes in a spirit of continuous improvement, the provision of views from a variety of perspectives – particularly customers of an individual's services – are to be welcomed as a means to enhanced performance.

- With flatter organisations and greater spans of control it is more difficult for any one manager to appraise a large number of staff with any degree of accuracy or knowledge. It aligns with the shift from management-driven to employee-driven performance management processes.

- Subordinates are often in closer contact with their managers than senior staff and are on the receiving end of his or her actions. Also, it is expected that involving staff in appraisals of their supervisors and other colleagues may well enhance their commitment to the organisation.

- If employees have greater access to their personal files, there is a need to ensure that the appraisee knows the results of appraisal. Having a more open approach, which draws upon a wider range of viewpoints, facilitates this and lessens the likelihood of legal action.

- The concept fits well with notions of employee involvement and empowerment and open organisational cultures, and encourages self-awareness.

Problems relating to 360-degree appraisal centre on whether the information gathered is accurate, valid and meaningful. Questions may be poorly worded, or open to wide interpretation – for example, 'Does the manager deal with problems in a flexible manner?' Additionally, external customers are often excluded from the process. In common with other methods, the process can be time-consuming, expensive and bureaucratic. Finally, the process assumes that managers will accept feedback and amend their behaviour accordingly – but Redman (2001: 67–8) suggests that there is a dearth of evidence that this actually happens. Conditions that inhibit and enhance the use of 360-degree feedback are given in Table 36. The most important enhancer is having an open culture, although this does not always mean that negative feedback is received constructively. As with all appraisal systems, dealing with negative feedback is the most difficult aspect, and unless it is handled supportively and sensitively, could result in demotivation.

Examine the list of inhibitors and enablers in the table below. How do they apply to your organisation? If there are problems, what – if anything – is being done to address them?

Table 36   Inhibitors and enhancers of 360-degree feedback

Inhibitors	Enhancers
360-degree feedback is discouraged/promoted because it is perceived as	
Part of a 'blame culture'	A means to a useful end
Merely lip service	Involving genuine support for
Involving conflicting priorities	development
A 'bolt-on' HR tool	Usefully making and taking time
Involving conflicting performance management	Involving 'ownership' of the feedback process
Not helping to manage negative feedback	A means of putting awareness into action
	Giving rise to worthwhile personal reflection

Adapted from Chivers W. and Darling P. *360-Degree Feedback and Organisational Culture.* CIPD, 1999

One of the major problems with all systems of performance appraisal is that they are used for many different and conflicting purposes, the pursuit of one often creating obstacles that prevent the achievement of others. There are further problems that centre on whether the review is forward- or backward-looking. In the case of developmental reviews, the focus tends to be on future learning needs. Conversely, when related to performance rewards, they are typically a review of the previous year and development needs are often overlooked (Lowry, 2002: 132; Fletcher, 1999: 7–8). This conflict of purpose is not the only criticism that can be made of performance appraisals in practice. Yet another problem is that many line managers regard appraisals as a bureaucratic and irksome exercise that is done solely to satisfy the personnel and development function (Redman, 2001: 73; Grint, 1993: 62). Some organisations have developed paperless or computer-based systems that require employees to do the bulk of the work, but where there is concern about the fundamental purpose of appraisal, they do not solve this particular problem. In too many instances the event is debased and becomes meaningless to all parties, but the paperwork is duly completed, sent to the personnel department and filed. In the absence of any follow-up, it is not surprising that systems fall into disrepute and fade away (Redman, 2001: 74). Appraisal is perceived as a practice that does not 'add value' to the organisation, and appraisers are neither rewarded nor recognised for conducting appraisals on time. Only if appraisals are seen to be worthwhile, leading to change and demonstrable outputs, can HR practitioners ever hope that line managers will see them as a key contributor to a high-commitment performance-oriented culture.

Additional problems surround measurements in terms of objectivity, equity, and meaningfulness. It may be the case that what is meaningful is not measurable. For example, advice that covers all angles – on the basis that the customer does not know what he or she doesn't know – may be difficult to measure. What is measurable may not be meaningful – for example, answering the telephone within five rings. There are additional problems in the ratings that are given by appraisers. Grint (1993: 63) describes the 'distortions' likely to occur in assessments of performance. The 'halo' effect leads to over-estimation, whereas the 'horn' effect results in a lower assessment than might otherwise be expected. The 'crony' effect is caused by closeness of the personal relationship between appraiser and appraisee; the 'Veblen' effect results in central tendencies, so named after the tutor's habit of giving all his students C grades irrespective of their quality. Finally, the 'doppelganger' effect occurs when appraisers reward similarities between themselves and appraisees, whereas differences lead to adverse ratings. This obviously has significant equal opportunities implications in view of the fact that in traditional top-down appraisals women and ethnic minorities have been prone to lose out due to imbalances in the hierarchical structure of organisations. Managers have also been seen to manipulate ratings for their own ends – for example, by downgrading graduates to 'show them that they didn't know everything' and by giving high ratings in order to get rid of weak performers (Redman, 2001).

Appraisers also face problems when confronted with appraisees who have not performed well during the year, especially if appraisal is linked to financial rewards. Ratings drift occurs because managers often feel uncomfortable in dealing with the poor performers, and even in an organisation that is itself not performing particularly well, a large pro- portion of its staff may still end up with above-average ratings. Redman (2001: 71–2) cites studies showing that appraisers are ill-prepared, talk too much, base much of the discussion on third-party complaints and rely on 'gut feelings'. On a more fundamental note, Redman (2001: 62) and Redman *et al* (2000: 48) suggest that there is little evidence that the systems actually improve performance. The allegation is that the system becomes a means of control, particularly where customers, peers, subordinates, and colleagues are potential appraisers. Peer review systems are labelled as 'screw-your-buddy' and managers who 'fail' appraisal may find themselves dispensed with. To illustrate this last point, Redman gives the example of Semco, a Brazilian company, in which managers are upwardly appraised regularly and are given a mark out of 100. The results are made public and those who regularly under- perform eventually disappear.

Despite numerous problems associated with performance appraisal, Redman (2001: 75) suggests that many managers have found such sys- tems valuable and that many problems have been resolved. He suggests that much of the damning research was carried out with 'hard and uncompromising models' which are now less common, and concentrated on the ineffective way in which many organisations implement appraisal. Certainly the empirical work carried out by Redman *et al* (2000) in a National Health Service Trust demonstrated that many of the managers and professionals valued the appraisal process; few suggested that it should be scrapped – rather that refinements should be made.

Think about the appraisal/review processes within an organisation with which you are familiar. What are the main aims of the process, and how well does it work in practice?

Reinforcing performance standards: managing poor performance

Much of the literature on new HRM styles describes situations in which employees have shown willing to work well beyond their contractual obli- gations for the employer in order to achieve competitive advantage. Examples include the hotel porter who used initiative to return a briefcase to a guest, the secretary who redrafted a letter to incorporate new information while his boss was away, or the production worker who ignored instructions and changed a machine setting to override a fault. Although such examples are quoted regularly, they are probably less extensive than the number of cases where employees fall short of targets or, worse still, fail to turn up for work at all. Performance management generally tends to be seen in terms of positive reinforcement and the identification of weaknesses to aid setting development targets. In contrast, relatively little has been written about the management of ineffectual performance although reviews are bound to expose those whose performance is poor, and who are unable or unwilling to meet standards required. Where this occurs, most of the literature emphasises the role of organisational inadequacies that may contribute to ineffective performance. These may include problems relating to recruitment and selection, promotion, working conditions, inadequate job descriptions, poor managers, work overload, stress and work organisation, and lack of appropriate training and development (Leopold, 2002: 143–4; Armstrong and Baron, 1998: 342–3). The issue of managing poor performance is considered below in relation to two issues: capability and attendance/absence.

It should be acknowledged that mistakes could be made at interview or at the point of promotion, and that where the problem is capability, use of procedures leading to dismissal can be used. According to Lewis and Sargeant (2000: 255–6), 'capability' is assessed by reference to 'skill, aptitude, health or any other physical or mental quality' just as inflexibility or lack of adaptability is assessed by reference to 'aptitude and mental qualities'. Stress is placed on the importance of early identification of problems as well as an investigation into the causes of poor performance. The ACAS Handbook suggests the following action where poor performance is identified:

- The employee should be asked for an explanation and the explanation checked.

- Where the reason is lack of the required skills, the employee should, wherever possible, be helped through training and given reasonable time to reach the required standards.

- Where the employee is then unable to reach the required standards, it should be considered whether alternative work might be found.

- Where alternative work is not available, the position should be explained to the employee before dismissal proceedings begin.

It is important to recognise that workers should not normally be dismissed because of poor performance unless warnings and a chance to improve have been given. Moreover, if the main cause of poor performance is the changing nature of the job, employers should assess whether the situation should be dealt with through redundancy rather than capability (ACAS, 2002). If individuals are not prepared to work as required – as opposed to not being able to – the case is likely to be dealt with as misconduct (Lewis and Sargeant, 2000: 257).

> How are capability issues dealt with in your organisation (or in one with which you are familiar)? How *should* such issues be addressed?

Where the problem relates to ill health, the basic issue is whether the employer could be expected to wait any longer for the employee to recover, as well as whether the contract has been frustrated. In cases of long-term illness, the ACAS Handbook recommends the following:

- The employee and employer should maintain regular contact.

- The employee should be kept informed if employment is at risk.

- The employee's GP should be asked when a return to work is likely, and the sort of work which the employee might then be capable of.

- Using the GP's report, the employer should consider whether alternative work is available.

- The employer is not expected to create a special job, but to take action on the basis of the medical evidence.

- Where there is doubt about the ill health, the employee should be asked if he or she is willing to be examined by a medical expert employed by the company.

- Where an employee refuses to co-operate in providing medical evidence or to be examined, the employee should be told in writing that a decision will be taken on the basis of the information available, and that this may result in dismissal.

- When the employee's job can no longer be kept open and no suitable alternative work is available, the employee should be informed of the likelihood of dismissal.

- Where dismissal takes place, the employee should be given the period of notice to which he or she is entitled and informed of any right of appeal.

When there are intermittent absences owing to ill health, the employer does not have to rely on medical evidence but can overview the employee's history of employment. This should take into account factors such as the types of illness and likelihood of recurrence, lengths of absence, the employer's need for that particular employee, the impact of the absences on the workforce and how far the employee was made aware of his or her position. In such cases dismissal may take place at a time when the employee is fit and in work (Lewis and Sargeant, 2000: 257–9). In practice, many managers tend to duck the capability issue by ignoring or side-stepping the problems. This can include moving the person to another department or establishment as a damage-limitation exercise, or having a quiet word about inadequate performance and the prospect of capability/disciplinary proceedings in the hope that the person will leave.

Recent research investigating best practice in relation to teacher capability, carried out by Earnshaw *et al* (2002), suggests that an increased willingness to tackle capability issues has emerged due to a culture change within the profession which has meant that poor performance is no longer tolerated by management or by peers. It is likely that this change came about as a result of the introduction of performance indicators combined with a rigorous inspection regime making teachers 'performance-aware'. The research found that in just under half of the cases, capability issues were resolved informally outside the established procedures, although in some cases work on the problems had lasted several years. Most often the capability procedures were genuinely supportive and gave the teachers opportunity to improve, with adequate resources deployed. However, many of the teachers found the stress of the procedures too great and took time off sick as a result, and many more went into denial unable to accept that they were lacking in capability. Because a large number of the teachers had been in the profession for many years without any system of assessment, it is hardly surprising that their initial reaction was to deny any shortcomings. The clearest message arising from the research was that capability issues should be addressed at an early stage, because in such cases there is a higher likelihood of improvement. Cases that dragged on simply prolonged the agony for all concerned, and were no more likely to produce a positive result. The research found that just under a quarter of the teachers improved. Of the rest, the majority resigned and a small proportion (less than 5 per cent) were dismissed on capability or ill-health grounds (Earnshaw *et al*, 2002: *ii*). Some of the most effective managers, upon identification of a problem, immediately triggered capability procedures in order to give maximum support to the individual and a framework for improvement. This ensured transparency and fairness throughout, and meant that the situation was resolved quickly, hopefully by improvement, but otherwise by quickly moving through the procedures.

Readers should note that this section merely provides a brief overview of disciplinary procedures. For further information refer to Lewis and Sargeant (2000: 255–9) and Taylor (1998: 176–8), as well as to Chapter 6.

Reinforcing performance standards: managing attendance

The management of attendance is a topic that is also an integral aspect of HRM. There are links with other parts of employee resourcing in terms of induction, welfare and counselling, and with employee development regarding training sessions for line managers who are required to handle attendance issues. Questions regarding sick pay, pension schemes and attendance payments link it with employee reward, and there are a multitude of connections with employee relations – in addition to being closely concerned with disciplinary procedures, the causes of absence have much to do with morale, commitment and conflict at work. Also, employers are increasingly aware of the need to ensure a 'duty of care' for employees, with the threat of litigation as a key pressure (IRS *Employee Health Bulletin* 22, August 2001).

Data from a CIPD survey (2001i) showed that the mean rate of sickness absence among 1,466 surveyed organisations was 3.8 per cent per annum, equivalent to 8.7 working days of absence per person – in addition to statutory and paid holidays. The cost of this absence in 2000 was estimated to be £12 billion. Since not all respondents included indirect costs (for example, of replacement labour), the actual costs are likely to be higher, and research from the Institute for Employment Studies (Bevan, 2001) also suggests that most employers underestimate the true costs of sickness absence. Of course, the calculated costs are based on *reported* absences, and there is evidence that not all absences are reported (Dunn and Wilkinson, 2002: 21), particularly managers' own absences (CIPD, 2001i: 8). Not all employers attempt to calculate such costs. The CIPD estimates that one fifth of employers do not know the level of sickness absence in their organisation (CIPD, 2001i) and the Industrial Society (IRS *Employee Health Bulletin* 22, August 2001) reports that only 41 per cent of employers calculate the costs of absence.

Does your organisation keep absence records on computer? If so, what information is hold, what is it used for, and who has access to these records? How could the system be improved so that line managers could play a greater role in the management of attendance?

If your organisation does not use a computerised system, how are records kept, how easy is it to identify problem cases, and what problems have emerged due to the lack of IT in this area?

Financial costs are not the only factor in the management of attendance. There is evidence that managers see employee morale (seen to be low where workers have to cover for others whom they see as 'pulling a fast one'), their own credibility, and loss of efficiency as being of greater concern than the immediate financial costs (Dunn and Wilkinson, 2002: 9). The indirect costs of poor levels of attendance are evident in inadequate levels of customer service, cancelled commuter trains, unanswered telephone calls, and overworked staff who cover for absent colleagues only to run into problems when attempting to complete their own work on time. Absence records may indicate the level of organisational health.

It is important to define clearly what is meant by absenteeism, to identify measures of absence, and to understand its main causes in order to set up effective control systems. Absence measures do not normally include anticipated and legitimate spells away from work – such as holidays, jury service, or attendance at a training course. Other forms of absence are typically divided between authorised and unauthorised. Broadly, authorised absences comprise situations in which employees are genuinely unwell and have a valid medical certificate, whereas unauthorised cases are those in which it is not clear if the employee is actually unwell or indeed has any genuine reason for being away from work. Self-certification has blurred the distinction between these two categories, although they may have to be dealt with in different ways. For example, if an employee has been absent for a series of single days over a specified period, a quiet word may lead to improved attendance patterns. Conversely, if an employee has been off sick for several months, a warning is hardly likely to speed up his or her return to work.

Despite the seeming importance of absence management, only 80 per cent of respondents to the recent CIPD survey had a written absence management policy, and this was the more likely the larger the organisation. Similarly, only 38 per cent of organisations benchmarked against other employers within their sector, and 23 per cent benchmarked within their region. However, parts of the public sector use benchmarking extensively, 87 per cent of local authorities and 79 per cent of health employers doing so (CIPD, 2001i). The reasons given for not measuring the cost of absence according to the Industrial Society (IRS *Employee Health Bulletin* 22, August 2001) are: absence is not a problem (37 per cent); too time-consuming (32 per cent); no computerised personnel system (20 per cent); benefits not worthwhile (18 per cent); other (16 per cent); no accurate attendance records (13 per cent); do not know how to measure costs (7 per cent). The CIPD study estimated that over half of all absence is short-term (that is, of five days or fewer), with this figure rising to two-thirds in firms with less than 100 employees. Even though there are relatively few incidents of long-term absence, it accounts for 38 per cent of lost time according to the CBI (IRS *Employee Health Bulletin* 22, August 2001).

According to the CIPD survey, absence levels have decreased recently, mainly due to 'tightened policy for reviewing attendance' and 84 per cent of employers thought it possible to reduce levels yet further. However, just under half of the surveyed employers had targets for decreasing sickness absence, typically aiming at about 3 per cent of working time or around 7 days per employee per year. Because absence rates are amenable to reduction as a result of intervention, it is apparent that not all 'sickness' absence is due to ill health. The actual causes of absence are difficult to ascertain, for workers are unlikely to report low morale, alcoholism or personal problems as valid reasons for absence. The CIPD survey found that the most commonly-reported reason for both short- and long-term absences for manual and for

Table 37   Employers' perceptions of the causes of absence, ranked 1 to 9

Causes as ranked by employers of manual workers	Rank	Causes as ranked by employers of non-manual workers
General sickness	1	General sickness
Paid sickness absence seen as entitlement	2	Home and family responsibilities
Personal problems	3	Personal problems
Lack of commitment	4	The impact of long hours
Home and family responsibilities	5	Paid sickness absence seen as entitlement
Work-related accidents/illnesses	6	Poor workplace morale
Poor workplace morale	7	Lack of commitment
Drink/drug problems	8	Work-related accidents/illnesses
The impact of long hours	9	Drink/drug problems

Source: IRS *Employee Health Bulletin* 22, August 2001

non-manual employees was minor illness such as a cold or flu. For absences of more than five days, stress was the main cause for non-manual staff, and back pain for manual workers. Table 37 presents data on employers' perceptions of the main causes of absence.

The surveys reveal that disciplinary approaches are widely used to deal with the problem, whereas the general trends from the case study material point to the prevalence of softer approaches that allow line managers a wide degree of discretion. Many employers appear to avoid negative sanctions, preferring to use a sensitive approach based on concern for the welfare of staff. This is supported by informal chats, counselling, return to work interviews, and the provision of medical support services. Dunn and Wilkinson (2001: 14–17) found only one example of the disciplinary approach, and in this case, the stringent application of disciplinary rules resulted in the reduction of absence rates from 11 per cent to 2 per cent, but there were also concerns about the resulting reduction in morale within the workplace. Delbridge's work in Nippon CTV (1998: 46–7) describes how it is made crystal clear at induction that absenteeism will not be tolerated by the company. Anyone who is absent for three times in three months is likely to be dismissed, and staff are encouraged to visit the doctor at work. In short, new staff are told, 'Don't be ill – it's easier that way!' Alarmingly, he goes on to describe how one worker was brought in and propped up on the assembly-line with a bucket placed near by (Delbridge, 1998: 127–8). This is clearly far from ideal, but for those organisations determined to use the ultimate sanction of dismissal, dismissals for sickness absence can be fair and reasonable in certain conditions and where procedures are followed (Stevens and Fitzgibbon, 2001; Lewis and Sargeant, 2000: 257–60). As the CIPD research reported, disciplinary procedures are the most common tool used for absence management,

Table 38   Absence-management tools

| Most effective tool (cited by over 10% of respondents) for managing | | | |
| short-term absence | | long-term absence | |
Most effective part of short-term strategies	Percentage of organisations (n = 1,277)	Most effective part of long-term strategies	Percentage of organisations (n = 1,277)
Return-to-work interviews for all absences	43	Occupational health involvement	43
Line manager involvement	27	Line manager involvement	21
Disciplinary procedures	20	Return-to-work interviews for all absences	12
Providing line managers with sickness information	19	Return-to-work interviews for long-term absence	10
Restricting sick pay	15	Restricting sick pay	10

Source: CIPD. *Employee Absence: A survey of management policy and practice*. London, CIPD. 2001i

and are one of the most common triggers of disciplinary action – together with performance and time-keeping (Taylor, 1998: 176).

The return-to-work interview is perceived as the most effective way of managing short-term absence, and the third most effective tool for long-term absence. It provides a useful opportunity to enquire about the reasons for absence, to follow up any serious problems, to suggest further assistance if required, or to make it clear that attendance is expected unless there are good reasons for absence. It focuses attention specifically on the absence, helping to generate an attendance culture, one in which genuine illness is acknowledged but malingering is dealt with severely. As with all people management issues, this message is important not only for the individual concerned but also for other workers, many of whom suffer the immediate consequences of colleagues' absence by having to undertake extra work as well as do their own. Interestingly, where shopfloor employees have been given responsibility for overall team performance (including absence control), they have often taken a firmer line than their supervisors.

The reporting of sickness absence information to line managers (81 per cent) and involving line managers in absence management (78 per cent) are also widely-employed strategies. However, the CIPD survey found that in only 44 per cent of organisations had line managers been trained in handling absence, and only 7 per cent had a nominated case manager to take responsibility for individual absence cases. The work by Dunn and Wilkinson throws light on some of the problems faced by line managers. In the absence of clear procedures there can be confusion as to whether line managers or the HR function should take responsibility for dealing with absence. Where line managers deal with the problems, they may use totally different approaches, resulting in allegations of unfair treatment. In the Dunn and Wilkinson study, some managers did not have the time to carry out return-to-work interviews, or they avoided any confrontation because they were so relieved to have the person back to help with work pressures. Many managers felt that absenteeism was not an issue for them, particularly where staff 'struggled in' or made up time. When managers knew that their workers would make up the time, they frequently did not record the absences, or did not read the absence reports. Absence of training is clearly an issue, as is the need for line managers to preserve good working relations (Dunn and Wilkinson, 2002).

Respondents to the Industrial Society survey (IRS *Employee Health Bulletin* 22, August 2001) thought that motivating staff was the most effective way to manage attendance. Strategies could include the offering of positive incentives such as attendance bonuses, although the CIPD survey found this was rarely used. Because they imply that workers should be paid a bonus simply for turning up to work, while those who are genuinely ill are penalised, attendance bonuses are not overly popular, and negative sanctions feature more than financial

CASE STUDY: Sickness absence policy in action

A small Norfolk firm, Tollit & Harvey suffered from 8 per cent absence as well as chronic lateness. The firm used questionnaires about job satisfaction, stress levels and other work-related issues to investigate this problem. The questionnaires showed that workers with long service who believed that the company spent time and effort on their training needs took fewer days off sick, and that employees underestimated the amount of time they took off by as much as one half. The majority of complaints centred on problems with the work environment, training issues and internal communications, suggesting that company morale was low. Managers at the time thought that introducing monitoring and review systems, as well as disciplinary procedures and reduced sick pay might reduce absenteeism, but they were persuaded to focus on a more holistic HR approach. Absence monitoring was introduced together with return-to-work interviews, and the company put out a statement saying that lateness would not be tolerated. Several people who had been responsible for

most of the long-term sickness absence were encouraged to leave. At the same time the company made a switch to multi-skilling and job rotation with greater emphasis on training. The changed work arrangements meant that boredom and upper limb disorders were both reduced, and this had a knock-on effect on absence levels. Additional changes included increased development of career paths, improvements to the environment, and extra channels of communications with supervisors and union representatives. Following a request from the shop floor, a four-day week was introduced, and this increased attendance rates which, following the changes, are now 98–99 per cent among production workers, compared with 90–92 per cent two years earlier. Tollit & Harvey estimate that this is saving the company £60,000–£80,000 per annum in direct benefits, with productivity gains as an added bonus.

Adapted from Arkin A. 'A Norfolk Broadside'. *People Management*, 19 April 2001b

incentives. The most common sanctions are withdrawal of sick pay – used by nearly half of the employers in the CIPD survey – and reducing annual leave entitlement, with dismissal as the ultimate sanction. Triggers may be established at a set level of absence (in terms of the number of days off in a given period, the number of absences, or both) beyond which action is taken. A major problem with this system is that setting a trigger of, say, 10 days, may encourage individuals to take up to nine days off. Despite this, some employers agree 'accepted' levels of absence with recognised trade unions. The Dunn and Wilkinson study (2002) found that common strategies included non-payment of sick pay on the first day of illness in order to curb one-day absences, restrictions on overtime, and absence league-tables. Once the line manager has been alerted that sickness absence has triggered concern, organisations vary on the use of discretion allowed to them.

Much of the research on absence management concentrates on what is seen as 'preventable' short-term absence. It is generally assumed that long-term absence is more likely to be genuine, although that is not always the case. Measures to reduce it are often not pursued actively, despite the fact that long-term absence accounts for a disproportionate amount of lost time (38 per cent), according to the recent CBI survey (IRS *Employee Health Bulletin* 22, August 2001). Countries adopting strategies that support employees returning to work have shown that they can be effective in reducing absence and thereby reducing the proportion of unemployed workers reliant on state sickness benefits. In the UK the proportion of 16- to 44-year-olds with long-standing illness rose from 16 per cent to 41 per cent between 1975 and 1995, and 3,000 people move from statutory sick pay to incapacity benefit each week (Bevan, 2001). According to a TUC report *Creating a Healthier Nation: Getting Britain back to work*, only one in ten victims of serious accidents returns to work compared with one in two in Sweden. The government is clearly concerned about the levels of workplace absenteeism as well as the UK's poor record in preventing job losses resulting from disability or ill health (James, Dibben and Cunningham, 2000). Within the public sector alone it is estimated that ill-health retirement costs £1 billion a year. The government is taking action to reduce levels of ill health and minimise the number of ill-health retirements by establishing targets in the public sector. For example, the target for the Civil Service is to reduce the 1999 sickness absence of 10 days per employee to 8 days by the end of 2001 and 7 days by 2003 (IRS *Employee Health Bulletin* 21, 2001).

Cunningham and James (2000: 34–5) point out that the lack of return-to-work strategies renders UK employers poorly equipped to deal with the requirements of the Disability Discrimination Act (1996) to make 'reasonable adjustments' for disabled employees. Their research with 77 HR professionals found that the most common 'reasonable adjustments' were alteration of working hours (46 per cent), transfer to other work (38 per cent) and transfer to light work (40 per cent). Most organisations did not offer occupational therapy, rehabilitation or home employment, and only 19 per cent used rehabilitation specialists to support a return to work. The majority used internal non-specialists to support the return-to-work process – usually line managers or HR staff. There was often a lack of consultation with the individual, with the union, and with personnel, and where line managers were used, there was a need for more training on how best to make workplace adjustments, as well as a budget to support such arrangements (James *et al*, 2000).

> It is essential that line managers deal with absence control in order to ensure that it is taken seriously. Compare the experiences at your own organisation with the material in this section of the book and suggest ways to improve your systems.

Counselling and support

The previous section hinted that problems emerging in the working environment may have their roots outside work, and problems at work can affect other spheres of an individual's life. For example, issues outside work to do with childcare or family responsibilities, alcohol and drug abuse, depression brought about by changes in life stage, or marital problems, all have an impact on the way in which an individual performs at work. Similarly, problems at work – due to racial or sexual harassment, bullying, post-traumatic stress, or blocked career opportunities – all have an impact on relations outside work.

Most managers, although not trained in counselling, use listening skills as part of their daily work. In addition, a number of organisations have made available to their employees access to professional counselling services for more personal and/or deep-seated problems. The ethos of counselling is that people have the ability within themselves to resolve their own problems when enabled to do so through the assistance of a professionally-trained counsellor. It would be highly unusual for a counsellor not to be accredited by the professional association – the British Association for Counselling and Psychotherapy – and all practitioners should adhere to strict BACP guidelines. Major among these is confidentiality, whether services are offered face-to-face, by telephone, or by e-mail. Use of e-counselling is spreading, and is particularly useful in dispersed organisations. It would seem that some people, initially at least, prefer the more distanced relationship in order to open up a discussion of problems (Bryson, 2001). It is beyond the scope of this book to go into great detail about counselling. Those who want more information should refer to BACP publications such as *A Framework for Good Practice* (2002) and *Code of Ethics* (1996), as well as texts on workplace counselling (www.bacp.co.uk). Other useful texts are Berridge *et al* (1997) and MacMahon (1997).

Counselling provision is often the central plank of Employee Assistance Programmes (EAPs). These are relatively new to Britain and were modelled on the US experience. The role of the EAP is to attempt to solve organisational and individual problems by integrating the programme into the management culture of the organisation, perhaps by using line managers for performance management purposes. The Employee Assistance Professionals' Association (EAPA) defines an EAP as 'a work-site-focused programme to assist in the identification and resolution of employee concerns which affect, or may affect, performance'. This can include personal matters related to issues such as health, relationships, family, financial, emotional, legal, mental ill health and addictions, as well as employment matters such as work demands, relationships, personal and interpersonal skills, and stress. The aim is to enhance individual performance in the workplace for the benefit of the individual and of the organisation. Counselling can be integrated into the organisation through the use of stress awareness surveys. Results from these can be used to help with the training of line managers and shop stewards in defining, identifying and confronting 'troubled' employees; agreeing protocol for no-blame referral to the EAP, and links with the firm's disciplinary system (Berridge, 2002).

Evaluation of EAPs suggests that they provide many benefits for the individuals concerned as well as for their employers. Individual employees find they are able to function more effectively both within and outside work, to operate with reduced stress levels, to work better within teams, and to produce better-quality work if they are not worried about personal or work-related problems. Employers may benefit through lower levels of labour turnover, reduced absenteeism, higher productivity, and better customer service, all of which can make an important contribution to higher profitability and competitive advantage. According to Hopkins (1998), the benefits of establishing an EAP may include:

- enabling managers to refer to specialists rather than waste their time attempting to resolve problems with which they are not competent to deal

- extending the processes of managing attendance, return-to-work initiatives, stress management, harassment and bullying policies, and disability management

- providing support for staff during periods of change

- satisfying health and safety requirements, including the 'duty of care'

- helping to retain key staff and attract highly skilled employees

- demonstrating that the organisation is a good employer.

The majority of those organisations that set up EAPs hope that the intervention will mitigate the cost of work-related absence – particularly stress – which the Institute of Management suggest costs £7 billion per annum (Wustemann, 2000). It is estimated by the International Labour Organisation (2000) that 10 per cent of European and North American workers suffer from depression, anxiety, stress or burnout. It is also noted that work-related stress is increasing, and that 5 per cent of working age people in the UK are experiencing major depression at any one time. Larger organisations like Boots and Marks & Spencer have put in place mental health policies as part of their EAP to promote mental well-being, and to help employees experiencing stress or other mental health problems (Briner, 2000: 8). However, stress and the effectiveness of stress-management strategies are hotly debated (James and Huffington, 1998: 7–10). Briner (2000: 9–17) suggests that a common definition should be used before attempting to analyse the most effective approaches for application in a work context. Evidence of the success of counselling and EAP services is offered by Hopkins (1998), who cites the four-year research conducted by the HSE and UMIST which concluded that there was a positive relationship between the use of EAP services and reductions in absenteeism. The BACP has also recently published research on the impact of EAPs and counselling at work (McLeod, 2001) which concludes that all published studies of the economic costs and benefits of workplace counselling have reported that provision more than covers its costs. Moreover, some studies have found substantial positive cost-benefit ratios. The research also offers convincing arguments for the positive effect of counselling interventions (www.eapa.org.uk):

- Counselling interventions are generally effective in alleviating symptoms of anxiety, stress and depression. Two-thirds of studies

CASE STUDY: Post Office counters stress

The Post Office estimated that stress-related absence was costing approximately £6.5 million per year, despite its extensive employee health-care programmes, and that stress-related absence doubled between 1993 and 1998. An absence management policy (the responsibility of line managers) and an Employee Health Service (EHS) were already in use. The EHS provided employees with information on health, personal, or work-related problems and help with stress management. The Post Office commissioned a research project to identify the causes of stress. The aim was to reduce reliance on treating the effects of stress and to integrate preventative measures into daily procedures so that they could become embedded in the organisational culture. The research recommendations included additional initiatives such as including stress-related hazards in health and safety risk assessments, the introduction of flexibility over working hours and work schedules, increasing the profile of the EHS, adjustments to job design and restructuring, and making stress-management training available to all.

Adapted from Sanders D. (1999), *Post Office Counters Stress*. IRS *Employee Health Bulletin* 12, December 1999

have shown that following counselling, levels of work-related symptoms and stress return to the 'normal' range for more than 50 per cent of clients.

- Counselling has been shown, in the majority of studies, to reduce sickness absence rates in clients by 25 to 50 per cent.

- Significant benefits for clients can be achieved in three to eight sessions of counselling.

Whatever the results of research into the benefits of EAPs, very few have closed and increasing numbers are now being established, indicating their value to employers.

One of the most important questions involved in the setting up of an EAP is whether or not it should be run internally or externally. The decision may depend on the size of the organisation, in that the EAPA suggests that one full-time counsellor is required to meet the needs of 3,000 employees (Hopkins, 1998). The EAPA estimated that by 1998 over 75 per cent of programmes were provided externally, covering over 700 organisations and 5 per cent of the working population, and that the average cost of a programme is £20–£30 per employee per annum. On the other hand, the major advantage of dealing with issues in-house is that counsellors are aware of existing organisational cultures and may be in a better position to influence changes in company policy if needed. The British Chapter of the EAPA lays down rules and standards for members and requires the maintenance of agreed client–counsellor ratios. It also insists that counsellors have professional qualifications, abide by the Data Protection Act, offer full training to specific groups of managers in the companies served, and have adequate indemnity and insurance. The address of the EAPA is 85 High Street, Witney, Oxfordshire, OX28 6HY; telephone 0800 783 7616; website www.eapa.org.uk.

Is it appropriate for counselling to be provided in-house rather than by an independent consultant, or is it advantageous to the employees concerned to have their problems dealt with by an outsider?

Do you think online counselling is likely to work? Why/why not?

CONCLUSION

Performance Management Systems (PMSs) are now much more widespread than they were in the early 1990s, and in some cases they are seen as synonymous with 'new' ways of managing human resources. They revolve around four stages: defining performance standards, reviewing and appraising performance, reinforcing performance standards, and supporting individuals to meet performance expectations. Several of these issues are taken up in later chapters in the book – for example, during our analysis of learning organisations and performance-related pay. Each stage of a PMS is important, but often too little attention is paid to the critical role which induction can play in creating the right cultural expectations among new recruits. Employers who are serious about their PMS have to realise that this stage of the cycle makes a significant contribution to the socialisation of new staff, and it is much more than a routine administrative exercise. PMSs also must be designed so that performance that is below standard can be dealt with in an appropriate way – that is, through counselling and assistance if an employee has a genuine problem, or through disciplinary procedures if the employee is unable or unwilling to meet performance standards.

Useful reading

BACH S. 'From performance appraisal to performance management', in S. Bach and K. Sisson (eds), *Personnel Management: A comprehensive guide to theory and practice.* Oxford, Blackwell. 2000.

BRINER R. 'Stress management: one in 10 Western workers laid low by stress'. IRS *Employee Health Bulletin* 10, December 2000. pp8–17.

Chartered Institute of Personnel and Development. *Employee Absence: A survey of management policy and practice.* London, CIPD. 2001.

DUNDON T., GRUGULIS I. *and* WILKINSON A. 'New management techniques in small and medium-sized enterprises', in T. Redman and A. Wilkinson (eds) *Contemporary Human Resource Management: Text and cases.* London, FT/Prentice-Hall. 2001.

DUNN C. *and* WILKINSON A. 'Wish you were here: managing absence'. *Personnel Review,* Vol. 31, No. 2. 2002.

FLETCHER C. *Appraisal: Routes to improved performance.* London, CIPD. 1999.

FOWLER A. *Induction.* London, CIPD. 1999.

MABEY C. 'Closing the circle: participant views of a 360-degree feedback programme', *Human Resource Management Journal*, Vol. 11, No. 1. 2001. pp41–53.

REDMAN T. 'Performance appraisal' in T. Redman and A. Wilkinson (eds), *Contemporary Human Resource Management: Text and cases.* London, FT/Prentice-Hall. 2001.

TAYLOR S. *People Resourcing.* London, CIPD. 2002.

Maximising the Skills and Contributions of People

Introduction

Organisations have traditionally employed specialists whose job was merely to *instruct* and *teach* people how to work more efficiently. Nowadays, the emphasis is on learning, both from the standpoint of the individual and from the organisation. The most progressive organisations now engage in facilitating learner development, in encouraging people to enhance their skills and knowledge, and fostering their creativity and initiative as part of a drive for continuous improvement. Of course, this is not necessarily undertaken for philanthropic reasons, but in order to improve productivity, performance, and knowledge-development so that organisations can compete more effectively. For the individual, the benefits are meant to be increased personal competence, adaptability, and the likelihood of continuous employability. As we saw in Chapter 6, the shift from training to learning and development is also emphasised by the CIPD through its Continuing Professional Development Policy.

This chapter looks at ways in which to maximise the skills and contributions of people by looking at the effect of government intervention on vocational education and training (VET) in the UK. It examines the way in which government policies have changed over the years, focusing in particular on the impact of these at workplace level through schemes such as Modern Apprenticeships. Investors in People (IIP) has been one of the best-known initiatives in the last decade and its principles are now well established in a large number of organisations. Not all assessments of IIP are positive however, and there is a body of research that suggests many schemes are little more than 'badging', having little direct impact on employee motivation or organisational performance. The learning organisation is a concept that has also attracted plenty of interest, but it is more difficult to find concrete evidence that it has been applied systematically and effectively to change significantly the way in which organisations operate. Trade unions also have a clear interest in training, and we analyse this in the chapter as well, before assessing the contribution that VET makes to skill improvement in Britain. Compared with some of our international competitors, the judgement is not all that positive as we saw in chapter 4.

The great skills debate: government, employers and education

The National Skills Task Force's (NSTF) first report *Towards a National Skills Agenda* (1998) acknowledged that many UK firms operate a low-skills equilibrium by producing low-added-value products or services that need low skill levels. The Task Force view was that these firms should be a minority, and that it would be economic suicide for the UK to be complacent about the situation. Because the developing world has access to far lower labour costs and similar levels of technology to the UK for the foreseeable future, the UK would be unable to compete on this basis. The Task Force's stated aim was to create an effective education and training system and a culture of lifelong learning in order to create a high-skill high-added-value economy in which innovation and growth were encouraged (NSTF, 1998: 11):

> *At the centre of this transformation lies the progression from the industrial society, based at its heart upon the physical capital of land, plant and machinery, to an information- and knowledge-based society built upon intellectual capital, the knowledge, imagination and creativity of our people. To compete effectively on the world stage, employers need access to the best-educated and best-trained workforce; to compete effectively in a dynamic labour market, individuals must acquire the skills needed, while education and training providers, and [the] government must be responsive to those requirements.*

The report differentiated between *skill shortages* (where there is a shortage in the accessible labour market and difficulties in recruitment), *skill gaps* (where there are skill shortages within the existing workforce), and *skills for the long term*. It recognised that there ought to be a coherent national strategy for the planning and delivery of education and training.

It is widely believed that lifelong learning is the key to governmental, corporate, and individual success. As Peter Honey (1998: 28) says in his introduction to *A Declaration on Learning*, drawn up by key-players in the field of learning:

Changes are bigger and are happening faster, and learning is the way to keep ahead. It is also the way to maintain employability in an era when jobs-for-life have gone. It enables organisations to sustain their edge as global competition increases. Learning to learn is increasingly being acknowledged as the ultimate life skill.

Compared with its major competitors, the UK has a poor record of investment in VET. The main concerns are that although our educational record has improved over recent years in terms of the numbers who attain GCSE passes and who enter higher education, in comparison with Europe the UK is particularly poor at delivering intermediate level 3 vocational qualifications (NSTF, 1998). The DfEE skill audit in 1996 showed only 30 per cent of the UK workforce was skilled to level 3 compared with 75 per cent in Germany (Harrison, 2000: 27). In Germany, increases in wages and career prospects are linked to training and qualifications, and young people are not as prone to be lured by the prospect of high pay in the short term. An additional problem is that UK firms distribute significantly more of their profits to investors and less to employees than do firms in Europe. This leads to a lower investment in research, development and training, and employees have less sense of ownership (Harrison, 2000: 62). At lower levels, Europe's educational standards compare well with the USA's, but unfavourably when compared with those of the Pacific Rim countries. At higher levels the comparison with the USA is unfavourable: approximately 30 per cent of Europeans move into tertiary education as opposed to almost 70 per cent in the USA. This leaves Europe less competitive in the high-tech market when compared with USA and Japan (Harrison, 2000: 64). It is thought that Japan also gains the edge because of the integration and coherence of business strategy and training and development (Harrison, 2000: 15). Of course, a lot depends on the equivalence of qualifications, and there may be differences between countries, between universities, and over time. The fact that a much higher proportion of people go to university may be due to changes in entry standards, as well as to improved levels of attainment. It is beyond the scope of this book to analyse the situation relating to VET in leading industrialised nations, but readers who want more depth on the subject are referred to Holden (2001: 343–9) and Harrison (2000: 60–77).

Since Labour came to power in 1997, there have been an increasing number of VET initiatives. Lifelong learning is seen as a panacea for low productivity and maintaining global competitiveness, as well as generating greater social inclusion and cohesion. In his speech delivered to the CBI in 1998, the Chancellor of the Exchequer, Gordon Brown, stated that the UK had a 'productivity gap' of 20–30 per cent with France and Germany, and 40 per cent with the USA. He promised change through use of employment policy, welfare, education, taxation and social security policies. Another factor is thought to be lack of investment in equipment, infrastructure, technology and skills. According to the DTI, for every £100 invested per worker in the UK between 1983 and 1994, £140 was invested in Germany, £150 in France, and £160 in Japan (Eiro on-line, 2000).

The education system is the first building-block for a culture of lifelong learning and skill enhancement. Those who have experienced initial success at school are more likely to be natural lifelong learners, and best able to take on board rapidly increasing changes in the knowledge and skills required of them. In the UK the divide between the knowledge-rich and the knowledge-poor starts and widens through school. The class system still has a major influence on access to higher levels of educational opportunities and qualifications, and therefore to those jobs and careers that bring additional learning opportunities. In comparison, those with poor experiences in the education system are most likely to be found in the low-pay low-skill sector of the labour market, without access to training and development and most at risk from unemployment.

Since 1985 there have been many changes to the education system aimed at improving quality and coherence. There has been a range of major changes. These include:

- the introduction of the national curriculum, A/S levels and SATs testing in line with national literacy and numeracy strategies

- local management of schools, a policy of naming and shaming schools which have poor results, and the replacement of failing schools with autonomous City Academies

- a national system of inspection (OFSTED) and the establishment of Educational Action Zones.

In addition, the decision has been taken to ignore parts of the national curriculum at key stage 4 (14–16 age-group) to provide a work-related programme for certain students. In order to promote a more coherent VET policy, the School Curriculum and Assessment Authority (which was responsible for GCSE and A-levels) merged with the National Council for Vocational Qualifications (which was responsible for NVQs) to form the Qualifications and Curriculum Authority (QCA) in 1997. Specific policies on vocational training include the introduction of GNVQs (see Chapter 4) and modern apprenticeships (see below). The number of young people who stay on in further and higher education is now higher than ever before. The proportion of 16–18-year-olds in full-time education rose from 33 per cent to 55 per cent in the decade to 1998. The number going into higher education has risen from approximately 15 per cent at the beginning of the 1990s to 30 per cent in 2000, and by 1998 a growing number of those applying to university or college held GNVQ qualifications (DfEE, 2000).

Despite such achievements, problems remain. The 2000 Report from the Chief Inspector of Schools commented that one in seven 16-year-olds leaves school without a basic-level qualification in English and maths. The final National Skills Task Force Report (DfEE, 2000) recommended that the education system become realigned with the needs of the economy and business. There is also concern because the impact of educational change on the national skills supply is unclear. The number of applications for degrees regarded as relevant for filling skill shortages (for example, physical, material, and environmental sciences) is declining, and at the same time many graduates find themselves unable to find appropriate jobs. In the meantime, chronic skill shortages remain a feature of the labour market and employers continue to complain that the education system does not equip young people with the skills they require (Harrison, 2000: 49–50). Additionally, the social mix of those who attend UK universities has not changed significantly since the 1960s, although one of the government aims is to address issues of equality and social cohesion. For fuller information on the educational context in relation to VET, refer to Harrison (2000: 39–59) and Ashton and Felstead (2001: 165–89).

What can be done to increase the proportion of young people from poorer backgrounds going on to higher education? What can be done to encourage students to apply for courses that fill the longer-term skills gap (such as physical, material, and environmental sciences)?

Finally, there remain concerns about those who leave school at the age of 16 and enter low-skill work without any opportunity for further training. In order to address this issue, modern apprenticeships were launched in 1993, and in 1997 legislation gave all those 16–17-year-olds who left full-time education training credits of up to £1,000 to spend on VET together with the statutory right to paid time off for study.

Modern apprenticeships – Foundation and Advanced

As well as the general concern over low-skill equilibrium, there is particular concern over intermediate level VET (level 3). Prior to the introduction of modern apprenticeships, training for craftworkers in the UK had been in decline and was restricted to a small number of occupational sectors. The UK position compared unfavourably with the German system where the apprenticeship scheme had long been held in high regard as providing excellent training. In large part this is because of the German culture which regards vocational training as equal to academic routes: nearly three-quarters of young people take up vocational (as opposed to academic) training. The infrastructure is also much stronger in that the training curriculum was devised by a consortium of training bodies, trade unions and teachers. Qualified instructors – who are legally required to stay up-to-date – deliver on-the-job training, and companies without excellent training facilities make use of training centres or other firms. Once the training has ended, trainees can progress to *Meister* level that allows them to become trainers or to set up in business. In the UK, there is neither such a supportive culture nor the same level of commitment from employers, and young people become demoralised because of lack of high-quality entry routes to particular industrial sectors. Gray and Morgan (1998: 126–7) argue that this has led to a vicious cycle by which employers absorb 16–17-year-olds drawn to them by short-term financial gains and use them as cheap labour, so perpetuating the low-skills equilibrium.

The Conservative government in 1995 launched Modern Apprentice-ships. The aim of re-marketing apprenticeships was to harness the high quality traditionally associated with the word, to extend training to sectors previously excluded, to give a viable alternative to the academic route, and to fill the intermediate skills gap. There was concern that young people were no longer choosing vocational training and that large numbers were being failed by the education route – as illustrated by the high numbers who dropped out before gaining any qualifications (Fuller and Unwin, 1998: 153–4). The modern apprenticeship combines elements of past schemes with new approaches, and in 2002 covers 80 industrial sectors. It is funded by the state, the employer, and the trainee who accepts relatively low wages while training.

Between 1995 and 2000 over a quarter of a million young people took part in Modern Apprenticeships. The structure of the modern apprenticeship system has been adjusted since its inception, and from 2000 has been divided into two levels. The Foundation level (these used to be National Traineeships and are still known as such in Wales) leads to NVQ level 2 and is offered in over 40 industry and service sectors. The Advanced level is offered in over 80 sectors and leads to NVQ level 3. Employee status is compulsory for the Advanced Modern Apprenticeships and recommended for the Foundation level.

According to Gospel and Fuller (1998: 5–6), the main features of the modern apprenticeship are that:

- It alternates work with on- and off-the-job training.

- SSCs (initially NTOs) design appropriate frameworks (in collaboration with employers and Learning and Skills Councils) which can be supplemented to meet local need.

- There is no longer a time-served element and they are open to those aged 16 to 24.

- Key skills (numeracy, communication, IT, problem-solving, and teamworking) form part of the scheme, thereby providing transferable skills.

- It is planned to allow progression to further or higher education.

Gospel (1998) and Gospel and Fuller (1998) suggest that there are many advantages to this new system, and that it has been generally well received by employers and trainees. However, they identified several problems including:

- variability between sectors in delivery of both NVQs and key skills, and variability within sectors for delivery of key skills – they questioned whether the NVQ3 in IT is equivalent to NVQ3 in business administration, for example, and whether the standards operating in one organisation were the same as those achieved at another

- concern about the NVQ framework and the notion of competency – in particular, how far theoretical understanding is ignored

- inadequate demand from employers (possibly due to fears of poaching)

- better able young people opting for the academic routes

- the numbers of 16–18-year-olds in apprenticeship training (approximately 10 per cent) not rising over the period 1992–1997

- the majority of the apprenticeships being concentrated in traditional sectors, with very small proportions in IT, chemicals, and telecommunications – engineering and business administration making up 25 per cent of all traineeships (Warner, 2000: 11)

- serious concerns remaining in relation to equality issues

- problems in relation to the quality of trainers and assessors, some of whom lacked experience of delivering key skills training.

They also noted that there was inadequate employer input into the schemes in some sectors, and that success seemed to depend on the industry framework. Where this was strong, as with the engineering industry, the system worked well. Another factor that influenced the success of modern apprenticeships was the degree to which they were integrated into the organisation's overall HR strategy. Gospel and Fuller (1998: 5–19) were able to cite a number of larger firms which had successfully achieved cohesion. Of the small and medium-sized firms that had achieved this, the majority were members of local and industry employer networks which provided support, reduced fear of poaching, and facilitated cost-sharing.

A particularly worrying criticism is the fact that approximately two-thirds of the Modern Apprentices did not reach NVQ level 3, the target that the government was particularly keen to hit. The reasons given for the low completion rate were promotion to jobs involving other forms of training and endemic high turnover rates in certain sectors (Warner, 2000: 14). This criticism is possibly the most problematical, because the CBI estimates that at least half of the jobs in the economy already require skills at level 3 or above, and the proportion is rising (Warner, 2000: 11). Part of the problem is that the traditional view – that the more able young people should take the academic route – is still very influential. The less academic are more likely to be persuaded to take the vocational route, but are also less likely to attain NVQ level 3.

> In order to fill the intermediate skills gap (at level 3) in the UK, vocational routes must become as attractive as academic routes to able young people. Do you agree with this statement, and do you think that Modern Apprenticeships will achieve this aim? If not, why not?

Despite criticism, the Modern Apprenticeship has been a welcome addition to VET, valued by many employers and young people alike. It has given many sectors the opportunity to structure their youth training and put in place a system which is certified, structured with planned pro-gression routes, and offers transparency and transferability. Gospel (1998: 448) suggests that 'the new apprenticeship may also be positive in that it provides a stepping-stone and a basis for further training'. Examples are cited from Sainsbury's that used it as a route to manage-ment positions, and Rover where it provided opportunities for switching between craft, technician and student schemes (Huddleston, 1998).

In February 2000 the government provided extra money for Foundation and Modern Apprenticeships in order to counter criticisms. The aim was to raise entry requirements, improve completion rates, provide more off-the-job training, and link with the new two-year foundation degrees (Warner, 2000: 13–14). It is hoped they will come to be regarded as equal to academic routes, and perhaps even meet the target suggested by the final National Skills Task Force Target of increasing the proportion of 25-year-olds with level 3 qualifications from 41 per cent to 70 per cent.

Because of the pace of change in this area, readers are referred to the website for up-to-date information: www.dfes.gov.uk/modapp/

CASE STUDY: Modern Apprenticeships take off

Westwind Air Bearings is a firm that produces specialist high-speed drills. In 2001 it won a special National Training Award for its Modern Apprenticeship and adult training schemes. Because of its rural location the firm offers higher-than-average wages and takes roughly seven apprentices each year. Recruitment is rigorous, and most entrants have maths and science GCSEs before starting on their five-year apprenticeship which confers either HNC in engineering or City and Guilds qualifications. The apprenticeship is much longer than most, and it includes a first year

of foundation engineering skills, three years on the modern apprenticeship scheme, followed by the fifth 'journeyman*' year with further day release. 'When they finish, our guys* are the bees' knees.' Westwind also offers adult training, and 25 of its existing workforce have trained to NVQ level 3 within a six- to eighteen-month time-frame.

*Westwind regrets the lack of women applicants.
Adapted from Littlefield D. 'Doing their bit',
People Management, 11 January 2001.
pp30–31

Investors in people

To date, the initiative that has probably had the greatest impact on the promotion of a learning society has been the Investors in People (IIP) initiative launched in 1991 in order to persuade employers to invest in training. It is designed for all types of organisation whether large or small, private or public sector, manufacturing or service industry. As the literature from IIP UK (2001) states:

> The Standard provides a national framework for improving business performance and competitiveness through a planned approach to setting and communicating business objectives and developing people to meet these objectives. The result is that what people can do, and are motivated to do, matches what the organisation needs them to do. The process is cyclical and should engender the culture of continuous improvement.

Although the government handed control over to IIP UK in 1993, IIP is still viewed as the government's main tool for increasing workforce training and development. IIP UK is now the national owner of the Standard and is responsible for its promotion, quality assurance, and development. The organisations in Northern Ireland, Wales, and Scotland are respectively known as Training and Education and Learning, Education and Learning Wales, and Scottish Enterprise. By 2001, about one quarter of the UK workforce worked in the 24,000 organisations that had been accredited. This included quite a number that had been recognised twice. According to IIP, 91 per cent of the organisations that gain accreditation remain with the Standard.

IIP is based on four key principles that incorporate a total of 12

Table 39   The Investors in People Standard

Principles	Indicators
Commitment An Investor in People is fully committed to developing its people in order to achieve its aims and objectives.	1 The organisation is committed to supporting the development of its people. 2 People are encouraged to improve their own and other people's performance. 3 People believe their contribution to the organisation is recognised. 4 The organisation is committed to ensuring equality of opportunity in the development of its people.
Planning An Investor in People is clear about its aims and objectives and what its people need to do to achieve them.	5 The organisation has a plan with clear aims and objectives which are understood by everyone. 6 The development of people is in line with the organisation's aims and objectives. 7 People understand how they contribute to achieving the organisation's aims and objectives.
Action An Investor in People develops its people effectively in order to improve its performance.	8 Managers are effective in supporting the development of people. 9 People learn and develop effectively.
Evaluation An Investor in People understands the impact of its investment in people on its performance.	10 The development of people improves the performance of the organisation, teams and individuals. 11 People understand the impact of the development of people on the performance of the organisation, teams and individuals. 12 The organisation becomes better at developing its people.

Source: www.investorsinpeople.co.uk

assessment indicators against which organisations are measured – for details see Table 39.

Once the IIP award has been made, there are regular reviews no more than three years apart. Although there is a charge for assessment, the main cost of accreditation is the staff time involved. In 2001, this was approximately £550 a day, the number of days required for accreditation varying according to the size and complexity of the organisation. IIP Quality Centres are responsible for assessment and quality assurance, and the Learning and Skills Councils (LSCs) are responsible for giving advice and support to organisations that wish to work towards accreditation (the LSC consultancy rates vary).

In 2000 IIP UK responded to feedback by making several changes. These included cutting down the bureaucracy involved, and giving companies and assessors greater flexibility in the way evidence is provided and assessed. The main changes were:

- The language of the Standard was changed to 'plain English'.

- Indicators of Investment in People were reduced from 23 to 12.

- An explicit commitment was made to equal opportunities.

- Companies and assessors were given more flexibility in the way they provide and assess evidence, with assessment emphasis on results rather than on processes.

- Assessors were required to give more feedback.

- Recognised companies were given a choice of a yearly audit or re-recognition every three years.

- The paperwork for employers was reduced.

A new requirement in relation to equal opportunities was added and this was thought likely to impact on equal access to training for part-time employees. In addition, IIP UK has been working with *learndirect* to improve IT literacy among small businesses and to pilot a small business helpline (Rana, 2000). In another new development, and in response to criticism about the Standard's lacking a developmental approach, 'stretch modules' were added for those organisations that are already accredited. The first example of this is the Recruitment and Selection Module (available from 2001) which was developed in co-operation with the CIPD, employers, and practitioners as a self-assessment tool. The format is similar to that of the IIP base standards, and it is assumed that additional modules will follow. The company has also taken on an overseas role with the launch of a European Standard by 2006. Other aims include examining future people management needs over the next decade and to broaden the range of accredited companies, in particular encouraging more small and medium-sized enterprises (SMEs) to attain the Standard.

The benefits of IIP

The benefits of IIP, according to the company, are:

a. Benefits accruing to the organisation as a result of the Standard:

- improved earnings, productivity and profitability – skilled and motivated people work harder and better, and productivity improves

- reduced costs and wastage

- enhanced quality

- improved motivation and retention rates, reduced absenteeism, readier acceptance of change, and identification with the organisation beyond the confines of the job

- customer satisfaction – IIP helps employees to become customer-focused
- public recognition, thereby helping to attract the best job applicants
- competitive advantage through improved performance.

b. *Benefits accruing to the organisation from the process:*

- the opportunity to review current policies and practices against a recognised benchmark
- a framework for planning future strategy and action
- a structured way to improve the effectiveness of training and development activities.

c. *Benefits to employees:*

- high-quality training when it is needed
- improved job satisfaction
- better communication
- career development opportunities
- increased responsibility and involvement
- a better working environment
- recognition
- pride in being part of a successful organisation.

d. *Benefits to customers:*

- better customer care
- satisfactory service
- confidence in the organisation's ability to meet their needs.

Source: www.investorsinpeople.co.uk

Several pieces of research conclude that the majority of those organisations accredited benefit from the IIP Standard. For example, the 2001 CIPD survey of national training and development practices among its members – the sample is drawn from different industrial sectors and all size-bands above 25 employees in the UK – found that 55 per cent had achieved the Standard. In these cases, the respondents felt that IIP had an impact on both organisational change and improving performance irrespective of either the size of the establishment or the industrial sector.

Alberga *et al* (1997) reported that recognised organisations were more likely to have all the best practices in place, and that the process of becoming recognised was likely to raise the profile of training and development issues. Additionally, there was a perceived association between

Figure 11   The impact of IIP on organisational performance

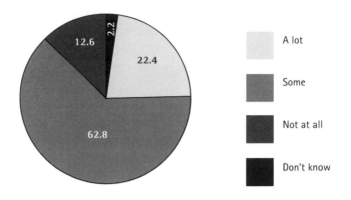

Source: CIPD, 2001i: 12

improved business performance in terms of increased productivity, better customer service, a reduction in workforce turnover, and improved employee motivation. Those companies that had sought re-recognition were particularly positive about the benefits, although that may be because the longer organisations are accredited, the more likely they are to see the benefits. All of Alberga *et al*'s respondents felt they had benefited in different ways, but they all agreed that the greatest benefit accrued from identification of areas where improvements would enhance performance. The 2000 IRS Survey also found that IIP had improved the quality of training and reinforced the link between training and business needs, resulting in positive publicity and a boost to staff morale. Research by Spilsbury *et al* (1995: 55) similarly confirmed that a majority of organisations believed that IIP had positively contributed to increased business benefits. More recently, Hoque (2001) concludes that 'On balance, training practice is better within workplaces with IIP accreditation than in those without.' Similarly, Down and Smith (1998: 154) found that many of the organisations that achieved IIP were those with the least to change, and therefore the least to gain, but nevertheless, the majority felt that they had gained 'significant benefits'. They reported that training became more focused and cost-effective. Moreover, communications and employee responsibility improved, and increased openness and self-sufficiency of staff was achieved through greater understanding of their role in the organisation and of the financial implications of their actions. A minority of the surveyed organisations reported labour cost reductions and reduced labour turnover as well as improvements in flexibility and productivity.

Is your own organisation IIP accredited? If it is, evaluate the advantages that accreditation has brought. If it is not, do you feel that it should be, and can you list the potential advantages?

Although there is plenty of evidence to suggest that the majority of those organisations committed to the Standard reap benefits, a number of concerns have emerged from recent research. Firstly, there is the issue of uneven distribution. According to Cully *et al* (1999: 58), under a third of all workplaces employing 25 or more people are accredited. A further 16 per cent had applied but were unsuccessful, but slightly over half had never applied. Accreditation was very closely associated with size – 62 per cent of the largest organisations were accredited – and those in the public sector were more likely to apply for the award. Ram (2000) reported that only 4 per cent of small firms had attempted to achieve the IIP Standard. His research showed that the commitment of time and money is extremely difficult for small firms which tend to operate in a dynamic and *ad hoc* way in response to market demands. In his survey, the small companies were often inspired to gain the Standard in response to demands from their main clients, particularly where the client was the TEC. The firms obtained the Standard by hastening through the paperwork, with the result that IIP made little difference to their operation. Hoque (2001) also investigated the imbalance between sectors, concluding that single independent workplaces, the private sector, and workplaces with a personnel specialist are *less* likely to have secured IIP. The sectors more likely to have acquired the Standard are: manufacturing; electricity, gas, and water; wholesale and retail, motor vehicle repair; hotels and restaurants; and financial institutions.

The second issue relates to the 'badging' process. It is alleged that a large number of organisations, particularly those in the initial waves of accreditation, used the process to 'badge' their current systems, already having good HR systems and procedures in place. Spilsbury (1995), Ram (2001), and Hill and Stewart (1999) all show that many small firms apply for accreditation as a marketing device. They add that small firms take *informal* training seriously, but that the informality and the reactive, *ad hoc* nature of training in small firms may make IIP unsuitable. Down and Smith (1998) agree, and suggest that the organisations with the most to gain – those with poor training and development – are those least likely to adopt IIP. None of the companies in their research had set out to *improve* training through IIP, but they became accredited in order to confirm the quality of training and HR standards, to measure the organisation against an external benchmark; and to gain recognition of excellence.

More recently, Hoque (2001) concluded that training practice is better within workplaces with IIP accreditation than in those without. However, in a large minority of accredited workplaces there was failure to engage in best-practice training activity (these were often the smaller workplaces), and there was little guarantee that IIP accreditation secured long-term improvements in those companies. He concluded that in these instances it may be that accreditation represents nothing more than 'a plaque on the wall' making the process merely a paper exercise, all training reverting to what it had been in the past once the award had been achieved. Hoque speculated that this was because the assessments for the awards were not carried out properly. In that the TECs' assessment carried out prior to 2001 had to meet performance targets in relation to the number of firms accredited, there was an incentive for them to pass as many firms as possible. Assessment is now the responsibility of IIP Quality Centres.

A third area of concern relates to the link between training and IIP, Douglas *et al* (1999) finding little perception of this among lower-level employees. Grugulis and Bevitt (2001) go further in stating that there were no benefits whatsoever from the badging process. Their research took place in a NHS Trust in which the workforce was already highly motivated and committed to their work and employer, and most of the best-practice systems were already in place. They commented that as the interests of employees and employers diverge, IIP may in effect set a ceiling on skill development for unskilled and semi-skilled workers as well as downplaying the role of informal training. The IIP audit emphasises formal qualifications and training methods, especially NVQ – an approach which they criticise because of its 'narrow focus and lack of developmental opportunities' – whereas many employees prefer on-the-job training. They conclude that:

> *If what is desired is really a general increase in the national skills base, as well as an increase in employee motivation and commitment, then focusing on employers' needs may not be the way to achieve it. A national system that emphasised individual needs as well as corporate ones could provide a more convincing step.*

The most significant concerns, however, relate to the connection between IIP and profitability, especially as IIP involves costs for employers. The Industrial Relations Services (*Employee Development Bulletin* 127, 2000) found that few employers believed that IIP helped to boost profits or income, although they agreed that IIP had improved the quality of training and the link between training and business needs. IIP UK questioned the validity of these findings, because their own investigation had found that 70 per cent of respondents believed that IIP had boosted productivity and competitiveness (Mahoney, 2000: 8–9). However, the link between productivity, profitability and training is notoriously hard to establish (Mahoney, 2000). In any case, some of the earlier research indicates that not all organisations sign up to the Standard for this purpose – reasons cover a range of HR and other objectives, including public relations. Down and Smith (1998: 143–54) found that the majority of organisations in their survey were initially unable to quantify the benefits of IIP, and that the link between IIP and performance was not regarded as relevant by many of the companies. However, on more intensive questioning, the majority were subsequently able to identify a wide variety of benefits including improved communications and employee responsibility, increased labour flexibility and productivity resulting in reduced labour costs. They concluded that there were significant measurable business benefits resulting from the IIP process, but that employers did not usually quantify them or even recognise them as such.

Other researchers have questioned the links between IIP and motivation and morale, and the benefits supposedly accruing in terms of reduced absenteeism, labour turnover, and workforce injuries. Although most studies seem to confirm that there are improvements in employee attitudes, particularly in terms of motivation and morale, Grugulis and Bevitt (2001) point out that much of this relies on employers' responses rather than those of employees. In addition, tangible evidence of increases in morale and motivation is difficult to find. Alberga *et al* (1997) conclude that using indicators such as absenteeism/sick leave, labour turnover, and workplace accidents/injuries, the companies that are accredited are only marginally better than those that are not. Only 3.8 per cent of employers reported reduced employee absenteeism/sick leave, 7.6 per cent reported lower levels of employee turnover, and 6.7 per cent reported lower levels of workplace accidents and injuries.

A question remains over whether or not IIP is able to attract a broader market, particularly small businesses, without an element of compulsion or financial incentives, and whether the emphasis on training for *current* business needs will be sufficient to meet the *future* demands of the economy. Unfortunately, the concern persists that for companies with accreditation, 'there is plenty of scope for these companies – should they choose to do so – to treat it as a paper exercise that will have no long-term effect on training once accreditation has been secured' (Hoque, 2001).

For up-to-date information, visit the IIP website: www.investorsinpeo ple.co.uk

CASE STUDY: IIP harnessing skills and managing change

A Warner Holidays leisure complex was about to go through a substantial refurbishment and transformation into an upmarket hotel and leisure complex. The result was intended to be the employment of full-time, rather than temporary, seasonal staff and to put an emphasis on staff development and quality. It was decided that the firm would benefit from IIP accreditation and the introduction of NVQs to facilitate the changes. IIP was introduced through the use of a working group including chefs, housekeepers, and entertainers who steered the process through each department. It was felt that perceptions of how IIP should be implemented would be more insightful if they came from the bottom up. IIP accreditation has had a major impact on the commitment of the staff as well as on the staff turnover rate. As the head chef commented, 'We used to go through the motions of training people. Now the company is making serious efforts to improve things. It has made me more determined to stay here.'

Adapted from Merrick N. 'The leisure principle'. *People Management,* 11 June 1998

Trade unions, training and learning

Throughout the 1960s and 1970s Britain operated a tripartite model under which it was agreed that trade unions, employers, the government and educationalists should all have a say in vocational education and training. This disappeared during the Thatcher years, and during the 1980s and 1990s the training agenda was dominated by employer views. It was market-driven and run by employers who, it was assumed, knew what their training needs were. The unions had a very low profile.

Since the Labour government came to power in 1997 there has been a shift to a more participative management style with emphasis on partnership, including the unions. Sutherland and Rainbird (2000: 189) state that 'strong co-operative relations between trade unions and management have been seen as central to the work modernisation agenda, both in managing processes of change in the workforce and in contributing to workers' employability in the wider labour market'. There were concerns that the voluntarist approach to training meant that the UK lacked the skills necessary to maintain economic competitiveness, and that standards of literacy and numeracy were particularly low. Sir Claus Moser's report (1999) estimated that there were 7 million people in the UK who had significant difficulties with literacy or numeracy, and he noted the powerful link between poor numeracy and poverty, and the high prevalence of poor literacy and numeracy among those who committed criminal offences.

The unions and government were united in seeing the need to promote learning to improve competitiveness, but also in recognising the role of lifelong learning as a citizenship issue – that is, as a means of promoting a more equal society and combating the ills associated with social exclusion. Evidence of the government's thinking can be seen in the Green Paper *The Learning Age: A Renaissance for a New Britain*. The UK government's attitude became more closely aligned to the social partnership model adopted by other EU member states. Indeed, the 1997 Treaty of Amsterdam requires member states to ensure employability and work modernisation through social partnership, and the Employment Relations Act (1999) asks that employers consult with trade union representatives on their training policy. Rana (2001a: 30), writing on the relationship, cites Rainbird:

> *One of the most striking things about the British context is that there is no formal role for the employee's voice in our training system ... This sets our system apart from all other European training systems.*

She argues that it is very difficult for those in jobs with no access to training and development to do anything about it, but that union involvement can be effective in bringing about change.

The TUC established its 'Learning Service' in 1994, funded from the European Social Fund (ESF), DfES, and other partners. Its Learning Mission is 'to represent all employee interests in securing the learning and skills they require to maintain their employability, enhance their career progression and guarantee social inclusion'. The aim was 'to create a learning culture in every workplace and for every worker to be a lifelong learner'. The Learning Service involves training learning representatives, setting up 'bargaining for skills' projects, and the establishment of the Union Learning Fund. Because the unions have approximately 7 million members, they are well placed to promote lifelong learning, with learning representatives as the backbone of the scheme. See the box below.

The role of the learning representative

- to generate demand for learning among members
- to give advice and guidance about learning
- to identify the learning needs of individual members
- to negotiate agreements that incorporate learning
- to set up and contribute to joint training or learning committees or to forums with a remit similar to safety committees'
- to work with employers to introduce, implement and monitor initiatives that can have benefits for members – eg Modern Apprenticeships, IIP, New Deal
- to argue for and take joint ownership of employee development schemes which may be based on workplace learning centres
- to liase with providers of training to secure resources and support for workplace learning.

Source: Learning Services Task Group Report, TUC 1998

To date, more than 2,000 learning representatives have received training in bargaining skills, front line advice and guidance, learning needs analysis, NVQs and assessment. Most learning representative courses carry Open College Network (OCN) accreditation, and the advice and guidance modules carry additional options that can lead to NVQ qualifications.

Considerable research (particularly by organisations such as the National Institute of Adult and Continuing Education – NIACE) focuses on the difficulty in attracting non-traditional learners. NIACE (McGivney, cited in Keep and Rainbird, 1997) found that 60 per cent of adults had not engaged in any learning activity in the previous three years, and that those least likely to participate were older workers (especially skilled and unskilled manual workers) and the unemployed. Because it is likely that employees are more willing to discuss basic skills problems with a colleague than with a manager, learning representatives can play a significant role in engaging with their members in a non-threatening way, and by giving them confidence to return to learn. This is not a new concept, for UNISON has for many years run a 'Return to Learn' course for those with few qualifications, having negotiated opportunity for paid time off with public sector organisations.

The government has welcomed union involvement and recognises that learning representatives have been especially successful in reaching the lowest-skilled workers and those with literacy and numeracy problems – traditionally, the hardest non-participants in learning to reach. Rana (2001a) reports how learning representatives were able to negotiate basic skills training for bakery workers at Newcastle British Bakeries in advance of their having to take a compulsory health and safety training course. She reported that workers were not keen to admit basic literacy problems to managers but happy to discuss them with the learning representative. The basic skills courses enabled workers to meet the challenge of the health and safety courses with confidence and success. Since the training of 2,000 learning representatives, approximately half have helped colleagues to attend courses. In addition, 35 per cent have facilitated access to funds for learning, over 60 per cent have carried out learning needs assessments, approximately two-thirds have given advice and guidance on learning, and over two-thirds have promoted the benefits of learning (Rana, 2001a).

However, the TUC reports that the majority of representatives are facing barriers, mainly due to lack of formal recognition, and that there is currently an intense debate about whether this should be provided (Rana, 2001a: 26). The TUC and the government feel that statutory recognition will help to promote their activities further, but employers have been unanimous in demanding voluntary agreements. Employers may well be reluctant to concede statutory support because unions are keen to promote 'lifelong learning' as well as learning that is job-specific or company-specific. Even basic literacy and numeracy is often seen as meeting personal development needs rather than organisational needs, and employers do not always see immediate benefits from basic skills training. This is particularly true in smaller companies.

Apart from the establishment of learning representatives, the TUC has been active in setting up 'Bargaining for Skills' projects and a Union Learning Fund, as well as working in partnership with other key players in the field of training and development. Brief details of these initiatives are outlined below.

Bargaining for Skills projects were set up from 1994 to raise awareness of training issues and to promote joint action with employers. The *Union Learning Fund* was set up in 1998 to pump-prime innovative and sustainable union activity in promoting equal access to lifelong learning. By 2000, the Learning Fund had funded the training of 6,700 workers and 1,600 union learning representatives, and 26 learning centres had been opened to provide 91 accredited courses/qualifications. The TUC has also worked with the Basic Skills Agency and employers on almost 20 union-led projects, backed by the Fund. Examples of initiatives include providing access to learning for shift-workers such as long-distance lorry drivers and expanding the Ford Employee Development and Assistance Programme (EDAP) to include family members of employees, on-site contract workers, and workers from a local retail park (TUC, 2000). TUC Education develops a wide range of courses for shop stewards, health and safety representatives, and pension-scheme trustees. A wide range of individuals use TUC Education services, and a significant number are previous 'non-participants' who have not sampled education since school. A TUC report (*Learning That Works: Accrediting the TUC Programme*) found that approximately one fifth of learners had no qualifications, and only 7 per cent of the participants had high levels of academic qualifications (HND/C, degrees, post-graduate level).

Trade unions have thus evidently played a very active role in the training renaissance in the workplace, particularly in working with the 'skills poor' – those who are least confident in their learning and least likely to sign up for education and training. However, it has to be remembered that almost a half of all workplaces with more than 25 employees are non-unionised, and that there is still difficulty in promoting training activity in the SMEs, and with the self-employed. The government consultation paper (DfES, 2001) states that 91 per cent of larger firms offer training to employees, but only 25 per cent of the smallest do. This raises major questions about whether or not training should be made compulsory.

> How might trade union representatives be able to help with the training renaissance, especially for the 'skills poor'?

Readers are referred to the TUC website for detailed up-to-date information on its learning initiatives: www.tuc.org.uk

Establishing a culture of lifelong learning in the workplace: beyond the learning organisation

Much has been written about workplace learning and the importance of maximising the skills and contributions of people through training and development. Harrison (2000: *ix*) states that 'People hold the key to more productive and efficient organisations. The way in which people are managed and developed at work has major effects upon quality, customer service, organisational flexibility and costs.' Many employers require their employees to have high levels of education in order to meet increasingly rigorous demands. Employees are variously expected to be able to use IT, to continuously learn and update skills, to take responsibility for their own learning, to understand their role in the organisation, to be able to work autonomously, to have the ability to solve problems, to change, and to anticipate the future.

Training and development has responded and is no longer a matter of teaching traditional craft or management skills, but has become involved with teaching people how to learn, and encouraging them to become lifelong learners. Keep and Rainbird (2000: 175) point out 'instead of training and skills being a bolt-on extra, learning moves to centre-stage and becomes the chief organisational principle around which business strategy and competitive advantage can be developed'. Stern and Sommerlad (1999: xi) reinforce the centrality of learning by stating that learning becomes 'part of the process of production and integral to the way in which work is organised'.

However, for many organisations, training is not centre-stage: there is a reluctance to train for fear that those newly trained will thereupon be poached, and training is too often seen as a cost rather than an invest-ment. Firms tend to buy in skills rather than train in-house, so perpetu-ating a short-term approach. Despite this, it is estimated that UK businesses spend £16 billion on training and developing their employees each year (Rana, 2000a).

Ashton and Felstead (2001: 181) and Stern and Sommerlad (1999: xi–xii) suggest that training provisions can be categorised in three ways:

- those that rely on *incidental* learning and do not invest unless forced to (for example, health and safety training) – Cully *et al* (1999) suggest that this comprises approximately 40 per cent of UK establishments

- those that provide training as *a response to specific events* – such as the introduction of IT or work reorganisation. In these cases, training is *ad hoc*, but is delivered systematically. These are thought to comprise approximately 40 per cent of UK establish-ments.

- those committed to becoming a learning organisation (LO) in which learning is continuous and is part of the business, enabling the organisation to continuously transform itself. Training is institu-tionalised with a budget, and training needs are assessed and eval-uated. Among most of them there is a belief on the part of senior management that training, employee development, motivation, accountability, and the ability to be self-managed are all vital to company success. Cully *et al* (1999) estimate that those aspiring to the title LO are those which have an HRM approach to training and comprise approximately 20 per cent of UK establishments.

> Using the above categorisations, analyse the training provision within
> your organisation (or in one with which you are familiar).

The model of the learning organisation has been the subject of interest
for a number of years. The ability of the LO to transform itself is perceived as important to those organisations attempting to compete in
the global marketplace for value-added goods and services, and in which
rapid responses are seen as critical. The concept of the LO was initially
articulated by academics such as Morgan (1986), Senge (1990), and
Pedler *et al* (1991). The Pedler *et al* definition (1991: 1) is succinct, capturing the essential principle that it is 'an organisation that facilitates
the learning of all its members *and* continuously transforms itself'.
Senge's definition (quoted in Keep and Rainbird, 2000: 174) concentrates more on the contribution of the employees. He says that the
learning organisation is one 'where people continually expand their
capacity to create the results they truly desire, where new and expan-
sive patterns of thinking are nurtured, where collective aspiration is set
free, and where people are continually learning to learn together'.

Drawing from a variety of sources, but mostly Pedler *et al* (1991:
18–23), the principal characteristics of a learning organisation are:

- the creation of opportunities for learning, not just in a formal
  sense, but also from everyday actions which are debated,
  reviewed and questioned

- the design of structures and cultures which ensure that all
  employees feel that they are encouraged to learn, to question
  existing rules and practices, and to experiment with new ideas,
  and are empowered to contribute to decisions at all levels

- the development of managers who are totally committed to facilitating learning by the adoption of open and participative
  approaches to decision-making

- the acceptance that mistakes will be made, but that they are an
  essential part of the learning process

- the provision of learning opportunities for *all* employees – not just
  managers – and the assumption that, with appropriate guidance,
  each employee should assume responsibility for his or her own
  learning and development

- the implementation of systems (for example, accounting and other
  data-processing) designed to be accessed by users rather than by
  experts

- the breaking down of barriers between different individuals and
  departments to encourage open communication and ways of

working, and the creation of internal supplier–customer relationships.

Ashton and Felstead (2001: 182) analysed current research and concluded that in general terms those organisations with a higher-than-average commitment to training were likely to have certain characteristics. These included a strong commitment to training by senior management, product innovation and differentiation, and they tended to be larger organisations that recognised trade unions and operated incentive schemes such as profit sharing. Finally, HRM has a bearing on training provision, and there is a strong correlation between high-performance work organisations and training – see Chapter 7 for more on this.

Despite the abundance of literature on the subject, there is considerable debate about the typology and extensiveness of learning organisations within the UK. Keep and Rainbird (2000: 177–91) state that the LO model is idealistic on a number of grounds, and that this may be the reason that models of knowledge management have begun to supersede it. Certainly, few firms would be able to meet all of the criteria for qualification, and there is little case study material that provides evidence of LOs – most examples come from the NHS and Rover. Additionally, the LO assumes the empowerment of workers, whereas evidence points to the continued existence of 'command-and-control' styles of management. There is a paucity of evidence of increased training activity in firms, and some evidence that many employers do not value the potential of their workforce. Dench *et al* (1998: 61) report that many firms prefer their workers just to get on with the job, and that 'working harder' was valued above 'working smarter'.

Community education: a learning organisation?

Michelle was a clerical worker in a small rural Community Education Centre. She was studying for an HNC in Business Studies at the same time as bringing up her young family alone. Her line manager was off for a long period, during which time she covered for him and instituted radical improvements to the fabric of the Centre and to the educational programme offered. She also devised a monitoring system for externally-funded projects that was subsequently adopted across the whole Service. She requested support for the second year of her course, but this was refused, and although there was some discussion of an honorarium for the additional responsibilities that she assumed, it was not forthcoming. Michelle left the Service to take up a job in a college where she hoped her ability and commitment would be recognised and rewarded.

How might this situation have been tackled differently, and what would be the advantages to all concerned?

Keep and Rainbird (2000: 190) conclude that there are too many factors inhibiting the growth of workplace learning in the UK. These include cost-based competition, Fordist production techniques, hierarchical management and low-trust relationships. In addition, there is a belief that people are a cost and therefore disposable, and a culture of blame. They suggest a range of activities that could boost workplace learning, including structured on-the-job training, mentoring and coaching, job rotation, work shadowing, teamwork and project work, and greater use of professional networks. Finally, they suggest that so long as UK managers see themselves as doers rather than 'reflective practitioners' the opportunities for change are limited.

> How far is your organisation along the road to becoming a learning organisation, and what more could be done to embed a culture of learning?

As noted earlier, the debate has shifted from the model of the LO to that of knowledge management (KM). Scarbrough *et al* (1999: 50) stress the importance of knowledge in advanced economies and argue that although the cost-benefits are hard to quantify, they can be enormous. They cite an article in the *Financial Times* on 14 July 1997 in which two recent examples were reported: Rank Xerox claimed to have saved £125 million from one KM project, and Dow Chemicals announced savings of £25 million through improved analysis of patents.

Scarbrough and Swan (1999: 1) use a broad definition of KM as 'any process or practice of creating, acquiring, capturing, sharing and using knowledge, wherever it resides, to enhance learning and performance in organisations'. KM is used to promote 'continuous innovation' and to keep up with rapid shifts in products, markets, and employment practices. Where there is rapid change, workers ought to become the source of competitive advantage. Of course, use of knowledge is not new, but what is new is the way that knowledge feeds on itself and creates the impetus for innovation. Castells (1996: 32) notes that 'for the first time in history, the human mind is a direct productive force, not just a decisive element of a production system'. Prusak (1997) suggests that knowledge production is not restricted to high-tech firms but becomes central across many organisations as a result of more flexible production processes which demand higher levels of information about changing customer requirements, delivery times, and so on.

Scarbrough *et al* (1999: 6) credit Drucker with the description of knowledge workers as those with high levels of education and specialist skills combined with the ability to apply these skills to identify and solve problems. Because knowledge workers therefore become the central plank of the production process, HRM takes up a critical role in appointing, retaining, and harnessing their skills to the full. Drucker (1988) likens managers to orchestra conductors in that their role is to co-ordinate the activities of knowledge workers. Scarbrough *et al* (1999) suggest that despite the fact that people management practices were crucial, even more so than use of information technology, few HRM specialists have been involved in KM initiatives. They argue that information technology has been used for relatively low-level exchanges but that human interaction was the preferred way to share knowledge. This recognises that tacit knowledge is as important as explicit knowledge, and that sharing tacit knowledge requires verbal communications.

Historically, research into KM was led by specialists in information technology, but the model has since been developed to include the human interface. Scarbrough *et al* (1999: 87–8) are forceful in stating that KM does not equal technology, and that installing IT does not equal implementing KM:

 Implementation of KM is not a technical exercise but a question of leading and managing change, involving as it does a broad range of responsibilities for those involved and a wide range of outcomes in terms of behaviour and business performance.

Figure 12   Knowledge management and learning organisations in context

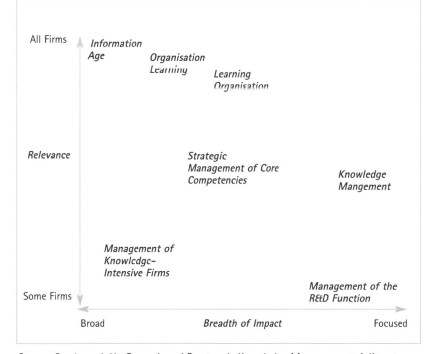

Source: Scarbrough H., Swan J. and Preston J. *Knowledge Management: A literature review,* London, CIPD, 1999a, p4

More recently Swart and Kinnie's (2001) research into expanding knowledge-intensive SMEs has contributed to the case study literature on KM. They suggest that the main characteristic of the knowledge-intensive firms is their growth pattern, in that they are usually born out of an innovative idea to fit a niche market need, and tend to grow fast. They also suggest that HRM is critical, and that HR procedures should 'grow from within' and become embedded in 'the way we do things'.

Assessing the contribution of VET to skill improvement

A recurrent theme throughout this chapter – and indeed the whole book – has been that the UK is trying to move from a situation where training has been *ad hoc* and fragmented to one where the focus is on learning and knowledge management. While such moves are to be welcomed, the UK VET system continues to face a number of challenges. Problems remain in relation to:

- the supply of and demand for high-level skills

- the amount and quality of training that firms provide

- the extent to which firms' training simultaneously meets the government's, individuals' and future skill needs as well as their own

- whether pump-priming the supply of highly-educated highly-skilled workers will be sufficient to enable the UK to escape from the low-skill equilibrium.

We examine each of these issues in turn below.

Firstly, there is a consensus that Britain has operated in a low-skills equilibrium, producing low-added-value goods. For long-term economic progress, it is argued that a shift must be made to a high-skill, high-value-added system based on a more highly-educated and flexible workforce. However, this is a broad-sweep approach, making the assumption that all high-value-added production and services require a highly-educated and skilled workforce. It is estimated that by 2010 almost one third of all *new* jobs will be in knowledge-based employment (Harrison, 2000: 3). But there is disagreement over the proportion of jobs in knowledge-based sectors that demand highly-skilled workers as well as the speed at which these sectors are developing and generating the demand. It is accepted that the demand for jobs in 2010 will not solely be for a highly-educated and highly-trained workforce (see *The demand for jobs in 2010* box early in Chapter 10). 80 per cent of the UK workforce is now employed in the service sector, much of which is not exported, and not subject to the same global market pressures as manufacturing. The 1998 WERS survey suggested that routine, low-skill, low-autonomy jobs are prevalent in the UK economy, and that high-skill, high-knowledge workplaces may account for only 2 per cent of the workforce. Crouch (1997) also argues that only a minority of the work-force is involved in producing internationally traded goods and services in which competitive advantage is critical. He adds that there are few high-skills export sectors in the UK – the main ones being information technology, pharmaceuticals, some branches of chemicals, aircraft manufacture, and some aspects of insurance and finance – but that together these account for a small proportion of UK exports. In most of the developed world, the main employers of highly-educated and trained employees are in the public sector in health, education, and welfare. He concludes that high-level skills are not universally needed, even in those organisations that operate in the high-skills sectors in which they may only be located in the R&D, design and product management roles. Keep (2001) calls this a 'spiral of skill' in which policy-makers forecast that higher levels are needed, and so individuals and firms skill up, thereby perpetuating an inflationary cycle. Keep gives the example of shop workers who are now defined as 'skilled', whereas 20 years ago they would have been 'unskilled'. Questions arise about whether or not they really are more skilled, and whether we get a better service as a customer, or a service user. Warhurst and Thompson (1998: 5) support this assessment, citing examples in the financial sector in which 'knowledge workers' in information transfer or in call centres have to use 'standardised quality' responses so that their work is routinised and lacks autonomy.

Keep (2001) also recognises the continued existence of large numbers of low-paid, boring, insecure jobs that require limited training. However, he suggests that it is not always the case that high-tech, high-skill firms train, and low-tech, low-skill firms do not. He also points out the problem that UK employers (particularly small firms) are not demanding as high an entry-level qualification as other developed counties that look for a level 3 qualification (*People Management*, 9 August 2000). Some of the evidence of increased vocational skill levels in the UK is based on growth in NVQ level 1 qualifications, a level that would be considered too basic to be taken into account in most of Europe.

One result of rising skill levels on the supply side (particularly the number of graduates entering the labour market) is that there is an under-utilisation of these skills. Keep and Rainbird (2000: 183) suggest that there is widespread underemployment and under-utilisation of existing skills within the workforce. They cite work by Green *et al* (1997) noting that 32 per cent of degree-holders believed they were in jobs that did not require that qualification, 30.6 per cent of those with sub-degree qualifications felt that they were over-qualified, and 22.4 per cent of workers with qualifications were in jobs where no qualifications were required.

Secondly, we can look at the amount and quality of training provided. Keep and Rainbird (2000: 173) suggest that in the absence of mandatory arrangements for training, many employers do not train. If they are short of particular skills, they poach or outsource, so reinforcing a short-term approach. A vicious circle is established by which companies persuade themselves that training and development is a luxury, and this leads to short-term financial gains overriding long-term capital investment in training and development. Because most employers in the UK operate in the low-pay economy and their competitive advantage is based on a low-skill equilibrium, this can make short-term economic sense and perpetuates the cycle. Additionally, in the UK training and development is still seen as an extra, non-strategic activity that is not fully integrated into the work of the firm. In comparison, Japanese managers regard the development of their staff as one of the highest priorities (Keep and Rainbird, 2000: 190). Harrison (2000: 26–7) suggests a further three factors that inhibit investment in training in the UK: the dominance of the financial sector, the culture of shareholders' expectations of high returns, and the lack of hard evidence that links training and development to productivity.

There is considerable debate over the amount of training being offered, with some evidence that it is not increasing as much as the literature would lead us to believe. Felstead *et al* (1997) contend that although the numbers of workers being trained is increasing, the average length of training has decreased, so that the overall level has remained constant. Ashton and Felstead (2001: 184) report that the amount of training has increased, but it is not as intense as in the past and it remains unequally distributed, most of it provided for those who are already highly-educated and working full-time in relatively highly-paid jobs. The picture is further complicated by the fact that some in high-tech organisations do not train whereas some in low-tech markets do because their senior managers are committed to the concept of training. Others train only when forced to by government requirements (eg health and safety regulations) or by customer requirements (eg to achieve ISO 9000 before supplying a large retail firm).

The third factor is – who gains from training? Harrison (2000: 4) stresses the importance of aligning workplace training with strategic business objectives, but laments that it does not always happen. At the centre of much of the debate is the problem of definition. The meaning of 'skill' has become much broader over time, and it now includes issues to do with behaviours, attitudes and personal characteristics (Sturdy *et al*, 2001). Yet it is important that there is clarification about the nature of skill – whether it is for high-value knowledge work, soft skills for service sector, key skills in terms of literacy, numeracy and IT, or general employability skills such as co-operation, motivation, and initiative (Keep, 2001). It is also important that skills are specified. Keep (2001) points out that 'If skills are the target, we need to know the shape and size of the target as well as the distance which we have to travel.' He suggests that definitions have altered mainly in response to sectoral changes that have taken place over recent years as reported in the NSTF's 2000 report:

- the shift from manual to non-manual work

- the decline in manufacturing and rise in service sectors

- the relative decline in craft skills and the rise in professional skills

- technical changes such as the use of IT

- growing international competition

- new forms of work organisation such as teamworking.

Keep (2001) makes three key points in relation to the definition of skills. Firstly, employers find it difficult to define the types of skills that they want. They are often vague, confused and contradictory. Because most organisations lack any HR planning, accuracy of definition is made even more difficult, with the result that we have little real knowledge about the extent of skill shortages and gaps. Keep suggests that this will make the work of the LSC and the SSDA in forecasting national, sectoral, regional, and local skill needs exceedingly difficult. Secondly, individual definitions of skill vary, particularly in relation to core or generic skills. There has been a move away from traditional 'hard' skills such as literacy and numeracy which are easily tested, to soft skills such as teamworking, which are harder to assess. The government's six key skills include hard and soft skills: IT, numeracy, communications, problem-solving, improving one's own learning and performance, and teamworking. DfES defines key skills as 'generic skills which individuals need in order to be effective members of a flexible, adaptable and competitive workforce'. As such they are integrated into GNVQs and Modern Apprenticeships, and attempts have been made to integrate them into A-levels, NVQs, and even degree courses. Finally, many jobs now look to aesthetic skills such as accent, social class, appearance, deportment and style. Many of these may not be amenable to training but are personal/life-chance traits, and as such raise major ethical and equal opportunity issues (Warhurst and Nickson, 2001).

It can be argued that generic skills should be provided by the education system, and Keep suggests that there is need for further debate on the division of responsibility between education and work in providing skills. A further problem is the increased use of line managers in the delivery of training. This raises the question of how skills can remain intricately linked to business strategy and whether this is too much to ask of managers, particularly as some of the new skills are behaviourally-based. In addition, as we have seen in Chapter 9, line managers are already faced with many conflicting priorities at work, and there is often a general disdain for HR issues.

Crouch (1997: 367–91) is concerned that because individual firms are the providers of training, training is usually organised to meet their specific needs, and may therefore not equate with the needs of individuals and society more generally. In fact, the majority of firms offer training only to a minority of employees, and since this tends to be firm-specific, it fails to contribute to overall labour market flexibility. It may provide skills for the *status quo*, but not for the future. Because education standards are supposedly rising, employers assume that they can easily hire suitable staff who already have the required skills.

Since one of the stated government aims for additional VET relates to social cohesion and inclusion, equal access to employment offering training is clearly a major issue. Speaking at the CIPD's Future of Learning for Work conference in 2001, Andy Westwood, DfES adviser and the Industrial Society's head of policy and research, (Cooper, 2001c: 11) stated that 'We have an underskilled, under-productive, and underemployed workforce.' He went on to criticise companies for allocating too much of their training budgets to managers and professionals who were five times more likely to receive training at work than those with no qualifications and/or in unskilled jobs. Ashton and Felstead (2001: 175) also stress that this leads to increased polarisation as training and skill levels rise for technicians, supervisors, administrators, professionals and managers, whereas there remain very few training opportunities for semi-skilled and unskilled manual workers. Crouch also reminds us that the deregulative approach adopted in both the UK and the USA makes it easy to dispose of workers. This has lead to polarisation between those who work in highly-paid jobs – who are likely to receive training – and those unemployed or in low-pay work at the edge of the labour market. There is evidence that age, gender, ethnicity, educational background, hours of work and employment status are all major determinants of access to workplace learning (Keep and Rainbird, 2000: 181). Sturdy *et al* (2001: 186–7) pointed out that aesthetic skills are also creating divisions. They showed that Glasgow residents were not 'posh' enough for many of the jobs requiring aesthetic skills, and that 'style' jobs were being taken by students and suburban commuters to the exclusion of inner-city youth. These factors operate to accentuate polarisation, rather than to ameliorate it.

This brings us to the final point. Finegold (1999: 79) suggests that increasing the supply of highly-educated and skilled workers is merely one element in the move to a high-skill economy, and probably the easiest to tackle. However, he maintains that it is unlikely to work on its own without addressing other issues. He looks at the prerequisites for creating high-skill ecosystems in California, and although he admits that they cannot simply be transferred wholesale to the UK context, he suggests that some elements might be. These include increased funding for basic research and pre-venture capital, more courses on starting up new businesses – especially for scientists and engineers – strategies to retain the talents of overseas students, and increased regional networks (including research universities) to promote sector clusters and sector networks.

CONCLUSION

During the last few years, there has been an unprecedented amount of change in the fields of education and training, and the national VET infrastructure has been almost totally rebuilt. Over this time, there have been improvements in UK skill levels, partly due to increased participation in higher education and partly due to employers contributing through IIP. There is also evidence that new organisational forms associated with higher skill levels and higher levels of training are increasing (Ashton and Felstead, 2001: 184). However, although the government regards training as a panacea, this is less than evident at the level of the organisation. It is still the case that few organisations live up to the image of the 'learning organisation' or the 'knowledge-intensive firm'. Compared with other European countries – such as France and Germany – the amount of investment in training and development in Britain remains low, and the proportion of people – managers and non-managerial staff – with formal qualifications is below that of our national competitors. Too many employees receive no training at all, even in the most basic forms of instruction about how to do their jobs, let alone in how to develop their skills or improve their contribution to organisational success. At the same time, there is evidence that existing stocks of skills and knowledge are under-utilised. The 1999 TUC Report stated that the UK had more poorly-qualified employees and fewer young people in training than most of its European competitors. Despite many changes, the government remains committed to voluntarism, although there is considerable doubt whether employers' voluntary commitment to training will be sufficient to plug the current skills gaps, let alone whether they will provide for longer-term skills needs to secure improved competitiveness. In any case, there is recognition that the supply of and demand for educated and skilled workers is only one part of the jigsaw in raising the competitive standing of UK organisations and will not in itself be sufficient to transform the low-skills equilibrium that has typified the UK.

Useful reading

ALBERGA T., TYSON S. *and* PARSONS D. 'An evaluation of the Investors in People Standard'. *Human Resource Management Journal,* Vol. 7, No. 2, 1997. pp47–60.

ASHTON D. *and* FELSTEAD A. 'From training to lifelong learning: the birth of the knowledge society?', in J. Storey (ed.), *Human Resource Management: A critical text,* London, Thomson. 2001.

DEPARTMENT FOR EDUCATION AND EMPLOYMENT. *Skills for all: Research for the National Skills Taskforce,* London, DfEE. 2000.

GOSPEL H. *and* FULLER A. 'The modern apprenticeship: new wine in old bottles?' *Human Resource Management Journal,* Vol. 8, No. 1, 1998. pp5–22.

HARRISON R. *Learning and Development.* London, CIPD. 2002.

INVESTORS IN PEOPLE UK. *The Benefits of Being an Investor in People.* www.investorsinpeople.co.uk. 2001.

KEEP E. *and* RAINBIRD H. 'Towards the learning organisation', in S. Bach and K. Sisson (eds) *Personnel Management.* Oxford, Blackwell. 2000.

MAHONEY C. 'Firms fail to see how IIP boosts profits'. *People Management,* 3 August 2000. pp8–9.

SCARBROUGH H., SWAN J. *and* PRESTON J. *Knowledge Management: A literature review.* London, IPD. 1999.

STERN E. *and* SOMMERLAD E. *Workplace Learning, Culture and Performance.* London, IPD. 1999.

Managing the Learning and Development Process

CHAPTER OBJECTIVES

By the end of this chapter, readers should be able to:

- utilise appropriate information from within and beyond the organisation in order to identify training priorities

- design and deliver learning and training initiatives to support organisational goals

- evaluate the effectiveness of training and learning initiatives both for the organisation and for individuals.

In addition, readers should understand and be able to explain:

- the differences between education, training, learning, and development

- the methods used to deliver training that are most appropriate to specified situations

- the ways in which e-learning can contribute to a systematic and well-developed training strategy.

Introduction

We have seen how the lack of training and development in most organisations is due to the short-termism so characteristic of British employers. But some is also due to an imperfect understanding of how adults learn, and many learners are themselves wary or dubious about further training and development opportunities, given their unsatisfactory experience in formal educational settings. Equally, many line managers regard the provision of 'learning opportunities' for manual workers or clerical staff as pampering the workforce, and as an unwarranted distraction from their departmental targets and duties.

In earlier chapters, we have emphasised the role that learning and development is expected to play in organisations which regard their employees as an important resource. Although recruiting and selecting staff is an effective way in which to transform the nature of the workforce, the opportunities for it are limited except in organisations that are expanding rapidly and/or opening new sites. In any case, apart from the costs of recruitment, it is not always possible to buy in the required skills (certainly not company-specific skills), and because of the speed of change it is not feasible to continually buy in these resources

(Sisson and Storey, 2000: 146–7). For the majority of larger organisations – especially those in the public sector and in manufacturing – the learning and development of existing employees offers a much greater opportunity for generating improvements in productivity and quality. Since it is estimated that UK businesses spend approximately £16 billion on training each year, it is clearly important that this money is spent effectively, and that the results are carefully evaluated (Spurling and Trolley, 2000: 46).

Definitions and terminology

Although terms such as 'training', 'development', 'learning' and 'education' are often used interchangeably, it is essential to be aware of the major distinctions between them, at least in their pure form. In reality, of course, some of the distinctions are less clear-cut – there is sometimes overlap between the concepts, and one may feed into another. For example, the educational process ought to involve learning, hopefully leads to development, and may even contain some training in specific techniques. In addition, as the use of NVQs spreads, the distinction between education and training is likely to become even more blurred.

Education is the system which aims to develop people's intellectual capability, conceptual and social understanding and work performance through the learning process. *Training* is a narrower concept and usually involves planned instructional activities, or other developmental activities and processes (Harrison, 2000: 2). The differences between education and training are not always obvious, and just because a two-day course (in negotiating skills, for example) takes place away from the employer's premises, it need not qualify as education unless it comprises part of a wider product, such as a professional qualification or an MBA. Similarly, full-time students on a Masters' programme in HRM who take part in an outdoor-based development programme undertake this as an element in their education even though the course may be run by trainers. Education and training typically refer – albeit implicitly – to the process by which an individual's attitudes, behaviour or performance is changed. By contrast, *learning* focuses explicitly on the changes which take place within the individual and to the process by which the learner acquires knowledge, develops a skill, or undergoes a transition in attitudes. Whereas training may be seen typically from the perspective of the deliverer (the trainer), learning starts out from a different standpoint – that of the learner.

There is less agreement among writers about the definition of *development*. Collin (2001: 295–6) views development as 'the process whereby, over time, the individual becomes more complex and differentiated through the interaction of internal and external factors'. Harrison (2000: 2) defines it as:

learning experiences of any kind, whereby individuals and groups acquire enhanced knowledge, skills, values or behaviour. Its outcomes unfold through time, rather than immediately, and they tend to be long-lasting.

Others see employee development in the same way as the CIPD – as the blanket term to describe the employer's strategy for managing the learning and training process. For example, Reid and Barrington (2001: 8) suggest that it is part of HRM and involves:

 the planning and management of people's learning – including ways to help them manage their own – with the aim of making the learning process more effective, increasingly efficient, properly directed and therefore useful.

Formalised learning has to have some purpose, typically measured by a series of outcomes, as is evident from the standards for the CIPD Professional Development scheme. By the end of a module, the learner should be able to perform a set of skills, display understanding of particular issues, and demonstrate competencies in specified areas. In addition, however, it is important to remember that most learners come to a new learning situation with existing skills, understanding and competencies. These are referred to as 'tacit' skills and knowledge.

Skill and understanding are those aspects of behaviour which are practised in the work situation, and which individuals must be able to perform at an acceptable level in order to do the job satisfactorily. They comprise motor skills, manual dexterity, social and interpersonal skills, technical skills, analytical skills, and so on. Skills are frequently seen in terms of a hierarchy, in which the lower levels are perceived as prerequisites for the higher levels – for example, Bloom's taxonomy (reproduced in Collin, 2001: 287) views learning as a series of building-blocks:

a) knowledge (simple knowledge of facts, terms, theories, etc)

b) comprehension (understanding the meaning of this knowledge)

c) application (ability to apply this knowledge and comprehension in new situations)

d) analysis (breaking down material into constituent parts and seeing relationships between them)

e) synthesis (reassembling the parts into a new and meaningful relationship)

f) evaluation (the ability to judge the value of the material).

Understanding and knowledge, and the ability to explain things to other people are therefore incorporated within the term 'skill'. For most observers, however, *skill* has a common-sense, everyday meaning, typically connected with these lower levels, and seen in the application of motor skills rather than the powers of analysis, synthesis and evaluation. It is also important to recognise that 'skill' is a socially con-structed phenomenon rather than some objective characteristic of an individual or task. For example, the skills that are valued are likely to be very different if your car has broken down in the desert from those that are regarded as useful when negotiating in a foreign language or man-aging a superstore (Sturdy *et al*, 1992: 4).

Tacit skills and knowledge are hard to define, and are frequently over-looked when considering the outcomes of learning. These refer to 'know-how' (Collin, 2001: 285), the ability to perform a task without being able to explain how it is being done. For example, female catering workers and homecare staff often undervalue their acquired skills and knowl-edge, regarding them as instinctive and natural. Because this know-how is typically acquired through experience rather than through formal instruction, it can be hard to specify and quantify. There is little doubt, however, that 'tacit skills can explain much of the high performance and excellent results achieved by the business' and 'because they are unique to the people of the particular organisation ... they give competitive advantage' (Harrison, 2000: 228). As we saw in Chapter 2, employees may use tacit skills in a variety of ways, both to assist management in the performance of duties and to resist managerial instructions. In relation to the former, employees may choose to override what they know to be faulty computer signals on chemical plants, whereas in respect of the latter, secretarial staff often cover up for their man-agers' failings. These are skills which are essential to organisational effectiveness but are rarely the subject of training courses or (apart from in Collin's work) considered in texts on employee development.

> Do you think it is possible for people to learn without being aware that they are learning? Do they need to consolidate the learning or relate it to theoretical principles for learning to be effective?

'Competency' is a newer term than 'skill', and has been growing in importance since the publication of *The Competent Manager* by Boyatsis in 1982. The competence/competency terminology has been widely used in Britain in recent years, but there is considerable confu-sion over it. According to Woodruffe (1992: 17), 'competency' is 'the set of behaviour patterns that the incumbent needs to bring to a position in order to perform its tasks and functions with competence'. In other words, 'competency' is concerned with the individual and his or her behaviour, whereas 'competence' is related to dimensions of the job or task in question.

At issue is whether or not it is possible to derive a list of generic com-petencies which are appropriate to all situations, or whether they are organisation- or function-specific. A number of lists of generic manage-ment competencies have been published, containing similar sorts of headings, albeit with different titles. The competency framework provides a set of performance criteria at organisation and individual levels, and identifies the expected outcomes of achieving those criteria. The National Management Standards are a framework based on the management of activities, resources, people, information, energy, quality, projects. Most such frameworks include the following competencies:

- breadth of awareness and strategic perspective

- oral and written communication

- leadership, decisiveness and assertiveness

- teamworking and the ability to work with others

- analysis and judgement

- drive and persistence

- organisation and planning

- sensitivity to others' viewpoints

- self-confidence and persuasiveness

- flexibility and adaptability.

> How adequately do you think this list of competencies relates to the personal characteristics required to perform your particular job satisfactorily?

For a fuller discussion of management development see Harrison (2000: 359–78), and for more information on competency frameworks see Whiddett and Hollyforde (1999).

The process of learning

The way in which people learn is of obvious importance to all HR professionals, in view of its centrality to most aspects of organisational life. Presented here is a brief overview of some of the different learning-process theories. There is neither the space nor the need to discuss them in detail at this point; readers who want a fuller explanation of these theories are referred to McKenna (2000) and to Stewart (2002: 169–86).

Gagne's (1977) classification is one of the better-known, seeing learning in terms of a hierarchy, moving from lower- to higher-order skills. Although it is suggested that this sequence forms the optimal conditions for learning, it does not mean that learning can take place only in this order. Gagne's eight classes of learning are:

- signal learning (see below)

- stimulus-response learning (see below)

- chaining (two or more stimulus-response connections)

- verbal association (learning chains that are verbal)

- discrimination learning (making different responses to different stimuli)

- concepts learning (making a common response to a class of stimuli that may differ in physical appearance)

- rule learning (a chain of two or more concepts)

- problem-solving (the combination of two or more rules via a process of thinking).

Association

The first category is *learning by association* or the behaviourist approach incorporating signal and other type of stimulus-response learning. Signal learning is most obviously apparent in the behaviour of household pets, which run to the kitchen when they hear food being placed in a dish on the floor (Gagne, 1977: 77). It is the classical conditioned response that has been popularised by the Pavlovian dogs experiment, although it might also be found in the fixed smile that appears on a salesperson's face the moment a customer walks through the door. Conditioning can be either classical (whereby the stimulus automatically leads to a response) or operant, in which case a desired response is rewarded and reinforced after it has been delivered. In the latter event, the behaviour may be natural and unconditioned, in the sense that it has not been trained into the individual, in which case appropriate behaviour is often learned by a process of trial and error. This is regularly used in training young children who are rewarded with a chocolate or a cuddle for using their potty. In organisations, operant conditioning can be seen in the recognition shown by a line manager to high-quality performance by a new recruit, and this can then act as a powerful reinforcement for learning how to do the job well. It is also apparent in bonus schemes where employees are rewarded for achieving high production figures or low reject rates, in the hope that they will learn about the importance of good levels of performance. Even in adults, reinforcement must occur soon after the event for it to be meaningful, and without appropriate reinforcement learning soon becomes extinct.

Stimulus-response reinforcement paradigms have been extremely influential in psychology, but there are serious concerns that they fail to account for all types of learning. In particular, given that the experiments were originally conducted on animals, the paradigm does not give sufficient weight to the dynamic and interactive complexity of human beings. Also, in the light of the range of stimuli in a work (as opposed to a laboratory) situation, it may prove difficult to determine the precise influence of one stimulus over a defined response.

How adequately do you think theories of learning based on laboratory experiments – on animals or human beings – can account for learning at work?

Cognition

The second category is *cognitive learning*, which is based not upon stimuli and responses but upon making connections between two or more stimuli. The classic example here is of a chimpanzee locked in a cage with a piece of fruit some distance away. The chimp first tries to escape in order to get the fruit. It then tries to use a short stick placed near the cage to reach the fruit. Eventually, the chimpanzee realises that the short stick could enable it to reach a longer stick with which it can pull the fruit towards the cage (Hilgard *et al*, 1979: 208–9). The idea of insight – known as the 'aha' experience – is central to cognitive learning, although in many situations we take insights for granted. But the pleasure of gaining an insight acts as a powerful reinforcer of learning, and a significant stimulus to memory. A good example of this is the case study that helps learners to link theories and practical applications, or group problem-solving which can have a highly positive effect on team-building if properly structured. Whereas stimulus-response applications might be suitable for training in basic practical skills, cognitive learning is more appropriate for mental skills. These types of theory rely on learners connecting together different concepts or actions to form a chain of stimuli enabling them to arrive at the ultimate goal (McKenna, 2000).

Cybernetics

Cybernetics represents the third strand of theories that attempt to explain the process of learning. This approach regards learning as an information-processing system in which a signal containing information is passed along a communication channel subject to interference from a variety of sources (Collin, 2001: 289). Stammers and Patrick (1975: 27–35), drawing upon earlier work by Crossman, outline the essential elements of this communication process. Signals have to be encoded to enable them to be transmitted along the communication channel, and decoded before they can be received. All messages are subject to 'noise' which acts as an obstacle to learning – this does not mean just audible noises but any factors that also interfere with the transmission process. Learning may be hindered, therefore, by the presence of other stimuli which interfere with the receipt of messages and cause them to be confused or imperfectly picked up (stress is a good example of this). There are also limits to the amount of information that can be transmitted along a channel. Feedback is an important aspect of these models. It may be intrinsic to the learning itself, in which case the individual is aware of it during the acquisition or application of the skill, or it may be extrinsic, in which case it becomes available at a later date and can influence future performance. This form of feedback may be derived from the individual learner or it may be provided by a trainer, or a set of figures which demonstrate the impact of learning upon performance, as shown in the box about RHP Precision below.

RHP Precision

RHP Precision won a special National Training Award for using training to tackle high failure rates in one of its key operations. The plant manufactures bearings, but there was a 20 per cent rejection rate. When business demands rose, management were prepared to invest in new machinery and additional staff. Thanks to the intervention of a new trainer who had been promoted from the shop floor this did not happen. He studied the way in which people worked and realised that most staff worked in different ways. Training for semi-skilled jobs was through 'sitting next to Nellie', and unfortunately this meant that some of the more experienced operators, who had high failure rates, were doing the training. The trainer retrained all staff individually, so as to avoid creating antagonism, and individuals' rejection scores were placed on the noticeboard. The strategy worked – failure rates went down to 1 per cent, saving £72,000 per year on labour costs alone.

Can you think of problems in your own organisation that could be remedied through training? How should the training be carried out and evaluated? Do you think there might be any negative reactions to placing results on a noticeboard?

Adapted from Littlefield D. (1999) 'To be precise', *People Management*, 14 January 1999. pp38–39

Social learning

The final category is *social learning theory*, in which the principle of learning comprises imitation (Bandura, 1977). This means that individuals learn to do specific tasks by watching other people perform them before trying for themselves and generalising from this as appropriate. Long ridiculed as 'sitting next to Nellie', these forms of learning may enable the transfer of 'tacit' skills from one employee to another, and they can result in more effective work performance. Many basic skills can be learned in this way, although reinforcement through doing (often repeatedly) is crucial to their success. Social and interpersonal skills may also be learned through this process, and often such tacit skills are acquired without the individual being aware that learning has actually taken place. One of the major problems with unstructured training (social learning), which does not incorporate feedback or evaluation, is that people may learn inefficient ways of working or may fail to take on board some of the tacit skills used by experienced workers. There are also dangers that individuals learn behaviour by imitation that is not welcomed by management or society – for example, bullying or aggressive behaviour, fiddles and scams, racism and sexism.

> Keep a diary for a week, and note all the times when you learned something new, either at work or elsewhere. Categorise these learning experiences according to the different theories outlined above. Make sure that you include *all* learning events, not just those that take place at work.

Experiential learning, cycles and styles

Much of the mainstream psychological literature has focused on what is seen as 'traditional' learning – the importance of building-blocks, hierarchies of skills, and reinforcing theory with examples. Clearly, this may

Figure 13 The learning process

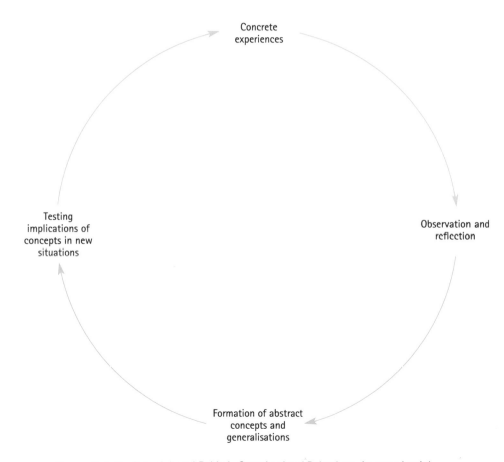

Source: Kolb D., Osland J. and Rubin I. *Organisational Behaviour: An experiential approach*. 6th edition. New Jersey, Prentice-Hall, 1995, p49

be particularly appropriate to educational situations and in child development, but it may be less appropriate for adults because not all individuals learn in the same manner. Carl Rogers (1969: 5) is the major proponent of experiential learning, which he sees as having the following components: personal involvement, self-initiation, pervasiveness, and evaluation by the learner. The essence of experiential learning resides in its meaning to the learner. This makes it quite different from traditional learning, and potentially exciting for employees who left school early and feel threatened by the classroom situation. Because it puts the responsibility for learning on the individual employee, it can also require skilful management of the learning situation by professional staff. As Mumford (1988: 171–2) warns, experiential learning can be 'a very inefficient, hit-or-miss operation ... guidance helps the process to be both quicker and easier'. The experiential approach is best known in the HR field through the work of Kolb, and Honey and Mumford, on the learning cycle, and it forms a centrepiece of the CIPD's guidance for continuing professional development (CPD). Kolb, Osland and Rubin (1995: 49) view the learning process as both active and passive, concrete and abstract, and conceive of it as a four-stage cycle. The model is displayed in Figure 13.

Kolb developed a Learning Styles Inventory based upon the four stages of the learning process. He argues that effective learners rely on four different learning modes, and every individual has an orientation toward one or more of these:

- An orientation towards *concrete experience* means that individuals adopt an intuitive stance, relying upon their personal judgement rather than on systematic analysis. These individuals enjoy relating to people, being involved in real situations, and adopt an open-minded approach to life.

- An orientation towards *reflective observation* leads individuals to view situations carefully, considering their meaning, and drawing out the implications of ideas. These people prefer to reflect on issues rather than acting, looking at questions from different points of view, and they value patient and thoughtful judgement.

- An orientation towards *abstract conceptualisation* implies that learners prefer to rely on the use of logic, ideas and concepts, opposing intuitive judgements. These individuals are good at systematic planning and quantitative analysis, and they value precise formulations and neat, conceptual systems.

- An orientation towards *active experimentation* means that individuals enjoy practical applications, active involvement in change, and a pragmatic concern with what works in practice. Achieving results is important for this group, and they value having an impact on their working environment.

Honey and Mumford (Mumford, 1988: 175–7) developed an instrument similar to that of Kolb, also comprising four learning styles, with norms based on the scores of management educators and trainers. Their Learning Styles Questionnaire categorises people into the following types:

- *activists*, who learn best by active involvement in concrete tasks, and from relatively short tasks such as business games and competitive teamwork exercises

- *reflectors*, who learn best by reviewing and reflecting upon what has happened in certain situations, where they are able to stand back, listen and observe

- *theorists*, who learn best when new information can be located within the context of concepts and theories, and who are able to absorb new ideas when they are distanced from real-life situations

- *pragmatists*, who learn best when they see a link between new information and real-life problems and issues, and from being exposed to techniques which can be applied immediately.

Readers who want more information on how to use this instrument are referred to Honey and Mumford (1986).

This focus on learning cycles and learning styles has major implications for the training and development process, and for the choice of particular techniques and learning technology. If a group comprises theorists alone, these individuals are likely to feel less comfortable with case studies or role-play situations, whereas a group of pragmatists would find this a particularly fruitful way in which to learn. Similarly, whereas reflectors only really make sense of a situation after they have had time to evaluate its impact, activists are keen to put ideas into practice at the earliest possible opportunity, getting frustrated if too much time is spent reviewing previous learning situations. Of course, it is more likely that groups contain a mix of different types of learners – in which case the tutor must be able to design learning situations to maximise strengths and improve on areas of weakness.

Despite their value, there are doubts about the use of learning styles questionnaires. Because the four categories represent 'ideal types', it is unlikely that people conform totally or even principally to a single learning style, and they may be strong on two apparently dissimilar axes. The precise questions asked of individuals are also capable of differing interpretations, depending upon the context in which they are set. For example, an individual may be a reflector in response to certain questions or situations, and a pragmatist in others. Moreover, the combination of people in a working group may lead individuals to adopt styles other than they might do in a formal learning situation. For example, a group of theorists may be cajoled into action, or a set of activists encouraged to reflect on their proposed course of action. This implies that people's preferred learning styles may alter over time rather than remaining static.

Determining learning styles

Sangita is a senior research scientist who runs a small team of professionals and technicians working for a large chemical company. She has a PhD in biochemistry, and spent many years working at the bench before being promoted to more senior jobs. She reports directly to the research and development director, who has been very successful in promoting the development of profitable new products in the past but requires a lot of convincing before agreeing to proceed. Sangita also works closely with line managers and shopfloor employees in trying to exploit the practical application of new ideas.

Which learning styles do you think are most likely for each of the groups/individuals (her boss, line managers, shopfloor employees) with whom Sangita deals, and what advice would you give her on how to approach these different sets of people?

An alternative conception of the learning cycle is developed by Engeström (1994: 32–5). This is termed 'integral learning', and it comprises six steps, each of which demands specific learning actions. The six steps are:

- motivation – the awakening of interest in the subject

- orientation – the formation of preliminary hypotheses on the subject which explain the principles and structure of the knowledge necessary for problem-solving; by fashioning a 'lens' through which to assimilate information, the learner creates an active model which enables essential points and linkages to be made

- internalisation – new knowledge is added to enrich and extend the model, as well as render it meaningful to the learner

- externalisation – applying the model to solve concrete problems, in so doing testing and evaluating its utility in a practical situation; application enriches and corrects theory, raising new questions and stimulating creativity

- critique – a critical evaluation of the validity and applicability of the model, identifying situations in which it might be useful or inappropriate

- control – by examining the way in which learning has taken place, the learner evaluates its effectiveness and tries to improve his or her learning methods.

The learning and development process in theory

The training process system comprises four steps:

- the identification of training and learning needs
- devising a learning plan
- delivery
- evaluation.

This is the framework adopted for the remainder of this chapter (see Figure 14). Harrison's (2000: 261–2) 'learning event' is based on the training process system. She defines the 'learning event' as 'any learning activity that is formally designed in order to achieve specified learning objectives'. She suggests that there are eight stages in the inception, design and delivery of planned learning events:

1   Establish needs.

2   Agree on the overall purpose and objectives for the learning event.

3   Identify the profile of the intended learning population.

4   Select the strategy, and agree on the direction and management of the learning event.

5   Select the learners and produce detailed specification for the learning event.

6   Confirm the strategy and design the event.

7   Deliver the event.

8   Monitor and evaluate the event.

In this approach emphasis is on the early stages of the training process, and relatively little on the choice of techniques and learning strategies that might be employed by HR professionals. There are clear advantages in using structured and sequential models for describing the training process, especially if they establish a framework within which managers can operate. These models are applicable irrespective of organisational context, but for large employers in particular they provide a way in which to subdivide training and development tasks between individuals so that their input can be monitored. In addition, they enable a valuable quality-assurance check on the progress of training, and a systematic framework into which new trainers can easily slot.

On the other hand, there is a feeling that these models represent an 'ideal' state of affairs rather than conveying an accurate and realistic picture of organisational practice. The idea that training and development regularly follow this logical and sequential cycle is open to question, and – as with other aspects of human resource development (HRD) – there is likely to be rather more *ad hoc* and reactive management of

Figure 14   The training process model

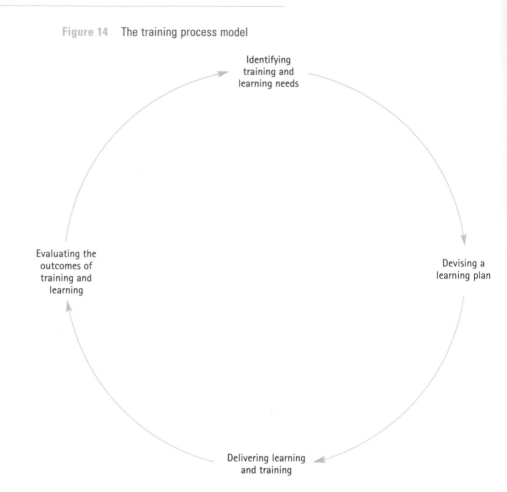

training than planned and proactive strategies (Reid and Barrington, 2001: 105–8). A more serious concern is that training and development often lapses into a 'closed' cycle, in which there are few, if any, links with other aspects of HR, let alone with broader business plans and objectives. This can result in efficient rather than effective training. In other words, the effectiveness of training is assessed against the training needs identified by the trainers themselves, and not measured in relation to their contribution to business goals.

Identifying training and learning needs

Using the traditional approaches, the first stage in the training cycle is an identification of training needs (ITN), which is often reviewed in conjunction with a training needs analysis (TNA). Although used interchangeably on many occasions, ITN is concerned with the process required to detect and specify training needs at an individual and organisational level, whereas TNA refers to the process of examining training needs to determine how they might actually be met. A training need exists when:

- there is a gap between the future requirements of the job and the current capabilities of the incumbent, whether this is measured in terms of skills, attitudes or knowledge

- it is anticipated that systematic training will overcome the deficiency or barrier (Arnold *et al*, 1998: 361).

We have to be certain, however, that training represents the best or the only solution to these problems, and that it is not being suggested as a panacea for all organisational ills. In some circumstances training may not be the most effective option, and the choice of a specific pro-gramme might be totally inappropriate. The problem may reside else-where, and there are dangers that employers may prescribe training as a universal solution ('Training is the answer, irrespective of the ques-tion!') without considering any alternative lines of action. Endeavours such as job redesign, better systems of communication and involve-ment, adjustments to organisational cultures and structures, and disci-plinary action to tackle a gap between actual and required performance, may be more appropriate. It may even make sense to do nothing (Bee and Bee, 1994: 59), because there are often as many dangers in pro-viding too much training as there are in providing too little. For example, excessive levels of training cost money and use up valuable resources, and may even result in job dissatisfaction if employees are unable to practise their new-found skills back at the workplace (Arnold *et al*, 1998: 361). Indeed, training can often become an end in itself, a closed loop, which is not measured against its contribution to broader organis-ational goals.

Training can be used in a range of different circumstances and con-texts, and this clearly has an effect on the design of programmes. Drawing on Harrison (1992: 283), there are broadly three principal cat-egories. First, training is used as a *socialisation initiative*, a mechanism for inducting new employees, and for ensuring that they learn about the job/tasks they are to undertake, as well as about the organisation and department of which they are a part. In these circumstances, making employees aware of the broader cultural norms of the organisation may be just as important as any specific skill or knowledge transfer. As we have already seen in Chapter 7, effective and comprehensive induction programmes are an important element in the shift by some employers to a high-commitment HRM philosophy. Second, training can be used as a *development initiative* – for example, by preparing employees for pro-motion, by helping them cope with new technology, or as part of an organisational change programme. In this situation training may be part of a formalised and well-established system within an organisation. These programmes – often referred to as 'the sheep-dip' approach to training – may give little consideration to the needs of individual members of staff compared with pressures to meet organisational requirements. Third, training is used as a *way in which to correct unsatisfactory performance*, perhaps as part of a disciplinary initiative in cases where individuals are found to be working below acceptable quality, output or customer service standards. The training need in these circumstances may be concerned with technical skills, such as how to operate a piece of machinery, or with highlighting problems in an individual's attitudes or behaviour (see Chapters 11 and 15). For example, a manager who has been harassing or bullying his staff might require very careful and sensitive training in how to relate to women employees.

Using the concepts of the learning organisation and knowledge-intensive firms (see Chapter 12) learning takes on a totally different approach. The emphasis is on *personal development*, the responsibility for learning placed firmly with individuals and their line managers. Within those workplaces that can claim to be learning organisations there should be systematic, whole-organisation learning that takes place continuously.

> These examples demonstrate some of the links between training and other parts of HRM and emphasise the important of horizontal integration. Try to identify three links relevant to your own organisation.

Training needs can be identified at three different levels – organisational, job/occupational, and personal – and it is assumed that all three can be integrated. Most publications stress the importance of commencing the ITN process with a review of *organisational training needs* in order to establish how specific training programmes may contribute to broader strategic goals (see, for example, Harrison, 2000: 98–9). Walters (1983: 181) outlines nine sources of information which help to identify training priorities. These are:

- organisational goals and corporate plans, which guide the trainer toward the direction in which the organisation is moving, and to the implications for future training and development

- human resource and succession planning, which provides information about future training needs for key managers, and indicates areas of priority

- personnel statistics, which provide information regarding labour turnover and absence, for example, which directs the trainer to possible sources of problems – this includes training, but may also suggest other reasons

- exit interviews, which may highlight information about potential management and supervisory training needs

- consultation with senior managers, which provides an understanding of the views of key opinion-formers and of organisational culture

- data on productivity, quality and performance, which provides clues about the relationship between actual and required performance

- departmental layout changes, which provide information about future developments and can highlight training needs (skills or knowledge) at an early stage

- management requests, which indicate perceived needs and ideas for further development

- knowledge of financial plans, which is essential to determine whether or not training requirements are likely to be adopted by senior management, and may encourage fresh approaches if resources are limited.

The principal advantage of such lists is that they highlight the importance of locating training and development firmly in its corporate context, and ensure that this aspect of HRM can be undertaken with broader strategic goals in mind. The list also provides a useful template against which to assess the contribution of learning and development to organisational objectives. In short, it offers a logical and sequential process for establishing training needs within realistic organisational parameters. But there are also shortcomings with this top-down approach, especially if it is conducted as part of a wide-ranging formal review of training activity. It can be time-consuming and expensive, and the data may be difficult to collect in the time available (Reid and Barrington, 2001: 175). If the review takes a long time, there are bound to be questions about the prioritisation of training over the period during which the organisational analysis takes place.

The second level is *job or occupation analysis*, the purpose of this stage being to identify more specific training needs. There are many similarities here with job analysis, which we dealt with in Chapter 10. Harrison (2000: 263) terms this 'job-training analysis' in order to differentiate it clearly from its recruitment and selection counterpart. This is the 'process of identifying the purpose of a job and its component parts, and specifying what must be learned in order for there to be effective work performance'. A range of methods can be used to collect information at the job training analysis level, including an examination of job descriptions and job specifications, the use of questionnaires, group discussions, observation of the task in hand, work diaries, and even getting analysts to do the job themselves. Interviews are particularly useful, not just with the job-holder but also with his or her supervisor, as well as with internal or external customers or clients. Reid and Barrington (2001: 219) note the value of self-observation as a technique for identifying training needs at the job level, and in some respects this is one of the best ways to determine precisely what the job entails. However, they note that there are problems with this methodology. For example, individuals may be too close to their jobs to identify training needs effectively, they may not keep an accurate record of events during the course of the day, and they may over-emphasise certain aspects of the job they enjoy or dislike in order to gain training. There is also the problem that confusions arise between training needs which are identified for the job, irrespective of who undertakes it, and those which relate to the person who is currently in the post.

The final stage is a *person-level analysis*, which has some similarities with the methods discussed above. This frequently involves the use of interviews and questionnaires, observation and work sampling, and testing the knowledge of job-holders on specific issues. It may also involve the use of performance appraisal and assessment centres for identifying development needs. Harrison (2000: 86) considers appraisal to be 'at the heart of training and development', which is true, but it is also at the heart of other aspects of HRM, where it has quite different connotations. The key point about appraisals is one of purpose: in training they are used to identify development needs, whereas in performance management or selection they tend to be used as part of an assessment process and may be linked with reward packages or with disciplinary matters. Where appraisal is linked to rewards, it is unlikely to unearth training needs that can lead to improvements in customer service or product quality. Conversely, when appraisal is part of a development initiative and is conducted with this as its clear purpose – as in an organisation which purports to operate with a 'blame-free' environment, for example – then the whole process is likely to be more open. If employees are encouraged to acknowledge that there are areas of their work which are not being performed at full capacity, or are being carried out with inadequate knowledge or skills, appraisal interviews may help to identify important training and development needs.

CASE STUDY: Training solutions at UKHO

The UK Hydrographic Office (UKHO) has been in business since 1795. In the 1990s it faced a range of new demands including the challenge to become self-financing, able to respond more quickly to demands, yet without having recourse to redundancies. Changes were effected using technology and training and development managed by HR specialists. A majority of the 900 staff participated in training activities over a one-year period. Managers were trained in groups with people from different grades, functions and departments. Several of the groups identified projects to work on – identifying problems and devising solutions. As a result, some have been formalised as tar-geted action groups (TAGs) looking at issues such as improving customer service. Despite initial cynicism about training, most of the managers have been converted to the values of training and improved communications:

'Close liaison with people whom we'd never had much working contact with before was a real benefit, especially with all these changes in the air ... now we've learnt to look for solutions instead of griping about difficulties.'

Adapted from Golzen G. 'Voyage of discovery', *People Management,* 11 January 2001. pp32–36

Training is most likely to be effective when three conditions apply. These are that training is seen as important for the future, that there is a need for training to meet individual job and development goals, and that there is a likelihood of recognition or reward by the organisation. In many cases, the last condition is left unmet, and employers express surprise that training has made such a limited impact on the organisation. For training to be truly effective, it must receive a positive reception at the workplace and trainees must feel that the training has been worthwhile and can be incorporated into future plans and actions. Too often, of course, individuals return from a training programme full of ideas only to encounter blocks and barriers within the organisation, and suspicion or derision from workmates.

Devising a learning plan

The traditional approach to devising training plans focuses on the need to determine clear aims and objectives that are relevant to the learners concerned and that enable any performance gap to be bridged. Both Harrison (2000: 278–82) and Arnold *et al* (1998: 364) make similar distinctions between aims and objectives in devising learning programmes. Aims are expressions of general intent, such as 'to grasp the basic principles of x' or 'to be aware of the influence of y on z', and they make no attempt to specify measurable outcomes. Objectives, on the other hand, are more precise, giving a clear focus for the learning in terms of competencies, abilities, or understanding at the end of the training event. Harrison (2000: 282) suggests that the most helpful objectives are those which describe not only the kinds of behaviour to be achieved but also the conditions under which that behaviour is expected to occur, and the standards to be reached in that behaviour. The expression of standards in the CIPD Professional Development scheme, for example, is phrased in terms of learning outcomes (objectives) with a broad statement about each of the modules (aims).

A major feature to consider when devising learning plans is the characteristics of the trainees themselves, and the 'baggage' they bring with them to the learning event – their prior knowledge, skills, attitudes, motivations and expectations. Trainees may well differ, *inter alia*, in terms of their level of educational achievement, their attitude towards learning, their ability to absorb new ideas or maintain concentration, and their teamworking skills. They are likely to have very diverse reasons for being involved in the learning event. Some may be there because they enjoy learning, while others may have a clear instrumental purpose, such as enhancing their chances of promotion. Yet others may attend a formal training programme because it is deemed to be their turn, or because a colleague dropped out at the last minute. Some may be there under duress, determined to put little effort into the sessions, and keen to demonstrate their lack of interest at every possible opportunity. There may also be variations in the extent to which trainees have been briefed beforehand about the learning event or in the amount of preparation undertaken before the workshop gets under way, for example. In order to be effective, and for learning to transfer back to the workplace, training and development has to be embedded in the norms and cultures of the organisation involved. This is particularly important with off-the-job training and with longer courses.

Obviously it is important to establish the aims and objectives for a learning event, and to take into account factors which influence the choice of training methods to be employed – such as the characteristics of the learners, and their motives for attending training sessions. But for effective learning to occur it is also crucial that HR professionals gain agreement for their recommendations from key decision-takers, and that this learning is located in its organisational context. Unfortunately, this political dimension to training is often overlooked. There are major issues in relation to gaining agreement and support from key managers on dealing with negative reactions to training, and on the costs and benefits of training interventions. In other words, there is more to training than choices about the most appropriate methods for establishing training needs or learning techniques.

Being aware of costs and benefits associated with training is something for which HR practitioners are not renowned. It is relatively easy to reel off a list of general benefits from training, especially those which relate to other aspects of HR, but it is less easy to quantify them financially. Reid and Barrington (2001: 195–200) suggest that a list of benefits might include:

- that training helps new staff to learn jobs more quickly

- that trained staff are less likely to make costly errors or to have accidents at work

- that an organisation with a reputation for training may find it easier to recruit high-quality staff

- that trained workers are likely to be more flexible and able to undertake a range of jobs

- that trained employees may be more committed to the organisation and less likely to leave for other jobs

- that training can help to focus employee attention on how to achieve high levels of quality and customer service.

It is hard to demonstrate unequivocally that training has a direct and measurable impact on organisational performance levels, although this does not stop people making the claim. For example, it could be argued that training led to an increase in market share from x to y, or it has ensured that 95 per cent of trains will arrive within five minutes of published time. Political skills might help the HR practitioner to identify measures regarded as relevant to business objectives that may be accepted by a senior manager. But it might prove difficult to sell these

Table 40   Learning pays: the value of learning and training to employers

	Average company	IIP-accredited company	Gain
Rate of return on capital (RRC)	9.21%	16.27%	77%
Pre-tax profit margins	2.54%	6.91%	172%
Average salary	£12,590	£14,195	13%
Turnover/sales per employee	£64,912	£86,625	33%
Profit per employee	£1,815	£3,198	76%

Source: National Advisory Council for Education and Training Targets, 1999

solutions on more than one occasion, or to convince senior managers who want to have 'hard' estimates of costs and benefits. Gibb and Megginson (2001: 138) analyse National Advisory Council for Education and Training Targets to compare UK companies with and without IIP so as to demonstrate the value of learning and training. See Table 40.

Costs are easier to calculate than benefits, although much depends on the items to be included in the equation. First, there are overhead or fixed costs such as permanent accommodation or training equipment, charges for heating and lighting, and managerial and administrative salaries. Obviously, these account for a much higher proportion of costs in an organisation with its own training centre than for one which sub-contracts all or most of its training activities. The second item is fixed costs that are allocated over the lifetime of a training programme, such as the salaries and on-costs of trainers and/or consultants. Included in this would also be the cost of developing training materials as well as evaluation tools. Finally, there are direct or variable costs, which vary according to the amount of training that is undertaken and include the costs of travel and residential costs, costs of duplicated training materials, and so on. It is more difficult to decide whether or not to include the costs of delegates in the figures, either as a pro rata element of their wage and salary bill or the costs of replacements.

Calculating the opportunity costs of *not* training is rather more difficult (Reid and Barrington, 2001: 199–200). These costs may include items such as payments to employees when learning on-the-job, the costs of wasted materials or rejected products due to less-than-competent employees, or the time which supervisors and other employees spend in correcting mistakes or dealing with problems caused by untrained staff. In other words, to consider the costs of training fully we have to be aware of the costs of not training, and of relying on informal, *ad hoc* and potentially inefficient methods for improving performance.

It may also be useful to make comparisons with the amount spent by other organisations on training and development. We have already seen that employers in Britain spend relatively little on training compared with many of their foreign competitors, but comparisons should also be made with similar types of organisations in the same sector or area of the country. If figures are low, this information may prove helpful to HR professionals seeking to justify training expenditure – or if comparisons are favourable, it may prove helpful in public relations terms. The judicious use of benchmarking is just as useful in the training field as it is in other areas of HR activity.

> How much does training cost your organisation, and how does it compare with the costs of other organisations either in the same sector or in the same area of the country? How can this information be used to make training and development activity more effective?

Delivering learning and training

There are a multitude of methods that can be used to train and develop staff, both on- and off-the-job, ranging from the relatively unstructured and informal – such as 'sitting next to Nellie' – through to the carefully programmed and structured – such as computer-assisted learning and project management. Most texts on the subject provide lists of different methods, their nature and meaning, their advantages and shortcomings (see, for example, Reid and Barrington, 2001: 239–55). Although useful at one level, these lists are lacking in two respects. First, they are not organised into any coherent conceptual framework which differentiates between techniques according to learning principles or the characteristics of the learning situation. This makes it difficult for readers to 'locate' different methods within a structure, and to recall them. The second problem is that although the lists describe concisely the key features of different methods, and outline their major advantages and disadvantages, there is little attempt to identify the conditions under which particular techniques may be appropriate for facilitating effective learning.

It is important to recognise therefore that no one method is inherently superior to any other, but that different methods are suitable for different sets of circumstances. Choosing when to employ the right methods, and why, is a much more critical consideration than being able to note the advantages and disadvantages of each method in the abstract. Although the lecture may be inappropriate for most training situations, it may be the ideal technique for a newly-appointed marketing director to open the annual sales conference and so set the tone for the detailed sessions which follow. Conversely, computer-based training can be very effective for reinforcing basic language skills but it offers rather less towards the development of teamworking and group problem-solving.

Rather than produce yet another list, here we review training methods in four distinct categories, differentiated according to the main approach adopted, and by whether the training is for individuals or group-based. Snape *et al* (1994: 73) make the distinction between 'andragogical' and pedagogical approaches to training and development. The 'andragogical' approach, more accurately described as 'auto-didactic', is essentially self-directed and participative, the trainer providing a facilitative or supportive role. The latter, by contrast, is largely trainer-driven and allows little room for student input into the learning situation. The second distinction is between individual and group-based training. This categorisation is illustrated in Figure 15, with an example of each type of training for illustrative purposes.

The top left-hand quadrant includes methods that are principally pedagogically-oriented and individually-based, such as one-to-one instructional techniques and simulations. These are particularly useful for the acquisition of standard programmable skills, and for the transfer of routine information and ways of working, but which also require practice and application in real-life situations. This can span the extremes of the scale in terms of traditional job levels. At one extreme might be simulators for pilots in the early stages of training when they need to learn basic operating rules and principles. At the other extreme would be the basic stages of an assembly operation or the standard scripts that are given to workers in call centres. The major point behind these techniques is that there is seen to be no room for discretion or creativity, or for employee input into the choice of how to speak to potential customers, fix together parts of a piece of equipment, or land planes safely. Of course, once employees actually start to do the work themselves and become more experienced, there may be much more room for autonomy and use of initiative.

Figure 15   Categories of training and learning methods

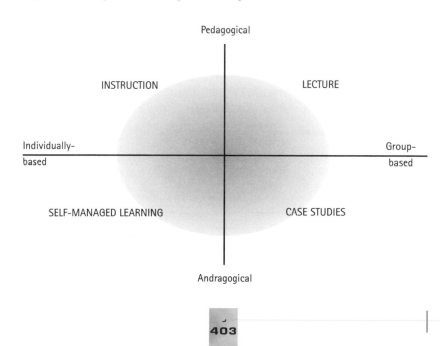

The basic principles of these kinds of training intervention are of the 'tell-show-do-review' variety, in which skills, knowledge and operating routines are transferred progressively to trainees until they have mastered the task. The trainer decides how quickly to move to a position of trust when he or she feels confident that the learner has acquired sufficient skills and knowledge, and has demonstrated sufficient competence in them to progress to the next stage of the instruction process. There is no room for vagueness or confusion in the instruction, especially if it relates to tasks that can have serious health or safety consequences. On the other hand, instructing staff to follow established routines may lead to motivational problems if the employees concerned feel that they already have the required skills or they do not share senior management's commitment to them. This has sometimes been a source of annoyance for staff in customer service organisations who feel sceptical about the messages they are told to convey.

The top right-hand quadrant includes methods which are pedagogically- and group-based, such as lectures, presentations and videos, and these are particularly appropriate in situations when a large number of people have to be given information at the same time, or when it is cost-effective to deliver training in this way. Most learners have been subjected to lectures at some times during their lives, and are often fully aware that there are limits to the amount that can be retained during a session. Estimates vary, but it is reckoned that less than a quarter of what is said is recalled, and the maximum concentration span is typically less than 20 minutes. Given that many lecturers have not received professional training in how to deliver lectures, and many more seem incapable of conveying information or ideas, let alone enthusing their learners, it is to be wondered why this technique is still practised so widely. However, it is a cost-effective way of providing information, at least to the extent of class contact hours, although whether or not it represents a cost-effective way of learning is another matter. On the other hand, most of us will have listened to an individual speak for an hour or more, and been enthralled. Some management gurus are renowned for keeping audiences transfixed for a couple of hours without interruption using few, if any, visual aids. But for most lecturers it is essential to use overhead projections or slides, distribute short summaries of the lecture, and litter the talk with examples and anecdotes to ensure that some retention takes place. Enthusiasm and knowledge of the subject matter are also essential, as is an awareness of learner needs, an ability to present information in a clear and concise manner, and a recognition that tone and cadence must vary to sustain attention.

One of the major problems with lectures and presentations is that they are often used inappropriately, transmitting information that can more easily be distributed electronically or as written documents or videos. These are now common as teaching aids, and can provide a useful interlude in the training programme to facilitate learning. But there are dangers with these techniques as well. They have to be chosen carefully to ensure that they are specifically directed at the issue in hand, they must be realistic and relevant, and they have to be contextualised in the programme with specific learning outcomes attached to them.

Choose what you think has been a successful lecture, or someone whom you feel to be a good lecturer, and identify the attributes of both that have led to that evaluation. Can these attributes be taught to other people? Why/why not?

The bottom right-hand quadrant is the 'andragogical'/group-based category, which includes case studies, projects, group role-playing exercises (such as in a negotiating exercise), and business games, some of which are managed through the use of computerised models. The basic point about this set of techniques is that they are essentially team-oriented and allow the group to propose its own solutions and ideas to problems with a minimum of trainer intervention during the process. The job of the trainer is to support the team, help it to arrive at conclusions, and generally facilitate the process of learning through a sharing of ideas. In effect, learning should take place through a process of induction, in which examples and incidents are generalised to arrive at a better understanding of the principles and processes which underpin management issues. This set of methods allows for the development of the core competencies regarded as central to any manager's job. These include decision-making, planning and time management, drive and persistence, the ability to work under pressure, oral and written communication, flexibility and adaptability, self-confidence and persuasiveness. In the case of projects that are initiated during a formal training course, but which are then continued back at work, other skills are developed as well, especially the ability to persuade senior managers that the project is worthy of time and effort.

Case studies provide a good avenue for 'real-life' problem-solving, for working out solutions in teams, and for presenting recommendations to other people. Like any other training technique, they must be well-managed, have clear learning outcomes associated with them, and be relevant to the needs and abilities of the trainees. They should be of an appropriate length and degree of difficulty for the student group, and contain sufficient information and enough flexibility to allow for competing solutions between different teams. There are problems associated with group-based training. Individuals working together in a team may come into conflict, or one or more individuals may dominate discussion in a way that excludes others and may lead to unsatisfactory solutions. Some learners often feel dissatisfied with the amount of information provided by the trainer, either becoming stressed because they feel that there is too much to analyse in the time provided, or insecure because they reckon there is too little from which to make a recommendation.

The final set of methods is the individually-based self-directed category, and this is where the use of computer-based training (CBT) has come to the fore. This group of techniques includes language laboratories and computer-assisted learning. Perhaps the principal point about these forms of training is that they are typically self-managed and can be undertaken at a pace, time, and possibly location that suits the individual concerned. With access to electronic media both at work and at home, and new generations of computers that use artificial intelligence to interact with learners, the opportunities for this type of training are considerable. Such techniques have the major advantage of being responsive to individual needs in a way that allows for a better fit between learning and domestic or work commitments. The self-management of learning is especially appropriate for the acquisition of impersonal systems (such as accounting or computing), the development and reinforcement of basic language skills, and for gathering information for reports. Although these techniques have been used for interpersonal skills training, it is unlikely that their use will become extensive in view of the importance of face-to-face contact for improving these skills. In this sort of situation, role-playing (either with a colleague or with a friend/partner) offers a much better solution to learning how to cope with, say, an aggressive senior manager or in counselling a poor performer.

E-learning
E-learning is increasingly being used by many organisations so that they can deliver information and training to all of their employees much faster and more efficiently. Examples include IBM which delivers half of its internal training online (Harrison, 2000: 207); Chartered Trust delivers three-quarters of its training online; Barclays Bank delivers e-training to its 2,000 small business advisers; the Royal Bank of Scotland provides e-learning for service centre team leaders and to induct service centre staff (Sanders, 2000b: 6–8); and the BBC is shifting to 30-per-cent e-learning (Cooper, 2000c: 6). Tom Peters stated at the American Society of Training and Development 2001 (Sloman, 2001a: 57) that 90 per cent of all training should be delivered by new technology by 2003. The UK has shown steady development in the use of Internet and intranet respectively for training purposes (Sanders, 2000b).

E-learning or computer-based learning (CBL) is delivered or received mainly through the Internet, intranets, extranets or the web, and is increasing across all sections of society. Tony Blair announced that he wanted all schools linked to the Internet by 2002 and universal access by 2005. The Higher Education Funding Council is aiming to develop an UK e-university which will be marketed worldwide (O'Shea, 2000: 10–11), and it is estimated that there are already around 1,600 corporate universities globally, around 200 of them in the UK (Arkin, 2000: 42–6).

Experience in the UK, USA and Scandinavia would seem to indicate that e-learning actually generates greater demand for training (Hammond,

2001: 26–31). The DfES exemplifies this, the use of its learning centres more than trebling between 1998 and 2000, with the expectation that the performance management training will be accessed by 2,500 managers (Merrick, 2000). The Director of Cisco's Internet Learning Solutions Marketing has said, 'We cannot build the classrooms or labs to train people fast enough to keep pace,' and added, 'The world of business has changed. IT is less like an ocean cruise and more like white-water rafting. We believe that e-learning is the way to turn the pace of change into a competitive advantage.' Cisco switched from 90-per-cent classroom-based learning to 80-per-cent e-learning in just one year, allowing its 30,000 partner organisations and customers access to its system (Hammond, 2001: 29).

The main advantages are that training can be accessed at times and locations to suit learners, who can work at their own pace, and that the training is consistent and methodical, and does not rely on variations between trainers. Most e-learning incorporates tests to check the learners' understanding and combines human interaction with work on the computer. It is regarded as particularly critical for multinational companies where new knowledge (for example, about a new product) has to be quickly disseminated worldwide and/or across many sites (Sanders, 2000b).

CASE STUDY: A case study for high-flyers: British Aerospace

BAe is a high-tech knowledge-based organisation that wants to be seen to be ahead in a highly competitive global market. In 1997, BAe set up its virtual university by working with over 70 colleges and universities throughout the country. Courses vary from MSc in Aircraft Engineering to development programmes in health, safety and the environment. The university is open to employees and their families, suppliers, partners and the local communities. In 1997 BAe spent £34m on off-the-job training, and it now plans to spend £22b in learning, research and development through the virtual university in the next decade. BAe's emphasis on learning started in 1994 when it focused on five 'values': people, customers, technology and innovation, partnership, and performance – the first four determining the fifth. The MD and vice-chancellor of the virtual university said, 'Creating a corporate university will ensure that education, training, research and development, technology and acquisition are right at the heart of the company's growth strategy and contribute towards company cohesiveness.' BAe is also looking at how the various educational and research initiatives taking place in pockets of the organisation can be made accessible to all employees. One of the aims of the virtual university is to catalyse, capture, communicate, and embed best practice in learning, research, and development and technology acquisition. One example of a course is the BAe Certificate in Management. This was developed in partnership with the Open University Business School and Lancaster University Management School. The modular course is expected to be taken by 5,000 employees and delivered through a combination of face-to-face and distance learning.

Adapted from Industrial Relations Services. 'Virtual lift-off for BAe's corporate university', IRS *Employee Development Bulletin* 110, February 1999. pp5–9

Jarvis Hotels introduced an e-learning induction programme in 1999. In view of the company's high staff turnover rates, and because many staff worked part-time on shiftwork, it was thought that e-learning would be highly beneficial. The training was planned so that human contact with local information was built in. It was a huge success in that the scheme reduced the cost of training from £40 per head to £7: the result was a reduction in staff turnover, greater customer satisfaction, and increased revenue.

Adapted from Sanders D. 'The pros and cons of computer-based learning', IRS *Employee Development Bulletin* 123, March 2000. pp6–8

However, e-learning is costly to develop, and it is not always the most appropriate training solution. The CIPD Guide on Training Technology (1998) summarised the most cost-effective circumstances for its use:

- where the course content is likely to remain relatively stable and not to require frequent revision

- where the content is largely to be concerned with knowledge – for example, company procedures

- where there is a long-term training need and thus a sufficient period in which to recoup the investment

- where the trainees are scattered geographically, so leading to potential savings in travel and subsistence

- where large numbers have to be trained in a relatively short time

- when unusual, expensive or dangerous situations have to be simulated.

Situations in which it may not be appropriate include:

- where it is not the most cost-effective solution

- where lead times are short

- where learners are not comfortable using computers

- where learning styles are more attuned to learning with others in groups

- where practical, hands-on skills are to be taught.

One of the main criticisms aimed at e-learning is the absence of the human interface. However, proponents maintain that use of computerised systems was never meant to replace this. Sloman (2001a: 57) is concerned that e-learning was hyped as an alternative to traditional training when it would have been better to make clear that the two may be regarded as complementary. He says that e-learning is most effective when it forms part of an overall strategy involving the classroom and on-the-job learning, and when the learner is given comprehensive and timely support. Sanders (2000b) also states that a mix of learning methods works best. She uses the example of a company in which staff are not used to using computers. In this case, face-to-face training can be used to introduce them to computers and ensure that they are all at the same knowledge-base before progressing to computer-based learning. Evidence suggests that in most cases classroom learning and/or human interaction is now offered alongside computer-based learning. As Paul Turner, the CIPD vice-president training and development, has declared (Rana, 2001b: 14):

> *The convergence of e-learning and technology with personal intervention – that's the future. There is a massive demand for e-learning opportunities, but I don't think it's the only solution. New learning technologies, combined with expert personal coaching and instruction, will give the training community the chance to offer individuals a total solution to their needs.*

This lesson has also been taken on board by *learndirect*, who in 2002 brought in tutors to supplement computerised learning.

How can e-learning be used in your organisation to improve training strategies and organisational performance?

A further criticism is that there are still very large numbers of people without access to computers and who are unfamiliar with them. Even in the financial services sector six out of ten people do not know how to use one, and until those people can be persuaded of the benefits of computer familiarity it will be difficult for them to e-learn (Hammond, 2001: 31). On a more worrying note, there is concern that some trainers are also reluctant to embrace e-learning. The CIPD Training and Development Report (2000b) found that only 17 per cent of respondents reported that they were using new technology 'a lot', most of them (70 per cent) saying they were making 'some' use of it. Sloman (2001b: 31) argues forcefully that HR training professionals risk finding themselves marginalised if they do not do so. However, he also warns that although trainers must be confident in the use of e-learning as an additional tool in their kitbag, they should be aware that it is not a universal solution, and that there are occasions when it is not the most appropriate training tool. As Sadler-Smith *et al* (2000: 474–90) report, e-learning is unlikely to replace 'learning by doing', whereby managers learn from interaction with others (for example, peers and customers) and from solving problems through feedback, making mistakes, and experimenting.

The conference paper we will never see: Lakin Scott Golding

Lakin Scott Golding is a firm with 3,000 employees at two manufacturing sites and its headquarters. It was decided that a switch would be made from classroom training to e-learning, delivered initially through computer-based technology and later through the company intranet. The result was chaos. The training manager reported major problems. These included:

- incompatibility of IT systems and chosen products, three times causing the postponement of the introduction of training

- the learning café degenerated into a spare meeting-room

- many of the soft-skill modules came to be seen as trivial in content and were in any case difficult to access

- managers sent their staff off on unauthorised external courses because of the failure of the e-learning experiment.
Adapted from Sloman M. *The E-learning Revolution: From propositions to action.* London, CIPD. 2001c

Evaluating the outcomes of training and learning

Whatever the method of training used, it is widely acknowledged that the evaluation of training is one of the most critical steps in the process, and one that is frequently carried out in neither a comprehensive nor systematic manner. Methods of evaluation most commonly used include informal feedback from line managers and trainees rather than tests or formal evaluations conducted some time after the training is completed. In other words, as with many other aspects of HRM, the extent of formal and systematic evaluation is limited, although the CIPD Training and Development Survey, April 2001j showed that evaluation is one of the most important issues for the following two years.

Evaluation deals with the overall benefits of training and often includes validity (Arnold *et al*, 1998: 371). Bee (2000: 42) suggests that it be called 'learning evaluation' because this implies concern with the whole process, from identification of learning needs through to application. She suggests that the best time to plan evaluation is when analysing learning needs because this will have a 'powerful influence on ensuring a well-designed training event'. There are a number of reasons why evaluation is necessary. They include improving the quality and effectiveness of training courses, and providing the trainers and the trainees with feedback, in terms of the design and relevance of the course in the achievement of individual learning objectives. It can enable organisations to establish whether training offers the most cost-effective and relevant solution to problems, instead of other HR actions such as recruitment or dismissal. It should also be part of the learning cycle, not only in causing trainees to reflect on what has been learned, but also in assisting them and their managers to identify future learning and development needs.

Once it is established why evaluation is being undertaken, it should then be possible to determine what should be evaluated, and when and how it might be done. Most ideas in this area stem from the work of Kirkpatrick (1967), who differentiated between four levels of evaluation: reaction, immediate, intermediate, and ultimate. Although each of these is considered in turn, it is important to recognise that evaluation at all levels must be undertaken in order to form a full picture of training effectiveness. Of course, the most important level of evaluation may differ according to the circumstances and the needs of different stakeholders. For example, whereas trainers may be more interested in how well they are performing in front of the group, the finance director may be more concerned about the cost-effectiveness of training programmes, and the departmental manager may be keen to assess the precise impact of training on job performance.

The *reaction level* is the evaluation generally gauged during or at the end of a course, and is often termed the 'smile sheet' since it assesses the performance of trainers in both absolute and relative terms. This form of evaluation aims to establish the views of one stakeholder, the learners themselves, about the training event, and these judgements are particularly relevant for assessing the adequacy of facilities and the overall organisation. Views are typically elicited through short questionnaires completed at the end of the training session or soon after it is completed. Such views can be highly useful to trainers, provided they see them as valuable and are prepared and able to act upon them. It is a system that is well-established in North America, has long been used on management courses, and is now commonly used in the UK higher-education system. Concerns about 'smile sheets' include worries that students merely react to the quality of the performance, the lecturer's ability to maintain surface-level interest or tell jokes to the class, so setting up expectations amongst both parties which may be of dubious educational merit. There are also doubts about the ability of learners to evaluate training in its wider context, as part of a broader educational programme or for its relevance to future performance in work (Reid and Barrington, 2001: 258). Indeed, it might be argued that there is no reason why positive reaction-level assessments should provide any indicator of subsequent job performance and the transfer of learning into the workplace.

Secondly, there is the *immediate level* of evaluation, which attempts to measure directly the extent to which training objectives have been achieved, in terms of knowledge, skills and attitudes. The Bees (1994) provide an example of questions that can be used to assess whether or not standards have been achieved following the completion of a disciplinary skills training course. The alternatives are:

- a list of true/false statements (such as 'the sole purpose of discipline is punishment')

- a forced-choice questionnaire where trainees must select one answer from three or four options (such as 'The main purpose of discipline is: a) punishment, b) teaching a lesson, c) improved performance, and d) don't know')

- a series of questions which require short five-minute-length answers, such as 'What information should be included in the record of the disciplinary hearing?'

The last of these options now forms one part of the final examination assessment portfolio in the CIPD Professional Development scheme. Forced-choice or true/false questions are seen by some to be superior to essays or more open questions, although there are problems with them. They guide the student towards an answer by providing signposts and parameters that are typically lacking in a management environment. In industry and commerce, for example, employees (and especially professionals) are asked for answers to general questions and problems (for example, What should we do about *x*?), which are then translated into terms of reference that guide subsequent activity. It is highly unlikely that managers will be provided with a series of forced-choice options, and asked to indicate which represents the best solution. Instead, they are asked to come to a judgement after researching the issue properly and systematically. Indeed, this is probably the best way to encourage creativity in organisations that preach continuous improvement and empowerment.

The third level of evaluation is the *intermediate level*. This refers to the impact of training on job performance and how effectively learning has been transferred back into the workplace. As the Bees (1994: 233) note, there is little point engaging in training if transfer does not take place, unless of course the objective is to keep employees away from work! But evaluation at this level is much less common than at the first two levels, in many cases because it is harder to undertake, but also because of problems in isolating the impact of training from the effect of other variables. Intermediate-level evaluation takes many forms, including interviews, self-report questionnaires, diaries, and observation. Observation may be effective for evaluating the transfer of technical skills (such as changing the wheel on a car), but may be more difficult to use to assess the extent of changes in time-management skills when a diary or a series of verifiable outputs might provide better data. For interpersonal skills a mixture of observation and self-reporting may be the most useful approach, in the light of the fact that part of the training objective is to encourage greater self-awareness of how relationships are handled. Evaluating the impact of training on a manager who has been accused of bullying may be even more difficult to determine, especially if victims lack the confidence to report incidents, or if the manager concerned refuses to recognise the problem. The chances of successful evaluation can be enhanced by a clear statement of objectives for the training, consultation with all those involved, and a careful design and testing of assessment instruments (Bee and Bee, 1994: 244). Arnold *et al* (1998: 373) point out that transfer of learning is severely limited where the trainee returns to an unsupportive setting in which changes in behaviour are not rewarded and may even be ridiculed.

Finally, there is *ultimate-level* evaluation, which attempts to assess the impact of training on departmental or organisational performance, and on the individual's total job. The distinction between intermediate- and ultimate-level evaluation is somewhat blurred, but the former usually refers to performance in a particular task or set of tasks for which training has been provided, whereas the latter evaluates the impact of training on overall results. The best indicators for ultimate-level evaluation vary enormously depending upon what are deemed to be key performance criteria, but typical examples might include:

- the number of customer complaints or rejects

- the level of sales, turnover, or productivity

- the number of accidents or lost employment tribunal cases

- the level of unauthorised absenteeism or labour turnover

- the proportion of letters answered within two days.

As the name implies, ultimate-level evaluation is the most difficult to do, and therefore the most problematical to use to determine the precise impact of training on performance. In some situations there may be no clear and simple measures to employ, or data may not be collected in a form which allows for evaluation to take place. There are many factors other than training which could affect the evaluation, especially at higher levels in the organisation when external influences can have a significant impact – for example, the influence of unemployment on labour turnover. In addition, only a small proportion of staff within a department or establishment might have been trained, and although their performance may have improved, that may have had relatively little overall effect. For many analysts, training interventions that can be proved to have had an impact at the ultimate level are what really matters – but Holly and Rainbird (2000: 280) rightly point out that there are dangers in becoming obsessed with organisational needs to the neglect of those relating to personal development. Nevertheless, they admit that 'the more the intervention is related to individual development and the process of learning itself ... the harder evaluation becomes'. As we saw in the previous chapter, learning organisations attempt to satisfy both these demands at the same time, and organisations with a claim to practise high-commitment HRM look for links between training and other areas of people management, as well as assessing its impact on performance.

CONCLUSION

In this chapter we have stressed the importance of having a systematic and well-organised structure for managing learning and development in organisations. Although there are a number of models and frameworks that can be used, each covers broadly the same cycle: identifying training and learning needs, devising learning plans, delivery, and evaluation. It is worth reiterating that there is no single best approach to training interventions since the most suitable method depends on its purpose, its subject matter, the size of the audience, and the finance available. Instead, HR practitioners must be able to choose the approach that is most appropriate for the specific circumstances in which the training is to be undertaken. At the same time, however, a thorough evaluation of training is critical, especially in assessing transfer back to the workplace for courses which take place off-the-job.

As Mayo (2000: 532) states, 'Developing human capital will be seen as a fundamental competitive issue, and aligning the activities associated with it as a critical business process. Employee development has a vital strategic part to play ... ' As with other components of HRM, the training arena is changing rapidly, not just through the availability of technology but also in terms of meeting organisational requirements (CIPD, 2001j: 37).

Useful reading

BEE F. 'How to evaluate training', *People Management*, Vol. 6, No. 6, 2000. pp42–45.

CHARTERED INSTITUTE OF PERSONNEL DEVELOPMENT. *Training and Development Survey*. London, CIPD. April 2001j.

COLLIN A. 'Learning and development', in I. Beardwell and L. Holden (eds) *Human Resource Management: A contemporary approach*. London, FT/Prentice-Hall. 2001.

HARRISON R. *Learning and Development*. London, CIPD. 2002.

MAYO A. 'The role of employee development in the growth of intellectual capital', *Personnel Review*, Vol. 29, No. 4, 2000. pp521–533.

MCKENNA E. *Business Psychology and Organisational Behaviour*. 3rd edition. Hove, Psychology Press. 2000.

REID M. *and* BARRINGTON H. *Training Interventions: Promoting learning opportunities.* London, CIPD. 2001.

SANDERS D. 'The pros and cons of computer-based learning', IRS *Employee Development Bulletin* 123, March 2000. pp6–8.

SLOMAN M. *The E-learning Revolution: From propositions to action.* London, CIPD. 2001c.

SPURLING M. *and* TROLLEY E. 'How to make training strategic', *People Management,* 13 April 2000. pp46–48

14 • Structures and Processes for Effective Employee Relations

> ## CHAPTER OBJECTIVES
>
> By the end of the chapter, readers should be able to:
>
> - provide management with advice on employee relations objectives that are appropriate for their own organisation
>
> - design an employee relations policy explaining how trade unions and collective bargaining will be dealt with, or how a non-union strategy will be effected
>
> - provide advice on the appropriateness of adopting different forms of employee involvement within their organisation.
>
> In addition, they should understand and be able to explain:
>
> - the way in which effective employee relations can contribute to increased employee potential and commitment
>
> - the processes of union recognition and derecognition
>
> - the nature and meaning of collective bargaining and employee involvement, and their place within the employee relations framework.

Introduction

Employee relations issues are central to work. Indeed, the way in which employers choose to manage their employees has for a long time been a source of interest to academics and practitioners alike. Different approaches have gained prominence in line with a variety of internal and external pressures on the employing organisation: these include the growth of trade unionism, changing product and employment market conditions, labour law, and new technology.

During the 1970s employers were encouraged to recognise and work with trade unions, required to improve the floor of employment rights for workers, and prompted to conciliate with rather than confront staff. However, during the 1980s the climate became more hostile for unions, and changes in the political and legal context removed much of their statutory support leaving many workers with little employment protection by continental standards. Moreover, the government encouraged employers to reassert their control, while high levels of unemployment in the United Kingdom further contributed to the shift in the balance of power. Some commentators then talked of 'the new employee relations' which reflected a fundamental shift in the nature of the employment relationship. Farnham's (2002: 69) view was thus that:

> *employee relations is the contemporary term for the field of study which analyses how the employment relationship between employers and employees is organised and practised.*

The late 1990s marked a new shift in the pattern of employee relations with a new Labour government (re-elected in 2001) more sympathetic to trade unions, and this has since been reflected in statutory recognition procedure. The policy environment has also become more animated, involving notions of employee rights (or in the EU case, citizenship) supported by new legal regulations (Ewing, 2002). Although the current government has remained committed to labour flexibility and considerable management 'choice' regarding employment practices, it has been prepared both to regulate independently on behalf of employees and to commit the UK more to European social policy.

The decline in union membership to less than a third of the workforce, (see Chapter 4) contributed significantly to the new employee relations terrain. Collective bargaining now has lower levels of coverage and scope than at any time since the 1930s, and trade unions have lost their national prominence and voice to an extent that would not have been thought possible in the 1970s. In addition, the extent of industrial action has also fallen dramatically, with days lost through strikes at a very low level, and a whole generation of HR managers now unaccustomed to dealing with collective disputes at work. In 1998 the number of incidents of industrial action of all kinds was two per 1,000 workplaces, and 94 per cent of workplaces experienced no industrial action of any kind in the previous five years (Cully *et al*, 1999: 298).

In this chapter we first examine management's role in employee relations, and in particular, management objectives. Secondly, we take up the subject of union recognition and the nature of union and non-union workplaces. Thirdly, we discuss how the 'rules' of employee relations are made through a process of negotiation and bargaining. Fourthly, we examine the processes by which workers are consulted or informed about change without collective negotiations.

Management's role in employee relations

The centrepiece of employee relations is the relationship between employers and employees, and it is part of this relationship that there are both common and divergent interests (see Chapter 2). Co-operation can serve employers and employees alike, since employees get the wage they require to sustain their living standards and employers receive in return the product of their work, whether in the form of a manufactured product or a service. It is in neither party's interest for the organisation to perform poorly with consequent negative effects on profits (for the employer) and on wages (for the employee). However, if there are clearly common goals there are also divergent interests. In simple terms, the employer generally wants to buy in labour at the lowest possible price or cost so as to maximise profits, whereas employees wish to sell their labour at the highest possible price. This produces a conflict of interests that does not necessarily result in open conflict but means that the arrangements reached may be unstable depending on relative bargaining power. Because employees are relatively weaker than employers, employees are likely to gain from organising themselves into trade unions in order to boost bargaining power.

Employee relations are thus characterised by both conflict and co-operation. Some people regard such relations as inextricably linked with conflict, since it is almost solely through conflict that employee relations have in the past obtained considerable media coverage. Yet it is now accepted that the so-called 'British disease' of industrial conflict in the 1970s was largely a myth, and that Britain had a record no worse than that of many other developed countries. Conflict may manifest itself through a strike or it may be contained or institutionalised through procedures (see Chapter 15).

> Write two lists, one specifying the common interests of employers and employees, and the other specifying divergent interests. Compare these lists with your own organisation's circumstances and culture, and see if the comparison helps you to evaluate the quality of employee relations.

However, the notion of two sides is also too simplistic. Firstly, neither side is consistently unified, so that a good deal of bargaining and disagreement takes place inside each party as well as between them. Within management there are likely to be conflicting objectives between different functions and between different levels – for example, the objectives of the sales team may conflict with those of the production function. Similarly, the demands placed upon line managers in terms of adherence to procedure agreements may cause conflict between them and the HR function. To some extent, though, the overriding objective of companies to secure profitability can help integrate the various sub-objectives. On the union side matters are even more complex, involving potential conflict between members in different departments and in different trade unions, as well as between different levels in the shop steward hierarchy. There may also be differences between different trade or interest groups or between the leadership and the ordinary rank-and-file members.

It is also inappropriate to conceive of only two parties in employee relations, for there may well also be third-party government intervention.

This can take several different forms. For example, legislation on employee relations has developed considerably since the 1960s, and it played a key role during the 1980s – legislation on the closed shop, industrial action, and ballots, for example, as we saw in Chapter 3. The government has also played a part in pay regulation since World War II. This has been particularly the case when it has pushed through a formal mechanism, such as the incomes policy of the 1960s and 1970s, or the imposition of cash limits for the public sector in the 1980s and the establishment of the minimum wage in 1998. The government has a second role, however – that of a key employer, with a managerial function. In addition, via the agencies of independent tripartite bodies such as ACAS, it has been intimately concerned with the resolution of disputes in both the public and private sectors.

Before looking at employee relations objectives, we should remind ourselves of the nature of management itself, and especially of the sharply differing contexts within which employee relations are enacted. Three aspects are worthy of mention. First, there is the distinction between different types of sectors (for example, manufacturing or service) and ownership (private or public). This leads to a categorisation of four types of employing organisation: private businesses, public corporations, public services, and voluntary bodies (Farnham, 2000). Second, there are major differences between employment in large, multi-establishment enterprises and small single-unit firms. Third, we must be aware of the influence of employee relations decisions compared with other corporate-level issues.

A number of writers in the USA have developed a 'strategic choice' model by which employers are seen as the key movers of change, and industrial relations policies are seen as strategic in that they form part of a long term plan (Kochan et al, 1986). This is important in recognising both the element of choice which faces managements, and also the extent to which management is able to set the agenda to which other actors – eg trade unions – then react (Purcell and Boxall, 2000).

It might be expected that employee relations objectives would be in line with corporate strategy, although this does assume that employers are proactive enough to have devised such strategies, and are not just muddling through. Even if it is assumed that employers have some idea about what they are doing, and why they are doing it, their objectives may be implicit rather than explicit, and in many cases not committed to paper. In any event, employee relations objectives typically include:

- reducing unit labour costs, though not necessarily wages

- achieving greater stability in employee relations by channelling discontent through agreed procedures

- increasing productivity and the utilisation of labour

- increasing co-operation and commitment so as to increase the likely acceptance of change

- increasing control over the labour process

- minimising disruption at work and reducing the likelihood of overt conflict.

Some of these objectives do not make sense in isolation. For example, although management clearly wants to minimise disruption, it can hardly be at the expense of high productivity. Yet high productivity might perhaps be achieved in the long term by engineering a strike so as to confront inefficient working practices. Equally, some of these objectives may be more appropriate at certain stages in an organisation's development, or for some types of employer.

Think of examples of conflicts in your organisation between parties who have different objectives. To what extent do objectives change over time?

Over the last 30 years a variety of bodies have argued that managements must adopt a more strategic approach to employee relations, largely because 'fire-fighting' with short-term *ad hoc* solutions seems only to store up trouble for the future. In contrast, it was suggested that devising a strategy could provide a greater likelihood of success in that it would increase consistency and harness commitment (Donovan, 1968; ACAS, 1981; Thurley and Wood, 1983; Tyson, 1995; Schuler *et al*, 2001). However, research suggests instead that managers have adopted an opportunistic and pragmatic approach to managing employees rather than the strategic approaches extolled by the strategic human resource management texts (Bach and Sisson, 2000). Companies tend to consider HR issues at the implementation stage of decisions, rather than at the point where the decisions themselves are initially being taken.

To try to understand management's approach to employee relations, it is useful to draw upon the concepts of 'frames of reference' developed by Alan Fox (1966) in his research paper for the Donovan Commission. These embody the main selective influences that cause managers to supplement, omit and structure what they see. It is in such a way that two people may see the same event in a completely different manner, and may judge its meaning, significance and outcomes in contrasting ways. The *unitary* frame of reference sees the organisation as a team (like a football team), the employees striving as a body towards a common goal. All members of the team are assumed to work to the best of their ability, to accept their place in the hierarchy, and to follow their appointed leader. There is no room or reason for factions. In that unions are unnecessary (since everyone is on the same side), conflict is seen as pathological or abnormal, the result of misunderstanding, caused by troublemakers. In contrast, *pluralism* conceives of the organisation as a number of miscellaneous groups with common and divergent interests, and management's job as to balance these competing demands. Trade unions may be regarded as a natural reflection of varied interests, rather than a cause of conflict. Conflict is not perceived as illegitimate but should be channelled or managed through rules and procedures (Ackers, 2002a, 2002b).

In simple terms, the two frames of reference have different perspectives on management prerogatives. Managers with a unitary perspective would expect employees to trust them to make the 'correct' decision, and because everyone supposedly has the same interests, there should be no conflict between what is best for the company and what is best for employees. In contrast, the pluralist, who accepts the role of a union in the workplace, believes in a policy of gaining the support of unions and employees to achieve an 'acceptable' solution. Pluralists believe that shop stewards should be consulted about changes that may have a fundamental effect on employees. On many occasions the substantive outcome of joint decision-making may be little different from that which would have been achieved by direct management action. However, the procedural element is different, and is critical.

Compare and contrast the unitarist and pluralist viewpoints on changes in employee relations. Do they contradict each other, or are both perspectives valid?

Bacon (2001: 194) notes that:

In the 1998 Workplace Employee Relations Survey (WERS 98) most managers (54 per cent) were 'neutral' about union membership, whereas 29 per cent were 'in favour', with 17 per cent 'not in favour' (Cully et al, 1999: 87). However, when managers are asked more directly whether they prefer to manage employees directly or through unions, then unitarist preferences emerge. For example, 72 per cent of managers agreed with the statement 'We would rather consult directly with employees than with unions', whereas only 13 per cent disagreed (ibid: 88). Consequently, management approaches to industrial relations are often characterised as a mixing and matching between unitarism and pluralism in the 'time-honoured British fashion'.

Individual managers may vary in their willingness to accept a curbing of managerial rights, to some extent depending on the subject matter under consideration. For example, managers may well be willing to

CASE STUDY: The 1997 dispute at BA: the right to manage?

By the end of the 1990s many of the structural factors that had provided the basis for BA's success were under threat. BA proposed £1 billion of cost savings from within the organisation. Much of this was to come from staff savings, including 5,000 voluntary redundancies and staff to be replaced by newly-hired employees on lower pay. This policy of reducing labour costs was also extended to 'core' BA staff, and BA attempted to change the structure of payments to cabin crew. It was proposed that the existing employees would be 'bought out' of their series of allowances (petrol, overnight stay, etc) by receiving a higher basic wage. BA offered a three-year guarantee that no crew member would earn less under the new system, but nothing beyond that – and it was clear to cabin crew staff that the measure was launched with the explicit aim of saving money. When negotiations failed, one union – the TGWU – threatened strike action (Cabin Crew 89, a small breakaway union, had already accepted management's offer). Both the TUC and *The Economist* felt that BA's management used bullying tactics. Members of the cabin crew were warned not to strike, and BA managers were instructed to tell discontented staff that anyone taking industrial action would be summarily sacked, then sued for damages. Any who simply stayed away would face disciplinary action, be denied promotion, and lose both pension rights and staff discounts on flights for three years. BA was also reported to be filming pickets.

The subsequent strike ballot had an 80 per cent turnout and 73 per cent of employees voted in favour of strike action. The TGWU called a series of 72-hour strikes, the first of them scheduled for 9 July 1997. In response, temporary staff and an alternative workforce of 'volunteer managers' were given training to perform the key tasks of the ground handling staff (*The Herald*, 26 June 1997), and BA threatened to take legal action over claimed discrepancies in the ballot. On the eve of the first day of action airline cabin crew were telephoned at home and warned that 'they had a duty to co-operate with their employer' (*The Times*, 8 July 1997).

These managerial actions certainly influenced the impact of the strike. On the first scheduled day of action fewer than 300 workers declared themselves officially on strike, but more than 2,000 called in sick. The company's threats and 'replacement workers' notwithstanding, more than 70 per cent of flights from Heathrow were cancelled (*The Economist*, 12 July 1997). It seemed that BA's macho approach had ensured only that collective action took the form of collective illness.

Ironically this 'mass sickie' served to make things worse for BA. Not only did the pre-strike ballots (conducted to comply with legislation designed to discourage union activities) compound the effects of the strike by providing customers with advance notice of it, but those employees who had called in sick stayed away in droves for longer than the official 72-hour strike. BA insisted that sick employees provide a doctor's note within 48 hours instead of the normal seven days – but many employees still stayed off for the full two weeks that their sick notes allowed, throughout which time services were cancelled and passengers turned away. One undercover employee publication, aptly named *Chaos*, gave advice on ways of maximising payments by delaying aircraft. These included throwing duvet feathers into the engine, supergluing down the toilet seat and poisoning the pilot. 'A particularly obnoxious captain can be made to suffer all the symptoms of violent food poisoning by emptying eye-drops from the aircraft's medical kit into his salad or drink' (*The Guardian*, 8 November 1997). The strike was costly. Airline seats are a particularly perishable form of consumer product, and aircraft scheduling is easily disrupted. When Bill Morris, the General Secretary of the TGWU, announced that he had written to BA boss Bob Ayling suggesting that they resume negotiations, Ayling agreed before even receiving the letter.

Source: Grugulis I. and Wilkinson A. *Managing culture at British Airways: hype, hope and reality.* Long Range Planning, 2002

negotiate on matters relating to payment methods, job design and work practices, but be unwilling even to consult about matters such as investment and pricing policy, or product development. At any event, while management may be willing to consult, involve, and even bargain, they will also insist that they have a 'prerogative' to make the final decision. This is why, in certain areas of employee relations – such as promotion and training – management prerogative is invariably exercised. In organisations where unions are absent, management is better able to vary the terms and conditions of employment at will.

The extent and nature of union recognition

The issue of union recognition lies at the very heart of employee relations, and policies and practices in this area have changed more than most in the last two decades. In the mid-1970s it was assumed that most employers would automatically recognise and deal with trade unions, support their activities in the workplace, and attempt to build close working relationships with senior shop stewards so as to lubricate relations at work and minimise the likelihood of disruption to business. By the 1990s many employers introduced new working patterns without even consulting, let alone negotiating with, union representatives. Although derecognition has not been widespread, the lack of new recognition has been seen as more significant (Cully *et al*, 1998: 16). However, work by Gall and McKay (1999) suggests that there has been a marked change in the relative incidences of derecognition and recognition, and that recognition agreements now outnumber cases of derecognition. They put forward five possible explanations. Firstly, the number of companies likely to derecognise are becoming fewer because most of those who might want to do it have done it. Secondly, notions of 'partnership' have been important in providing employers with a more positive view of unions. Thirdly, some companies were waiting to see what legislation was to be enacted, and as a result of the legislation are now more likely to recognise unions. Fourthly, trade unions have put more resources into various campaigns to increase recognition. Finally, employers have adapted to the developments in European legislation in terms of consultation (see also Sargeant, 2001).

Until recently there was no legally enforceable recognition route in order to obtain recognition. This made the British system different from those operating in many other industrialised countries in Europe and North America. In theory it meant that if they so desired, British employers could choose to grant recognition to a union that had no members in the workplace. Indeed, this is precisely what happened at some of the greenfield sites when deals with a single union were signed before any employees were recruited, as at Nissan (Wickens, 1987: 129–37). Conversely, employers could choose not to recognise a union at a workplace where all employees were union members – although this is more of a hypothetical situation and in practice would be difficult to sustain. In

Table 41   Indicators of union presence, by workplace size and management attitudes

	Percentage of employees who are members of a union	Percentage of workplaces that have any union members	Percentage of workplaces that grant full union recognition
Workplace size			
25 to 49 employees	23	46	39
50 to 99 employees	27	52	41
100 to 199 employees	32	66	57
200 to 499 employees	38	77	67
500 or more employees	48	86	78
Management views on union membership			
In favour	62	98	94
Neutral/not an issue	23	50	29
Not in favour	7	16	9
All workplaces	36	53	45

Base: all workplaces with 25 or more employees
Source: Cully M., Woodland S., O'Reilly A., Dix G., Millward N., Bryson A. and Forth, J. *The 1998 Workplace Employee Relations Survey: First Findings*, London, Department of Trade and Industry. 1998. p15

other words, the ultimate decision to grant recognition remained the prerogative of management. As noted in Chapter 3, the 1999 Employment Relations Act changed this by making legal provision for statutory trade union recognition.

In broad terms, there seems to be an increasing distinction between (a) those workplaces where unions have maintained a presence and where they appear to be supported by managements, (b) those where they are being edged out and are perhaps in danger of becoming extinct, and (c) non-union workplaces. The critical importance of management attitudes is shown graphically by the WERS data. Unions were recognised in 45 per cent of workplaces overall, but in 94 per cent of workplaces where management had a favourable view of unions, and in only 9 per cent of workplaces where management had an unfavourable view (Cully *et al*, 1998: 15). We examine these three options above.

Working with the unions

The proportion of workplaces in Britain that recognise a union fell from 66 per cent in 1984 to 45 per cent in 1998, although there is still sub-stantial sector variation (Cully *et al*, 1998: 28; Millward *et al*, 2000: 264). For example, 25 per cent of all private sector organisations recognise a trade union, whereas in the public sector recognition is 95 per cent. Union recognition appears also to be a function of organisational size. Recognition thus ranged from 33 per cent in the smallest workplaces to 76 per cent in the largest. It is also important to note that recognition is variable in both scope and depth (Brown *et al*, 1998), in that employers recognise unions for specific activities – such as discipline, grievance or health and safety representation – but not necessarily for full-blown collective bargaining. For example: at Sainsbury's unions are recognised for individual grievances, while at ICI unions are involved in business planning (Sisson and Storey, 2000: 190). According to WERS, there are no union members at all in 47 per cent of workplaces, compared with 36 per cent in 1990. The decline in the incidence of union recognition from 1980 was largely a private sector phenomenon, and after 1990, entirely so (Millward *et al*, 2000: 97).

There are a number of reasons why employers choose to work with, rather than against, unions at the workplace. Firstly, management may regard trade union representatives as an essential part of the communications process in larger workplaces. Rather than being forced to establish a system for dealing with all employees or setting up a non-union representative forum, management may perceive the trade unions as a channel that allows for the effective resolution of issues concerned with pay bargaining or grievance-handling. It is also the case that reaching agreement with union representatives, in contrast to imposing decisions, can furnish decisions with a legitimacy that would otherwise be lacking. The decisions made can be 'better' decisions as well. Even if this method of decision-making appears more time-consuming than the simple imposition of change, less time is spent trying to correct mistakes or to persuade employees after the event of the efficacy of management ideas.

Secondly, employers may decide that it is more important to achieve long term stability in employee relations even though their power advantage might allow them to impose changes on the unions. It is argued that management is better able to persuade unions to observe procedures if they have also conformed to previous agreements. As a *quid pro quo*, employers have to be prepared to use procedures themselves for resolving differences at work, especially in the area of disciplinary matters. Indeed, it can be argued that 'responsible' workplace union organisation and 'responsive' management is mutually reinforcing.

Thirdly, some employers have taken the view that unionisation is inevitable because of the nature of their workforce, the industry, and the region in which establishments are located. The new recognition procedure means that where there is sufficient support for a union, employers may feel it is far better to reach an agreement with a preferred union from the outset rather than to suffer from poor employee relations and consequent low employee morale through defiance. This was the case at Airflight – a charter airline – which, in the context of having acquired a unionised company, and with legislation on recognition imminent, decided that it made sense to recognise BALPA, the pilots union (Marchington *et al*, 2001: 77). It is also important to keep the trade union issue in perspective. Employers have many concerns other than those relating to trade unions, and provided the unions do not present a major obstacle to the realisation of more important goals, a union presence can be tolerated or even promoted. Finally, even if employers did wish to reduce the role of unions at the workplace, they may lack the power to carry through their intentions because of local constraints. For example, skill shortages may make wholesale dismissals unrealistic in that the tacit skills of workers would be lost, with the consequence of less effective and less efficient organisations. Moreover, it is often forgotten that trade unions perform a number of functions in the workplace that often assist the management of employee relations. In a non-union organisation following complete derecognition the onus falls upon management to perform an even greater range of tasks, and there are suggestions that it has proved difficult to sustain alternative representation arrangements as well as satisfy employee expectations.

Most people join trade unions primarily for instrumental reasons – for example, for protection against arbitrary management decisions or for

CASE STUDY: A package deal: TGWU success at UPS

UPS entered the UK in 1992, and took over Carryfast, then the UK's largest private parcels service. The company continued Carryfast's practice of negotiating with union representatives at depots where the TGWU had a solid presence, but refused to hold talks with the union at a national level. 'They negotiated with one or two depots and then rolled out the terms they'd agreed across the company, which was less than adequate because few people were involved in the negotiations,' according to Danny Bryan (the TGWU national secretary for road transport).

UPS argued that the union did not have enough members in the company. The TGWU responded by campaigning successfully to increase membership and then asking managers if they could talk informally with them about pay and conditions. The firm agreed in 1994, and in 1997 managers signed a deal to bargain nationally with the representatives of its 2,000-plus drivers and loaders, and also gave the TGWU the right to appoint shop stewards to negotiate on local issues. According to Bryan: 'We'd spent three years demonstrating to them that we could be a serious partner.'

Nigel Goodson, HR director for the firm's UK operation, admits that it had originally not seen the point in dealing with the union nationally, and had been preoccupied in its early years in the UK with 'integrating a number of businesses that had come from different origins'. However, in the longer run managers were persuaded that 'it was the right time and in everybody's interests' to negotiate. 'We wanted to adopt a national set of terms and conditions, which we did with the union in 1996. Signing the deal in 1997 was merely formalising a *de facto* situation that had existed for a year.'

In 2000 the company and the union signed a three-year agreement on pay and conditions. According to the HR director, the move has allowed workers to know where they stand in the longer term and enabled the company to budget for improvements to terms and conditions, including union requests for a reduction in the working week.

Adapted from Cooper C. Union recognition feature, *People Management*, 13 September 2001d. p41

insurance against accidents (see Chapter 4). They may not necessarily believe in the notion of collective action but join for individual defensive purposes. The insurance function in the event of discipline, dismissal, injury or dispute may be central. On the other hand, some people may join unions because of peer-group pressure or because they feel it is morally right to be in a union. The predominantly instrumental attitude partly explains why participation in union affairs is generally so low, although it does increase considerably if there is a concrete problem or specific issue in employee relations (Waddington and Whitson, 1997). It also explains why unions tend to be seen in local and economic terms, since that is where the union performs its service and is most visible to the ordinary member, especially through the activities of its lay representatives. This 'local' perspective helps us understand why people agree that 'unions in general are too strong' and at the same time feel 'that unions at [the individual's workplace] are not strong'. However, Millward *et al* (2000: 89) note that in recent years there has been an increased unwillingness to become union members even in situations where the employer encourages unionisation.

Why do people join unions? Discuss the factors that influence the decision to join or not to join a union.

After a period during the 1980s in which it appeared that the notion of working with the unions disappeared from the employee relations agenda, there has been a recent revival of interest in notions of 'partnership' (Involvement and Participation Association, 1993; Ackers and Payne, 1997; Guest and Peccei, 2001). This refers to a situation in which management are prepared to support the activities of the trade union(s), and for their part employees are more likely to regard union membership as an important aspect of their employment conditions. A good example of this is the Involvement and Participation Association (IPA) report (*Towards Industrial Partnership*, 1993), which is publicly endorsed by leading trade union and management representatives as well as a number of well-known academics. While not seeking to deny differences of opinions and goals, the report recognises the high degree of common interests shared by employers and unions, and stresses the need to accept the legitimacy of representative institutions. WERS provided a fillip to collectivism by reporting that the combination of union recognition and high-commitment management (HCM) practices had a significantly positive effect on performance. As Cully *et al* (1999: 135) note: 'Workplaces with a recognised union and a majority of the HCM practices ... did better than the average, and better than workplaces without recognition and a minority of these practices.'

Edging out the unions

Whereas some employers have sought to develop their relationship with unions, others have opted for marginalisation or derecognition. In these situations employers have decided that their objectives are more likely to be achieved by reducing or removing the union presence. In some workplaces there may have been disputes that slowed down or prevented changes in working practices, or managers may have been concerned about whether or not they could work with trade unions. Others may simply have taken advantage of a superior power-base to remove or restrict the activities of unions, to reduce wage costs, and to enforce a stricter managerial regime. Some of the reduction in union influence has occurred as part of a broader management strategy rather than as an attack on unions as such, and the removal of the union is undertaken in conjunction with a shift to more direct methods of employee involvement. For example, some employers place considerable emphasis on cultures that stress individualism and performance-related pay schemes rather than collectively-negotiated rates. In short, management is seeking to deny, rather than legitimise, the unions.

Even when trade unions are marginalised, they retain a presence in the workplace, and in many cases maintain the right to collective bargaining. In these situations, even though the institutions of collective employee relations remain in place, they represent a much less important aspect of human resource policies and practices. A number of changes are typically associated with marginalisation:

- Substantial reductions are made in the number of shop stewards at establishment level.

- There is a severe tightening-up on access to time off for trade union activities and facilities for undertaking union-related work.

- Full-time shop steward positions are withdrawn, often subsequent to the dismissal (usually through redundancy or early retirement) of the existing role-holders.

- Support for deduction-of-(union-)contributions-at-source (DOCAS) arrangements fades away entirely.

- A lower priority is accorded to collective bargaining with unions, followed by the upgrading of consultative committees.

- A greater emphasis is placed on individualism and direct communications from line managers to all employees.

Certainly in recent years, as unions have become less able and willing to take industrial action, employers have pruned the collective bargaining agenda and relied more heavily on written and oral communications to all staff, as opposed to going through union channels alone. As Marchington *et al* (2001: 64) recount:

> *The production director at a carpet manufacturer reflected on recent changes. Ten years ago, managers would meet the shop steward who would then roll information out. 'We'd never dream of that now. It's crazy when you think back. We used to not talk [directly] to our employees, only through a union representative.'*

WERS 1998 confirmed that the trend to 'hollow out' collective agreements was continuing. Even where worker representatives were present, no negotiations occurred over any issues in half of these workplaces (Cully *et al*, 1999: 110). In a further 13 per cent of workplaces negotiations occurred only on non-pay issues, in 17 per cent they only covered pay, and in 22 per cent negotiations occurred over pay and one other issue. Managers in many workplaces appear to regard certain HR issues as 'off limits' to union representatives, and do not even involve unions by providing them with information (Bacon, 2001: 198).

Employers can take this strategy further and try to derecognise unions – an idea that entered the vocabulary of British employee relations only in the 1980s (Gall and McKay, 1999). It is important to appreciate at the outset that derecognition is not a homogeneous concept (Dundon, 2002). In its most straightforward form derecognition refers to the *complete* withdrawal of collective bargaining rights and trade union organisation for some or all employees at a workplace or throughout an entire employing organisation. In other words, no trade union is recognised for the employees involved, even though by law they retain the right to join unions of their choice. Alternatively, derecognition can mean the removal of bargaining rights for *one or more* unions in a multi-union environment, while allowing for, and even encouraging, the transfer of membership to other unions in the workplace. In this situation management might seek to simplify existing arrangements and reduce the number of unions with which it deals, and the end-result could well be levels of union membership little different from before the derecognition. Whereas one union loses, another gains.

The extent of union derecognition is difficult to gauge. WERS shows that the decline in union membership cannot be explained by the marginal rise in derecognition, which is insignificant compared to other sources of membership decline – such as shifts in employment from areas of high to low union density. Furthermore, it is important to note that a number of problems often occur after derecognition. Line managers have reported increased workloads caused by the added responsibility for individual communication and consultation post-derecognition. Other issues include shopfloor tension and deteriorating employee attitudes toward management (Dundon, 2002b). Gall (1998) reported on two areas of publishing and printing in which there was the introduction of a two-tier wage structure and the elimination of institutional voice. Although manual workers have been affected by derecognition, it is to a lesser extent than non-manual, professional and managerial staff have been. The main triggers for derecognition over recent years relate to ownership changes, a move to personal contracts, relocation and reorganisation (Gall and McKay, 1999: 608).

What are the advantages and disadvantages of union recognition for employers?

Managing without unions

As with derecognition, non-unionised firms did not receive much attention in publications prior to the 1980s. It was well known that there were large numbers of small, usually independent, companies which did not recognise or deal with trade unions, but they were generally labelled 'traditionalist', unitarist or 'sweatshop' employers, and castigated (usually quite rightly) for their poor treatment of staff. It was only with the growing awareness of what Beaumont (1987: 117) refers to as the 'household name' group – companies such as IBM, Marks & Spencer, Hewlett Packard – that academic and practitioner interest started to blossom. These companies were praised for their employee relations policies, which were designed to offer employees more than could be achieved by trade unions through negotiations. At last it appeared that non-unionised firms could actually feel proud of their approach to employee relations, and these companies later began to be seen as fertile ground for the development of HRM in the UK.

Non-unionism is more extensive in certain parts of the country (such as the south-east of England) and in certain sectors of the economy (such as retailing, professional services, and hotels and catering) than in others. Younger and smaller establishments are also more likely to be non-union, and there has been some debate as to whether the high-technology sector is adding to the stock of non-unionism (Farnham, 2000: 183). But non-unionism can take many different forms, varying from the sophisticated, and arguably more pleasant, employment practices that characterise the 'household name' group through to the sweatshops and 'bleak houses' (Sisson, 1993) of 'Dickensian' employers. One of the problems with studies of non-union firms has been the lack of differentiation between these highly contrasting forms of employee relations, which have little in common beyond the refusal by employers to recognise trade unions for collective bargaining. Guest and Hoque (1994a) argue that the term 'non-unionism' is actually limiting, in that firms are only analysed in relation to unionisation. They suggest a categorisation of non-union firms into the good, the bad, the ugly and the lucky – here we focus on the first three of these.

First, and most celebrated by commentators, are employers who are probably leaders in their product market, who would be classified by Guest and Hoque as 'good'. These are often large employers, who have a clear strategy for managing people and operate with a wide range of human resource policies. These employers have tended to operate a 'union substitution' policy (Beaumont, 1987; Blyton and Turnbull, 1998) that offers a complete employment package intended to be perceived by employees as an attractive alternative to trade union membership. Such an approach might include:

- a highly competitive pay and benefits package that is typically in excess of those offered by other firms in the same labour market

- a comprehensive battery of recruitment techniques (including psychometric tests) designed to select individuals who 'match' organisational norms and discard those who do not fit with the company profile (eg those with a history of union activism)

- a high priority accorded to induction programmes geared up to socialising employees into the company ethos

- a stress on training and development opportunities, related both to the employees' work and more broadly to their role in the company and society (eg employee development and assistance programmes and career counselling)

- a focus on employee communications and information-sharing within the enterprise, such as through team briefing

- a system enabling employee concerns and anxieties to be dealt with by management (rather than a union), as well as for employee contribution of ideas that may help to improve organisational efficiency

- a commitment to provide employees with secure and satisfying work while they are employed by the organisation, often involving regular moves to different types of job

- single-status and harmonised employment policies between blue- and white-collar employees

- an individualised pay and appraisal system differentiating between staff in terms of previous performance and future potential, designed to reward those who contribute most to organisational success, (eg performance-related or merit pay).

The HR practices used by these 'good' firms – see Chapter 7 as well – certainly look attractive to employees. Assess whether or not they represent a cost-effective alternative to trade unions.

However, such organisations have not escaped criticism. It could be argued that 'sophisticated' employment practices are merely an illusion designed to obscure the true nature of HRM regimes, or that workers are merely 'conned' by their overt appeal into working harder, not for their own benefit but for that of the company. Similarly, it has been suggested that employers may continue to provide superior employment practices only under favourable economic and competitive conditions, and that product market problems will lead to their permanent or temporary withdrawal. In other words, the supposed employer commitment to employees as their 'most valuable resource' is both superficial and trite. In the case of a steel plant that widely publicised the introduction of an HRM approach and subsequently derecognised trade unions, employee gains proved illusory, with managerial strategy geared towards compliance, work intensification and the suppression of any counterbalancing trade union activity (Bacon, 1999). There is also an argument that these sophisticated non-union organisations offer good benefits only because of the previous and continuing efforts of trade unions across the economy as a whole.

The second type of non-union firm is the traditional sweatshop employer, often a small independent single-site company operating as a supplier to one of the sophisticated non-union organisations analysed above. Managements that deliberately deprive workers of their rights are categorised as 'ugly', whereas those that offer poor terms and conditions without such manipulative intentions are referred to as 'bad'. The subordinate position many of these small suppliers fulfil in relation to a larger company – dependent, dominated and isolated – leaves them with little control over their own destiny and places a primacy on labour flexibility. Such firms are under considerable pressure to control costs and increase flexibility, goals many of these employers believe to be achievable only without what they see as interference by trade unions. In these circumstances pay rates are likely to be low, while formal fringe benefits and welfare arrangements may be virtually non-existent. The regime in these small firms tends to be highly personalised (Scott *et al*, 1989; Dundon and Wilkinson, 2002). Recruitment practices are also likely to reflect the owner/managers' deep distrust of unions. The lack of formal disciplinary procedures means that employee protection is haphazard and arbitrary at best, totally absent at worst (Wilkinson, 1999). Guest and Conway (1999) described a firm without a union presence or high-commitment HRM as 'a black hole', noting the lack of employee satisfaction and commitment and the high propensity of employees to quit. In a study by Dundon *et al* (1999: 258–62) a personnel manager took the view that 'communicating to employees can be a dangerous thing. The current system of withholding information is a strategy that has been built up over the years and is used to keep employees on their toes.'

At the same firm, one of the employees noted that the 'The firm is run by "family-men". What they say goes. It's as simple as that ... and I can't see them giving that control up.' The WERS study noted much lower levels of sanctions and dismissals in workplaces where unions were recognised, suggesting unions' success in defending against arbitrary dismissal (Cully *et al*, 1999: 28).

Collective bargaining

Collective bargaining has been a significant component of British employee relations from the end of World War I through to the 1980s. It was the principal method by which wages and conditions were determined for a majority of the workforce, although it has been described as a 'hollow shell' (Hyman, 1997). In addition, collective bargaining out-comes (in terms of wage levels, hours worked and holiday entitlements, for example) also influenced the terms and conditions of employees whose pay was determined by management alone. One reason why sophisticated paternalist employers offer terms and conditions of employment superior to those negotiated by trade unions is to ensure that they remain union-free. In recent years, however, the prominence of collective bargaining has declined. Collective bargaining is by no means restricted to formal confrontation. Indeed, the mass of negotiations take place continually between shop stewards, supervisors/line man-agers and personnel managers at workplace level, incorporating a wide range of matters concerned with working conditions, health and safety, discipline and grievance cases, and welfare/social concerns. It is an all-pervasive social process that may be overt or covert, and informal or formal (Gospel and Palmer, 1993: 180). Collective bargaining is thus a process that occurs principally – in terms of the time involved and the number of issues dealt with – at workplace level through unwritten deals and custom and practice. Conversely, some of the more important and long-term decisions about pay and working conditions are the sub-ject of infrequent company-wide or multi-employer negotiations.

Collective bargaining is concerned with both *substantive* (on what is determined) and *procedural* issues (on how decisions are made). Many of the blockages in bargaining occur not because of disputes about sub-stantive matters (such as marginal increases in pay) but due to dis-agreements about how employee relations are to be managed in the future – for example, over union derecognition. In short, collective bar-gaining is both an adversarial and a co-operative process, one in which employees not only state their opposition to managerial plans with which they disagree but alternatively put forward suggested improve-ments on management decisions they feel are inadequate. In rare cir-cumstances unions may unilaterally set the rules – the very opposite of management prerogative. This was seen historically with the craft soci-eties, which imposed their own employment rules on employers, often insisting on a specific period of apprenticeship and requiring all new workers to have a union card. It is also evident today in professions, such as lawyers and accountants, whose bodies operate in a similarly restrictive fashion.

The overall distribution of formal collective bargaining can be estimated from the WERS data. This shows that the proportion of employees (in establishments which employ 25 or more people) with recognised unions whose terms and conditions are formally negotiated by collective bargaining fell from 70 per cent of all employees in 1984 to 41 per cent by 1998 (Cully *et al*, 1999: 241–2). Sweeping changes in the political and legal environment in the last 20 years together with changes in sec-toral employment and unemployment have had a major impact on work-place union organisation. The distinctive British system of adversarial collective bargaining is no longer characteristic of the economy as a whole. As Millward *et al* (2000: 234–5) note, 'The system of collective relations, based on the shared values of the legitimacy of represen-tation by independent trade unions and on joint regulation, crumbled ... to such an extent that it no longer represents a dominant model.'

The shape and character of collective bargaining varies considerably between workplaces, particularly in relation to the level at which bar-gaining takes place and the size/structure of the unit of employees who are covered by any agreement. The concept of bargaining level refers to the point(s) at which collective bargaining takes place, and it can range from workplace/section through to establishment, division, company and industry/multi-employer at its most complex. In many cases terms and conditions are the subject of negotiation at more than one level in the hierarchy, as for example with the setting of holiday entitlements at industry level, pension arrangements at the company level, and wages and flexibility issues locally. In other words, bargaining can take place on both a multi- and a single-employer basis, as well as at a range of levels within a multi-establishment organisation.

Since the 1980s managements have rediscovered their prerogative (Sisson and Storey, 2000) and are more prepared to make use of their superior bargaining power. Multi-employer bargaining has been replaced by single-employer bargaining, and now decentralised unit-specific arrangements associated with organisation-based employment systems are more common. In these new systems the role of the union may be marginalised as the employer focuses on direct communication with individual employees and the implementation of HR practices, such as performance-related pay, which are managerially determined. In short, the scope of managerial prerogative has been extended (Tailby and Winchester, 2000; Guest 2001b).

> How are pay and working conditions determined at your organisation (or an organisation of your choice), and has this changed in the last few years? Why has it changed, or why has it not changed? Review your answer after completing this section.

For a large part of the twentieth century, and certainly until the 1950s, multi-employer bargaining was considered to be the norm in the UK, and in some industries there was very little difference between the nationally-negotiated wage rate and an individual's actual pay. Overall, the last 20 years has seen a significant reduction in the extent of multi-employer bargaining – from 60 per cent of workplaces in 1980 to 42 per cent in 1990 and 29 per cent in 1998. Inevitably, this has been influ-enced by pressures from increasingly competitive international product markets, the growth in large multi-divisional corporations, with profit and cost-centre management (Sisson and Storey, 2000: 197), and the fact that trade unions have been less able to resist moves to decentralise negotiations in recent years. Government policies have also provided triggers for the abolition of multi-employer arrangements. This has occurred following the privatisation of major utilities such as water and electricity, or indirectly through the encouragement of local deals which more closely reflect company or plant-specific problems, such as in the ports following the abolition of the National Dock Labour Scheme in the late 1980s. In the public sector, privatisation and contracting-out has shrunk the range of bargaining activities. In other parts of the sector – eg teaching, local government and healthcare – there has been reform and in some parts of the sector pressure to decentralise pay bargaining. Within the private sector as a whole, the decline has been rather more pronounced. Multi-employer agreements have all but disappeared, and pay has been set at enterprise level by managers rather than by joint regulation (Millward *et al*, 2000: 221).

A second trend has seen shifts within organisations away from centralised bargaining arrangements towards a greater emphasis on site and unit-level negotiations. The aim has been to encourage units to take decisions themselves, reflecting devolved responsibility for financial control, although Sisson and Storey (2000: 201) note that such control is often an illusion, because key issues of employment policy may still be decided at high levels in the organisation. Interest in recent years has focused on increasing the width of bargaining units, especially at workplace or company level, and the supposed attractions of single-table bargaining (STB). It is apparent that both management and unions can gain from STB. For the unions, the advent of STB can prevent 'divide-and-rule' tactics on the part of management and, provided the unions have clear objectives, help to develop closer working relationships and reduce the likelihood of inter-union disputes. The rationalisation of unions at establishment level, by which some of the smaller unions (in terms of membership levels at the establishments involved) lose representative rights to larger unions, can also increase the effectiveness of union organisation and cohesiveness on the ground. There is additionally a feeling that STB deals have prevented the concluding of employer-driven single-union arrangements, and they have gained a measure of TUC support.

From industrial democracy to employee involvement

Interest in the subject of employee participation has swung dramatically over the last 30 years. The 1970s model of participation reached its high point with the 1977 Bullock Report on 'Industrial Democracy', which addressed the question of how workers might be represented at board level. This emerged in a period of strong union bargaining power and the Labour government's 'Social Contract'. The Bullock Committee's approach to industrial participation had several distinctive features. It was partly union-initiated, through the Labour Party, and based on collectivist principles that saw trade unions playing a central part in future arrangements. In addition, it was wedded to the general principle of employee rights established on a statutory basis (Ackers *et al*, 1992: 272).

In contrast, the last 20 years have produced a quite different agenda for participation, retitled 'employee involvement' (EI). The context initially was reduced union power under an anti-corporatist Thatcher government, which resisted statutory blueprints and encouraged firms to evolve the arrangements that best suited them. It was an agenda that differed from the one of the 1970s in several ways. First, it was management-initiated, often from outside the industrial relations sphere, and with scant reference to trade unions. Second, EI was individualist, and stressed direct communications with individual employees. Third, it was driven by business criteria concerning economic performance and the 'bottom line', with an emphasis on employee motivation and commitment (Ackers *et al*, 1992: 272). Dutiful compliance and following rules no longer described the 'good worker'. Instead, management demanded employee commitment, working beyond contract, and the exercising of initiative. The notion of high-commitment practices (Pfeffer, 1998) made the case even more forcefully that long-term competitive advantage could only be achieved through people (see Chapter 7).

Unlike notions of industrial democracy, which are rooted in notions of employee rights, EI stemmed from an economic efficiency argument. It is seen to make business sense to involve employees, for a committed workforce is likely to understand better what the organisation is trying

Table 42   The use of 'new' management practices and EI schemes

'New' management practice/ EI scheme	Percentage of workplaces
Most employees work in formally-designated teams	65
Workplace operates a system of team briefing for groups of employees	61
Most non-managerial employees have performance formally appraised	56
Staff attitude survey conducted in the last five years	45
Problem-solving groups (eg quality circles)	42
'Single status' between managers and non-managerial employees	41
Regular meetings of entire workforce	37
Profit-sharing scheme operated for non-managerial employees	30
Workplace-level joint consultative committee	28
Employee share-ownership scheme for non-managerial employees	15
Guaranteed job security or no compulsory redundancies policy	14
Most employees receive minimum of five days' training per year	12
Individual performance-related pay scheme for non-managerial employees	11
Workplace operates a just-in-time system of inventory control	29
Most supervisors trained in employee relations skills	27
Attitudinal test used before making appointments	22

Base: all workplaces with 25 or more employees
Adapted from Cully *et al*, 1998. p10

to do and be more prepared to contribute to its efficient operation. But management decides whether or not employees are to be involved and how they are to be involved. EI in its most limited forms could be characterised as a move away from 'You will do this' to 'This is why you will do this' (Wilkinson *et al*, 1993: 28). There was a sizeable growth in direct EI and communications during the 1980s as managements stepped up their communication with employees as a whole (Millward *et al*, 1992: 175). The 1990 WERS confirmed the growth in EI and communication (Cully *et al*, 1998). Teamworking was practised in 65 per cent of all workplaces, team briefing in 61 per cent, staff attitude surveys in 45 per cent, and problem-solving groups formed in 42 per cent. Regular meetings of the entire workforce occurred in 37 per cent of these workplaces and were more extensive than workplace-level consultative committees (see Table 42). As in all surveys, however, this tells us relatively little about the character of EI as experienced by ordinary employees.

EI takes a number of forms in practice:

- *downward communication* from managers to employees, the principal purpose of which is to inform and 'educate' staff so that they accept management plans – This includes techniques such as team briefing, informal and non-routinised communications between managers and their staff, formal written media such as employee reports, house journals or company newspapers, and videos which are used to convey messages to employees about the organisation's financial performance or to publicise some new managerial initiative. These techniques provide employees with greater amounts of information from managers than most enjoyed previously. In theory, employers gain because employees are 'educated' about the needs of the business and utilise their greater knowledge-base to improve customer service or product quality, so helping to sustain competitive advantage.

- *upward problem-solving*, which is designed to tap into employee knowledge and opinion, either at an individual level or through small groups – The objective of these techniques is to increase the stock of ideas within an organisation, to encourage co-operative relations at work, and to legitimise change. These include quality circles or action teams, suggestion schemes and attitude surveys (Wilkinson, 2001). In theory these schemes offer employees the prospect of greater opportunities to contribute to discussions about work-related issues, and employers the possibility of higher levels of productivity and quality.

- *task participation and teamworking*, in which employees are encouraged or expected to extend the range and type of tasks undertaken at work – As with the previous categories, these are also a form of direct EI of an individualist nature, some of which have their roots in earlier quality-of-working-life experiments in the

1960s and 1970s (Procter and Mueller, 2000). Examples of task participation are horizontal job redesign, job enrichment and teamworking, each of which has figured in a number of chemical and vehicle components companies which operate their production systems on a teamwork and relatively autonomous basis. Task-based participation is probably the most innovative method of EI, in that it is focused on the whole job rather than comprising a relatively small part of an employee's time at work. In addition, unlike team briefing or quality circles, which can be viewed as additional or incidental to working arrangements, this is integral to the work itself.

- *financial involvement*, which encompasses schemes designed to link part of an individual's reward to the success of the unit or enterprise as a whole – The object of much attention since the 1980s, this takes a variety of forms in practice, ranging from profit-sharing and employee share-ownership schemes through to employee share ownership plans (ESOPs) which emerged in Britain in the 1980s (Pendleton, 2000; Wilkinson *et al*, 1994). Financial involvement shares similar objectives to the techniques already discussed but also operates under an assumption that employees with a financial stake in the overall success of the unit/enterprise are more likely to work harder for its ultimate success.

EI schemes can thus be seen as a rejection of the classical school of management which emphasised a strict division of labour, with workers as 'machine-minders', carrying out fragmented and repetitive jobs (Wilkinson, 1998). They imply a neo-unitarist win-win approach, which is moralistic in tone, and which is 'represented as squaring the circle of organisational needs for high levels of employee performance and employees' demands for autonomy and self-expression in work' (Claydon and Doyle, 1996: 13). There is a danger that these programmes are viewed solely in a positive and upbeat manner, so ignoring the more contested and mundane nature of much participation. For example, rather than leading to autonomy and self-management, they may merely produce greater work intensification, increased stress levels, and redundancies (Wilkinson, 2001). There is a fear that employers are exchanging strong union-centred forms of participation for EI initiatives that are 'weak on power'. As one HR manager noted in a recent study (Marchington *et al*, 2001: 24), 'There are plenty of vehicles for staff to have a voice, but the question is whether [the] voice is being heard and whether action is being taken as a result of this. And that's debatable.'

What forms of employee involvement operate at your organisation? What purpose is served by each form of EI, and could its practice be improved?

The rise of EI has coincided with the decline of indirect, representative participation such as joint consultative committees (JCCs). By 1998, JCCs were to be found in under a third of all workplaces, being especially prevalent in the public service sector (Millward *et al*, 2000: 109). Unlike the methods of direct EI discussed in the previous section, JCCs are built upon the notion of indirect participation and worker representation in joint management–employee meetings. The scope of joint consultation is typically wider than collective bargaining – and may, for instance, include financial matters – although the issues discussed are not formally negotiated. For some, they represent a diluted form of collective bargaining, and the shift in interest towards consultation reflects a decline in collectivism. However, JCCs can take a number of forms, often contrasting sharply with each other in terms of their objectives, structures and processes (Marchington, 1994: 669–72). Some researchers suggest that joint consultation has been revitalised in order to cover issues traditionally dealt with through collective bargaining, and to involve employee representatives more closely with management issues in order to convince them of the 'logic' of their decisions. Others have argued that the committees have largely been concerned with trivia and are thus marginal to the employee relations processes of the organisation. Consequently, in some organisations JCCs can act as a safety-valve (ie an alternative to industrial action) through which to address more deep-seated employee grievances, while in others they can be used as a device to hinder the recognition of trade unions or to undermine union activities in highly unionised workplaces. The relationship between collective bargaining and joint consultation in unionised workplaces can be a source of tension, particularly if management is trying to edge out the unions and there has been a failure to engage in meaningful consultations.

> Do JCCs exist in your organisation? If so, what forms do they take, and are they successful? How could they be improved? If there are no JCCs, what mechanisms are in place to consult with the workforce? Would a JCC be useful? Why/why not?

Employee voice and social partnership

Recent research (Marchington *et al*, 2001) found 'voice'   the term used by employers as an alternative to 'consultation', 'communication' or 'say' – to describe a forum of two-way dialogue. This enabled staff to influence events at work and bring together collective and individual structures. Human resource managers typically play an important role in the choices made about employee voice. Their expertise may be brought to bear in identifying the options available, forming alliances with line managers and devising strategies for implementation. In terms of the influences that shape managerial choice, there was generally a broad mix of factors. For some managers the idea of rational choice was often related to satisfying employee expectations, particularly when faced with tight labour markets. Other respondents equated choice with their own understanding of corporate and organisational objectives. In the smaller and family-run enterprises this related to the personal styles and characteristics of owner-managers. A further group of managers made the point that in reality they had no choice, either because employees 'demanded a say' or due to market pressures and new legislative requirements. On the whole, however, management decides whether or not workers have a voice, and it is managers rather than employees who decide what mechanisms to utilise.

Different external influences shaped management choice, evident across both large and small as well as single- and multi-site organisations. Legislation for trade union recognition or the requirement to establish a European Works Council is one pressure, meaning that choices are made merely to comply with new or forthcoming legislation. However, in a broader context, the research found that external influences also open up new options for managers, and regulation seemed to encourage more creative managerial thinking about the choices available. There were obstacles to voice as well, as the box below shows.

Barriers to employee voice

CIPD research (Marchington *et al*, 2001) identified three particular barriers to employee voice – a partial lack of employee enthusiasm, an absence of necessary skills, and issues concerning line managers. In a few of the case studies employees lacked enthusiasm to participate in voice arrangements. At some of the larger and multi-site organisations, managers noted that although employees demanded a greater say, it was not always forthcoming in practice. At Airflight, management had to work hard to get representatives involved in the employee consultative forum, and at Midbank some staff council seats were unfilled. There was also an issue of low employee response rates in some organisations to surveys that made it difficult to interpret employee voice. Of course, much depends on managerial support for voice and the range of issues open to employees. An apparent lack of employee interest in voice may thus have to do with the specific mechanisms in place rather than with a generalised disinterest in voice *per se*.

There was evidence that some managers lacked the necessary skills to implement and manage employee voice programmes, and this seems a more important barrier than a lack of employee enthusiasm. The view was expressed, mainly among larger and multi-site establishments, that voice should be built up gradually, with the confidence and skills of individuals found lacking on occasions.

Related to the issue of available skills and competencies is the role of middle managers. In several organisations support for employee voice from the top was critical. In a majority of cases, middle managers acted as a blockage either through choice or ignorance. In several organisations line managers viewed HR issues as secondary to operational matters. However, unlike earlier studies on employee involvement, this report identifies a major cultural change over time. The generation of 'cops' and 'giving orders' had much diminished, and the departure of the old guard through restructuring and redundancy was a feature at several sites. It was also apparent that the use of new technology and electronic forms of employee voice allowed employers to bypass middle managers more easily.

Source: Marchington M., Wilkinson A., Ackers P. and Dundon A. *Management Choice and Employee Voice*. London, CIPD. 2001

The research by Marchington *et al* (2001) on employee voice also found that it could have a positive impact, in three general ways. The first is valuing employee contributions. This might lead to improved employee attitudes and behaviours, loyalty, commitment and co-operative relations. The second impact relates to improved performance, including productivity and individual performance, lower absenteeism and (in a few cases) new business arising from employee voice. The final impact relates to improved managerial systems. This incorporates the managerial benefits from tapping into employee ideas, the informative and educational role of voice along with improved relations with recognised trade unions.

Towards social partnership?

If EI looks as if it is here to stay, there are signs that – under New Labour – it has been joined by a revival of representative participation. The public policy context of employee participation has changed markedly in recent years with the concept of social partnership – a term rarely used in the 1980s (see Ackers and Payne, 1998; Brown, 2000; Tailby and Winchester, 2000). The European Union concept of social dialogue centres on partnership between employers and employees, through representative bodies, notably trade unions and works councils. It also advocates participation as an extension of employee citizenship rights and not just business expedience.

An important contemporary issue in this area is the *European Works Council* (EWC) *Directive*. The centralist philosophy underpinning this initiative is in sharp contrast to the voluntarist approach promulgated by successive Conservative governments since the early 1980s. Since Britain entered the EU in the early 1970s there have been a number of attempts to create a more coherent and uniform 'social' framework, and to harmonise certain standards of employment and company law across the member states (see Chapter 3). More recently, further attempts have been made to harmonise policies in the areas of information, consultation and participation.

The EWC Directive requires employers to set up an EWC or equivalent information and consultation procedure if they have at least 1,000 employees within the states covered by the Directive (including at least 150 employees in at least two of these countries). There is scope for the negotiation of customised agreements, but in the event of failure to agree, a standard package will apply. In broad terms this provides a template for the composition of the EWC and its remit, as well as a stipulation that an annual meeting should take place. The EWC is informed and consulted about the enterprise's progress and prospects in a number of areas, including the broad financial and employment situation, as well as trends in employment and any substantial changes in working methods.

The Directive seeks to ensure that employees in large and medium-sized multi-national organisations are informed and consulted about the organisations in which they work. Some see this Directive as one of the most far-reaching and important developments in European industrial relations, whereas others regard it as far too weak to make any substantial difference. On the positive side, EWCs have been seen as an opportunity for management to communicate corporate strategy, to facilitate discussion of change, to encourage international contact, to facilitate employee identification with the company, to build a 'European' culture and to enhance management-union partnerships. Trade unions and employee representatives in turn gain access to useful company information to facilitate collective bargaining (Cressey, 1998). Trade union criticisms have centred on the limited capacity of EWCs to effectively influence managerial prerogative in multi-national companies. Some research reports employers paying lip-service to their EWCs – for example, announcing major plant closures within days of an EWC meeting at which there was no discussion of such issues (Stirling and Fitzgerald, 2001). Criticism from employers have been that EWCs have not added any value to their pre-existing employee involvement practices but have merely added another layer to the communications process. New EWCs in particular face a number of challenges to their effectiveness. They are being introduced in a very competitive and fast-moving marketplace with organisational restructuring involving mergers, acquisitions, joint ventures and divestments giving rise to problems of continuity for EWCs. EWC delegates also face difficulties in setting up effective communications and reporting-back systems to inform those whom they represent about issues that arise in discussions (Redman, 2002: 81–2).

> Do you think that employers have much to fear from works councils?
> What impact would an EWC have on your organisation or one with
> which you are familiar?

An increasing number of organisations have been responding to the
new public policy framework, including Welsh Water, Blue Circle, Tesco,
and Legal and General who have struck voluntary partnership deals
with trade unions. Others, like the non-union Marks & Spencer, have
had to accept EWCs. British Airways, following the 1997 industrial dispute, also issued a statement about the principles of partnership. By
and large these agreements balance the EI agenda, with a greater
emphasis on employment security and employee representation
through consultative committees and trade unions. The price for the
latter is to eschew adversarial bargaining and reactive conflict for consultation and proactive co-operation, following the trade union style of
Scandinavia and Germany. The TUC and the IPA have promoted a more
positive-sum relationship between trade unions and management which
transcends 'arms-length adversarialism' and connects representative
and direct forms of participation (Ackers and Wilkinson, 2000). A practical manifestation of this is the TUC's positive attitude to EWCs,
despite their potentially non-union character (see Monks, 1998). Finally,
according to work by Wood and Fenton O'Creevy (1999: 44), multinationals which relied *only* on direct EI involved their employees less
than those prepared to also consult or negotiate. Although the union
was the channel for only a limited number of issues, the overall level of
involvement was still higher on average in unionised operations. This
may be because unions put managers under pressure to inform and
consult via other channels or because management involves staff in
other channels in order to counter or bypass the union. A third possibility is that managements which are favourably inclined towards unions
are more likely to be well-disposed to other forms of EI as well. In any
case, employees enjoyed more genuine participation when trade unions
were present. Whether partnership will provide the way forward
remains to be seen. Bacon (2001: 204) takes a cautious view, noting
that 'there is little evidence that employers are able to offer the job
security guarantees that unions seek, or that trade unions are able to
prevent managers unilaterally imposing changes in work organisation'.

CASE STUDY: The Co-operative Bank

The Co-operative Bank is a clearing bank with regional roots employing around 4,000 staff in over 100 locations in the UK. Like most financial institutions, the company provides HR support from a centralised base, although many HR processes, in respect of the management of staff, have been devolved to line managers. New performance management tools have recently been agreed with the union for the call centres which provide better terms and conditions, and have resulted in reduced staff turnover, increased productivity and improved career progression.

A single union has sole negotiating rights for staff, and membership is well over 70 per cent. Union presence in the workplace is in the form of local representatives and there is also a full-time seconded representative. National joint partnership meetings are held monthly, supported by local and departmental partnership forums between the union and management representatives. These local forums concentrate on jointly resolving local business-related matters without the need to progress these to national level. This enables the national partnership team to concentrate on wider issues. A further consultation forum is the company's Staff Council. This enables elected representatives from all areas of the business to meet with senior managers to discuss bank-wide business-related matters. This forum is separate from the union partnership meetings.

The Co-operative Bank recently won a *Sunday Times* award for its commitment to best-practice HRM and employee involvement. Voice has been given much greater emphasis since the 1980s as the bank has changed its approach to managing staff. A number of employee involvement activities were driven from the centre in the 1980s, including quality circles and TQM. Communication with staff is now provided through various staff and business briefings. All these have been designed as part of the human resource strategy to explain to staff the changes that are taking place within the organisation and to raise commercial awareness while at the same time getting staff to appreciate the importance of internal customers. A further form of communication is the well-established quarterly company newspaper, to which staff are encouraged to contribute. Attitude surveys, focus groups and suggestion schemes – one member of staff recently received £25,000 – are also regular features. The Co-operative Bank's partnership approach commits it to measuring and reporting on issues that staff themselves identify as important.

Adapted from Marchington M., Wilkinson A., Ackers P. and Dundon A. *Management Choice and Employee Voice*. London, CIPD. 2001

CONCLUSION

It is important to reiterate that employee relations, like all aspects of HR, are characterised by conflict and co-operation. At certain times, and in certain workplaces, one of these assumes predominance. This sometimes gives the misguided impression that employee relations at one site or at one point in time are solely about conflict, whereas at other establishments or times they are seen only in terms of co-operation. Furthermore, just because conflict is not expressed overtly, this does not mean that it is absent, and neither can it be assumed that the workplace is a haven of consensus.

It would appear that employee relations are becoming increasingly bifurcated, not so much between union and non-union organisations, but within each of these broad categories. Given the degree to which labour markets have been deregulated over the last 20 years, employers now have greater flexibility in choosing appropriate styles and structures for managing employee relations, as well as a greater opportunity to integrate people management strategies with those affecting the business as a whole. To do this effectively, however, requires employers to embrace a more strategic and externally-focused approach to the management of employee relations, to be aware of the techniques which are adopted by other employers, and to disregard the latest fads and fashions if these are inappropriate for their own workplace. How many do this, of course, is another question.

It should be clear from this chapter that the 'rules' of employee relations can be made and influenced in many ways. Although most analyses have focused on collective bargaining as the main rule-making institution, it must not be forgotten that some rules are made unilaterally by managements. The various WERS surveys clearly chart the decline in the collective institutions of joint regulation (Cully *et al*, 1999: 246). However, these do not appear to have been replaced by any single new model of employee relations, but rather by alternative approaches in different workplaces in different parts of the country.

Despite the decline in union influence, Cully *et al* (1999: 296) note that 'an engagement with a union presence is still part of the work experience for two out of three employees, even if only half that number are actually union members'. However, the representation gap identified by Towers (1997) has certainly increased since 1990. As Cully *et al* (1999: 297) note, there was an enormous gap between the percentage of workplace management who said they consulted employees about changes at the workplace (70 per cent) and the percentage of employees who agree with them (30 per cent). Millward *et al* (2000: 135) point out that while employees may not have lost their 'voice', the notion of *voice* had changed significantly. There has been a major shift from channels involving representatives – usually able to call upon the resources of independent trade unions – to channels where managers communicate directly with employees as and when they see fit. But they also note that:

> the combined presence of a recognised trade union and union representation on a formal consultative committee was the only formulation to be independently associated with employees' perceptions of fair treatment by managers.

In this chapter we have sought to emphasise that patterns of collective bargaining vary greatly between workplaces and between organisations, and that HR managers are able to exercise some degree of choice and influence over their eventual shape. In order to do this, however, HR practitioners must be aware of the different types of bargaining arrangement that exist, and their suitability for particular organisational contexts. It is important not to be seduced by the latest fads and fashions but to make informed decisions about which bargaining levels and units are most appropriate for each employment situation. Similar options are also available for the mix of EI arrangements which might 'fit' with the needs of employers as well.

Useful reading

BACON N. 'Employee relations', in T. Redman and A. Wilkinson (eds), *Contemporary Human Resource Management*, FT/Pearson. 2001.

BLYTON P. *and* TURNBULL P. *The Dynamics of Employee Relations*. 2nd edition. London, Macmillan. 1998.

CRESSEY P. 'European works councils in practice', *Human Resource Management Journal*, Vol. 8, No.1, 1998. pp67–79.

CULLY M., WOODLAND S., O'REILLY A., DIX G., MILLWARD N., BRYSON A. and FORTH, J. *The 1998 Workplace Employee Relations Survey: First findings*, London, Department of Trade and Industry. 1998.

EWING K. 'Industrial relations and labour law', in P. Ackers and A. Wilkinson (eds), *Reworking Industrial Relations*, Oxford, OUP. 2002.

GENNARD J. *and* JUDGE G. *Employee Relations*. 3rd edition. London, CIPD. 2002.

MARCHINGTON M., WILKINSON A., ACKERS P. *and* DUNDON A. *Management Choice and Employee Voice*. London, CIPD. 2001.

MARGALIS A. 'Spirited response', *People Management*, 13th September 2001. pp32–38.

TAILBY S. *and* WINCHESTER D. 'Management and trade unions: towards Social Partnership', in S. Bach and K. Sisson (eds) *Personnel Management*. 3rd edition. Oxford, Blackwell. 2000.

WILKINSON A. 'Empowerment' in T. Redman and A. Wilkinson, *Contemporary Human Resource Management*. London, FT/Pitman. 2001.

CHAPTER

15 • Using Employee Relations Procedures to Resolve Differences and Engender Commitment

CHAPTER OBJECTIVES

By the end of the chapter, readers should be able to:

- devise procedures that help to achieve fairness and consistency at work

- advise line managers on how to handle disciplinary and grievance cases

- contribute to the collective bargaining process.

In addition readers should understand and be able to explain:

- the value of procedures in helping to create a positive psychological contract

- the principal components of, and differences between, disciplinary and grievance procedures

- the way in which HR specialists may provide support for line managers in operating procedures.

Introduction

Policies and procedures are defined as 'formal, conscious statements' that support organisational goals. They are the official way companies disseminate their policies as the *leitmotif* of acceptable practice (Storey and Sisson, 1993). However, there is a difference between a 'policy' and a 'procedure'. As Dundon (2002c: 196–7) notes:

Policies are written documents that outline defined rules, obligations and expectations for managers and employees. Typically, policy statements cover areas such as discipline, grievance, redundancy, reward, recruitment or promotion. The policy may be a statement of intent, such as 'it is the policy of this company to promote and reward high achievers'.

Procedures outline the details of how to enact a policy. For example, having a policy of 'rewarding high achievers' would require some guidance on how managers implement the policy, such as the criteria for promotion or how much they can reward an individual. Similarly, a discipline procedure would outline possible sanctions, areas of conduct and so on. 🔳🔳

The scope and depth of HR policies and procedures can be used as a gauge of management style. The absence of policies and procedures may indicate an informal managerial approach, whereas very detailed policies and procedures might point to a formalised managerial style. Procedures are often seen as a product of the employee relations environment of the 1960s and 1970s in which there was a more explicit struggle for control at the workplace. This had two principal effects. First, it produced the need for clear procedures so that all employees were aware of works rules and the action that could be taken against them if those rules were flouted. Second, it made for greater clarity and consistency in management action.

In contrast, the environment today is one in which trade unions are weaker and managers have greater freedom to avoid some of the so-called 'bureaucratic' rules that supposedly constrained their ability to manage. Moreover, as the principal activities of many HR practitioners have shifted away from employee relations to employee development, employee resourcing and employee reward, the main guides to management action are seen as business need, flexibility and commitment, rather than adherence to rules and procedures (Storey, 2001). Previous appeals to consistency, compromise and regulations have been displaced by a new language of competitiveness, customers and commitment. Storey's classic research (1992: 178) highlighted the following criticisms of procedures.

> *From the hard side of [HRM] comes the criticism that the long-drawn-out appeals and referrals are simply inappropriate in a fiercely competitive and fast-changing climate. From the soft side ... the regulator's arguments about due process and about honouring agreements and observing custom and practice are anathema.*

However, this interpretation contains a number of problems. It is by no means obvious that an emphasis on rules and procedures is outdated. Indeed, a belief in consistency and fairness is central to gaining the commitment of employees in any organisation (Clark, 1993). Moreover, what may appear as flexibility to managers may seem unfair and arbitrary treatment to an employee. As Renwick and Gennard (2001: 168) observe, issues to do with rights and responsibilities of employer and employees are:

> *a logical consequence of the employment relationship itself. Not all the interests of both employers and employees necessarily coincide, and inappropriate actions and transgressions on either side raise the issue of the satisfactory resolution of those differences within the parameters of both the organisational context and the law. These interests are expressed in both parties' rights and responsibilities to each other in legal contracts of employment.*

Even the new ideas of HRM do not necessarily mean the absence of procedures. For example, recruitment, selection, training and appraisal are much more formalised now than in previous eras. As Torrington (1998: 501) notes:

> *The formality of procedure provides a framework which avoids the risk of inconsistent ad hoc decisions and the employee knows at the outset how the matter will be handled. The key features of procedure are fairness, facilities for representation, procedural steps and management rules.*

This chapter examines the role of procedures in the management of human resources, explains the functions which procedures serve, and provides guidance on how to assess them. It discusses how procedures are designed and how they operate in practice.

The nature and extent of procedures

A government social survey in 1969 found that only 8 per cent of establishments operated a formal disciplinary and dismissal procedure. The Donovan Commission (1968: 30) took up the cause of procedural reform, wanting 'procedures which are clear where the present procedures are vague, comprehensive where the present procedures are fragmented, speedy where the present procedures are protracted, and effective where the present procedures are fruitless'. It was felt that a lack of proper procedures was a major cause of industrial disputes. Consequently, procedures – if followed – could stabilise important areas of employee relations within the firm and could be beneficial to them (Scott *et al*, 1989: 97; Dundon and Wilkinson, 2002).

There is evidence that procedural reform has taken place, at least formally. 'The 1970s saw a massive spread of formal disciplinary and dismissal procedures across British industry and commerce,' so that by the 1980s they had become 'almost universal in all but the smallest workplaces' (Millward *et al*, 1992: 212). Over 90 per cent of workplaces have disciplinary and grievance procedures. Today, even in smaller workplaces (25–49 employees), 88 per cent have a disciplinary procedure and 87 per cent have a grievance procedure (Cully *et al*, 1998: 14). Part of this growth has been caused by the increasing involvement of the law (see Chapter 3), notably the Industrial Relations Act 1971, which introduced the notion of unfair dismissal as a landmark. Since then there has been considerable formalisation, largely due to the growth in cases being taken to employment tribunals. Earnshaw *et al* (1998: 549) note that research in the 1970s and 1980s reported considerable employer hostility to procedures among small business owners. However, this was much less apparent by the end of the 1990s. They conclude that the unfair dismissal legislation – now in operation for over 25 years – as well as the emphasis given by tribunals to procedural matters have helped bring about attitudinal change. There are now frequent references made to the benefits such procedures have for managers (such as clarifying authority, indicating processes to be followed), which suggests that they may have acquired greater managerial acceptance than at the time of earlier research.

A procedure agreement can be defined (Hawkins, 1979: 132) as:

> *a set of rules whose purpose is to influence the behaviour of management, employees and trade union representatives in a defined situation. The rules are, in effect, an agreed code of voluntary restraints on the use of power.*

Procedures can be adopted in a number of different areas:

- *recognition* – specifying the rights of unions to recruit, organise and represent defined groups of staff in the workplace. Details may be included covering bargaining units and the facilities for, and duties of, shop stewards.

- *disputes* – indicating the route to be followed in the event of a collective or departmental issue, including reference to agreements between employers' organisations and trade unions

- *grievance* – indicating what is to be done in the event of an individual issue or complaint

- *disciplinary* – setting the standards of conduct expected from employees, specifying what is to be done following behaviour or conduct deemed unsatisfactory

- *redundancy* – specifying the organisation's approach to consultation about redundancy, methods of selection, compensation and assistance in finding other employment

- *equal opportunities* – outlining the organisation's commitment to, and provision of, equal opportunities regardless of gender, race or disability (see Chapter 6).

Of course, this list is not exhaustive but merely indicative of the most common procedure agreements to be found in organisations (see also Farnham, 2000: 76–81). The main objective of any procedure is to establish an agreed set of rules so as to channel any discussion or discontent through the appropriate mechanisms for its resolution. However, it is important to remember what procedures *cannot* do. Thomson and Murray (1976: 84) note that a procedure:

> *cannot solve the underlying causes of conflict ... it is very limited in the extent to which it can institutionalise conflict if there is not a basic consensus about the legitimacy of the roles of the parties. It cannot itself make up for deficiencies in the structure of the relationship.*

> Write down three procedures operating at your workplace and explain their purpose. How successful are they in meeting their purpose?

In relation to equal opportunities, the WERS data (Cully *et al*, 1998: 13) is enlightening:

> *One way in which employers may strive to give practical effect to these laws is by establishing policies and practices designed to combat discrimination and promote equal treatment.*

Some two thirds of workplaces (64 per cent) are covered by formal written equal opportunities policies which address equality of treatment or discrimination. The areas covered by such policies include sex (98 per cent), race (98 per cent) and disability (93 per cent), religion (84 per cent), marital status (73 per cent) and age (67 per cent). Of the workplaces without a formal written policy half claimed that it was not written down or that they were aiming to be an equal opportunity employer. In a third of workplaces without a policy, managers saw them as unnecessary. A further 2 per cent said that they did not need a policy because their workplace employed few or no people from disadvantaged groups (Cully *et al*, 1998)!

There is also a relationship with size. Workplaces without a policy were predominantly small: larger units increase the complexity of the management task. Cully *et al* (1998: 14) again:

> *The more complex the management task, the greater the need for rules and procedures to achieve consistency of behaviour on the part of individual managers. The greater the need for rules and procedures, the greater the need for workers and workers' representatives to accept this legitimacy.*

In Table 43, Cully *et al* compare practices employed at workplaces with and without a policy. It is clear that those workplaces with a formal equal opportunities policy are much more likely to have a range of procedures and practices to support equal treatment.

Table 43   Equal treatment practices

Organisational practice	Percentage of workplaces with a formal equal opportunities policy	no equal opportunities policy
Keeping employee records with ethnic origin identified	48	13
Collecting statistics on posts held by men and women	43	13
Monitoring promotions by gender and ethnicity	23	2
Reviewing selection procedures to identify indirect discrimination	35	5
Reviewing the relative pay rates of different groups	17	15
Making adjustments to accommodate disabled employees	42	16
None of these	27	67

Base: all workplaces with 25 or more employees
Source: Cully M., Woodland S., O'Reilly A., Dix G., Millward N., Bryson A. and Forth, J. *The 1998 Workplace Employee Relations Survey: First findings*. London, Department of Trade and Industry, 1998. p13

The case for procedures in employee relations

There are a number of reasons why employers implement employee relations procedures in the area of employee relations. These are:

- They help to clarify the relationship between the two parties, and recognise explicitly the right of employees to raise grievances. This helps to focus conflict within agreed mechanisms and facilitates its resolution. In short, it can create a framework for good employee relations.

- They provide a mechanism for resolution by identifying the individuals or post-holders to whom the issue should be taken initially, and by specifying the route to be followed should there be a failure to agree at that level.

- They act as a safety-valve and provide time within which to assess the issue that has been raised. They can consequently 'take the heat out of the situation' by providing time to reflect.

- They help to ensure greater consistency within the organisation. They can reduce reliance on word-of-mouth or custom and practice, and minimise arbitrary treatment.

- They lead to more systematic record-keeping, and consequently to improved management control and information systems.

- If written down and applied appropriately, and if they meet the criteria of natural justice, they are important in employment tribunal cases.

● The process of drawing up procedures involves both parties working together to decide on the agreed mechanisms. Thereafter, joint ownership of an agreed procedure may promote a willingness to make it work.

As with all lists, this one must be read with caution, for the potential advantages may not operate in all situations and at all times. It is also likely that different levels of management have conflicting perspectives on the need for operating such procedures. For example, line managers may regard procedures as little more than red tape and bureaucracy, seeing all procedures as detracting from their main role of production or service. Equally, they may feel that the disciplinary process is long-winded – for example, by taking too much time to get rid of unsatisfactory employees. It is up to senior managers, and especially HR professionals, to train line managers in how to use procedures and explain their value. For instance, it can be stressed that arbitrary or hasty action can lead to unfair dismissal claims, and damages existing notions of the psychological contract in the organisation.

For procedure agreements to be of value, the parties have to be willing to use them rather than settling their differences through other means (such as strike action) before procedures have been exhausted. If, for example, managers continually flout the spirit of a procedure (perhaps by unilateral changes to working practices), it would not be a surprise if union representatives then adopted a similar attitude. In short, if procedures are to be successful they require a degree of normative agreement as to their utility. In general terms, procedures have to reflect current practice. If the process of grievance resolution is vastly different from the formal requirements, it is likely that people will ignore procedures and try to resolve issues in an *ad hoc* and arbitrary manner. Because of this it is not surprising that the language of procedures tends to be broad and general, and the duties and obligations that are placed on the parties remain imprecise.

There are two main criteria for assessing procedural adequacy: acceptability and appropriateness (Marsh and McCarthy, 1968: 3). Firstly, for a procedure to operate effectively it must be broadly *acceptable* to all parties. Clearly, it is unlikely to operate to the complete satisfaction of each party since there may well be differing expectations. For example, managers may be more interested in 'the consistency of decisions' and for the procedures to filter out 'local' matters so enabling the more important issues to move upwards. However, unions and employees may desire speedy resolutions to problems as well as the opportunity to participate in the operation of procedures. Secondly, a procedure has to be *appropriate* to the structure of the industry and group within which it operates, and has to be related to the levels of decision-making within such a group. So it may not be sensible for organisations always to impose a uniform procedure on departments or subsidiaries if these are in a wide range of differing industrial contexts. Indeed, it may well be that in such circumstances – where the procedure is perceived to be inappropriate within a particular context – the procedure itself becomes a cause of conflict.

Ultimately, however, the procedure is not an end in itself, and there may be times when it is sensible to short-circuit the procedure to sort out a pressing problem. For example, some stages may be missed out or employee representatives may be brought in even before line managers are formally involved in resolving grievances. Similarly, procedures might be avoided altogether, or trade union or employers' association officials may be consulted at an early stage.

Although procedures reflect circumstances that are appropriate for different organisations and workplaces, they retain a remarkable similarity in terms of the main components. There are three points to be made here about procedures, with reference to the spirit in which they are introduced, the role of the HR function, and third-party involvement.

The preamble and 'spirit' behind agreements

Most procedures contain an introduction or preamble outlining the principles behind the scheme and the spirit in which it is to operate. For example, some refer to the agreement being in the mutual interests of both parties while others emphasise the need for a speedy resolution of differences. Some procedures make specific reference to the stage at which industrial action is allowed, and it is common to state that neither party should invoke sanctions prior to the exhaustion of procedures. Although such provisions are not legally binding, the clause is in effect seen as a gentleman's agreement. Management often accepts a mutual obligation to process issues through the relevant procedure as speedily as possible, with time-limits specified to ensure that issues do not get bogged down and slow the resolution of the problem or grievance. The main aim behind the inclusion of a time-limit is to demonstrate the employer's commitment to speedy resolution after allowing the heat to be taken out of the situation. Having said that, time-limits can also be used as a stalling device by management.

The role of the HR function

HR specialists are often seen as the guardians or custodians of procedures. Grievances and disputes are usually seen as a line management responsibility but with personnel specialists available to provide advice and assistance when required. In that the HR function may have been instrumental in designing the procedures, it usually has an influence over arrangements whether or not it has been formally involved at each stage.

> What is the division of responsibility between line managers and HR specialists in relation to disciplinary practice and procedures in your organisation? How well does this work – and what could be improved, if anything?

It may be important that HR specialists are involved at an early stage if line managers lack human resource and legal skills. However, if line managers see HR only as providing information or interpreting procedures, this may not happen. In the light of this, HR specialists must ensure that they have a good idea of what is happening at ground level, as well as understanding the legislation and the customs and practices of a particular workplace. Where this is lacking, they may be excluded from decision-making and relegated to a back-seat role, so that their involvement in issues of grievance or conflict resolution is sought after rather than before the conflict has arisen. Their contribution to organisational effectiveness may then be perceived as limited. As we saw in Chapter 9, a common criticism of the HR function is that it 'always passes the buck' and is 'out of touch with reality' in the workplace. Consequently it is important that HR specialists have good relationships with line managers and that lines of responsibility are clear (Renwick and Gennard, 2001).

The role of external third-party involvement

Some procedures provide an automatic role for third-party intervention from the Advisory, Conciliation and Arbitration Service (ACAS), whereas others may be tied to an agreement between employers' organisations and trade unions. Yet others make use of an independent arbitrator on an *ad hoc* basis. Intervention by a third party can be in one of three forms: conciliation, mediation or arbitration. With conciliation and mediation, assistance is provided when the parties have reached an impasse but the parties themselves must resolve the issue. With conciliation, the third party must confine itself to facilitating discussion, whereas in mediation it can actually come up with specific recommendations. Arbitration involves the third party (such as ACAS) coming up with a decision to resolve the issue. It ought to be noted that ACAS should not be used as a substitute for the establishment of joint union–management procedures for dispute resolution because this allows the parties to avoid taking responsibility, and employee relations can be damaged if commitment to agreed procedures withers away.

Disciplinary procedures

We have already noted that the concept of unfair dismissal was first introduced by the Industrial Relations Act 1971 – amended subsequently in the Employment Protection (Consolidation) Act 1978 (EPCA) and the Employment Rights Act (ERA) 1996. The ERA 1996 obliges employers to ensure that the principal statement of employment conditions makes reference to rules, disciplinary and appeals procedures (Farnham, 2000: 421). The ACAS Code of Practice (ACAS, 2000: 6) states that:

disciplinary procedures should not be viewed primarily as a means of imposing sanctions. Rather they should be seen as a way of helping and encouraging improvement amongst employees whose conduct or standard of work is unsatisfactory.

Minor misconduct is usually dealt with by informal warnings – so being five minutes late, for example, is very unlikely to lead to dismissal. Clearly, actions must be appropriate to the circumstances. Managers should not look simply to punish employees but to counsel them, especially over inadequate performance. If performance is not up to standard, management should investigate the reasons rather than just deal with the 'offence'. Employee performance may vary for reasons other than employee laziness or ineptitude. Lack of training, or problems at home must be considered, and employees should be supported to improve rather than simply punished. As we saw in Chapter 11, counselling should be seen as a positive rather than punitive action.

Where employees feel that they have been dismissed unfairly, they can refer the case to an employment tribunal (provided that they have one year's continuous service) which determines whether or not the dismissal is fair or unfair. There are five potentially 'fair' reasons for dismissal within the Act:

- lack of capability (including health or qualifications) for performing work of the kind the employee was employed to do – the Disability Discrimination Act requires employers to make 'reasonable' adjustments to employment arrangements (Gennard and Judge, 1999: 268–9)

- misconduct

- redundancy

- duty or restriction imposed under or by a legal enactment

- some other substantial reason of a kind to justify the dismissal (eg reorganisation of business).

Once the substantive case has been established, the question of whether the dismissal was fair or unfair can be determined, having regard to the reason given by the employer. Fairness depends on whether in the circumstances – which include the company's size and administrative resources – the employer acted reasonably.

No question of 'reasonableness' arises, and no qualifying period is required, if dismissal is for an automatically unfair reason such as:

- pregnancy and/or maternity

- trade union involvement

- whistle-blowing (Public Interest Disclosure Act, 1998)

- asserting a statutory right

- raising health and safety issues

- working in contravention of the Working Time Regulations 1998.

Although the legislation provides for unfairly dismissed employees to be reinstated or re-engaged, in practice they tend to be awarded compensation. This normally comprises a basic award of up to £6,300 and a compensatory award of up to £50,000, although where dismissal is for whistle-blowing or raising health and safety issues, the compensatory award has no ceiling (Earnshaw, 2002: 262–3).

The ACAS Code of Practice first appeared in 1977 and was revised in 2000. Although the code in itself is not binding, in the absence of other procedures, or despite the existence of poorly-designed ones, it can be admissible in evidence to an employment tribunal that is attempting to determine the fairness of the dismissal. It recommends that disciplinary procedures should:

- be in writing

- specify to whom they apply

- provide for matters to be dealt with quickly

- indicate the disciplinary actions that may be taken

- specify the levels of management which have the authority to take the various forms of disciplinary action, ensuring that immediate superiors do not normally have the power to dismiss without reference to senior management

- provide for individuals to be informed of the complaints against them and to be given an opportunity to state their case before decisions are reached

- give individuals the right to be accompanied by a trade union representative or by a fellow employee

- ensure that, except for gross misconduct, no employees are dismissed for a first breach of discipline

- ensure that disciplinary action is not taken until the case has been carefully investigated

- ensure that individuals are given an explanation for any penalty imposed

- provide a right of appeal and specify the procedure.

In addition, disciplinary procedures should:

- apply to all employees, irrespective of their length of service

- be non-discriminatory and applied irrespective of sex, marital status or race

- ensure that any period of suspension for investigation is with pay, and specify how pay is to be calculated during such a period (if, exceptionally, suspension is to be without pay, this should be provided for in the contract of employment)

- ensure that where the facts are in dispute, no disciplinary penalty is imposed until the case has been carefully investigated and it is concluded on the balance of probability that the employee committed the act in question.

Think of an attempt at disciplinary action by an employer that went wrong, and explain how it occurred. What could have been done to stop it going wrong?

It should also be remembered that indiscipline at work can have wider ramifications for the management of employee relations, for dismissal and other disciplinary measures can be a cause of strike action. It is important to appreciate that discipline at work also involves self-discipline and peer discipline as well as managerial discipline, and that the first two have been given greater attention in recent years (Edwards 2000; Dunn and Wilkinson, 2002).

The disciplinary procedure at Komatsu

1. General
It is mutually agreed by the Company and Union that management have a positive role in encouraging and ensuring that all employees perform responsibly and effectively at work. The process detailed below is designed to make the individual employee aware as early as possible of a need for improvement in performance so that serious disciplinary action is taken only after opportunities for improvement have not been satisfactorily responded to by the employee. While the emphasis is on correction, in the interest of the company as a whole, disciplinary action will be taken where it is necessary to uphold the high standards of performance.

2. Principles
The following general principles will apply in all cases where disciplinary action is contemplated. The procedure will:
a) be generally known and available
b) be seen to be fair and effective by all employees
c) provide adequate opportunity for the employee to make the necessary improvement in performance required

d) provide for the employee to have the right to state his case before a decision is made

e) provide for the employee to have the right to be accompanied by a representative on request at any stage of the procedure

f) provide for previous recorded verbal and written warnings to be disregarded if the specified time period has elapsed without further disciplinary action

g) except for gross misconduct, ensure that no one will be dismissed for a first offence

h) provide for a right of appeal to all formal disciplinary action.

3. Process

a) *Informal stages*

By normal day-to-day corrective action and by individual counselling and advice, management will make employees aware of the improvements in standard required. Minor offences will be reprimanded by management informally but formal written records will not be kept at this stage. It is hoped that most matters can be speedily and effectively resolved at this level. However, in the event of failure to improve conditions to the required level, the following procedure will be invoked.

b) *Formal procedure*

While the procedure below will be followed in normal circumstances, the entry level for disciplinary action will be determined by careful consideration by management of the severity of the offence. The procedure may therefore be commenced directly at Stages II and III without previous warning.

At each stage, the offences will be comprehensively investigated by the appropriate members of management, and there will be full provision for the employee to hear the case against him, or her, and give his, or her, own explanation of the circumstances leading to the investigation. Following the enquiry, disciplinary action may be invoked at any of the following stages.

Stage I – Formal oral warning

Personnel normally present: the employee's immediate boss; the employee; if requested by the employee, his, or her, representative

Procedure

The immediate boss will make it clear to the employee that this is the first stage of the formal procedure and then will discuss the matter concerned with the employee explaining fully what is required and, where appropriate, what time period is given for corrective action. An opportunity will be given to the employee to put his/her point of view. The employee will receive a copy of the Warning. The Formal Verbal Warning will also be recorded on the employee's personal file. If the employee fails to improve his performance to the required standard, Stage II of the formal procedure will follow. A Formal Verbal Oral Warning will remain in force for six months.

Stage II – Formal written warning (final warning)

Personnel normally present: the employee's immediate boss and his boss; the employee; a member of the personnel department; if requested by the employee, his representative

Procedure

If improvements are not made or there are other incidents of a failure to sustain standards or of a serious first offence, a Formal Written Warning will be issued by the immediate boss's boss. This will fully specify the problem, the corrective action necessary and the consequences if performance is not improved to the required standard. An opportunity will be given to the employee to put his/her viewpoint. The employee will receive a copy of the Formal Written Warning. The Formal Written Warning will also be recorded on the employee's personal file. If improvements are not made, the final stage of the procedure will follow. A warning at this stage will remain in force for 12 months.

Stage III – Final stage – dismissal

Personnel normally present: a senior member of the personnel department; the employing manager; the employee; if requested by the employee, a representative

Procedure

A full investigation into the circumstances of the case will precede the decision. This will consider all relevant factors including previous employment record and allow the employee concerned to state his/her case with the involvement of his/her representative.

4 Right of appeal

All employees have the right to appeal against any formal disciplinary action to the next level of management. The appeal must be in writing and lodged with the personnel department within three working days of the date of the hearing.

5. Investigation/Hearing

If the employee's representative cannot attend on the set date and time, the hearing may be postponed for one week on the request of the employee.

6. Representation

At the request of the employee his/her representative will be present at any meetings held with the employee to investigate the offence or issue a decision on the disciplinary action. A representative is/may be:

- someone who is employed by a trade union of which he/she is an official
- an official of a trade union whom the union has reasonably certified

in writing as having experience at disciplinary and grievance procedures, ie shop steward, branch officer; another of the employer's workers.

The representative is permitted to address the hearing, but not answer questions on the employee's behalf. The employee and the representative will be allowed to confer during the hearing.

7. Gross misconduct

Serious offences which constitute gross misconduct will result in the final stage of the disciplinary procedure being activated without previous warnings or notice of termination. The employee will be regarded as suspended if appropriate with pay until the hearing takes place. Examples of offences which will be regarded as gross misconduct include:

- theft, or attempted theft, of company or employee property
- use of or threat of violence
- falsification of company documents
- serious disruptive or abusive behaviour
- being under the influence of drugs or alcohol on company premises
- wilful neglect or damage to company or employee property
- serious breaches of safety regulations
- disclosure of confidential information
- prolonged unauthorised absence
- serious negligence of duty
- gross insubordination or persistent refusal to carry out a reasonable working instruction
- refusal to be stopped and searched
- inappropriate use of computers/information technology.

This list is by no means exhaustive but merely provides examples of behaviour which will be regarded as gross misconduct.

Source: Komatsu UK Handbook, 2001

An IRS survey (IRS *Employment Trends* 727, 2001: 7) of 46 organisations found that the majority had rewritten their disciplinary procedures during the previous three years. This had been brought about by changes to the law specifically allowing for an employee to be accompanied by a fellow worker or a trade union representative, as well as to respond to the revised ACAS Code of Practice issued in 2000. There were also 'internal' reasons for reviewing procedures, principally to ensure that required standards of conduct were communicated to employees, that the place of counselling and oral warnings were clarified, and that lists of the type of behaviour that constitute misconduct were provided.

The offences that most commonly result in disciplinary action (IRS *Employment Trends* 727, 2001, p7) are:

1	absenteeism
2	poor performance
3	bad time-keeping
4	theft/fraud
5	refusal to obey instructions
6	aggression/verbal abuse
7	health and safety infringements
8	alcohol/drug abuse
9	assault
10	sexual/racial harassment

Absenteeism was ranked as the first or second most common reason by more than two-thirds of private sector firms and about half the public sector organisations. Poor performance, time-keeping problems and theft/fraud were also singled out by quite a number of organisations as a common reason for instigating disciplinary procedures. Once again, this tended to be more marked in the private than in the public sector. The remaining six offences were cited rather less often. For further details, see IRS *Employment Trends* 727 (2001).

Grievance procedures

A grievance is a complaint made by an employee about management behaviour (Gennard and Judge, 1999: 276). In the UK, grievance procedures tend to be used widely and embrace both collective and individual issues reflecting the idea that the line between grievance (individual) and dispute (collective) can sometimes be a blurred one. However, in general, grievance procedures are used for handling individual issues, while collective issues are usually dealt with by disputes procedures. In practice some organisations have a combined procedure which reflects the fact that grievances are often likely to affect more than one employee, and others allow for grievances which can be referred to the collective disputes procedure. A grievance procedure is a parallel mechanism to the disciplinary procedure (Rollinson, 2002: 98–9).

Problems can arise if agreements and rules are not written down because custom and practice is likely to produce ambiguity. Often it is possible to separate disputes of interest (what *should be* in the agreement) from disputes of right (what *is* in the agreement). During the 1960s and 1970s, grievance procedures formed part of national agreements, which led to problems because of the time it took to take a grievance to the end of the procedure. Consequently, industrial action sometimes took place before the procedure had been exhausted. Nowadays, however, it is much more common to have local grievance procedures to cover establishments or single employers. As Renwick and Gennard (2001: 171) observe, although a formal grievance procedure is not legally required, employers who do not have a formal grievance procedure can fall foul of the law. Furthermore, as Gennard and Judge (1999: 210–11) note:

> the benefits of having procedures for handling employee grievances are also clear from the case of Chris Metcalf Ltd v Maddocks (1985). The industrial tribunal ruled that a grievance procedure would have enabled employees to articulate their worries and anxieties, and would thus have prevented the problems occurring. An appeal by the firm against the decision failed.

The aim of a grievance procedure is to prevent issues and disagreements from leading to major conflict, and to prevent employees from leaving. Even if an employee's grievance is the result of a fellow employee's action – as in racial or sexual harassment – the grievance procedure is taken against management for failing to provide protection. As with discipline, the spirit with which the grievance procedure is approached is significant. It may be easy for management simply to follow the letter of the procedure, making it a hollow sham, but once that becomes known, employees will not bother to refer issues to the procedure. Consequently, it is important that HR professionals encourage the proper use of procedures to uncover any problems particularly where line managers wish to hide them through the fear that such problems show them in a bad light. Open-door systems operate in some organisations that allow workers to take up grievances with managers directly rather than follow a lengthy procedure. However, this relies on managers taking the system seriously and being prepared to devote time and effort to keep it going.

Disputes procedures specify how collective grievances should be dealt with. The chain of complaint may go from the supervisor, or immediate line manager, to the departmental manager or personnel manager to senior management. It may provide for matters to be referred to a third party such as ACAS if matters are not resolved. It is also important that the procedure is efficient and relatively quick. Clearly, there is a balance between the time needed to reflect on the issue at hand while ensuring that it is not 'lost' in the process because of the length of time involved. The basic elements of a grievance procedure are contained in the box below.

The basic elements of a grievance procedure

These include:

- There should be a formal, written procedure.
- The procedure should be agreed with employees or union representatives.
- Where there is a separate disputes procedure, the two procedures should be linked.
- An individual grievance should be settled as close to the point of origin and within as short a time-scale as possible.
- The right to be accompanied should be addressed.
- Confidentiality should be assured.

Source: Farnham D. *Employee Relations in Context*. 4th edition. London, CIPD. 2000. p415

According to WERS 1998, almost all workplaces (91 per cent) had a formal procedure for dealing with individual grievances raised by employees. Only in stand-alone sites (74 per cent) was the incidence substantially below the average. Almost all the public sector workplaces had a procedure in place (99 per cent). Where workplaces operated without a procedure, managers were asked how problems were resolved. Typically, the answer was 'They come to me and we sort it out.' Employees were made aware of the existence and content of these procedures through the letter of appointment (47 per cent), a staff handbook (55 per cent) or via a notice-board (19 per cent). In the small number of workplaces without a written procedure, it was claimed that employees were made aware of their rights either when they started work or at some other time by their line manager or supervisor. On this point Cully *et al* (1999: 77) noted that although most employees had access to a formal procedure for grievances, they might be reluctant to raise a grievance without some form of support. Consequently, relatively little use was made of grievance procedures. At workplaces with procedures, only a third (30 per cent) said that the procedure was utilised. The interpretation of this is complex: either employees had nothing to complain about, or the procedure was not regarded as a particularly effective mechanism for resolving problems. Comments on the lack of use included (Cully *et al*, 1998: 77–8):

'Because we are quite happy to listen to them at any time and deal with problems before they develop' (quote from private sector, 'other business services', 500+ employees).

'It's not part of the culture of this company' (quote from private sector, construction company, 500+ employees).

'They haven't felt the need. If there is anything, they can usually sort it out without resorting to the procedure' (quote from private sector, financial services, 50–100 employees).

'Probably because they imagine nothing will change – lack of confidence in the procedure' (quote from private sector, health, 100–200 employees)'

Get a copy of your own organisation's grievance procedure, and compare it with one from another organisation of your choice. What are the major differences between them? How might your procedure be adapted, if at all, to make it work better?

Employers are not required by law to have a grievance procedure but are required in the terms and conditions of employment to provide the name/job-title of someone to whom employees can apply (Employment Relations Act 1996). The ERA 1999 included a stipulation on reasonable requests to be accompanied during hearings. From 2000, a worker asked to attend a disciplinary or grievance hearing can 'reasonably request' to be accompanied by a lay trade union official or a fellow-worker. Although 'reasonable' is not defined, the ACAS Code suggests that it would not be reasonable to request to be accompanied by someone who might prejudice the hearing or who might have a conflict of interest; or someone from a distant location when someone suitable is on site. The 'companion' may not act in the same way as a representative, who may actually present the case on the subject's behalf. However, the companion can address the hearing – but not answer questions – and can confer with the worker (IRS *Employment Trends* 726, 2001: 8). Aikin (2000) suggests that employers must consider precise rules rather than leaving questions of reasonableness to individual managers who may well reach different conclusions. In view of the introduction of the right to be accompanied, it is important for employers to be clear what constitutes counselling, coaching or an informal warning – where the right does not apply – and what is part of the disciplinary procedure (Pitt, 2000: 256). The Public Interest Disclosure Act 1998 amended the ERA 1996 to 'the opportunity for workers to raise concerns such as workplace malpractice, suspicion of criminal acts, miscarriages of justice, and dangers to health and safety (Farnham, 2000: 415) within the grievance procedure.

An IRS Survey (IRS *Employment Trends* 726, 2001) of over 100 employers found that all but two had written procedures – very much in line with the WERS results. Over half of the organisations first introduced these procedures more than 10 years ago. There was strong support for the argument that grievances should be dealt with quickly and fairly at the lowest possible level in the organisation, and this was best done informally between the worker and his or her immediate line manager. Although the number of stages in the procedure varied between organisations, three stages was the most common, and it was rare for there to be fewer than this. The most common causes of grievances (IRS *Employment Trends* 726, 2001: 7) are:

1	pay and grading
2	terms and conditions
3	working practices
4	discipline
5	work allocation
6	bullying
7	discrimination

Broadly, pay and grading issues are the most typical, and this was particularly marked in the NHS. Concerns about other terms and conditions of employment, working practices and work allocation also featured prominently as sources of grievance. Complaints about the handling of disciplinary cases and bullying were also noted by quite a number of organisations, although grievances about sexual harassment were relatively rare. For further details, see IRS *Employment Trends* 726 (2001).

The IRS respondents (*Employment Trends* 726, 2001: 16) suggested that six pieces of advice were relevant to other employers when designing and operating grievance procedures. These are:

- Emphasise quick and informal procedures.

- Keep policies simple.

- Liaise with and involve employee representatives.

- Communicate the policy to employees and managers.

- Provide training for line managers.

- Be consistent when applying procedures.

Line managers and the use of procedures

So far in this chapter we have discussed the importance of procedures, stressing the value of being proactive, taking the initiative, and estab-lishing/reinforcing their use. Management has been treated as if it comprised a unified group, sharing common interests and perspectives. However, in reality, there may well be conflict between the perspectives held by HR specialists and line managers. In practice, it seems likely that operational pressures take priority over HR considerations, and that directives from HR specialists tend to have less force than those coming from a production director. This helps to explain why line man-agers are often hostile to rules that appear to emanate from the HR specialists, who may well then find themselves castigated for 'not living in the real world'. A personnel policy that appears well formulated, embodies the basic rules of good management practice, and ensures uniformity and consistency may thus seem to be a very different kettle of fish when viewed from the position of the line manager. Under such circumstances, HR specialists must be able to persuade line managers that procedures are valuable tools and guidelines rather than mill-stones. One argument might be that the procedures are no more than the codification of good practice. So, for example, the disciplinary pro-cedure represents a helpful prompt to some managers encouraging them to follow actions they should be taking in any case. Moreover, by not following procedure they potentially lay themselves and their employer open to the likelihood of appeals, time spent at an employment tribunal, and ultimately financial penalties. A short-cut by line managers may cost dearly later. A second argument might be that breaking rules or condoning new custom and practice merely lays down the seeds of greater trouble thereafter. For example, for line managers to concede to employees' demands in exchange for their greater co-operation in meeting a production target might create an expectation that all extra effort will be so rewarded. Thirdly, the observance of procedures sets the tone for dealing with other issues in the workplace. If managers are seen to be fair and prepared to follow procedures, it is much more likely that employees will behave likewise if they are unhappy with some aspect of management behaviour. Rather than taking industrial action to settle differences, employees are encouraged to ensure that pro-cedures are exhausted first. This allows employers to maintain produc-tion or services while resolving problems at work.

Procedures therefore have a role in giving line managers a clear per-spective on the direction in which the organisation is moving, its objec-tives, and the general standards applied in relation to all aspects of the employment relationship. Although line managers may not have the time to become experts in all these matters, they should know the broad par-ameters of actions, as well as where and when to look for advice. Personnel specialists clearly play a key role both in providing information and acting as a sounding-board.

The IRS research into managing discipline at work (IRS *Employment Trends* 727, 2001) demonstrated that line managers were increasingly taking responsibility for disciplinary procedures. Over half of the 46 respondents (20 in the public sector and 26 in the private sector) reported that line managers spent up to 5 per cent of their time on disciplinary issues, and about one fifth estimated that line mangers spent about 10 per cent of their time on disciplinary issues. Despite this, discipline still makes up a significant portion of the workload of HR staff. Over half of the respondents estimated that it took up 5 per cent, and approximately one fifth that it took up 20 per cent or more of HR staff time (IRS *Employment Trends* 727, 2001: 8).

How can HR practitioners convince line managers that it is worth using procedures and that procedures can make a contribution to organisational success?

Many employers reviewed their disciplinary procedures following the 1987 House of Lords decision in the case of *Polkey v A. E. Dayton*. This made it clear that a dismissal is likely to be seen as unfair if a fair procedure is not followed. Recent changes in disciplinary procedures focus on sexual and racial harassment, smoking at work, and the need to differentiate between appraisal and disciplinary process. It is also now required that sanctions against employees – for example, in the event of a misdemeanour – are set out in the disciplinary procedure so as to form part of the employment contract. Renwick and Gennard (2001: 170) argue that all managers must be trained properly to handle grievance and discipline cases so that they can draw a distinction between unjustified employee complaints and those that are justified under the organisation's procedure, collective agreement or work rules. Where a dismissal has occurred, in investigating whether or not the employee has a genuine grievance against their employer, tribunals test the issues of fairness and reasonableness by asking whether procedures applied 'conform to the concepts of natural justice'.

CASE STUDY: Procedures in action

Drawing on CIPD legal helpline experience, Firth explains the range of issues that must be considered when disciplining staff, citing a specific case involving a worker in a call centre.

A worker who was two weeks short of the qualifying period allowing him to take out an unfair dismissal claim had been deleting client data. The worker's line manager wanted to dismiss him immediately. The HR manager advised that the disciplinary process must be fair and that there was a risk that the employee could claim breach of contract on two grounds if the procedures were not followed. This was, firstly, because the firm's disciplinary procedure was incorporated into its employees' contracts. Secondly, the worker was

two weeks short of qualifying for the right to claim unfair dismissal. The tribunal might decide that had the company followed the correct procedure, the employee's period of employment would have continued for a further two weeks so that the employee achieved the qualifying period. This would create a situation in which the employee could potentially claim damages for loss of the opportunity to claim for unfair dismissal. The case of *Raspin v United News Shops Ltd* (1999) established this principle. The HR manager advised that the company's disciplinary procedures should be used.

Adapted from Firth J. 'Sack full of sorrows',
People Management, 17 June 1999. p25

The contribution of HR specialists to the bargaining process

Gennard and Judge (1999: 311–27) examine in detail the preparation for bargaining, and in this section we outline the key elements relating to the roles of HR practitioners. Typically, a bargaining team includes three roles. These are leader (spokesperson and negotiator), note-taker (recording proposals, ensuring all issues are addressed), and strategist (to monitor strategies and seek common ground). It is important for the team to maintain discipline throughout the process and not provide opportunities for the other side to exploit any lack of coherence. The HR function would normally take a key role in this process – according to WERS over 90 per cent of HR/personnel managers have a responsibility for pay and conditions of employment (Millward *et al*, 2000: 63). There are a number of stages in the bargaining process.

Analysis

This stage is concerned with collecting and analysing relevant information to support a claim/proposal. In preparing for this stage, the managers are likely to gather a range of information from both internal and external sources. Many of these fall within the province of HR managers. Internal sources may cover issues such as:

- labour productivity trends

- profitability

- labour turnover

- absenteeism

- total sales

- investment

- pay changes

- orders pending

- the cash-flow position.

External sources include information from employers associations (see Chapter 4), the trade press such as *People Management* and *Personnel Today*, as well as industry-specific journals. UK government and other literature is particularly helpful. Examples include *Labour Market Trends*, *New Earnings Survey*, *Industrial Relations Services Pay and Benefits Bulletin*. Another useful source is Incomes Data Services, which produces reports on pay statistics and a pay directory.

The identification of tradeable items

Also important when preparing for negotiations is identifying the key issues on which management may be prepared to trade. For example, changes in basic pay or to the working week may be ruled out, whereas variable pay such as bonuses and certain aspects of working conditions may be used as trade-offs. The team also must assess what they believe the other party may be willing to trade to see if there is any basis for agreement. In that HR managers are more likely to spend time with worker representatives than most other managers, their assessment of the situation is likely to be very important.

Aims and strategy

Management should examine what they are seeking to achieve in terms of what is ideal, what is realistic, and what is the minimum acceptable. This can be done in relation to all the items on the 'shopping list' of each of the parties, and by putting these together they should be able to see if there is likely to be any basis for agreement. Key issues might include:

- Are employees willing to take industrial action?

- What is the degree of organisation and solidarity amongst employees?

- What is the quality of leadership amongst union representatives?

- Have employees imposed sanctions previously, and if so, what was the result?

- What type of industrial sanctions did they use? What tactics did they use?

- What is the degree of substitutability for products and services produced by employees?

- Can an alternative supply of labour be obtained?

- How crucial is the group of employees in the production/service supply process?

- How long will it take for industrial sanctions, if imposed, to have an adverse effect on the operation of the organisation?

Presenting the proposal

The proposal should briefly summarise the main issues to be discussed and then present the case in detail along with supporting evidence. At this early stage management will set out their ideal position with an opening statement. There are advantages in opening from an extreme position because it provides more room for movement in bargaining and it can lower expectations. The potential downside is that it may not be treated seriously by the unions or it might trigger an equally extreme response. Much depends upon context and existing relationships.

Confirmation of common ground

Once the original presentations by both sides have been completed, it will be much clearer what the main sources of contention are. At this early stage there may be little common ground, but the meeting should reach the point at which it is decided to identify what common ground there is and to make an effort towards possible agreement, and thus keep the momentum of the bargaining session going, leaving the more difficult issues to be returned to later.

Adjournment

Apart from normal scheduled breaks, there are constructive uses for adjournments. Firstly, an adjournment gives the parties a chance to withdraw and review progress. Secondly, it can provide a break if negotiations have reached an impasse. Thirdly, it provides an opportunity for one or two members from each side to talk informally with each other away from the negotiating tables without any formal commitment (Fowler, 1996).

Factors to consider in concluding the agreement

Management have to be satisfied with the issues that have been discussed and agreed, and satisfied too that both sides understand and are committed to what has been accepted. If this is not achieved or there is some ambiguity, problems will arise later when either party may accuse the other of misapplying the agreement. Secondly, management have to convince the other party that the final offer is indeed the end of the process or it risks undermining credibility. Thirdly, management should not rush into concluding a final agreement. It is vital to have an adjournment to ensure that everybody concerned has all the information and that no problems have been forgotten. Gennard and Judge (1999: 325–6) note that once oral agreement has been reached, the agreement can be written up in draft form stating the following:

- the names of the parties to the agreement
- the date on which the agreement was concluded
- the date upon which the agreement will become operative
- the groups/grades that are covered by the agreement
- the exceptions (if any) to the agreement
- the contents (clauses) of the agreement
- the duration of the agreement
- whether the agreement can be reopened before this finish date, and if so, in what circumstances
- whether the agreement can be terminated if it has no end date, and, if so, how
- the manner in which disputes over its interpretation and application will be settled (will it be the existing grievance/disputes procedure?)
- which, if any, other agreements it replaces.

The written agreement should contain the signatures of representatives of the parties covered by the agreement. Once both sides are happy with the wording, the agreement can be formally signed.

HR managers play an important role as policy actors and 'hidden persuaders' (Wilkinson and Marchington, 1994) in the bargaining process (see Chapter 9). They are expected to interpret new employment regulations, to prepare the organisation for 'best-practice' initiatives like Investors in People, to form alliances with general managers in search of recipes to enhance employee contribution, and to help line managers incorporate human resources dimensions into operational schemes such as teamworking. Increased regulation may therefore offer an important opportunity for the HR specialist. It provides them with opportunities to introduce new systems and processes into their organisations, and it lends them greater legitimacy as experts. The creation of a new institutional baseline of employee rights and a changed normative framework can provide management with an opportunity to exercise creativity. Without this framework, there is a danger that employees may choose instead to articulate their views through litigation or high labour turnover rather than through constructive internal channels.

CONCLUSION

In this chapter we have reviewed a number of the procedures to provide a framework for employee relations, and which have grown extensively in coverage during the last 25 years. In the current climate – where concepts of flexibility, empowerment and de-layering reign supreme – procedures are seen by some commentators as an anachronism, a legacy of the so-called 'old' collectivist and bureaucratic industrial relations of the 1970s. But we ought to remember why procedures were introduced in the first place, and the purposes they have been expected to serve. One of the major rationales behind the emergence of unfair dismissal legislation was to reduce the likelihood of employees taking industrial action to protect fellow-workers whom they felt had been badly treated by management. The procedures established as a result of this legal intervention helped to change attitudes and behaviour, and few HR managers (or their line management colleagues) would welcome a return to the days of industrial disputes. As we noted in Chapter 2, many employees now feel that the psychological contract is too one-sided. Although workers may lack the resources or the will to engage in industrial action, a perception of being unfairly treated can easily translate into demotivation, a lack of interest in quality and customer care, and feelings of exclusion and powerlessness.

Procedures are an essential element of good employment relations and HR practice (see Chapter 7), because they provide a clear framework within which issues can be resolved. In the absence of procedures, each new problem has to be tackled from first principles, and managers and employee representatives might then have to spend considerable amounts of time trying to derive common ground rules before being able to resolve the issues. As noted by Renwick and Gennard (2001: 169), there is a business case for procedures:

> That business case rests on the assumption that if discipline and grievance issues are dealt with properly, employee dissatisfaction should decrease and motivation increase, labour turnover should decline and retention rates increase, and a reservoir of discontent from employee against employer would thus be avoided.

Without procedures, there would be no incentive for managers or employees to attempt to resolve disputes in an orderly manner. The end-result would be that both parties would seek to use the most formidable elements of their bargaining power to impose their own preferred solutions on the other. Procedures help to create a positive psychological contract by emphasising the importance of fairness.

Useful reading

AIKIN O. 'Strictly invitation only', *People Management*, 6 July 2000. p20.

ADVISORY, CONCILIATION *AND* ARBITRATION SERVICE. *ACAS Code of Practice Disciplinary Practice and Grievance Procedures at Work*. London, HMSO. 2000.

CUNNINGHAM I. *and* HYMAN J. 'Devolving human resource responsibilities to the line: beginning of the end or a new beginning for personnel?', *Personnel Review*, Vol. 28, No, 1/2, 1999. pp9–27.

EARNSHAW J., GOODMAN J., HARRISON R. *and* MARCHINGTON M. *Industrial Tribunal Workplace Disciplinary Procedures and Employment Practice*, Employment Relations Research Series No 2, DTI. 1998.

EDWARDS P. 'Discipline: towards trust and self-discipline', in S. Bach and K. Sisson (eds), *Personnel Management*, 3rd edition. Oxford, Blackwell. 2000.

INDUSTRIAL RELATIONS SERVICES. 'Managing discipline at work', IRS *Employment Trends* 727, May 2001. pp5–11.

INDUSTRIAL RELATIONS SERVICES. 'Airing a grievance: how to handle employee complaints', IRS *Employment Trends* 726, April 2001. p9.

GENNARD J. *and* JUDGE G. *Employee Relations*. 2nd edition. London, IPD. 1999, Part Four.

RENWICK D. *and* GENNARD J. 'Grievance and discipline' in T. Redman and A. Wilkinson (eds), *Contemporary Human Resource Management*. FT/Pitman. 2001.

● Motivating Staff and Rewarding
Contributions

CHAPTER OBJECTIVES

By the end of this chapter, readers should be able to:

● provide advice about how to motivate and reward people so as
to maximise employee contributions to organisational
performance

● advise management on the circumstances under which
different payment systems may be appropriate for their
organisation

● outline the case for and against the introduction of
performance-related pay and specify the conditions under
which it is appropriate.

In addition, readers should understand and be able to explain:

● the principal differences between types of pay scheme

● the importance of linking the pay system to wider
organisational goals and other HR strategies

● how effective reward management practice can contribute to
enhanced employee motivation and satisfaction at work.

Introduction

The sight of employees sprinting away from the workplace as the factory
hooter sounds suggests that well-motivated staff are not necessarily
the norm in UK industry. Studies also show that even where labour
turnover – one indicator of employee satisfaction – is limited, this may
obscure deep-rooted discontent when employees feel they have little
choice but to remain with their current employer because of the economic situation or their lack of transferable skills. The WERS survey
found that all but 7 per cent of workplaces had some workers who were
not satisfied with their jobs (Cully *et al*, 1999: 298).

In the light of the increased emphasis in recent years on people as a key
source of competitive advantage, it is not surprising to see corporate
initiatives introduced to 'buy' employee commitment. But how successful are such campaigns, and on what assumptions are they based? It
seems sensible to take a step back and try to understand the complexities of motivating people at work. This is important at three levels. First,
it is important for management, who clearly need to know and

understand what motivates people because it affects work perform-ance, recruitment and retention. Second, employees should think through what expectations they have of work and whether they are happy with their lot. Finally, for HR professionals, issues such as these influence the design and implementation of reward structures and sys-tems which they implement or monitor.

Money is certainly a factor that can motivate people at work, but even here things are not straightforward. Many people are motivated to work hard regardless of financial reward, and for some the level of monetary reward is important symbolically – as recognition of worth. Clearly, there are other benefits from being at work as well as money – such as activity, variety, status and social contacts. In recent years there has been a growing emphasis in the literature that reward should be utilised as a strategic tool to manage corporate performance and to influence corporate values and beliefs (Armstrong, 1999; Lewis, 2001) rather than just as a technique to recruit, retain and motivate staff. Armstrong and Brown (2001: 5) define reward strategy as:

a business-focused statement of the intentions of the organis-ation concerning the development of future reward processes and practices, which are aligned to the business and human resource strategies of the organisation, its culture and the environment in which it operates.

This is very much a phenomenon of the last 20 years, with an associ-ated upbeat rhetoric, and it is often set against an alleged backcloth of earlier approaches criticised for being inflexible and bureaucratic. Reward management is a key element in the strategic approach to HRM for a number of reasons. Firstly, it is a mechanism by which employers aim to elicit effort and performance; secondly, the actual payment system may require adjustment to develop motivation; and thirdly, it is often a significant part of the employer's financial strategy (Hendry, 1994: 343).

Such an approach ties in well with the HRM ideal, which sees policies designed around strategic choices rather than simply reflecting environmental pressures. This means that there is unlikely to be a state-of-the-art 'one size fits all' set of practices suitable for all organis-ations, and managers must develop a 'fit' between remuneration poli-cies and the strategic objectives of the organisation (Lawler, 1985; Brown, 2001). However, the extent to which remuneration is used as a strategic tool in practice is more open to doubt. Management tends to assess or reassess one part of the remuneration package but often fail to analyse the whole system. Furthermore, management has a whole host of objectives for their remuneration policy, but these sometimes contradict one another, and their wider implications are not always clearly thought through.

In this chapter we examine the varieties of reward system and the different elements in the reward package as well as the different types of pay schemes that can be implemented. It is important that the reward philosophy and policy reflects the overall objectives of the employer, and that the different elements of the package send a clear and consistent message to employees. Moreover, as organisations become flatter and promotion opportunities are reduced, this places even greater emphasis on the recognition and reward elements of the pay system.

Motivation and rewards

Most texts on social psychology divide theories of motivation into content theories and process theories. Content theories focus on what are seen as fundamental human needs (for example, physiological, food and safety needs), whereas process theories try to understand the psychological processes involved in motivation (Bowey and Thorpe, 2000; Mullins, 2001).

F. W. Taylor, the father of scientific management, viewed employees as rational and economic in their approach but basically lazy and having to be motivated by management through the pay system. Because employees were motivated primarily by money, it was important to ensure that the jobs they were doing were capable of providing the opportunity to maximise earnings. Accordingly, jobs had to be examined scientifically through time-and-motion studies, broken down into their constituent parts, and then put back together in the most efficient manner. This 'best' method was devised by observing the 'best' workers on each particular task. Once the 'best' method had been established, it could then be taught to other workers, who could be retrained if necessary. However, his approach has been widely criticised, in particular for his tendency to equate people with machines, his assumption that there was one universal best method, and his contention that the single incentive to earn money is the primary motivating factor at work (Rose, 1978: 62). Others have noted that his conception of the rational-economic person led to a self-fulfilling prophecy to the effect that if employees are expected to be motivated solely by economic incentives, the management approach used to deal with them is likely to train them to behave in exactly that way. Taylor's ideas ('Taylorism') can be seen clearly in payment-by-results schemes – notably in piecework – which make explicit the link between reward and effort.

The human relations movement emerged by the 1920s, presenting a picture of 'social man' against the 'economic man' of the scientific management school. This idea developed originally from research (known as the Hawthorne experiments) on fatigue and its link with productivity. The groups at the plants under investigation were studied over a period of time, and changes were introduced relating to alterations in rest periods, refreshments, starting and finishing times, payment schemes and environmental conditions such as lighting. However, in contrast with the prevailing wisdom, variations in these conditions did not appear to correlate with productivity. Even when the experiment ended and conditions returned to their original state, production was some 30 per cent higher than at the start. These results were then interpreted as resulting from increased worker satisfaction through being given special attention, working as a close-knit group, and being involved in decision-making. It was clear that workers did not always respond to incentive schemes as managers had expected, often having their own goals (as a group) which acted against management objectives. However, as with scientific management, the human relations school has been criticised for its unitarist philosophy, for its 'one best way' approach, and for its methodology. The implications of this approach for reward strategy are not that payments are irrelevant, but that new payment schemes may have a once-and-for-all Hawthorne effect which may increase productivity. Yet this school of thought suggests that rewards should be seen in a broader work context – one in which employee objectives other than the simple maximisation of earnings are important.

> What motivates you at work? List the factors that affect your feelings about the job, and rank them. Which tasks are you motivated to do well, and which do not motivate you? Explain your conclusions.

By the 1940s Maslow had developed the 'hierarchy of needs' approach to motivation. To some extent this incorporated the previous two theories of motivation, and rather than identifying a single source of motivation it suggested an ascending hierarchy of needs. The theory claims that people are motivated by a number of factors at work, aiming to satisfy one particular need before moving on to attempt to satisfy the next in the hierarchy. Thus, basic security needs such as food, jobs and housing have to be achieved before individuals begin to consider their social and affiliative needs. Once these needs are satisfied they can then look to satisfy their personal needs for ego-satisfaction and self-actualisation. One implication of the 'hierarchy of needs' approach is that for those on low wages, and consequently operating at the lower end of the hierarchy, money may loom more significantly than for those earning considerably more. The latter have satisfied their basic needs, and may have moved on to higher-level needs. However, the ongoing controversy over executive rewards – which led to the Cadbury and Greenbury Reports – might appear to contradict this notion (see the *'Fat cats'* box below). There is little research evidence to support the notion of a universal hierarchy of needs. It is also apparent that, on the same day, employees may demand not only more money but also more satisfying work, and are thus operating at more than one level of hierarchy at one time. Maslow's work is also reflected to some extent in McGregor's

(1960) distinction between theory X and theory Y managers. Theory X managers believe workers are lazy and uninterested in their work, and must therefore be highly controlled and offered incentives to get them to work harder. In contrast, theory Y managers believe workers can be motivated by goals of self-esteem and the desire to do a good job; consequently, management's role is to facilitate this.

'Fat cats'

The debate over 'fat cats' continues to the present day with concerns that bosses are being overpaid relative to performance. Indeed, according to the Co-operative Insurance Society (CIS) six out of ten of Britain's biggest companies are not following best practice to control and monitor directors' pay and bonuses. In short, they flout government guidelines laid down to ensure the highest standards of boardroom behaviour. The guidelines, enshrined in the combined code, have been put together over ten years by the Cadbury, Greenbury and Hampel committees (the *Guardian*, 2 May 2001).

According to Towers Perrin/*Business Week* (cited by the *Guardian*, 23 August 2000), US chief executive officers earn 475 times more than the average worker, whereas in Germany the ratio is 15:1, in the UK 24:1 (the biggest gap in Europe) and in Japan 11:1. However, the message that wage compression can help performance is not one of the lessons that British managers have been keen to promote! Of course this depends on the view one takes on what high pay is for. According to Lazear (1998):

> American CEOs have recently come under attack for their very high salaries, particularly in comparison to their European and Japanese counterparts. Whilst their salaries may be too high, focusing on their salaries alone misses the entire point of the compensation structure. The CEO's salary is there not so much to motivate the CEO as it is to motivate everyone under him [sic] to attempt to attain that job.

UK criticism ('Profits down, top pay up': the *Guardian*, 16 July 2001) suggests that bosses all too easily downplay the performance link in favour of a self-serving market rate justification (Caulkin, 2001). Concerns about high payments at troubled Marks & Spencer have kept the debate going (the *Guardian*, 4 July 2001), and at Railtrack the chief executive who resigned after the Hatfield crash received a £1.4m payoff.

Herzberg's two-factor theory of motivation was very influential in the 1960s, especially with large companies such as ICI. His research found that satisfaction and dissatisfaction were not necessarily related, and that just because a person did not feel satisfied about a particular aspect of his or her work it did not mean that he or she was necessarily dissatisfied. Equally, if workers did not feel dissatisfied, this did not imply automatic satisfaction. The motivators that tended to be identified with the good feelings included factors such as achievement, responsibility, recognition, advancement and the work itself. The so-called 'hygiene' factors – associated with bad feelings – included company policy, working conditions, supervision and pay. So if an employee spoke about feeling good, it was related to having achieved something or having been granted recognition. Conversely, when speaking about feeling bad, the reference was to factors such as poor supervision or insufficient pay. However, the key point here is that unless the hygiene factors are satisfied, motivators are of little use, and Herzberg felt that many firms did not even satisfy the hygiene factors. If this theory holds true, then it has similar implications to Maslow's work, in that pay is only significant as a 'hygiene' factor and that an appropriate level must be found which meets employee expectations. But there will be no motivating effect by paying above this level. The theory also has implications in relation to the need to restructure or enrich jobs to provide satisfying work, for 'true' motivation is seen to derive from factors associated with the job itself and opportunity for achievement, involvement and recognition. We return to this concept in the next chapter when we deal with non-financial rewards and recognition. Bowey and Thorpe (2000: 84) observe that much of this literature was written from an 'upstream' position focusing on the potential for these ideas; there are few 'downstream evaluations' of what has actually happened to organisations following the implementation of a particular theory or idea.

Later literature has posited that people are complex animals. This does not provide us with any automatically universal picture of the employee, for as Rollinson et al (1998: 184) notes, 'the needs and values of individuals are highly diverse, and the organisations in which people work are very different'. Goldthorpe and his colleagues (Goldthorpe et al, 1968) found in their research a group of manual workers, termed 'instrumental', who appeared to want little else from work other than enough money to enable them to enjoy life to the full outside the workplace. Few of the respondents seemed particularly satisfied with their work but neither were they dissatisfied; work was simply not a priority in their lives – it was unimportant. They came to work for purely instrumental reasons and their attachment to workmates, company and union was of a similar order. Other workers – while valuing their pay – also stressed the importance of the work group and the sense of achievement in their work.

In contrast to the content approaches, the process approach explores the psychological processes that are involved. Expectancy theory is based on the expectations that people bring with them to the work situation, and the context and way in which these expectations are satisfied (Vroom, 1964). This is not a static model, and there may well be different sets of expectations at different times. Expectancy theory implies that management must demonstrate to employees that effort will be recognised and rewarded, in both financial and non-financial terms. The importance of this theory is that the onus is on management to establish schemes to reward the behaviour it wants. Moreover, it helps to explain why employees do not always respond in the desired way because they do not believe management's word that, for example, co-operation in the introduction of new technology will not lead to job losses.

Three concepts are central to this theory. Firstly, performance–outcome expectancy: this means that employees believe that if they act in a particular way, there are foreseeable consequences. For example, employees might believe that, if they exceed work quotas they will get bonuses, or if the target is not met pay will be docked. Secondly, the concept of valence, which refers to the value to the employee of an outcome that derives from behaviour. For example, one employee might value being promoted, whereas another would prefer to continue working doing the same job within the same department because he or she places a strong value on friendship at work. Thirdly, there is effort–performance expectancy, which is the employee's perception of the likelihood of achieving the desired objective. For example, if an employee believes it is impossible to meet a sales target because the product is not a good one or because the target is simply unrealistic, he or she may not even deem it worth the effort to try. In simple terms, employees focus on three questions:

- Can I perform at this level if I try?

- If I do manage to perform at the set level, what are the consequences?

- What do I feel about the consequences of that action?

The theory implies that low motivation will be the product of jobs where there is little worker control. Nadler and Lawler (1979) draw out the implications for managers and their organisations. They must:

- discover what outcomes/rewards are valued (have higher valence) for each employee – and whether it is monetary reward or recognition, for example

- design tasks and jobs so that employees can satisfy needs through work

- individualise reward systems, including their work and benefits, possibly using a cafeteria-style approach

- be specific about the desired behaviours

- ensure that performance targets are attainable – otherwise, employees may not bother to try very hard

- ensure that there is a direct, clear and explicit link between desired performance and rewards; if staff value intrinsic rewards, such as interesting work, then management can concentrate on redesigning jobs rather than increasing pay

- check that there are no conflicting expectancies

- ensure that changes in reward/outcome are significant, for as Nadler and Lawler (1979: 227) put it, 'Trivial rewards will result in trivial amounts of effort and thus trivial improvements in performance', or, in more popular language, 'If you pay peanuts, you get monkeys'

- check that everyone is treated fairly by the system.

A central concept of expectancy theory is the view that other approaches to motivation – such as advocated by Taylor, Mayo (the Human Relations movement) or Maslow – are based on the assumption that all employees are alike, motivated by money, recognition or whatever. In addition, all situations are alike and hence there is one best way to motivate employees (Rollinson *et al*, 1998: 145–84).

Do you think that workers are (or should be) prepared to put up with dull, boring jobs if they are paid high wages?

Reward management in context

When trying to understand the strategic choices made by management about reward policies, the broader political and economic context is clearly important. In the 1960s and 1970s, for example, Bowey *et al* (1982: 37–53) found that the main reason employers introduced incentive schemes was to provide a way of giving workers pay increases at a time of government restraints. Because of the lack of long-term strategic intent, few employers achieved reduced costs and less than half increased output. In the 1980s and 1990s the Conservative government's free-market philosophy and its attempt to cultivate an 'enterprise culture' influenced remuneration policies. This produced an ideological shift in ideas towards the concept of paying people for their performance rather than for their attendance. There was a more direct impact brought about by changes in taxation policy – such as lower rates of income tax, heavier taxation of fringe benefits, and new fiscal incentives for share ownership. In terms of the economic context, lower levels of inflation in the last few years have reduced the significance of general cost-of-living pay rises, and hence provided greater scope for the individualisation of annual pay increases. Product market developments also provided an impetus for change, especially with the intensification of international competition, privatisation, deregulation, and competitive restructuring.

There are several factors which influence salary and wage levels (Curnow, 1986). Firstly, job 'size' has traditionally been the main determinant of pay. This includes factors such as responsibility, level in the organisational hierarchy, required knowledge, skills or competencies, external contacts, complexity, and decision-making. In this way, the individual's hierarchical position in large organisations has been central to the design of internal pay structures, his or her performance rewarded by promotion. However, job size is now regarded as less important than individual contribution. In other words, having a large staff or control of larger budgets does not in itself indicate a significant contribution that merits extra reward. Secondly, individual characteristics – such as age, experience, qualifications and special skills, contribution and performance – are also significant factors. Thirdly, labour market factors – such as the supply and demand of particular skills both locally and the 'going rate' in the particular labour market – are important. Fourthly, product market conditions and the employer's cost structure – such as its position in the market, profitability and market ambitions and strategies – have a major influence on pay strategy. Finally, the remuneration philosophy of the organisation also has an influence on wage and salary levels. An organisation with the reputation for being a 'good employer', and wishing to attract the most able staff, is likely to offer higher wages than one in which staff are valued less positively.

According to Lawler (1984: 128), reward systems can influence a number of HR processes and practices which in turn have an impact on organisational performance. Firstly, rewards influence recruitment and retention – 'those organisations that give the most rewards tend to attract and retain the most people' (Lawler, 1984: 128). High wages attract more applicants, which allows greater choice over selection and hiring decisions, which in turn may reduce labour turnover. In addition, better performers have to be rewarded more highly than poor performers. The type of payment system – not just the level of rewards – also has an effect on recruitment and retention, so performance-based systems are more likely to attract high-performers.

Secondly, employees see reward systems as signalling the importance the employer places on various activities or behaviours. Reward systems thus have a motivational impact and must be integrated with the corporate behaviour being sought. A key strategic issue is how to use the reward system to overcome the tendency towards short-termism. If rewards are tied too closely to annual performance, managers may not devote time and energy to long-term objectives and may 'mortgage the future for present performance'.

Thirdly, the way in which employees are rewarded has a major influence on corporate culture. For example, reward systems that provide benefits for long-serving staff are likely to shape the existing culture into one in which loyalty is perceived as central to the corporate ideology. In contrast, a system that rewards innovative behaviour is more likely to help create a creative and innovative culture.

Fourthly, the reward system can help to define the status hierarchy and the decision-making structure. For example, if rewards are related directly to position in the hierarchy, horizontal career mobility is unlikely to be valued by staff because they do not see it as a reward. Wage compression can produce high performance because there is less incentive to waste time on 'gaming the system' – ie spending time ingratiating oneself with a supervisor or trying to affect the criteria for reward allocation (Pfeffer, 1994: 50–1). De-emphasising pay can also help enhance other bases of satisfaction with work.

Finally, cost is a key factor in reward systems, and for service-sector organisations labour costs are a significant proportion of their overall costs. If an organisation is under financial pressure, the employer might wish to achieve flexibility so that labour costs can be brought down. Having a lower cost ratio than competitors might be another aim. However, lower wages do not always mean lower labour costs because that depends on productivity, and high wages may be correlated with higher levels of performance (Pfeffer, 1998: 195–202).

Review the reward strategies at your workplace in the light of the five areas identified by Lawler as having an impact on organisational performance. How might you redesign your reward strategy to take account of them?

Integration or contradiction in reward structures

The fact that management aims may conflict with or contradict each other is a particular danger if those responsible for remuneration policy are unclear about its specific objectives. For example, Armstrong (1999: 11) lists a number of possible management objectives – ensuring that firms can attract, retain and motivate the appropriate quantity and quality of staff; communicating organisational values; underpinning organisational change; providing value for money; supporting the realisation of key values; and encouraging behaviour to achieve the organisation's objectives.

Another potential problem is that there may well be differences in the expectations of different groups of workers from the payment system, as we saw from the section on expectancy theory earlier in this chapter. Although much of the literature discusses the functional and dysfunctional role of reward systems, it is not always matched by discussion of the strategic role of such systems. It is usual to regard the reward system as dependent on the business strategy and the management style of the organisation concerned. Yet, as we have seen from the previous section, existing human resources and reward systems may also exercise a constraint on corporate strategy, so the relationship is not simply one-way.

The 'New Pay' is Lawler's term for an approach that asserts the need for an understanding of the organisation's goals, values and culture and the challenges of a global economy when formulating reward strategy (Armstrong, 1999: 14). This has now become the orthodoxy in pay ideas (Lawler, 1990; Schuster and Zingheim, 1992). The business strategy of the organisation determines the behaviours employees must demonstrate in order to ensure that goals may be implemented effectively. These behaviours may, in part, be delivered by the reward strategy (Lewis, 2001: 102). However, Lewis points out that there are a number of assumptions that underlie the model. First, it assumes that business strategy is a rational top-down process and that HR goals can be simply matched to it (see Chapter 8). Second, the model is 'essentially unitarist' in that it assumes that employees will endorse business strategy and demonstrate the behaviours it implies. Third, it is deterministic – it assumes that an effective reward strategy will have a direct impact upon organisational performance. Fourth, it assumes that pay will motivate employees to behave in a way in which they might not otherwise do. As Lewis observes:

> *Clearly, caution needs to be exercised in assuming that the implementation of strategic reward management will lead to a reward strategy that will automatically change employee behaviours in line with the organisation's business strategy. There are far too many variables which may conspire against such a straightforward cause-effect relationship. However, it would be foolish to abandon the possibility that reward strategy may play a role in contributing to organisational change.*

There are two dimensions to consider in the strategic design of reward systems (Lawler, 1984: 131). First, there is a structural content dimension (formal procedures and practices), and second, there is a process dimension (communication and decision process parts).

In relation to the *structural decisions*, there are several issues to address:

- the basis for rewards – Are people to be paid for the jobs they do (ie through job evaluation techniques) or for their skills or competencies? Skills-based pay is regarded as more appropriate for those organisations that have a flexible, relatively permanent workforce that is oriented towards learning.

- pay for performance – Should staff be paid on the basis of seniority or performance? Because of the problems in implementing performance-based schemes, some believe that individual pay should be based on seniority, as in Japan, with motivation to be achieved through other means (such as personal growth or recognition). If managements decide to pursue the performance route, decisions must be made on the behaviours to be rewarded and how they are to be rewarded (for example, by individual or group plans).

- the market position – The market position and stance of an organisation influence the organisational climate. If management feel it is important to be a leading player with pay levels set above those of competitors, there is likely to be a different reward system from one in which staff are regarded as less critical to business success.

- internal–external pay comparisons – Management needs to decide the extent to which they value internal equity – someone doing similar work is paid the same even if they may be in different regions or in different businesses – or external equity, which focuses on the labour market as the key determinant of levels of pay. This issue depends on the extent to which the organisation wishes to have an overall corporate identity (eg everyone working for a multinational chemical company to have similar conditions of service) or to preserve product market differentiation (eg bulk chemicals and pharmaceuticals to be treated as distinct business or product lines).

- a centralised–decentralised reward strategy – Organisations with a centralised strategy usually have a corporate HR department that develops standardised pay and wage guidelines. This creates a feeling of internal equity and shared values. In decentralised organisations, flexibility allows for local options.

- a degree of hierarchy – Managements can choose whether they employ a hierarchical approach to reward – by which people are rewarded according to their position in the hierarchy and are often also provided with symbols of their status – or a more egalitarian approach by which the climate is more team-based and there are fewer status symbols.

- the reward mix – This refers to the type of rewards given to individuals (benefits, status symbols, etc) or, indeed, the choice employees are given through a cafeteria-style approach by which individuals can make up their own package (see Chapter 17). Again, the form of rewards should reflect the culture or climate the employer wishes to create and reinforce.

Assess where your organisation fits with regard to the eight structural issues raised by Lawler, and whether they support or contradict one another. Explain why this is the situation and how greater horizontal and vertical integration may be achieved.

In relation to the *process dimensions* of reward systems there are two key issues:

- communications policy – How far the employer wants to have an open or closed policy on rewards depends on its philosophy. In some organisations, disclosure of salary is a dismissible offence.

- decision-making practices – The issue here is whether or not to involve employees in system design and administration. Involvement can lead to important issues being raised and expertise being provided, which is not always the case if a top-down approach is adopted. Moreover, involving employees and their representatives increases the acceptance of any changes because there is a greater sense of legitimacy bestowed on decisions. Cox (2000: 363) presents the argument for involvement in pay scheme design thus:

> *Seeking information from employees may provide a fuller perspective on whatever problems exist in the operation of the current pay scheme, thus increasing the chance that they will be resolved in the design of the new system. Furthermore, this may also ensure that the rewards offered are commensurate in timing and kind with the rewards employees desire. Full explanations of the reasons for changing the system may make employees more likely to accept the new system. The consultation process may allow the opportunity to identify any individuals or groups likely to be adversely and unfairly affected and to take action to prevent this before the scheme is implemented. Some authors argue that the process itself of involving as many parties as possible in the development of a new scheme makes them more committed to its success.*

There is no right or wrong approach, so what matters is choosing a position which supports the culture and systems, and which produces the behaviour necessary to enhance organisational effectiveness. Lawler (1984: 145) takes up the theme:

> *Reward system design features are not stand-alone items. There is considerable evidence that they affect each other and, as such, need to be supportive of the same type of behaviour, reflect the same overall managerial philosophy, and be generated by the same business strategy.*

He illustrates this by showing how two contrasting management philosophies call for two quite different approaches to reward practices – see Table 44.

Table 44   Appropriate reward system practices

	Traditional, or Theory X	Participative, or Theory Y
Reward system		
Fringe benefits	Vary according to organisation level	Cafeteria – same for all levels
Promotion	All decisions made by top management	Open posting for all jobs; peer group involvement in decision process
Status symbols	A great many, carefully allocated on the basis of job position	Few present, low emphasis on organisation level
Pay		
Type of system	Hourly and salary	All salary
Base rate	Based on job performed; high enough to attract job applicants	Based on skills; high enough to provide security and attract applicants
Incentive plan	Piece-rate	Group and organisation-wide bonus, lump-sum increase
Communications policy	Very restricted distribution of information	Individual rates, salary survey data, all other information made public
Decision-making locus	Top management	Close to location of person whose pay is being set

Source: Lawler E. 'The strategic design of reward systems', in C. Fombrun, N. Ticky and A. Devanna (eds), *Strategic Human Resource Management*, New York, Wiley, 1984. p146 (Reprinted with permission of John Wiley & Sons, Inc.)

Moreover, the congruence or fit has to be consistent with the HR system as a whole. As Lawler (1984: 145-6) notes, this 'means that the reward system needs to fit such things as the way jobs are designed, the leadership style of the supervisors, and the types of career tracks available in the organization ... ' Unless this kind of fit exists, the organisation will be replete with conflicts and, to a degree, the reward system practices will potentially be cancelled out by the practices in other areas. In short, a contingency approach – which takes into account particular organisational and environmental factors – is likely to be superior to an off-the-shelf solution which reflects current fads and fashions.

Much of the literature in the field tends to be prescriptive. We are told how management should tackle the subject of reward management but not what actually happens in practice. Kessler's (2001: 268) research suggests that the overwhelming impression was one of incremental change in approach to pay. Changes in reward policy appear to have been driven by short-term cost considerations and the need to respond to immediate labour market pressures rather than by any strategic intent. A major concern is that few managements attempt to evaluate their pay schemes in any real depth. They appear not to have clear criteria against which the schemes can be evaluated, but instead tend to rely on a 'gut feel' assessment that, for example, because of its performance emphasis a performance-related pay (PRP) system must be conducive to good performance (Sisson and Storey, 2000). Conversely, any contra-indications or difficulties are dismissed as mere 'teething problems' which relate to issues of implementation. An interesting study of how HR professionals attempted to align reward strategy with business strategy at BOC Gases (UK) was described in *People Management* (Collerton and Bevan, 1998). It emphasised the need not simply to show how employees can contribute to business success but how they can also share in the spoils.

Different types of payment scheme

According to Torrington (1993: 149), arrangements for payment have since the 1940s had one or two underlying philosophies. First, *the service philosophy* emphasises the acquisition of experience, implying that people become more effective as they remain in a job so that their service is rewarded through incremental pay scales. These scales are typically of five to eight points, encouraging people to continue in the post for several years while there is still some headroom for salary growth. Second is *the fairness philosophy*, which emphasises getting the right structure of differentials. The progressive spread of job evaluation from the 1960s onwards was an attempt to cope with the problems of relative pay levels that were generated by increasing organisation size and job complexity. Legislation on equal value in the 1970s gave further impetus to this approach.

Accompanying the growth of pay systems emphasising service and fairness, was a steady decline in incentive schemes. These were developed almost entirely for manual workers from the early part of the twentieth century until the late 1960s, but faded back following years of battling with union representatives, through employees using their ingenuity in outwitting the work-study officer, and because of changes in production technology. More recently there has been a return to the incentive idea and a new performance philosophy has arisen. Length of service is useful, fairness is necessary, but what really matters is *the performance* of the employee (Torrington, 1993: 149).

It is important that HR professionals do not see the payment system solely as something in its own right, but also see that it has links with organisation strategy and other human resource practices. Simply adopting a policy of selecting a scheme because it is the latest thing to do is likely to be a recipe for failure. Nor should managements regard the adoption of a payment system as the complete and final solution to problems of pay policy. Indeed, there is a view that every scheme that is implemented, however satisfactory, contains the seeds of its own destruction (Watson, 1986: 182–3). As individuals or groups bring their own interests to bear on the system, the system subsequently becomes very difficult to manage as those interests become embedded. The system then starts to serve certain groups rather than the organisation as a whole. Furthermore, as technology, business objectives, work organisation and labour supply alter, it and other systems may have to be re-evaluated. In short, pay systems are not for ever (Sisson and Storey, 2000: 141).

Describe the payment systems that exist in your organisation, and explain their rationale.

It is also crucial to understand that the choice of payment system depends on the particular circumstances of the organisation, the technology, the characteristics of the labour market and employee attitudes. Accordingly, managers must think carefully about the conditions under which a scheme will operate and the messages it will send to various audiences. A contingency approach, in which managers pick a scheme appropriate to their organisational needs, is more likely to be successful (Taylor, 2000: 15–18). For example, an employer who stresses the importance of quality is likely to undermine this philosophy by the introduction or maintenance of a payment-by-results scheme (such as piecework) which transmits the message that output is the key aim of the employer. Equally, an organisation that is not doing well financially may find it difficult to introduce a system of performance-related pay (PRP) because employees are likely to see few benefits for themselves. Indeed, research suggests that PRP schemes require to be 'greased in' to facilitate a trouble-free introduction. Moreover, the paucity of systematic evidence on the incentive effects of various payment systems should urge us to be wary of swallowing a consultant's line that their package will improve performance where other schemes or strategies have failed.

Payment according to time

Time-based rates are usually expressed as an hourly rate, a weekly or monthly wage, or an annual salary. Some three-quarters of British employees are paid on straightforward time-based rates, although in some cases a payment by results component may be added. There are two forms of time-based rate. The first is a flat rate per period of time. The second incorporates fixed scales, with increases based on length of service (Lynch, 2000: 275). Such schemes are simple and cheap to administer, are easily understood by employees, and are unlikely to cause disputes in themselves. Nonetheless, they are limited in providing work incentives (ACAS, 1991). Time-based rates are often found in managerial and white-collar work, although many managers put in more than their contractual hours, or in complex and process industries (such as in chemicals) where it is difficult to measure individual contributions to performance. With time-based systems, work effort and work quality has to be guaranteed by supervisory control or through well-established systems of custom and practice.

There has been a shift from simple wage systems, with a single rate attached to all jobs of the same description, to salary systems where there is a range of pay for each job grade. Salary systems with pay progression reflect a view that experience is important and should be rewarded, so that progression through salary scales is based on length of service or age (Thompson, 2000: 127). However, there have been problems with traditional incremental systems, which in theory can provide both 'carrot' and 'stick' by withholding or offering increments. In practice, the lack of a systematic appraisal system and high employee expectations means that automatic increments tend to be the norm. This means that staff bunch at the top of a grade, so making it expensive for employers to fund. Within the NHS there are proposals to abolish the automatic, service-based incremental programmes in favour of one based on responsibilities and competencies as the route to progression (Hatchett, 2001: 37). Different rules apply for movement *within* grades, which typically use an incremental system, from those for promotion *between* grades, where a more demanding system is typically employed (Brown and Walsh, 1994: 451). Whereas time-based rates should be simple, in practice additional payments for overtime add complexity. An additional problem with time-based rate schemes is grade drift by which – over time – jobs bunch up in the higher ranks of the structure. Also, there can be a proliferation of job grades, because new grades are used to 'buy' employee acceptance to a change in the job, which then requires restructuring every few years in order to simplify the structure. However, Brown and Walsh (1994: 454) argue that allowing grade drift in order to facilitate change – knowing there will be restructuring at a later period – is preferable to haggling over 'fair' cash shares from productivity improvements. In other words, one-off payments are granted in return for productivity improvements.

Payment by results (PBR)

The philosophy here is to establish a link between reward and effort as a motivational factor. Such schemes reflect the ideas of F. W. Taylor, the father of scientific management who, by standardising work processes through time and motion studies, laid the groundwork for such schemes to operate. As we saw earlier, views that workers are motivated solely by money led to the introduction of payment schemes that had been designed to reflect that.

Individual PBR schemes vary in practice, and they can relate either to the whole of the employee's pay or be part of an overall pay package. Actual payment may vary according to output, or there may be payment of a fixed sum on the achievement of a particular level of output. Most schemes have fallback rates and guarantee payments for downtime. The principal advantage of individual PBR schemes is that the incentive effect should be strong because workers can see a direct link between individual effort and earnings. By way of contrast, the major disadvantages of individual PBR are that they are expensive to install and maintain, often requiring a dedicated team to establish the system. Moreover, standards are often disputed and considerable effort may be made on both sides to apply the appropriate standards, or to renegotiate in the light of any changes, as perhaps caused by new technology or by problems with components supplied. Finally, there is often friction between employees because of the emphasis on personal performance. Employees may also point to external factors that impact on performance but are not within their own control.

The most popular form of individual PBR is piece-work. Piece-work (or piece-rate) schemes have a long tradition in British industry, in particular in the textiles, footwear and engineering industries. They are based upon work-study methods by which the employee is simply paid a specific rate or price per unit (ie piece) of output. Although piece-work survives in some industries, such as clothing (Druker, 2000: 115), few new schemes are being introduced and their importance has declined since the 1960s (Millward *et al*, 2000: 213). Such schemes are regarded as incompatible with the emphasis on team-based forms of work organisation – eg cellular manufacturing. Outside the production arena, PBR was once common in the form of commission paid to sales staff in sectors such as insurance and estate agencies. However, commission-based pay was badly hit by scandals over the mis-selling of pensions in the 1990s, when this form of payment was perceived as a major contributor to the problem.

Three major issues must be considered in relation to PBR schemes: control, erosion and complexity. It has been argued that under PBR, less personal or direct supervision is necessary because it is in the worker's own interest to be productive. The age-old problem of buying workers' time but not their effort is supposedly eliminated. On the other hand, the system encourages speed, not quality (Druker, 2000: 115) so supervisors are obliged to watch for short-cuts that may result in lower quality or in health and safety risks or hazards. With frequent changes in technology, management now need closer control over production, and for that reason individual PBR has become less popular.

Schemes can degenerate through rate drift as a result of a learning curve, new technology (which does not always lead to the remeasuring of jobs), and various worker fiddles which can hide slack rates. One other key issue relates to problems of leapfrogging and poor morale as a result of changes in rates that other workers then try to negotiate. PBR can rarely be applied uniformly to all employees in an organisation, and may well therefore seem out of place in a harmonised environment.

For PBR to operate properly, standards of performance have to be set. In the past, rate-fixers who had expertise in the industry would set standard prices or times. More recently, standards have tended to be set by using work-study techniques. This requires both work study and the dedication of part of the personnel function, not to mention a quality-monitoring department. However, changes in product, material, specification or method are likely to require a new set of standards, which in turn may stimulate a bargaining process that can lead to employee relations problems, especially when workers who have become proficient in a specific task resist new methods.

A variation is group PBR, which is often used where the production process makes it difficult to attribute performance to any one individual, so it is based around the group. Considerations that apply here are similar to those that apply with individual PBR, but it is also important to recognise that a group scheme is likely to have a more positive effect if it is based on a natural work group, in which cohesiveness and solidarity can reinforce the scheme. However, the motivational effect of group PBR schemes is likely to decline as group sizes increase, the group loses its ethos, and there is a greater distance between effort and earnings.

Can you think of any jobs in your organisation for which a form of PBR might be suitable? What *makes* it/them suitable? Could PBR rise again?

Plant/enterprise-based schemes

Whereas PBR can be effective for particular industries or groups, it may do little for overall performance, especially if there is friction between different groups. Enterprise or plant-wide bonus schemes (sometimes called *gainsharing*) encourage staff to identify more widely with the organisation as a whole, attempting to make work appear to be a win-win situation, both employees and the organisation deriving direct financial success from the operation (Bowey, 2000: 330). Gainsharing (a minority practice in the UK) differs from profit-sharing schemes in that it takes account of the fact that profits may be affected by external factors such as interest rates or the increased price of raw material. Gainsharing thus recognises that profits may bear little resemblance to productivity gains that reward employees for their efforts towards increasing their performance, and establishes a link between the achievement of corporate objectives and increased reward (Morley, 2002: 93–4).

Scanlon plans – named after their inventor, an ex-union-official who was responsible for a number of schemes in the US steel industry in the 1930s and 1940s – are based on the ratio of total payroll costs to sales value of production. A norm is estimated from an inspection of the figures over a representative period prior to the introduction of the technique. The smaller the ratio, the higher the bonus. The payment aspect of Scanlon plans is supplemented by a participation element often incorporating both a suggestion scheme and some form of consultative structure at departmental and/or unit level.

The *Rucker plan* (like its UK variant, the *Bentley plan*) is similar in many respects, but the wage calculation is based on the ratio of payroll costs to production value added (PVA) – that is, the difference between the sales value of output and the cost of materials, services and supplies. It represents the commercial value of the process of conversion from raw (or bought-in) materials to the finished product, so that value added is then available for the payment of all potentially internally-controlled costs such as wages, profits and investment. The amount that constitutes wages is a proportion of the value added, fixed at a rate determined after the inspection of records over the preceding years. For example, assume that for every £1,000 received for the sales value of output £500 is spent on the cost of materials, supplies and services. The £500 which remains is the production value added. An inspection of previous accounts suggests that labour's share of PVA is 40 per cent – that is, wages have typically taken £200 of the £500 value added. Wages will then increase or decrease in future depending upon the absolute size of PVA, and this can be increased by greater sales value of output or lower costs of services, supplies and materials. Either of these will increase the amount available for distribution as wages, profits and investment. Increasing the sales value of output can be achieved by higher sales or prices, and costs of materials can be reduced among other actions – by greater control over their usage, a higher proportion of output which is 'right first time', more efficient utilisation of energy, and so on. The incentive for employees to improve these aspects of their work is recognised in an explicit manner and can be rewarded by higher payments; gainsharing is therefore institutionalised and becomes a non-negotiable bonus for the employee. In addition, so as to protect workers against loss-sharing, minimum wage levels are set, and a reserve account is set up to cope with this eventuality.

However, the payment element is only one part of the scheme. Central to the whole scheme is a structure enabling employee representatives to contribute to decision-making via a works council or Joint Consultative Committee (JCC) arrangement. IDS (1999) reports a gainsharing plan for workers at Philips Components in Durham where payment reflects local labour market rates, technical performance and an annual bonus. The plan operates as a production rather than team bonus linked to factors both team and plant-based (Druker, 2000: 16). Managers are charged with the responsibility of ensuring that employees understand the figures, and with listening to worker suggestions about the operation of the system and its establishment. A key feature of the scheme thus formalises the relationship between employee participation in decision-making, organisational efficiency and individual reward.

In general such schemes have the advantage that employees see their contribution to the total effort of the enterprise and do not see themselves as individual units. In this way it can facilitate achievement of corporate identity. As this form of financial participation is often part of a wider consultation process, this can lead to a greater understanding of business issues as employees take more interest in the overall performance of the enterprise. There may be a greater willingness on the part of employees to accept and even push for change; managers may feel more able to discuss issues with workers; and greater productivity and efficiency can be achieved.

Set against the advantages, there are some potential disadvantages. Firstly, although gainsharing plans are implemented on the assumption that employees perceive the connection between their own efforts and the rewards generated by the scheme, in many cases the employees have little control over the size of the bonus. External factors – such as increased costs of raw materials or services – may limit the bonus, as may management decisions to delay an increase in prices due to competitive pressures. Secondly, rather than encouraging co-operation between different groups in the organisation, the schemes may increase inter-group hostility and recriminations if the bonus levels fail to meet employee expectations. Not only can this be problematical for employers and run counter to their objectives, it can also create conflicts within and between unions. Thirdly, some unions fear that gainsharing plans will lead to a progressive marginalisation of their role. This could occur because collective bargaining is likely to become less important in determining wage levels, or because employees will develop greater commitment to the goals of the company and 'give away' hard-fought-for gains.

Probably most important of all, some schemes may fail because managers are not prepared to accept a modified role, listen to employee suggestions for improvements, and act upon these ideas. A reassertion of managerial prerogative is likely to undermine employee commitment to the scheme.

In view of the current vogue for empowerment and the gaining of employee commitment to organisational goals, why are establishment-wide incentive schemes not more popular?

Performance-related pay (PRP)

The early 1990s have seen employers from both the private and the public sectors putting a much greater emphasis on 'paying for performance' and attempting to 'incentivise' remuneration in order to improve individual and organisational performance and create a new performance-based culture. These schemes base pay on an assessment of the individual's job performance. Although such schemes are not identical, they provide 'individuals with financial rewards in the form of increases to basic pay or cash bonuses which are linked to an assessment of performance, usually in relation to agreed objectives' (Armstrong, 1999: 268). Accordingly, pay is linked to performance measured by a number of specific objectives (for example, sales targets or customer satisfaction). This reflects a move towards rewarding output (rather than input), using qualitative (rather than quantitative) judgements in assessing performance, a focus on working objectives (rather than personal qualities), and an end to general annual across-the-board pay increases (Fowler, 1988).

PRP became popular as a reflection of the 'enterprise culture' in the late 1980s but continues to find favour in two-thirds of organisations up to the present day, particularly in the eyes of managers and professional staff. However, WERS indicates that whereas non-managerial employees had some form of appraisal in more than half of workplaces, in only 11 per cent were these on individualised PRP schemes (Cully *et al*, 1998: 10). PRP has also become more widely used in the public sector (for example, local government, the NHS, the Civil Service, and more recently, teachers), for which governments of both political complexions have promoted the concept. Similarly in sectors such as financial services it was felt that the traditional system of reward valued seniority and long service, but not performance (Lewis, 1998).

Teachers and performance-related pay

The teachers' case is interesting because it reflects the imposition of PRP on an unenthusiastic workforce. As part of a wider set of changes in the education sector designed to enhance skills, salaries have been raised 'substantially but selectively' by introducing a threshold (which is based on an application form with evidence of knowledge) on the top of the experience-related salary scales. Once teachers pass this they are then able to enter a new pay range based on annual performance review (Marsden, 2000). Those who pass the threshold immediately receive £2,000, and later payments could take salaries up to £30,000 (see Cooper, 2000d).

However, the scheme has been attacked by the NUT and NAS/UWT who have claimed it will lead to jealousy and loss of morale. The academic David Guest stated that 'For performance-related pay to work, you have to have a situation where the employees have control over the outcome. If they don't have control, the whole thing becomes a farce.' And consultants such as Duncan Brown pointed to the failure to consult (Cooper, 2000e). Guest noted, though, that teachers would

---

be pragmatic and that 'most will overcome their distaste and see that the government is offering a free gift they might as well go for'. In research conducted at the London School of Economics, Marsden (2000) noted that because teachers are strongly attached to the principle that their pay should reflect job demands, there is a feeling that all teachers deserve a pay rise. Whatever the unfairness and inconsistencies of the old system, it is suggested that the proposed link between pay and performance will do little to improve fairness. Although the government stressed the positive arguments for improving rewards and incentives, teachers' responses are likely to be conditioned by what they believe are its true objectives. There is general scepticism about the professed goal of raising pupil achievements, and a strong suspicion that there is a hidden agenda towards minimising the cost of uprating teachers' salaries, and towards getting more work out of them (Marsden, 2000). The headlines and debates have continued as almost all teachers who have applied for the bonus have been successful (only 3 per cent of applicants failed to qualify), and over £12 million has been spent on external assessors to verify that heads had correctly awarded bonuses (Cassidy, 2001).

Read Armstrong's article in People Management, *12 October 2000. Do you agree with him that the teachers' case is a lesson in 'how not to'?*

PRP is different from the types of incentive scheme that we have examined so far in this chapter, in that many traditional incentive schemes in manufacturing are collectively-negotiated and based on standard formulae whereas PRP is designed on an individual and personal basis. Accordingly, some workers do better than others – and some do worse – and it is this that makes PRP for manual workers a recent phenomenon. A common approach has been to have PRP on top of a general award, so that, say, 2 per cent is awarded to all employees to cover inflation, and additional payments are made to reward above-average performance. Alternatively, there may be no across-the-board increase but all pay increases are dependent on performance.

According to Armstrong (1999: 276–7), PRP offers the following potential benefits:

- It motivates people and therefore improves individual and organisational performance.

- It acts as a lever for change.

- It encourages line managers to see the process of objective-setting as part of their approach to managing their department or unit.

- It delivers a message that performance generally or in specified areas is important, and that good performance is paid more than poor performance.

- It links reward to the achievement of specified results that support the achievement of organisational goals.

- It helps the organisation to attract and retain people through financial rewards and competitive pay, and reduces the 'golden handcuff' effect of poor performers staying with employers.

- It meets a basic human need – to be rewarded for achievement.

> What are the principal benefits that employer and employees gain from PRP? Does this general list correspond with experience in your own organisation? Which of these reasons do you believe are the strongest ones? Do any of these relate to your own organisation?

It is hard to find definitive evidence to measure the achievements of PRP. Indeed, isolating one aspect of HR and linking it to performance is problematical. Although PRP has been widely promoted, and practitioners in particular seem to retain great faith in its merits, in recent years there has been a more cautious, not to say critical, evaluation of the ideas behind PRP. Brown and Armstrong (1999) claimed that there were at least as many studies suggesting PRP can reinforce and contribute to organisational and individual performance as those suggesting that it cannot. The studies cited tend to be based on employer perceptions (often the personnel managers responsible for introducing the scheme) rather than employees (Hendry et al, 2000). The best 'proxy' indicator is likely to be employee reactions. As Lewis (1998; 74) notes:

If employees are generally in agreement with both the principle and practice of PRP, then they will be motivated to better job performance and beneficial organisational outcomes will follow. Conversely, if they are not in agreement with either the principle or the practice of PRP, then they will not be motivated to perform more effectively in their jobs and such organisational outcomes will not follow.

Lewis argues for more attention to the softer element of the PRP process, such as greater involvement in agreeing objectives, feedback of results in a developmental way, although he observes that in the financial service organisations he examined, managers tended to impose objectives on staff.

One of the most cited studies is by Marsden and Richardson (1994) who analysed the Inland Revenue's introduction of PRP on the grounds that it should act as a motivator. They questioned over 2,000 staff about the impact of PRP on their own behaviour as well as on others Judgements concerning performance were made through the staff appraisal system, which involved three key stages. Firstly, there was an annual discussion of individual work objectives for the coming year between each staff member and his or her supervisor. Secondly, there was a review of achievements in relation to job plans which sometimes led to producing a revised plan. Finally, there was evaluation of staff performance at the end of year according to thirteen criteria. These included standard of work (quality and quantity), personal skills (planning, problem-solving, negotiation, decision-making), management (of staff and resources), communication (oral and written), working relationships (with colleagues and the public), and knowledge (both professional and technical). Staff were placed in one of five categories – outstanding performance, performance significantly above requirements, performance that meets the normal requirements, performance that is not fully up to requirements, and unacceptable performance. Payments were made in the form of additional increments, which were usually permanent even if in principle they could be withdrawn after unsatisfactory performance. The research found that a majority of Inland Revenue staff (57 per cent) supported the principle of PRP, although a significant minority (40 per cent) felt hostile to it. Marsden and Richardson also found that any positive motivational effects had at best been 'very modest', and it was 'by no means implausible that the net motivation effect so far has been negative', as Table 45 illustrates.

Evidence was also gathered from those staff who carried out appraisals. That evidence confirmed the earlier results, and indeed it seemed that the appraisers were even more sceptical of the system than the employees. The obvious demotivation among staff was worrying for proponents of PRP: 55 per cent believed it had helped to

Table 45   PRP in the Inland Revenue

Has performance-related pay led you to:	Percentage	
	Yes	No
improve the quality of your work?	12	80
increase the quantity of your work?	14	78
work harder?	9	71
work beyond the job requirements?	21	70
give sustained high performance?	27	63
improve your priorities at work?	22	64
show more initiative?	27	61
express yourself with greater clarity?	13	67
be more effective in dealing with the public?	9	68
improve your sensitivity?	14	63

Source: Marsden D. and Richardson R. 'Performing for pay? The effects of "merit" pay on motivation in a public service', British Journal of Industrial Relations, Vol. 32, No. 2, 1994. p251

undermine staff morale, and 62 per cent said it had caused jealousy between them. The main reason for the failure to motivate was the perception that the allocation of performance payments was unfair. Awards were given only to those who had received good ratings, but many respondents felt the appraisal system had been corrupted. Some staff felt that the amount of money involved was not large enough to justify a change in behaviour. It is worth noting that Lawler (1990) suggests that anything less than 10 per cent of salary is too little for PRP. Finally, many staff felt that they were unable to improve their performance. The experience at the Inland Revenue appears to have also been reflected in the public sector more generally (Marsden and French, 1998). The Makinson report (see IRS *Pay and Benefits Bulletin* 499, 2000) subsequently examined the criticisms of PRP in the civil service and suggested replacing it with team bonuses.

There are many other criticisms directed at PRP – the difficulty of appraisal, the difficulty of formulating objectives, the risk of bias or perceived bias, the inevitable inflationary tendency, the high costs of administration, the dubious impact on performance, the problems associated with a focus on the individual, and the difficulty of organising and delivering the necessary degree of managerial commitment (Torrington *et al*, 2002: 604–5). Furthermore, performance pay stimulates high expectations. People respond to it because there is the prospect of more money, and the prospect has to be of significantly more money if it is to be attractive. Management therefore often introduces the scheme by indicating how much one can expect. An enthusiastic, performance-enhancing response (which is the sole purpose of the exercise) will bring with it a widespread expectation of considerably more money. A theme echoed widely in the PRP literature is that people think it is a good practice in principle, and indeed it is difficult to object to the view that hardworking and effective employees should get more than those who are less hardworking or effective. However, they are likely to disagree with how the scheme operates in practice – a factor that may lead to continual changes to the schemes. Other concerns include the fact that managers are unhappy at marking staff below average, feeling that all their staff are above average. One way to prevent this is to allocate quotas for each category, to avoid ratings clustering at a central point, but this can seem arbitrary. As Purcell (2000: 41) notes:

> *Most people in receipt of IPRP [individual performance-related pay] are in the middle range of performance. We can expect 10 per cent of staff to be in the top-performing bracket and 5 per cent to be in the poor-performer category. The rest – all 85 per cent of them – will get average awards that are similar to the going rate. Most of them have no prospect of getting into the top bracket next year, so the incentive is minimal. We could live with this if the outcome of the pay system was neutral, but often it is negative, costing more than any benefit achieved.*

According to an IPD survey (1998b) manual trade unions have been particularly unenthusiastic about PRP, dismissing such systems as unfair and divisive, and the public sector respondents were more negative, possibly reflecting a feeling of imposition combined with a view that the schemes are primarily concerned with control. Although PRP is declining in popularity, it is still widely utilised. Cox (2000: 372) describes this as puzzling in view of the negative findings, categorising PRP as 'almost universally condemned as unworkable and ineffective in the UK'. The IRS *Pay and Benefits Bulletin Report* 501 (2000) found that 'all new' schemes were increasingly rare and that companies which had PRP were now looking at flexible reward systems that took account of team performance.

In the performance assessment process, which lies at the heart of individual PRP, there are complaints about subjectivity and inconsistency (leading to accusations of favouritism). This is often compounded by lack of attention to the training of managers in carrying out appraisal and to the administrative procedures for monitoring arrangements. Furthermore, the links between performance and the level of pay are not always clear and effective. It is also apparent that individual PRP sits rather uneasily with a number of other policies which managers profess to be pursuing – especially the emphasis on teamwork.

There is a concern that PRP – with its emphasis on annual individual performance leads to a short-termist approach by which individuals look for quick returns from small-scale projects rather than addressing more fundamental problems. Of course, it is possible to argue that this simply suggests that care must be exercised in the choice of performance objectives. If sales targets are regarded as the only real objective, it is likely that long-term customer relationships, as well as management–staff relations, may be threatened. On the other hand, if the latter are highlighted as key priorities in the targets, the issue of measurement may be problematical.

Another key issue relates to equal opportunities. As Armstrong notes, there is ignorance of the Danfoss (1989) ruling under the EC Equal Pay Directive which states that 'The quality of work carried out by a worker may not be used as a criterion for pay increments where its application shows itself to be systematically unfavourable to women.' As Armstrong (1998: 280) comments, 'There is a possibility that assessments made by managers (the majority of whom are still male) of their female staff could be biased.' Druker (2000: 123) also observes that 'Payment *for the job* failed to deliver equal pay for women workers but, given a legacy of workplace gender discrimination, there is a risk that payment *for the person* will counter rather than advance the cause of pay equity.'

> Prepare a paper on PRP for your management team, making suggestions on whether it is appropriate for your organisation. Justify your recommendations.

Financial participation and employee share ownership

From the 1980s there was substantial growth in the field of financial participation (sometimes termed 'people's capitalism') fuelled by a number of developments in the area. It included the Conservative government's interest in extending financial involvement on a voluntary basis as opposed to other more radical forms of participation. In addition the Social Chapter makes reference to employee participation in the capital or profits/losses of the European company. Unlike the current British provisions, however, it goes further in requiring a scheme to be negotiated between the management board of the enterprise and the employees or their representatives. There are a number of objectives behind the introduction of financial involvement – such as education, recruitment and retention, performance and paternalistic ideas – although it is likely that several of these are combined (Hyman, 2000: 180–1).

There was major growth in employee share ownership schemes in the 1990s, which can be attributed partly to tax incentives in order to make them more attractive to companies. The 1998 WERS survey showed that over 40 per cent of employees received profit-related payments or bonuses, and that nearly 30 per cent were entitled to Save As You Earn (SAYE) share options (Arthurs, 2002b: 200). Such payments are on the increase in Europe, with British companies leading the way (Pendleton and Brewster, 2001), and there is some evidence to suggest that organisations in which employees have a financial stake perform better (Freeman, 2001).

Some 2 million employers are involved in more than 1,800 Inland-Revenue-approved schemes, through SAYE share options, employee share ownership programmes (ESOPs) or a corporate personal equity plan (PEP). SAYE share option schemes allow employees to buy shares in their company on a specified future date at the (often discounted) share price at the start of the contract. Employees enter a savings scheme for three, five or seven years, using the proceeds to purchase the shares. For the standard ESOP the organisation sets up an employee benefit trust linked to a share participation scheme. The trust then either borrows money or receives contributions from the company with which to purchase shares for distribution to employees. A Single Company PEP provides tax advantages for employees in approved profit-sharing or SAYE schemes with reduced capital gains tax. A new type of all-employee scheme was introduced in 2000–2001 that involved tax relief arrangements on up to £3,000 of free shares awarded on the basis of performance. Other proposals involved 'partnership' or 'matching' shares, currently known as 'BOGOF' (Buy one, get one free). All such shares are free of income tax, National Insurance contributions (NICs) and capital gains tax if held for five years (Stredwick, 2002: 70–1).

A number of problems are apparent in profit-sharing and employee share-ownership schemes. Firstly, schemes do not usually provide any real control because employees are unable to influence to any great extent the level of profits or the quality of management decision-making within the enterprise. Secondly, investing savings in the firms for which they work can increase employee insecurity. If the employer goes out of business or suffers cutbacks, individuals not only stand to lose their jobs, they might also lose some or all of their savings (Heery, 2000: 65). The 2002 Enron scandal in the USA exemplifies this. A further major problem with financial involvement is that it does not link effort to reward in a clear and unambiguous manner, nor is the payout made at regular enough intervals to act as a motivator of staff. Because profits or share prices are affected by many factors other than employee performance, it is difficult to conceive of this as a reward for effort. Indeed, due to factors beyond the control of employees, an individual who has worked extra hard during the year may be 'rewarded' with a negligible profit share, or one that has hardly bothered may receive a bonanza. In any case, by the time the share announcement is made, so much time has passed since the beginning of the financial year that it is difficult to recall how hard one had been working. All of these problems are especially marked in multi-divisional businesses. This leads to the dis-embodiment of profit-sharing from its alleged motivational base making shares/bonuses nothing more than an extra payment that leads to more or less satisfaction depending upon the amount. Some would argue that employers would be better advised using this money to reward specific individuals, say, through a performance-related pay scheme, rather than through a standardised, all-embracing system.

> Why are employees not always keen to engage in profit-sharing? How might you seek to persuade staff in your organisation that profit-sharing is a good idea?

New payment initiatives

Skills-based pay (sometimes referred to as competence-based pay or pay-for-knowledge) schemes have become more prominent in organisations (Hastings, 2000). This approach emerged from the USA in the 1980s to provide incentives for technical staff. Core competencies or skills are built into the pay system, and rewarded according to the standard or level achieved, so inputs *and* outputs are considered, rather than just outputs – which has become a criticism of PRP – and it is forward-looking rather than retrospective. Such an approach encourages skill development and should widen and deepen the skills-base of the organisation. Furthermore, it may increase job satisfaction, break down rivalries between groups or units, and increase flexibility as well. This in turn could reduce the costs of absenteeism. Competence-based pay is actually wider than skills-based pay because it incorporates behaviour and attributes, rather than simply skills alone, for which reason some writers suggest that skills-based pay is for manual workers, whereas competency pay is for white-collar workers. In many respects this system represents a rejection of ideas encountered in job evaluation because, unlike job evaluation, it evaluates the person rather than the job. There are potential problems with such systems, in that managements have to think some years ahead about future skill requirements. It may create high and unfulfilled expectations among employees if they reach the top of the skills-based pay structure. As Lewis (2001: 108) notes:

The more the approach moves from one where identifying discernible skills and outputs is possible, the more subjective the measurement process becomes. As yet, little empirical research has been done on the operation of competence-related pay but it would be surprising were it to uncover anything other than the same sort of employee dissatisfactions as PRP. However, the measurement criteria themselves may be more acceptable to employees than in the case of PRP. This is often because there is some form of employee involvement in the development of the competence statements, albeit that line managers are making the assessment of the extent to which they have been demonstrated. This is unlike PRP where it is usually the manager who defines the performance objectives and assesses performance.

CASE STUDY: Competence-based pay at Adams

The key aims of the competence-based pay-for-skill scheme for store managers were to:

- give managers a clear understanding of their role and responsibilities

- identify objectives for individuals to give them a clear direction

- provide managers with feedback on how they are performing

- reward staff for their performance

- facilitate succession planning for the company

- change the organisational culture.

Competencies were largely based on personal effectiveness and business management, with a strong retail focus, and were part of a broader process, starting with managers defining expectations by:

- agreeing to roles and responsibilities
- identifying performance indicators
- formulating their own performance-developed plan.

Before their final review meeting store managers have to assess their own performance, decide what they have achieved and think about their future training and development needs. At the appraisal interview each store manager and regional manager discuss and agree on a score for every element of every competency, set new objectives for the next six months, and update the personal development plan. Employees are therefore assessed against a combination of personal and technical competencies and agreed objectives. Each competency has three levels.

Personal effectiveness

Store manager competencies

1 Leadership and influencing

Demonstrates a willingness to accept responsibility for directing others, balancing a goal-focused approach to achieving Adams' business needs with an ability to maintain staff morale, being able to gain trust, inspire confidence, persuade and to communicate clearly with people at all levels.

2 Motivating

Socially confident, self-motivated and enthusiastic role model, with the ability to be perceptive, tolerant and objective in reading and understanding staff, and open and warm in giving praise to others to build a desire to achieve.

3 Developing

Self-assured, willing to delegate, trust and rely on others, demonstrating patience, empathy and tolerance in coaching, and having the capacity to think strategically about the benefits of developing others.

4 Drive and results-orientation

Having high energy levels, a need to succeed, a 'can do' attitude, proactive in taking the initiative, being able to adapt to change and having the ability to manage a number of different and demanding issues at any one time. Having a willingness and desire to learn, to seek opportunities for self-development, to go forward with the brand, and to deliver business results.

Business manager competencies

1 Customer focus and market awareness

Maximising sales by understanding mums' needs and kids' wants, by demonstrating an in-depth knowledge of the Adams brand, the local marketplace and the broader retail environment, having the ability to convey this knowledge and understanding to others.

2 Visual merchandising skills

Able to demonstrate a clear understanding of visual merchandising principles, having the ability to logically and commercially interpret company guidelines and to adopt to own store configuration to drive sales. Conscientious in maintaining high visual merchandising standards.

3 Stock management

Having a practical, methodical and efficient approach to stock management, with the ability to understand, implement and monitor controls to minimise stock loss at the same time as maximising sales opportunities.

4 Planning and organising

Consistent in thinking and planning own and others' activities taking account of day-to-day and longer-term business needs, well-organised in managing Adams' administration procedures, exercising good time management and adopting a flexible approach, able to build a business plan for the store.

5 Problem-solving and decision-making

Confident and calm in assuming decision-making responsibility, having the ability to objectively analyse information and formulate logical solutions which ensure that opportunities are maximised and risks minimised.

Adams decided to implement the option of a percentage on top of salary for competency. To avoid having a large reward gap between the different levels of competency the company opted to include extra stages within each level, and this has created more of an incentive. It means that someone who is deemed to be working towards a level 2, but has not yet attained it, will get more than an individual who scores a straight level 1.

The new pay-for-skill scheme replaces the annual cost-of-living increase. Adams wants to change store managers' perception of viewing their pay review as an automatic cost-of-living increase and build a greater pay-for-performance mentality within the organisation.

Adapted from 'Retail rewards: competency-based pay at Adams', IRS *Pay and Benefits Bulletin* 480, September 1999

Competence-based pay is regarded as more applicable for organis-ations which are experiencing rapid technical change and in which a high degree of involvement already exists so that the new scheme can be introduced with the co-operation of employees and the exchange of necessary information (Cox, 2000). There is little evidence of its impact in the UK, and it appears more written about than practised (Thompson, 2000: 143). The 1998 IPD survey reported that the system was used for 6 per cent of managers and 11 per cent of non-managers. Furthermore, as Druker (2000: 119) notes:

There are constraints as well as benefits in the use of SBP. It requires a careful analysis of skill needs and a clear commit-ment to training opportunities. Whilst skills-based payment sys-tems seem to facilitate an open-ended commitment to upward mobility, employers are concerned with the application as much as with the acquisition of skill. There is a concern to avoid paying for skills that are not used. The scope for advancement through skills acquisition is likely to be inhibited both by the training budget and by employer willingness to accommodate increased wage costs, unless it is an integral and necessary aspect of organisational change.

'Reward management interventions do more harm than good in build-ing trust, commitment and motivation.' Read the debate on the sub-ject in *People Management*, 3 February 2000, and decide who you agree with.

CONCLUSION

It is clear that there are fads and fashions in the reward area that are influenced by prevailing theories of motivation, as well as external and internal contingencies. In this chapter we reviewed the way in which dominant reward philosophies tend to reflect the views of leading management writers who make significantly different assumptions about what motivates workers. Accordingly, incentive schemes are typically founded upon the assumption that money is the sole motivating force, while time-based systems are more likely to reflect the view that employees have hierarchies of needs. By way of contrast, some of the process theorists argue that motivation is a highly personal concept, and reward policies must therefore be flexible, allowing for cafeteria benefits and individualised packages. External contextual factors – such as incomes policies, taxation systems, and the management of the economy – also have an important influence over the choice of appropriate reward systems, as does the employer's overall business strategy and position in the product market.

We have reviewed a range of different payment systems, considering objectives and purpose, countrywide distribution, and advantages and disadvantages in practice. The point has been made that no one type of system is superior to the others because so much depends upon the context in which each scheme is to function. In this respect, the history and traditions of the workplace and the industry are critical, as too are the attitudes of management and employees. It is argued that the pay package represents a powerful potential lever in facilitating employee contributions to organisational success, but too often employers adopt pay systems without a full and systematic analysis of the options available. Rather than being commonplace, strategic reward management is a rarity, and all that seems to happen is that employers 'shuffle the pack' (Kessler, 1994), moving from one scheme to another when deterioration sets in. Furthermore, pay is a double-edged sword in view of its centrality to the employment relationship. It *can* be seen as a lever for change – but the importance of pay means that the consequences of getting it wrong are serious (Kessler, 2000). But we must also recall that the reward package is somewhat more than the payment system alone, incorporating a range of financial and non-financial benefits: these are considered in the next chapter.

Useful reading

ARKIN A. 'Mutually inclusive', *People Management*, 20 March 1997. pp32–34.

ARMSTRONG M. *Employee Reward*, 3rd edition. London, CIPD. 2002.

ARMSTRONG M. *and* BROWN D. *New Dimensions in Pay Management*, London, CIPD. 2001.

BROWN D. *Reward Strategies: From intent to impact*, London, CIPD. 2001.

CHARTERED INSTITUTE OF PERSONNEL AND DEVELOPMENT, *The Future of Reward*. London, CIPD. 2001.

CONKERTON S. *and* BEVAN S. 'Paying hard to get', *People Management*, 13 August 1998. p40.

LEWIS P. 'Reward management' in T. Redman and A. Wilkinson (eds) *Contemporary Human Resource Management*. London, FT/Pearson. 2001.

THORPE R. *and* HOMAN G. (eds) *Strategic Reward Systems*. London, FT/Prentice-Hall. 2000.

WHITE G. *and* DRUKER J. (eds) *Reward Management: A critical text*. London, Routledge. 2000.

Introduction

In the previous chapter we examined a range of different types of payment systems and their relevance to particular organisational contexts. When examining the reward package as a whole, however, it is important to consider other benefits – financial and non-financial – that provide the total reward experience for employees. If we take into account the various schools of thought on motivation and reward (see Chapter 16), it is clear that pay is only one element of the total reward package. Too often benefits are not seen in a strategic way but taken as 'givens'. Expectancy theory, however, suggests that a more contingent view ought to be taken, and that it may make sense to individualise rewards – a notion that has led to considerable interest in 'cafeteria' benefits.

In the reward management literature most attention has been focused on pay because it is often seen as a key lever of change, and much less attention has been devoted to benefits such as pensions and sick pay. Indeed, the other benefits have often been regarded as fixed, despite the fact that many employers pay above the statutory minimum. The benefits package has itself been subject to fads and fashions, many employers merely reacting by adjusting benefits to address short-term problems such as recruitment and retention, rather than adopting a long-term approach. For example, in the field of pensions, probably the largest item in the benefits package, there has been an absence of strategic thinking (Smith, 2000). It should be apparent from our examination of motivation that terms and conditions beyond pay can be very significant in the overall reward package.

The employment relationship assumes that employees will give their time to the organisation in return for a reward, which will certainly include money but may also include other factors such as status or job satisfaction. However, this is by no means a simple process in that the actual work is often not specified and/or different employees may expect different rewards. Because many factors are not specified in the contract – work intensity and supervision, for example – the effort bargain can only be established over time by custom and practice. Yet the effort bargain is potentially unstable because factors change, and the relationship may come to be perceived by one or other party as compromised. For example, at a time of recession managers may attempt to change working practices to increase productivity, whereas workers may perceive this as a breach of custom and practice, so leading to potential conflict (Baldamus, 1961). The achievement of fairness is central to the issue of payment, and however well the bonus scheme or payment is devised it is unlikely to be effective if it is perceived to be unfair – see Chapter 2 on the psychological contract. As Brown and Walsh (1994: 443) observe, 'the prudent personnel manager devotes far less time to devising new pay incentives than to tending old notions of fairness'. Even so, as they point out 'there is nothing absolute about fairness in pay', for it is 'a normative idea' based on comparison. Equity theory suggests that people will be better motivated if they feel they are treated equally, and demotivated if they are treated unequally. This has been referred to as the 'felt-fair' principle (Armstrong 1999: 52–3).

The remainder of this chapter is organised as follows: Firstly, we discuss job evaluation and equal value. Secondly, we look at benefits other than pay, examining pensions so as to illustrate our theme. Thirdly, we analyse the steps taken by employers to harmonise conditions, which includes benefits such as pensions and sick pay, but also the removal of barriers such as separate car parks, canteens or toilets. Fourthly, we discuss non-financial recognition, and the importance of involvement, autonomy and responsibility, before moving on to examine job redesign. As Devanna et al (1984: 48) note, 'Organisations tend to think of rewards in a fairly limited way as pay, promotion and benefits ... There are many other rewards that the organisation has to offer that individuals value.'

Before reading the remainder of this chapter, gather information about the pay levels for a sample of five occupations – for example, Member of Parliament, train driver, checkout operator, nurse, HR manager. Place these in rank order. Do you consider these pay levels to be fair in relation to each other? Why/why not? Discuss notions of fairness and differentials with your colleagues.

Job evaluation

Job evaluation can be defined as a process by which jobs are placed in a rank order according to overall demands placed upon the job-holder. It therefore provides a basis for a fair and orderly grading structure, but it is best regarded as a systematic rather than a scientific process. It is a method of establishing the relative position of jobs within a hierarchy, which is achieved by using criteria drawn from the content of the jobs. However, there is sometimes considerable confusion concerning the process. The process of writing job descriptions (which was dealt with in Chapter 10) is central to job evaluation, but it is not designed to evaluate the person or job-holder on his or her performance, or to establish the pay for the job. Job evaluation has existed since the 1920s but was given considerable impetus in the 1960s and 1970s because of government incomes policies. Job evaluation in some form is to be found and probably used in 50–75 per cent of organisations (Thompson and Milsome, 2001: 9), and its incidence increases with establishment size. Job evaluation has a number of benefits. It provides a formula for dealing with grievances about pay, and decisions are likely to be more acceptable if there is a formal system rather than only *ad hoc* ways of dealing with pay issues.

According to Arthurs (2002c: 131–2), employers normally have some or all of the following objectives in seeking to introduce job evaluation:

- to establish a rational pay structure

- to create pay relationships between jobs which are perceived as fair by employees

- to reduce the number of pay grievances and disputes

- to provide a basis for settling the pay rate of new or changed jobs

- to provide pay information in a form that enables meaningful comparisons with other organisations to be made (see also Armstrong, 1999: 108).

In broad terms job evaluations fall into two types of scheme – *non-analytical* and *analytical*.

Non-analytical schemes

Non-analytical schemes use a simple ranking method – jobs are placed in rank order – and no attempt is made to evaluate or compare parts of each job. Such schemes have fallen from favour in recent years because they are unlikely to constitute a defence in an equal-value claim at a tribunal. There are various forms of non-analytical scheme.

Job ranking
Under this system, job descriptions or titles are placed in a rank order or hierarchy to provide a league-table. It is a very simple method

because the job is considered as a whole rather than broken down into constituent parts. It is usually seen as suitable for small organisations in which the evaluation team is likely to know all the jobs. Simple and cheap to implement, it tends however to be very subjective. Furthermore, whereas job Y may be identified as being more difficult to do than job X, it is not clear *how much* more difficult it is (Duncan, 1992: 277; Smith and Nethersell, 2000: 219). For example, the following represents a simple categorisation.

Grade 1
Supervised manual labour

Grade 2
Unsupervised manual labour following prescribed procedures

Grade 3
Tasks involving interpretation of procedures

Grade 4
Tasks involving interpretation of procedures and responsibility for work groups

---

Paired comparison

This approach is similar to the above but more systematic in that each job is compared with every other job, and points are allocated depending on whether the complexity of it is less than, equal to, or more than the other jobs. The points are added up to provide a league-table. The system is more objective than job ranking but can be time-consuming unless there is computer support, in view of the comparisons that have to be made

Job classification

This is the reverse of the above process in that, under this technique, the number of grades is first decided upon, and a detailed grade definition is then produced. Benchmark (representative) jobs are evaluated with non-benchmark jobs before being slotted in on the basis of the grade definitions. The main drawbacks are that complex jobs may be difficult to assess because they may stretch across grade boundaries, and because the system works best in cohesive, stable and hierarchical organisations, its appeal today is limited (Smith and Nethersell, 2000: 219).

The main drawback of these 'whole job' approaches is that they are highly subjective. In view of the fact that the jobs themselves are not analysed systematically, it is likely that implicit assumptions about the worth of jobs may be left unquestioned. Physical strength, for example, may be given extra weight, which has significant implications for equal opportunities, in that 'women's' jobs may be rated lower than 'men's' jobs for historical reasons.

Analytical schemes

By contrast, analytical schemes involve a systematic analysis of jobs by breaking them down into constituent factors. There are two principal categories of analytical scheme.

Points rating

This is the most popular technique of all. It involves breaking down jobs into a number of factors, usually between 3 and 12, to include factors such as skill, judgement, knowledge, experience, effort, responsibility and pressure. Each factor receives weighting, which is then converted to points, and the total number of points determines the relative worth of a job. It is more objective than non-analytical methods, and by breaking down the jobs helps to overcome the danger of assessing people rather than jobs (Smith and Nethersell, 2000: 220). However, it is a time-consuming process that is prone to provoking grievances when small changes in job content lead to re-grading issues.

Factor comparison

This attempts to rank jobs and attach monetary values simultaneously. Jobs are analysed in terms of factors (mental and physical requirements, responsibility, etc) and benchmark jobs are examined, one factor at a time, to produce a rank order of the job for each factor. The next step is to check how much of the wage is being paid for each factor. Where employees are shown to be overpaid for the job they do, the usual practice is 'red-circling', which keeps the individual's pay in the post as it is (sometimes for a set period of time) although a successor would be paid the newly-evaluated (lower) rate. This system is not popular in Britain, partly because the allocation of cash values to factors is perceived as too arbitrary, and it assumes that a pay structure already exists. Factor comparison was the basis of the development of the Hay Guide chart profile method, the most widely-used around the world (Smith and Nethersell, 2000: 221).

Despite the growth of more 'scientific' forms of job evaluation, ultimately the process is subjective, in that assumptions are made about the design of the scheme, the factors and weights chosen, as well as the judgement of those doing the evaluating. Because of this, employee involvement in the scheme is important to lend credibility to something that would otherwise be seen as management-driven.

Criticisms of job evaluation

Armstrong and Murlis (1998) suggest a number of reasons why job evaluation is in a transitional phase. Firstly, equal-pay legislation has meant that it has been necessary to re-examine schemes to ensure they are analytical and gender-neutral. Secondly, new technology is changing roles, eliminating job differences and introducing new skills – for example, by reducing the emphasis on physical skills and increasing the relevance of more conceptual skills. Thirdly, there is now greater flexibility in working arrangements, and a growth in teamworking, for example. Fourthly, de-layering has meant that decisions are being made by employees lower down the hierarchy. In this way, more is being demanded of employees, and their horizons may be narrowed rather than widened by job descriptions that define a single job. Fifthly, labour market pressures due to skill shortages can lead to comparisons based on external relativities rather than on internal relativities. Finally, the notion of individual contribution is growing more important – a trend that is apparent in relation to performance-related pay schemes (see Chapter 16).

> What are the main strengths and weaknesses of job evaluation in your organisation?

Traditional criticisms of job evaluation have pointed to its costly and bureaucratic nature as well as its lack of flexibility. It is argued that job descriptions assume stability and hierarchy in the world of work – a situation that no longer appears to exist – and that job evaluation may not be compatible with employers' attempts to develop high-performance workplaces (Rubery, 1995). We have already noted that formal job evaluation processes began in the 1960s and 1970s, when, for many organisations, the main interest was in establishing internal equity, with a focus on jobs rather than on people. External labour markets were regarded as relatively homogeneous, and issues of individual performance and contribution were to a large degree optional extras, or accommodated by highly-structured systems in which employees gained automatic progression. In addition, traditional job evaluation has difficulties in coping with jobs based on knowledge work and teamworking, as well as with flatter structures. Conventional job evaluation was seen as exaggerating small differences in skill and responsibility by the attachment of points in a way that impeded flexibility. Management stressed the need to evaluate employees and not just jobs. However, rather than abandoning job evaluation, it appears that there is a movement to make it more flexible so as to reflect internal and external worth (Pickard and Fowler, 1999).

Current developments

There is some evidence that employers are developing simultaneously more flexible forms both of work organisation and of systems for job evaluation (Kessler, 2000). Strategies to achieve this include the creation of generic job descriptions and broad bands, the development of career progression linked to the attainment of key skills or competencies, the development of 'growth structures' involving clear career paths, and the integration of manual and non-manual structures. However, Whitfield and McNabb (2001) note that there is evidence that such schemes raise employee expectations, and that the conflict between new forms of work organisation and job evaluation is not readily resolvable. Nevertheless, employers are pursuing flexibility with flatter structures and fewer grades, but with wider bands attached to each grade. Rather than abandoning job evaluation, it has provided the foundation for major changes to pay structure in the NHS and local government in order to deal with equal-pay and single-status issues (Thompson and Milsome, 2001: 7). Work by Armstrong and Brown (2001) also concluded that the death of job evaluation had been greatly exaggerated, although they do acknowledge that new perspectives are evolving – such as competence-based job evaluation associated with broadbanding. With de-layering and the growth of teamworking, employers appear to be attempting to value jobs in ways that fit with the need for operational and role flexibility. Hence there has been a growth of broadbanding or job-family pay structures, which reward people who adapt to new challenges and expand their roles.

Broadbanding

Broadbanding involves the compression of a hierarchy of pay grades or salary ranges into a number of wider bands. Each of the bands normally spans the pay opportunities previously covered by several separate grades and pay ranges (Armstrong and Brown, 2001: 55). Armstrong's work (2000b: 35) suggests that broadbanding has not replaced analytical job evaluation because job 'sizing' was regarded as a basis for designing the structure, ensuring that internal equity is maintained, subject to market rate issues. However, with the structure established, job evaluation then plays a support role. Broadbanding is driven by twin pressures of the need to replace complex pay structures and organisational changes in structure and has now become the leading approach to pay structure (Thompson and Milsome, 2001; Armstrong and Brown, 2001). Not all employees are likely to be enthusiastic because it adds uncertainty to pay determination, unlike the transparency and predictability of service-related increments.

The key features of broadbanding, according to Armstrong and Brown (2001: 61), are:

- typically no more than five or six bands for all employees covered by the structure, although some organisations describe their structures as being broadbanded when they have as many as eight or nine grades

- wide pay spans, which can be 80 per cent or more above the minimum rate in the band

- emphasis on external relativities; market pricing may be used to define reference-point or 'target rates' for roles in the band, and to place jobs in the band

- less reliance on conventional and rigidly-applied analytical job evaluation schemes to govern internal relativities

- focus on lateral career development and competence growth

- increased devolution of pay decisions to line managers who can be given more freedom to manage the pay of their staff in accordance with policy guidelines and within their budgets by reference to information on market rates and relativities within their departments

- less emphasis on hierarchical labels for bands

- less concern for structure and rigid guidelines, and more concern for flexibility and paying for the person rather than the job.

Research also indicates that *competence-based factors* are being added to existing points-factor schemes and/or replaced existing factors. Job descriptions are being replaced by generic role definitions setting out core competencies, a move that has been encouraged by the take-up of NVQs (see Chapters 10 and 12). If a role requires a particular level of competence, that level can then be translated into a standard of competence performance for the individual in that role. A 'family' of closely-related jobs – such as research scientists, for example – can be constructed as a hierarchy of levels, the employees paid according to the range and depth of their competencies (Armstrong, 1999: 192–4). However, managements are interested in outputs such as bottom-line results or employee contributions, and not just inputs such as competency levels.

Equal-value considerations

The Equal Pay Act 1970 which came fully into operation in 1975 gave men and women the right to equal treatment in contracts of employment, and was concerned with wages as well as with other terms and conditions. In simple language, this meant that an employer was required to employ women and men doing the same work on the same terms and conditions. The Equal Pay Act did not originally provide for equal pay for work of equal value. It envisaged dealing with situations where men and women were doing the same or broadly similar work (which meant that the scope of comparison was narrow), where a voluntary job evaluation scheme had evaluated the work as equal, or where terms and conditions were laid down in collective agreements, employers' wage structures or statutory wage orders. Although the earnings gap between men and women has narrowed since 1970, the 1998 New Earnings Survey showed that women's average gross hourly earnings excluding overtime were 80 per cent of men's (Armstrong, 1999: 155). The Kingsmill Report in 2001 found the earnings gap to be 18 per cent. The minimum wage may be expected to reduce the gap over time because women are disproportionately represented in the low-pay sector.

The Equal Pay (Amendment) Regulations 1983 broadened the scope of the original 1970 Act. A woman or man is entitled to 'equal pay for work of equal value' (in terms of the demands made on a worker under various headings – for instance, effort, skill, decision-making). So if a woman is doing work of the same value as a man, even if it is a different job, she can claim equal pay (Equal Opportunities Commission, 2000). The change means that women performing jobs in which traditionally few men have been employed are now within the scope of the Act (or the reverse – the Act gives the same rights to men), whereas prior to this, women could not claim equal pay because they were doing jobs not done by men employed by the same employer. Equal-value claims can be made across sites, provided employees are deemed to be in the same employment (that is, working for the same or an associated employer). For example, in *Leverton v Clwyd County Council* (1989), the House of Lords ruled that establishments were covered by the same 'purple book' agreement, even if there were variations in individual terms and conditions.

The equal-pay case-file

The following cases exemplify some of the most significant decisions in this field.

1988: Hayward v Cammell Laird – Julie Hayward, a cook, won the first case to be taken after the 1984 equal-value amendment to the Equal Pay Act 1970. She claimed equal pay with tradesmen at the shipyard.

1995: Ratcliffe and others v North Yorkshire County Council – Three catering assistants and 1,300 other catering workers, mainly women, compared pay and conditions with those of a number of other employees, including a school crossing attendant. They had been made redundant and re-employed on reduced pay following the Council's successful in-house bid for its school catering service. The Council's claim that the difference in pay was due to the external labour market was discounted by an industrial tribunal, a decision upheld in the House of Lords. The Lords held that the market rate reflected the fact that the women found it hard to find work that fitted in with their childcare responsibilities, and was therefore discriminatory.

1996: School catering staff v Cleveland County Council – More than 1,500 women settled for sums ranging from £200 to £1,300. They claimed equal pay with that of male ground maintenance staff. Their salaries had, in effect, been reduced to prepare for competitive tendering.

1997: Enderby v Frenchay Health Authority and the Secretary of State for Health – Pam Enderby, a former speech therapist, filed a claim in 1986 comparing her work to that of a senior pharmacist and a senior psychologist, which are both male-dominated occupations, whereas speech therapy is a female-dominated field. The European Court of Justice ruled in 1991 that where significant statistics disclosed an appreciable difference in pay between two jobs of equal value, one of which is carried out almost exclusively by women and the other predominantly by men, the employer must show that the difference is based upon objectively-justified factors. Collective bargaining was not held to be a sufficient objective justification. The Department of Health conceded the case in April 1997.

Among 1,500 other speech therapists pursuing equal value cases, Margaret Evesham had her claim upheld by an industrial tribunal. It preferred the methodology of the independent expert to that of the employer's expert – who came from Hay Management Consultants. According to the tribunal, the overall problem with the Hay scheme for assessing whether jobs are of equal value is that the jobs must be assessed against the standard scheme, however adapted. The tribunal considers it preferable to identify factors that arise directly from the job functions being assessed.

1998: School catering staff v Bedfordshire County Council – Nearly 400 school catering staff settled their sex discrimination and equal-pay claims for a total of £1.5 million. Most will receive between £2,000 to £4,000 in back pay, although kitchen managers could receive up to £15,000.

Source: Pickard J. and Fowler A. '1999 grade expectations'. *People Management*, 11 February 1999. pp32–38. (Note: For new cases see www.cipd.co.uk)

Equal-pay regulations have far-reaching implications for organisations and their pay systems, and many employers have sought to introduce a new scheme or reassess their existing job evaluation system. Clearly job evaluation systems should reflect published objective criteria which can enable the employer to justify why particular rates are being paid to men and women. However, it is important to ensure that the scheme itself does not reflect discriminatory values, perhaps by overrating 'male' characteristics such as strength. In *Bromley and others v H and J Quick Ltd* (1988), the Court of Appeal held that paired comparisons in a whole job approach was inadequate, and a valid job evaluation scheme must be 'analytical'. It is believed that an integrated-analysis job evaluation scheme (applying to all employees) is the most defensible, and the case is helped if the system has been negotiated with a trade union and there is employee involvement in the operation of the scheme.

However, it has been argued that job evaluation seems to reinforce existing hierarchies rather than be independent and objective. This

Table 46   Is your job evaluation scheme free of gender-bias? Job evaluation (in points) using discriminatory and non-discriminatory factors

Discriminatory factors	Maintenance fitter	Company nurse
Skill		
experience in job	10	1
training	5	7
Responsibility		
for money	0	0
for equipment and machinery	8	3
for safety	3	6
for work done by others	3	0
Effort		
lifting requirement	4	2
strength required	7	2
sustained physical effort	5	1
Conditions		
physical environment	6	0
working position	6	0
hazards	7	0
Total	**64**	**22**

Non-discriminatory factors	Maintenance fitter	Company nurse
Basic knowledge	6	8
Complexity of task	6	7
Training	5	7
Responsibility for people	3	8
Responsibility for material and equipment	8	6
Mental effort	5	6
Visual attention	6	6
Physical activity	8	5
Working conditions	6	1
Total	**53**	**54**

Source: Equal Opportunities Commission, *Good Practice Guide: Job evaluation schemes free of sex bias*. Manchester, EOC. 2000

effect is partly the result of the aims of job evaluation, which tend to emphasise stability and acceptability, and hence endeavour not to disrupt established differentials (Armstrong, 1999). Non-analytical schemes are particularly prone to bias because they produce a 'felt-fair' rank order that can be based on stereotypes. Yet even with analytical schemes, problems can occur in factor choice and weighting. For example, caring and human relations skills are often missed or misunderstood. Table 46 illustrates that the choice of different factors can produce quite a different (points) rank order for the same jobs.

Rubenstein (1992) argues that the work women do tends to be undervalued (because women perform it), with the effect that traditional job evaluation (which emphasises acceptability) can merely perpetuate the status quo. Job evaluation may therefore not get rid of pay discrimination against women but merely make pay discrimination more subtle and difficult to prove.

An employer can justify differences in pay only where the variation between the terms and conditions is due to a 'material' (ie significant and relevant) factor, and not difference in gender. That is, even when 'like work' is proved, a woman has no right to equal pay if an employer can show that there is a material difference (not based on sex) between the two employees which justifies the difference in payment. Material factors held by case law to justify a difference in pay are market forces (for example, increasing the pay of a particular job to attract candidates), and 'red-circling' – ie where a job is downgraded but pay is not reduced (Shaw and Clark, 2000: 211 – 12). Other material differences could be experience or a qualification. However, this is to be evaluated on a one-by-one basis, because experience may be deemed relevant in one instance but irrelevant in another. For example, if a man is being paid more than the comparator because of certain skills he has which the applicant does not, it must be shown that these skills are necessary for the current job and do not represent, for example, a past pay agreement. The basis of comparison is each individual term of the contract. In *Hayward v Cammell Laird*, a cook claimed equal pay with a painter, joiner and insulation engineer. The report by the independent expert noted that her work was of equal value and should be paid at the

Table 47   Job titles that can result in sex discrimination

Male job-title	Female job-title
Salesman	Shop assistant
Assistant manager	Manager's assistant
Technician	Operator
Office manager	Typing supervisor
Tailor	Seamstress
Personal assistant	Secretary
Administrator	Secretary
Chef	Cook

Source: Equal Opportunities Commission, *Good Practice Guide: Job evaluation schemes free of sex bias*. Manchester, EOC. 2000

same rate. The argument that some of Hayward's terms and conditions were more favourable than those of the comparators, and therefore could offset the difference in pay rates, was ultimately rejected by the House of Lords (Armstrong, 1999: 160).

Equal value cases cannot be defended on the ground of implementation costs or of the impact on employee relations. Moreover, in *North Yorkshire County Council v Ratcliffe and others*, the House of Lords ruled that a local authority which paid women catering workers less than a group of male workers doing equivalent work – so that it could compete with a commercial firm for a tender – had not established that the difference in pay was due to a material factor other than gender.

Pensions

Pensions can be seen as a form of deferred pay. They are probably the most widespread of all fringe benefits and the most costly element of the remuneration package, especially for older workers. Half of the entire working population are members of occupational schemes, despite the fact that reward management evinces little interest in this area (Taylor, 2000b). Occupational pensions developed during the nineteenth century as part of a broader paternalistic-driven personnel policy in gas and public-service organisations, in conjunction with various other benefits such as paid leave, sickness and accident benefits. Paternalism was not simply the act of benevolent employers, but was initially apprehended as a means of managing retirement, and later of attracting and retaining a good, loyal labour force (Smith, 2000: 154–6). After World War II, pension schemes began to develop as more employees became liable to tax, thus making the tax-relief aspects of pensions especially attractive.

There are two main types of pension scheme. First, and most widespread, are defined-benefit (DB) schemes, in which the level of pension is calculated as a percentage of the retiring individual's final salary. The second are defined-contribution (DC) money-purchase schemes, in which regular payments are made (by employee and employer) to a pension fund, which are then invested – the employee eventually receives a pension based on the final value of the investment. DC schemes represent a minority of schemes. The result of the Social Security Acts 1985 and 1986 led to employees no longer being required to join a scheme, as well as to reduced penalties for those leaving. Those who do leave can take their pension with them – hence the terminology of 'portable' pensions. The incentive to stay with a particular firm is reduced, although in practice final salary revaluation tends to result in a pension that is less than the employees would have received if they had remained (Taylor, 2000b). The view that pensions were a 'golden handcuff' because of poor transfer values when changing schemes now has less force. Employees can begin personal pension plans on which they

Table 48   Comparisons of final salary (DB) and money-purchase (DC) schemes

Final salary (DB)	Money-purchase (DC)
Benefits are defined as a fraction of final pensionable pay	Benefits are purchased by accumulation of contributions invested
Benefits do not depend on investment returns or annuity rates	Benefits are dependent on investment returns, contributions and cost of annuities at retirement
Employer contributes necessary costs in excess of employee contributions	Employer contributions are fixed
Employer takes financial risk	Employee takes financial risk
Early leavers often suffer a loss because benefits are broadly linked to prices rather than to earnings	Early leavers generally do not suffer a loss because their account remains invested within the scheme
Benefits are designed for long-serving employees with progressive increases in pensionable pay	Benefits are designed for short-serving employees or those whose pensionable pay fluctuates

Source: IPD Key Facts 1999

receive a National Insurance rebate. Employers may currently even feel a need to improve their schemes to ensure that they have a retention/attraction value.

The European Court of Justice judgement in 1990 that required employers to equalise pension ages has led to the introduction of flexible pension ages, but this makes it more difficult for employers to use their schemes to determine the age at which employees will retire. Furthermore, the net result will be a rise in the cost of pension provision, which may lead some managements to re-evaluate the aims of their funds. The pressures of an ageing population, greater flexibility in working patterns and retirement age, the changing balance between private and public pension provision and increased pension regulation are all having an impact on traditional ideas about pension provision, and a shift is beginning to become apparent towards DC and away from DB.

The main objectives of occupational pension provisions are: retention, attracting new staff, improving employee relations, and managing the time and manner in which employees retire (Taylor, 2000b; Morley, 2002). Research suggests that senior management objectives rarely go beyond using pensions to attract new recruits, and many are not defined at all (Smith, 2000). Strategic intent is seen to be missing, thus reflecting the distinction between the management of remuneration (which is seen as strategic, and requiring to be actively managed) and that of pensions, which is perceived quite separately and considered closer to welfare.

Occupational or company schemes usually involve contributions from both the employer and the employee, although there are non-contributory schemes (that is, in which only the employer contributes), especially for managerial staff. Pensions may be seen as a form of deferred payment. About 4.5 million people in the UK already receive pensions from private sector occupational pension schemes, and a further 8.5 million people are paying into occupational schemes (Morley, 2002: 186–7). The Inland Revenue approves schemes (for tax relief) and sets limits on the level of benefits payable – a maximum pension at two-thirds of the employee's final salary. In the UK, annual contributions add up to around 15–20 per cent of an employer's annual wage bill, so they represent a significant proportion of labour costs.

> How much consideration did you give to the pension scheme when you started work with your current employer, and did it have any influence over your decision to take up employment there? Why do most people treat pensions in a non-strategic way?

Changes in UK legislation in the late 1980s and 1990s and judgements of the European Court of Justice, (for example, *Barber v Guardian Royal Exchange*) have each had important implications. In particular, it seems likely that the government will try to shift some of its current responsibility for old-age pension provision to the private sector. As individuals become more responsible for their old age, they may look more closely at employer provision in this area (Taylor, 2000b). However, the research evidence suggests that employees are either partly or wholly ignorant about the pension scheme provided by employers. There are also implications for HR professionals who may need to evaluate organisational objectives regarding pension schemes (Terry and White, 1998). The Pensions Act (1995) attempted to further increase the involvement of employees (or pensioners) by giving them a right to nominate or select a number of trustees, which established the need for an internal communications campaign to explain various details of the scheme. Because women have normally had shorter working lives, their pensions can be significantly lower than those of men, and it was for this reason that new legislation for sharing pensions was introduced in the Welfare Reform and Pensions Act 1999. The regulations allow for both private and state additional pensions to be shared by couples who divorce after 1 December 2000 (Morley, 2002: 186–7).

Flexible benefits

There are many other benefits which employees may value – such as sick pay, company cars, health insurance and holidays, but there is not the space to review each of them here. Perhaps one of the most valued benefits in these uncertain times is job security. Although few organisations today guarantee such benefits, some prescribe a lengthy process to be followed before redundancies are invoked, and this may provide some reassurance that terms will be fair and generous. (For a wider examination of benefits, see Armstrong, 1999: 391–407.)

In recent years there has been great interest in the notion of 'cafeteria' and flexible benefits (IDS, 1998; Clarke, 1998). The main reason for such an approach is to maximise flexibility and choice, particularly in the area of fringe benefits which can make up a high proportion of the total remuneration package. Under this system staff are provided with 'core' benefits – including salary – and are offered a menu of other costed benefits (company car, health insurance, childcare, length of holiday entitlement, etc) from which they can construct a package of benefits, up to a total value. The emphasis is on choice. Such schemes have been popular in the USA but have not been widely taken up in the UK as a result of administrative complexity and taxation issues, as well as inertia within organisations (Smith, 2000: 385). Smith argues that a preoccupation with simplicity and performance-related pay in Britain seems to act as a barrier to the lateral thinking required to evaluate flexible plans. Some of the ideas on cafeteria benefits sit well with the motivation literature, which stresses that different individuals have different needs and expectations from work. IDS identified 50 firms that operated comprehensive flexible benefit packages, including Walker's Snack Foods, the Burton Group and the Mortgage Corporation, but studies suggest that only a small minority of organisations currently operate a flexible benefits package.

How could cafeteria benefits be applied in your organisation?

According to the 1998 IDS report:

- Flexible benefits schemes are no longer the preserve of senior managers, and now cover a wider spectrum of employees.

- Dental insurance, holidays and private medical insurance are the three most common flexible benefits, but other common options include childcare vouchers, health screening, private car-leasing, retail vouchers, and life assurance.

- The reasons most often given by companies for introducing flexible benefits are the freedom it gives employees to create a mix of benefits that suits their personal circumstances (particularly in view of the growing number of dual career couples) and the longer-term potential to contain expenditure on benefits.

- The opportunity to vary benefit packages seems to be popular with employees; in some firms over 80 per cent of employees are now flexing their benefits to at least some extent.

CASE STUDY: Banking on a total reward package

The Royal Bank of Scotland offers a 'total reward' benefits package which was produced after staff consultation. 20 per cent of staff chose new preferences, and this proportion is expected to increase over time. The package is divided into six groups: private health cover, insurance (including life assurance for spouses and partners), savings such as voluntary contributions to pension schemes, 'lifestyle features' – which include the manager's company car, childcare vouchers and retail vouchers for use at Whitbread and Safeway – basic salary, and holiday. Innovative features include the facility to buy or sell up to three days' leave, the provision of a legal rights helpline, and the availability of an additional car-leasing scheme to all employees. Many more benefits are now extended to spouses and partners, and even the Christmas bonus can be traded in for a different benefit.

There are still some core benefits that are not part of the value account, although their worth is still included in the total reward statement that everyone receives each year. These include the basic pension scheme, the group profit-share scheme, death-in-service benefit, and any performance-related bonus. Eligibility for loans, the bank's Sharesave scheme and the house-purchase scheme are also not included on the flexible menu. Flexible benefits are increasingly regarded as a tax-efficient method of rewarding staff now that profit-related pay has ended.

Adapted from: Blackman T. 'Trading options', *People Management*, 6 May 1999. p42, and Clarke A. 'Flexible friends', *Personnel Today*, 5 November 1998. pp28–30

Harmonisation

Recent years have seen considerable discussion about the advantages of harmonising benefits to remove status differentials – for example, separate pension or sick-pay provision – because such differentials send out a message that some employees are second-class citizens, with a different and inferior set of rights. Harmonisation is concerned with the process of reducing differences, normally between manual and non-manual workers. The ultimate aim is to eliminate differences based on the status of employees – hence the term 'single-status', or sometimes 'staff-status' (see Chapter 7).

Conditions of employment offering scope for harmonisation may include:

- payment systems and methods of payment
- overtime and hours of work

- shift premiums

- actual times of work

- clocking or other time-recording procedures

- sick-pay schemes

- holiday entitlement and holiday pay

- pension arrangements

- period of notice (above the statutory minimum)

- redundancy terms

- lay-off/guaranteed week

- canteen facilities

- fringe benefits such as health insurance and company cars.

What differences in terms and conditions still exist between groups of workers in your organisation? Do you think that it is possible to justify them to a trade union official? If so, how?

The 1980s witnessed an increase in harmonisation, particularly inspired by the practices of Japanese new entrants, and especially on greenfield sites where there was an acceptance among all parties that common terms and conditions were a good idea. At Nissan, Wickens (1987: 7) argues that single-status is a misnomer:

It is simply not possible for everyone to have the same status in an organisation – the plant manager has a different status to the supervisor to the line worker simply because of the position held ... What we can do, however, is to eliminate many of the differences in the way we treat people and end up with the same or similar employment packages. Thus the term 'common terms and conditions of employment' is more accurate.

It is becoming increasingly difficult to present a coherent case for continuing distinctions between manual and non-manual workers in terms of separate car parks, toilets and canteens. The roots of such distinctions are deep and historically-based, and in some cases the process of reform has been slow although accelerated as a result of downsizing and restructuring over the last 20 years (Druker, 2000). Harmonisation was also perceived as one facet of employer initiatives to enhance high commitment on the shop floor (Wood, 1996), and WERS reported that single-status was strongly associated with teamworking and job security (Cully *et al*, 1998: 11).

In the UK, fringe benefits have typically been dependent on the status of the employee, so reflecting class structure, and as such the status divide has proved to be especially resistant to change (Price and Price, 1994: 527). During the Industrial Revolution in the nineteenth century it became impossible for the single entrepreneur to carry out all the management responsibilities, and so employees were brought in to take over some of these responsibilities. Two key features of this industrial bureaucracy emerged. Firstly, the hierarchy of control was associated with non-manual status, a division of brain from brawn (Arthurs, 1985). Secondly, the number of controlling tiers of bureaucracy was associated with the idea of a 'career' with which loyal and good performance would be rewarded with promotion (Price and Price, 1994). At the same time, the application of scientific management principles was applied to the shop floor allowing workers little discretion within highly specific work tasks, pay tied to output, and close discipline, all of which created a low-trust environment (Fox, 1974). By contrast, in the civil service and local government, the greater size of the non-manual workforce, the absence of a manufacturing environment, and the influence of a public sector ethos created less of a divide, and as a result, manual workers have tended to share better pension and sick-pay benefits.

Research in the late 1960s found particular disparities in relation to working hours, attendance, discipline and holidays. Manual workers had to operate according to stricter rules, and the penalties applied to them were more frequent and severe. Manual workers were disadvantaged in a number of ways: a longer working week, shorter holidays, more likelihood of suffering deductions in pay, greater irregularity of earnings, pay linked to physical capacity, greater job insecurity, few promotions, stricter rules and discipline, and separate facilities such as canteens, toilets and car parks (Wedderburn and Craig, 1974; Price and Price, 1994).

Identify the obstacles preventing harmonisation from being put into effect, and explain what can be done to overcome them.

However, reviewing the evidence some quarter of a century later, Price and Price (1994: 531) report that 'There has been a clear trend towards a narrowing or elimination of differences in treatment.' In particular, leave arrangements (holidays, sick pay and special leave), occupational pensions, and some fringe benefits (product discounts, canteen facilities) appear to have been harmonised. There has also been progress in relation to methods of recording attendance (because clocking has either been abolished or been replaced by computerised time-keeping for all employees) and a limited reduction of differences in the working week. However, payment systems and grading structures (with the exception of the introduction of cashless pay) have been more resistant to harmonisation.

As Storey and Sisson (2000: 128) argue, many of the differences 'cannot be justified and make little sense', and also make it difficult to win commitment and co-operation as demanded by HRM. Although managers were keen to wax lyrical about the importance of people and the creation of a new corporate culture, demonstrating this in practice has proved to be somewhat more elusive. In a context where common interests are emphasised, it would seem somewhat odd if some groups of workers were treated differently. Important icons in the 1980s were the high-profile Japanese implants such as Nissan, Komatsu and Toshiba, whose apparent success in achieving a committed and productive workforce made them leading-edge companies. The emphasis which managements at these companies have placed on single status – with the removal of separate canteens, car parks and even different types of clothing – caught the headlines. The logic of treating people differently has never been obvious, nor has the curious message about the value of different staff. As one union representative pointedly remarked to us, 'Does the fact that we get less bereavement leave than white-collar workers mean we grieve less, or do managers believe we are a lesser breed of humanity?'

At Komatsu, for example, single status was described as one of the biggest lessons to be learned from Japan. This was not simply a matter of having a single works canteen but meant that each member of staff had the same appraisal system and criteria. Similarly, the reward structure was also consistent with this message, all employees (from board to shop floor) on performance-related pay schemes. Pfeffer (1994: 48) refers to such initiatives as 'symbolic egalitarianism', and suggests that they have a role to play in reducing 'them and us' attitudes, and achieving competitive advantage through people. According to Morton (1994: 49), the demonstration of single status was a precondition for flexibility at Komatsu. He argues that if employees do not feel threatened by losing an employable skill, resistance will disappear. The strong emphasis on teamworking was also a significant factor, with employees recruited for their flexibility and team-orientation. The work siren to start and end the shift was abandoned in favour of individual and supervisor responsibility. Demonstration by example was seen as central and described as 'wearing a hairshirt with sincerity'. This included the entire staff wearing the company uniform, using the same canteen and car park, working in open-plan offices, and even taking lunch together at the same time (Morton, 1994: 82).

Most employers have adopted a gradualist approach to change, but some have gone for fundamental reform with wide-ranging reviews of terms and conditions. However, the more extensive programmes are more commonly found on greenfield sites, where great care is taken with the whole HR package so as to help create an appropriate culture. At the Rolls-Royce aircraft engine plant at Derby harmonisation was implemented in several stages to take account of changes in the shift premium, the abolition of clocking off, and movement to staff terms for sickness. These were followed by consolidation of shift pay, a reduction in the working week and flexible work hours (IDS, 1998; Druker, 2000: 120). When Price Waterhouse and Coopers & Lybrand merged in 1998, a commitment to harmonise conditions was central to the plan, a key feature being flexible benefits (Franks and Thompson, 2000). This was seen as important because it firmly recognised staff differences and diversity, it provided a good recruitment edge, and it facilitated the alignment at the two existing arrangements. In some cases, as at BP Chemicals, single status has been part of a major change in management philosophy that has included continuous improvement and the rhetoric of individualising employment relations through to non-union consultation schemes (Tuckman, 1998).

There are a number of factors that promote harmonisation. Firstly, new technology cuts across existing demarcation lines (craft, skilled and semi-skilled), and status differentials tend to impede flexibility. Harmonisation is sometimes introduced as a way of 'buying out' old work practices. The introduction of technology also increases demands and responsibilities on manual workers who are required to be more co-operative rather than compliant, in effect to take on multi-skilling and technician roles. In such circumstances harmonisation can play a key role in trying to make blue-collar workers part of the corporate team. Moreover, with such changes it may be difficult to make clear distinctions between blue-collar and white-collar (Sisson and Storey, 2000: 128).

Secondly, the legislation on sex discrimination and equal pay has narrowed differences between blue- and white-collar workers and has also extended rights – such as maternity pay – to all workers who have sufficient length of service. Some employers used to provide these benefits solely to white-collar workers. Moreover, as the European Commission continues to press ahead in its moves to harmonise terms and conditions across Europe, the UK will appear even more out of step if it maintains different conditions for different groups of workers. There is some evidence that firms attempting to individualise employment contracts also tend to standardise non-pay terms and conditions (see Brown *et al*, 1998).

Thirdly, the growth in single-table bargaining and the recent spate of union mergers have also been important forces for change, as well as saving management time and reducing conflict between work groups. Fourthly, changes in employment structure in recent years have had an impact on lower-level white-collar jobs, which have become increasingly routinised and deskilled, involving lower prospects for pay and promotion. A gap is now more apparent between clerical employees and professional workers, with little movement between the two. At the same time, many blue-collar jobs have been re-skilled due to technological demands which require technical training. As a result, there is often little to distinguish manual from non-manual jobs. Similarly, now that many unions (such as UNISON) represent both manual and non-manual workers, it seems anachronistic to maintain status differentials between different groups of workers.

The WERS data provides an opportunity to assess how far harmonisation has actually progressed. Table 49 shows what managers and non-managerial employees were entitled to in 1998. Putting together these items, Cully *et al* (1999: 73–4) conclude in a summary measure that 41 per cent of workplaces were single-status. Such workplaces were more common where there was a recognised trade union at the workplace (45 per cent), where there was a personnel specialist (48 per cent), and where the workplace was covered by an integrated employee development plan (46 per cent).

The largest harmonisation agreement, covering 1.2 million council workers, was announced in 1997, merging the administrative, professional, technical, clerical and manual grades. Although there was local flexibility, there was a national pay spine (upon which council-level grading structures are based) and agreed terms on issues such as working-time and leave. Overall, IRS (*Employment Trends* 710, 2001: 10) conclude that progress has been slow and patchy because the complexity of the task coupled with cost pressures means that few councils have instituted new pay and grading structures. Most have nevertheless made significant changes in other areas – in particular, the harmonisation of basic working hours.

Despite being part of the conventional wisdom of 'good employee relations' (Arthurs, 1985: 17), there are a number of potential pitfalls to

Table 49   Entitlements to non-pay terms and conditions, by sector

| | Percentage of workplaces | | | | | |
| | in the private sector | | in the public sector | | all together | |
	Managers	*Employees*	*Managers*	*Employees*	*Managers*	*Employees*
Employer pension scheme	78	62	93	93	82	71
Company car or car allowance	63	12	33	17	55	14
Private health insurance	61	22	7	2	46	16
Four weeks or more paid annual leave	91	81	96	95	92	85
Sick pay in excess of statutory requirements	83	64	77	76	81	67

Source: Cully M., Woodland S., O'Reilly A. and Dix G. *Britain at Work: As depicted by the 1998 Workplace Employee Relations Survey*. London, Routledge. 1999. p74

harmonisation. Firstly, there may be cost issues. It may well be expensive to equalise notice periods, for example, especially in times where constant change puts an emphasis on flexibility. Although in the short run costs may well increase, it is anticipated that the longer run offers more benefits. In local government progress on the implementation of single status has been slow partly as a result of costs (Hatchett, 2001: 38). Secondly, workers may be unwilling to see cashless pay as a benefit, so making it necessary to 'buy out' cash payments. However, there could be cost savings in areas of capital costs (two different canteens replaced by a large one, for example), and reducing the administrative costs involved in operating two systems. Thirdly, as with many other management initiatives, supervisors and middle managers are often wary, partly because of confusion over what 'harmonisation' is designed to achieve and also because of insecurity and concern about their 'new' responsibilities and issues (Marchington and Wilkinson, 2000).

Non-financial rewards and recognition

According to Herzberg (1987: 30):

Managers do not motivate employees by giving them higher wages, more benefits, or new status symbols. Rather, employees are motivated by their own inherent need to succeed at a challenging task. The manager's job, then, is not to motivate people to get them to achieve; instead, the manager should provide opportunities for people to achieve so they will become motivated.

It is important to consider the role which non-financial rewards and recognition play in motivating staff, and in this section we examine a number of them. Having said that, there is often lip-service paid to their significance – and it is interesting to note that Armstrong's CIPD work (1999) contains a mere six pages on it within a 500-page text. Semler's (1993) story of his company and management style in Brazil is a good example of how employees accept responsibility when they are treated in such a way as to be made aware that they are highly valued. The desire of many individuals to seek opportunities for personal growth through their work is very powerful (Lewis, 2001).

> Think of jobs you have done in the past. What factors made them satisfying?

How do job characteristics combine to motivate, reward and recognise good employee performance? According to Ford (1969), 'Perhaps they have the effect of a shotgun blast; it is the whole charge that brings the beast down' (quoted in Robertson *et al*, 1992: 62). A 'job characteristics model' has been developed by Hackman and Oldman (1976) which incorporates the five core job characteristics they believe are involved in job satisfaction and motivation. These characteristics are:

- skill variety – the range of skills and talents required

- task identity – the extent to which the completion of a whole piece of work is required

- task significance – the impact of the task on others

- autonomy – freedom and discretion in selecting methods and hours of work

- feedback – clear information provided on performance.

According to these writers, if jobs are designed in a way that maximises these core dimensions, three psychological states can occur:

- experienced meaningfulness at work, which is the result of skill variety, task identity and task significance

- experienced responsibility for work outcomes, which is the result of autonomy

- knowledge of results of work activities, which is the result of feedback.

If these do occur, work motivation and job satisfaction will be high and other behavioural outputs – such as attendance – may also be positively affected (Rollinson *et al*, 1998: 244–6). Equally, employees with high 'growth-need strength' (GNS) are more likely to experience changes in their critical psychological state when core job dimensions are improved. It is also important to realise that simply having a highly-motivated employee does not necessarily equate with good job performance. Employees also need the necessary skills and the tools and materials to do a good job. Obviously, a motivated but unskilled employee is unlikely to do a job to the required standard, but neither is a motivated and skilled employee who has had inadequate training or is provided with inappropriate raw materials.

> What can be done within your organisation to redesign work in order to change core job dimensions?

Today it is perhaps more appropriate to take a less universalistic approach when considering motivation at work. Managements should try to assess the subjective priorities of their employees rather than assume and enforce a particular view. It is also the case that attitudes and priorities may change over time, so managers have to be flexible.

There are two common themes relating to non-financial reward and motivation. These are:

- recognition and feedback
- involvement autonomy and responsibility.

Recognition and feedback

Employees' work has to be valued by employers and for that reason recognised by them – a line that is taken up by a number of the Total Quality Management gurus such as Crosby and Deming. According to Crosby (1980: 218):

> *People really don't work for money. They go to work for it, but once the salary has been established, their concern is appreciation. Recognise their contribution publicly and noisily, but don't demean them by applying a price-tag to everything.*

He argues that it is much more important to recognise achievements through symbolic awards and prizes. However, Kohn (1993: 55) states that research shows that tangible rewards, as well as praise, can actually lower the level of performance, particularly in jobs requiring creativity. According to him, studies show that intrinsic interest in a task (the sense that it is worth doing for its own sake) tends to decline when the individual concerned is given an external reason for doing it. Extrinsic motivations are not only less effective than intrinsic motivations, they can also corrode intrinsic motivation. People who work in order to get a reward tend to be less interested in the task than those who are not expecting to be rewarded. According to Kohn (1993: 55), when we are led to do something in order to get a prize, we feel that the goal of the prize controls our behaviour and this deprivation of self-determination makes tasks seem less enjoyable. Moreover, the offer of an inducement sends a message that the task cannot be very interesting, otherwise it would not be necessary to bribe us to do it.

Others have argued that providing praise for good work, rather than criticism for poor work, is important. Managers should 'catch staff doing it right'. Token prizes/awards can also play a role because they have symbolic worth even if they are low in financial value (Crosby, 1980: 218). There has been growing interest in this field in recent years, and some employers have moved beyond seeing non-financial recognition solely as the watch or clock presented on retirement (Hilton, 1992). Thames Water, for example, has a Values in Practice (VIP) award designed to celebrate outstanding achievements (Trapp, 2001b). These are believed to be more motivating than cash, and can provide important feedback. Feedback itself must be regular, timely and relevant based on the principle of positive reinforcement. In other words, employees have to be given feedback more than once a year in a formal appraisal. As far as possible it should relate to a recently-completed task, and it should also be directly relevant to the employee's work effort/output figures (the establishment as a whole may be too removed from the individual employee).

Stredwick (2002: 208–9) identifies two types of formal recognition scheme. The first was developed from long-established suggestion schemes. He sees key aspects of such schemes as:

- encouraging employees to participate by inculcating a culture of 'continuous improvement' so employees think about how the work processes could be improved

- training employees in putting forward their proposals

- having a committee drawn from all levels and activities in the company who will help to sift major ideas and encourage participation in their areas

- ensuring swiftness in decision-taking, including instant awards and a guaranteed response for all ideas

- making worthwhile awards, which can include a proportion of the saving and the opportunity to be entered in draws for various events

- encouraging teams to apply themselves so that an idea can represent the thinking of a number of people in an area

- ensuring good publicity and recognition on success through company magazines

- instigating campaigns which integrate with company strategy over issues such as health and safety, quality, and the environment.

The second type is where tokens are used to acknowledge staff going beyond the call of duty. Prizes are limited in value – eg vouchers, badges. Recognition can also be through holidays, and day-trips to other organisations which supply raw materials or market the finished goods. The absolute cost of these sorts of reward is likely to be small, but they have a powerful symbolic significance.

Involvement, autonomy and responsibility

Research that links participation to higher levels of satisfaction and increased productivity is to be found in the social science literature (Pfeffer, 1994: 42). People value the ability to have influence over their work. Modern HRM literature appears to endorse this, arguing that employees come to work motivated and interested but are soon alienated by the web of rules and constraints which govern their working lives. If only management could find ways to release and tap employees' creativity – for example, via employee involvement (EI) – their commitment to organisational goals would follow. It works upon the assumption that common interests are achievable in organisations, although most management fail to capture the interest of their staff, partly because communications are ineffective but also because contributions are not welcomed. It is stressed that employees should have the opportunity to satisfy their needs for involvement, autonomy and responsibility through

CASE STUDY: Using reward strategically: an illustration

Richer Sounds is a specialist hi-fi separates retailer in the UK, which sees customer service as the driving philosophy behind the company. Employees are encouraged to help the customer buy rather than go for the 'hard sell'. Management argues that the company's basic principles are quality products and branded names, value for money and customer service. It is argued that while the first two can be controlled by head office, the latter is very much in the hands of the ordinary branch employee or 'colleague' as he or she is known.

The company sees reward very broadly in that there is both a payment and a recognition aspect (ie a non-financial aspect) to its approach. Pay is above-average for the industry, comprising a basic rate supplemented by commission, profit-share and a customer service bonus. A customer service index (CSI) is calculated, such that individuals are assessed on several indicators, the main one being customer feedback on service quality. Each customer receipt includes a freepost questionnaire, in which the customer is invited to assess the level of service provided by the salesperson, who is identified by payroll number on the form.

The individual's bonus is related to the feedback. So if a customer ticks 'excellent', the sales assistant receives an extra £3, if 'poor', a deduction of £3 takes place. These are totalled up at the end of each month and a bonus is paid. The company is at pains to point out that any deductions are far outweighed by the bonuses. Indeed, it is unlikely that anyone with a stream of negative feedback would actually retain the job at Richer Sounds, although management reports a relatively high voluntary turnover of new staff, some of whom find that they are uncomfortable with this approach. The peer group is seen as crucial in encouraging good performance, and managers are provided with the results on each individual's performance, which are distributed internally. Although many of the incentives focus on the performance of the individual, and staff wear name-badges to encourage greater individual responsibility, company performance is also rewarded with a profit-sharing scheme.

The company also believes non-financial recognition is important in motivating staff and has an array of initiatives designed to make working for the company satisfying and enjoyable. Staff performing above and beyond the call of duty receive gold aeroplanes in recognition of their achievement, while wooden spoons are given to staff for acts of amazing stupidity. A suggestion scheme does have a small financial component from between £5 and £25, but the key element is a dinner or other non-monetary award for the best two suggestions each quarter. The company receives 20 suggestions per employee per year – the highest number in the UK. Branches and departments compete in the 'Richer Way League'. This is based on customer service standards and profit, and provides the use of a Rolls-Royce or a Bentley for a week as the prize for the top performing branch. Teamwork is thus emphasised, and branch staff are encouraged to socialise outside the workplace as a way of consolidating the team identity.

Adapted from: Golzen G. 'Award scheme comeback', *The Times*, 13 April 2000. p19; and Marchington M., Wilkinson A., Ackers P. and Dundon T. *Management Choice and Employment Voice*, CIPD Report. 2001

work, perhaps through participation in quality circles or merely by being involved more in day-to-day matters, so that they can agree actions to be taken and be more positive in implementing such measures. Management styles might well have to be addressed as well.

How might these states be achieved? Clearly some of these aspects of management can be integrated into day-to-day management activity, and recognition and feedback can be made part of the corporate culture. However, to illustrate the variety of ways an employer might achieve such goals, we examine the practice of *job redesign*.

Job redesign

Job redesign is concerned with the allocation of task functions among organisational roles, and has been defined as 'any attempt to alter jobs with the intent of increasing the quality of work experience and productivity' (Wilson, 1999: 13). While early work in this area was largely concerned with matters of efficiency and rationalising work, breaking it down into tiny components in line with Taylor's ideas, modern job redesign has broader aims and looks to balance efficiency and job-satisfaction goals. Because there has been increasing recognition that extrinsic rewards (such as pay) are insufficient on their own to motivate employees, more emphasis has been put on intrinsic factors such as job content. Drawing on expectancy theory, the aim is to design jobs which satisfy employee needs so that the work can be performed to a high standard, so enabling both employee and organisational goals to be satisfied (Robertson *et al*, 1992: 73). Job redesign can take a wide variety of forms in practice.

Job rotation is perhaps the most basic type of job redesign. It involves workers moving from job to job (with similar levels of skill) in an attempt to alleviate boredom. In a supermarket, for example, it might involve shelf-stacking, checkout-operating and counting boxes in the warehouse. However, the common criticism is that job rotation is little more than swapping one boring job for another – it can actually be demotivating if it affects a bonus pattern, or breaks up a work group.

Job enlargement involves widening a job so that one or more related tasks are added to the existing one at a similar level of responsibility. This can reduce the repetitiveness of performing jobs of short-cycle operations and may add to motivation for employees if they can see their contribution to the final product or service. However, Herzberg (1968: 18) writes of job enlargement as doing no more than 'enlarge the meaninglessness of the job', and it can actually add to work intensification. It has also been suggested that whereas a worker can 'switch off' from one boring job, doing a number of different relatively mundane tasks requires concentration, which is resented if the job is monotonous.

Job enrichment involves a more radical design of the job, perhaps replacing skills designed by job re-designers in an earlier era. New responsibilities are added, as when production workers take on some responsibility for maintenance or take on decision-making roles in respect of work scheduling. In some cases employees acquire a complete job so that they can see a real purpose to what they are doing.

Autonomous work groups extend job enrichment in that not only is there a wider range of operative/production skills but groups of employees also acquire responsibility for management tasks, such as choosing work methods, regulating the pace of work, and allocating and scheduling work. Self-supervision is stressed, and this encourages autonomy. In some cases, groups may even take responsibility for training and recruitment.

Teamworking is perhaps the most recent manifestation of job redesign and involves a group of multi-capable workers who switch between tasks, organise and allocate work, and are responsible for all aspects of production, including quality (Mueller and Proctor, 2000). High-performance work teams operate without supervision and have wide-ranging responsibilities for production and maintenance. Other changes may also take place to support teamworking, including open-layout, flexitime, the removal of clocking, and a new open management style. This raises a central issue about the extent to which such initiatives might have to be supported by changes in management style and HR practices (Marchington and Wilkinson, 2000).

Do you think that job redesign has made work more satisfying by rewarding and recognising employee contributions, or has it just made work more intensive and stressful?

CONCLUSION

When reviewing reward systems, care must be taken not only with the choice of suitable payment schemes and benefits packages, but also with the processes by which they are implemented. There are a number of key factors that managements have to take into account when implementing reward systems. This is based on the view that a careful systematic analysis which addresses potential problems is more likely to succeed than an *ad hoc* approach. Firstly, it is important to analyse what is wrong with the existing reward system and separate out symptoms from causes, and establish whether or not the scheme is fundamentally flawed or just plagued by implementation problems. Secondly, it is essential to involve employees and their representatives in the process of change because they may add useful knowledge on the issues which affect them and about which management is unaware. It also allows management to sound out employee opinion and so assess the feasibility of their plans, while employees who have been involved are more likely to accept and understand the system rather than reject it as an arbitrary management imposition. For example, for job evaluation, working parties or panels are usually set up to conduct the actual process of evaluation, which ensures that there is greater legitimacy to the decisions (subjective as they are) that have been taken. Thirdly, it is important to prepare the way by communicating the system, taking care to explain how it is intended to work, and outlining the implications for each group of workers. Finally, it is not enough simply to install the system. It must be monitored and reviewed to ensure that it operates in the way that was intended, and that it is judged against established criteria. Because all reward systems tend to have unintended consequences and decay over time, regular review is critical. There is no such thing as an ideal scheme that can operate for many years without modification (Thorpe *et al*, 2000: 247–73).

At times when it is difficult for employers to fund pay increases above the rate of inflation and provide a range of generous financial benefits (such as pensions and sick-pay arrangements), attention may have to turn to non-financial recognition and reward. This includes the harmonisation of certain terms and conditions such as clocking on and off, single canteens and car parking arrangements, none of which is likely to be as expensive as financial rewards. It can also include initiatives designed to make work more satisfying and fulfilling, and to seek increases in variety, involvement, autonomy and responsibility through job redesign and Total Quality Management. The gains to be made from these can be extensive and contribute directly to the achievement of organisational success.

Perhaps most important of all, at least for employees, is the idea that reward systems should be fair and equitable, that overall benefits and payments should be consistent with what is perceived as the quality of the individual's contribution, in comparison with the contributions of other people, both internal and external to the organisation. The ongoing debate about the reward packages of top managers and executives sums this up well. Most manual and non-manual workers would deem it reasonable that such people should earn rather more than they do themselves, although there may be disagreements about the precise ratio. However, they would consider it totally unfair that these individuals are not subject to an open regulatory system, and that they are able to benefit from well-designed share option schemes and gain perks which appear excessive, especially if their organisations are not performing well.

Useful reading

ARMSTRONG M. *Employee Reward*, 3rd edition. London, CIPD. 2002.

ARMSTRONG M. *and* BROWN D. *New Dimensions in Pay Management*, London, CIPD. 2001.

ARMSTRONG M. 'Feel the width', *People Management*, 3 February 2000. pp35–38.

EQUAL OPPORTUNITIES COMMISSION, *Good Practice Guide: Job evaluation schemes free of sex bias*. Manchester, EOC. 2000.

FRANKS O. *and* THOMPSON D. 'Mix 'n match', *People Management*, 17 February 2000. pp40–43.

SMITH P. *and* NETHERSELL G. 'Job Evaluation', in R. Thorpe and G. Homan *Strategic Reward Systems*. FT/Prentice-Hall, 2000.

TERRY N. *and* WHITE P. 'Occupational pension schemes and their interaction with HRM', *Human Resource Management Journal*, Vol. 8, No. 4, 1998. pp20–36.

THOMPSON P. *and* MILSOME S. *Reward Determination in the UK*. London, CIPD. 2001.

TRAPP R. 'Main attraction', *People Management*, 25 October 2001b. pp44–46.

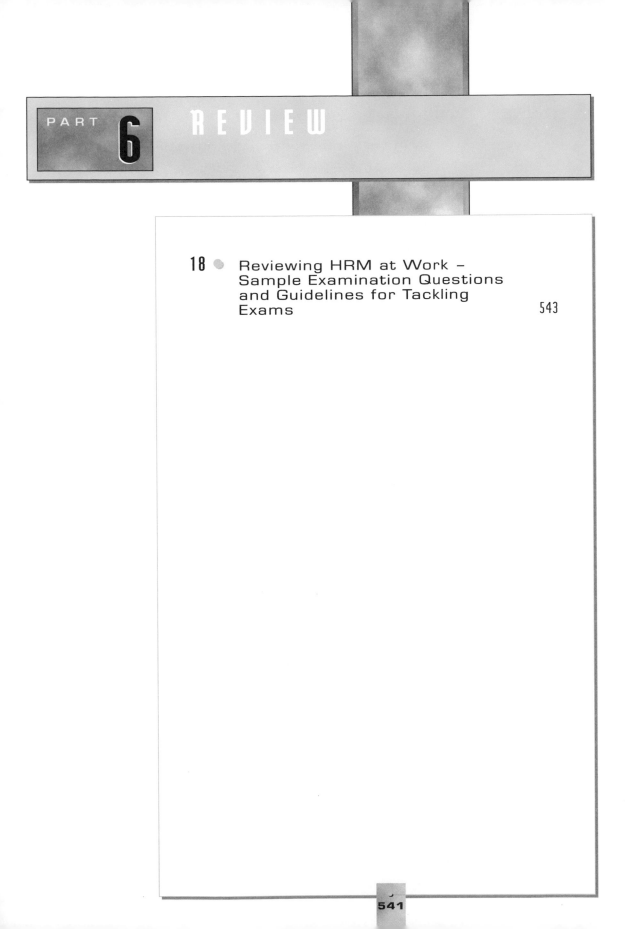

Reviewing HRM at Work – Sample Examination Questions and Guidelines for Tackling Exams

Introduction

The purpose of this final chapter is to review readers' knowledge and understanding of the major issues dealt with in the book. This chapter should prove especially useful for those studying for the CIPD Standards in the area of People Management and Development, in that it provides similar questions to those likely to be found on the nationally-set examination paper. At the same time, however, it should also prove beneficial to those studying for internally-set examinations, either for CIPD-accredited programmes or for business and management degree courses, because it provides a framework for revision. It might also prove useful for those practitioners interested in posing questions about HR practices in their own organisation.

The chapter comprises three sections in all. The first two follow the format of the CIPD national examination paper in People Management and Development, and a third section provides general advice on how to tackle examinations.

The first section contains six questions drawn from the material that appears in the book and the standards, which require students to produce reports or similar assignments relating general principles to specific features of organisational practice. *Approximately one hour should be allocated for each question*.

The second section includes 25 questions designed to test knowledge and understanding through short answers, typically a few paragraphs in length, *each of which should be completed in less than 10 minutes*. This style of question has now been used since 1996, not just in People Management and Development but throughout the whole Professional Qualification Scheme (PQS) standards.

There is a major and very explicit difference with the Professional Development Scheme (PDS) Standards introduced in 2002, however – their positioning at the postgraduate or M-level. This means that answers must demonstrate a critical and evaluative approach rather than rely on description, and there must be a review of the wider issues surrounding the question. Answers must also indicate an understanding of organisational realities and the contribution that HRM or people management and development can make to improvements in performance. For example, it is not enough to argue that 'high-commitment management' is the way forward without placing it in the context of the organisation's objectives, product and labour market position and size/sector. This may indicate that the implementation of so-called 'progressive' techniques may be problematical and/or may require to be introduced carefully because such techniques are likely to be resisted by some managers. Furthermore, answers must show clearly and concisely that the student is able to present ideas and information in a way that is likely to convince other managers of its value. This should be reflected not only in the relevance of the advice provided in an answer but also in the quality of the writing and its layout as text presentation.

Section A: reports and presentations

(Remember that where a question below refers to 'your organisation', you may if you wish regard it as referring to 'an organisation of your choice'.)

1   As part of your organisation's drive for external accreditation, you have been asked to review your existing HR policies and assess the extent to which they are integrated with each other and with broader organisational objectives. In particular, you are required to demonstrate how these HR policies contribute to improved levels of performance.

2   Write a background paper for your general manager (or his or her equivalent) on the desirability of devolving more HR activities to *either* line managers *or* a well-known firm of management consultants. Provide examples to support your argument.

3   As part of your organisation's management development programme, you have been asked to deliver a 15-minute talk to new graduate trainees on 'The contribution of learning and development to organisational success.' Prepare an outline of your talk, provide examples as appropriate, and explain briefly how you would aim to get your message across to the audience.

4   It has come to your notice that line managers are ignoring organisational guidelines on recruitment and selection, and you have decided to organise a short training session to remind them of those. Provide an outline of what you would include in this session, paying particular attention to how you might persuade line managers of the merits of following the guidelines, and alerting them to the dangers of not doing so.

5   Critically review your organisation's existing employee relations policy and evaluate the degree to which it manages to deliver a positive psychological contract. Pay particular attention to how it helps to enhance employee commitment and loyalty as well as provide fairness and employee voice for staff.

6   You have been asked to take part in a discussion session for full-time students at a local university or college about the advantages and limitations of performance-related pay. You have been asked to make a 10-minute contribution to this session. What would be your main themes, what evidence would you bring forward to support your point of view, and how would you ensure that the students gained a good understanding of the complexities of organisational life?

Section B: questions requiring short answers

(Remember that where a question below refers to 'your organisation', you may if you wish regard it as referring to 'an organisation of your choice'.)

1   Evaluate how changes in the political, legal and economic environment have affected your organisation in recent years.

2   Has there been a growth of 'atypical' forms of employment – such as part-time and temporary work – in your organisation over the last five years? Explain why this has happened/not happened, and assess whether or not it has made a difference to organisational costs and effectiveness.

3   To what extent do you think that recent changes in the infrastructure for vocational education and training (VET) are likely to deliver a more highly-skilled workforce in practice?

4   Identify and evaluate the research skills and information sources needed when preparing a report on *either* the recruitment problems facing your organisation *or* how induction training might be improved.

5   Discuss the meaning of the term 'the management of diversity'? How and why could 'the management of diversity' make a difference in your organisation.

6   Critically assess how 'high-commitment' or 'best-practice' HRM is supposed to contribute towards improvements in organisational performance.

7   A number of organisations claim to offer employment security for their employees. What does this mean in practice, and does it contribute to enhanced levels of employee commitment and motivation?

8   Assess whether or not one of the models for linking business strategy to HRM can be applied to your own organisation. *(Choose one of the models reviewed in Chapter 8.)*

9   Analyse *three* major obstacles that prevent the conversion of

management strategy into practice, and explain how these obstacles might be overcome.

10 Critically review the 'business partner' model of HRM (Ulrich, 1998) and assess whether or not it could be applied to your organisation.

11 Drawing on recent surveys, explain which HR activities are most likely to be devolved to line managers, and assess how HR professionals can ensure that line managers undertake these activities effectively.

12 Identify and justify criteria suitable when selecting management consultants to use in the area of people management and development. Provide examples – if appropriate, from your own organisation – to illustrate your answer.

13 Critically review *three* of the principal measures that are used to evaluate the contribution of the HR function to organisational performance.

14 Outline briefly the most widely-used methods of recruitment and selection in your organisation, and review whether or not they are cost-effective.

15 What is meant by the term '360-degree performance review'? Assess whether or not it would help to motivate staff in your organisation to improve their performance.

16 To what extent can an attendance management policy 'add value' to the organisation?

17 Specify the main principles underpinning the Investors in People (IIP) Standard, and critically assess how successful IIP has been in maximising the skills and contributions of people in practice.

18 Analyse how continuing professional development (CPD) might be important both for employing organisations and for their staff.

19 Review the measures used to evaluate the contribution of any learning and development initiative to organisational success.

20 Do the employee involvement (EI) practices used in your organisation contribute to improved performance? How and why do they/don't they?

21 Assess whether or not partnership agreements between employers and trade unions can contribute to effective employment relations in organisations.

22 How can grievance procedures be designed to ensure that employees feel that their concerns are being addressed by management in a way that gains their commitment?

23 Discuss whether or not there are any circumstances under which individual performance-related pay is likely to motivate employees.

24 Explain briefly the meaning of the term 'non-financial rewards and recognition'. Do you think that these are likely to motivate staff and reward their contributions in your organisation? Why/why not?

25 Analyse how job evaluation schemes can be designed to deliver equity, fairness and effectiveness in organisations.

Examination guidelines

The purpose of this final section is to provide students with some guidance on how to tackle examination questions on the People Management and Development paper. A number of general comments are appropriate, in view of the fact that students tend to make similar mistakes on each part of the paper, but these are supplemented with more specific observations about Sections A and B. Such errors are not made just by CIPD candidates, of course, so the guidance should be useful for students at different levels and on different types of programme.

Four general points are worth making:

- Many candidates fail to answer all parts of a multi-part question, particularly in Section A. Typically, many of those who fail do not provide any detail of the costing of projects or the gains that employers might make, even when that information is specifically demanded in the question. Students must remember that they are unlikely to gain more than half the available marks if they answer only half the question!

- Many candidates fail to address the question that has been set, preferring to base their answer on what they wish to tell the examiner. While this can be very interesting, it also demonstrates a failure to appreciate the requirements of a 'customer' – if examiners can be seen in that light. Similarly, it is common for students to write an essay rather than a report or a draft talk when it is a report or draft talk that has been requested. One of the skills the examiners are trying to assess is the ability of students to write in a concise, convincing and focused manner.

- Many candidates seem to lose sight of the overall objective when answering a question, and provide an unbalanced answer that devotes far too much time to one part of the question, with the result that too little time is spent on other parts. This problem can be reduced if clear planning is undertaken before starting to write the answer. On some occasions, students seem to feel that making references to well-known academics demonstrates that they understand the principal issues; this is all very well if the references are relevant and appropriate, and do not appear to be bolted on to a somewhat peripheral answer.

- Many students fail to locate their answer in the wider commercial and environmental context, showing little appreciation of national trends or longer-run developments in the economy as a whole or HRM in particular. There is often a temptation to assume that current fads and fashions offer superior solutions to organisational problems, and little recognition that they may be superficial and trite. Moreover, students often fail to recognise the force of existing cultural norms and traditions when putting forward recommendations, somehow assuming that all options are feasible. It is important to show some awareness of the constraints (financial or otherwise) as well as the opportunities when answering questions. The Professional Development Scheme – like its predecessor – aims to develop in students the ability to persuade line managers of the utility of specific recommendations in response to specific organisational problems.

Taking a more positive slant, there are certain guidelines which candidates should bear in mind when preparing for examinations, some of which build upon what has been said in the previous paragraphs. These are:

- Make sure that the material in the whole syllabus is understood, at least to the extent of being able to provide short paragraph-length answers to the questions in Section B. In addition, when addressing the specific questions in Section A, students must be able to demonstrate a holistic appreciation of HRM and its contribution to organisational performance.

- Provide examples as appropriate to support a particular answer and argument. These may be drawn from any organisation, not only the one for which the student currently works, and it is useful if contemporary examples are provided because they show that the student is up-to-date and is reading the professional journals.

- Write concisely and clearly, providing signposts to an answer. There is nothing worse for an examiner (or any reader, for that matter) than having to re-read an answer several times in order to try to identify precisely what the student is trying to say. A clear introduction stating explicitly what will be contained in the answer helps considerably. So too does the use of paragraphs, sections and numbering. The precise technique used matters less than the overall impact, and students should therefore use the approach with which they feel most comfortable.

- Ensure that the examination is timed so that an attempt can be made at all sections and all questions. It is worthwhile reiterating that approximately one hour should be allocated to each section on the examination paper. This means that in Section B, each question should take between five and 10 minutes to answer.

These guidelines should not be regarded as a somewhat idiosyncratic attempt to impose unrealistic academic standards on CIPD or any other students, but as indicating skills that are central to all aspects of managerial work. These include: addressing the question posed; choosing from alternatives to formulate a realistic answer; justifying and costing a recommendation; and writing in a clear and well-structured manner that succeeds in convincing the reader.

In Section A, which is notionally allocated one hour, students have a choice of *one* from four questions. They are required to write a report or provide details on some other practical assignment – such as designing a training session, preparing the outline for a talk, taking part in a debate or writing a letter to a newspaper. It is crucial that the format specified is observed, so that an outline for a talk is presented, or the notes for a paper are drawn up, or the training session is designed. Students who write essays in response to questions in this section are not going to pass, irrespective of the quality of their answer. However, it is imperative that an analytical and evaluative approach is taken that considers the question in relation to the wider business environment and the body of literature on the subject, and that it provides examples of practice in other organisations as appropriate.

Section B comprises *10* questions from which *seven* must be addressed – again with the assumption that the whole section will take an hour to complete. Each question is capable of being answered in seven or eight minutes through relatively short answers. These questions are drawn from any part of the PM&D Standards, and require students to present fairly basic core information in order to demonstrate their knowledge and understanding. The answers in this section must be concise, but they can usefully be supplemented with examples to illustrate the students' wider understanding of the issue. It is critically important that all seven questions are tackled. As with Section A, it is essential that a critical review is undertaken rather than just a regurgitation of irrelevant theory or a description of practice in the student's own organisation.

Bibliography

ACKERS P. 'Pluralism', in T. REDMAN and A. WILKINSON (eds), *The Informed Student Guide to Human Resource Management*, London, Thomson Learning. 2002a.

ACKERS P. 'Unitarism' in T. REDMAN and A. WILKINSON (eds), *The Informed Student Guide to Human Resource Management*, London, Thomson Learning. 2002b.

ACKERS P. 'Employment ethics' in T. REDMAN and A. WILKINSON (eds), *Contemporary Human Resource Management*. London, FT/Prentice Hall. 2001.

ACKERS P., MARCHINGTON M., WILKINSON A. *and* GOODMAN J. 'The use of cycles: explaining employee involvement in the 1990s', *Industrial Relations Journal*, Vol. 23, No. 4, 1992. pp268–283.

ACKERS P. *and* PAYNE J. 'British trade unions and social partnership: rhetoric, reality and strategy', *The International Journal of Human Resource Management*, Vol. 9, No. 3, 1998. pp529–550.

ACKERS P. *and* PRESTON D. 'Born again: the ethics and efficacy of the conversion experience in contemporary management development', *Journal of Management Studies*, Vol. 34, No. 5, 1997. pp677–701.

ACKERS P. *and* WILKINSON A. 'From employee involvement to social partnership: Changing British management approaches to employment participation', *Croners Employee Relations Review*. Vol 14 2000 pp3–10.

ACKROYD S. *and* HUGHES J. *Data Collection in Context*. London, Longman. 1992.

ACKROYD S. *and* PROCTER S. 'British manufacturing organisation and workplace industrial relations: some attributes of the new flexible firm', *British Journal of Industrial Relations*, Vol. 36, No. 2, 1998. pp164–183.

ADAMS K. 'Externalisation versus specialisation: what is happening to personnel?', *Human Resource Management Journal*, Vol. 1, No. 4, 1991. pp40–54.

ADVISORY, CONCILIATION AND ARBITRATION SERVICE HANDBOOK. *Discipline at Work*. www.acas.org.uk 2002.

ADVISORY, CONCILIATION AND ARBITRATION SERVICE. *Annual Report 2000–2001*, London, ACAS. 2001.

ADVISORY, CONCILIATION AND ARBITRATION SERVICE. *ACAS Code of Practice on Disciplinary Practice and Grievance Procedures at Work*. London, HMSO. 2000.

ADVISORY, CONCILIATION AND ARBITRATION SERVICE. *Introduction to Payment Systems*, ACAS Advisory Booklet No.2. London, HMSO. 1991.

ADVISORY, CONCILIATION AND ARBITRATION SERVICE. *Improving Industrial Relations: A joint responsibility.* London, HMSO. 1981.

AHLSTRAND, B. *The Quest for Productivity: A case study of Fawley after Flanders*, Cambridge, Cambridge University Press. 1990.

AIKIN O. 'Strictly invitation only', *People Management*, 6 July 2000. p20.

ALBERGA T., TYSON S. *and* PARSONS D. 'An evaluation of the Investors in People Standard'. *Human Resource Management Journal*, Vol. 7, No. 2, 1997. pp47–60.

ANDERSON N. *and* OSTROFF C. 'Selection as socialization'. In N. ANDERSON and P. HERRIOT (eds), *International Handbook of Selection and Assessment.* Chichester, John Wiley & Sons. Ltd. 1997.

APPLEBAUM E., BAILEY T., BERG P. *and* KALLEBERG A. *Manufacturing Competitive Advantage: The effects of high-performance work systems on plant performance and company outcomes.* Ithaca, NY, Cornell University Press. 2000.

ARKIN, A 'Central intelligence', *People Management*, 22 November 2001a. pp38–41.

ARKIN A. 'A Norfolk broadside', *People Management*, 19 April 2001b. pp36–39.

ARKIN A. 'Combined honours', *People Management*, 12 October 2000. pp42–46.

ARKIN A. 'Mutually inclusive', *People Management*, 20 March 1997. pp32–34.

ARMSTRONG M. 'Feel the width', *People Management*, 3 February 2000b. pp35–38.

ARMSTRONG M. 'A lesson in how not to', *People Management*, 12 October 2000. p57.

ARMSTRONG M. *Employee Reward.* 2nd edition. London, CIPD. 1999.

ARMSTRONG M. *Employee Reward.* London, IPD. 1998.

ARMSTRONG M. *Using the Human Resource Consultant: Achieving results, adding value.* London, Institute of Personnel Management. 1994.

ARMSTRONG M. *Personnel and the Bottom Line*, London, Institute of Personnel Management. 1989.

ARMSTRONG M. *and* BARON A. *Performance Management: The new realities.* London, CIPD. 1998

ARMSTRONG M. *and* BROWN D. *New Dimensions in Pay Management.* London, CIPD. 2001.

ARMSTRONG, M. *and* MURLIS, H. *Reward Management.* 4th edition. London, Kogan Page. 1998.

ARMSTRONG M. *and* MURLIS H. *Reward Management.* 3rd edition. London, Kogan Page. 1995.

ARNOLD J., COOPER C. *and* ROBERTSON I. *Work Psychology: Understanding human behaviour in the workplace.* 3rd edition. London, FT/Pitman Publishing. 1998.

ARTHUR J. 'Effects of human resource systems on manufacturing performance and turnover', *Academy of Management Journal*, Vol. 37, No. 3, 1994. pp670–687.

ARTHUR W., WOEHR D., *and* GRAZIANO W. 'Personality testing in employment settings: problems and issues in the application of typical selection practices', *Personnel Review*, Vol. 30, No. 6, 2001. pp657–76.

ARTHURS A. 'The National Minimum Wage' in T. REDMAN and A. WILKINSON, *The Informed Student Guide to Human Resource Management*. London, Thomson Learning. 2002.

ARTHURS A. 'Profit-related pay' in T. REDMAN and A. WILKINSON, *The Informed Student Guide to Human Resource Management*. London, Thomson Learning. 2002b.

ARTHURS A. 'Job evaluation' in T. REDMAN and A. WILKINSON, *The Informed Student Guide to Human Resource Management*. London, Thomson Learning. 2002c.

ARTHURS A. 'Towards single status', *Journal of General Management*, Vol. 11, No.1, 1985. pp17–28.

ASHTON D. *and* FELSTEAD A. 'From training to lifelong learning: the birth of the knowledge society?', in J. STOREY (ed.), *Human Resource Management: A critical text*. London, Thomson. 2001.

ATKINSON J. 'Flexibility or fragmentation? The United Kingdom labour market in the eighties', *Labour and Society*, Vol. 12, No. 1, 1987. pp87–105.

ATKINSON J. 'Manpower strategies for the flexible organisation', *Personnel Management*, August 1984. pp28–31.

ATKINSON J. *and* MEAGER N. 'Is flexibility a flash in the pan?', *Personnel Management*, September 1986. pp26–29.

BACH S. 'From performance appraisal to performance management', in S. BACH and K. SISSON (eds), *Personnel Management: A comprehensive guide to theory and practice*. Oxford, Blackwell. 2000.

BACH S. *and* SISSON K. (eds), *Personnel Management: A comprehensive guide to theory and practice*. Oxford, Blackwell. 2000.

BACON N. 'Employee relations', in T. REDMAN and A. WILKINSON (eds), *Contemporary Human Resource Management*. London, FT/Prentice-Hall. 2001.

BACON N. 'Union derecognition and the new human relations: A steel industry case study', *Work, Employment and Society*, Vol. 13, No.1, 1999. pp1–17.

BAKER B. *and* COOPER J. 'Occupational testing and psychometric instruments: an ethical perspective'. In D. WINSTANLEY and J. WOODALL (eds), *Ethical issues in contemporary HRM*. London, Macmillan. 2000. pp59–84.

BALDAMUS W. *Efficiency and Effort*. London, Tavistock. 1961.

BANDURA A. *Social Learning Theory*. New Jersey, Prentice-Hall. 1977.

BARCLAY J. 'Improving selection interviews with structure: organisations' use of "behavioural" interviews', *Personnel Review*, Vol. 30, No. 1, 2001. pp81–101.

BARKER J. 'Tightening the iron cage: concertive control in self-managing teams', *Administrative Science Quarterly*, Vol. 38, 1993. pp408–437.

BARLOW G. 'Deficiencies and the perpetuation of power: latent functions in management appraisal', *Journal of Management Studies*, Vol. 26, No. 5, 1989. pp499–517.

BARNEY J. 'Firm resources and sustained competitive advantage'. *Journal of Management*, Vol. 17, No. 1, 1991. pp99–120.

BARRICK M., MOUNT M. *and* JUDGE A. 'Personality and performance at the beginning of the new millennium: what do we know and where do we go next?' *International Journal of Selection and Assessment*, Vol. 9, No. 1–2, 2001. pp9–30.

BAXTER B. 'Consultancy expertise: a post–modern perspective', in H. SCARBROUGH (ed.), *The Management of Expertise*. London, Macmillan. 1996.

BEARDWELL I. *and* HOLDEN L. (eds), *Human Resource Management: A contemporary approach*. 3rd edition. London, FT/Prentice-Hall. 2001.

BEAUMONT Report. 1996.

BEAUMONT P. *The Decline of Trade Union Organisation*. London, Croom Helm. 1987.

BECKER B. *and* GERHART B. 'The impact of human resource management on organizational performance: progress and prospects'. *Academy of Management Journal*, Vol. 39, No. 4, 1996. pp779–801.

BEE F. 'How to evaluate training', *People Management*, Vol. 6, No. 6, 2000. pp42–45.

BEE R. *and* BEE F. *Training Needs Analysis and Evaluation*. London, Institute of Personnel and Development. 1994.

BEER M., SPECTOR B., LAWRENCE P., QUINN MILLS D. *and* WALTON R. *Human Resource Management: A general manager's perspective*. Glencoe, Free Press. 1985.

BELL J. *Doing your Research Project*. Milton Keynes, Open University Press. 1987.

BENNETT R. *Research Guides for Higher Degree Students*. Oxford, Thomson Publications. 1983.

BERG P. 'The effects of high performance work practices on job satisfaction in the United States steel industry', *Relations Industrial/Industrial Relations*, Vol. 54, 1999. pp111–35.

BERRIDGE J. 'Employee Assistance Programme' in T. Redman and A. Wilkinson (eds) *The Informed Student Guide to Human Resource Management*, London, Thomson Learning, 2002.

BERRIDGE J., COOPER C. *and* HIGHLEY-MARCHINGTON C. *Employee Assistance Programmes and Employee Counselling*. Chichester, John Wiley & Sons. 1997.

BEVAN S. 'Counting the cost of absence'. IRS *Employment Review* 739, 1 November 2001. pp46–47.

BIRD A. *and* BEECHLER S. 'Links between business strategy and HRM strategy in US-based Japanese subsidiaries: an empirical investigation', *Journal of International Business Studies*, First quarter 1995. pp23–46.

BLACKMAN T. 'Trading options', *People Management*, 6 May 1999. p42.

BLYTON P. *and* TURNBULL P. *The Dynamics of Employee Relations*. 2nd edition. London, Macmillan. 1998.

BLYTON P. *and* TURNBULL P. *The Dynamics of Employee Relations*, London, Macmillan. 1994.

BONE A. 'Working time' in T. REDMAN and A. WILKINSON (eds), *The Informed Student Guide to Human Resource Management*. London, Thomson Learning. 2002

BONE A. 'Employment law update', *Croners Employee Relations Review*, No.2, 1999. pp2–9.

BOWEY A. 'Gainsharing', in R. THORPE and G. HOMAN, (eds), *Strategic Reward Systems*. London, Financial Times/Prentice-Hall. 2000.

BOWEY A. *A Guide to Manpower Planning*. London, Macmillan. 1975.

BOWEY A. *and* THORPE R. 'Motivation and reward', in R. THORPE and G. HOMAN, (eds), *Strategic Reward Systems*. London, Financial Times/Prentice-Hall. 2000.

BOWEY A., THORPE R., MITCHELL F., NICHOLLS G., GOSNOLD D., SAVERY L. *and* HELLIER P. *The Effects of Incentive Payment Systems: UK 1977–1980*. Department of Employment Research Paper No. 36. London, HMSO. 1982.

BOXALL P. 'The strategic HRM debate and the resource-based view of the firm'. *Human Resource Management Journal,* Vol. 6, No. 3. 1996. pp59–75.

BOXALL P. *and* PURCELL J. *Strategy and Human Resource Management*. London, Palgrave. 2002.

BOXALL P. *and* PURCELL J. 'Strategic human resource management: where have we come from and where should we be going?', *International Journal of Management Reviews*, Vol. 2, No. 2, 2000. pp183–203.

BOXALL P. *and* STEENEVELD M. 'Human resource strategy and competitive advantage: a longitudinal study of engineering consultancies'. *Journal of Management Studies*, Vol. 36, No. 4, 1999. pp443–63.

BOYATSIS R. *The Competent Manager: A model for effective performance*. New York, Wiley. 1982.

BRAMHAM J. *Human Resource Planning*. London, Institute of Personnel and Development. 1994.

BRAMHAM J. *Practical Manpower Planning*. London, Institute of Personnel Management. 1975.

BRAVERMAN H. *Labour and Monopoly Capital*. New York, Monthly Review Press. 1974.

BREWERTON P. *and* MILLWARD L. *Organizational Research Methods, A Guide for Students and Researchers*. London, Sage. 2001.

BREWSTER C., GILL C. *and* RICHBELL S. 'Industrial relations policy: a framework for analysis', in K. THURLEY and S. WOOD (eds), *Industrial Relations and Management Strategy*. Cambridge, Cambridge University Press. 1983.

BRINER R. 'Stress management: one in 10 Western workers laid low by stress'. IRS *Employee Health Bulletin* 18, December 2000. pp8–17.

BRITISH ASSOCIATION FOR COUNSELLING AND PSYCHOTHERAPY. *A Framework for Good Practice*. www.bacp.co.uk 2002

BRITISH ASSOCIATION FOR COUNSELLING AND PSYCHOTHERAPY. *Code of Ethics*. BACP. 1996.

BROWN D. *Reward Strategies: From intent to impact*, London, CIPD. 2001.

BROWN W. 'Putting partnership into practice in Britain', *British Journal of Industrial Relations*, Vol. 38, No. 2, 2000. pp299–316.

BROWN W. *Piecework Bargaining*. London, Heinemann. 1973.

BROWN D. *and* ARMSTRONG M. *Paying for Contribution*. London, Kogan Page. 1999.

BROWN W., DEAKIN S., HUDSON M., PRATTAN C. *and* RYAN, P. 'The individuali-sation of employment contracts in Britain', *DTI Employment Relations Research Series*, No. 4. London, DTI. 1998.

BROWN W. *and* WALSH J. 'Managing pay in Britain', in K. SISSON (ed.), *Personnel Management*. 2nd edition. 1994.

BRYMAN A. *Research Methods and Organisation Studies*. London, Unwin Hyman. 1989.

BRYSON V. 'Online counselling at work: issues and ethics'. IRS *Employment Review* 740, 19 November 2001. pp43–44.

BUCHANAN D. *and* BODDY D. *The Expertise of a Change Agent*. Hemel Hempstead, Prentice-Hall. 1992.

BUCHANAN D., BODDY D. *and* McCALLUM J. 'Getting in, getting on, getting out and getting back', in A. BRYMAN (ed.), *Doing Research in Organisations*. London, Routledge. 1988.

BUCKINGHAM, M. 'What a waste', *People Management*, 11 October 2001. pp36–40.

BURAWOY M. *Manufacturing Consent; Changes in the labour process under monopoly capitalism*. Chicago, University of Chicago Press. 1979.

BURCHELL, B., LADIPO D. *and* WILKINSON F. (eds), *Job Insecurity and Work Intensification*. London, Routledge. 2002

BURCHELL B., DAY D., HUDSON M., LADIPO D., MANKELOW R., NOLAN J., REED H., WICHERT I. *and* WILKINSON F. *Job Insecurity and Work Intensification: Flexibility and the changing boundaries of work*. York, Joseph Rowntree Foundation. 1999.

BURGESS S. *and* REES H. 'A disaggregate analysis of the evolution of job tenure in Britain', *British Journal of Idustrial Relations*, Vol. 36, No. 4, 1998. pp629–655.

BURN D. *and* THOMPSON L. 'When personnel calls in the auditors', *Personnel Management*, January 1993. pp28–31.

BURNES B. *Managing Change*. London, Pitman Publishing. 2000.

BUYENS D. *and* DE VOS A. 'Perceptions of the value of the HR function', *Human Resource Management Journal*, Vol. 11, No. 3, 2001. pp53–89.

CALDWELL R. 'Champions, adapters, consultants and synergists: the new change agents in HRM', *Human Resource Management Journal*, Vol. 11, No. 3, 2001. pp39–52.

CALLAGHAN G. *and* THOMPSON P. '"We recruit attitude": The selection and shaping of routine call centre labour', *Journal of Management Studies*. Vol 39, No. 2, 2002 pp233–54.

CARROLL M., COOKE F. L., GRUGULIS I., RUBERY J. *and* EARNSHAW J. 'Analysing diversity in the management of human resources in call centres', paper presented to HRMJ conference, 2001a.

CARROLL M., COOKE F. L., HASSARD J. *and* MARCHINGTON M. *Pottering Around with Outsourcing: The future of core manufacturing activities in the UK ceramic industry*, Future of Work Working Paper Series. 2001b.

CARROLL M. *and* MARCHINGTON M. *The Recruitment and Retention of Drivers: Evidence from small UK road haulage firms.* Manchester School of Management Working Paper 9912, UMIST. 1999.

CASSELL C. 'Managing diversity', in T. REDMAN and A. WILKINSON (eds), *Contemporary Human Resource Management.* London, FT/Prentice-Hall. 2001.

CASTELLS M. *The Rise of the Network Society.* Oxford, Blackwell. 1996.

CASSIDY S. 'Teachers' pay bonus schemes wasteful', *The Independent*, 14 July 2001.

CAULKIN S. 'The time is now', *People Management*, 30 August 2001. pp32–34.

CENTRAL ARBITRATION COMMITTEE. *Annual Report 2000–2001.* London, CAC. 2001.

CERTIFICATION OFFICER. *Annual Report of the Certification Officer 2000–2001.* London, ACAS. 2001.

CHANDLER A. *Strategy and Structure: Chapters in the history of the American industrial enterprise.* Cambridge, MIT Press. 1962.

CHANG E. 'Career commitment as a complex moderator of organizational commitment and turnover intention', *Human Relations*, Vol. 52, 1999. pp1257–1278.

CHARTERED INSTITUTE OF PERSONNEL AND DEVELOPMENT. Professional Standards for the Professional Development Scheme, London, CIPD

CHARTERED INSTITUTE OF PERSONNEL AND DEVELOPMENT. *Working Time Regulations: Have they made a difference?* Survey Report. London, CIPD. 2001a.

CHARTERED INSTITUTE OF PERSONNEL AND DEVELOPMENT. *Consolidated Membership Statistics at Year End.* London, CIPD. August 2001b.

CHARTERED INSTITUTE OF PERSONNEL AND DEVELOPMENT. *Requirements of the Applied Personnel and Development Standards.* London. CIPD. 2001c.

CHARTERED INSTITUTE OF PERSONNEL AND DEVELOPMENT. *Performance Through People: The new people management.* London, CIPD. 2001d.

CHARTERED INSTITUTE OF PERSONNEL AND DEVELOPMENT. *The Case for Good People Management: A summary of the research.* London, CIPD. 2001e.

CHARTERED INSTITUTE OF PERSONNEL AND DEVELOPMENT. *Labour Turnover.* London, CIPD. 2001f.

CHARTERED INSTITUTE OF PERSONNEL AND DEVELOPMENT. *Recruitment Report.* London, CIPD. 2001g.

CHARTERED INSTITUTE OF PERSONNEL AND DEVELOPMENT. *Psychological Testing. Recruitment and Selection Quick Facts.* www.cipd.co.uk. 2001h.

CHARTERED Institute of Personnel and Development. *Employee Absence: A survey of management policy and practice.* London, CIPD. 2001i.

CHARTERED INSTITUTE OF PERSONNEL AND DEVELOPMENT. *Training and Development Survey.* London, CIPD. April 2001j.

CHARTERED INSTITUTE OF PERSONNEL AND DEVELOPMENT Executive Briefing, *The Future of Reward*. London, CIPD. 2001k.

CHARTERED INSTITUTE OF PERSONNEL AND DEVELOPMENT *Recruitment Report*. London, CIPD. 2000a.

CHARTERED INSTITUTE OF PERSONNEL AND DEVELOPMENT. *Training and Development Report*. London, CIPD. 2000b.

CHARTERED INSTITUTE OF PERSONNEL AND DEVELOPMENT. *The Changing Role of the Trainer*. London, CIPD. 1999.

CHARTERED INSTITUTE OF PERSONNEL AND DEVELOPMENT. *Key Facts: Age and employment*. London, CIPD. 1999b.

CHARTERED INSTITUTE OF PERSONNEL AND DEVELOPMENT. *Managing Diversity: Evidence from case studies*. London, CIPD. 1999c.

CHARTERED INSTITUTE OF PERSONNEL AND DEVELOPMENT. *Guide to Training Technology*. London, CIPD. 1998.

CHIVERS W. *and* DARLING P. *360-Degree Feedback and Organisational Culture*. London, CIPD. 1999.

CHRYSSIDES G. *and* KALER J. *An Introduction to Business Ethics*. London, Chapman & Hall. 1993.

CLARK J. 'Procedures and Consistency versus Flexibility and Commitment in Employee Relations: a comment on Storey', *Human Resource Management Journal*, Vol. 4, 1993. pp79–81.

CLARKE A. 'Flexible friends', *Personnel Today*, 5 November 1998. pp28–30.

CLAYDON T. *and* DOYLE M. 'Trusting me, trusting you? The ethics of employee empowerment', *Personnel Review*, Vol. 25, No.6, 1996. pp13–25.

COFF R. 'Human assets and management dilemmas: coping with hazards on the road to resource-based theory', *Academy of Management Review*, Vol. 22, No. 2, 1997. pp374–402.

CULLERTON S. *and* BEVAN S. 'Paying hard to get', *People Management*. 13 August 1998.

COLLIN A. 'Learning and development', in I. BEARDWELL and L. HOLDEN (eds), *Human Resource Management: A contemporary approach*. London, FT/Prentice-Hall. 2001.

COLLING, T. 'Tendering and outsourcing: working in the contract state?', in S. CORBY and G. WHITE (eds), *Employee Relations in the Public Services*. London, Routledge. 1999.

COOK M. *Personnel Selection : Adding value through people*. 3rd edition. Chichester, Wiley. 1998.

COOKE F., EARNSHAW J., MARCHINGTON M. *and* RUBERY J. 'For better and for worse? Transfer of undertaking and the reshaping of employment relations', *International Journal of Human Resource Management*. Forthcoming 2002.

COOPER C. 'A package deal', *People Management*, 13 September 2001d. p41.

COOPER C. 'Long-awaited dispute plan promises to cut tribunals', *People Management*, 17 May 2001a. p7.

COOPER C. 'Win by a canvas', *People Management*, 25 January 2001b. pp42–43.

COOPER C. 'Rolling with it', *People Management*, 28 September 2000a. pp32–34.

COOPER C. 'Is education really to blame for the Great British skills famine?', *People Management*, 9 August 2000b. pp10–11.

COOPER C. 'BBC signals switch to intranet learning', *People Management*, 8 June 2000c. p6.

COOPER C. 'Employment experts slate performance pay for teachers', *People Management*, 11 May 2000e. p6.

COOPER C. 'Teachers' anger fuelled by lack of consultation, *People Management*, 11 May 2000d. p11.

COOPER D. *and* ROBERTSON I. *The Psychology of Personnel Selection*. London, Routledge. 1995.

COUSSEY M. *Getting the Right Work–Life Balance*. London, CIPD. 2000.

COWLING A. *and* WALTERS M. 'Manpower planning – where are we today?', *Personnel Review*, Vol. 19, No. 3, 1990. pp3–8.

COX A. 'The importance of employee participation in determining pay effectiveness', *International Journal of Management Reviews*. Vol. 2, No. 4, 2000. pp357–372.

CRAWSHAW M., DAVIS E. *and* KAY J. '"Being Stuck in the Middle" or "Good Food Costs Less at Sainsbury's"', *British Journal of Management*, Vol. 5, No. 1, 1994. pp19–32.

CRESSEY P. 'European works councils in practice', *Human Resource Management Journal*, Vol. 8, No.1, 1998. pp67–79.

CRICHTON A. *Personnel Management in Context*. London, Batsford. 1968.

CROSBY P. *Quality is Free*. New York, Mentor. 1980.

CROUCH C. 'Skills-based full employment: the latest philosopher's stone', *British Journal of Industrial Relations*. Vol. 35, No.3, 1997. pp367–391.

CULLY M., WOODLAND S., O'REILLY A. *and* DIX G. *Britain at Work: As depicted by the 1998 Workplace Employee Relations Survey*. London, Routledge. 1999.

CULLY M., WOODLAND S., O'REILLY A., DIX G., MILLWARD N., BRYSON A. *and* FORTH, J. *The 1998 Workplace Employee Relations Survey: First findings*. London, Department of Trade and Industry. 1998.

CUNNINGHAM I. *and* HYMAN J. 'Devolving human resource responsibilities to the line: Beginning of the end or a new beginning for personnel?', *Personnel Review*, Vol. 28, No, 1/2, 1999. pp9–27.

CUNNINGHAM I. *and* HYMAN J. 'Transforming the HRM vision into reality: the role of line managers and supervisors in implementing change', *Employee Relations*, Vol. 17, No. 8, 1995. pp5–20.

CUNNINGHAM I. *and* JAMES P. 'Absence and return to work: towards a research agenda'. *Personnel Review,* Vol. 29, No. 1/2, 2000. pp33–47.

CURNOW B. 'The creative approach to pay', *Personnel Management*, October 1986. pp70–75.

CURRIE G. *and* PROCTER S. 'Exploring the relationship between HR and middle managers', *Human Resource Management Journal*, Vol. 11, No. 3, 2001. pp53–69.

CURTIS S. *and* LEWIS R. 'A coincidence of needs? Employers and full-time students', *Employee Relations*, Vol. 23, No. 1. 2001. pp38–54.

DARWIN J., JOHNSON P. *and* McAULAY J. *Developing Strategies for Change*. FT/Prentice-Hall. 2002.

DAVIES J. 'Labour disputes in 2000', *Labour Market Trends*, Vol. 109, No. 6, 2001. p302.

DEEPHOUSE D. 'To be different, or to be the same? It's a question (and theory) of strategic balance', *Strategic Management Journal*, Vol. 20, 1999. pp147–166.

DELANEY J. *and* HUSELID M. 'The impact of human resource management practices on perceptions of organizational performance'. *Academy of Management Journal*, Vol. 39, 1996. pp349–69.

DELBRIDGE R. *Life on the Line in Contemporary Manufacturing: The workplace experience of lean production and the 'Japanese' model.* Oxford, Oxford University Press. 1998.

DELERY J. *and* DOTY H. 'Modes of theorising in strategic human resource management: tests of universalistic, contingency and configurational performance predictions', *Academy of Management Journal*, Vol. 39, No. 4, 1996. pp802–35.

DENCH S., PERYMAN S. *and* GILES L. *Employers' Perceptions of Key Skills.* IES *Report* 346. Sussex, Institute of Employment Studies. 1998.

DENHAM N., ACKERS P. *and* TRAVERS C. 'Doing yourself out of a job? How middle managers cope with empowerment', *Employee Relations*, Vol. 19, No. 2, 1997. pp147–59.

DENSCOMBE M. *The Good Research Guide.* London, Open University Press. 1998.

DENZIN N. *The Research Act.* Aldine, Chicago 1970.

DEPARTMENT FOR EDUCATION AND EMPLOYMENT. *Providing Statutory Rights for Union Learning Representatives.* London, DfEE. 2001.

DEPARTMENT FOR EDUCATION AND EMPLOYMENT. *Skills for All: Research for the National Skills Taskforce.* London, DfEE. 2000.

DEPARTMENT FOR EDUCATION AND EMPLOYMENT. *The Learning Age: A Renaissance for a new Britain.* London, DfEE. 1998.

DEPARTMENT OF TRADE AND INDUSTRY. *Fairness at Work.* Cm3968. 1998.

DEVANNA M., FOMBRUN C. *and* TICHY N. 'A framework for strategic human resource management', in C. FOMBRUN, N. TICHY and A. DEVANNA (eds), *Strategic Human Resource Management.* New York, Wiley. 1984.

DICKENS L. 'Doing more with less: ACAS and individual conciliation', in B. TOWERS and W. BROWN (eds), *Employment Relations in Britain: 25 years of the Advisory, Conciliation and Arbitration Service.* Oxford, Blackwell. 2000.

DICKENS L. 'Beyond the business case: a three-pronged approach to equality action', *Human Resource Management Journal*, Vol. 9, No. 1. 1999. pp9–19.

DICKENS L. 'Wasted resources? Equal opportunities in employment', in K. SISSON (ed.), *Personnel Management in Britain*. Oxford, Blackwell. 1994.

DICKENS L. *and* HALL M. 'The state: labour law and industrial relations', in P. Edwards (ed.), *Industrial Relations: Theory and practice in Britain*. Oxford, Blackwell. 1995.

DIMAGGIO P. *and* POWELL W. 'The iron cage revisited: institutional isomorphism and collective rationality in organisational fields', *American Sociological Review*, Vol. 48, 1983. pp147–60.

DIPBOYE R. 'Structured selection interviews: Why do they work? Why are they underutilized?', in N. ANDERSON and P. HERRIOT (eds), *International Handbook of Selection and Assessment*. Chichester, John Wiley & Sons Ltd. 1997.

DONOVAN. *Royal Commission on Trade Unions and Employers Associations* 1965–68 Report. Cmnd 3623. London, HMSO. 1968.

DOOGAN K. 'Insecurity and long-term unemployment', *Work, Employment and Society*. Vol. 15, No. 3. 2001. pp419–441.

DOUGLAS A., KIRK D., BRENNAN C. *and* INGRAM A. 'The impact of Investors in People on Scottish local government services', *Journal of Workplace Learning*, Vol. 11, No. 5, 1999. pp164–9.

DOWN S. *and* SMITH D. 'It pays to be nice to people: Investors in People – the search for measurable benefits'. *Personnel Review*, Vol. 27, No. 2, 1998. pp143–155.

DRUCKER P. *Post-Capitalist Society*. Oxford, Butterworth-Heinemann. 1993.

DRUKER J. 'Wages systems', in G. WHITE and J. DRUKER (eds), *Reward Management: A critical text*. London, Routledge. 2000.

DRUKER J. *and* STANWORTH C. 'Partnerships and the private recruitment industry', *Human Resource Management Journal*, Vol. 11, No. 2, 2001. pp73–89.

DUNCAN C. 'Pay, payment systems and job evaluation', in B. TOWERS (ed.), *A Handbook of Industrial Relations Practice*. 3rd edition. London, Kogan Page. 1992.

DUNDON T. 'Recognition' in T. REDMAN and A. WILKINSON (eds), *The Informed Student Guide to Human Resource Management*. London, Thomson Learning. 2002a.

DUNDON T. 'Trade union de-recognition', in T. REDMAN and A. WILKINSON (eds), *The Informed Student Guide to Human Resource Management*. London, Thomson Learning. 2002b.

DUNDON T. 'Policies and procedures', in T. REDMAN and A. WILKINSON (eds), *The Informed Student Guide to Human Resource Management*. London, Thomson Learning. 2002c.

DUNDON T. *and* WILKINSON A, 'Employment relations in SMEs', in B. TOWERS (ed.), *Handbook of Employment Relations Law and Practice*. London, Kogan Page. 2002.

DUNDON T., GRUGULIS I. *and* WILKINSON, A. 'New management techniques in small and medium-sized enterprises', in T. REDMAN and A. WILKINSON (eds), *Contemporary Human Resource Management*. London, FT/Prentice-Hall. 2001.

DUNDON T., GRUGULIS I. *and* WILKINSON A. 'Looking out of the black hole: non-union relations in an SME', *Employee Relations*, Vol. 21, No.3, 1999. pp251–266.

DUNN C. *and* WILKINSON A. 'Wish you were here: managing absence'. *Personnel Review*, Vol. 31, No. 2. 2002. pp228–246.

EARNSHAW J. 'Contract of employment', in T. REDMAN and A. WILKINSON (eds), *The Informed Student Guide to Human Resource Management*. London, Thomson Learning. 2002.

EARNSHAW J. 'Unfair dismissal' in T. REDMAN and A. WILKINSON (eds), *The Informed Student Guide to Human Resource Management*. London, Thomson Learning. 2002.

EARNSHAW J., GOODMAN J., HARRISON R. *and* MARCHINGTON, M. *Industrial Tribunal Workplace Disciplinary Procedures and Employment Practice*, Employment Relations Research Series No.2. London, DTI. 1998.

EARNSHAW J., MARCHINGTON M. *and* GOODMAN J. 'Unfair to whom? Discipline and dismissal in small establishments', *Industrial Relations Journal*, Vol. 31, No. 1, 2000. pp62–73.

EARNSHAW J. RITCHIE E. MARCHINGTON L. TORRINGTON D. *and* HARDY S. *Best Practice in Undertaking Teacher Capability Procedures*. London, DfES. 2002

EASTERBY SMITH M., THORPE R. *and* LOWE A. *Management Research: An introduction*. London, Sage. 1996.

THE ECONOMIST. 'A Wapping mess', *The Economist*, 12 July 1997. pp54–56.

EDWARDS P. 'Discipline: towards trust and self-discipline', in S. BACH and K. SISSON (eds), *Personnel Management*. 3rd edition. Oxford, Blackwell. 2000.

EDWARDS P. (ed.), *Industrial Relations: Theory and practice in Britain*. Oxford, Blackwell. 1995.

EDWARDS P. *and* WRIGHT M. 'Human resource management and commitment: a case study of teamworking', in P. SPARROW and M. MARCHINGTON (eds), *Human Resource Management: The new agenda*. London, Pitman. 1998.

EDWARDS, R. *Contested Terrain*. London, Heinemann, 1979.

EIRO ONLINE [European industrial relations observatory online] *The UK productivity gap*. UK9805121F. www.eiro.eruofound.ie/ 2000

EMPLOYMENT TRIBUNAL OFFICE *Annual Reports*.

ENGESTRÖM Y. *Training for Change: New approach to instruction and learning in working life*. Geneva, International Labour Office. 1994.

EQUAL OPPORTUNITIES COMMISSION. *Facts about Women and Men in Great Britain 2001*. 2001. www.eoc.gov.uk

EQUAL OPPORTUNITIES COMMISSION news releases. 5 December 2001 www.eoc.gov.uk

EQUAL OPPORTUNITIES COMMISSION, *Good Practice Guide: Job evaluation schemes free of sex bias*. Manchester, EOC. 2000.

EQUAL OPPORTUNITIES COMMISSION, *Equality in the 21st Century: A new approach*. Manchester, EOC. 1998.

EQUAL OPPORTUNITIES COMMISSION, *Code of Practice: For the elimination of discrimination on the grounds of sex and marriage and the promotion of equality of opportunity in employment.* London, HMSO. 1985.

ETHICAL CONSUMER. Vol 74, January 2002. p 7.

EUROPEAN FOUNDATION FOR THE IMPROVEMENT OF LIVING AND WORKING CONDITIONS *Working Conditions in Atypical Work.* Dublin, European Foundation for the Improvement of Living and Working Conditions. 2000.

EWING K. 'Industrial relations and labour law', in P. ACKERS and A. WILKINSON (eds.) *Reworking Industrial Relations.* Oxford, OUP. 2002.

FAGAN, C. and WARREN, T. *Gender, Employment and Working Time Preferences in Europe.* European Foundation for the Improvement of Living and Working Conditions. postmaster@eurofound.ie 2001.

FAIRCLOUGH M. and BIRKENSHAW C. 'Employee rights and management wrongs – *mastering people management*', *Financial Times*, 26 November 2001. pp4–5.

FARNHAM D. 'Employee relations', in T. REDMAN and A. WILKINSON (eds), *The Informed Student Guide to Human Resource Management.* London, Thomson Learning. 2002.

FARNHAM D. *Employee Relations in Context.* 4th edition. London, CIPD. 2000.

FARNHAM D. *Personnel in Context.* London, Institute of Personnel Management. 1990.

FELSTEAD A., GREEN F. and MAYHEW K. *Getting the Measure of Training: A report on training statistics in Britain.* Leeds, Centre for Industrial Policy and Performance. 1997.

FELSTEAD A., JEWSON N., PHIZACKALEA. A. and WALTERS S. 'Working at home: statistical evidence for seven key hypotheses', *Work, Employment and Society*, Vol. 15, No. 2, 2001. pp215–231.

FENTON O'CREEVY M. 'HR practice – vive la différence', *Mastering People Management, Financial Times*, 26 November 2001a. pp6–8.

FENTON O'CREEVY M. 'Employee involvement and the middle manager: saboteur or scapegoat?' *Human Resource Management Journal*, Vol. 11, No. 1 2001b. pp24–40.

FERNER A. and QUINTANILLA J. 'Multinational, national business systems and HRM: the enduring influence of national identity or a process of Anglo-Saxonisation', *International Journal of Human Resource Management*, Vol. 9, No. 4, 1998. pp711–731.

FERNIE S., METCALF D. and WOODLAND S. *Does HRM Boost Employee–Management Relations?* London School of Economics, Centre for Economic Performance and Industrial Relations Department. 1994.

FINCHAM R. and EVANS M. 'The consultants' offensive: reengineering – from fad to technique', *New Technology, Work and Employment*, Vol. 14, No.1, 1999. pp32–44.

FINEGOLD D. 'Creating self-sustaining high-skill ecosystems', *Oxford Review of Economic Policy*, Vol. 15, No. 1, 1999. pp60–79.

FINEMAN S. and MANGHAM I. 'Data meanings and creativity', *Journal of Management Studies*, Vol. 20, No. 3, 1983. pp295–300.

FIRTH J. 'Sack full of sorrows', *People Management*, 17 June 1999. p25.

FLETCHER C. *Appraisal: Routes to improved performance*. London, CIPD. 1999.

FLETCHER C. 'The implications of research on gender differences in self-assessment and 360-degree appraisal'. *Human Resource Management Journal*, Vol. 9, No. 1, 1999b. pp39–46.

FLETCHER C. 'A deciding factor', *People Management*, 26 November 1998. pp38 40.

FOMBRUN C., TICHY N. and DEVANNA M. (eds), *Strategic Human Resource Management*. New York, Wiley. 1984.

FORDE C. 'Temporary arrangements: the activities of employment agencies in the UK', *Work, Employment and Society*, Vol. 15, No. 3. 2001. pp631–644.

FOWLER A. *Writing Job Descriptions*. London, CIPD. 2000.

FOWLER A. *Induction*. London, CIPD. 1999.

FOWLER A. 'How to conduct a disciplinary interview', *People Management*, 21 November 1996. pp41–7.

FOWLER A. 'New directions in performance-related pay', *Personnel Management*, Vol. 20, No. 11, 1988.

FOX A. *Beyond Contract*. London, Faber & Faber. 1974.

FOX A. *Industrial Sociology and Industrial Relations*, Royal Commission Research Paper No.3. London, HMSO. 1966.

FRANKS O. and THOMPSON D. 'Mix 'n match', *People Management*, 17 February 2000. pp40–43.

FRASER J. M. *Employment Interviewing*. London, McDonald and Evans. 1966.

FREEMAN R. 'Upping the stakes, *People Management*, 8 February 2001. pp24–29.

FREIDSON E. (ed.), *The Professions and their Prospects*. London, Sage. 1973.

FRIEDMAN M. *Effective Staff Incentives*. London, Kogan Page. 1990.

FRIEDMAN M. 'The social responsibility of business is to increase its profits', *The New York Times Magazine*, 13 September 1970. Reprinted in G. CHRYSSIDES and J. KALER (eds.), *An Introduction to Business Ethics*. London, Chapman Hall. 1993.

FROBEL P. and MARCHINGTON M. *Team Effectiveness: A cross-national and cross industry perspective*. Fifth International Workshop on Teamworking, Leuven. September 2001.

FULLER A. and UNWIN L. 'Reconceptualising apprenticeship: exploring the relationship between work and learning', *Journal of Vocational Education and Training*, Vol. 50, No. 2, 1998. pp153–173.

GAGNE R. *The Conditions of Learning*. New York, Holt Saunders. 1977.

GALL G. 'Back to terms', *People Management*, 13 September 2001. pp40–42.

GALL G. 'In place of strife?', *Personnel Management*, 14 September 2000. pp26–30.

GALL G. 'The changing social relation of production: union recognition and industrial relations in the UK magazine industry', *Industrial Relations Journal*, Vol. 29, 1998. pp151–161.

GALL G. *and* McKAY S. 'Development in recognition and union derecognition in Britain, 1994–1998', *British Journal of Industrial Relations*, Vol. 37, No. 4, 1999. pp601–614.

GALLIE D., WHITE M., CHENG Y. *and* TOMLINSON M. *Restructuring the Employment Relationship*. Oxford, Oxford University Press. 1998.

GEARY J. *and* DOBBINS A. 'Teamworking: a new dynamic in the pursuit of management control', *Human Resource Management Journal*, Vol. 11, No. 1, 2001. pp3–23.

GENNARD J. 'Europe is about far more than beef bans', *Employee Relations*, Vol. 22, No. 2, 2000. pp117–120.

GENNARD J. 'Labour government: change in employment law', *Employee Relations*, Vol. 22, No. 1, 1998. pp12–25.

GENNARD J. *and* JUDGE G. *Employee Relations*. 3rd edition. London, CIPD. 2002.

GENNARD J. *and* JUDGE G. *Employee Relations*. 2nd edition. London, IPD. 1999.

GENNARD J. *and* JUDGE G. *Employee Relations*. London, IPD. 1997.

GENNARD J. *and* KELLY J. 'The unimportance of labels: the diffusion of the personnel/HRM function', *Industrial Relations Journal*, Vol. 28, No. 1, 1997. pp27–42.

GENNARD J. *and* KELLY J. 'Human resource management: the views of personnel directors', *Human Resource Management Journal*, Vol. 5, No. 1, 1994. pp15–32.

GIBB S. 'The state of human resource management: evidence from employees' views of HRM systems and staff', *Employee Relations*, Vol. 23, No. 4 2001. pp318–36.

GIBB S. *and* MEGGINSON D. 'Employee development', in T. REDMAN and A. WILKINSON (eds), *Contemporary Human Resource Management*. London, FT/Prentice-Hall. 2001.

GILES E. *and* WILLIAMS R. 'Can the personnel department survive quality management?', *Personnel Management*, Vol. 23, No. 4, 1991. pp28–33.

GILL J. *and* JOHNSON P. *Research Methods for Managers*. London, PCP. 1997.

GLASER B. G. *and* STRAUSS A. L., *The Discovery of Grounded Theory: Strategies for qualitative research*. New York, Aldine De Gruyter. 1967.

GLOVER C. 'The taking stock market', *People Management*, 6 December 2001. pp44–45

GLOVER I. *and* HUGHES M. (eds), *The Professional–Managerial Class: Contemporary British management in the pursuer mode*. Aldershot, Avebury. 1996.

GOLDTHORPE J., LOCKWOOD D., BECHOFER F. *and* PLATT, J. *The Affluent Worker: Industrial attitudes and behaviour*. Cambridge, Cambridge University Press. 1968.

GOLZEN G. 'Voyage of discovery', *People Management*, 11 January 2001. pp32–36.

GOLZEN G. 'Award scheme comeback', *The Times*, 13 April 2000. p19.

GOODMAN J. 'Building bridges and settling differences: collective concili-ation and arbitration under ACAS', in B. TOWERS and W. BROWN (eds), *Employment Relations in Britain: 25 years of the Advisory, Conciliation and Arbitration Service*. Oxford, Blackwell. 2000. pp31–65.

GOSPEL H. 'The revival of apprenticeship training in Britain?', *British Journal of Industrial Relations*, Vol. 36, No. 3, 1998. pp435–457.

GOSPEL H. *and* FULLER A. 'The Modern Apprenticeship: new wine in old bottles?' *Human Resource Management Journal*, Vol. 8, No. 1, 1998. pp5–22.

GOSPEL H. *and* PALMER G. *British Industrial Relations*. 2nd edition. London, Routledge. 1993.

GOSS D. *Principles of Human Resource Management*. London, Routledge. 1994.

GRANT D. *and* OSWICK C. 'Of believers, atheists and agnostics: practitioner views on HRM', *Industrial Relations Journal*, Vol. 29, No. 3, 1998. pp178–193.

GRATTON L., HOPE-HAILEY V., STILES P. *and* TRUSS C. *Strategic Human Resource Management*. Oxford, Oxford University Press. 1999.

GRAY D. *and* MORGAN M. 'Modern Apprenticeships: filling the skills gap?', *Journal of Vocational Education and Training*, Vol. 50, No. 1, 1998. pp123–134.

GREEN F. 'It's been a hard day's night: the concentration and intensifica-tion of work in late twentieth-century Britain', *British Journal of Industrial Relations*, Vol. 39, No. 1. 2001. pp53–80.

GREEN F., ASHTON D., BURCHELL B., DAVIES B. *and* FELSTEAD A. *An Analysis of Changing Work Skills in Britain*. Paper presented to the Low Wage Employment Conference of the European Low Wage Employment Research Network, CEP, LSE. December 1997.

GRIFFITHS W. 'Profession knowledge and research update', *People Management*, 11 May 2000. pp57–60.

GRIMSHAW D. *and* RUBERY J. *The Gender Pay Gap: A research review*. Manchester, EOC. 2001.

GRIMSHAW D., VINCENT S. *and* WILLMOTT H. 'New control modes and emer-gent organisational forms: private–public contracting in public admin-istration and health service provision', *Administrative Theory and Praxis*, Vol. 23, No. 2. 2001. pp407–430.

GRINT K. 'What's wrong with performance appraisals? A critique and a suggestion', *Human Resource Management Journal*, Vol. 3, No. 3, 1993. pp61–77.

GRUGULIS I. 'The management NVQ: a critique of the myth of rel-evance'. *Journal of Vocational Education and Training*, Vol. 52, No. 1. 2000.

GRUGULIS I. *and* BEVITT S. *The Impact of Investors in People*. Paper pre-sented at ESRC seminar: The Changing Nature of Skills and Knowledge. UMIST 3–4 Sept 2001. Forthcoming in *Human Resource Management Journal*.

GRUGULIS I. *and* WILKINSON A. 'Managing Culture at British Airways: hype, hope and reality', *Long-Range Planning*, April 2002.

THE GUARDIAN. 'Profits down, top pay up', *The Guardian*, 16 July 2001. p20.

THE GUARDIAN. 'Railtrack directors given share options worth 2m', *The Guardian*, 4 July 2001. p2.

THE GUARDIAN. 'Most firms flout pay code', *The Guardian*, 2 May 2001. p21.

THE GUARDIAN. 'Rewarding the boardroom: gazing in awe at executive salaries', *The Guardian*, 23 August 2001. p27.

THE GUARDIAN. 'BA fights sabotage call', *The Guardian*, 8 November 1997. p10.

GUEST D. 'Human resource management: when research confronts theory', *International Journal of Human Resource Management*, Vol. 12, No. 7, 2001. pp1092–1106.

GUEST D. 'Industrial relations and human resource management', in J. STOREY (ed.), *HRM: A critical text*. London, Thomson Learning. 2001b.

GUEST D. *Why Do People Work?*, Presentation to the Institute of Personnel and Development National Conference, Harrogate, October 1995.

GUEST D. 'Personnel management: the end of orthodoxy?', *British Journal of Industrial Relations*, Vol. 29, No. 2, 1991. pp149–75.

GUEST D. *and* CONWAY N. *Public and Private Sector Perspectives on the Psychological Contract*. London, CIPD. 2001.

GUEST D. *and* CONWAY N. *The Psychological Contract in the Public Sector*. London, CIPD. 2000.

GUEST D. *and* CONWAY N. 'Peering into the black hole: the downside of the new employment relations in the UK', *British Journal of Industrial Relations*, Vol. 37, No. 3, 1999. pp367–389.

GUEST D. *and* CONWAY N. *Fairness at Work and the Psychological Contract: Issues in people management*. London, IPD. 1998.

GUEST D. *and* HOQUE K. 'The good, the bad and the ugly: employment relations in new non-union workplaces', *Human Resource Management Journal*, Vol. 5, No. 1, 1994a. pp1–14.

GUEST D. *and* HOQUE K. 'Yes, personnel does make a difference', *Personnel Management*, November 1994b. pp40–44.

GUEST D. *and* KING Z. *Voices from the Boardroom: Senior executives' views on the relationship between HRM and performance*. London, CIPD. 2002.

GUEST D. *and* KING Z. 'Personnel's paradox', *People Management*, 27 September 2001.

GUEST D. *and* PECCEI R. 'Partnership at work: mutuality and the balance of advantage', *British Journal of Industrial Relations*, Vol. 39, No. 1, 2001. pp207–236.

GUEST D. *and* PECCEI R. 'The nature and causes of effective human resource management', *British Journal of Industrial Relations*, Vol. 32, No. 2, 1994. pp219–242.

GUEST D., MICHIE J., SHEEHAN M. *and* CONWAY N. *Employment Relations, HRM and Business Performance: An analysis of the 1998 workplace employee relations survey*. London, CIPD. 2000a.

GUEST D., MICHIE J., SHEEHAN M., CONWAY N. and METOCHI M. *Effective People Management: Initial findings of the Future of Work study.* London, CIPD. 2000b.

HACKMAN J. and OLDHAM G. 'Motivation through the design of work: test of a theory', *Organisation Behaviour and Human Performance*, Vol. 16, 1976. pp250–79.

HALL L. and TORRINGTON D. 'Letting go or holding on – the devolution of operational personnel activities', *Human Resource Management Journal*, Vol. 8, No. 1, 1998. pp41–55.

HAMMOND D. 'Reality bytes', *People Management*, 25 January 2001. pp26–31.

HAMMOND SUDDARDS. *Legal Essentials: Disability discrimination.* London, CIPD. 2000.

HANDY, C. *Inside Organisations: 21 ideas for managers.* London, BBC Books. 1991.

HARRISON R. *Employee Development.* 2nd edition. London, CIPD. 2000.

HARRISON R. *Employee Development.* London, IPD. 1992.

HART T. 'Human resource management – time to exorcise the militant tendency'. *Employee Relations*, Vol. 15, No. 3, 1993. pp29–36.

HASTINGS S. 'Grading systems and estimating value', in G. WHITE and J. DRUKER (eds) *Reward Management: A critical text.* London, Routledge. 2000.

HATCHETT A. 'A test of determination', *People Management*, 8 February 2001. pp36–40.

HAWES W. 'Setting the pace or running alongside? ACAS and the changing employment relationship', in B. TOWERS and W. BROWN (eds), *Employment Relations in Britain: 25 years of the Advisory, Conciliation and Arbitration Service.* Oxford, Blackwell. 2000.

HAWKINS K. *A Handbook of Industrial Relations Practice.* London, Kogan Page. 1979.

HEERY E. 'Trade unions and the management of reward', in G. WHITE and J. DRUKER (eds) *Reward Management: A critical text.* London, Routledge. 2000

HEERY E. 'The re-launch of the Trades Union Congress', *British Journal of Industrial Relations*, Vol. 36, 1998. pp339–360.

HEERY E. and SALMON J. 'The insecurity thesis', in E. HEERY and J. SALMON (eds), *The Insecure Workforce.* London, Routledge. 2000.

HEERY E., SIMMS M., DELBRIDGE R., SALMON J. and SIMPSON D. 'The TUC's organising academy: an assessment', *Industrial Relations Journal*, Vol. 31, No. 5, 2000. pp400–415.

HELLER F., PUSIC E., STRAUSS G. and WILPERT B. *Organisational Participation: Myth and reality.* Oxford, Oxford University Press. 1998.

HENDRY C. *Human Resource Management: A strategic approach to employment.* London, Butterworth. 1994.

HENDRY C., WOODWARD S., BRADLEY P. and PERKINS S. 'Performance and rewards: cleaning out the stables', *Human Resource Management Journal*, Vol. 10, No.3, 2000. pp46–62.

THE HERALD. 'Turbulence and hot air ahead', *The Herald*, 26 June 1997. p2.

HERRIOT P. 'The role of the HRM function in building a new proposition for staff', in P. SPARROW and M. MARCHINGTON (eds), *Human Resource Management: The new agenda*. London, FT/Pitman. 1998.

HERRIOT P. 'The management of careers', in S. TYSON (ed.), *Strategic Prospects for Human Resource Management*. London, Institute of Personnel and Development. 1995a.

HERRIOT P. *Why Do People Work?*, Presentation to the Institute of Personnel and Development National Conference, Harrogate. October 1995b.

HERZBERG F. 'Worker's needs: the same around the world', *Industry Week*, 21 September 1987. pp29–32.

HERZBERG F. 'One more time: how do you motivate employees?', *Harvard Business Review*, Jan/Feb 1968. pp53–62.

HERZBERG, F. *Work and the Nature of Man*. Cleveland, World Publishing. 1966.

HICKS-CLARKE D. *and* ILES, P. 'Climate for diversity and its effects on career and organisational attitudes and perceptions', *Personnel Review*, Vol. 29, No. 3. 2000. pp324–45.

HIGGINBOTTOM K. 'BP learns outsourcing lesson', *People Management*, 8 November 2001. p8.

HIGGINBOTTOM K. 'DDA changes should be unveiled now, says disability rights body', *People Management*, 11 October 2001. pp16–19.

HILGARD E., ATKINSON R. L. *and* ATKINSON R. C. *Introduction to Psychology*. 7th edition. New York, Harcourt Brace Jovanivich. 1979.

HILL R. *and* STEWART J. 'Investors in People in small organisations: learning to stay the course?', *Journal of European Industrial Training*, Vol. 23, No. 6, 1999. pp286–299.

HILTON P. 'Using incentives to reward and motivate employees', *Personnel Management*, Vol. 24, No. 9, 1992. pp49–51.

HOGARTH T., HASLUCK C., PIERRE G., WINTERBOTHAM M., *and* VIVIAN D. 'Work–life balance 2000: results from the Baseline study', IRS *Labour Market Trends*, July 2001. pp 371–373.

HOLDEN L. 'Human resource development: the organisation and the national framework', in I. BEARDWELL and L. HOLDEN (eds), *Human Resource Management*. London, FT/Prentice-Hall. 2001.

HONEY P. 'The debate starts here', *People Management*, 1 October 1998. pp28–29.

HONEY P. *and* MUMFORD A. *The Manual of Learning Styles*. 3rd edition. Maidenhead, Peter Howey. 1986.

HOLLY L. *and* RAINBIRD H. 'Workplace learning and the limits to evaluation', in H Rainbird (ed.), *Workplace Learning*. London, Macmillan Press. 2000.

HOPE-HAILEY V., GRATTON L., McGOVERN P., STILES P. *and* TRUSS C. 'A chameleon function? HRM in the 90s', in *Human Resource Management Journal*, Vol. 7, No. 3, 1997. pp5–18.

HOPKINS R. 'Choosing an employee assistance programme', IRS *Employee Health Bulletin* 6, December 1998. pp4–7.

HOQUE K. 'All in all it's just another plaque in the wall', *Journal of Management Studies*, May 2003.

HOQUE K. *All in all, it's just another plaque on the wall. The incidence and impact of the Investors in People Standard*. Paper presented at the 6th European Congress, International Industrial Relations Association, Oslo 25–29 June, 2001. Forthcoming in *Journal of Management Studies*.

HOQUE K. *Human Resource Management in the Hotel Industry*. London, Routledge. 2000.

HOQUE K. 'Human resource management and performance in the UK hotel industry', *British Journal of Industrial Relations*, Vol. 37, No. 3, 1999. pp419–443.

HOQUE K. *and* NOON M. 'Counting angels: a comparison of personnel and HR specialists', *Human Resource Management Journal*, Vol. 11, No. 3, 2001. pp5–22.

HOSKISSON R., HITT M., WAN W., *and* YIU, D. 'Theory and research in strategic management', *Journal of Management*, Vol. 25, No. 3, 1999. pp417–56.

HOWARD K. *and* SHARP J. *The Management of a Student Research Project*. Aldershot, Gower Publishing. 1983.

HUDDLESTON P. 'Modern Apprenticeships in college: something old, something new', *Journal of Vocational Education and Training*, Vol. 50, 1998. pp1–10.

HUNTER L., McGREGOR A., MacINNES J. *and* SPROULL A. 'The flexible firm, strategy and segmentation', *British Journal of Industrial Relations*, Vol. 31, No. 3, 1993. pp383–407.

HUSELID M. 'The impact of human resource management practices on turnover, productivity and corporate financial performance', *Academy of Management Journal*, Vol. 38, No. 3, 1995. pp635–72.

HUSELID M. *and* BECKER D. 'Methodological issues in cross-sectional and panel estimates of the HR-firm performance link', *Industrial Relations*, Vol. 35, 1996. pp400–422.

HUSSEY D. *Strategic Management; From theory to implementation*. Oxford, Butterworth Heinemann. 1998.

HUTCHINSON S. *and* WOOD S. 'The UK experience', *Institute of Personnel and Development, Personnel and the Line: Developing the New Relationship*. London, IPD. 1995. pp3–42.

HUTTON W. *The Stakeholding Society*. Cambridge, Polity Press. 1998.

HYMAN J. 'Financial participation schemes', in G. WHITE and J. DRUKER (eds), *Reward Management: A critical text*. London, Routledge. 2000.

HYMAN R. 'The future of employee representation', *British Journal of Industrial Relations*, Vol. 35, No. 3, 1997. pp309–336.

ICHNIOWSKI C., SHAW K. *and* PRENNUSHI G. 'The effects of human resource management practices on productivity: a study of steel finishing lines', *American Economic Review*, Vol. 87, 1997. pp291–313.

ILES P. 'Employee resourcing' in J. STOREY (ed.), *Human Resource Management: A critical text*. London, Routledge. 2001.

ILES P. *and* ROBERTSON I. 'The impact of personnel selection procedures on candidates', in N. ANDERSON and P. HERRIOT (eds), *International Handbook of Selection and Assessment*. Chichester, John Wiley & Sons Ltd. 1997.

INCOMES DATA SERVICES. *Bonus Schemes*, Study 655. March 1999.

INCOMES DATA SERVICES. *Flexible Benefits*. July 1998.

INDUSTRIAL RELATIONS SERVICES. 'Benchmarking the HR function: the IRS guide', IRS *Employment Review* 742a, 17 December 2001. pp6–14.

INDUSTRIAL RELATIONS SERVICES. 'Flexible working – new rights for parents, more work for tribunals'. IRS *Employment Review* 742b, 17 December 2001. pp46–49.

INDUSTRIAL RELATIONS SERVICES. 'Graduate recruitment 2001/02: diversity and competition,', IRS *Employment Review* 742c, 17 December 2001. pp31–40.

INDUSTRIAL Relations Services. 'Benchmarking labour turnover 2001/02, Part 1', IRS *Employment Review* 741, 3 December 2001. pp31–38.

INDUSTRIAL RELATIONS SERVICES. 'The skill of the chase', IRS *Employment Review* 740, November 2001, pp34–38.

INDUSTRIAL RELATIONS SERVICES. 'Developing HR policies: a case of reinventing the wheel?', IRS *Employment Review* 740, 19 November 2001. pp7–15.

INDUSTRIAL RELATIONS SERVICES. 'Businesses behaving responsibly', IRS *Employment Review* 739. November 2001. pp6–11.

INDUSTRIAL RELATIONS SERVICES. 'Managing disability at work', IRS *Employment Review* 738, October 2001a. pp 6–14.

INDUSTRIAL RELATIONS SERVICES. 'Employer direct: a virtual network', IRS *Employment Review* 738, October 2001b. pp15–18.

INDUSTRIAL RELATIONS SERVICES. 'Unions focus on recruiting and retaining members', IRS *Employment Trends* 737, October 2001. pp2–3.

INDUSTRIAL RELATIONS SERVICES. 'Part-time working options and arrangements', IRS *Employment Trends* 735, September 2001. pp4–16.

INDUSTRIAL RELATIONS SERVICES. 'Employers report steady decrease in absence', IRS *Employee Health Bulletin* 22, August 2001. pp4–6.

INDUSTRIAL RELATIONS SERVICES. 'Single status: the story so far', IRS *Employment Trends* 710, August 2001. pp2–11.

INDUSTRIAL RELATIONS SERVICES. 'Think local: using jobcentres for recruitment', IRS *Employment Development Bulletin* 139, July 2001. pp12–16.

INDUSTRIAL RELATIONS SERVICES. 'Recruiting and training young employees 2001', IRS *Employment Development Bulletin* 138, June 2001. pp4–16.

INDUSTRIAL RELATIONS SERVICES. 'Civil Service absence is static', IRS *Employee Health Bulletin* 21, June 2001. pp14–16.

INDUSTRIAL RELATIONS SERVICES. 'Managing discipline at work', IRS *Employment Trends* 727, May 2001. p5–11.

INDUSTRIAL RELATIONS SERVICES. 'Airing a grievance: how to handle employee complaints', IRS *Employment Trends* 726, April 2001. p9.

INDUSTRIAL RELATIONS SERVICES. 'Phone a friend: using bounty hunters in the search for staff', IRS *Employment Development Bulletin* 135, March 2001. pp6–7.

INDUSTRIAL RELATIONS SERVICES. 'Dial–up HR at Scottish and Newcastle', IRS *Employment Trends* 721, February 2001.

INDUSTRIAL RELATIONS SERVICES. 'Access all areas', IRS *Employment Trends* 708, July 2000. pp5–16.

INDUSTRIAL RELATIONS SERVICES. '360-degree feedback: a rounded view', IRS *Employment Review* 705, June 2000. pp5–9.

INDUSTRIAL RELATIONS SERVICES. 'Work–life: the state of play', IRS *Employment Trends* 704, May 2000. pp12 16.

INDUSTRIAL RELATIONS SERVICES. 'In-store personnel managers balance Tesco's scorecard', IRS *Employment Trends* 703, May 2000. pp13–16.

INDUSTRIAL RELATIONS SERVICES. 'Human resources consulting: friend or foe?', IRS *Employment Trends* 698, February 2000. pp7–12.

INDUSTRIAL RELATIONS SERVICES. 'Effective selection tools: adapt and survive', IRS *Employee Development Bulletin* 124, April 2000. pp5–10.

INDUSTRIAL RELATIONS SERVICES. 'The interview: its role in effective selection', IRS *Employment Development Bulletin* 122, February 2000. pp12–16.

INDUSTRIAL RELATIONS SERVICES. 'The truth about merit pay', IRS *Pay and Benefits Bulletin* 501, August 2000. pp5–9.

INDUSTRIAL RELATIONS SERVICES. 'Civil Service pay – from individual to team rewards', IRS *Pay and Benefits Bulletin* 499, July 2000. pp5–9.

INDUSTRIAL RELATIONS SERVICES. 'Retail rewards: competency-based pay at Adams', IRS *Pay and Benefits Bulletin* 480, September 1999.

INDUSTRIAL RELATIONS SERVICES. 'The business of selection: an IRS survey', IRS *Employment Development Bulletin* 117, September 1999. pp5–16.

INDUSTRIAL RELATIONS SERVICES. 'Privatising personnel', IRS *Employment Trends* 684, July 1999. pp5–11.

INDUSTRIAL RELATIONS SERVICES. 'British managers need to get a life', IRS *Employment Trends* 688, September 1999. p2.

INDUSTRIAL RELATIONS SERVICES. 'Ethics at the workplace', IRS *Employment Trends* 675, March 1999. pp6–13.

INDUCTRIAL RELATIONS SERVICES. 'Virtual lift–off for BAe's corporate university', IRS *Employee Development Bulletin* 110, February 1999. pp5–9.

INDUSTRIAL RELATIONS SERVICES. 'What do employers' associations offer to members?', IRS *Employment Trends* 653. 1998. pp11–16.

INDUSTRIAL RELATIONS SERVICES, 'NVQ survey', IRS *Employee Development Bulletin* 40, April 1993, pp2–15.

INSTITUTE OF PERSONNEL AND DEVELOPMENT. *The IPD Guide on Outsourcing*. London, Institute of Personnel and Development. 1998a.

INSTITUTE OF PERSONNEL AND DEVELOPMENT. *Executive Summary: Performance pay survey*. London, IPD. 1998b.

INSTITUTE OF PERSONNEL AND DEVELOPMENT KEY FACTS. *Strategic Issues in Occupational Pensions*. London, IPD. April 1999.

INTERNATIONAL LABOUR ORGANISATION. *Mental Health in the Workplace*. October 2000. www.ilo.org

INVESTORS IN PEOPLE UK. *What is Investors in People?*, www.investorsin-people.co.uk. 2001.

INVOLVEMENT AND PARTICIPATION ASSOCIATION. *Sharing the Challenge Ahead: Informing and consulting with your workforce. A guide to Good Practice*. London, IPA. 2001.

INVOLVEMENT AND PARTICIPATION ASSOCIATION. *Towards Industrial Partnership: A new approach to relationships at work*. London, IPA. 1993.

JAMES K. *and* HUFFINGTON C. 'Organisational stress: targeting resources more effectively', IRS *Employee Health Bulletin* 6, December 1998. pp7–10.

JAMES P. 'Disability discrimination', in T. REDMAN and A. WILKINSON (eds), *The Informed Student Guide to Human Resource Management*. London, Thomson Learning. 2002.

JAMES P., DIBBEN P. *and* CUNNINGHAM I. 'Missing persons', *People Management*, 23 November 2000. pp41–2.

JOHNSON G. *and* SCHOLES K. *Exploring Corporate Strategy*. London, Prentice-Hall. 2002.

JOHNSON R. 'Import duty', *People Management*, 8 March 2001. pp25–29.

JOHNS T. *Report-Writing as an Exercise in Persuasion*. London, IPD. 1996.

KAHN-FREUND O. 'Industrial relations and the law: retrospect and prospect', *British Journal of Industrial Relations*, Vol. 7, 1965. pp301–316.

KAHN-FREUND O. 'Labour law', in M. GINSBERG (ed.), *Law and Opinion in England in the 20th Century*. London, Stevens. 1959.

KAMOCHE K. 'Strategic human resource management within a resource-capability view of the firm', *Journal of Management Studies*, Vol. 33, No. 2, 1996. pp213–233.

KANDOLA R. *and* FULLERTON J. *Diversity in Action: Managing the mosaic*. London, IPD. 1998.

KEEP E. *If it moves, it's a skill – the changing meaning of skill in the UK context*. Paper presented at ESRC seminar: The Changing Nature of Skills and Knowledge. UMIST. 3–4 Sept 2001.

KEEP E. *and* RAINBIRD H. 'Towards the learning organisation', in S. BACH and K. SISSON (eds), *Personnel Management*. Oxford, Blackwell. 2000.

KELLIHER C. *and* PERRETT G. 'Business strategy and approaches to HRM: a case study of new developments in the UK restaurant industry', *Personnel Review*, Vol. 30, No. 4, 2001. pp421–437.

KELLY JAMES. 'Union militancy and social partnership', in P. ACKERS, C. SMITH and P. SMITH (eds), *The New Workplace and Trade Unionism*. London, Routledge. 1996.

KELLY JOHN. *and* GENNARD J. 'Getting to the top: career paths of personnel directors', *Human Resource Management Journal*, Vol. 10, No. 3, 2000. pp22–37.

KESSLER I. 'Reward system choices', in J. STOREY (ed.), *Human Resource Management: A critical text*. London, Routledge. 2001.

KESSLER I. 'Remuneration systems', in S. BACH and K. SISSON (eds), *Personnel Management*. 3rd edition. Oxford, Blackwell. 2000.

KINGSMILL REPORT. *Report on Women, Employment and Pay*. London, DFEE. 2001.

KINNIE N., HUTCHINSON S. *and* PURCELL J. 'Fun and surveillance: the paradox of high-commitment management in telephone call centres', *International Journal of Human Resource Management*, Vol. 11, No. 5, 2000. pp63–78.

KIRKPATRICK D. 'Evaluation of training', in R. CRAIG *and* L. BITTELL (eds), *Training and Evaluation Handbook*. New York, McGraw-Hill. 1967.

KIRSCHENBAUM A. *and* MANO-NEGRIN R. 'Underlying labour market dimensions of "opportunities": the case of employee turnover', *Human Relations*, Vol. 52, 1999. pp1233–1255.

KLEIN J. 'Why supervisors resist employee involvement', *Harvard Business Review*, September/October, 1984. pp87–95.

KOCHAN T. *and* BAROCCI T. *Human Resource Management and Industrial Relations*. Boston, Little Brown. 1985.

KOCHAN T., KATZ H. *and* CAPPELLI R. *The Transformation of American Industrial Relations*. New York, Basic Books. 1986.

KOCHAN T., MCKERSIE R. *and* CAPPELLI P. 'Strategic choice and industrial relations theory', *Industrial Relations*, Vol. 23, No. 1, 1985. pp16–39.

KOHN A. 'Why incentive plans cannot work', *Harvard Business Review*, September/October, 1993. pp54–63.

KOLB D., OSLAND J. *and* RUBIN I. *Organisational Behaviour: An experiential approach*. 6th edition. New Jersey, Prentice-Hall. 1995.

KOMATSU UK Handbook, 2001.

LABOUR MARKET TRENDS (monthly), Central Statistical Office. London, HMSO.

LANE C. *Management and Labour in Europe*. Aldershot, Edward Elgar. 1989.

LANSBURY R., BAMBER G. *and* WAILES N. *International and Comparative Employment Relations*. Sydney, Allen & Unwin. 2002.

LAWLER E. *Strategic Pay: Aligning organisational strategies and pay systems*. San Francisco, Jossey-Bass. 1990.

LAWLER E. 'The strategic design of reward systems', in C. FOMBRUN, N. TICKY and A. DEVANNA (eds), *Strategic Human Resource Management*. New York, Wiley. 1984.

LAZEAR E. *Personnel Economics*. Cambridge, Mass, MIT Press. 1998.

LEGGE K. 'The ethical context of HRM: the ethical organisation in the boundaryless world', in D. WINSTANLEY and J. WOODALL (eds), *Ethical Issues in Contemporary Human Resource Management*. London, Macmillan Business. 2000.

LEGGE, K. *Human Resource Management: Rhetoric and realities*, London, Macmillan. 1995.

LEGGE K. *Power, Innovation and Problem-Solving in Personnel Management*. London, McGraw-Hill. 1978.

LEIGHTON P. *and* PROCTOR G. *Legal Essentials: Recruiting within the law*. London, CIPD. 2001.

LENGNICK Hall C. *and* LENGNICK HALL M. 'Strategic human resource management: a review of the literature and a proposed typology', *Academy of Management Review*, Vol. 13, No. 3, 1988. pp454–470.

LEONARD D. *Wellsprings of Knowledge: Building and sustaining the sources of innovation*. Boston, Harvard Business School Press. 1998.

LEOPOLD J. *Human Resources in Organisations*. London, Prentice-Hall. 2002.

LEWIS D. *Essentials of Employment Law*. 3rd edition. London, IPM. 1990.

LEWIS D. *and* SARGEANT M. *Essentials of Employment Law* 7th edition. London, CIPD. 2002.

LEWIS P. 'Reward management', in T. REDMAN and A. WILKINSON (eds), *Contemporary Human Resource Management*. London, FT/Prentice-Hall. 2001.

LEWIS P. 'Managing performance-related pay based on evidence from the financial service sector', *Human Resource Management Journal*, Vol. 8, No.2, 1998. pp66–77.

LEWIS P. *Practical Employment Law*. Oxford, Blackwell. 1992.

LIEVENS F. *and* KLIMOSKI R. 'Understanding the assessment centre process: where are we now?', *International Review of Industrial and Organizational Psychology*, Vol. 16. 2001. pp245–286.

LIFF S. 'Manpower or human resource planning: what's in a name?', in S. BACH and K. SISSON (eds), *Personnel Management: A comprehensive guide to theory and practice*. Oxford, Blackwell. 2000.

LIFF S. 'Diversity and equal opportunities: room for a constructive compromise?', *Human Resource Management Journal*, Vol. 9, No. 1. 1999. pp65–75.

LITTLEFIELD D. 'Doing their bit', *People Management*, 11 January 2001. pp30–31.

LITTLEFIELD D. 'To be precise', *People Management*, 14 January 1999. pp38–39.

LOVAS B. *and* GHOSHAL S. 'Strategy as guided evolution', *Strategic Management Journal*, Vol. 21, No. 9, 2000. pp875–96.

LOWE J. 'Teambuilding via outdoor training: experiences from a UK automotive plant', *Human Resource Management Journal*, Vol. 2, No. 1, 1992. pp42–59.

LOWRY D. 'Performance management', in J. LEOPOLD (ed.), *Human Resources in Organisations*. London, Prentice-Hall. 2002.

LSC Strategic Framework to 2004: Corporate Plan: www.lsc.gov.uk

LUPTON B. 'Pouring the coffee at interview? Personnel's role in the selection of doctors', *Personnel Review*, Vol. 29, No. 1, 2000. pp48–68.

LUPTON B. *and* SHAW S. 'Are public sector personnel managers the profession's poor relations?', *Human Resource Management Journal*, Vol. 11, No. 3, 2001. pp23–38.

LYNCH P. 'Time-based pay', in R. THORPE and G. HOMAN (eds), *Strategic Reward Systems*. London, Financial Times/Prentice-Hall. 2000.

MABEY C. 'Closing the circle: participant views of a 360-degree feedback programme', *Human Resource Management Journal*, Vol. 11, No.1. 2001. pp41–53.

MABEY C., SALAMAN G., *and* STOREY J. *Human Resource Management: A strategic introduction*. London, Blackwell. 1998.

MacDuffie J. 'Human resource bundles and manufacturing performance: organizational logic and flexible production systems in the world auto industry', *Industrial and Labor Relations Review*, Vol. 48, 1995. pp197–221.

Machin S. 'Union decline in Britain', *British Journal of Industrial Relations*, Vol. 38, No. 4, 2000. pp631–645.

MacMahon G. 'Counselling in private practice', in S. Palmer (ed.), *Handbook of Counselling*. 2nd edition. London, Routledge. 1997.

Madsen D. *Successful Dissertations and Theses*. 2nd edition. San Francisco, Jossey-Bass. 1992.

Mahoney C. 'Glass ceiling as tough as it was 10 years ago', *People Management*, 12 October 2000. p13.

Mahoney C. 'Firms fail to see how IIP boosts profits', *People Management*, 3 August 2000. pp8–9.

Makin P., Cooper C. and Cox C. *Managing People at Work*. London, Routledge. 1989.

Mant, A. 'Changing work roles', in S. Tyson (ed.), *Strategic Prospects for HRM*. London, IPD. 1995.

Marchington M. 'Employee involvement at work', in J. Storey (ed.), *Human Resource Management: A critical text*. 2nd edition. London, Thomson. 2001.

Marchington M. 'Teamworking and employee involvement: terminology, evaluation and context', in S. Procter and F. Mueller (eds), *Teamworking: Issues, concepts, and problems*. London, Blackwell. 1999.

Marchington M. 'The dynamics of joint consultation', in K. Sisson (ed.), *Personnel Management in Britain*. Oxford, Blackwell. 1994.

Marchington, M. 'Managing labour relations in a competitive environment', in A. Sturdy, D. Knights and H. Willmott (eds), *Skill and Consent: Contemporary studies on the labour process*. London, Routledge. 1992. pp149–84.

Marchington M. and Grugulis I. '"Best practice" human resource management: perfect opportunity or dangerous illusion?', *International Journal of Human Resource Management*, Vol. 11, No. 4, 2000. pp905–925.

Marchington M. and Parker P. *Changing Patterns of Employee Relations*. Hemel Hempstead, Harvester Wheatsheaf. 1990.

Marchington M. and Wilkinson A. 'Direct participation' in S. Bach and K. Sisson (eds), *Personnel Management in Britain*. 3rd edition. Oxford, Blackwell. 2000.

Marchington M. and Wilkinson A. *Core Personnel and Development*. London, CIPD. 1996.

Marchington M., Goodman J. and Berridge J. 'Employment relations in Britain', in G. Bamber and R. Lansbury (eds), *International and Comparative Employment Relations: A study of industrialised market economies*. 2nd edition. Sydney, Allen & Unwin. 2002.

Marchington M., Wilkinson A. and Ackers P. 'Waving or drowning in participation?', *Personnel Management*, March 1993a. pp30–33.

MARCHINGTON M., WILKINSON A. *and* DALE B. 'The case study report', in A. BARON (ed.), *Quality: People management matters*. London, Institute of Personnel Management, 1993b.

MARCHINGTON M., WILKINSON A., ACKERS P. *and* DUNDON A. *Management Choice and Employee Voice*. London, CIPD. 2001.

MARGALIS A. 'Spirited response', *People Management*, 13 September 2001. pp32–38.

MARSDEN D. *Teachers before the 'Threshold'*, London, Centre for Economic Performance Working Paper. 2000.

MARSDEN D. *and* FRENCH A. *What a Performance: PRP in the public sector*. London, Centre for Economic Performance Working Paper. 1998.

MARSDEN D. *and* RICHARDSON R. 'Performing for pay? The effects of "merit" pay on motivation in a public service', *British Journal of Industrial Relations*, Vol. 32, No. 2, 1994. pp243–262.

MARSH A. *and* McCARTHY W. *Disputes Procedures in Britain Royal Commission*. Research Paper No.2, Part 2. London, HMSO. 1968.

MARTIN R., FOSH P., MORRIS H., SMITH P. *and* UNDY R. 'The decollectivisation of industrial relations? Ballots and collective bargaining in the 1990s', *Industrial Relations Journal*, Vol. 22, No.3, 1991. pp197–208.

MASLOW A. 'A Theory of Human Motivation', *Psychological Review*, Vol. 50, 1943, pp370–396.

MAUND L. *An Introduction to Human Resource Management: Theory and practice*. Basingstoke, Palgrave. 2001.

MAYAN-WHITE B. 'Problem-solving in small groups: team members as agents of change', in C. MABEY and B. MAYAN-WHITE (eds), *Managing Change*. 2nd edition. London, PCP. 1993.

MAYO A. 'The role of employee development in the growth of intellectual capital', *Personnel Review*, Vol. 29, No. 4, 2000. pp521–533.

MAYO A. 'Called to account', *People Management*, 8 April 1999. p33.

MAYO A. 'Economic indicators of human resource management', in S. TYSON (ed.), *Strategic Prospects for Human Resource Management*. London, IPD. 1995.

McGOVERN P., HOPE-HAILEY V., STILES P. *and* TRUSS C. 'Human resource management on the line?', *Human Resource Management Journal*, Vol. 7, No. 4, 1997. pp12–29.

McGREGOR D. *The Human Side of Enterprise*. New York, Harper & Row. 1960.

McKENNA E. *Business Psychology and Organisational Behaviour*. 3rd edition. Hove, Psychology Press. 2000.

McLEOD J. *Counselling in the Workplace: The facts*. Rugby, BACP. 2001.

MEGGINSON D. 'Style counsel revisited', *People Management*, 6 December 2001. p57.

MERRICK N. 'Learning zone', *People Management*, 22 June 2000. pp44–48.

MERRICK N. 'Premier division', *People Management*, 19 August 1999. pp38–41.

MERRICK N. 'The leisure principle', *People Management*, 11 June 1998, pp56–57.

MILES A. *and* HUBERMAN A. *Analysing Qualitative Data: A source book for new methods*. London, Sage. 1984.

MILES M. 'Qualitative data as an attractive nuisance: the problem of analysis', *Administrative Science Quarterly*, Vol. 12, No. 4, 1979. pp590–601.

MILES R. *and* SNOW C. *Organisational Strategy, Structure and Process*. New York, McGraw-Hill. 1978.

MILLER P. 'Strategy and the ethical management of human resources', *Human Resource Management Journal*, Vol. 6, No. 1. 1996. pp5–18.

MILLWARD N., BRYSON A *and* FORTH J. *All Change at Work: British employment relations 1980–1998, as portrayed by the Workplace Industrial Relations Survey series*. London, Routledge. 2000.

MILLWARD N., STEVENS M., SMART D. *and* HAWES W. *Workplace Industrial Relations in Transition*. Aldershot, Dartmouth Publishing. 1992.

MINTZBERG H., AHLSTRAND B. *and* LAMPEL J. *Strategy Safari: A guided tour through the wilds of strategic management*. London, Prentice-Hall. 1998.

MINTZBERG H. 'An emergent strategy of direct research', *Administrative Science Quarterly*, Vol. 24, No. 4, 1979. pp582–589.

MINTZBERG H. 'Patterns in strategy formation', *Management Science*, Vol. 24, No. 9, 1978. pp934–948.

MITCHELL J. 'Case and situation analysis', *Sociological Review*, Vol. 31, No. 2, 1983. pp187–211.

MONKS J. 'Trade unions, enterprise and the future', in P. SPARROW and M. MARCHINGTON (eds) *Human Resource Management: The new agenda*. London, FT/Pitman. 1998.

MONKS, K. 'Models of personnel management: a means of understanding the diversity of personnel practices?', *Human Resource Management Journal*, Vol. 3, No. 2, 1993. pp29–41.

MORGAN G. *Images of Organisation*. Newbury Park, Sage. 1986.

MORLEY M. 'Gainsharing' in T. REDMAN and A. WILKINSON (eds), *The Informed Student Guide to Human Resource Management*. London, Thomson Learning. 2002.

MORLEY M. 'Pensions', in T. REDMAN and A. WILKINSON (eds), *The Informed Student Guide to Human Resource Management*. London, Thomson Learning. 2002.

MORRELL K, LOAN-CLARKE J. *and* WILKINSON A. 'Unweaving leaving: the use of models in the management of employee turnover', *International Journal of Management Reviews*, Vol. 3, No. 3, 2001. pp219–244.

MORRIS J., WILKINSON B. *and* MUNDAY M. 'Farewell to HRM? Personnel practices in Japanese manufacturing plants in the UK', *International Journal of Human Resource Management*, Vol. 11, No. 3, 2000. pp1047–1060.

MORRIS T. *and* PINNINGTON A. 'Continuity and change in professional organisations: evidence from British law firms', in D. BROCK, M. POWELL and C. HININGS (eds), *Restructuring Professional Organisations*. London, Routledge. 1999.

MORTON C. *Becoming World Class*. London, Macmillan. 1994.

MOSER C. *A Fresh Start*. www.lifelonglearning.co.uk/mosergroup/ 1999.

MUELLER F. 'Societal effect, organisation effect and globalisation', *Organisation Studies*, Vol. 15, 1994. pp407–428.

MUELLER, F. 'Human resources as strategic assets: an evolutionary resource-based theory', *Journal of Management Studies*, Vol. 33 No. 6, 1996. pp757–785.

MUELLER F. *and* PROCTOR S. (eds), *Teamworking*. London, Macmillan. 2000.

MULLINS L. *Management and Organisational Behaviour*. 6th edition. London, FT/Pitman. 2001.

MULLINS L. *Management and Organisational Behaviour*. 5th edition. London, FT/Pitman. 1999.

MUMFORD A. 'Enhancing your learning skills – a note of guidance for managers', in S. Wood (ed.), *Continuous Development*. London, Institute of Personnel Management. 1988.

NADLER D. *and* LAWLER E. 'Motivation: a diagnostic approach', in M. STEERS and L. PORTER (eds), *Motivation and Work Behaviour*. 2nd edition. New York, McGraw-Hill. 1979.

NATIONAL SKILLS TASK FORCE. *Towards a National Skills Agenda*. www.dfee.gov.uk/skillrep/ 1998.

NEWELL S. *and* SHACKLETON V. 'Selection and assessment as an interactive decision–action process', in T. REDMAN and A. WILKINSON (eds), *Contemporary Human Resource Management*. London, FT/Prentice-Hall. 2001.

NEWELL S. *and* SHACKLETON V. 'Recruitment and selection', in S. BACH and K. SISSON (eds), *Personnel Management: A comprehensive guide to theory and practice*. Oxford, Blackwell. 2000.

NEWELL S. *and* TANSLEY C. 'International uses of selection methods', *International Review of Industrial and Organizational Psychology*, Vol. 16. 2001. pp195–213.

NIVEN M. *Personnel Management, 1913–1963*. London, Institute of Personnel Management. 1967.

NOON M. *and* BLYTON P. *The Realities of Work*. London, Macmillan Business. 2002.

NOLAN J. 'The intensification of everyday life', in B. BURCHELL, D. LADIPO and F. WILKINSON (eds), *Job Insecurity and Work Intensification*. London, Routledge. 2002.

O'DOHERTY D. 'Human resource planning: control to seduction?', in I. BEARDWELL and R. HOLDEN (eds), *Human Resource Management: A contemporary approach*. London, Pitman. 2001.

OGBONNA E. *and* WHIPP R. 'Strategy, culture and HRM: evidence from the UK food retailing sector', *Human Resource Management Journal*, Vol. 9, No. 4, 1999. pp75–90.

OLIVER C. 'Sustainable competitive advantage: combining institutional and resource-based views', *Strategic Management Journal*, Vol. 18, No. 9, 1997. pp697–713.

O'SHEA T. 'E-asy does it'. *Guardian Education*, 10 October 2000. pp10–11.

OWEN D., REZA B., GREEN A., MAGUIRE M. *and* PITCHER J. 'Patterns of labour market participation in ethnic minority groups', *Labour Market Trends*, November 2000. pp505–510.

PALMER M. 'Very testing testing', *People Management*, 10 January 2002. pp18–19.

PATTERSON M., WEST M., LAWTHOM R. *and* NICKELL S. *The Impact of People Management Practices on Business Performance*. London, IPD. 1997.

PEARN M. *and* KANDOLA R. *Job Analysis*. London, Institute of Personnel Management. 1993.

PECK S. 'Exploring the link between organisational strategy and the employment relationship: the role of human resource policies', *Journal of Management Studies*, Vol. 31, No. 5, 1994. pp715–36.

PEDLER M., BURGOYNE J. *and* BOYDELL T. *The Learning Company: A strategy for sustainable development*. London, McGraw-Hill. 1991.

PENDLETON A. 'Profit sharing and employee share ownership', in R. Thorpe and G. Homan (eds), *Strategic Reward Systems*. Harlow, FT/Prentice-Hall. 2000.

PENDLETON A. *and* BREWSTER C. 'Portfolio workforce', *People Management*, 12 July 2001. pp38–40.

PENROSE E. *The Theory of the Growth of the Firm*. Oxford, Blackwell. 1959.

PEOPLE MANAGEMENT. 'Keep HR strategy in-house, warn outsourcing leaders', *People Management*, 5 April 2001. p13.

PETTIGREW, A. 'Contextualist research and the study of organisational change processes', in E. LAWLER (ed.), *Doing Research That Is Useful in Theory and Practice*. New York, Jossey-Bass. 1985.

PETTIGREW A. *The Politics of Organisational Decision-Making*. London, Tavistock. 1973.

PFEFFER J. *The Human Equation: Building profits by putting people first*. Boston, Harvard Business School Press. 1998.

PFEFFER J. 'Pitfalls on the road to measurement: the dangerous liaison of human resources with the idea of accounting and finance', *Human Resource Management*, Vol. 36, No. 3, 1997. pp357–365.

PFEFFER J. *Competitive Advantage Through People*, Boston, Harvard Business School Press. 1994.

PICKARD J. 'Taking it on the chin', *People Management*, 8 November 2001. p14.

PICKARD J. 'A sell-out strategy', *People Management*, 23 November 2000. pp32–36.

PICKARD J. 'The truth is out there', *People Management*, 3 February 2000. pp48–50.

PICKARD J. *and* FOWLER A. 'Grade expectations', *People Management*, 11 February 1999. pp32–38.

PITT G. *Employment Law*. 4th edition. London, Sweet & Maxwell. 2000.

PLUMBLEY P. *Recruitment and Selection*. London, Institute of Personnel Management. 1991.

PORTER M. *Competitive Advantage: Creating and sustaining superior performance*. New York, Free Press. 1985.

PRAHALAD C. 'How HR can help to win the future', *People Management*, 12 January 1995. pp 34–36.

PRICE R. *and* PRICE L. 'Change and continuity in the status divide', in K. SISSON (ed.), *Personnel Management in Britain*. Oxford, Blackwell. 1994.

PROCTER S. *and* MUELLER F. (eds), *Teamworking*. London, Macmillan. 2000.

PROCTER S. *and* CURRIE G. 'The role of the personnel function: roles, perceptions and processes in an NHS trust', *International Journal of Human Resource Management*, Vol. 10, No. 6, 1999. pp 1077–1091.

PRUSAK L. *Knowledge in Organisations*. Oxford, Butterworth Heinemann. 1997.

PURCELL J. 'After collective bargaining? ACAS in the age of human resource management', in B. TOWERS and W. BROWN (eds), *Employment Relations in Britain: 25 years of the Advisory, Conciliation and Arbitration Service*. Oxford, Blackwell. 2000.

PURCELL J. 'The search for best practice and best fit in human resource management: chimera or cul-de-sac?' *Human Resource Management Journal*, Vol. 9, No. 3, 1999. pp 26–41.

PURCELL J. 'The impact of corporate strategy on human resource management', in J. STOREY (ed.), *New Perspectives on Human Resource Management*. London, Routledge. 1989.

PURCELL J. *Good Industrial Relations: Theory and practice*. London, Macmillan. 1980.

PURCELL J. *and* AHLSTRAND B. *Human Resource Management in the Multi-Divisional Company*. Oxford, Oxford University Press. 1994.

PURCELL J., BROWN D. *and* SANDRINGHAM J. 'Pay per view', *People Management*, 3 February 2000. pp 41–43.

QUINN J. *Strategies for Change: Logical incrementalism*. Homewood, Illinois, Irwin. 1980.

RAM M. 'Investors in People in small firms', *Personnel Review*, Vol. 29, No. 1, 2000. pp 69–89.

RAMSAY H. *and* SCHOLARIOS D. 'Selective decisions: challenging orthodox analyses of the hiring process', *International Journal of Management Reviews*, Vol. 1, No. 4. 1999. pp 63–89.

RAMSAY H., SCHOLARIOS D. *and* HARLEY B. 'Employees and high-performance work systems: testing inside the black box', *British Journal of Industrial Relations*, Vol. 38, No. 4, 2000. pp 501–531.

RANA E. 'Low skills, low interest', *People Management*, 13 September 2001a. pp 24–30.

RANA E. 'Take initiative on online learning, trainers urged', *People Management*, 25 January 2001b. p 14.

RANA E. 'IIP revamp aims to cut back on bureaucracy', *People Management*, 13 April 2000. pp 14.

RANDELL G. 'Employee appraisal', in K. SISSON (ed.), *Personnel Management in Britain*. Oxford, Blackwell. 1994.

REDMAN T. 'European Works Councils', in T. REDMAN and A. WILKINSON (eds), *The Informed Student Guide to Human Resource Management*. London, Thomson Learning. 2002.

REDMAN T. 'Performance appraisal', in T. REDMAN and A. WILKINSON (eds), *Contemporary Human Resource Management*. London, FT/Prentice-Hall. 2001.

REDMAN T., SNAPE E., THOMPSON D., *and* KA-CHING YAN F. 'Performance appraisal in an NHS hospital', *Human Resource Management Journal*, Vol. 10, No. 1, 2000. pp.48–61

REDMAN T. *and* WILKINSON A. (eds), *The Informed Student Guide to Human Resource Management*. London, Thomson Learning. 2002.

REDMAN T. *and* WILKINSON A. (eds), *Contemporary Human Resource Management*. London, FT/Prentice-Hall. 2001.

REID M. *and* BARRINGTON H. *Training Interventions: Promoting learning opportunities*. London, CIPD. 2001.

REID P. 'Legislative straitjacket', *People Management*, 22 June 2000. p59.

REID P. 'EU Social Policy', *CIPD Quick Facts*. 2000b.

REID P. 'EU Social Policy: after Amsterdam', *CIPD Quick Facts*. 2000c.

REILLY P. *and* PICKARD J. 'HR service centres: called into question', *People Management*, 6 July 2000. pp26–36.

RENWICK D. *and* GENNARD J. 'Grievance and discipline', in T. REDMAN and A. WILKINSON (eds), *Contemporary Human Resource Management*. London, FT/Prentice-Hall. 2001.

RICHARDSON R. *and* THOMSON M. 'The impact of people management practices on business performance: a literature review', *Issues in People Management*. London, Institute of Personnel and Development. 1999.

RIPPIN S. *and* DAWSON G. 'How to outsource the HR function', *People Management*, 27 September 2001. pp42–43.

RITSON N. 'Corporate strategy and the role of HRM: critical cases in oil and chemicals', *Employee Relations*, Vol. 21, No. 2, 1999. pp159–175.

ROBERTS G. *Recruitment and Selection: A competency approach*. London, Institute of Personnel and Development. 1997.

ROBERTSON I. 'Undue diligence', *People Management*, 22 November 2001. pp42–43.

ROBERTSON I., SMITH M. *and* COOPER D. *Motivation*. London, IPM. 1992.

ROBINSON P. 'Explaining the relationship between flexible employment and labour market regulation,' in A. FELSTEAD and N. JEWSON (eds), *Global Trends in Flexible Labour*. London, Macmillan. 1999.

ROCHE W. 'In search of commitment-oriented human resource management practices and the conditions that sustain them', *Journal of Management Studies*, Vol. 36, No. 5. 1999. pp653–678.

RODGER A. *The Seven-Point Plan*. London, National Institute for Industrial Psychology. 1952.

ROGERS C. *Freedom to Learn*. Ohio, Charles and Merrill Publishing Company. 1969.

ROLLINSON D. 'Grievance', in T. REDMAN and A. WILKINSON (eds), *The Informed Student Guide to Human Resource Management*. London, Thomson Learning. 2002.

ROLLINSON D., BROADFIELD A. *and* EDWARDS D. *Organisational Behaviour and Analysis*. London, Addison-Wesley. 1998.

ROSE M. *How Far Can I Trust It? Job satisfaction data in the WERS98 Employee Survey*, ESRC Future of Work Paper Number 6. Swindon, ESRC. 2000.

ROSE M. *Explaining and Forecasting Job Satisfaction: The contribution of occupational filing*, ESRC Future of Work Paper Number 3. Bath, ESRC. 1999.

ROSE M. *Industrial Behaviour*. Harmondsworth, Penguin. 1978.

ROYLE T. 'Recruiting the acquiescent workforce: a comparative analysis of McDonald's in Germany and the UK', *Employee Relations*, Vol. 21, No. 6. 1999. pp540–555.

RUBENSTEIN M. 'Making visible the invisible – rewarding women's work', *Equal Opportunities Review*, 1992. pp23–32.

RUBERY J. 'Performance-related pay and the prospects for gender equity', *Journal of Management Studies*, Vol. 35, No.5, 1995. pp637–654.

RUBERY J. *and* GRIMSHAW D. *Employment Policy and Practice*. London, Palgrave. 2002.

RUBERY J., EARNSHAW J., MARCHINGTON M., COOKE F. *and* VINCENT S. 'Changing organisational forms and the employment relationship', *Journal of Management Studies*, Vol 39, No 5, 2002 pp645–72.

RUMMEL R. *and* BALLAINE W. *Research Methodology in Business*. New York, Harper & Row. 1963.

SADHEV K., VINNICOMBE S. *and* TYSON S. 'Downsizing and the changing role of HR', *International Journal of Human Resource Management*, Vol. 10, No. 5. 1999. pp906–923.

SADLER-SMITH E. *and* BADGER B. 'The HR practitioner's perspective on continuing professional development', *Human Resource Management Journal*, Vol. 8, No. 4, 1998. pp66–75.

SADLER-SMITH E., DOWN S. *and* LEAN J. '"Modern" Learning Methods: Rhetoric and Reality', *Personnel Review*, Vol. 29, No. 4, 2000. pp474–490.

SALAMON M. *Industrial Relations: Theory and practice*. 4th edition. Harlow, FT/Prentice-Hall. 2000.

SANDERS D. 'Improving retention and performance through induction', IRS *Employee Development Bulletin* 130, October 2000a. pp13–14.

SANDERS D. 'The pros and cons of computer-based learning', IRS *Employee Development Bulletin* 123, March 2000b. pp6–8.

SANZ-VALLE R., SABATER-SANCHEZ R. *and* ARAGON-SANCHEZ A. 'Human resource management and business strategy links: an empirical study', *International Journal of Human Resource Management*, Vol. 10, No. 4, 1999. pp655–671.

SARGEANT M. 'Employee consultation', *Employee Relations*, Vol. 27, No. 5, 2001. pp483–497.

SAUNDERS M., LEWIS P. *and* THORNHILL A. *Research Methods for Business Students*. 2nd edition. London, FT/Prentice-Hall. 2000.

SCARBROUGH H. (ed.), *The Management of Expertise*. London, Macmillan. 1996.

SCARBROUGH H. *and* SWAN J. *Case Studies in Knowledge Management.* London, CIPD. 1999.

SCARBROUGH H., SWAN J. *and* PRESTON J. *Knowledge Management: A literature review.* London, CIPD. 1999.

SCASE R. *and* GOFFEE R. *Reluctant Managers: Their work and lifestyles.* London, Unwin Hyman. 1989.

SCHEIN E. *Organisational Psychology.* New Jersey, Prentice-Hall. 1965.

SCHMIDT F. *and* HUNTER J. 'The validity and utility of selection methods in personnel psychology: practical and theoretical implications of 85 years of research findings', *Psychological Bulletin*, Vol. 124, No. 2. 1998. pp262–274.

SCHMITT N. *and* CHAN D. 'The status of research on applicant reactions to selection tests and its implications for managers', *International Journal of Management Reviews*, Vol. 1, No. 1. 1999. pp45–62.

SCHULER R. 'Strategic human resource management and industrial relations', *Human Relations*, Vol. 42, No. 2, 1989. pp157–184.

SCHULER R. *and* HUBER S. *Personnel and Human Resource Management.* 5th edition. New York, West Publishing. 1993.

SCHULER R. *and* JACKSON S. 'Linking competitive strategies with human resource management', *Academy of Management Executive*, Vol. 1, No. 3, 1987. pp207–219.

SCHULER R., JACKSON S. *and* STOREY J. 'HRM and its link with strategic management', in J. STOREY (ed.), *Human Resource Management: A critical text.* 2nd edition. London, Thomson Learning. 2001.

SCHUSTER J. *and* ZINGHEIM P. *The New Pay: Linking employee and organisational performance.* New York, Lexington. 1992.

SCOTT M., ROBERTS I., HOLROYD G. *and* SAWBRIDGE D. *Management and Industrial Helations in Small Firms*, Department of Employment Research Paper, No.70. London, HMSO. 1989

SEMLER R. *Maverick!* London, Arrow Business Books. 1993.

SENGE P. *The Fifth Discipline: The art and practice of the learning organisation.* London, Century. 1990.

SHAW S. 'Commission for Racial Equality', in T. REDMAN and A. WILKINSON (eds), *The Informed Student Guide to Human Resource Management.* London, Thomson Learning. 2002.

SHAW, S. 'Equal Opportunities Commission', in T. REDMAN and A. WILKINSON (eds), *The Informed Student Guide to Human Resource Management.* London, Thomson Learning. 2002.

SHAW S. *and* CLARK M. 'Women, pay and equal opportunities', in R. THORPE and G. HOMAN (eds), *Strategic Reward Systems.* Harlow, FT/Prentice-Hall. 2000.

SILVERMAN A. *Interpreting Qualitative Data.* London, Sage. 1993.

SISSON K. 'Human resource management and the personnel function', in J. STOREY (ed.), *Human Resource Management: A critical text.* 2nd edition. London, Thomson Learning. 2001.

SISSON K. 'In search of human resource management', *British Journal of Industrial Relations*, Vol. 31, No. 2, 1993. pp201–210.

SISSON K. *and* STOREY J. *The Realities of Human Resource Management.* Milton Keynes, Open University Press. 2000.

SISSON K. *and* TIMPERLEY S. 'From manpower planning to strategic human resource management?', in K. SISSON (ed.), *Personnel Management: A comprehensive guide to theory and practice in Britain.* Oxford, Blackwell. 1994.

SLOMAN M. 'Plug but no play', *People Management*, 13 September 2001a. p57.

SLOMAN M. 'Forewarned is forearmed', *People Management*, 5 April 2001b. pp26–33.

SLOMAN M. *The E-learning Revolution: From propositions to action.* London, CIPD. 2001c.

SMITH I. 'Flexible plans for pay and benefits', in R. THORPE and G. HOMAN (eds), *Strategic Reward Systems.* Harlow, FT/Prentice-Hall. 2000.

SMITH M. 'Personnel selection research', *International Journal of Organisational and Occupational Psychology*, 2002.

SMITH M. *and* ROBERTSON I. *The Theory and Practice of Systematic Personnel Selection.* Basingstoke, Macmillan. 1993.

SMITH P. *and* MORTON G. 'New Labour's reform of Britain's employment law: the devil is not only in the detail but in the values and policy too', *British Journal Industrial Relations*, Vol. 39, No. 1, 2001. pp119–138.

SMITH P. *and* MORTON G. 'Union exclusion and the decollectivisation of industrial relations in contemporary Britain', *British Journal of Industrial Relations*, Vol. 31, No. 1, 1993. pp97–114.

SMITH P. *and* NETHERSELL G. 'Job evaluation', in R. THORPE and G. HOMAN (eds), *Strategic Reward Systems.* Harlow, FT/Prentice-Hall. 2000.

SNAPE E., REDMAN T. *and* BAMBER G. *Managing Managers: Strategies and techniques for human resource management.* Oxford, Blackwell. 1994.

SPILSBURY M., MORALEE J., FROST D. *and* HILLAGE J. *Evaluation of Investors in People in England and Wales.* Institute of Employment Studies, Research Report 263. 1995.

SPURLING M. *and* TROLLEY E. 'How to make training strategic', *People Management*, 13 April 2000. pp46–48.

STAIRS M., KANDOLA B. *and* SANDFORD-SMITH R. 'Slim picking', *People Management*, 28 December 2000. pp28–30.

STAMMERS R. *and* PATRICK J. *The Psychology of Training.* London, Methuen. 1975.

STANSFIELD L. 'Continuing professional development', in T. REDMAN and A. WILKINSON (eds), *The Informed Student Guide to Human Resource Management.* London, Thomson Learning. 2002.

STERN E. *and* SOMMERLAD E. *Workplace Learning, Culture and Performance.* London, CIPD. 1999.

STEVENS P. *and* FITZGIBBONS E. 'How to tackle long-term sick leave', *People Management*, 12 July 2001.

STEWART J. 'Individual learning', in J. LEOPOLD (ed.), *Human Resources in Organisations.* Harlow, FT/Prentice-Hall. 2002.

STILES P. 'The impact of the board on strategy: an empirical investigation', *Journal of Management Studies*, Vol. 38, No. 5, 2001. pp627–650.

STIRLING J. *and* FITZGERALD I. 'European Works Councils: representing workers on the periphery', *Employee Relations*, Vol. 23, No.1, 2001. pp13–25.

STOREY J. (ed.), *Human Resource Management: A critical text.* 2nd edition. London, Thomson Learning. 2001.

STOREY J. *Developments in the Management of Human Resources.* Oxford, Blackwell. 1992.

STOREY J. *and* SISSON K. *Managing Human Resources and Industrial Relations.* Buckingham, Open University Press. 1993.

STOREY M. *and* WRIGHT J. 'Recruitment and selection', in I. BEARDWELL and L. HOLDEN (eds), *Human Resource Management: A contemporary approach.* London, FT/Prentice-Hall. 2001.

STORR F. 'This is not a circular', *People Management*, 11 May 2000.

STREDWICK J. 'Employee share schemes' in T. REDMAN and A. WILKINSON (eds), *The Informed Student Guide to Human Resource Management.* London, Thomson Learning. 2002.

STREECK W. 'The uncertainties of management and the management of uncertainty: employers, labour relations and industrial adjustment in the 1980s', *Work, Employment and Society*, Vol. 1, No. 3, 1987. pp281–308.

STURDY A., GRUGULIS I., *and* WILLMOTT H. (eds), *Customer Service: Empowerment and entrapment.* London, Palgrave. 2001.

STURDY A., KNIGHTS D. *and* WILLMOTT H. (eds.), *Skill and Consent: Contemporary studies on the labour process.* London, Routledge. 1992.

SUTHERLAND J. *and* RAINBIRD H. 'Unions and workplace learning: conflict or cooperation with the employer?', in H. RAINBIRD (ed.), *Training in the Workplace, Critical Perspectives on Learning at Work.* Basingstoke, Macmillan Press Ltd. 2000.

SUTTON R. *and* SHAW B. 'What theory is not', *Administrative Science Quarterly*, Vol. 40, No. 3, 1995. pp371–384.

SWART J. *and* KINNIE N. *Human Resource Advantage Within a Distributed Knowledge System: A study of growing knowledge-intensive firms.* Paper presented at ESRC seminar: The Changing Nature of Skills and Knowledge. UMIST. 3–4 Sept 2001.

TAILBY S. *and* WINCHESTER D. 'Management and trade unions: towards social partnership', in S. BACH and K. SISSON (eds), *Personnel Management.* 3rd edition. Oxford, Blackwell. 2000.

TANG T., KIM J. *and* TANG D. 'Does attitude toward money moderate the relationship between intrinsic job satisfaction and voluntary turnover?', *Human Relations*, Vol. 53, 2000. pp213–245.

TAYLOR P. *and* BAIN P. '"An assembly line in the head": work and employee relations in the call centre', *Industrial Relations Journal*, Vol. 30, No. 2, 1999. pp101–117.

TAYLOR R. *The Future of Employment Relations.* Swindon, ESRC. 2002.

TAYLOR S. *People Resourcing.* London, CIPD. 2002.

TAYLOR S. 'Debates in reward management', in R. THORPE and G. HOLMAN (eds), *Strategic Reward Systems*. Harlow, FT/Prentice-Hall. 2000.

TAYLOR S. 'Occupational pensions', in R. THORPE and G. HOLMAN (eds), *Strategic Reward Systems*. FT/Prentice-Hall. 2000b.

TAYLOR S. *Employee Resourcing*. London, CIPD. 1998.

TERRY N. *and* WHITE P. 'Occupational pension schemes and their interaction with HRM', *Human Resource Management Journal*, Vol. 8, No.4, 1998. pp20–36.

THIETART R.A. *et al. Doing Management Research*. London, Sage. 2001.

THOMASON G. *A Textbook of Industrial Relations Management*. London, Institute of Personnel Management. 1984.

THOMPSON M. 'Salary progression schemes', in G. WHITE and J. DRUKER (eds), *Reward Management: A critical text*. London, Routledge. 2000.

THOMPSON M. *Pay and Performance: The employer experience*. Brighton, Institute of Manpower Studies, Report No. 218. 1992.

THOMPSON P. *and* McHUGH D. *Work Organisations: A critical introduction*. 3rd edition. London, Palgrave. 2002.

THOMPSON P. *and* MILSOME S. *Reward Determination in the UK: Research report*, London, CIPD. 2001.

THOMSON A. *and* MURRAY V. *Grievance Procedures*. Farnborough, Saxon House. 1976.

THORPE R. *and* HOLMAN G. (eds), *Strategic Reward Systems*. London, FT/Prentice-Hall. 2000.

THORPE R., BOWEY A. *and* GOODRIDGE M. 'Auditing a remuneration system', in R. THORPE and G. HOLMAN (eds), *Strategic Reward Systems*, London, FT/Prentice-Hall. 2000.

THURLEY K. *and* WOOD S. (eds), *Industrial Relations and Management Strategy*. Cambridge, Cambridge University Press. 1983.

THE TIMES. 'Passengers grab rivals' seats to beat BA strike', *The Times*, 8 July 1997. p3.

TOPLIS J., DULEWICZ V. *and* FLETCHER C. *Psychological Testing: A manager's guide*. London, Institute of Personnel Management. 1994.

TORRINGTON D. 'Discipline', in M. POOLE and M. WARNER (eds), *IEBM Handbook of Human Resource Management*. London, International Thomson Press. 1998.

TORRINGTON D. 'How dangerous is human resource management: a reply to Tim Hart', *Employee Relations*, Vol. 15, No. 5, 1993. pp40–53.

TORRINGTON D. 'Human resource management and the personnel function', in J. STOREY (ed.), *New Perspectives on Human Resource Management*. London, Routledge. 1989.

TORRINGTON D. 'How does human resource management change the personnel function?', *Personnel Review*, Vol. 17, 6, 1988. pp3–9.

TORRINGTON D. *and* HALL L. *Personnel Management: Human resource management in action*. London, Prentice-Hall. 1995.

TORRINGTON D., HALL L. *and* TAYLOR S. *Human Resource Management*. London, Prentice-Hall. 2002.

TOWERS B. *The Representation Gap: Change and reform in the British and American workplace.* Oxford, Oxford University Press. 1997.

TRAPP R. 'Main attraction', *People Management*, 25 October 2001b. pp.44–46.

TRAPP R. 'Virtue and reality', *People Management*, 11 October 2001a. pp28–34.

TRUSS C., GRATTON L., HOPE-HAILEY V., McGOVERN P. *and* STYLES P. 'Soft and hard models of human resource management: a reappraisal'. *Journal of Management Studies*, Vol. 34, No. 1, 1997. pp53–73.

TUC. *Learning in Partnership.* November 2000.

TUC. *Learning Services Task Group Report*, www.tuc.org.uk. 1998

TUC. *Black Workers Deserve Better.* www.tuc.org.uk. 2001

TUCKMAN A. 'All together better? Single status and union recognition in the chemical industry', *Employee Relations*, Vol. 20, No.2, 1998. pp132–149.

TURNER H. A. *Trade Union Growth, Structure and Policy: A comparative study of the cotton unions.* London, Allen & Unwin. 1962.

TWOMEY B. 'Disability and the labour market: results from the Summer 2000 Labour Force Survey', *Labour Market Trends*, May 2001. pp241–252.

TYSON S. *Human Resource Strategy: Towards a general theory of human resource management.* London, Pitman. 1995.

TYSON S. *and* FELL A. *Evaluating the Personnel Function.* London, Hutchinson. 1986.

ULRICH D. *Human Resource Champions: The next agenda for adding value and delivering results.* Boston, Harvard Business School Press. 1997.

ULRICH D. 'A new mandate for human resources', *Harvard Business Review*, Jan-Feb 1998. pp125–134.

VAN MAANEN J. 'The fact of fiction in organisational ethnography', *Administrative Science Quarterly*, Vol. 24, No. 4, 1979. pp539–550.

VISSER C., ALTINK W. *and* ALGERA J. 'From job analysis to work profiling – do traditional procedures still apply?', in N. ANDERSON and P. HERRIOT (eds), *International Handbook of Selection and Assessment.* Chichester, John Wiley & Sons Ltd. 1997.

VROOM V. *Work and Motivation.* Chichester, John Wiley & Sons Ltd. 1964.

WADDINGTON J. 'United Kingdom: recovering from the neo-liberal assault', in J. WADDINGTON and R. HOFFMAN (eds), *Trade Unions in Europe: Facing challenges and searching for solutions.* Brussels, European Trade Union Institute. 2000.

WADDINGTON J. *and* HOFFMAN R. (eds), *Trade Unions in Europe: Facing challenges and searching for solutions.* Brussels, European Trade Union Institute. 2000.

WADDINGTON J. *and* WHITSON C. 'Why do people join unions in a period of membership decline?', *British Journal of Industrial Relations*, Vol. 35, No. 4, 1997. pp515–546.

WALKER, J. *Human Resource Strategy.* New York, McGraw-Hill. 1992.

WALSH J. 'A happy reunion', *People Management*, 8 Nov 2001. pp33–36.

WALTERS B. 'Identifying training needs', in D. GUEST and T. KENNY (eds), *A Textbook of Techniques and Strategies in Personnel Management*. London, Institute of Personnel Management, 1983.

WALTON R. 'From control to commitment in the workplace', *Harvard Business Review*, Vol. 63, March-April 1985. pp76–84.

WARD K., GRIMSHAW D., RUBERY J. *and* BEYNON H. 'Dilemmas in the management of temporary work agency staff', *Human Resource Management Journal*, Vol. 11, No. 4, 2001. pp3–21.

WARHURST C. *and* NICKSON D. *Looking Good, Sounding Right: Style counselling in the new economy*. London, The Industrial Society. 2001.

WARHURST C. *and* THOMPSON P. 'Hands, hearts and minds: changing work and workers at the end of the century', in P. THOMPSON and C. WARHURST (eds), *Workplaces of the Future*. London, Macmillan Press. 1998.

WARNER J. 'Improving the quality of Modern Apprenticeships', IRS *Employee Development Bulletin* 124, April 2000. pp11–16.

WATSON TOM. 'Recruitment and selection', in K. SISSON (ed.), *Personnel Management: A comprehensive guide to theory and practice in Britain*. Oxford, Blackwell. 1994.

WATSON TONY. 'Managing, crafting and researching: words, skill and imagination in shaping management research', *British Journal of Management*, Vol. 5, Special issue, June 1994. pp77–87.

WATSON TONY. *Management, Organisation and Employment Strategy*. London, Routledge & Kegan Paul. 1986.

WATSON TONY. *The Personnel Managers: A study in the sociology of work and employment*. London, Routledge & Kegan Paul. 1977.

WEDDERBURN, LORD. 'Collective bargaining or legal enactment – the 1999 Act and union recognition', *Industrial Law Journal*, Vol. 26, No. 1, 1997. pp1–42.

WEDDERBURN D. *and* CRAIG C. 'Relative deprivation in work', in D. WEDDERBURN (ed), *Poverty, Inequality and Class Structure*. Cambridge, Cambridge University Press. 1974.

WERNERFELT B. 'A resource-based view of the firm', *Strategic Management Journal*, Vol. 5, No. 2, 1984. pp171–180.

WHIDDETT S. *and* HOLLYFORDE S. *The Competencies Handbook*. London, Institute of Personnel and Development. 1999.

WHITE G. *and* DRUKER J. (eds), *Reward Management: A critical text*. London, Routledge. 2000.

WHITFIELD K. *and* McNABB R. 'Job evaluation and high-performance work practices: compatible or conflictual?', *Journal of Management Studies*, Vol. 38, No. 2, 2001. pp.293–312.

WHITTAKER J. 'Remaking the grade', *People Management*, 27 September 2001. pp44–46.

WHITTINGTON R. *What Is Strategy and Does It Matter?* London, Routledge. 1993.

WICHERT I. 'Job insecurity and work intensification: the effects on health and well-being', in B. BURCHELL, D. LADIPO and F. WILKINSON (eds), *Job Insecurity and Work Intensification*. London, Routledge. 2002.

WICKENS P. *The Road to Nissan: Flexibility, quality, teamwork*. London, Macmillan. 1987.

WILKINSON A. 'Empowerment', in T. REDMAN and A. WILKINSON (eds), *Contemporary Human Resource Management*. London, FT/Prentice-Hall. 2001.

WILKINSON A. 'Employment relations in SMEs', *Employee Relations*, Vol. 21, No. 3, 1999. pp206–217.

WILKINSON A. 'Empowerment: theory and practice', *Personnel Review*, Vol. 27, No.1, 1998. pp40–56.

WILKINSON A. *and* MARCHINGTON M. 'Total Quality Management: instant pudding for the personnel function?', *Human Resource Management Journal*, Vol. 5, 1, 1994. pp33–49.

WILKINSON A., GODFREY G. *and* MARCHINGTON M. 'Bouquets, brickbats and blinkers: total quality management and employee involvement in practice', *Organization Studies*, Vol. 18, No. 5, 1997. pp799–819.

WILKINSON A., MARCHINGTON M. *and* ACKERS P. 'Strategies for human resource management: issues in larger and international firms', in R. HARRISON (ed.), *Human Resource Management*. London, Addison-Wesley. 1993.

WILKINSON A., MARCHINGTON M., ACKERS P. *and* GOODMAN J. 'ESOPS fables: a tale of a machine tool company', *International Journal of Human Resource Management*, Vol. 5, No. 1, 1994. pp121–143.

WILLIAMS, A. 'Uncertain freedoms', *People Management*, 14 September 2000. pp18–19.

WILLIAMS R. S. *Performance Management*. Thomson Business Press. 1998.

WILSON F. *Organisational Behaviour: An introduction*. Oxford, OUP. 1999.

WINSTANLEY D. *and* WOODALL J. *Ethical Issues in Contemporary Human Resource Management*. London, Macmillan Business. 2000.

WITCHER B. *and* WILKINSON A. *What a Research Thesis Should Look Like*. Department of Management Working Paper, University of East Anglia. 2002.

WOOD S. 'Learning through ACAS: the case of union recognition', in B. TOWERS and W. BROWN (eds), *Employment Relations in Britain: 25 years of the Advisory, Conciliation and Arbitration Service*. Oxford, Blackwell. 2000.

WOOD S. 'Human resource management and performance', *International Journal of Management Reviews*. Vol. 1, No. 4, 1999a. pp367–413.

WOOD S. 'Getting the measure of the transformed high-performance organization', *British Journal of Industrial Relations*, Vol. 37, 1999b. pp391–418.

WOOD S. 'High-commitment management and payment systems', *Journal of Management Studies*, Vol. 33, No. 1, 1996. pp53–77.

WOOD S. 'The four pillars of human resource management: are they connected?' *Human Resource Management Journal*, Vol. 5, No. 5, 1995. pp49–59.

WOOD S. *and* ALBANESE M. 'Can we speak of a high-commitment management on the shop floor?', *Journal of Management Studies*, Vol. 32, No. 2, 1995. pp1–33.

WOOD S. *and* FENTON O'CREEVY M. 'Channel hopping', *People Management*, 25 November 1999. pp42–45.

WOOD S. *and* DE MENEZES L. 'High-commitment management in the UK: evidence from the Workplace Industrial Relations Survey and Employers' Manpower and Skills Survey'. *Human Relations*, Vol. 51, No. 4, 1998. pp485–515.

WOOD SUE. *Continuous Development*. London, Institute of Personnel Management. 1988.

WOODRUFFE C. *Development and Assessment Centres: Identifying and assessing competence*. London, IPD. 2000.

WOODRUFFE C. 'What is meant by a competency?', in R. BOAM and P. SPARROW (eds), *Designing and Achieving Competency*. Maidenhead, McGraw-Hill. 1992.

WORMAN D. 'Press home the advantage', *People Management*, 22 November 2001. p25.

WRIGHT P. M., McMAHON G. C. *and* McWILLIAMS A. 'Human resources and sustained competitive advantage: a resource-based perspective', *International Journal of Human Resource Management*, Vol. 5, No.2, 1994. pp301–326.

WUSTEMANN L. 'How to get the best from an EAP', *People Management*, 12 October 2000.

YEUNG A. *and* BERMAN B. 'Adding value through human resources: reorienting human resource measurement to drive business performance', *Human Resource Management*, Vol. 36, No. 3, Fall 1997. pp321–335.

YIN R. *Case Study Research: Design and methods*. London, Sage. 1984.

YIN R. 'The case study crisis: some answers', *Administrative Science Quarterly*, Vol. 26, No. 1, 1981. pp58–65.

YONG J. *and* WILKINSON A. 'The state of total quality management: a review', *International Journal of Human Resource Management*, Vol. 10, No. 1, 1999. pp137–161.

YOUNDT M., SNELL S., DEAN J. *and* LEPAK D. 'Human resource management, manufacturing strategy, and firm performance'. *Academy of Management Journal*, Vol. 39, 1996. pp836–66.

• Index